NEW ENGLAND ROAD TRIP

Miles Howard

NEW ENGLAND
Road Trip
Burlington
Montpelier
Green Mountain National Forest
Adirondack Park
New Hampshire's White Mountains
Franconia
White Mountain National Forest
Southern Vermont
Woodstock
Plymouth
Lebanon
VT
NH
Grafton
Concord
Green Mountain National Forest
Bennington
Brattleboro
Schenectady
Troy
Albany
NY
The Berkshires
Williamstown
North Adams
Lowell
Boston
Lenox
Stockbridge
MA
Worcester
Springfield
Poughkeepsie
Hartford
Providence
RI
CT
Fall River
New Haven
Bridgeport
Stamford
Rhode Island
Yonkers
New York City
Newark
Jersey City
New York
Islip

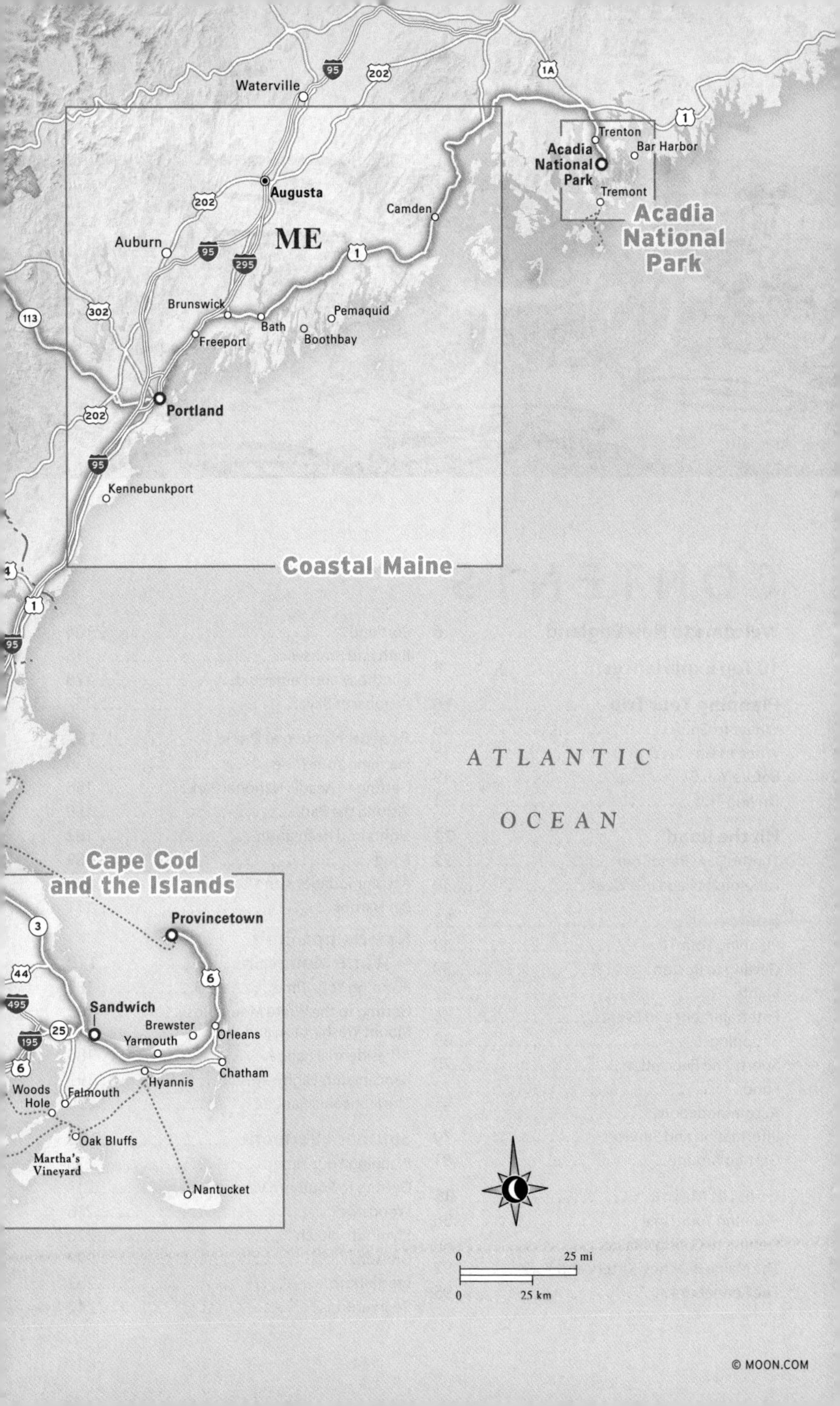

Waterville
95
202
1A
1
Trenton
Acadia National Park
Bar Harbor
Tremont
Acadia National Park
Augusta
202
Camden
ME
Auburn
95
295
1
Brunswick
302
113
Bath
Pemaquid
Boothbay
Freeport
Portland
202
95
Kennebunkport
Coastal Maine
1
95
ATLANTIC
OCEAN
Cape Cod and the Islands
3
Provincetown
6
44
495
Sandwich
Brewster
Orleans
25
195
Yarmouth
6
Chatham
Hyannis
Woods Hole
Falmouth
Oak Bluffs
Martha's Vineyard
Nantucket
0
25 mi
0
25 km
© MOON.COM

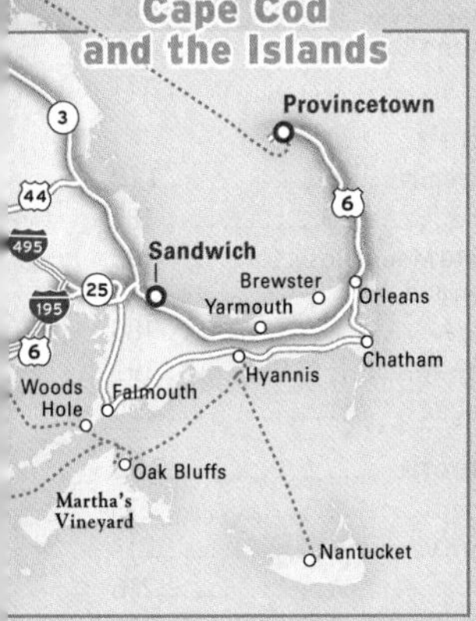

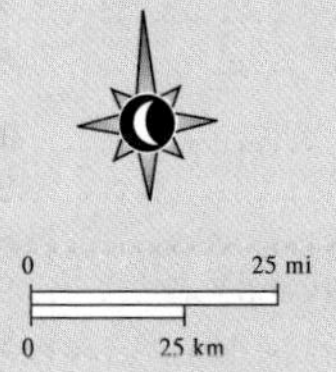

CONTENTS

WELCOME TO
New England

From cobblestone streets to moonlit coves, hilltop farms to award-winning clam shacks, a New England road trip is a drive through American history.

New England is one of those special places where the story of America began. The Wampanoag and Abenaki Indigenous people explored the thunderstruck mountains and hidden hollows here, long before ships from Europe first appeared on the coastline, whose lighthouses and villages are testaments to those who followed—pilgrims, whalers, academics, abolitionists, artisans and creators, and the founders of the United States.

But history is just the beginning.

Imagine being in a canoe on Walden Pond, gazing at the maples that seduced Thoreau. The trees seem frozen in time. But on the water, you can glimpse the reflection of those maples moving slowly. That's what traveling through New England feels like. There's a timelessness to the pebble beaches, Revolutionary War battlegrounds, windswept peaks, and colonial houses that color the landscape. But there's also an undercurrent of *active* history moving through here.

In New England today, you'll hear tales of cutting-edge research in medicine, nationally renowned culinary wizards, art festivals that attract visitors from around the world, and political activists working day and night to make life better for people here and afar. This is the enduring spirit of New England: always reaching, squinting at the horizon, but at the same time looking forward to a frosty ale and a big bucket of steamed blue mussels with friends, family, or strangers.

Pick and choose from the best the Northeast has to offer. Wander rooty trails or indulge in a farm-to-table feast. Put your feet up next to the ocean. Plan an expedition to the literal edge of the map. This book is an invitation to hit those roads and make a trip that's all your own—with a dash of New England spontaneity and oddities for good measure.

10 TOP EXPERIENCES

1 Scrambling up to a waterfall or wandering through a flowering forest on the region's **best hikes** (page 28).

2 Finding fantastic **fall foliage** as New England's deciduous trees paint the landscape (page 30).

3 Soaking up the sun along the **Cape Cod National Seashore** (page 351).

4 Following the footsteps of New England legends on the **Freedom Trail** (page 42) and the **Black Heritage Trail** (page 44).

5 Witnessing an outdoor spectacle at **Tanglewood** (page 270), Providence's **WaterFire festival** (page 313), or the **Boston Marathon** (page 68).

6 Visiting the eye-popping **museum at the Rhode Island School of Design** (page 307).

7 Taking a delicious trip along the **Cheese Trail** in Vermont (page 229).

8 Sampling award-winning **craft beers** in the hopping brewery circuit of downtown **Portland** (page 114) and Boston's **Samuel Adams Brewery** (page 63).

9 Ascending **Mount Washington** via the historic cog railway, zigzagging auto road, or on foot (page 186).

10 Enjoying **New England cooking,** from fresh-caught fried clams in Wellfleet to Providence-style grilled pizza (page 25).

MT. WASHINGTON
FRIED 
SANDWICHES
SPECIALTIES
BEVERAGES
Come in WE'RE OPEN

PLANNING YOUR TRIP

Where to Go

Boston

Revolutionary history is layered with immigrant heritage and urban culture in this brassy, wisecracking city. Throw in some of the **best art museums** in the country, **world-class universities,** and the crack of baseball bats at **Fenway Park,** and Boston begins to feel like that "shining city upon a hill" Puritan settlers hoped to found—but with pizza and oysters on the half shell.

Coastal Maine

Maine's 3,478 miles (5,597 km) of coastline encompass **sandy beaches;** the vibrant downtown of Portland, the state's largest city; and endless **rocky coves.** Life happens on the water here: Cozy harbors bristle with the masts of sailboats, while many locals earn a living with fishing poles and lobster traps. Take to the sea to spot **humpback whales** and **puffin colonies,** paddle a **kayak** past wave-whipped points, and plunge into the icy North Atlantic.

Acadia National Park

Wild scenery meets classical elegance in this island park. Carriage trails wind between sun-splashed peaks, grand bridges traverse forest streams, and historic hotels overlook the tides. Make a predawn drive up **Cadillac Mountain** to catch the **country's first sunrise,** go tidepool-hopping on the Park Loop Road, then head into the town of **Bar Harbor** for a *very* Vacationland blend of tourist shops, ice cream, and lobster meals.

New Hampshire's White Mountains

The gentle Appalachians erupt into rugged peaks in the White Mountains, and **Mount Washington** towers above all. This range is remarkably accessible to visitors who can drive, ride, or walk to the top of **New Hampshire's highest peak** and hike along the blustery alpine ridge linking the iconic **Presidential Range.** And while the Granite State's Old Man of the Mountain crumbled in 2003, there's plenty of rock left, along with **roaring waterfalls, ancient caves,** and **scenic drives.**

Southern Vermont

Take back roads and byways through Vermont at its most bucolic, and slow down to the pace of life in this tiny state. The trip from the starchy, small-town center of **Woodstock** to the funky galleries of **Brattleboro** passes **picture-book villages** and winding rivers, rolling orchards, and destination-worthy **craft breweries.**

The Berkshires

This countryside retreat offers refreshing contrasts: Old-fashioned charm abounds, but the Berkshires overflow with **pioneering arts and culture,** including the glorious **Tanglewood Music Festival** in the summer months. In recent years, the Berkshires have become a **hot culinary destination,** and young chefs are drawing in crowds with New American fare sourced from regional farms and producers.

Rhode Island

Newport is an unlikely setting for Renaissance palazzos and Greek Revival chateaus, but when 19th-century U.S. elite built summertime "cottages," they piled their glamour and gaudery into this charming colonial city. Those sprawling mansions are remarkably well preserved, and a trip through the properties is a glimpse into **Gilded Age high society.** Meanwhile, just up the road, **Providence** offers its own contemporary renaissance, with **James Beard Award-winning chefs**

Clockwise from top left: *The Embrace* on Boston Common by sculptor Hank Willis Thomas; harbor seals in coastal Maine; kayaking near Stockbridge in the Berkshires and the transcendent **WaterFire** festival, wherein boats of torchbearers paint the nocturnal city with firelight.

Cape Cod and the Islands

Just a few hours from Boston, Cape Cod and the islands of **Nantucket** and **Martha's Vineyard** are a world unto themselves. Generations of artists, writers, and free spirits have escaped to their dune shacks and beach retreats, adding color to a centuries-old fishing community. Nantucket's cobblestone streets are infused with **whaling history.** The harbors of Martha's Vineyard's brim with old-fashioned schooners. Locals call Cape Cod's **Provincetown** "the end of the world." It remains an artsy, liberal haven—and the East Coast's hottest **LGBTQ+ party destination.**

New York City

Cue the Jay-Z (or the Sinatra) for a whirlwind trip through the Big Apple. While New York isn't part of New England, it's a **convenient gateway** to the region and offers a perfect contrast to the beaches, villages, and mountain charms of the Northeast with its **skyscrapers, museums,** and **monuments.** Leave room for bagels or a bowl of ramen.

When to Go

With its lazy days, balmy weather, and warmer water, New England's **peak season** is during the school vacation months, **early July-late August.** While cities can be swelteringly hot and hotels jam-packed, this is the ideal time to enjoy the **beaches** that stretch from Rhode Island to Acadia National Park.

Autumn is New England's showstopper, when deciduous forests shed their green for a lavish display of red, gold,

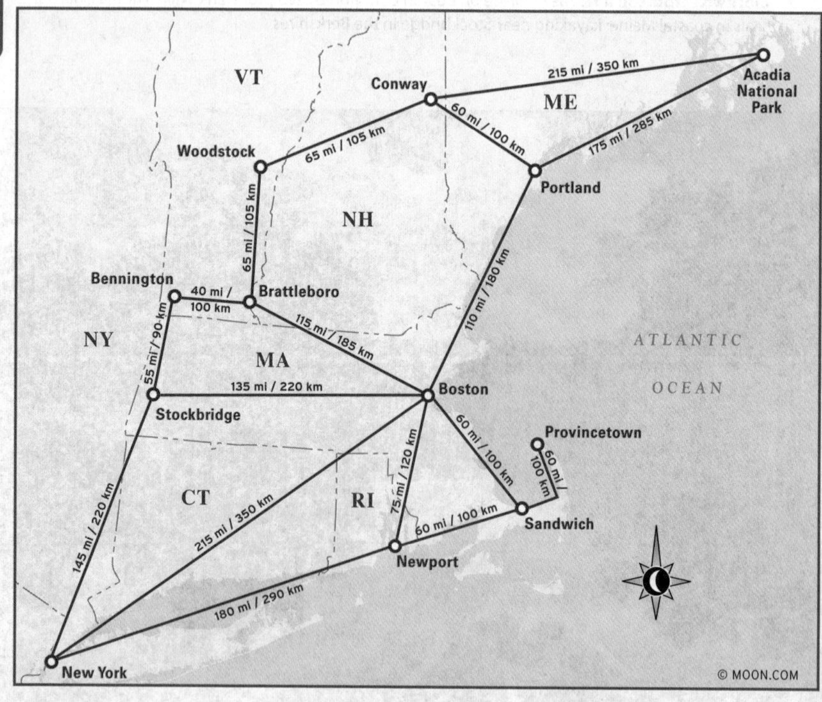

New England for Families

Get started on the ultimate kid-friendly road trip.

- **Boston Tea Party Ships and Museum, Boston:** Get a taste of Revolutionary history at a hands-on museum with costumed actors and interactive exhibits (page 60).

- **Dive-in Theater Boat Cruise, Acadia National Park:** Gaze beneath the surface in this kid-focused, splashy nature outing from Bar Harbor with Diver Ed, who brings up touchable critters like sea stars, lobsters, and sea cucumbers (page 169).

- **Mount Washington Cog Railway, New Hampshire's White Mountains:** Aspiring engineers and mountaineers will love the slow-moving, scenic trip on this 150-year-old mountain railway (page 187).

- **Scott Farm Orchard, Southern Vermont:** Pick apples in a scenic orchard by Rudyard Kipling's Vermont home (page 232).

Mount Washington Cog Railway

- **Cape Cod Baseball League, Cape Cod:** The free outdoor games held along the Cape are family-friendly ways to enjoy our national pastime without the crowds or hype—and you may just spot a future baseball legend (page 343).

and orange. **Fall color** depends on fickle weather conditions, but the season begins in **mid-September** in Vermont and New Hampshire, and spends two months working its way south, with Rhode Island peaking in the last two weeks of **October.**

For travelers hoping to ride the waves in Rhode Island and watch the turning of leaves in the White Mountains, the **last week of September** can offer the best of both worlds; plus, the beaches are far quieter when the kids are back in school. **Winter** and **spring,** while perfect for skiers and maple syrup aficionados, are notoriously terrible for driving, with roads stopped up by everything from snowdrifts to mud pits. By early **May,** most back roads have dried out and the first blossoms are opening up in the south—this is the ideal time to get bargain rates on hotels around the region. And if you're willing to gamble with rain conditions, **June** is a glorious time for wildflowers, scented lilacs, and pastures full of newborn calves and woolly lambs.

Before You Go

The easiest place to fly into and launch a New England trip is **Boston,** though **Portland, Maine,** and **Providence, Rhode Island,** are emerging as "port" cities themselves. While it adds an extra half day of driving on either end, beginning or ending a New England road trip in **New York City** adds a nice counterpoint. If you are renting a car in any of these cities, plan to pick it up *after* spending time there, as paid parking and crowded

Clockwise from top left: gingerbread cottages in Oak Bluffs, Martha's Vineyard; Acadia's Thunder Hole; a windjammer cruise in Acadia

streets make it easier to explore by public transport.

When visiting during **high season** or **fall foliage season,** it's essential to book **accommodations** and **rental cars** well in advance, though impromptu **campers** can usually find somewhere to sleep without much notice. Unless you're planning to dine at a handful of elite restaurants in Boston and New York, it's unnecessary to make reservations more than a few days ahead of time.

Whenever you come, bring ample **layers of clothing,** as the weather is often changeable. If your itinerary includes visiting the peaks of the White Mountains, keep in mind that **temperatures** can become quite chilly even in the middle of summer, and sailing in Maine, Massachusetts, and Rhode Island means blustery shore winds. On the other hand, you can't go far in New England before hitting an outdoor outfitter or thrift store—anything left at home will be easy to find in a dozen shades of plaid.

Driving Tips

In New England, the most memorable roads are winding, **two-lane highways** that define the "scenic route." When planning point-to-point drives, consider investing in a **detailed map of the area,** as the roads have a habit of merging, diverging, and changing names. Above all, don't assume you'll have **cell phone access,** as rural swaths of western Massachusetts, Vermont, New Hampshire, and inland Maine can have thin coverage.

Speed limits change regionally: Unless otherwise marked, assume a maximum of 65 miles (105 km) per hour on interstates and 45 miles (72 km) per hour on two-lane highways. Using a cell phone while driving can earn you a hefty fine, and seat belts are mandatory. Some New Hampshire, New York, Rhode Island, and Maine highways have **tolls** (ranging from $1-10), so it's worth traveling with cash. All Massachusetts tolls are now automated, so you can either bring or rent a transponder, or pay your tolls by mail or online upon receiving a bill.

Travelers with electric vehicles will be relieved to know that New England offers more than 97,000 charging stations at gas stations, grocery stores, and shopping centers throughout the region. Nearly half of these stations are clustered in Massachusetts, while less densely populated states like Maine and Vermont offer a more modest selection. Planning charging stops is essential for rural-bound road trips, and thanks to the charging station database at ChargeHub.com, you can easily search for stations by town and state before hitting the road.

HIT THE ROAD

The 14-Day Grand Tour

An epic loop through American history, high peaks, and picture-perfect countryside, this two-week trip is a "grand tour" in every sense. The full itinerary means quite a bit of time on the road, so those looking for a more leisurely vacation should snip out bits of this route in exchange for extra beach days, hikes, and free time to explore along the way. But if you've got an itchy pedal foot and the urge to put some miles on the odometer, this gives you the very best of New England.

Days 1-2

BOSTON

Get a crash course in Revolutionary history on the **Freedom Trail,** which stretches from the shiny dome of the **Massachusetts State House** to the **Bunker Hill Monument.** Don't tackle the whole thing at once—the trail isn't complete without a lunch break in the Italian American **North End** neighborhood. Try **Italian ice, cannoli,** or a classic **submarine sandwich** before crossing the Charles River toward the USS *Constitution.* Take a sunset stroll at Arnold Arboretum on the **Emerald Necklace** and find your way from there to **Jamaica Mi Hungry** for coconut shrimp and jerk pork shoulder.

On your second day, take a field trip from the city to **Walden Pond** for a serene swim. From there, backtrack to the city, grab a nourishing sandwich from **Flour Bakery + Café,** and spend the afternoon exploring **Back Bay**'s art and architecture; duck into the sanctuary of **Trinity Church,** soak up the scholarly atmosphere in the **Boston Public Library** reading room, then stand in the center of the world at the stained glass **Mapparium.** Spend the afternoon in one of Boston's world-class museums, taking in ancient artifacts and contemporary art at the **Museum of Fine Arts,** or head to the **Boston Tea Party Ships and Museum** to reenact the city's favorite piece of colonial-era civil disobedience. At dusk, saunter over to the South End for a glass of wine and succulent hand-made pasta at **MIDA.**

Days 3-5

COASTAL MAINE AND ACADIA

275 MI/443 KM, 6 HR

Stop by **Caffé Vittoria** in the North End for an old-world cappuccino before procuring some wheels and heading to **Portland,** an easy, two-hour drive up the interstate. Before you reach the city, make a detour to the **Wells Reserve at Laudholm** for a biodiverse stroll through maples and cedars, sandy beaches, and briny estuaries. The reserve is conveniently located just down the road from Kennebunkport favorite **Port Lobster.**

Get a taste of Portland's maritime life on a **boat tour of Casco Bay**—hop a historic **schooner** or take a ride on the **mailboat run** that connects the bay's islands to the mainland—then kick off the evening by visiting some of the city's award-winning microbreweries like **Bissell Brothers** and **Foundation.**

On your second day on the coast, enjoy a decadent breakfast at Portland's **Holy Donut,** then hit the road for lighthouse-hopping and harbor-strolling. Drive up to **Bath** and work your way through the **Maine Maritime Museum,** or go a bit farther to **Rockland** and take in three generations of Wyeths at the **Farnsworth Art Museum** before visiting nearby **Owls Head Light.** Pick up a picnic lunch to eat near **Rockport**'s idyllic harbor, then visit the nautical boutiques in downtown **Camden.** Make the final push to **Acadia National Park** on Mount Desert Island, recover with noshes and lager at **Mainely Meat BBQ,** and turn in early if you're planning to catch **sunrise on Cadillac**

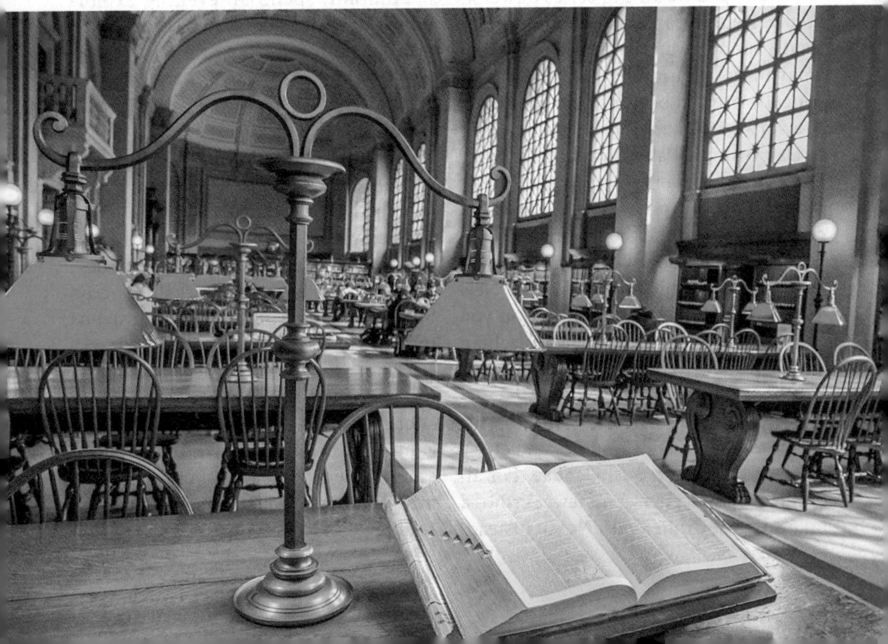

Clockwise from top left: seafood; Beehive Trail summit in Acadia National Park; the Bates Hall reading room at the Boston Public Library

Mountain, a pilgrimage place where you can see the first sunlight hit the coast.

After your morning's start, mountaintop sunrise or not, enjoy the rest of the day car-free in the national park; rent a bike, hop the free **Island Explorer shuttle,** and cruise the extensive network of **carriage trails** that link great stone bridges, viewpoints, and rolling mountains. For the real experience of a **Maine lobster dinner,** cross the island to **Thurston's Lobster Pound** to get one with all the fixings at the edge of a scenic harbor.

Days 6-7

WHITE MOUNTAINS

215 MI/346 KM, 4.75 HR

The route to the White Mountains crosses the dark, deep forests of inland Maine, ticking off a series of towns that recall the state's immigrant heritage: Pass Naples, Sweden, and Denmark on your way to the outdoor mecca of **North Conway.** Nab some thin-crust pizza from **Flatbread Company** and then stretch your legs after the long drive on the easy walk to **Diana's Baths,** a series of waterfalls perfect for an early evening dip (if there's enough water). Fortify yourself for a day in the mountains with dinner and a locally brewed beer at **Moat Mountain Brewery & Smokehouse.**

Day two is all about mountain peaks and rugged scenery: Chug to the top of **Mount Washington** on the 150-year-old **cog railway,** or hike the mountain yourself—on a clear day at the summit you'll have views stretching from Maine to New York's Adirondack Mountains, and you can watch a steady stream of Appalachian Trail through-hikers pose for photos at the top. And once you're back in the valley, you can motor over to Littleton for some savory riverside noodles and curry at **Taste The Thai & Sushi House.** For all of the bucolic scenery and fewer crowds, take a journey into **Evans Notch** instead, choosing from a series of gusty peaks with panoramic views of nearby valleys and mountain ranges.

Days 8-9

SOUTHERN VERMONT

165 MI/266 KM, 3 HR

Take the **Kancamagus Highway** for a swooping, scenic drive through the mountains on your way to **Woodstock,** where you'll find a classic village green, art galleries, and farm-to-table restaurants in a lush river valley. Hop a wagon ride, learn to churn your own butter, and get friendly with some Jersey cows at the **Billings Farm & Museum,** then spend the afternoon visiting classic **covered bridges.**

The drive from Woodstock to **Brattleboro** is another stunner, especially if you take the scenic route: Visit the **President Calvin Coolidge State Historic Site** to see his family homestead on your way to Route 100, then wind through pretty villages like **Grafton.** After culminating the day's journey with kebabs and springy salads at **Tulip Bar and Restaurant,** spend an evening exploring Brattleboro's **art galleries,** or catch a circus performance at the town's **New England Center for Circus Arts.**

Day 10

THE BERKSHIRES

80 MI/129 KM, 2 HR

Watch the mountains fade into gentle hills as you make your way south, and choose a couple of the region's best destinations for a classic Berkshires day: Spend the morning with adventurous modern art in **North Adams** at the **MASS MoCA** or follow in Thoreau's footsteps to the top of **Mount Greylock.** After lunch, continue south to **Lenox** to visit the elegant home of **Edith Wharton,** then spend a quiet evening in the **Brava** wine bar, mingling with musicians from nearby **Tanglewood.**

TOP EXPERIENCE

One Tasty Trip

lobster roll

You could spend a lifetime eating and drinking your way across New England. The clam shacks and lobster pounds that hug the coast epitomize New England cuisine at its most classic, stripped-down, and elemental, while newer waves of restaurants in Providence and Portland attract chefs from across the nation and offer globally inspired fare with creative twists.

- **Boston's North End:** Discover the city's **Italian** heritage in its tastiest form: cannoli, wood-fired pizza, and hearty submarine sandwiches (page 73).
- **Portland's Food Scene:** The little city that helped make **farm-to-table** and **dock-to-table cuisine** a New England obsession is one of the region's most reliable outposts for decadent food (page 112).
- **Maine's Lobster:** Maine's most famous crustacean is also its favorite meal: Try a lobster roll at **Port Lobster** (page 100), or get the full dinner experience at **Thurston's Lobster Pound** (page 170).
- **Straight from the Farm:** A farm-fueled catering service turned hot-ticket restaurant, Brattleboro's **A Vermont Table** (page 240) gives local produce a global twist. In **Williamstown** in the Berkshires, **Mezze Bistro + Bar** (page 260) celebrates the twists and turns of the season with ultra-fresh, ingredient-focused fare.
- **Cape Cod's Clam Shacks:** Seasonal clam-and-fry joints open their doors each spring with great piles of seafood. Two favorites: **Jim's Clam Shack** in Falmouth (page 336) and **Cap't Cass Rock Harbor Seafood** in Orleans (page 349).
- **International Fare:** Za'atar flatbreads with peppers and lamb at **Aleppo Sweets** (page 319), wood-grilled pizza at **Al Forno** (page 318), and locally caught ceviche at **Los Andes** (page 318) are just a few of the internationally rooted recipes one can seek out and savor in Providence.

Clockwise from top left: hiking Cadillac Mountain in Acadia National Park; Alpine Garden accommodations near Mount Washington; a steep climb in the White Mountains

Coastal Charm

Coast Guard Beach, Cape Cod

New England's got beaches for days...

- **Popham Beach, Coastal Maine:** This stretch of shoreline offers the best of Maine, a sandy beach at the end of a scenic peninsula and a little rocky island to explore at low tide (page 125).
- **Bar Island, Acadia National Park:** The path from Bar Harbor to this forested islet only becomes a beach at low tide, which makes it the perfect place to find stranded sea creatures and tidepools (page 168).
- **Sachuest Beach, Newport:** Catch an easygoing summer swell at Sachuest Beach, a favorite surf spot just outside of downtown Newport (page 301).
- **Coast Guard Beach, Cape Cod:** Endless sand lined with wild roses, dramatic cliffs, and windswept lighthouses make this one of the best beaches in the East, and it's a favorite place for watching whales without leaving dry land (page 351).
- **Race Point Beach, Cape Cod:** The far tip of Cape Cod is nothing but beach, rolling dunes, and hidden shacks—for the ultimate "end of the world" experience, sleep at the remote Race Point Light (page 361).

Day 11

NEWPORT AND PROVIDENCE

190 MI/306 KM, 3.5 HR

Keep pointing toward the coast and you'll wind up in the pretty port city of Newport, where the waterside **Cliff Walk** cuts past some of the grandest **Gilded Age estates** in New England. Pick a single mansion to explore before hitting the beach for **clam cakes,** sand, and sun. As the sun sets, zip up to Providence for a twilight meander on the **RiverWalk** and follow it with a parade of fresh-caught fish crudo at **Oberlin.**

Days 12-13

CAPE COD

120 MI/193 KM, 2.25 HR

Snag some fresh baklava at **Aleppo Sweets** and drive all the way to "the end

TOP EXPERIENCE

Best Hikes

the woods of the Wells Reserve

Hike White Mountain crags, walk a trail through rolling Cape Cod sand dunes, or catch America's first sunrise.

Boston

A pair of trails trace American history in Boston.

- **Freedom Trail:** Follow the red line on the sidewalk, and get a whiff of the Revolution (page 42).
- **Black Heritage Trail:** Learn about the separate struggle for freedom of African Americans on this path from memorial to museum (page 44).

Coastal Maine

- **Wells Reserve at Laudholm:** Wander mixed hardwood forests and bird-filled estuaries on a network of trails and boardwalks that lead to the sandy expanse of Laudholm Beach (page 93).
- **Megunticook Trail:** Gain elevation and mountaintop views of Camden Harbor on this hike (page 148).

Acadia National Park

- **South Ridge Trail:** This long, dreamlike passage through verdant forests and wetlands takes you to the top of Cadillac Mountain, where you can catch the country's first sunrise (page 164).
- **Beehive Trail:** Climb straight up a rock face, aided by iron rungs (page 166).
- **Bar Island Trail:** Take a low-tide stroll across the sandbar that links Bar Island to downtown Bar Harbor (page 168).

New Hampshire's White Mountains

Acadia's iron rung trails

- **Presidential Traverse:** Among the most ambitious hikes in New England is the trail that links every peak in the Presidential Range over almost 23 grueling miles (37 km), with views in every direction (page 192).
- **Diana's Baths:** A short stroll is the perfect warm-up for a dip in the waterfall-fed wading pools for which this easygoing trail is named (page 193).
- **Caribou Mountain:** Far less crowded than the Presidential and Franconia Ranges, this "little" mountain in Evans Notch boasts unbeatable views into New Hampshire and Maine (page 207).

Southern Vermont

- **Faulkner Trail:** Get an early start and catch sunrise from the summit of Mount Tom (page 222).
- **Quechee Gorge Trail:** Follow the mellow footpath into Vermont's deepest gorge (page 222).

The Berkshires

- **Bellows Pipe Trail:** Follow in the footsteps of Thoreau on this 9.6-mile (15.4-km) loop that links North Adams to the summit of Mount Greylock, or simply drive to the summit, where you can enjoy the most dramatic section as an out-and-back (page 266).
- **Monument Mountain Trails:** Pass carriage roads and crumbling stone walls on Mohican Monument Trail or Hickey Trail, both of which earn you views of the rolling southern Berkshires (page 282).

Newport

- **Cliff Walk:** Walk all 3.5 miles (5.6 km) of this path, or just snip off a section—you'll pass some of the grandest Gilded Age estates in New England and spot surfers off the rocky coast (page 294).

Cape Cod and the Islands

- **Snail Road Trail:** Trek across the sand in Provincetown on your way to a lonely beach, following a trail into the dunes (page 362).

of the world"—that's colorful, creative **Provincetown** to you—to spend your last days exploring **Cape Cod.** Make for the **Cape Cod National Seashore** when you arrive, where you'll find the finest beaches in New England, crumbling cliffs, and historic lighthouses, and spend a day wandering the sand.

The next day, get a taste of Provincetown's artistic heritage by strolling the **downtown galleries,** then join a tour of the rustic **artists' shacks** scattered through the rolling dunes. Power up for the evening with surf and turf cooking at the **Canteen,** see if you can keep up with the locals at a raucous **tea dance,** then spend a night on the town in true **P-town** style with tickets to a **drag show.**

Day 14

BOSTON

115 MI/185 KM, 2.25 HR

Start your last day of New England adventures with some pastries from the **Portuguese Bakery,** then hit the **Cape Cod Rail Trail** for a morning of exploring on two wheels. If you have time, break up the return drive to Boston with stops in one or more of the villages that line the Inner Cape: Visit **Chatham**'s pretty **lighthouse,** play a round of pirate-themed minigolf in **Yarmouth,** or see a classic **saltbox home** in old-fashioned **Sandwich.** And consider a "last supper" of golden fried clams at **Seafood Sam's** before crossing the bridge to the mainland.

Fabulous Foliage in a Week

TOP EXPERIENCE

Discover New England's brightest season on a seven-day leaf-peeping tour.

Day 1

NEW YORK CITY

Hit the Big Apple and enjoy classic NYC: Hop a ferry to the **Statue of Liberty,** get panoramic views from the **One World Observatory,** then pick up bagels and lox for a picnic in **Central Park,** which is stunning under a canopy of colorful leaves.

Days 2-3

THE BERKSHIRES

140 MI/225 KM, 2.75 HR

Follow the Hudson River Valley toward **Great Barrington,** Massachusetts, then leave the highway behind for the winding roads through the Berkshires. Stretch your legs on a hike up **Monument Mountain,** where you'll see bright leaves rolling through a series of quiet valleys. Visit the **Norman Rockwell Museum** for a glimpse of autumns past—many of his canvases feature bright New England falls. Settle into **Stockbridge** for a cozy evening of live music by the fire in the **Red Lion Inn's pub.**

Keep pointing north on back roads—or trade your car for a bike on the **Ashuwillticook Rail Trail**—leaving plenty of time to stop at **farm stands** along the way. Route 8 is particularly scenic from Pittsfield to **North Adams,** winding past the Cheshire Reservoir and slopes of Mount Greylock. In fine weather, drive all the way to the summit of **Mount Greylock,** which looks out over a landscape of brooding evergreens and colorful deciduous trees, but if you find yourself a cold, rainy afternoon, warm up in **MASS MoCA,** the sprawling modern art museum in the heart of workaday North Adams.

Days 4-5

SOUTHERN VERMONT

120 MI/193 KM, 2.25 HR

Visit the site of Vermont's most famous Revolutionary-era battle in little **Bennington,** then follow Route 9—whose changing elevation offers a varied palette of colors—to **Brattleboro,** the hippie heart of southern Vermont's creative

Top: fall foliage in Central Park, New York **Bottom:** view from Franconia Ridge in the White Mountains

Art and Culture

Newport Folk Festival

Join colorful crowds on gallery walks, or brush up on high culture at music festivals and museums.

- **Museum of Fine Arts, Boston:** Stroll from the art of ancient Egypt to Impressionist masterpieces in this enormous, exquisite museum (page 58).
- **Massachusetts Museum of Contemporary Art, the Berkshires:** Follow the twists and turns of modern art through the sprawling MASS MoCA, which occupies a former factory in tiny North Adams (page 262).
- **Tanglewood Music Festival, the Berkshires:** Stretch out on the grass at the summer home of the Boston Symphony Orchestra in Lenox, where picnics are raised to fine art (page 270).
- **Music Festivals, Newport:** Watch marquee names from around the world as well as up-and-coming artists at the town's two historic musical blowouts, the Newport Folk Festival and Newport Jazz Festival (page 300).
- **Provincetown Galleries, Cape Cod:** Explore the creative culture of P-town, long a haven for artists and writers (page 356).

culture. Try to catch a **circus show** or **gallery walk** while you're there, join a tasting of unusual sour beers at **Hermit Thrush Brewery,** or spend the afternoon **picking heirloom apples** at **Scott Farm Orchard,** which offers a magnificent combination of fall fruit and foliage.

Take a roundabout way toward the town of **Woodstock,** tracing a route that includes **tasting aged cheddar** in Grafton's time-warp village center. Skip across to scenic Route 100, which ducks through deep valleys and over rushing mountain streams on its way to the **President Calvin Coolidge State Historic Site.** The historic site is tucked into a quiet hollow that's stunning in autumn and a good place to hear Yankee lore about this Vermont presidential candidate. Then visit **Long Trail Brewing**

Company, which often features special **autumn brews** like the Harvest Barn Ale.

Day 6

WHITE MOUNTAINS

120 MI/193 KM, 2.75 HR

Take on the twists and turns of the **Kancamagus Highway,** where each roller-coaster dip brings fresh views of the rugged high-mountain landscape. There are plenty of trails and riverside picnic spots to relax at along the way, but save some daylight for an afternoon adventure: Peak baggers can zip to the top of **Mount Washington,** which feels like a slice of early winter with views of fall foliage in the surrounding valley floors. For a lower-elevation view of the trees, head to **Flume Gorge,** where a covered bridge glows bright red against a backdrop of vivid yellow and orange leaves. And as the sun goes down, make for the riverside patio at **Schilling Beer Company** for wood-fired pizza, real-deal bratwurst, and European lagers.

Day 7

BOSTON

145 MI/233 KM, 3 HR

Get an early morning start, and plan to drop your car off *before* exploring Boston on foot. With an afternoon in the city, plan to walk the **Freedom Trail,** winding from the bright trees of **Boston Common** through Revolutionary sites to the historic **North End** and concluding at the **Bunker Hill Monument.** From there, amble back to the city center and go bivalve wild in the history-steeped dining room at **Union Oyster House.**

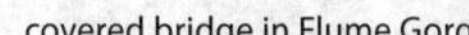

covered bridge in Flume Gorge

Boston

Highlights

★ **Historic Trails:** Follow the footsteps of history along the **Freedom Trail** (page 42) and **Black Heritage Trail** (page 44).

★ **Boston Common and Boston Public Garden:** Catch a ride on a swan boat or watch some summertime Shakespeare in the oldest park in the United States (page 47).

★ **Boston Public Library:** With masterpiece paintings and exquisite architecture, this landmark library is far more than books—but it's got millions and millions of those (page 56).

★ **Fenway Park:** From the Green Monster to the bleachers, this ball field is a pilgrimage place for baseball lovers (page 57).

★ **Museum of Fine Arts:** Discover Impressionist treasures and artifacts from around the world (page 58).

★ **Emerald Necklace:** Walk or bike five meandering miles of trees, flowers, and marshlands to an arboretum with hundreds of rare flora species (page 71).

★ **North End Cuisine:** Pick up a cannoli, slurp an Italian ice, then watch the neighborhood drift by over a perfect cappuccino (page 73).

Boston

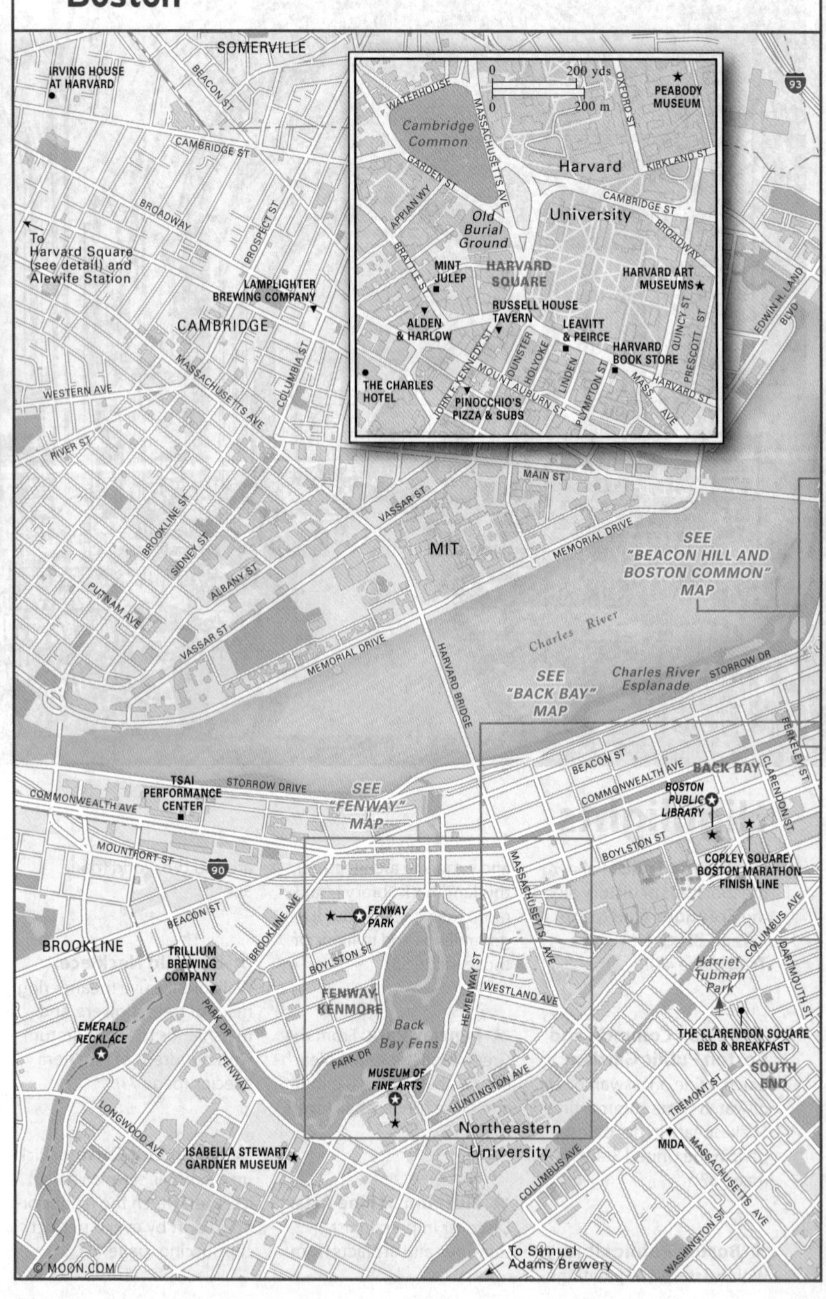

SOMERVILLE
IRVING HOUSE AT HARVARD
BEACON ST
CAMBRIDGE ST
BROADWAY
PROSPECT ST
To Harvard Square (see detail) and Alewife Station
LAMPLIGHTER BREWING COMPANY
CAMBRIDGE
MASSACHUSETTS AVE
COLUMBIA ST
WESTERN AVE
RIVER ST
BROOKLINE ST
SIDNEY ST
ALBANY ST
PUTNAM AVE
VASSAR ST
MEMORIAL DRIVE
MAIN ST
MIT
HARVARD BRIDGE
Charles River
SEE "BEACON HILL AND BOSTON COMMON" MAP
SEE "BACK BAY" MAP
Charles River Esplanade
STORROW DR
TSAI PERFORMANCE CENTER
STORROW DRIVE
COMMONWEALTH AVE
SEE "FENWAY" MAP
MOUNTFORT ST
90
BEACON ST
BACK BAY
BOSTON PUBLIC LIBRARY
CLARENDON ST
BERKELEY ST
BOYLSTON ST
COPLEY SQUARE/ BOSTON MARATHON FINISH LINE
BROOKLINE
TRILLIUM BREWING COMPANY
BROOKLINE AVE
FENWAY PARK
BOYLSTON ST
FENWAY-KENMORE
HEMENWAY ST
WESTLAND AVE
Harriet Tubman Park
COLUMBUS AVE
DARTMOUTH ST
THE CLARENDON SQUARE BED & BREAKFAST
EMERALD NECKLACE
PARK DR
FENWAY
Back Bay Fens
MUSEUM OF FINE ARTS
HUNTINGTON AVE
TREMONT ST
SOUTH END
LONGWOOD AVE
Northeastern University
MIDA
MASSACHUSETTS AVE
ISABELLA STEWART GARDNER MUSEUM
COLUMBUS AVE
WASHINGTON ST
EDWIN H. LAND BLVD
93
To Samuel Adams Brewery
© MOON.COM
0 200 yds
0 200 m
WATERHOUSE
Cambridge Common
MASSACHUSETTS AVE
OXFORD ST
PEABODY MUSEUM
Harvard
KIRKLAND ST
GARDEN ST
CAMBRIDGE ST
University
APPIAN WY
Old Burial Ground
BROADWAY
BRATTLE ST
MINT JULEP
HARVARD SQUARE
HARVARD ART MUSEUMS
RUSSELL HOUSE TAVERN
ALDEN & HARLOW
LEAVITT & PEIRCE
QUINCY ST
PRESCOTT ST
JOHN F. KENNEDY ST
DUNSTER
HOLYOKE
LINDEN
HARVARD BOOK STORE
THE CHARLES HOTEL
MOUNT AUBURN ST
PLYMPTON ST
MASS AVE
HARVARD ST
PINOCCHIO'S PIZZA & SUBS

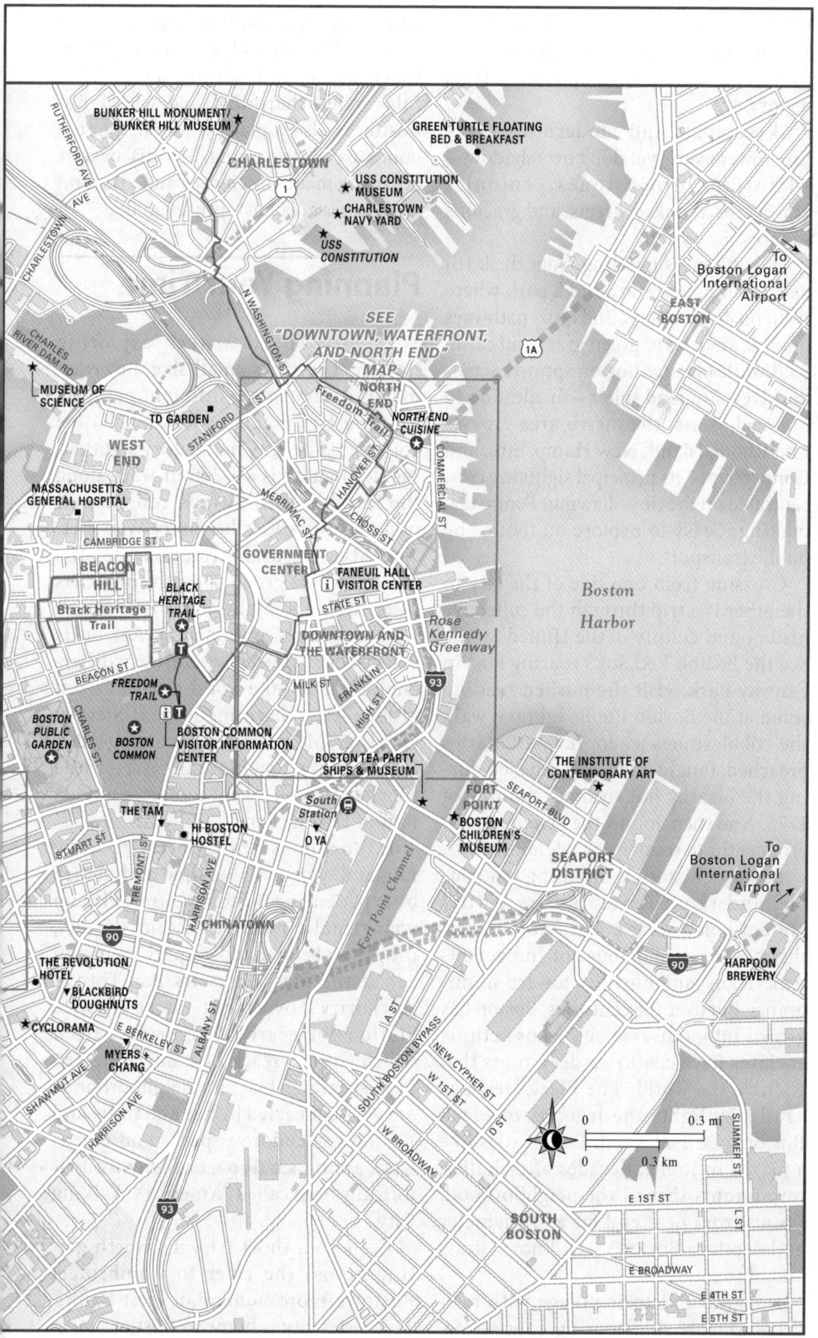
BUNKER HILL MONUMENT/
BUNKER HILL MUSEUM
CHARLESTOWN
GREEN TURTLE FLOATING
BED & BREAKFAST
USS CONSTITUTION
MUSEUM
CHARLESTOWN
NAVY YARD
USS
CONSTITUTION
RUTHERFORD AVE
CHARLESTOWN AVE
N WASHINGTON ST
To
Boston Logan
International
Airport
EAST
BOSTON
SEE
"DOWNTOWN, WATERFRONT,
AND NORTH END"
MAP
CHARLES RIVER DAM RD
MUSEUM OF
SCIENCE
TD GARDEN
STANIFORD
NORTH
END
Freedom Trail
NORTH END
CUISINE
WEST
END
MASSACHUSETTS
GENERAL HOSPITAL
MERRIMAC ST
HANOVER ST
CROSS ST
COMMERCIAL ST
CAMBRIDGE ST
BEACON
HILL
GOVERNMENT
CENTER
FANEUIL HALL
VISITOR CENTER
BLACK
HERITAGE
TRAIL
Black Heritage
Trail
STATE ST
Boston
Harbor
DOWNTOWN AND
THE WATERFRONT
Rose
Kennedy
Greenway
BEACON ST
FREEDOM
TRAIL
MILK ST
FRANKLIN
HIGH ST
BOSTON
PUBLIC
GARDEN
CHARLES ST
BOSTON
COMMON
BOSTON COMMON
VISITOR INFORMATION
CENTER
BOSTON TEA PARTY
SHIPS & MUSEUM
THE INSTITUTE OF
CONTEMPORARY ART
FORT
POINT
SEAPORT BLVD
THE TAM
HI BOSTON
HOSTEL
South
Station
O YA
BOSTON
CHILDREN'S
MUSEUM
STUART ST
TREMONT ST
HARRISON AVE
SEAPORT
DISTRICT
To
Boston Logan
International
Airport
Fort Point Channel
CHINATOWN
THE REVOLUTION
HOTEL
BLACKBIRD
DOUGHNUTS
HARPOON
BREWERY
CYCLORAMA
E BERKELEY ST
ALBANY ST
A ST
SOUTH BOSTON BYPASS
NEW CYPHER ST
MYERS +
CHANG
SHAWMUT AVE
W 1ST ST
HARRISON AVE
W BROADWAY
D ST
0
0.3 mi
0
0.3 km
SUMMER ST
E 1ST ST
SOUTH
BOSTON
L ST
E BROADWAY
E 4TH ST
E 5TH ST

Follow the Freedom Trail and the Emerald Necklace through Boston to find a city that's grown up alongside its history.

Skyscrapers and modern architecture tower over—yet don't overshadow—Victorian brownstones, colonial graveyards, crooked streets, and gracious squares.

Downtown is bustling from dusk till dawn, but it wraps around a park where swan boats, pavilions, and quiet pathways provide an oasis of green grass and calm. And while Greater Boston sprawls across four New England states—in addition to Massachusetts, the metro area crosses into Rhode Island, New Hampshire, and Connecticut—its principal sights are concentrated on the tiny Shawmut Peninsula, making it easy to explore on foot or by public transport.

Crossing from one side of the city to the other is a trip through the collective history and culture of the United States: See the Boston Red Sox's roaring fans in Fenway Park, visit the hushed reading room at the Boston Public Library, walk the cobblestones where revolutionaries preached, fought, bled, and rebelled during the blazing hot summer months of 1775. And then, follow the greener, flowering paths to residential neighborhoods.

Boston's history is anything but simple, and those Revolutionary battles are entwined with a legacy of slavery, the massacres and abuse of Indigenous Americans, and hostility toward immigrants. But over the centuries, Boston has grown into a diverse city whose ethnic enclaves have centuries-deep roots that encircle the world. The Black Heritage Trail highlights the legacies of Black Bostonians. The North End bustles like a piazza in Rome, decades after Italian immigrants shaped the neighborhood. Locals from near and far add character and depth to Boston's well-known brass and bluster.

Imagine a historic village with residents who are still laboring, innovating, and living, and you'll have an accurate picture of Boston today. Its architecture, sports scene, and salt-of-the-earth locals can feel charmingly old-school. But Boston is also a place where neighborhoods are transforming, new discoveries are being made in sciences and arts, and local tastes are constantly evolving.

Planning Your Time

You could spend a week exploring Boston. The city's small size, however, makes it easy to see different parts on the same trip, no matter how much time you have. The only mandatory sightseeing destination is a 1-2 hour walk along the Freedom Trail, which connects all of downtown's Revolutionary War sites. The city's cultural attractions, for the most part, are grouped on the outskirts of downtown in the Back Bay, South End, and Fenway districts. Art buffs can choose between several very different museums—the world-class Museum of Fine Arts, charming Isabella Stewart Gardner Museum, and cutting-edge Institute of Contemporary Art—while sports fans won't want to miss a guided tour of Fenway Park.

If Boston is your portal to New England, you can save time and money by experiencing Boston car-free. Pick up your rental car after exploring the city, drop it off beforehand, or park your own car at the Massachusetts Bay Transit Authority's overnight lot at Alewife Station (in nearby Cambridge, from which you can reach Boston via the Red Line subway). The city neighborhoods are well-connected by bus and train, and Boston's splendorous parks and greenways are no small part of why it's historically been called "America's Walking City."

Even on a short trip, it's worth getting across the river to Cambridge, Boston's more bohemian "left bank." This sister city is home to Boston's most

Best Restaurants

★ **Gene's Chinese Flatbread Café:** Broad, hand-pulled noodles are rolled in chili, garlic, and aromatic spices at this Chinatown landmark (page 73).

★ **Neptune Oyster:** The lobster rolls alone would make this chic North End restaurant a destination, and the raw bar is the best in the city (page 74).

★ **Modern Pastry:** The debate over the North End's best cannoli rages on, but the crispy, creamy version at this classic spot is a strong contender (page 74).

★ **MIDA:** Some of the most succulent handcrafted pasta in Boston awaits at this lively Mediterranean eatery (page 75).

★ **Tres Gatos:** Savor some Mexican and Middle Eastern-influenced tapas and then hunt for books and records at this unique Jamaica Plain eatery (page 76).

elite cultural institutions—Harvard University and the Massachusetts Institute of Technology. And to the south of Back Bay and the Fenway, the quieter community of Jamaica Plain boasts some of city's most stunning parks, such as Arnold Arboretum, while also reflecting Boston's residential diversity and salt-of-the-earth vibe. If you fancy a local ale alongside bona fide Bostonians, go here. Or better yet, walk here by taking the Emerald Necklace pathway that snakes from Boston Common, through the Fenway, to the edge of "JP," as locals call it.

Orientation

The bulk of Boston's downtown still takes up the Shawmut Peninsula, with Boston Common at the center. The downtown neighborhoods are organized around the Common, with Beacon Hill and the North End to the north, the Financial District and downtown to the east, and Back Bay and the South End to the west and south. East Boston, along with Logan International Airport, is across Boston Harbor to the northeast, while South Boston and the new Seaport District form a peninsula to the southeast. Across the river to the north are intellectual Cambridge and hip Somerville. And south of Boston's urban core, Jamaica Plain is home to activists, artists, and multigenerational families.

Getting to Boston

Driving from New York City

212 mi/346 km, 3.5 hr

Leave New York City heading north on **FDR Drive.** Use the left lane to access Exit 17 to the **Robert F. Kennedy Bridge** ($10.17 toll), then stay left to merge onto **I-278 East.** After 4.5 miles (7 km), I-278 East merges with **I-95 North** ($1.75 toll). Follow I-95 North 46 miles (74 km) to Exit 27A in Bridgeport, Connecticut; exit right onto **Route 8 North,** which you'll follow 5.5 miles (9 km) to Exit 9 and **Route 15 North.**

Take Exit 68 NE to merge onto **I-91 North** toward Hartford/Middletown, then stay right for Exit 29 and merge onto **Route 15 North** toward **I-84 East.** Use the left two lanes to continue onto I-84 East toward Boston. North of Sturbridge, I-84 East merges with **I-90** ($7.25 toll, no cash); stay right at the split for **I-90 East.** Take Exit 24A to South Station for all downtown Boston and North End destinations.

Best Accommodations

★ **HI Boston Hostel:** Meet travelers from around the globe in this ultramodern hostel that's steps away from downtown sights (page 77).

★ **Green Turtle Floating Bed and Breakfast:** Equal parts luxurious and offbeat, this trio of boats is moored at the Charlestown pier (page 78).

★ **The Verb:** Join a hip crowd of revelers at the pool, spin some vinyl on your personal turntable, and soak up the rock-and-roll vibe of Boston's edgiest boutique hotel (page 78).

★ **The Clarendon Square Bed and Breakfast:** Explore the South End in the morning and then enjoy views of nocturnal Boston from the rooftop hot tub at this elegant inn (page 79).

★ **Irving House at Harvard:** Simple, affordable rooms overlook the Harvard University campus in the heart of Cambridge (page 79).

Driving from Newport

75 mi/121 km, 1.25 hr

Follow West Main Road north from downtown Newport, which turns into **Route 114 North.** Merge onto **Route 24 North** for about 37 miles (59.5 km). Take Exit 21A for **I-93 North,** then take Exit 23 for all downtown Boston and North End destinations.

Driving from Cape Cod

60 mi/97 km, 1 hr

Starting at the **Sagamore Bridge,** which links Sandwich and Sagamore across the Cape Cod Canal, follow **Route 3 North.** Use Exit 20B to merge onto to **I-93 North,** remaining on it until Exit 23 for all downtown Boston and North End destinations.

Driving from Coastal Maine

110 mi/177 km, 1.75 hr

From Portland, take **I-295 South** ($1 toll) to **I-95 South** ($4 toll at York Toll Plaza, $2 toll in Portsmouth), which you'll remain on for about 84 miles (135 km); at Exit 46 merge onto **Route 1** South/Newbury St./ Newbury Turnpike, which loops around to join **I-93 South** into downtown Boston. For downtown and North End destinations, take Exit 24.

Driving from the Berkshires

135 mi/217 km, 2 hr

From **Stockbridge,** follow Route 102 East to Lee for about 5 miles (8 km), where you'll use the right lane to merge onto I-90 East. From **Lenox,** drive southeast on Walker Street/Route 183 North and stay right at Lee Road, following signs to Route 7 South. Merge onto **Route 7 South** to Lee.

From **Lee,** you'll take **I-90 East** ($10.90 toll, no cash), remaining on it for about 123 miles (198 km) before taking Exit 24 to merge onto **I-93 North.** Take Exit 23 for all downtown Boston and North End destinations (135 mi/217 km, 2 hrs).

If you're traveling from the northern part of the Berkshires, an alternate, more scenic route includes the Mohawk Trail: Leave **North Adams** on **Route 2 East** to Greenfield; when Route 2 bisects Interstate 91, continue straight onto **Route 2A,** which makes a sharp left turn before rejoining Route 2 a short distance later. From Greenfield through Erving, Route 2 and Route 2A are merged, but follow signs for the Mohawk Trail to continue on Route 2 when the roads diverge after Erving. After passing Concord, merge onto **I-95 South** using the ramp toward Attleboro, then take Exit 25 to

Two Days in Boston

Day 1

Start your day in America's oldest park, **Boston Common,** where you can sip a cup of coffee with a view of the gleaming, gilded **Massachusetts State House.** Get your bearings by following the **Freedom Trail** through the city's most important historic sites, with stops to pay your respects to Paul Revere and John Hancock at the **Granary Burying Ground,** visit the **Old State House** and site of the **Boston Massacre,** and stroll **Faneuil Hall.** By the time you reach the Italian American enclave of **North End,** you'll be ready for a sub sandwich with all the fixings from **Monica's Mercato** followed by a classic North End dessert—choose between a sugar-dusted cannoli from **Modern Pastry** or zesty Italian ice from **Polcari's Coffee** (or try them both).

Boston Common

Get back on the trail for an afternoon in **Charlestown,** where you can tour the **USS *Constitution*** and learn about real-life Rosie the Riveters, then climb to the top of the **Bunker Hill Monument** to get a patriot's-eye view of the entire city. Head back into downtown Boston the easy way, on a ferry ride from the **Charlestown Navy Yard** to the waterfront, then finish the night in one of downtown's creative eateries.

Day 2

Now that you've covered the city's essential sights, slow down at one of Boston's great museums: see Impressionist masterpieces at the **Museum of Fine Arts** and learn about a history-making art heist at the **Isabella Stewart Gardner Museum.** From either museum, walk or bike the **Emerald Necklace** to Jamaica Plain, where you can frolic among hundreds of tree species at **Arnold Arboretum** before refueling with some juicy coconut shrimp and sweet plantains from **Jamaica Mi Hungry.**

For your last afternoon in the city, stock up on picnic supplies for an alfresco lunch in the **Boston Public Garden,** where you can watch the city drift by from a shady patch of grass, then take a lazy turn around the duck lagoon on a classic **swan boat.** When the sun goes down, join the boisterous local scene at one of Boston's many dive bars, where dim lights and televised sports pair well with pints of cheap beer or Irish whiskey. Start at **The Tam** and see where the night takes you, or go colonial-era at **Union Oyster House,** whose stately, wood-accented dining room is the perfect place to slurp locally harvested oysters.

I-90 East ($3.55 toll, no cash). Take Exit 24A to South Station for all downtown Boston and North End destinations (142 mi/228.5 km, 2.75 hrs).

Getting There by Air, Train, or Bus

Air

Flights to Boston's **Logan International Airport** (www.massport.com/logan-airport) are available from almost all major cities. From Logan, ground transportation can be arranged from the information desk at baggage claim. The most efficient way to get into the city is via taxi, though expect to pay a minimum of $30 for downtown locations, or shared van service to downtown and Back Bay for $30-40 per person.

Far cheaper (and almost as quick) are the MBTA Silver Line bus and Blue Line subway (www.mbta.com). Inbound rides on SL1 from Logan Airport to Boston's South Station are free, and leave from stops directly in front of each terminal. Buses leave several times an hour 5am-1am, and reach South Station in 15-25 minutes. If you're continuing to downtown stops or Cambridge you can transfer to the Red Line here. For the Blue Line, which runs from 6am to 12:30pm daily, you can catch the free shuttle bus that offers direct service from the airport departures areas to nearby Airport station. Take the Bowdoin-bound train to State Street station ($2.40 fare, 10-15 minutes) for direct access to downtown Boston and connecting to the Orange Line.

Train

From most destinations, **Amtrak** (South Station, Summer St. and Atlantic Ave., 800/872-7245, www.amtrak.com) runs service to both the South Station and Back Bay Station. (Amtrak trains from all destinations in Maine run to the North Station.) The **Massachusetts Bay Transportation Authority** (617/222-5000, www.mbta.com) also runs commuter rail service from locations in Greater Boston for fares of up to $6.

Bus

Bus service arrives at the South Station. Most U.S. destinations are served by **Greyhound** (800/231-2222, www.greyhound.com). However, smaller bus companies also run from various locations around the region, such as the **FlixBus** (855/626-8585, www.flixbus.com), **Concord Coach Lines** (800/639-3317, www.concordcoachlines.com), and **Peter Pan Bus** (800/343-9999, www.peterpanbus.com).

Sights

Beacon Hill

Federal-style row houses and narrow brick sidewalks make this compact district one of the most charming historic neighborhoods. The Black Heritage Trail goes right through the neighborhood, which also contains some of the earliest stops on the Freedom Trail. It's worth taking some time to simply wander, discovering picturesque Acorn Street, spotting the characteristic rippled purple glass in some of Beacon Hill's oldest homes, and making like a local in a café on Charles Street.

TOP EXPERIENCE

★ Freedom Trail

John Hancock, Sam Adams, Paul Revere—history has given the names of America's revolutionaries a nobility and purpose that might have surprised those early Bostonians. In fact, the months leading up to the War for Independence must have seemed more haphazard insurrection than organized battle for freedom to those who lived through them. Even in today's Boston, the passionate men and women who agitated for independence are vivid and accessible. It's easy to get drawn into the stories—both those that have become legendary and those that are less known.

From the picnic greens of **Boston Common** to the towering sails of the **USS *Constitution*,** a red line on the sidewalk connects 16 historic sites, with frequent descriptive markers, on a 2.5-mile (4-km) walking trail ideal for getting your bearings in the city. Pick up a map at the **Boston Common Visitor Center** or the trail website (www.thefreedomtrail.org) and make your way from the common to a series of churches, graveyards, and other early landmarks in downtown, then continue through the Italian American neighborhood of **North End** to visit **Paul Revere's House** and the church where

Beacon Hill and Boston Common

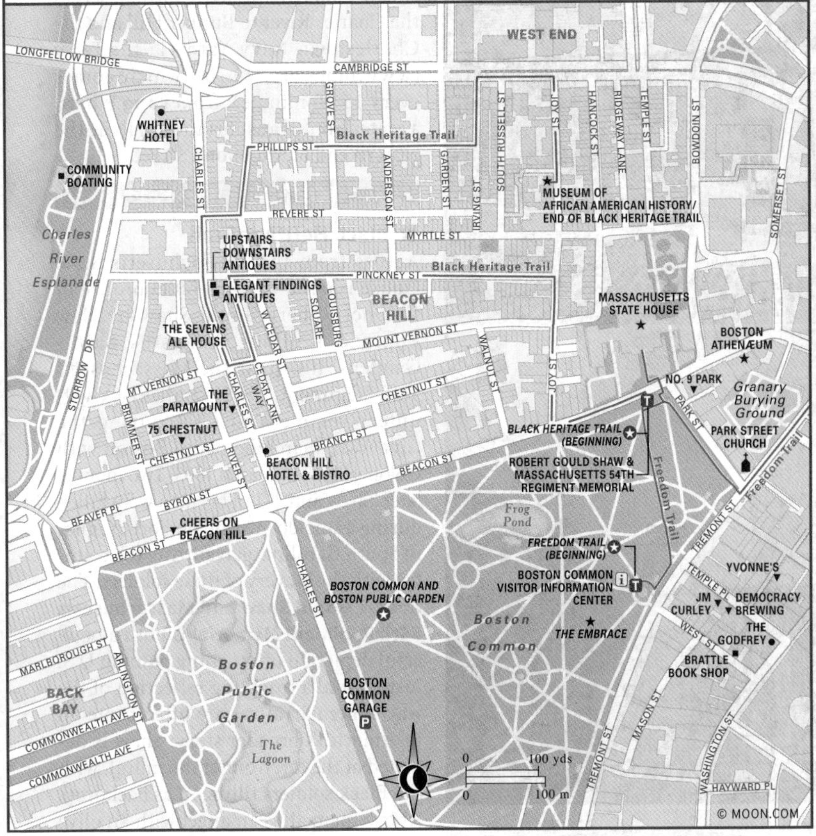

signal lights for Revolutionary commanders were hung.

The trail then crosses the Charles River to the **Charlestown Navy Yard** and **Bunker Hill Monument,** where climbing 294 steep steps earns you panoramic views of the city from the top of a giant obelisk.

Visitors can walk the line themselves or take a 90-minute **guided tour** offered by the Freedom Trail Foundation (Boston Common Visitor Information Center, 148 Tremont St., 617/357-8300, www.thefreedomtrail.org, $17 adults, $15 students and seniors, $8 children) that covers the first 11 sites along the route; guides are costumed actors playing lesser-known patriots. This is a good place to meet William Dawes, the "other" midnight rider; Abigail Adams, the intellectual letter writer and future first lady; or James Otis, who gave fiery, pro bono legal representation to colonists challenging British laws in court. The National Park Service (NPS, www.nps.gov/bost) also leads **free tours** and offers talks at sites along the Freedom Trail; check the website for schedules.

Perhaps the best way to take in the trail is to book the morning tour with the NPS

or the Freedom Trail Foundation, then stop for lunch and an Italian ice in the North End. After lunch, continue across the Charles River to Bunker Hill and the Charlestown Navy Yard via the **ferry** (www.mbta.org, $3.70), which comes every 15-30 minutes, from **Long Wharf,** a waterfront transportation hub at the eastern end of Richmond Street.

TOP EXPERIENCE

★ Black Heritage Trail

Across from the Massachusetts State House is a life-size bas-relief bronze of Colonel Robert Gould Shaw by New England sculptor Augustus Saint-Gaudens. It depicts the Massachusetts 54th Regiment, the first all-Black volunteer regiment to fight during the Civil War, marching out of Boston with Colonel Shaw in March 1863. Two months later, Shaw and 271 of his men were killed during a suicide mission on Fort Wagner in South Carolina, galvanizing the country with the bravery of these soldiers. The **Robert Gould Shaw and Massachusetts 54th Regiment Memorial** is both a powerful depiction of a turning point in U.S. history and a troubling reflection of the way white narratives are often centered in America's broader story: Shaw is depicted at the forefront of the mural, with the Black soldiers filling in as backdrop. Above them all is an angel with an olive branch, symbolizing peace, and poppies, symbolizing death, and the inscription *"Omnia Relinquit Servare Rempublicam,"* which means "He gives up everything to serve the republic."

The memorial is the beginning of the **Black Heritage Trail** (www.maah.org/boston_heritage_trail), which traces the separate journey to freedom of African Americans, nearly 100 years after the events of the first Freedom Trail. Plaques

Top to bottom: Paul Revere's House; interior of the African Meeting House; the Robert Gould Shaw and Massachusetts 54th Regiment Memorial

at historic houses en route detail the lives of abolitionists and orators who lived on the back side of Beacon Hill, where Boston's more than 1,000 free African Americans lived and worked by the turn of the 19th century. Follow the trail to the end to visit the **African Meeting House,** once headquarters of the New England Anti-Slavery Society. Considered the "Black Faneuil Hall," the church now houses the **Museum of African American History,** which has exhibits and films dedicated to the story of Boston's abolitionists. The trail is also part of the **Boston African American National Historic Site** (617/742-5415, www.nps.gov/boaf), and the National Park Service runs free 90-minute tours along the route. You can also pick up a map of the trail at the **Museum of African American History** (46 Joy St., 617/725-0022, www.maah.org, Tues.-Sat. 10am-4pm) or find one on the National Park Service app.

Museum of African American History

Small but fascinating, the **Museum of African American History** (46 Joy St., 617/725-0022, www.maah.org, Tues.-Sat. 10am-4pm, $10 adults, $8 seniors and youth 13-14, under 13 free) has exhibits and films dedicated to the story of Boston's abolitionists. See the pulpit where Frederick Douglass recruited for the Massachusetts 54th Regiment, learn about the lives of activist pastors, and trace the roots of some of the United States' most prominent African American writers and thinkers to local Boston neighborhoods. It's worth seeing this museum as part of the free, National Park Service-run tours of the **Black Heritage Trail** (617/742-5415, www.nps.gov/boaf).

Massachusetts State House

On a sunny day, the shimmering gold dome of the state's capitol building can be seen from miles around. The brick building beneath it is the tidy federal-style structure of the **Massachusetts State House** (24 Beacon St., 617/727-3676, www.sec.state.ma.us/trs, tours Mon.-Fri. 10am-3:30pm, free), designed by prominent Boston architect Charles Bullfinch and built in 1798. At the time, 15 white columns were pulled up Beacon Street in a procession of 15 white horses, one for each state. The wooden dome on top was sheathed in copper by Revolutionary renaissance man Paul Revere in 1802, then covered with 23-karat gold leaf in 1948. Two marble wings were added at the turn of the 20th century.

An impressive selection of statues graces the park side of the building. The towering statue of John F. Kennedy by the main entrance was created by local sculptor Isabel McIlvain and was recently moved closer to the street for better visibility. In front of the wings are statues of two prominent women colonists: Anne Hutchinson, a freethinking Puritan who was banished to Rhode Island after nettling local ministers, and Mary Dyer, a prominent Quaker minister condemned for her religion and hanged on Boston Common in 1660.

Boston Athenaeum

The center of Boston's intellectual life during the early 19th century, this private library was a favorite of scholars like Ralph Waldo Emerson and Oliver Wendell Holmes, who gathered to debate the political and philosophical issues of the day. Today, docents offer tours of the renovated **Boston Athenaeum** (10 Beacon St., 617/227-0270, www.bostonathenaeum.org, Mon.-Thurs. 9am-8pm, Fri.-Sat. 9am-5pm, $10 adults, $8 students and military, $5 children under 12), including the study where Nathaniel Hawthorne reportedly saw the ghost of onetime library regular Reverend Harris (Hawthorne mused that the good reverend might have stopped by to read his own obituary). Among the library's more unusual holdings are the private library of George Washington and one of the

That's Weird. . .

Massachusetts State House's golden dome

In Massachusetts, fish are a big deal, and not just on the culinary circuit. The Wampanoag people were hauling haddock and clams from the local waters long before European colonists showed up and initiated a more extractive, market-driven relationship with the natural world here. Over centuries, the fish has been a staple of New England culture and commerce. And you don't need to take my word for it. Look no further than the centuries-old relic hanging in the Massachusetts House of Representatives today (24 Beacon St., https://malegislature.gov). Known as the **Sacred Cod,** this five-foot-long (1.5-m) codfish sculpture, carved from pine and installed in 1784, is a shrine to New England's most iconic fish.

So beloved is the Sacred Cod that a 1933 theft (or "cod-napping") of the sculpture prompted state officials to dig through silt at the bottom of a local lake, on a tip that the Sacred Cod might have been chucked in! (To everyone's relief, it was eventually dropped off on the state house lawn in a flower box.)

The Sacred Cod isn't the only display of fishy dedication. Not to be outmatched for homage, the Massachusetts State Senate erected its own marine relic: a bronze fish casting that hangs from the chandelier in the Senate chamber. Its name? The Holy Mackerel.

Stop by the **Massachusetts State House** for all the fish-based enthusiasm mixed with local government you can handle.

world's largest collections of books about the Romany people. Art & Architecture tours of the library are offered Tuesday and Thursday at 3pm, Sunday at 1pm, and Monday at 5:30pm.

Park Street Church

The white-steepled church at the corner of Park and Tremont Streets looks particularly dramatic with a backdrop of downtown high-rises and has been a beloved landmark since its completion in 1809—the novelist Henry James once called it "the most interesting mass of brick and mortar in America." As legend has it, **Park Street Church** (1 Park St., 617/523-3383, www.parkstreet.org, mid-June-Aug. Tues.-Sat. 9:30am-3pm) was known as "brimstone corner" during the War of 1812 for the great stores of gunpowder in the basement, and the song "America (My Country 'Tis of Thee)" was sung on the steps of the church on July 4, 1831, its first public performance.

Granary Burying Ground

Three signers of the Declaration of Independence are interred in the tiny **Granary Burying Ground** (Tremont St. between School St. and Park St., daily 9am-4pm) surrounded by gleaming commercial buildings: Samuel Adams, John Hancock, and Robert Treat Paine. You'll also find Paul Revere, Ben Franklin's parents, and the victims of the Boston Massacre here, though this was far from being a cemetery for the elite—historians believe more than 5,000 people were buried here, some in mass burial sites like the crowded Infants Tomb. Many of the gravestones date from the 17th century, weather-beaten stone slabs inscribed with moving (and sometimes flippant) epitaphs and winged death skulls.

★ Boston Common and Boston Public Garden

Boston Common

Boston Common (139 Tremont St.) began its life as a sheep and cow pasture in 1634, just a few years after the city itself was founded. These days, the Common feels like the city's collective backyard, with space for throwing Frisbees, spreading out picnics, and playing in the grass.

Several monuments within the park are attractions in and of themselves. The stunning fountain located just a few steps down from Park Street toward Boylston is named **Brewer Fountain,** a bronze replica of a fountain exhibited at the Paris World's Fair of 1855. The objects on its base depict sea gods and goddesses Neptune, Amphitrite, Acis, and Galatea. Opposite the gold-domed statehouse is the **Robert Gould Shaw and Massachusetts 54th Regiment Memorial,** a bas-relief by Augustus Saint-Gaudens that depicts the

Top to bottom: sculpture at the Frog Pond in Boston Common by David Phillips; Boston Public Garden; swan boats

first all-Black volunteer regiment in the Union army. By the Park Street subway station at the east end of the Common, visitors regularly congregate around ***The Embrace,*** an enormous bronze sculpture by Hank Willis Thomas, which recreates the moment when Dr. Martin Luther King Jr. and Coretta Scott King held each other, arm-in-arm, upon learning that the former had just won a Nobel Peace Prize. Near the intersection of Park and Beacon Streets, the **Frog Pond** is an ice-skating rink in winter and a shallow fountain in summer, when it fills with kids cooling off. On the Tremont Street side, at the intersection with Boylston, the **Francis Parkman Bandstand** is used as the site for summer concerts, political rallies, and **Shakespeare in the Park** (www.commshakes.org).

Boston Public Garden

In contrast to Boston Common's open, parklike feel, the **Boston Public Garden** (4 Charles St.), right next door, is an intimate outdoor space, full of leafy trees and flower beds. Built on landfill in the 19th century, the garden was the country's first public botanical garden, envisioned by its creators as a respite from urban life. It's especially romantic at sunset, when the trees cast mysterious shadows over the walkways. The centerpiece is a lagoon, which is crossed by a fairy-tale bridge and surrounded by willow trees trailing their branch tips in the water—note the tiny island in the center of the lagoon, which is used by ducks that pad up out of the water on an adorable, ducks-only ramp. Tracing lazy circles in the lagoon are Boston's famous **swan boats** (617/522-1966, www.swanboats.com, mid-Apr.-mid-June daily 10am-4pm, mid-June-early Sept. daily 10am-5pm, $4.50 adults, $4 seniors, $3 children 2-15), a flotilla of six large paddleboats with the graceful white birds at the stern. The boats are a mandatory attraction if you are in Boston with children, as are the nearby bronze statues of Mrs. Mallard and her eight little ducklings. The statues pay homage to Robert McCloskey's children's book *Make Way for Ducklings,* which was partially set in the Boston Public Garden.

Downtown and the Waterfront

Downtown is where Boston's history and cutting edge coexist, an easily walkable district where colonial sites are densely packed amid skyscrapers. While not as picture-perfect as Beacon Hill, it's the heart of the action. The waterfront is pedestrian-friendly, lined with parks, restaurants, and attractions. Just east of Boston Common, the Downtown Crossing area has mega stores, boutiques, and landmark theaters.

King's Chapel

Boston's original Anglican church, **King's Chapel** (Tremont and School Streets, 617/523-1749, www.kings-chapel.org, Mon. and Wed.-Sat. 10am-5pm, Sun. 1:30pm-5pm, $5 suggested donation), was founded in 1686, but the current stone church building dates to 1749 and holds a bell cast by Paul Revere that is still rung before services. The adjoining graveyard is the oldest in Boston; as such, it contains the graves of some of the original colonists of Massachusetts, including Governor John "City on A Hill" Winthrop, and Anne Prine, said to be the real Hester Prynne on whom Nathaniel Hawthorne based his book *The Scarlet Letter.* There's a fascinating "Bells and Bones" **tour** of the church's bell tower and 200-year-old crypt (617/523-1749, tours at 10am, 11am, noon, 1pm, 2pm, 3pm, and 4pm, $10 adults, $8 seniors, students, and military, $5 children under 13).

Old South Meeting House

The Boston Tea Party may have ended in the harbor, but it started at the brick church building with a gray-shingled tower known as the **Old South Meeting House** (310 Washington St., 617/482-6439, www.oldsouthmeetinghouse.org,

Downtown, Waterfront, and North End

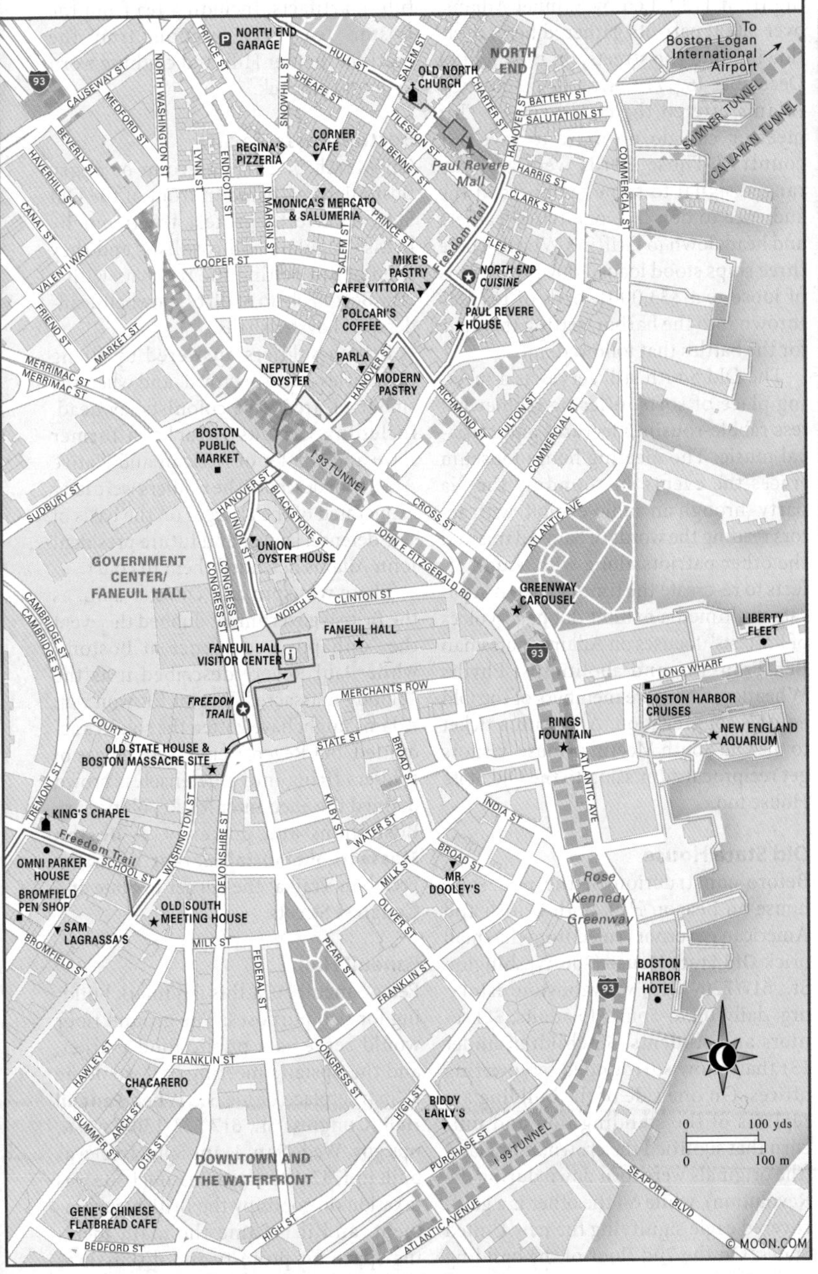

daily 10am-5pm, $15 adults, $14 seniors and students, $8 children under 13), dating from 1729. Led by Samuel Adams, over 5,000 patriots gathered here, overflowing into the streets, on the night of December 16, 1773. After fiery speeches, Adams uttered the code words: "This meeting can do no more to save our country." Those words were a prearranged signal to some members in the audience to don face paint and feathers and head down to Griffin's Wharf, where three ships stood loaded down with bins of loose tea; $33,000 worth of tea was thrown into the harbor, setting the stage for the battles that followed.

The Old South still serves as a meeting place of sorts, offering (somewhat less rabble-rousing) lectures and classical music. The meeting house museum traces the events surrounding the tea party through an audio exhibit, with actors reading the words of Sam Adams and the other patriots along with sound effects to re-create the time period. A separate multimedia exhibit dubbed "Voices of Protests" focuses on Adams, statesman Ben Franklin, and abolitionist Phyllis Wheatley, who were members of the Old South's congregation. And with a ticket to the Old South Meeting House, visitors get reciprocal admission to the Old State House too.

Old State House

Before construction of the new state house on Beacon Hill, both British and American governors ruled from the small brick **Old State House** (206 Washington St., 617/720-1713, www.bostonhistory.org, daily 10am-5pm, $15 adults, $14 seniors and students, $8 children under 13) that's now surrounded by towering offices. On one side of the building are replicas of the standing lion and unicorn that signified the crown of England (the originals were torn down during the Revolution), while on the other is a gold-covered eagle signifying the new United States. On the 2nd floor of the building is the headquarters for the Bostonian Society, which runs a small museum full of artifacts, including tea from the Boston Tea Party, weapons from the Battle of Bunker Hill, and clothing worn by John Hancock.

Boston Massacre Site

On March 5, 1770, a group of angry Bostonians gathered in front of the Old State House to protest treatment by British regulars and royalists, and they soon began pelting the redcoats with a *very* Boston blend of dirty snowballs, cinders, and oyster shells.

British soldiers answered by firing their rifles into the crowd, and when the smoke cleared, five colonists lay dead, including Crispus Attucks, a former slave and whaler of African and Native American descent. The soldiers were later exonerated of the charges on the basis of self-defense; lawyer and future president John Adams defended them in court.

There was spin and counter-spin, as the British government dubbed the event the "unhappy occurrence at Boston," while Paul Revere described it as the "bloody massacre." Patriot PR won out: Adams might have gotten the soldiers acquitted, but Revere's engraved images of soldiers firing into a defenseless crowd defined the encounter for Revolutionary Bostonians and posterity. A **Boston Massacre memorial marker** is on the Freedom Trail at the corner of State and Congress Streets.

Faneuil Hall

Peter Faneuil built this landmark building for two purposes: The ground floor would serve as a public food market, and the upstairs meeting hall would be a "marketplace of ideas." When **Faneuil Hall** (Congress St., 617/523-1300, www.nps.gov, Wed.-Sun. 11am-5pm, free) was built in 1742, the most pressing issue was taxation on goods by the British government, and it became the main meeting space for protests and discussions by the Sons of Liberty—earning it the nickname the "Cradle of Liberty." After it was expanded in size by architect Charles Bullfinch, the hall was also the main venue for talks by William Lloyd Garrison, Frederick Douglass, and other antislavery activists. Public talks and citywide meetings are still held in the upstairs hall, lent more gravitas by the huge mural of Daniel Webster arguing against enslavement that overlooks the stage. During the day, historical talks are given by National Park Service rangers every half hour.

New England Aquarium

The centerpiece of the massive waterfront **New England Aquarium** (Central Wharf, 617/973-5200, www.neaq.org, daily 9am-6pm, $34 adults, $32 seniors, $25 children 3-11, free children under 3, IMAX $10 adults, $8 seniors and children 3-11, whale watch $65 adults, $57 seniors, $45 children 3-11, free children under 3) is a 200,000-gallon tank full of sharks, sea turtles, and giant ocean fish that rises like a watery spinal column through the center of the building. A long walkway spirals around the tank, giving viewers a chance to see sealife on all levels of the ocean, from the toothy pikes that float on the surface to the 550-pound, 95-year-old sea turtle, Myrtle, often spotted snoozing on the floor. Other crowd-pleasers are the harbor seals in the courtyard and enormous open-air penguin pool, occupied by three dozen rockhopper, little blue, and African penguins who fill the building with their raucous cries. The aquarium even ventures out into the harbor itself for whale-watching trips, seeking out the humpbacks and right whales that make their way into Massachusetts Bay.

North End

Everyone from tour guides to locals will tell you the same thing about this historic neighborhood: "It's just like being in Italy!" The truth is, though, there's something essentially Bostonian about the Italian American North End—the home of the Celtics basketball team as well as numerous pastry shops, old-fashioned grocers, and classic red-sauce joints.

The area is the oldest part of the city, and its history overflows with Puritans and revolutionaries, including Paul Revere, whose house still stands. But by the mid-19th century it was run-down and crime-ridden. Poor Irish immigrants settled here after fleeing famines at home and were joined by a wave of Jewish immigrants and, finally, the Italians, who reshaped the neighborhood in the image of Genoa, Palermo, Milan, and Naples.

Even as it has gentrified over the years, the North End has retained its cultural identity, with third- and fourth-generation Italians returning on Italian feast days, when churches and community clubs try to outdo each other with lavish parades full of floats, bunting, and sizzling Italian sausage. It's a fascinating place to eat, drink, and explore: With a cannoli in hand, taking in colonial architecture and dodging Boston traffic, you wouldn't mistake it for anywhere else in the world.

Paul Revere House

Every town in New England claims to have a Paul Revere bell in its belfry or a dusty bit of Revere silver in its historical museum. The patriot who made the famous midnight ride to warn the suburbs of the British march, however, was virtually unknown until before the Civil War, when Massachusetts poet Henry Wadsworth Longfellow made him the subject of a poem to stir up passion for the Union cause. And he wasn't the only rider out that night. At least two other riders, William Dawes and Dr. Samuel Prescott, were also out warning the colonists.

Whatever the details of Revere's famous night, he was a riveting one-man band of the colonial world who earned his living as a silversmith, coppersmith, bell ringer, and dentist. He raised many of his 16 children in the house that still bears his name. The **Paul Revere House** (19 North Sq., 617/523-2338, www.paulreverehouse.org, mid-Apr.-Oct. daily 10am-5:15pm, Nov.-mid-Apr. 10am-4:15pm, $6 adults, $5.50 seniors and students, $1 children 5-17, free children under 5) is a typical example of 17th-century architecture and the oldest house still standing in downtown Boston. The house doesn't have many artifacts—the Museum of Fine Arts is the best place to go to see Revere silver—but it's an interesting window into the living quarters and implements of a typical family in colonial urban North America.

Old North Church

Paul Revere was a bell ringer in the landmark **Old North Church** (193 Salem St., 617/858-8231, www.oldnorth.com, Tues.-Sat. 10am-5pm, $5 adults, $5 seniors, military, and students, $3 children 6-8, free under 6) when he was a child, so he knew just where to hang his signal lights to warn the rebels that the British were moving by sea to Charlestown, then on to Concord and Lexington. The church sexton, Robert Newman, was the unsung hero in the story—he was arrested by the British the following morning and held in prison until freed by General George Washington in an exchange. Inside the church, reproductions of colonial flags hang from the ceiling, and every half hour a guide tells Revere's story from the pulpit.

Between Old North and Hanover Street is the **Paul Revere Mall,** with a huge bronze statue of Revere on his horse, keeping watch over pigeons and wizened Italian ladies. Look for the plaques along the wall that honor other patriots who grew up in the North End or tell the stories of some of the original Puritan settlers of the neighborhood, including theologians Cotton and Increase Mather, governor John Winthrop, and Ann Pollard, the first woman settler to arrive in Boston.

statue of Paul Revere and the Old North Church

Charlestown

The original settlement of the Puritans was named after the king they left behind. A swampy mess of a place without much access to fresh water, Charlestown was eventually abandoned when John Winthrop and company were invited over to the Shawmut Peninsula to found Boston. Charlestown, which is incorporated as a neighborhood of Boston, grew to be an important port in the 18th century. Then tragedy struck during the Revolutionary War, when the British fired cannonballs filled with incendiary oil across the channel and burned the city to the ground in retaliation for their losses at the Battle of Bunker Hill.

The city was rebuilt in the early 19th century about the same time as the brick mansions and brownstones were going up on Beacon Hill, and it shares that neighborhood's historic, cozy feel. Gas lamps, black shutters, and window boxes abound in the neighborhood that winds up toward the Bunker Hill Monument.

Bunker Hill Monument

High on the top of Breed's Hill stands the 221-foot (67-m) granite obelisk of the **Bunker Hill Monument** (Monument Square, 617/242-5641, www.nps.gov/bost/historyculture/bhm.htm, July-early Sept. Wed.-Sun. 10am-5:30pm, Sept.-Oct. Wed.-Sun. 11am-5pm, Nov.-May Wed.-Sun. 1pm-4:30pm, June Wed.-Sun. 11am-5pm, free) to mark the misnamed first major battle of the Revolutionary War. In it, the patriots—while defeated—inflicted such high casualties upon the British army that thousands rushed to the colonial cause to begin a protracted siege of Boston. Climb the 294 steep, winding steps to the top of the monument for fine views of Boston Harbor and the city skyline.

Across the street, the impressive **Bunker Hill Museum** (43 Monument Sq., June Wed.-Sun. 10am-5pm, July-early Sept. Wed.-Sun. 10am-5:30pm, early Sept.-Oct. Wed.-Sun. 10am-5pm, Nov.-May Wed.-Sun. 10am-4:30pm, free) opened in 2007 with two floors of exhibits about the battle. In addition to artifacts such as a British cannonball, the museum features two dioramas with miniature figurines that perpetually fight the battle over again with the help of a sound and light display. The highlight, however, is the beautifully painted "cyclorama" on the 2nd floor, depicting the battle in breathtaking 360 degrees.

USS *Constitution*

The oldest commissioned ship in the American Navy, the **USS *Constitution***—also known as "Old Ironsides"—was named by President Washington and launched in 1798. In 17 years of active duty, it racked up a battle record as celebrated as any ship of its time, defeating the heavier British ships *Guerrière* and *Java* during the War of 1812, and leading a blockade of Tripoli during the War of

the Barbary Coast. She's now docked at Charlestown Navy Yard, where sailors give tours every half hour; it's thrilling to stand behind a long cannon on the gun deck or sit at the gambrel table in the captain's quarters. The last time the *Constitution* detached from a tugboat to sail freely under its own power was in 1997 during its 200th anniversary; the ship, however, is towed out into Boston Harbor and turned around with a 21-gun salute every year on July 4. (Members of the public can sign up on the ship's website for a lottery to board the ship for these cruises.)

Get the background on the ships and the naval yard at the **Charlestown Naval Yard Visitors Center** (Charlestown Navy Yard, Building 5, 617/242-5601, www.nps.gov/bost/historyculture/cny.htm, June-Oct. Wed.-Sun. 10am-5pm, Nov.-May Wed.-Sun. 10am-4pm), which features a 10-minute video on the history of the yard, along with ropes, chains, uniforms,

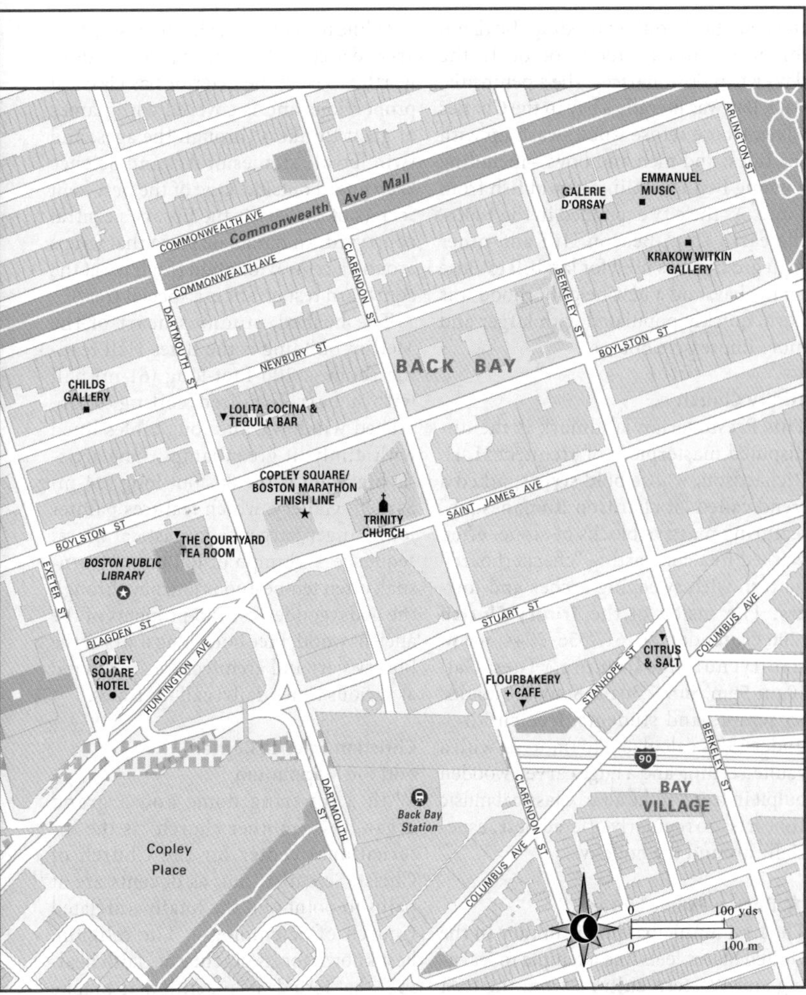

and other artifacts. Near the ship is a much larger **USS *Constitution* Museum** (Charlestown Navy Yard, 617/426-1812, www.ussconstitutionmuseum.org, daily 10am-5pm, $10 adults, $5 children) that displays swords, pistols, and cannonballs captured from the *Constitution*'s various engagements, along with a giant model of the ship under full sail. Kids love the upper floor of the museum, which features a cannon they can swab, wad, and "fire" against an enemy ship.

Fenway and Back Bay

Back Bay

In the most fashionable neighborhood in Boston, Back Bay's grand boulevards are lined with brownstones and large Victorian-style apartment buildings, linked by short side streets that are ordered alphabetically (Arlington, Berkeley, Clarendon...). Ironically, given how swanky the neighborhood has become, the area used to be one big disease-spreading swamp—it's no accident that the neighborhood's main drag, Boylston Street, is named after a doctor. In the days when Boston used to be a peninsula, Back Bay was literally a bay in the Charles River, where refuse would wash up with the tides, and men and boys—including a young Ben Franklin—would fish from shore. As the city expanded in the 1800s, the earth from Beacon Hill and other high ground was used for landfill to close up the bay, and a new neighborhood was born, quickly populated with larger and more impressive houses.

Trinity Church

This Presbyterian landmark is the undisputed masterpiece of architect H. H. Richardson, whose bold style sparked a trend called "Richardson Romanesque" featuring massive blocks of stone, often worked in a contrasting "checkerboard" pattern with sweeping arches and towers. The inside of the **Trinity Church** (206 Clarendon St., 617/536-0944, www.trinitychurchboston.org, Tues.-Sat. 10am-5pm, Sun. 7:30am-8pm, $10 adults, $8 seniors and students, free children under 13) is calculated to impress, with a vaulted ceiling and a huge carved wooden pulpit in front of the altar. Classical music concerts are regularly offered here, especially around the holidays.

★ Boston Public Library

The first municipal public library in the United States feels like a temple to learning and Western culture, from the bust of Athena watching over the entryway to stunning murals depicting vivid mythological scenes. The **Boston Public Library** (700 Boylston St., 617/536-5400, www.bpl.org, Mon.-Thurs. 9am-8pm, Fri.-Sat. 9am-5pm, Sun. 11am-5pm, free) fills two city blocks on the south side of Copley Square, dividing its treasures into two buildings. The original, designed by Charles McKim and opened in 1895, is now the research library, with a more modern building next door holding the circulating collection.

While the library's collection is vast, its art and architecture make it destination-worthy as well; the exterior has classical proportions and is covered with names of great thinkers through the ages, and twin female statues of Art and Science keep guard outside. One of the best-kept secrets of the city is the library's central courtyard, an Italianate plaza that wraps around a central fountain (high tea at the courtyard restaurant is a special treat).

The hushed, studious heart of the McKim building is the Bates Hall reading room, a 200-foot-long (61-m) hall with a barrel-vaulted ceiling; high, arched windows; and long tables lined with dimly lit green lamps. One artistic highlight is the 80-foot-long (24-m) Sargent Gallery, which features painter John Singer Sargent's fantastical mural sequence "Triumph of Religion," a sensual, often tempestuous journey through the gods, goddesses, and prophets of the ancient world. Free hour-long tours of the library's art and architecture are offered at various times daily; call for times.

Christian Science Center and the Mapparium

With a towering dome and a grand organ, this "mother church" is the international center for the Church of Christ, Scientist (not, as docents are at pains to point out, the totally unrelated Church of Scientology). The religion, best known for its practice of "faith healing" that forbids its practitioners to take medicine for illnesses, was founded in 1879 by Mary Baker Eddy—a leader of the early women's movement and a pioneering publisher who launched *The Christian Science Monitor* newspaper. The Christian Science Center features a unique homage to the global outreach of the *Monitor*. The **Mapparium** (200 Massachusetts Ave., 617/450-7000, www.marybakereddylibrary.org, Mon.-Sat. 10am-5pm, Sun. 11am-5pm, $6 adults, $4 seniors, students, and youth 6-17, free children under 6) is a 30-foot-diameter globe with the countries of the world (circa 1935) displayed in vibrant stained glass around the walls. Standing on a clear bridge in the center offers a remarkable perspective on a globe whose borders have been dramatically rewritten by more than 80 years of conflict. Twenty-minute tours of the Mapparium include a seven-minute light show with inspirational soundbites from Nelson Mandela, Eleanor Roosevelt, and other seminal thinkers.

Fenway

Upon first glance, the area of the city known as the Fenway doesn't seem to offer much. A gritty network of streets lined with pubs and discount stores, the neighborhood has traditionally been the stomping grounds for students of nearby Boston University. Scratch beneath the surface, however, and you'll find several of the city's premier cultural attractions, including the Museum of Fine Arts, the jewelbox Isabella Stewart Gardner Museum, and the crossroads of Boston's epic "Emerald Necklace" park network. The neighborhood gets its name from the Back Bay Fens, a winding, swampy greensward that serves as the drainage channel for the city. Today, the Fens is a rambling parkland, lined with ball fields and community gardens, including the hidden Kelleher Rose Garden, a dreamy garden full of vine-covered trellises and over 100 varieties of roses. The center of the neighborhood is Kenmore Square, a lively crossroads of student bars, discount stores, and burrito joints, just down the street from the historic home of the Boston Red Sox: Fenway Park.

★ Fenway Park

A new banner was flapping in the breeze here after the Red Sox's come-from-behind sprint to win the 2004 World

Top to bottom: game day at Fenway Park; courtyard at the Isabella Stewart Gardner Museum; Museum of Fine Arts

Fenway

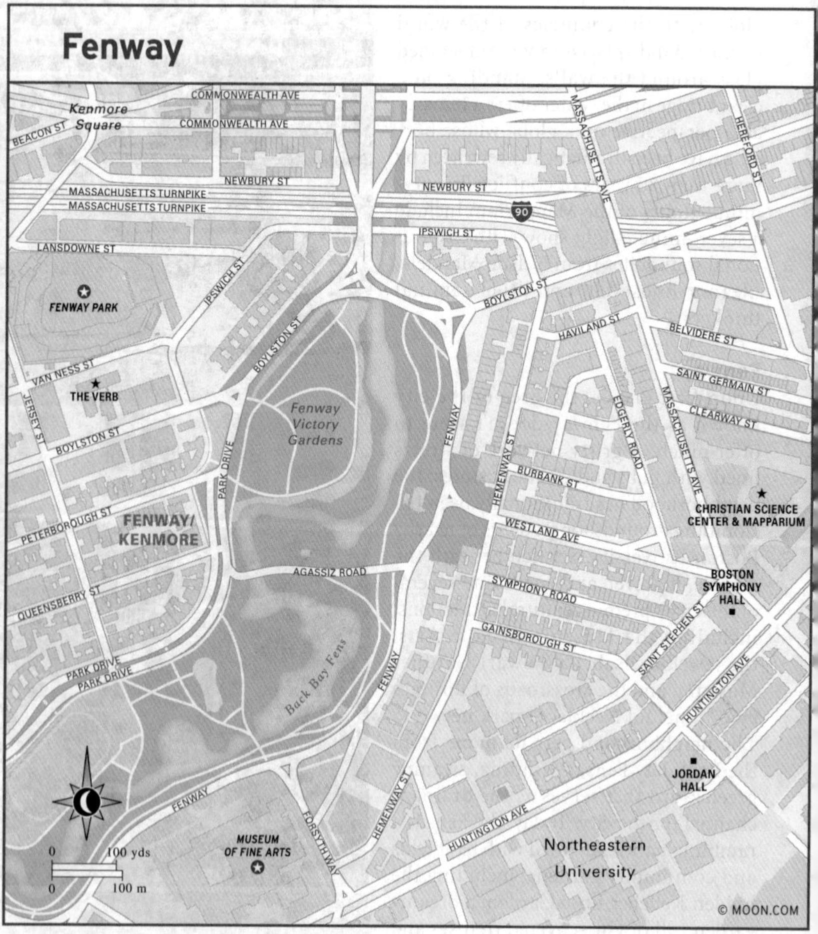

Series. While the high of that victory infused **Fenway Park** (4 Yawkey Way, 617/226-6666, www.redsox.com, tours Apr.-Oct. 9am-5pm, Nov.-Mar. 10am-5pm, hrs differ on game days, $25 adults, $17 military and children 3-12) with a new energy, Fenway has long been one of the most electric places to catch the national pastime. First opened in 1912, Fenway has a soul that none of the more modern parks can match. For the uninitiated, the geography of the park—with its Green Monster, Pesky's Pole, and Ted Williams's seat—can seem a little arcane, but you can get your bearings with a tour led by one of the Fenway faithful. As good as those tours may be, however, nothing quite beats taking a seat in the bleachers, grabbing a Sam Adams, and waiting for the first crack of the bat.

★ Museum of Fine Arts

This grand, neoclassical museum's art collection is one of the best and most beloved in the country. The MFA, as it's known, is particularly noted for its French Impressionist works, but it also has outstanding Asian and Egyptian collections, as well as many celebrated early American paintings and artifacts. The **Museum of Fine Arts** (465 Huntington Ave., 617/267-9300, www.mfa.org, Sat.-Mon. and Wed. 10am-5pm, Thurs.-Fri. 10am-10pm, $27 adults, $10 youth 7-17, free children under 7, active military, and veteran families from Memorial Day to Labor Day) began its life as the painting collection of the Boston Athenaeum, the private library on Beacon Hill. Under its current leadership, the museum has taken some gambles to bring more modern viewers into the galleries, staging artistic exhibitions of guitars and race cars alongside showstopping special exhibits featuring masterpieces by Monet, Van Gogh, and Gauguin.

At present, most visitors to the MFA make a beeline for the 2nd floor, which is home to several jaw-dropping rooms dedicated to works by French Impressionists Monet, Manet, Renoir, Van Gogh, and others. Less trafficked but equally rewarding are the American galleries, where you'll find what's arguably the most famous American painting ever: Gilbert Stuart's original unfinished painting of George Washington. The collection includes several paintings by John Singer Sargent, including the arresting *Daughters of Edward Darley Bolt,* as well as those by Boston's own adopted artist, John Singleton Copley, including his portrait of Paul Revere. Tours of various collections within the museum are offered free with admission throughout the day.

Isabella Stewart Gardner Museum

The small **Isabella Stewart Gardner Museum** (280 The Fenway, 617/566-1401, www.gardnermuseum.org, Mon. and Wed. 11am-5pm, Thurs. 11am-9pm, Fri. 11am-5pm, Sat.-Sun. 10am-5pm, $20 adults, $18 seniors, $13 students, free youth under 18) is filled with priceless European and American paintings. The most cherished work of art, however, may be the building itself, which is constructed around a plant-filled Italianate courtyard that may be the most pleasing indoor space in the city. The namesake socialite who built the museum was known as something of a brilliant eccentric who loved art and the Red Sox, and scandalized polite society by posing for a sensuous portrait by John Singer Sargent. On display in the museum, the portrait was exhibited only once in Gardner's lifetime due to the wishes of her husband.

The building, where Gardner lived, has four floors of artwork organized as a living house museum, with some of the original typed labels still in place. The museum made headlines around the world for what's often called the largest art heist in history: As St. Patrick's Day revelers filled the streets during the early hours of March 18, 1990, two thieves disguised as police officers stole 13 works of art, including two Rembrandts and a stunning Vermeer. The empty frames for the stolen paintings still hang on the wall, and a five-million-dollar reward has never been collected. Charmingly, anyone named Isabella gets free entry to the museum for life.

South End

Running along the southern edge of Fenway, Back Bay, and downtown, Boston's South End neighborhood doesn't have iconic sights, but with brick Victorian houses and a booming arts community, it's a fascinating place to wander. Pleasant parks with community gardens are filled with young families, and the hotel and restaurant options that spill out along the northern edge are a short walk away from downtown and Back Bay.

The Cyclorama

Not many people have experienced a cyclorama painting or photograph—a panoramic artwork that completely encircles the viewer, giving them a sense of 360-degree immersion in the art. Back in 1884, Boston-based cyclorama manufacturer Charles F. Willoughby commissioned a venue uniquely designed to display these massive, dramatic images. The resultant building was aptly named **The Cyclorama** (539 Tremont St., 617/426-5001, www.bostonarts.org, Mon.-Fri. 9am-5pm, closed to the public during private events). Located on one of the South End's busiest streets, and now under the care of the Boston Center for the Arts (BCA), The Cyclorama's interior is a stunning artwork itself. The circular exhibit hall's massive domed ceiling is festooned with twisted pipes and metal scaffolding, with a skylight at the center of the dome.

The Cyclorama's offerings have expanded far beyond cycloramas. On any given weekend at The Cyclorama, you could stumble into a performance by Boston's Huntington Theatre Company, a showcase of handmade quilts representing different faiths, or even gourmand gatherings like the Massachusetts Craft Brewers Festival (typically held in April). Much like a cyclorama painting, this place has a way of making you feel like you've traipsed into another world.

Harriet Tubman Park

One of the South End's pleasures is its innumerable little parklets nestled between the Victorian homes and brick buildings, blooming with flowers and often containing historic relics that many visitors breeze past. **Harriet Tubman Park** (450 Columbus Ave.), a shaded green space whose rotunda benches encircle a 10-foot (3-m) bronze statue of the history-making abolitionist, suffragette, and civil rights activist, is one such parklet. After escaping enslavement, Tubman found her way to Massachusetts and attended meetings in Boston with activists such as Frederick Douglass. This was done at great risk to her safety, as the Fugitive Slave Act would have allowed Tubman to be detained in Boston and sent back to the South. But Boston was where Tubman and her colleagues hatched plans to help more African Americans make the perilous journey to relative safe havens in the Civil War years. Fittingly, the Tubman memorial statue (designed by the late Boston sculptor Fern Cunningham) depicts Tubman leading a small group north. Not only is this one of Boston's most stirring statues, but it just so happens to be the first statue on city-owned property honoring a woman.

Seaport

Across Fort Point Channel from downtown, the South Boston waterfront district is a neighborhood in transition. For years, it has been home to New England's largest community of artists, who have taken advantage of the solid warehouses that once housed the stores for Boston's wool trade to build artist studios and performance spaces; the area itself is a visual artist's dream, with open spaces broken by iron girders and views of the harbor. It's now a darling of developers using the last bits of open space to create new hotels and condos.

Boston Tea Party Ships and Museum

The original three British ships that were the unwilling hosts to the Boston Tea Party were moored at Griffin's Wharf, which was later buried in landfill during the expansion of the city. The best estimate of the location is near the present-day corner of Atlantic Avenue and Congress Street, near South Station. Not far from that spot, the **Boston Tea Party Ships and Museum** (306 Congress St., 617/338-1773, www.bostonteapartyship.com, daily 10am-5pm, $34 adults, $25 children 3-12, free under 3) features replicas of the three original ships—the *Beaver, Dartmouth,* and *Eleanor*—but the real highlight is the vivid, and participatory, reenactment by actors in period dress.

Institute of Contemporary Art

The **Institute of Contemporary Art** (ICA, 25 Harbor Shore Dr., 617/478-3100, www.icaboston.org, Tues.-Wed. and Sat.-Sun. 10am-5pm, Thurs.-Fri. 10am-9pm, $20 adults, $17 seniors, $15 students, free children under 17, free to all Thurs. after 5pm) was once viewed as being on par with New York's Museum of Modern Art (MoMA) on the vanguard of experimental modern art. While MoMA decided to collect the artists it exhibited and now boasts the likes of Jackson Pollock and Jasper Johns, the ICA felt that it could better remain on the cutting edge by continually exhibiting new work. Making up for lost time, the ICA opened a new home on the waterfront in 2006, a space-age landmark that triples the size of the museum's old home in Back Bay, and more importantly adds a permanent collection for the first time. In its old location, the museum garnered a reputation for staging explosive exhibitions such as the first U.S. display of the photos of Robert Mapplethorpe in the 1980s; in recent years, however, its exhibits of contemporary multimedia installations and photography have had a more uneven reception. The new building, designed by edgy architectural firm Diller Scofidio + Renfro, has reinvigorated the museum, providing dramatic views of the waterfront from flexible gallery spaces, and adding a 325-seat performing arts theater overlooking the harbor.

Boston Children's Museum

Kids can get their hands into giant bubbles, colorful art projects, and science exhibits at the fun **Boston Children's Museum** (308 Congress St., 617/426-6500, www.bostonchildrensmuseum.org, daily 9am-noon and 1:30pm-4:30pm, $22, free children under 1), which is best suited for children under the age of 11. Budding construction workers can build

Top to bottom: Institute of Contemporary Art; The Museum of Science; Arnold Arboretum

skyscrapers and jackhammer them down in the Construction Zone; little monkeys can tackle a brightly colored maze of tunnels, towers, and walkways called the Climb; and the nautically inclined can float their boats in a 28-foot-long (8.5-m) model of the Fort Point Channel (visible outside the museum's walls) called Boats Afloat.

Cambridge

Two of the country's most iconic universities—Harvard and the Massachusetts Institute of Technology (MIT)—are just across the Charles River from downtown Boston in historic, quirky Cambridge. These are just the beginning of the over 100 colleges and universities in the greater Boston area, and a regular influx of students is part of what keeps Boston eternally young and energetic. Head across the river to get a taste of the intellectual scene; Cambridge is about three miles (5 km) from downtown Boston and easily reached on the MBTA Red Line (Harvard station).

Harvard University

Download an audio tour and map to take a self-guided trip around the Harvard campus, or start the trip like a prospective student on a **Harvard Campus Tour** (1350 Massachusetts Ave., Cambridge, 617/495-1573, www.harvard.edu, free tours Mon.-Sat. 9am-5pm) that takes in the best of the university's green quads, landmark libraries, and that famous Harvard Yard.

Three separate facilities make up the **Harvard Art Museums** (617/495-9400, www.harvardartmuseums.org, daily 10am-5pm, free), and Harvard's **Peabody Museum** (11 Divinity Ave., Cambridge, 617/496-1027, www.peabody.harvard.edu, daily 9am-5pm, $15 adults, $13 seniors, $10 children 3-18 and non-Harvard students with ID, under 3 free) is one of the oldest anthropological museums in the world.

Many of Boston and Cambridge's schools open their doors to the public for lectures by speakers from around the world. The **Harvard University *Gazette*** (www.news.harvard.edu/gazette) publishes a full schedule of talks, and Harvard's own "In the Community" page (community.harvard.edu/calendar/upcoming) also offers listings of campus events that are open to the general public. Contemporary readings and talks by authors are frequently held at the **Harvard Book Store** (1256 Massachusetts Ave., Cambridge, 800/542-7323, www.harvard.com).

Campus life spills into the streets at **Harvard Square** (Massachusetts Ave. and Brattle St.), a bustling plaza lined with shops and restaurants. Chain outlets have dimmed some of the spot's independent charm, but there are still enough buskers, artists, and studious undergraduates to make it an inviting destination.

The Museum of Science

Ask anyone who grew up in Boston to summon childhood memories and odds are they'll recall stargazing in the planetarium or standing in the shadows of the triceratops skeleton at the **Museum of Science** (1 Science Park, 617/723-2500, www.mos.org, daily 9am-5pm, $29 adults, $25 seniors, $24 children 3-11, under 3 free). Located in Science Park, a land bridge between the Boston and Cambridge sides of the Charles River, the Museum of Science is a labyrinth of interactive exhibits that offer visitors a window into the workings of the natural world, from the biological to the elemental. Museum classics include the largest Van de Graaff static electricity generator in the world, where you can watch enormous bolts of lightning crackling and dancing around the generator's metallic sphere. Another crowd pleaser is the New England Habitats Hall, whose life-sized dioramas depict the woods and waters of New England with stuffed critters and real trees and fauna sourced from around the region. (This particular exhibit may leave you raring to drive north to the White Mountains or the waters of Acadia.)

Then there's the cinematic entertainment. The offerings at the museum's **Charles Hayden Planetarium** include a journey to Mars and the birth of moons, as well as nature documentaries and occasional blockbusters shot in IMAX. And if you can handle a little vertigo, the stadium-style seating and five-story-tall domed screen of the Mugar Omni Theater adds a stomach-plunging thrill to IMAX images of Mount Everest or the underwater caves found in Mexico's Yucatán Peninsula. You can catch a show at either theater without paying the full museum admission price. Tickets are $10 for adults, $9 for seniors, and $8 for children 3-11.

Jamaica Plain

Tucked away from the concrete and cacophony of Boston's core, to the south side, Jamaica Plain (or "JP," as locals call it) is a lushly wooded oasis of residential streets and parks, where overlooked treasures await the more inquisitive traveler. Its denizens include decades-deep Bostonians, immigrants whose journeys encircle the globe, medical residents from nearby hospitals, and artists and progressive political activists. JP might just be Boston's most free-spirited and friendly community. Whether under a dogwood tree, or at a bar top over pints of local porter, you'll meet people here whose classic Boston saltiness is paired with sincerity and civic spirit that can feel fleeting in major cities.

Arnold Arboretum

More than 280 acres of North American and East Asian trees and woody plants are the romantic headlining attraction at **Arnold Arboretum** (125 Arborway, 617/524-1718, www.arboretum.harvard.edu, daily sunrise-sunset, free). Located a short walk away from Jamaica Plain's bustling Centre Street, the Arboretum is Harvard University's collection of common and rarefied trees, sourced from near and far. The on-site herbarium and library are open to the public, a must-see for anyone with a passing interest in herbology and regional flora. But one of the most vividly pleasurable ways to spend a late morning or afternoon in Jamaica Plain is simply to wander the winding pathways that weave through the arboretum's vast halls of maple, beech, and other seemingly limitless tree species. The arboretum grounds are replete with flowering quads, wooded hollows, chuckling streams, and grassy hillsides that are ideal for a picnic.

Summiting the hills offers a modest calf workout and lovely views of Boston's skyline to the north. **Bussey Hill,** the most well-tread, is a gently sloped behemoth that's close to the arboretum's main entrance, with plenty of meadows along the winding path to the top. Venture deeper and you'll find the best vista atop **Peters Hill,** near the southern end of the preserve. The tallest point in the arboretum, and the steepest climb, Peters Hill is a popular spot for watching Boston's Fourth of July fireworks. Quite often, though, your only companion up here will be the breeze itself.

TOP EXPERIENCE

Samuel Adams Brewery

If you've ever imbibed an American craft beer and wondered how domestic beer became this good, a visit to **Samuel Adams Brewery** (30 Germania St., 617/368-5080, www.samueladams.com, see website for weekly tour hours, $10) is a pilgrimage worth taking. The brewery's seminal Boston Lager, a malty German-style brew derived from a recipe from founder Jim Koch's grandmother, was one of the earliest craft beers to "catch on" in America's Bud- and Miller-heavy suds circuit during the 1980s. While most Sam Adams beers today are produced in factories in the Rust Belt, the Jamaica Plain brewery remains the company "test kitchen," where batches of pre-market Sam Adams beer are offered to visitors who attend brewery tours.

The tour here is the best in Boston's brewery scene, with wisecracking young guides who walk tour groups through the ingredients and fermentation equipment that it takes to brew beer, before pivoting into a taproom for pitchers of at least three Sam Adams beers. (If you're lucky, your guide might just throw a funkier fourth brew into the mix.) Any beer left over in the pitchers is "yours to keep" at the end of the tour, inviting you to top off your tasting glass and leaving you to decide whether you'd prefer to walk or stagger out of the brewery.

Franklin Park

Winding stone staircases, rustling woodlands, volleys of golf balls, and a zoo boasting animatronic dinosaurs as well as some of New England's most beloved western lowland gorillas: As Boston's largest green space, at a whopping 485 acres (196 ha), **Franklin Park** (www.boston.gov/parks) fires on all cylinders. The park bridges Jamaica Plain and the nearby neighborhood of Dorchester, making the space feel like a hub of the universe. On a summer day, families and friends gather on the park's central athletic fields to grill burgers and picnic on the fields.

Every turn of the path through Franklin Park invites you to ask, "What's up there?" Enter the **Franklin Park Zoo** (1 Franklin Park Rd., 617/541-5466, www.zoonewengland.org, Apr.-Sept. daily 9am-5pm, Oct.-Mar. daily 9am-4pm, $22 adults, $20 seniors, $15 children 2-12, free under 2) and you'll encounter school groups from across the Boston area, getting an up-close look at giant anteaters and adolescent hippos. Walk the park's stony trails to **Scarboro Pond** for some great blue heron-watching, then amble by the **William J. Devine Golf Course** (1 Circuit Dr., 617/265-4084, www.cityofbostongolf.com), where aspiring

Samuel Adams Brewery

Arnold Palmers come to practice their swing.

While not technically part of Franklin Park, there's also **Forest Hills Cemetery** (95 Forest Hills Ave., 617/524-0128, www.foresthillscemetery.com, see website for hours), a huge Victorian-era graveyard connected to the park's southwestern boundary. The cemetery features a hand-carved miniature village alongside the graves. Each village building is a representation of the home of a cemetery resident. A side trip here is a must if you plan on roaming Franklin Park.

Entertainment and Events

As a city that has always prided itself on culture, Boston rarely lacks for interesting arts and entertainment offerings. To find what's happening, check www.boston.com and www.thebostoncalendar.com, which has lots of free events. For tickets to theater performances, a great web resource is **BosTix** (617/262-8632, www.artsboston.org/sellbostix), which offers half-price tickets the day of the show.

Nightlife

Bars

Beacon Hill

Last call for the sitcom *Cheers* was in 1993, but the Beacon Hill bar where the exterior shots were filmed is still a serious destination. Life imitates art at **Cheers on Beacon Hill** (84 Beacon St., 617/227-9605, www.cheersboston.com, Sun.-Tues. and Wed. 11am-9pm, Thurs.-Sat. 11am-10pm), formerly the Bull & Finch Pub, where the upstairs has been reinvented as the fictitious television bar, complete with brass nameplates for the "regulars." There is a second location at Faneuil Hall, but it's worth heading to the original, which has a bit more charm to go with the cheese.

An oasis of blue-collar culture (or at least off-duty lawyers) with a tony address, **The Sevens Ale House** (77 Charles St., 617/523-9074, Mon.-Sat. 11:30am-1am, Sun. noon-1am) is a great spot to pull up a stool and savor a foamy black and tan.

The menu at **No. 9 Park** (9 Park St., 617/742-9991, www.no9park.com, Wed.-Thurs. and Sun. 5pm-9pm, Fri.-Sat. 5pm-9:30pm) includes hard-to-find bottles and old-world varietals that earned the wine program a James Beard Award. Though it's primarily a restaurant, the quiet bar is an elegant place to enjoy a glass and a snack from the à la carte menu.

Boston Common

The most iconic bars in Boston fall firmly into "dive bar" territory—the kind of sticky, beer-soaked neighborhood joints where St. Patrick's Day memories are forged (or erased). One classic of the genre is **The Tam** (222 Tremont St., 617/482-9182, Mon.-Fri. 10am-2am,

Sat.-Sun. 11am-2am, cash only), a morning-to-night destination for cheap beer, loud music, and a gruff crowd of locals. Another downtown favorite is **Biddy Early's** (141 Pearl St., 617/654-9944, Mon.-Fri. 10:30am-2am, Sat. 11am-2am, Sun. noon-2am), where Irish-themed decor and PBR sriracha chicken wings pair beautifully with dartboards and arcade games.

There's an excellent selection of beers from around New England at **jm Curley** (21 Temple Pl., 617/228-5333, Mon.-Sun. 4pm-2am), along with very credible cocktails and fresh bar food. Bacon popcorn is a favorite here.

Some of the finest cocktails in town are at the ultra-stylish, nostalgic **Yvonne's** (2 Winter Place, 617/267-0047, www.yvonnesboston.com, Sun.-Thurs. 5pm-1am, Fri.-Sat. 4pm-2am), a Downtown Crossing supper club with two great places to drink (and take selfies): Settle in at the grand mahogany bar or grab a spot in the "library," which is lined with designer-selected vintage titles.

Downtown and the Waterfront

Many of Boston's finest Irish bars are buried in hard-to-reach neighborhoods, but despite its downtown location, **Mr. Dooley's** (77 Broad St., 617/338-5656, www.somerspubs.com, Mon.-Fri. 11:30am-2am, Sat.-Sun. 9am-2am) is the real deal. Pints of Guinness and Jameson shots go well with live Irish music most weekend nights. Come ready to sing along to all the classics.

North End

Somewhere between chic Italian bistro and fantasy Prohibition-era speakeasy, **Parla** (230 Hanover St., 617/367-2824, www.parlaboston.com, Mon.-Fri. 4pm-midnight, Sat.-Sun. 10am-midnight) infuses its cocktail list with seasonal ingredients and offbeat flavors, but the gorgeous space alone is worth the visit.

The North End take on the Boston dive bar is **Corner Café** (87 Prince St., 617/523-8997, Mon.-Sat. 8am-2am, Sun. noon-2am), where locals scratch lottery tickets, drink cheap draft beer, and slurp up pudding shots (which are better than they sound). The real secret, however, is that Corner Café invites patrons to order food from outside, so you can grab a beer and call for a Regina's pizza.

Fenway and Back Bay

In the spirit of the raunchy, beer-loving poet, the **Bukowski Tavern** (50 Dalton St., 617/437-9999, Mon.-Thurs. 4pm-1am, Fri.-Sun. noon-1am) has a gleefully unreconstructed feeling, but with a good draft list that transcends the usual dive bar pours.

Think outside the margarita at the gothic-themed **Lolita Cocina & Tequila Bar** (271 Dartmouth St., 617/369-5609, Sun.-Thurs. 11:30am-1am, Fri.-Sat. 11:30am-2am), where tufted black leather and red lights meet a menu of sophisticated cocktails. Mixed drinks are fresh and fierce, but there's also an appealing menu of house-made nonalcoholic drinks. The dessert menu is legendary.

Cambridge

A modest brick facade in the heart of Harvard Square masks the beautiful and roomy subterranean bar at **Russell House Tavern** (14 JFK St., 617/500-3055, www.russellhousecambridge.com, Sun.-Mon. 4pm-10pm, Tues.-Thurs. 4pm-11pm, Fri.-Sat. 4pm-midnight). The decor is heavy on leather, marble, and dark wood. Hard-to-find draft beers like Harpoon's Irish stout are paired with classic cocktails and avant-garde mixology offerings, shaken and stirred by gregarious bartenders.

Inman Square, the crossroads of Cambridge and Somerville, is an unsung hotbed of watering holes. **Trina's Starlite Lounge** (3 Beacon St., Somerville, 617/576-0006, www.trinastarlitelounge.com, Sun.-Thurs. 5pm-1am, Fri.-Sat. 5pm-2am) strikes the balance between divey and classy, with reasonably priced cocktails served in a cozy candlelit space ideal for a first date, or some boozy Thomas Pynchon reading.

Jamaica Plain

In a city of Irish bars, Scottish libations and pub fare rarely get their due, but you'll find both at **The Haven** (284 Amory St., www.thehavenjp.com, Sun.-Wed. 5pm-11pm, Thurs.-Sat. 5pm-midnight). Decked out with authentic stag antlers on the wall, The Haven offers the expected bevy of peaty, smoky scotches, but dinner here is a prudent investment too. The haggis is as authentic as it comes.

Ancient guitars, vintage PBR signage, and multicolor holiday lights festoon the walls inside the **Midway Café** (3496 Washington St., 617/524-9038, www.midwaycafe.com, daily 5pm-2am). Arguably the hub of JP nightlife, the Midway offers an impressive roster of craft beers, ciders, and cocktails while also hosting shaggy soirees like Queeraoke—a LGBTQ+ karaoke showcase that turns into a raucous dance party—as well as Friday night's Hippie Hour, when multigenerational Deadheads gather to crush brews and make plans for the Dead & Company's next stop in Boston.

Breweries

Harpoon Brewery (306 Northern Ave., 617/456-2322, www.harpoonbrewery.com, Sun.-Tues. noon-8pm, Wed. noon-8:30pm, Thurs. noon-9pm, Fri.-Sat. noon-10pm) has spent decades concocting some of Boston's more adventurous brews—like a dragon fruit and hibiscus sour ale—at their vast facility. Seek out their flagship brewpub in the Seaport neighborhood, grab a spot at one of the communal beer hall tables, and be sure to order one of the hot, fluffy house pretzels, which are made with malted barley from the brewhouse.

For the most aggressive, in-your-face double IPAs in the Fenway area, try **Trillium Brewing Company** (401 Park Dr., 857/499-0078, www.trilliumbrewing.com, Mon.-Sat. 11am-midnight, Sun. 11am-8pm), where hazy and prodigiously hopped ales are the star offerings.

Savor some suds and conversations with fellow travelers steps away from Boston Common at **Democracy Brewing** (35 Temple Pl., 857/263-8604, www.democracybrewing.com, Mon. 4pm-8pm, Tues.-Wed. noon-9pm, Thurs.-Sat. noon-10pm, Sun. noon-8pm), whose English-style golden ales or extra special bitter ales are the real deal.

If you plan on checking out Harvard, fuel your scholarly foray with a Birds of a Feather New England-style IPA at **Lamplighter Brewing Company** (284 Broadway, Cambridge, 617/945-0450, www.lamplighterbrewing.com, Tues.-Sat. 11am-midnight, Sun.-Mon. 11am-10pm), which is housed in a mom-and-pop garage in Cambridge whose owners leased the building to the brewers.

Live Music

The South End's **Wally's** (427 Massachusetts Ave., 617/424-1408, www.wallyscafe.com) hosts jazz the way it was meant to be played, in a closet-sized room that heats up both on and off stage. Meanwhile, the nearby "Harvard of jazz," the Berklee School of Music, sponsors performances of both modern legends and up-and-coming prodigies at its **Berklee Performance Center** (136 Massachusetts Ave., 617/747-2261, www.berkleebpc.com), which also occasionally has folk and pop acts.

When it comes to live music, sound quality is everything. One of the country's first concert halls designed with the help of acoustic science experts is **Boston Symphony Hall** (301 Massachusetts Ave., 617/266-1200, www.bso.org). Built in 1899 and located at the nexus of Back Bay and the South End, Symphony Hall is home of the **Boston Symphony Orchestra,** whose concert season usually kicks off in September. While the venue's "shoebox" dimensions, high ceilings, shallow side balconies, and sloped stage walls keep the music unmuffled, the acoustic virtues of the hall are almost overshadowed by how visually resplendent Symphony Hall is. Replicas of Greek and Roman statues line the upper walls of the concert hall. Looking down at it all from the upper balcony, mid-concert, you can't help but feel like a part of a cultural tradition that's been passed down through centuries.

Weekend concerts are the hottest tickets offered, starting at around $45, but an excellent budget alternative is the BSO's Saturday morning open rehearsal performances, where tickets can be scored for as little as $21 apiece. A select number of BSO performances each season are also eligible for the $25 Under 40 promotion, wherein visitors ages 40 and under can score tickets for a bargain $25 each. (This is part of the Orchestra's effort to cultivate the next generation of members.)

In addition to Boston Symphony Hall, Boston has many excellent smaller halls that regularly offer classical concerts. These include: New England Conservatory's acoustically refined **Jordan Hall** (30 Gainsborough St., 617/585-1260, https://necmusic.edu/concerts) and Boston University's **Tsai Performance Center** (685 Commonwealth Ave., 617/353-8725, www.bu.edu/tsai).

A little-known choral gem, **Emmanuel Music** (15 Newbury St., 617/536-3356, www.emmanuelmusic.org) performs entire Bach masses on Sundays from September through May at Emmanuel Church. **Trinity Boston** (206 Clarendon St., 617/536-0944, www.trinitychurchboston.org) has half-hour organ recitals on Fridays at 12:15pm, as well as occasional choral concerts in one of the most beautiful settings in Boston—Copley Square's Trinity Church.

Festivals and Events

TOP EXPERIENCE

Boston Marathon

In April, runners come from around the world to compete in the **Boston Marathon** (www.baa.org), the oldest (and some say toughest) marathon in the United States. Spectators start lining the route to cheer along Beacon and Boylston Streets, all the way to Copley Square, where the finish line is painted in the street. Of course, the marathon itself is only part of the fun. The Boston Athletic Association, which is in charge of the event, also provides a race expo with over 200 vendors, a pre-race dinner, and a post-race party (presented by Samuel Adams).

If you're not interested in competing in the race, you can yell yourself hoarse, encouraging runners from the sidelines, or volunteer to support the participants by helping with registration or handing out much-needed cups of water along the route. The Boston Marathon is a treasured event in Boston. If you're in town in April, don't miss it.

Fourth of July

Americans from around the country tune in to the Boston Pops performance on the **Fourth of July,** when the esplanade becomes a gallery for a fabulous fireworks show. And on those sultry midsummer Friday nights, the South End's innumerable art galleries open their doors to the public for First Fridays, inviting all to come savor some art over a glass of pinot noir.

Shakespeare on Boston Common

Numerous (often free) events take place throughout the summer months, from **open-air Shakespeare on Boston Common** (www.commshakes.org) to **outdoor concerts.** A good resource for finding current listings is www.bostonusa.com.

Shopping

Beacon Hill

Charles Street

Charles Street in Beacon Hill has some 40 antiques stores crammed into one-third of a mile (0.5 km); one of the best is **Upstairs Downstairs Antiques** (93 Charles St., 617/367-1950, Mon.-Sat. 10am-6pm, Sun. noon-5pm), a warren of rooms stuffed with tableware, glassware, and other knickknacks from a dozen decades. Armchair explorers and treasure hunters alike thrill at the selection of antique hand-painted china, furniture, and jewelry at **Elegant Findings Antiques** (89 Charles St., 617/973-4844, www.elegantfindingsantiques.com, Thurs.-Sat. noon-5pm), which are sourced from around the world.

Back Bay

Newbury Street

The place to shop for high-end, stylish clothes is Back Bay's tony **Newbury Street,** which carries outposts of international designers from Armani to Zegna, alongside local boutiques.

Newbury Street also hosts the most prestigious art galleries in the city. The biggest name on the street is the **Krakow Witkin Gallery** (10 Newbury St., 617/262-4490, www.barbarakrakowgallery.com, Wed.-Fri. 10am-5:30pm), which draws nationally known contemporary artists. More traditional and opulent paintings spanning the 16th to 21st centuries are on display at the venerable **Galerie d'Orsay** (33 Newbury St., 617/266-8001, www.galerie-dorsay.com, Mon.-Sat. 10am-6pm, Sun. noon-6pm), which focuses on Impressionist work. The **Childs Gallery** (169 Newbury St., 617/266-1108, www.childsgallery.com, Tues.-Fri. 9am-6pm, Sat.-Sun. 11am-5pm) is home to one of

Top to bottom: Boston Marathon; a tribute to the classics at Brattle Book Shop; the Emerald Necklace

the city's greatest collections of pre-World War II American and European art.

The kind of shop where you can settle in with a coffee and a good read, **Trident Booksellers & Café** (338 Newbury St., 617/267-8688, www.tridentbookscafe.com, daily 8am-10pm) has a wonderful selection of titles and hosts frequent author events and reading.

Downtown

Downtown Crossing

Most of the shopping in this bustling district is of the big-name, big-store variety, with names like H&M and Primark lining Washington Street, Summer Street, and Winter Street. One long-standing exception to downtown's plate glass window displays is **Brattle Book Shop** (9 West St., 617/542-0210, www.brattlebookshop.com, Mon.-Sat. 9am-5:30pm), where three stories cannot contain a collection of books that spills beyond the bookstore and into the adjoining alley, whose brick walls are painted with the images of iconic authors. Barely five minutes from here, scribes with a taste for the decadent go wild for the luxury fountain pens and leatherbound writing cases at the **Bromfield Pen Shop** (49 Bromfield St., 617/482-9053, www.appelboom.com, Mon.-Sat. 10am-5pm).

Cambridge

Harvard Square

There are still some locally owned gems among the chain stores that have crept into this triangular plaza. With time-warp charm and all sorts of quirk, **Leavitt & Peirce** (1316 Massachusetts Ave., Cambridge, 617/547-0576, www.leavitt-peirce.com, Mon. and Wed.-Sat. 10am-6pm, Sun. noon-6pm) has been Harvard's tobacconist since 1884, but also stocks a trove of games and gentlemanly gifts like cuff links and shaving brushes. Another fun place to browse is **Mint Julep** (6 Church St., Cambridge, 617/576-6468, www.shopmintjulep.com, Mon.-Sat. 10am-7pm, Sun. 11am-6pm), a women's clothing boutique that has everything from Kentucky Derby hats to designer selvedge denim jeans.

Sports and Recreation

Hiking and Biking

Watch pink- and white-sailed dinghies tack and jibe along the shore from the **Charles River Esplanade** (www.esplanadeassociation.org), which has three miles (4.8 km) of waterfront trails that stretch from the Museum of Science to the Boston University Bridge. The trails are especially charming in the springtime, when blossom-laden cherry trees arch over the path.

When the "Big Dig" construction project put I-93 underground, it created 15 acres (6 ha) of surface-level space that's been transformed into the **Rose Kennedy Greenway** (www.

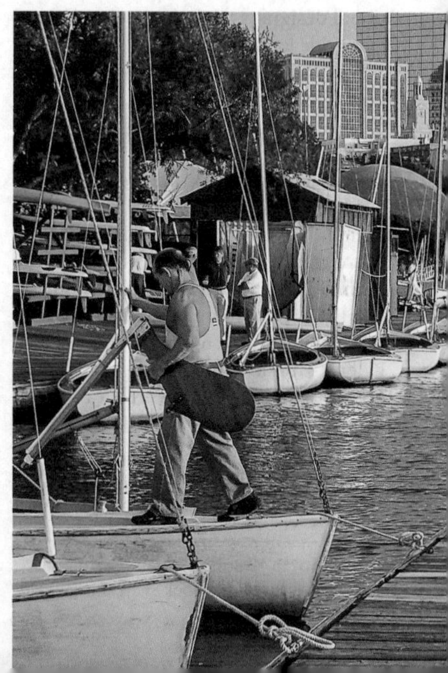

rosekennedygreenway.org), a slender line of parks that runs 1.5 miles (2.4 km) from the Chinatown Gate to North End Park. One highlight of the parks is the **Greenway Carousel** (Atlantic Ave. and Cross St., 888/839-7616, $4), whose colorful animals are all Massachusetts natives—don't miss the chance to ride a codfish, peregrine falcon, whale, or lobster. You'll also find some wonderful art along the way; exhibits change seasonally, but past installments have featured Chinese artist Ai Weiwei and abstract pieces with a focus on local history and nature. Many of the seven water fountains along the greenway are strategically designed for cooling off in the Boston summer. Favorites with the wading toddler crowd include the **Rings Fountain** (Central St. and Cross St.), **North & South Canal Fountains** (Cross St. and Hanover St.), and interactive **Harbor Fog Fountain** (High St. and Cross St.), whose movement sensors trigger great billows of cooling mist.

★ Emerald Necklace

The gentle pedestrian and bike paths that amble past the Fens' community gardens and reedy marshlands are actually part of much larger trail that links many of Boston's parks and greenways, called the **Emerald Necklace** (www.emeraldnecklace.org). Comprising 1,100 acres (445 ha) of green space, the Emerald Necklace begins at Boston Common and meanders south through Back Bay and the Fenway to Jamaica Plain's Arnold Arboretum and Franklin Park. Frederick Law Olmsted, the landscape architect behind some of America's most storied parks, designed the interconnected system. From above, the linked parks and greenways resemble a necklace hanging around the "neck" of Shawmut Peninsula. Today, from dawn to dusk, you'll encounter joggers, cyclists, dog walkers, and wanderers from near and far exploring the city via the Emerald Necklace's pathways.

From the Fenway, you'll have two

Community Boating

choices. Heading north on the necklace will take you to the Commonwealth Avenue Mall, a greenway that runs straight up the middle of Back Bay's Comm Ave., with shade trees and bronze-and-granite sculptures of figures like Alexander Hamilton. The mall leads to Boston Public Garden, bringing you back to the historic heart of Boston and the northern terminus of the necklace at around three miles (5 km). For a more intimate look at Boston's residential enclaves, take the Emerald Necklace pathway south from Fenway through corridors of oak trees to reach the rippling waters of Jamaica Pond and the hills of Arnold Arboretum and Franklin Park, all of which are located in Jamaica Plain. Franklin Park, the necklace's southern terminus, is a roughly four-mile (6.4-km) walk or bike ride from the Fenway.

Boating

Boston Harbor remains a transportation hub for the region, and **Boston Harbor Cruises** (www.bostonharborcruises.com) runs convenient boat service to **Salem** (1 hr, round-trip ticket $47 adults, $45 seniors, $38 children 3-11) and **Provincetown** (1.5 hrs, round-trip ticket $92 adults, $90 seniors, $78 children 3-11, $33 under 3) that are a good alternative to driving. To simply get views of the city from the water, though, take a turn on its **Narrated Historic Sunset Cruise** (1.5 hrs, tickets $48 adults, $44 children 3-11), which travels along the harbor shoreline to the USS *Constitution,* just in time for its cannon salute to commemorate the day's end.

Take in the harbor under sail with the **Liberty Fleet** (617/742-0333, www.libertyfleet.com, cruises $46-55 adults, $35-50 children under 12), which offers day sails, sunset sails, and a "Rum and Revelry" sail with costumed actors and drinks. The schooner *Liberty Clipper* is the flagship, a 125-foot (38-m) gaff-rigged replica of the Baltimore clipper-style ships prized by fast-moving privateers during the American Revolution and War of 1812. Her little sister is the 67-foot (20-m) *Liberty Star,* whose classic lines are modeled on 19th-century coastal schooners—crews on board both ships are friendly and experienced, and the sails can be as hands-on (or -off) as desired.

All those postcard-ready sailboats on the Charles River belong to **Community Boating** (21 Mugar Way, 617/523-1038, www.community-boating.org, Apr.-early June Mon.-Fri. 1pm-sunset, Sat.-Sun. 9am-sunset, mid-June-mid-Aug. Mon.-Fri. 3pm-sunset, Sat.-Sun. 9am-sunset, late Aug.-Oct. Mon.-Fri. 1pm-sunset, Sat.-Sun. 9am-sunset), an institution on the Charles River Esplanade since the 1940s. Experienced sailors can rent a sailboat for $85-119, and 2-hour kayak and paddleboard rentals are available at $34/person.

Spectator Sports

With baseball, hockey, and basketball, Boston has an almost year-round sports season, with fervor to match. Most iconic is the **Red Sox** (877/733-7699, www.redsox.com) baseball team based at Fenway Park. After suffering through the 86-year-long "Curse of the Bambino," it can finally bring home pennants again (the Red Sox sold the legendary player Babe Ruth to the New York Yankees after winning the 1918 championship, and didn't catch a break until the 2004 World Series). The hockey-playing **Bruins** (617/624-2327, www.bostonbruins.com), who call **TD Garden** home, are another passion-inspiring team and the oldest NHL team in the United States. And while the 1980s heyday of Larry Bird, Kevin McHale, and Robert Parish has not returned, the **Celtics** (866/423-5849, www.nba.com/celtics) still pack the TD Garden to the gills.

Food

Beacon Hill

The open kitchen at **The Paramount** (44 Charles St., 617/720-1152, www.paramountboston.com, daily 8am-4pm and 4:30pm-9pm, $12-30) slings fresh, flavorful diner fare at breakfast and lunch: Try caramel banana French toast, huevos rancheros, hefty salads, and sandwiches. Dinner gets a bit more grown-up with pasta dishes and entrées like coconut shrimp or lobster ravioli with curried tomato sauce. Lines can get long at this neighborhood favorite, so it's a good option to call ahead for sandwiches and have a picnic in nearby Boston Public Garden.

Tucked down a brick-lined side street, **75 Chestnut** (75 Chestnut St., 617/227-2175, www.75chestnut.com, dinner daily 5pm-11pm, brunch Sat.-Sun. 10:30am-3pm, $18-45) is a cozy neighborhood bistro that's refined enough for a romantic evening out. The dinner menu includes classic seafood dishes and pasta, salads, steaks, and a few burgers. Brunch is especially popular here, with a short but appealing menu and a Bloody Mary bar.

Downtown and the Waterfront

Daniel Webster downed brandy and oysters here, and John F. Kennedy loved to sip lobster bisque in booth 18; **Union Oyster House** (41 Union St., 617/227-2750, www.unionoysterhouse.com, Sun.-Thurs. 11am-9pm, Fri.-Sat. 11am-10pm, $13-40) is the oldest operating restaurant in the United States. Find all the classics here, from Boston baked beans to baked scrod, but if you just want to soak up the historic atmosphere, grab a drink and a half-dozen oysters at the downstairs raw bar or the darkly colonial-looking Union Bar.

One might never suspect this laid-back, counter service lunch place of having the "World's No. 1 Sandwiches," but **Sam LaGrassa's** (44 Province St., 617/357-6861, www.samlagrassas.com, Mon.-Fri. 11am-2pm, $11-16) has a passionate following that lines up for enormous deli sandwiches and chowder. Roast beef and Reubens are served in classic style here, piled high with deli meat, but it's the pastrami that made this place famous.

Find Chilean sandwiches piled with freshly grilled meat, veggies, and muenster cheese at **Chacarero** (101 Arch St., 617/542-0392, www.chacarero.com, Mon.-Fri. 11am-3pm, $12-16), a pocket-sized sandwich shop beloved by locals. The secret ingredient: green beans.

It *is* possible to order the namesake sandwiches at ★ **Gene's Chinese Flatbread Café** (86 Bedford St., 617/482-1888, www.genescafe.com, Mon.-Sat. 11am-6:30pm, $8-14), but the real draw is the hand-pulled noodles that come doused in fresh garlic, chili oil, cilantro, and green onions. The noodles are a chewy delight, and Gene's is one of the only places in New England where you can find traditional Xi'an Chinese food.

The sushi and Japanese small plates at **O Ya** (9 East St., 617/654-9900, www.o-ya.restaurant, Tues.-Sat. 5pm-8:30pm, $60-88) are both creative and exquisite, and meals here are consistently ranked among the best in the city. For an all-out feast, try the nightly tasting menu that includes one of the chef's signature dishes: hamachi nigiri, a squeaky fresh cut of yellowtail marinated in soy, draped over pressed rice, and finished with banana pepper mousse.

Boston Public Market (100 Hanover St., 617/973-4909, www.bostonpublicmarket.org, Mon. 8am-8pm, Tues.-Thurs. 8am-9pm, Fri.-Sat. 8am-10pm, Sun. 10am-8pm) is an indoor, year-round market space with dozens of local vendors selling prepared foods, products, and groceries.

★ North End

There's always a line out the door of **Regina Pizzeria** (11½ Thacher St., 617/227-0765, www.reginapizzeria.com,

Sun.-Wed. 11am-9pm, Thurs.-Sat. 11am-10pm, $16-29), but joining the line is part of the fun at this landmark destination. The kitchen turns out blistered, lightly blackened pies topped with traditional Neapolitan ingredients, but it's the crust that really shines: The pizzaoli in the open kitchen throw disks of dough that are chewy, thin, and just slightly uneven, truly some of the best in town.

Stop by **Monica's Mercato & Salumeria** (130 Salem St., 617/742-4101, www.monicasboston.com, daily 10am-8pm, $11-20) at lunchtime, and you'll order your sub alongside a line of North End cops, construction workers, and longtime locals—it's a good omen that doesn't disappoint. Sandwiches are layered with freshly sliced prosciutto, salami, and Italian cheeses, bathed in extra virgin olive oil and balsamic vinegar, and wrapped to go. There's no seating in this shoebox-size deli, but it's a five-minute walk to the North End Park, where you'll find shaded tables and park benches.

It would be easy to miss little **Polcari's Coffee** (105 Salem St., 617/227-0786, www.polcaris.com, Mon.-Fri. 11am-5pm, Sat. 10am-5pm, Italian ice $3-5), a shop that's weighed out the neighborhood's espresso beans and spices on a pair of great brass scales since 1932. In the warm months, though, Polcari's scoops cups full of fine-grained, lemony Italian ice that's unbelievably refreshing on a hot day.

Whether you're sipping a morning cappuccino or an amaro nightcap, the marble-topped tables at **Caffé Vittoria** (290 Hanover St., 617/227-7606, www.caffevittoria.com, daily 8am-midnight, $5-14) are perfect for watching North End life drift by. Every surface of this old-world café is covered in antique espresso machines, vintage Italian posters, and other memorabilia. Cappuccinos come under a melting layer of powdered chocolate, and the late-night menu of cordials—these include herbal amari and sweet sips like crema di limoncello—are perfect with traditional Italian desserts.

An island of contemporary style in the thoroughly old-school North End, ★ **Neptune Oyster** (63 Salem St., 617/742-3474, www.neptuneoyster.com, Mon.-Fri. 11am-10pm, Sat.-Sun. 11am-11pm, $25-35) gets a lot of hype and deserves every bit of it. The big, buttery lobster rolls are the best in Boston, but the creative seafood menu skims through the world's great coastal cuisines: Try whole mackerel with Basque piperrada, or Mozambique-style scarlet prawns. The line starts well before the doors open for lunch, and the tiny space can be cramped and loud.

Don't leave the North End without a string-wrapped box filled with traditional Italian sweets. The classic cannoli rivalry is between a pair of legendary shops geographically close enough to allow a head-to-head comparison. The versions at **Mike's Pastry** (300 Hanover St., 617/742-3050, www.mikespastry.com, daily 8am-10pm, $3-10) are hefty and sweet, overflowing with ricotta filling. ★ **Modern Pastry** (257 Hanover St., 617/523-3783, www.modernpastry.com, Sun.-Thurs. 7am-10pm, Fri.-Sat. 7am-midnight, $3-9) has a slight edge, serving smaller, more delicate cannoli that are filled on the spot.

Fenway and Back Bay

Another fabulous place for something sweet is **Flour Bakery +Café** (131 Clarendon St., 617/437-7700, www.flourbakery.com, Mon.-Fri. 7am-7pm, Sat.-Sun. 8am-6pm, $6-20), one of nine locations in the Boston area run by master pastry chef Joanne Chang. You'll find sandwiches and salads fine enough for an upstanding lunch, but it's the lusciously sugary tarts, rolls, and pies that bring in the crowds—a particular favorite is Chang's sticky bun, a mammoth treat that's surprisingly light beneath a coating of caramel and pecans.

Steps away from the Boston Public

Library in Copley Square, **Citrus & Salt** (142 Berkeley St., 617/424-6711, www.citrusandsaltboston.com, dinner Mon.-Tues. 5pm-11pm, Wed. noon-11pm, Thurs.-Fri. noon-midnight, Sat. 5pm-midnight, Sun. 5pm-11pm, brunch Sat.-Sun. 10:30am-3:45pm, $18-34) is worth the diversion. With its cream-colored interior draped in twinkling lights and an inventive drink menu featuring fruity pebble agave iced tea and soft-serve sorbet mimosas, this Baja-inspired culinary oasis revels in decadence. Chef Jason Santos's passion for Mexican coastal cuisine is palpable in specialties like the tamarind and habanero-glazed mahi-mahi. Come for the elaborate menu and return for in-house barbecue and cocktail classes offered each summer!

The Boston Public Library's Italianate courtyard is a glorious place to linger in the summer, but many visitors never discover the restaurant overlooking the space. Stop by **The Courtyard Tea Room** (700 Boylston St., 617/859-2282, www.thecateredaffair.com, Wed.-Thurs. and Sun. 11am-4:45pm, Fri.-Sat. 10am-4:45pm, afternoon tea $39 on weekdays and $45 on weekends) for the elegant high tea, and nibble on tiered platters of savory sandwiches, sweet petit fours, and scones with cream . . . and a freshly brewed pot of tea.

South End

The treats at **Blackbird Doughnuts** (492 Tremont St., www.blackbirddoughnuts.com, Wed.-Fri. 7am-4pm, Sat.-Sun. 8am-4pm, $4-8) are displayed individually on cake pedestals, and speared with miniature flags that make them look like tiny, recently discovered islands. Pillowy raised doughnuts come in flavors like salted toffee, passion fruit, and the oozing Peach Icebox Bismarck, but the namesake sweet is a vanilla bean-glazed cake doughnut. Pick up treats to go, as this tiny shop has no seating.

An "indie diner" with a colorful, irreverent attitude, **Myers + Chang** (1145 Washington St., 617/542-5200, www.myersandchang.com, dinner Sun.-Wed. 4pm-9pm, Thurs.-Sat. 4pm-10pm, dim sum brunch Fri.-Sun. 11:30am-2:30pm, $20-42) has a generous menu that ranges from dim sum brunch (on weekends) to noodle soup, Asian-influenced mains, home-style Indonesian food, and anything else that appeals to the talented kitchen. This is an especially good choice on Monday, Tuesday, and Wednesday's "great dates nights," with prix fixe menus for two priced $60-68.

The North End might be Boston's Little Italy, but some of the city's most succulent hand-crafted pasta and springiest insalata are lovingly prepared at ★ **MIDA** (782 Tremont St., 617/936-3490, www.midaboston.com, dinner Sun.-Thurs. 4pm-10pm, Fri.-Sat. 4pm-11pm, brunch Sat.-Sun. 10:30am-2:30pm, $19-37). Chef and owner Douglass Williams, one of *Food & Wine*'s 10 Best New Chefs in America 2020, serves up nourishing Mediterranean fare like melt-in-your-mouth short rib lasagna and poached tuna puttanesca. The outdoor patio is wonderful for watching South Enders glide by.

Cambridge

Harvard Square is jam-packed with places to recover from hard-core learning (and sightseeing). For something that transcends the budget student joints, **Alden & Harlow** (40 Brattle St., Cambridge, 617/864-2100, www.aldenharlow.com, Mon.-Fri. 5pm-11pm, Sat.-Sun. 10:30am-2:30pm and 5pm-11pm, $25-46) serves exquisite, ingredient-focused small plates like fried quail, bass crudo, and chicken liver pâté. Book a table around opening time to nab their hotly coveted "secret burger"; they only make a small handful of them each night.

Nostalgic alumni are sure to stop by **Pinocchio's Pizza & Subs** (74 Winthrop St., Cambridge, 617/876-4897, www.pinocchiospizza.net, Mon.-Thurs. 11am-1am, Fri.-Sat. 11am-2am, Sun.

noon-midnight, $4-15) for hefty, piping-hot slices of Sicilian-style pizza. Check out the "celebrity guest" photos on the wall and see how many Harvard grads you can recognize.

Jamaica Plain

Jamaica Plain's heady, irreverent atmosphere is epitomized at ★ **Tres Gatos** (470 Centre St., 617/477-4851, www.tresgatosjp.com, daily 5pm-10pm, brunch Sat.-Sun. 10:30am-3pm, $17-32), a cozy little bookstore and vinyl record shop that doubles as a restaurant with some of the tastiest Mexican and Middle Eastern-inspired tapas in New England. The blue cheese and almond-stuffed Medjool dates are a must, but if you're feeling famished, the paella with shrimp, clams, rabbit, and black garlic will carry you away on a saffron-scented cloud.

The international cuisine scene in both Jamaica Plain and Dorchester is large enough to spend months sampling, but an excellent gateway is **Jamaica Mi Hungry** (225 Centre St., 617/259-8017, www.jamaicamihungry.com, Mon.-Sat. 11am-9pm, $8-12). Chef Ernie Campbell has brought Jamaican cooking to several corners of New England, and his JP counter-service restaurant has grown a cult following thanks to staples like the fiery jerk pork shoulder with mango chutney, the root beer-braised oxtail, and of course, Jamaican-style beef "patty" pastries.

Accommodations

Because Boston is so compact, all the following listings are good choices for accessing the city's main sights and attractions. They won't come cheap—Boston is among the most expensive cities in the United States for hotels and

Top to bottom: Blackbird Doughnuts; the original Mike's Pastry in Boston's North End; a waterside view from the Boston Harbor Hotel

vacation rentals. There are some wonderful options, however, and it's worth booking well in advance to secure a spot.

Beacon Hill

$250-350

A quaint bed-and-breakfast on the back of Beacon Hill, the **Whitney Hotel** (14 Mugar Way, 888/673-3650, www.whitneyhotelboston.com, $229 s, $339 d) has spartan but comfortable rooms that were originally quarters for nurses at the nearby Massachusetts Eye and Ear Infirmary. There are small kitchenettes in each room and a continental breakfast is served in the common space. Parking is available at the nearby Charles Street garage ($84 for 24 hrs).

Over $350

The **Beacon Hill Hotel and Bistro** (25 Charles St., 617/865-8020, www.beaconhillhotel.com, $450-600) is right in the heart of the action in this fashionable, historic neighborhood. The rooms are smallish, but charming and sweetly decorated. A full breakfast is served in the downstairs bistro, or can be brought to your room. The real star of this boutique hotel is the rooftop terrace, which offers perfect people-watching down toward Charles Street. It's an ideal spot to bring a bottle of wine at the end of the day.

Downtown and the Waterfront

Under $150

On the edge of downtown, with a great location between the theater district and Chinatown, ★ **HI Boston Hostel** (19 Stuart St., 617/536-9455, www.bostonhostel.org, dorms $64-140, private rooms $245-289) sets the standard for large, urban hostels, and it's easily the best budget option in the city. Dormitory rooms range from eight-bed economy options to four-bed premium rooms, both gender-specific and co-ed, and the thoughtful design makes them comfortable spaces to sleep for all kinds of travelers. Beds have assigned lockers, small reading lights, and charging stations, and the shared hallway bathrooms are always immaculate; private rooms have en suite bathrooms and a spare, modern style. There's no parking on-site, but hostel staff directs guests to the **Boston Common Parking Garage** (0 Charles St., overnight $18), which is a 0.4-mile (0.6-km) walk from the hostel.

$250-350

Old-world elegance is faded but still enchanting at the **Omni Parker House** (60 School St., 617/227-8600, www.omnihotels.com, $290-470), one of downtown Boston's most storied hotels. The waitstaff have included Malcom X and Ho Chi Minh, both of whom presumably ferried countless baskets of the Parker House Rolls that were invented here. The hotel regularly lands on the list of Boston's most haunted places (paranormal activity is said to be particularly high on the 3rd floor). If you book Table 40 in the Parker Restaurant, you'll dine where J.F.K. proposed to the future Jackie Kennedy. In keeping with the historic building, rooms are rather small, and while they're pleasantly furnished, they're neither as historic nor as luxurious as the public spaces. Valet parking is available for $57.

Over $350

One of Boston's new crop of boutique hotels, **The Godfrey** (505 Washington St., 617/804-2000, www.godfreyhotelboston.com, $350-425) is chic and modern, and right in the thick of the Downtown Crossing shopping area. You'll find all the luxe amenities—valet parking, spa services, fitness center—along with rooted-in-Boston flourishes such as local art and designs. Splash out for a corner room for wraparound views of the city below.

A 60-foot (18-m) archway that perfectly frames the Atlantic is the first thing you see upon approaching the

Boston Harbor Hotel (70 Rowes Wharf, 617/439-7000, www.bostonharborhotel.com, $530-660). This five-star waterfront palace spares no luxury, with its fine linens, soothing rainfall showers, and stunning harbor views. To slather on the maritime ambience, make a dinner reservation for the in-house restaurant, The Rowes Wharf Sea Grille, and tuck into Scottish salmon and spiced Wellfleet oysters right next to the Boston Harborwalk, a 43-mile (69-km) public path that covers the shoreline of Boston Harbor. Self-parking is available for $49/night at the Rowes Wharf underground garage.

Charlestown

$250-350

Just across the bridge in Charlestown, ★ **Green Turtle Floating Bed and Breakfast** (1 13th St., Pier 8, 617/340-2608, www.greenturtlebb.com, $300-415) offers a novel solution to Boston's perennial lack of space. Accommodations are in a two-bedroom houseboat or a 45-foot (22-m) motor yacht, pulling off an unusual blend of luxury and quirk. Rooms are very comfortable and well appointed, a full breakfast is placed outside your room each morning by the friendly hosts, and the boats' kitchenettes are stocked with snacks and drinks. The bed-and-breakfast is a one-mile (1.6-km) walk from North End sights and close to the public ferry dock on Pier 4. From Logan, you can get here by water taxi for $20 per person (inquire at the airport).

Fenway and Back Bay

$150-250

With a quiet location, **Oasis Guest House** (22 Edgerly Rd., 617/267-2262, www.oasisguesthouse.com, shared bath $210-260, private bath $280-330, 3-person suite $279) is walking distance to Fenway Park and public transportation. The somewhat faded decor leans old-fashioned, but it's a perfectly tidy, friendly place to land, whether you're in the Oasis property itself or Adams Bed and Breakfast, a neighboring outpost with similar facilities and the same management. A small continental breakfast is served, limited parking is available on-site on a first-come, first-served basis for $25, and there's a public garage nearby with $38, 24-hour parking. Note that weekend reservations often require a two-night minimum.

Nestled in the heart of Back Bay in a historic 19th-century building, the 164-room **Copley Square Hotel** (47 Huntington Ave., 617/536-9000, www.copleysquarehotel.com, $190-260) offers simple elegance, surprisingly reasonable nightly rates for the area, and proximity to nearby destinations like Newbury Street and the Boston Public Garden. While it's received several facelifts over the years, the Copley Square Hotel is actually one of the longest-operating hotels in Boston, with over 120 years of welcoming visitors to the city. The communal kitchen offers free coffee and light bites each morning, and valet parking is available for $59 per day.

$250-350

A trio of Back Bay town houses are linked up to make the **Newbury Guest House** (261 Newbury St., 617/670-6000, www.newburyguesthouse.com, $300-440). This bed-and-breakfast is walking distance from an appealing array of shops and cafés. Breakfast includes hot options like eggs and bacon along with croissants, fruit and yogurt, and hot drinks. Rooms are clean, light, and airy, and some have in-room fireplaces—welcome on blustery fall evenings. A few parking spaces are available on-site for $30/night; call when booking to reserve.

Over $350

Achingly cool and Instagram-ready, ★ **The Verb** (1271 Boylston St., 617/566-4500, www.theverbhotel.com, $320-660) combines a colorful rock-and-roll aesthetic with high-end service and style. The poolside scene is fun and occasionally boisterous; the bar serves strong, creative cocktails; and you can browse the lobby's vinyl library for something to spin on your in-room Crosley record player. Before a stem-to-stern overhaul, this was a Howard Johnson hotel, and The Verb raises a glass to that history at Hojoko, its on-site Japanese tavern. Valet parking is $68 per night, and you're a baseball-throw's distance from Fenway Park.

South End

$150-250

There's still a roller-skating rink beneath the armchairs and coffee tables at **The Revolution Hotel** (40 Berkeley St., 617/848-9200, www.therevolutionhotel.com, $180-250), an enormous YWCA-turned hotel. The stylish rooms range from basic queen suites to bunk bed quads, and the shared solo-occupancy bathrooms are full of fresh towels. While all rooms are private, the overall effect is hostel-like, with a room for movie nights, games, and convivial common spaces. This is a good choice for families, as triples and quads are available with no additional charge for extra guests. Plus, guests can nab a discounted parking rate of $30 per day at the nearby garage at 100 Clarendon Street.

Over $350

★ **The Clarendon Square Bed and Breakfast** (198 W. Brookline St., 617/536-2229, www.clarendonsquare.com, $329-399) feels consciously designed for travelers looking to savor the cosmopolitan delights of Boston. Encased in a classic Boston brownstone, this charming boutique hotel offers deluxe queen bed guest rooms and more spacious suites where you can avail yourself of plush robes, down duvets, and Frette linens after a long day of sauntering around the city. Then there's the rooftop patio and hot tub, where you can enjoy a glass of wine or champagne while gazing out at the twinkling lights of nocturnal Boston. Public garages within five minutes' walking distance of the hotel charge an average parking rate of $39 per day.

Cambridge

$150-250

Want to try Harvard-style living for a few nights without coughing up a semester's worth of room-and-board fees? The ★ **Irving House at Harvard** (24 Irving St., Cambridge, 617/547-4600, www.irvinghouse.com, $130-320) offers budget-friendly B&B accommodations right next door to the campus itself. Many of the 44 homey rooms have private baths, and the simple furniture and interior designs are complemented by perks like wall-mounted flat-screen TVs and, in some rooms, nook-like bunk beds that are great for kids. A continental breakfast is served daily, and limited free parking is available first come, first served at the small adjacent lot.

Over $350

Rising above the Charles River like a giant brick-and-glass Rubik's cube, **The Charles Hotel** (1 Bennett St., Cambridge, 617/864-1200, www.charleshotel.com, $379-649) puts you right in the nucleus of Harvard Square, in suitably chic digs. Rustic Shaker furniture, marble bathrooms, and old-school New England wall art spruce up the guest rooms and suites here. The hotel is also host to Regattabar, one of Cambridge's hottest jazz clubs, and New England farm-to-table restaurant Henrietta's Table. The hotel's underground garage offers parking for $45 per night.

Information and Services

Information

A good place to get oriented is the **Boston Common Visitor Information Center** (148 Tremont St., 888/733-2678, www.

Side Trip to Walden Pond

Walden Pond

The writer **Henry David Thoreau** built a cabin by this small, wooded pond in **Concord** where he chronicled a year in the woods. *Walden*, his 1852 book, has become a classic of American literature, beloved by generations of naturalists and armchair homesteaders. Thoreau's minute observations of passing seasons and the natural world are particularly beautiful, and his social criticisms cut as deeply today as they did in the mid-19th century.

It might come as a surprise, then, to see the bustling boat ramp, swimming beach, and grassy slopes filled with picnicking families of today's **Walden Pond State Reservation** (915 Walden St., Concord, 978/369-3254, www.mass.gov, daily 5am-7:30pm, $30/vehicle). While it may no longer be the place to contemplate Thoreau's "tonic of wildness," you can follow a path through the woods to the former site of his cabin, now marked with granite posts, visit a reconstruction of the cabin, and learn the natural and literary history of Walden Pond at a new visitor center.

And if Thoreau would have grumbled about the fuss and crowds at Walden Pond (the writer was certainly fond of grumbling), scholars of his life often point out that even in his day the small woods were no howling wilderness. He frequently walked home to Concord to drop his laundry at his mother's house or raid her cookie jar, and he was rumored to have slipped away with pies left unguarded on windowsills. Thoreau enjoyed visitors at his one-room cabin and made frequent calls at the home of fellow writer Ralph Waldo Emerson. For Thoreau was not Concord's only great thinker: The small community was also home to Nathaniel Hawthorne and Amos Bronson Alcott, a political reformer and father of Louisa May Alcott, and the writers were part of a vibrant Transcendentalist community committed to self-reliance, social justice, and spiritual experiences.

After exploring Walden Pond, lovers of American literature can pick up the trail of Concord letters on the **Emerson-Thoreau Amble** (www.concordma.gov), a 1.7-mile (2.7-km) walking path that winds from Walden Pond to **Heywood Meadow** (Heywood St. at Lexington Rd.). The path goes by Thoreau's cabin site and bean field, a pond where Thoreau took the Alcott and Emerson children on berry-picking outings, and a partial view of Ralph Waldo Emerson's house.

Getting There from Boston

Follow I-93 North to Route 16 West and Route 2 West. In Concord, turn south onto Route 126. Walden Pond State Reservation is on the right (19 mi/30.5 km, 0.5 hr).

bostonusa.com, Mon.-Fri. 8:30am-5pm, Sat.-Sun. 9am-5pm), located in the park halfway between the Park Street and Boylston Street T stops. There you can pick up maps and guides, along with discount museum coupons and brochures for major attractions. It's also the starting place for the Freedom Trail and several trolley tours around the city. The National Park Service runs its own **Faneuil Hall Visitor Center** (1 Faneuil Hall, 617/242-5642, www.nps.gov/bost, July-early Sept. daily 11am-5pm, mid-Sept.-June Wed.-Sun. 11am-5pm), which includes a good collection of books on Boston and Massachusetts. If you are planning ahead, you can contact the **Greater Boston Convention & Visitors Bureau** (800/733-2678, www.bostonusa.com) for additional publications with the latest tourist information. The NPS also has a Boston-specific **app** with tours, maps, and info.

Attraction Passes

While many of Boston's most appealing experiences are free, seeing the city's museums and attractions can add up quickly. A couple of cards and passes bundle attractions under a single price, often with a dizzying array of variations: The app-based **Go City All-Inclusive Pass** (www.gocity.com, $79-159 adults, $49-114 children) has passes in increments ranging from a single day to a week and includes admission to many of the city's best sites, with no limits on the number you can visit each day. If you're a fast-moving sightseer and plan to check out classic Boston attractions like the New England Aquarium, the Paul Revere House, and Fenway Park, this is a great deal. For those who like to take more time at museums and historic sites, though, it might be hard to get enough value for the cost.

If just a couple of specific places are on your list, it's definitely worth purchasing tickets to them via the same company's **Explorer Pass,** where you select your destinations and save between 15 and 50 percent by purchasing in advance. Another option is the **Boston City Pass** (www.citypass.com, $79 adults, $67 children), which includes the New England Aquarium and the Museum of Science, plus two additional destinations of your choice: Franklin Park Zoo, the Harvard Museum of Natural History, a skyline observatory visit in Back Bay, or a harbor cruise. You'll have nine days to visit all of the sites included with your pass. Who it works for: anyone already planning to visit two of the higher-dollar attractions on a more relaxed schedule.

Services

Emergencies

For medical emergencies, call 911. Boston has many hospitals with 24-hour emergency rooms, including **Massachusetts General Hospital** (55 Fruit St., off Cambridge St., 617/726-2000, www.massgeneral.org) and **Tufts Medical Center** (800 Washington St., 617/636-5000, www.tuftsmedicalcenter.org).

Getting Around

Car

Ask local drivers about Boston's behind-the-wheel style, and they'll describe their competitive, fast-moving traffic as part of the city's Hobbesian soul. Ask anyone else in New England, and they'll explain how Bostonians earned their regional nickname: Massholes.

If you can get around without it, it's far easier and cheaper to leave your car in a garage while in Boston. Check with your accommodations first, as many often have a deal with a nearby location.

Parking

It's possible to find street parking in Boston, but regulations can be Kafkaesque, with varied time limits and many resident-only zones. If you do find on-street parking, meters are active Monday-Saturday, 8am-8pm, and most

The Places in Between: Lexington, Concord & Lincoln

sign in front of Hartwell Tavern at Minute Man National Historical Park

Boston may be a hub of history and recreation, but west of the city, the suburban towns of **Lexington, Concord,** and **Lincoln** add depth and color to the story of Massachusetts (and the country). Some of the earliest, most incendiary fights of the Revolutionary War happened here. Writers who would help define American literature made their homes in these hills and hollows. To this day, the melange of historic relics and timeless woodlands amid these "battleground towns" may just inspire you to reflect on the past—or to look creatively to the future.

Lexington: 14.7 miles/23.6 km from Boston

Lexington, linked to Boston and Cambridge via Massachusetts Avenue, is where the first American colonists shed blood in defiance of Great Britain in 1775. The inaugural shootout between Lexington's militia and recently arrived British soldiers went down on the **Lexington Battle Green** (1625 Massachusetts Ave., Lexington), located in the center of town and marked by Henry H. Kitson's iconic **Minuteman Statue.** (You might

take both coins and credit cards, as well as payment through the **ParkBoston app.**

In downtown, **Boston Common Garage** (0 Charles St., 617/954-2098, weekdays $28 for 3-10 hrs, $32 for 10-24; weekends $14 for 1-3 hrs, $16 overnight) is large, convenient, and affordable. The **North End Garage** (600 Commercial St., 617/723-1488, $29 for 2-10 hrs, $39 for 10-24 hrs) is close to TD Garden and North End sights. Prices fluctuate and some small lots offer good discounts: Parking app **SpotHero** (www.spothero.com) is an excellent way to search for nearby spots using custom time parameters, often at discounted prices—though some garages require you to print your pass. Most garages do not include "in and out" privileges.

One bargain option is to leave your car outside of the city entirely. Some MBTA stations have enclosed garages that are much cheaper than city parking: **Alewife Station** (11 Cambridgepark West, Cambridge, www.lazparking.com, overnight parking $9) is convenient and big, with 2,471 spaces in an enclosed garage. Alewife is at the end of the Red Line, and

recognize this from the back of the Massachusetts quarter.) The minutemen were so dubbed because they were expected to be ready for battle on a minute's notice.

Concord: 19.6 miles/31.5 km from Boston

You can follow in the footsteps of militia members and British soldiers by visiting **Minute Man National Historical Park** (978/369-6993, www.nps.gov/mima, free) and walking or biking the five-mile (8-km) **Battle Road Trail** from Lexington to Concord. You'll pass ancient stone walls, preserved buildings like the Hartwell Tavern, and monuments dedicated to important moments like Paul Revere's capture by the British. But there's more here than wartime mementos. **Nathaniel Hawthorne's former home,** a preserved colonial house called **The Wayside** (455 Lexington Rd., Concord, www.nps.gov/mima, Mon.-Sun. 9:30am-5:30pm, $7 adults, free 16 and under), still stands along the trail. And a short walk down Lexington Road, at the Battle Road Trail's terminus in Concord, you'll find **Louisa May Alcott's Orchard House** (399 Lexington Rd., Concord, 978/369-4118, www.louisamayalcott.org, Apr.-Oct. Mon.-Sat. 10am-5pm, Sun. 11am-5pm, Nov.-Mar. Mon.-Fri. 11:30am-3:30pm, Sat. 10am-5pm, Sun. 11am-5pm, $15 adults, $12 seniors and students with ID, $8 youth 6-17). This is where Alcott cranked out the first draft of *Little Women.* Thanks to decades of preservation efforts, every room inside looks just like it did when Alcott was crafting her opus—even the furniture, like the "shelf-desk" that Alcott's father built for her. Thirty-minute tours are offered every half hour.

Lincoln: 17.8 miles/28.6 km from Boston

Lincoln is shorter on historic buildings, but big on lush forests and natural oases like **Walden Pond.** It's the intuitive place for Bostonians to come wander, physically and mentally. The network of hiking trails at **Mount Misery** (Rt. 117, Lincoln, www.lincolnconservation.org) is far more resplendent than the name might suggest, bypassing steep hills and fields that bring to mind Terrence Malick's *Days of Heaven* at dusk. Even Walden itself boasts some overlooked and rugged side trails to spots like **Emerson's Cliff,** a rocky pinnacle where Thoreau's Transcendentalist pal had aspired to build a poet's lodge. But one particularly compelling house of creation that made it past the blueprint stage is the nearby **deCordova Sculpture Park and Museum** (51 Sandy Pond Rd., Lincoln, 781/259-8355, www.decordova.org, Mon.-Fri. 10am-4pm, Sat.-Sun. 10am-5pm, $14 adults, $12 seniors and students, free children under 13), whose art galleries overlook nearby Flints Pond and where massive sculptures lurk in the surrounding forest and gardens.

frequent trains make the 25-minute trip to downtown Boston.

Public Transit

Boston has some of the gnarliest traffic in America, ranking right up there with Los Angeles and Atlanta. For peace of mind (and to save on parking costs), use public transit whenever possible. The "T," which is short for MBTA or **Massachusetts Bay Transportation Authority** (617/222-3200, www.mbta.com), is cheap, safe, and easy to use. Subway fares are $2.40 with an e-ticket, cash, or a reloadable Charlie Card that you can pick up at major stations. All four of the MBTA's colored subway lines service Boston's downtown and historic neighborhoods. For Fenway, the Green Line is your best bet. The Orange Line extends to Jamaica Plain, while the Red Line crosses the Charles River and burrows into Cambridge. You can even catch the Blue Line from Logan Airport to reach downtown Boston. More out-of-the-way locations require taking an MBTA bus, which can be slowed by Boston's gridlock congestion but offer extensive coverage across the city. Fares are currently $1.70. Often overlooked as a means of transportation are the ferries that ply Boston Harbor. A trip from Charlestown Navy Yard to Long Wharf (perfect after completing the Freedom Trail) costs $3.70.

Taxi

Keep in mind that the MBTA doesn't run 12:30am-5:30am. The only option at that time is to take a taxi, which isn't cheap. Fares start at $2.60 for the first one-seventh mile (0.3 km), and add $2.60 for each additional mile (1.6 km), with $28 for each hour of waiting time. Also note that trips to Logan are saddled with an additional $2.75 for tolls.

Call a cab from the hybrid fleet of **Boston Cab Dispatch** (617/536-5010, www.bostoncab.us), which also has wheelchair-equipped cars, or try **Boston Logan Taxi Cab** (617/499-4800, www.bostonlogantaxicab.com), whose website allows pre-booking for airport pickups. **Uber** and **Lyft** services are also available in Boston.

Coastal
Maine

Highlights

★ **Whale-Watching:** Spot the humpback whales that spout and breach across the waves (page 98).

★ **Lighthouse Bagging:** Every rocky peninsula and outcropping has its very own lighthouse, from hidden gems to crowd favorites (page 104).

★ **Portland's Breweries:** Taste your way through microbreweries in a beer-obsessed city by the sea (page 114).

★ **Lobster Feast:** Dig into great piles of steamed lobster and clams at a rustic island dinner (page 134).

★ **Paddling Penobscot Bay:** The best way to see Maine's rocky coves and historic harbors is by boat, allowing you a seal's-eye view of the coast (page 147).

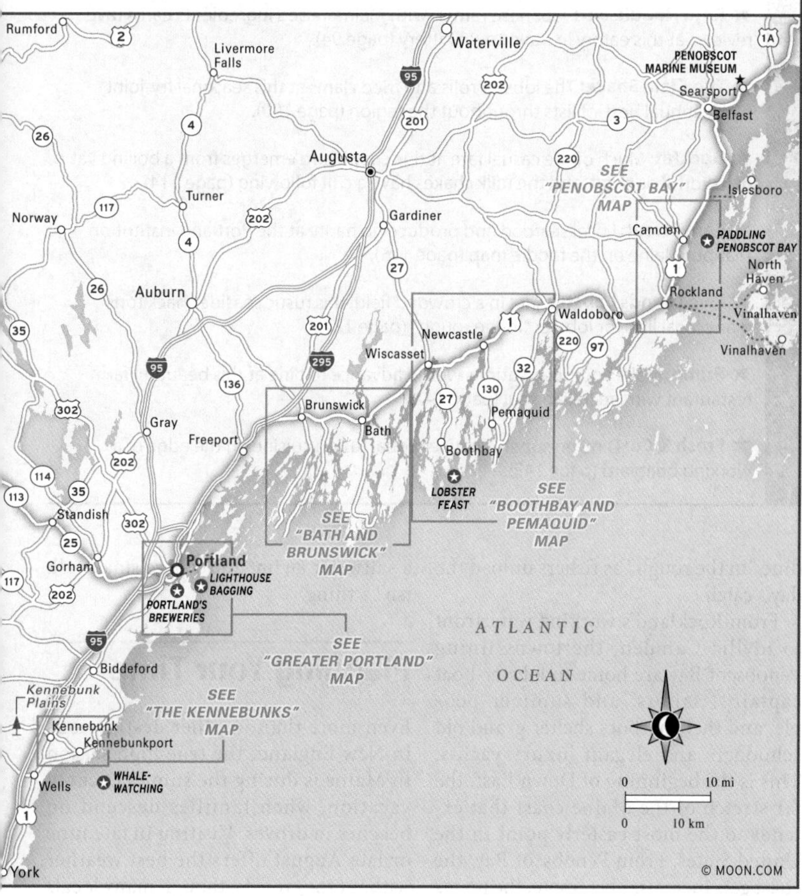

Trace a route along Maine's 3,500-mile (5,633-km) waterfront, and you'll find fishing towns, far-flung beaches, and one of New England's most vibrant small cities.

Within day-tripping distance from Boston, the south coast is a classic vacation getaway for city crowds who come to sail and socialize in grand seaside inns. This is the pinnacle of Maine beach chic, with perfect sand, gentle surf breaks, and elegant waterside dining. A few lighthouses up the coast, Portland is the cultural capital of the state, with a fabulous setting and quality of life that draw creative talent from around the country. Framed by a pair of scenic parks, downtown overflows with boat-to-table restaurants, microbreweries, and art.

Beyond Portland, the shoreline goes wild, fracturing into deep coves and bays; proud shipwright towns stand back from the sea on tidal rivers that sent merchant vessels and warships to every corner of the globe. Roads to the shore dead-end at seasonal lobster shacks where you can

Best Restaurants

★ **Anju Noodle Bar:** Japanese ramen with Maine-raised ingredients earns rave reviews at this eatery in downtown Kittery (page 94).

★ **The Clam Shack:** The lobster rolls and fried clams at this seasonal fry-joint make annual best-of lists throughout the region (page 100).

★ **Duckfat:** Much of the casual fare at this cozy bistro emerges from a boiling vat of flavorful duck fat, and the milk shakes have a cult following (page 114).

★ **Fore Street:** Local seafood and produce go haute at the Portland institution that put Maine on the foodie map (page 115).

★ **Five Islands Lobster Co.:** In a crowded field, this rustic seaside shack tops many local lists for lobster "in the rough" (page 127).

★ **Primo:** Make your reservations well in advance to dine at this beautiful farm restaurant with an Italian soul (page 142).

★ **Fresh & Co:** Dine on super-creative global fusion cuisine on the edge of a working boatyard (page 149).

dine "in the rough" as fishers unload the day's catch.

From Rockland's working waterfront to idyllic Camden, the towns lining Penobscot Bay are home to lobster-boat captains, sailors, and summer people, and their harbors shelter grand old schooners and elegant luxury yachts. This is the beginning of Down East, the far stretch of the Maine coast that extends to the most easterly point in the United States. From Penobscot Bay, the coast gets increasingly remote, the towns divided by long passages of deep forest and rugged shoreline leading onward to the scenic jewel of Acadia National Park.

Cerulean seas, balsam firs, ancient lighthouses, and buttery lobster rolls are just a few staples of New England's most postcard-perfect landscape. It seems to seduce everyone—even the most cynical New Englanders—and its menage of land-and-ocean can feel otherworldly. But the simpler way of life in coastal Maine is special, too. This is a place where dinners are savored, where a summer day's work is rewarded with a saltwater swim, and where small talk isn't a thing.

Planning Your Time

Even more than in other destinations in New England, the true high season in Maine is during the summer school vacation, when families descend on beaches in droves. Visiting in late June or late August offers the best weather without the crowds, though many locals say September is the finest month, with still-warm days and cooler nights. At any time of year, however, the weather can be unpredictable, and Maine can seemingly pass through multiple seasons in a single day, with sunshine giving way to fog and rain before turning again.

Experiencing the highlights of coastal Maine takes at least a week, especially when summer crowds turn Route 1 into a series of bottlenecks. Allot this much time, and you can take in the region in a series of clusters (with less time, perhaps

Best Accommodations

★ **Sandy Pines Campground:** Spend the night in a glamped-out Conestoga wagon or camper van on the banks of a gorgeous salt marsh (page 102).

★ **Seaside Inn:** Catch sunrise—and sunset—on the beach from this perfectly placed, old-fashioned hotel (page 103).

★ **Inn by the Sea:** Luxurious rooms, rescue puppies, and ecofriendly policies? A location on the south coast's best beach doesn't hurt either (page 116).

★ **Hermit Island Campground:** Fabulous campgrounds can be found up and down the coast, but this one's got an island to itself (page 127).

★ **Old Granite Inn:** Homey and historic, this laid-back inn is perfect for watching sails and seabirds drift by (page 144).

★ **16 Bay View:** Wake up to the sounds of schooner lines and lapping waves at a boutique hotel with a rooftop terrace (page 151).

focus on one, and avoid Route 1 when possible for expediency).

Spend a couple of days exploring south coast lighthouses, beaches, and restaurants from the Kennebunks—Kennebunkport and Kennebunk—or Portland, with time to visit the outdoors or comb the shelves of mom-and-pop shops. Make your second destination one of the towns of Maine's Midcoast, such as Brunswick, Bath, Wiscasset, or Damariscotta. Plenty of museums and historic downtowns are along Route 1, but don't miss the chance to get off the main road, following quiet highways to island communities and seaside lobster shacks.

After making its way through inland forests, Route 1 finds the coast in Penobscot Bay, where a trio of wonderful towns is perched on picturesque harbors: Rockland, Rockport, and Camden are ideal places to trade your car for a kayak or berth on a historic schooner and explore islands dotting the coast.

Orientation

Perched just before the coastline crumbles into a squiggly line of bays and peninsulas, Portland is the cosmopolitan hub and gateway to Maine's bounteous shoreline. Beyond the city, other destinations on the Maine coast lie along Route 1, a two-lane highway lined with banks of wildflowers and thick forest. Traffic often slows to a crawl in each of the towns along the way, where quieter coastal roads sheer off into fishing villages and deep inlets.

Getting to Coastal Maine

Driving from Boston

90 mi/145 km, 1.5 hr

To get to Maine's south coast from Boston, head out on **I-93 North,** then take Exit 37A to merge onto **I-95 North** ($2 toll in New Hampshire). For **Kennebunk,** take **Exit 25** ($4 toll), and follow **Route 35** into downtown (90 mi/145 km, 1.5 hrs). For **Portland,** stay on I-95 until **Exit 44** ($5 toll), merging onto **I-295.** Stay right and take Exit 7 for downtown locations (110 mi/177 km, 1.75 hrs).

Driving from New Hampshire's White Mountains

65 mi/105 km, 1.5 hr

Driving to coastal Maine from the White Mountains means a trip through rural farmlands and mountains on two-lane roads. To drive to **Portland** from **Conway, New Hampshire,** take **Route 113 East** until it merges briefly with **Route 25 East,** then make a slight right in Gorham to continue onto **Route 112 North.** When Route 112 intersects **Route 114 South,** turn right on Route 114, following it beneath the interstate. Turn left onto Mussey Road, which becomes West Broadway, following signs to **I-295 North.** Merge onto I-295 North for 3.3 miles (5.3 km) and take Exit 7 to downtown Portland.

To reach the Kennebunks from Conway, leave town on **Route 113 East** across the border into Maine, turning right in Fryeburg to continue onto **Route 113 South** for 18 miles (29 km). Turn right onto **Route 117 South/Route 5 South** into Cornish, where you'll turn left to stay on **Route 117.** After 2.5 miles (4 km), turn right to stay on Route 117 for another 16 miles (26 km), then turn right onto **Route 35 South** for 18 miles (29 km) into downtown **Kennebunk.** It's approximately 65 miles (105 km) and 1.5 hours of driving time to reach either Portland or Kennebunk from Conway.

Driving from New York City

295 mi/475 km, 4.5 hr

The drive from New York City to coastal Maine takes around 4.5-5 hours, though it can be significantly longer with traffic. Leave New York City heading north on **FDR Drive.** Use the left lane to access Exit 17 to the **Robert F. Kennedy Bridge** ($10.17 toll), then stay left to merge onto **I-278 East.** After 4.5 miles (7 km), I-278 East merges with **I-95 North** ($1.75 toll). Follow I-95 North 46 miles (74 km) to Exit 27A in Bridgeport, Connecticut; exit right onto **Route 8 North,** which you'll follow 5.5 miles (9 km) toward Exit 9 to **Route 15 North.**

Take Exit 68 NE to merge onto **I-91 North** toward Hartford/Middletown, then stay right for Exit 29 onto **Route 15 North** toward **I-84 East.** Use the left two lanes to continue onto I-84 East. North of Sturbridge, Massachusetts, I-84 East merges into **I-90** ($1.00 toll); stay right at the split for **I-90 East.** In Auburn, use the right two lanes to take Exit 10 to merge onto **I-290 East.** Use the left lane to take Exit 26B to **I-495 North,** then merge onto **I-95 North** at Exit 60. For **Kennebunk,** take **Exit 25** ($4 toll), and follow Route 35 into downtown (295 mi/475 km, 4.5 hrs). For **Portland,** stay on I-95 until **Exit 44** ($5 toll), merging onto **I-295.** Stay right and take Exit 7 for downtown locations (315 mi/507 km, 5 hrs).

Getting There by Air, Train, or Bus

Air

Maine's largest airport is **Portland International Jetport** (1001 Westbrook St., 207/774-7301, www.portlandjetport.org), with service from American Airlines, Delta, Frontier, JetBlue, Southwest, and United. There you'll find national car rental agencies Alamo, Avis, Budget, Dollar, Enterprise, Hertz, and National, and the **Greater Portland Transit District METRO** (207/774-0351, https://gpmetro.org), which has a bus from the airport to downtown Portland (Route #5, 6-15 buses daily).

Train

The Amtrak **Downeaster** (800/872-7245, www.amtrakdowneaster.com) runs from Boston to Brunswick five times a day. The Portland stop is at the **Portland Transportation Center** (100 Thompson's Point Rd.) two miles (3.2 km) outside of downtown, which you can reach by bus in 10-20 minutes (Route #1). Trolleys link **Wells Regional Transportation Center** with the Kennebunks, and the **Freeport**

Two Days in Coastal Maine

Rockland Breakwater and lighthouse

Day 1

Flip a coin: small-town escape or city experience? Choose the more urban option, and kick off your time in **Portland** with a trip to the **Portland Museum of Art,** taking in the Maine coast through the keen eyes of Edward Hopper and Rockwell Kent. Grab a quick cup of chowder in the **Old Port** before starting a tour of the city's excellent microbreweries. Shoppers should consider a side trip to the boutiques of **Exchange and Congress Streets,** and aspiring yachties can end the afternoon with a cruise on **Casco Bay;** either way, you'll have worked up an appetite for dinner at one of the city's many **boat-to-table** restaurants.

If your quarter came up small town, make a beeline for **Penobscot Bay.** Get the lay of the land by following a trail (or auto road) to the top of **Mount Battie** or **Mount Megunticook,** then descend to the coast for a seafood lunch on **Camden Harbor.** History buffs should make a detour to the **Penobscot Marine Museum,** but there's no better way to enjoy the coast than from a boat: Grab a paddle or head out on an afternoon sailing trip, then bring it back home for locally caught seafood at **Waterfront.**

Day 2

On day two, Portland adventurers can pick up pastries or doughnuts at one of the city's fabulous bakeries on their way to the lighthouses lining the rocky shoreline, then settle on pretty Crescent Beach at **Cape Elizabeth** for an afternoon of sun and sea. When the sun goes down, head back to the historic town center for dinner: Choose between gorgeous oyster joint **Eventide Oyster Co.** and upscale **Fore Street,** two of the best destinations for well-prepared seafood in coastal Maine. Rubbing shoulders with the colorful downtown crowd is part of the experience.

Small-town escapists can make their way to **Rockland** for a morning walk down the **Rockland Breakwater,** which crosses the harbor to a pretty brick lighthouse, then find a restaurant in the vibrant downtown. Explore paintings by three generations of Wyeths in the wonderful **Farnsworth Art Museum,** and take in a classic Maine sunset at **Owls Head Lighthouse.** Savor the magic hour in the Rockland hills with inventive Italian-inspired cuisine at Primo (reservations are a must).

station is within walking distance of downtown shops.

Bus

Concord Coach Lines (100 Thompson's Point Rd., Portland, 800/639-3317, www.concordcoachlines.com) operates buses from Boston and New York City; long-distance routes connect to Portland, then continue to many towns along Route 1, including Brunswick (16 Station Ave.), Bath (Mail It 4 U, 10 State Rd.), Rockland (Maine State Ferry Terminal, 517A Main St.), and Camden/Rockport (Maritime Farms, 20 Commercial St./Rte. 1, Rockport).

Greyhound (950 Congress St., Portland, 207/772-6588 or 800/231-2222, www.greyhound.com) has services to Portland and Brunswick from Boston.

The Maine Beaches: Kittery and York

The southern portal to coastal Maine is known as "the Maine Beaches"—a rather on-the-nose moniker of what awaits travelers here and farther north along I-95 and Route 1. Unlike the ritzy realm of the Kennebunks or the cosmopolitan bustle of Portland, the Maine Beaches' premier communities—Kittery and York—are home to some of the state's most overlooked natural amenities. The sandy expanse of York Beach, the barnacled rocks at Fort Foster Park, and the lookout tower atop Mount Agamenticus are worthy elements of a Maine expedition. But what really makes the Maine Beaches special is the lived-in atmosphere. Here, relative to other coastal enclaves, you're more likely to share a bar top, a hiking trail, or a stretch of beach with year-round Mainers whose livelihoods are rooted to the land and sea.

Fort Foster Park

Unlike the rest of Maine's coast, where lobster boats seem to come in all the colors of the rainbow, Kittery's waterfront is replete with naval docks and infrastructure. Kittery was a shipbuilding hub during the United States' colonial era and remains home to several battleships today. During World War II, the coastal landscape here was outfitted with artillery gun batteries and underwater minefields, in anticipation of invasion from the Axis Powers. Today, the old batteries are a neat feature of **Fort Foster Park** (Pocahontas Rd., Kittery, 207/439-2182, www.kitteryme.gov/fort-foster-park, late May-mid-Sept. daily 10am-8pm or dusk, whichever comes first, $20/vehicle), an 88-acre (35.6-ha) expanse of wooded trails and pebbly beaches where visitors can walk and climb through the detritus of New England maritime history. The park's centerpiece is a 565-foot (172-m) wooden pier that stretches out toward the horizon. It's the perfect place

to take in a sunset, with the nearby city of Portsmouth, New Hampshire, silhouetted across the water. The on-site charcoal grills and picnic tables are further reason to consider spending a summer evening here.

Shopping

When you're bound for Maine, chances are you'll find yourself wading through seaweed-laden salt water or swatting mosquitoes at dusk. Your best bet for the requisite outdoor gear and apparel is the sprawling **Kittery Trading Post** (301 Rte. 1, Kittery, 207/439-2700, www.kitterytradingpost.com, daily 9am-7pm), which is conveniently located a stone's throw off I-95. Featuring two floors of equipment for any conceivable Maine adventure, the "post" is also decorated with an impressive collection of taxidermy critters, including moose and bear. The staff can speak from plenty of experience when offering advice on what footwear or bug repellent to buy.

Sports and Recreation

A stopover to the Maine beaches demands some proper beach time. **Long Sands Beach** (Rte. 1A, May-mid-Oct., $2/hr parking kiosks) is a mile (1.6 km) of white sandy heaven located between the villages of York Harbor and York Beach. Here, amid the swell of beachgoers from the surrounding communities, you'll see it all: sunbathing, surfing, jogging, volleyball, and countless kids and parents splashing around in the surf, happy as clams. The entire beach is actually 15 miles (24 km) long, but the small sandy stretch is where most of the action is located. For a quieter beach day experience, drive 25 minutes north of York to the **Wells Reserve** (342 Laudholm Farms Rd., Wells, 207/646-1555, www.wellsreserve.org, daily 7am-dusk, $6 adults, $2 16 and under) and take the reservation's wildlife-rich trails one mile (1.6 km) past fields and apple trees to **Laudholm Beach,** a more secluded paradise buffered by briny estuaries. Since there's no public

the pier at Fort Foster Park

beachside parking at Laudholm, you're guaranteed relative solitude.

The popularity of coastal Maine overshadows the state's immense woods and craggy mountains deeper inland. But you don't have to leave the coastline to get a taste, thanks to York's own **Mount Agamenticus** (Mountain Rd., York, www.agamenticus.org, auto road access Apr.-Sept. daily 6am-dusk, Oct.-Mar. daily 7am-dusk). While "Big A" rises a modest 692 feet (211 m) above sea level, the dizzying list of trails that spiderweb up and down the mountain from all sides can be mixed and matched for a hike that will satisfy practically any taste. The **Ring Trail** and the **Sweet Fern** cutoff are especially worth considering, since they bypass several rusted ski lift towers that were once part of a winter resort that operated here through the early 1970s. There's also a free **auto road** that leads right to the top of Agamenticus, where visitors can enjoy an **observation deck** and tower that offers views of New Hampshire's White Mountains on a clear day.

Entertainment and Events

In a state where craft beer flows freely, **Tributary Brewing Co.** (10 Shapleigh Rd., Kittery, 207/703-0093, www.tributarybrewingcompany.com, Wed.-Sat. noon-7pm, Sun. noon-5pm) stands out for its cozy taproom and sun-splashed outdoor deck, and, more importantly, for the enviable quality of its ales and lagers. One brew in particular, a jet-black Russian imperial stout dubbed "Mott the Lesser" that's only offered a couple of times each year, draws a line of ravenous beer geeks that wraps around the building, rain or shine.

Food

Nothing says "Welcome to Maine" like a heaping basket of golden-fried whole belly clams, haddock, or shrimp from local roadside favorite **Bob's Clam Hut** (315 Rte. 1, Kittery, 207/439-4233, www.bobsclamhut.com, daily 11am-8pm, $14-25). A family-owned and decades-old stalwart for crispy fresh-caught seafood, Bob's has been applauded by everyone from *USA Today* food critics to Guy Fieri, the patron saint of American drive-in food. The coleslaw is some of the best in Maine: light on mayo and seasoned to savory perfection.

A popular spot is ★ **Anju Noodle Bar** (7 Wallingford Sq., Kittery, 207/703-4298, www.anjunoodlebar.com, Tues.-Thurs. and Sun. noon-9pm, Fri.-Sat. noon-10pm, $18-32), where big bowls of creamy chicken, pork, or vegetable-based ramen noodles are served in a minimalist wood-bound space that overlooks Wallingford Square, the center of Kittery's small downtown area. Be sure to leave room for a few appetizers like the miso-tahini-crusted cauliflower or the banh mi buns with local pork terrine.

If seaside sunsets, riesling wine, and a nice helping of lobster-stuffed chicken breast with Boursin sauce sounds like the cornerstone of a perfect day in Maine, call ahead and procure a table at the York Harbor Inn's **1637 Ocean View Restaurant** (480 York St., York, 207/363-5119, www.yorkharborinn.com/dining, Sun.-Thurs. 5pm-8pm, Fri.-Sat. 5pm-9pm, $18-40). Chef Gerald Bonsey is constantly putting his own spin on classic Maine seafood and farm-raised fare. True to its name, the restaurant offers some truly lovely views of the ocean from its softly lit dining room.

Accommodations and Camping

Camping

Steps away from Long Sands Beach is **Libby's Oceanside Camp** (725 York St., York, 207/363-4171, www.libbysoceancamping.com, mid-May-mid-Oct., pop-up camper sites $70, RV sites $105-130), which is just that: a collection of RV and pop-up tent sites beside the ocean. Have no illusions: You'll be sharing this space with many other campers. But the grounds and restrooms are well-maintained and the location is hard to beat for beach proximity.

Under $150

Routes 1 and 1A offer a seemingly endless buffet of motels, including national chains, but the better deals are often scored at indie lodgings like the **Coachman Inn** (380 Rte. 1, Kittery, 207/439-4434, www.coachmaninn.net, $90-180). The basic, understated rooms won't win any style awards, but that's not what you're here for: You're here to explore, and the Coachman is a well-situated base camp with comfortable beds, decent amenities, and competitive prices in the summer.

$150-250

Perched on the banks of the Piscataqua River, which flows along the Maine-New Hampshire border, the **Water Street Inn** (6 Water St., Kittery, 207/707-8855, www.waterstinn.com, $170-225) might just be the prettiest little nook for resting your head while in Kittery. Housed in a Victorian brick mansion and featuring eight sunny rooms with textiles and artworks that bring to mind the Maine landscape, the inn offers custom mattresses, keyless entry, and in-room climate controls among a generous list of amenities. Be sure to leave time to enjoy a complimentary morning coffee on the inn's front porch, where rocking chairs overlook plots of flowers.

Information

Stock up on maps and travel advice at the Maine Tourism Association's Kittery-based **visitor center** (I-95 and Rte. 1, Kittery, 207/439-1319, www.mainetourism.com, June-Sept. Sun.-Thurs. 8am-6pm, Fri.-Sat. 8am-8pm).

Getting Around

Street parking in both Kittery and York is free. The only likely place where you'll encounter metered parking is Long Sands Beach, where parking costs $2 per hour and is enforced daily from 8am to 10pm, mid-May through mid-October. Credit cards and cash are accepted at the parking kiosks.

The Kennebunks

The two towns that make up Maine's toniest seaside destination—Kennebunk and Kennebunkport—are filled with luxurious inns featuring platoons of beach chairs on the waterfront. A great, sweeping curve of beach in Kennebunk is one of the best on the southern coast, with plentiful sand and sunrise views of the bay. And the Kennebunk River, a spidering tidal waterway that divides the pretty villages, also offers places to swim and sit away from the blustering waves of the sea.

While the Kennebunks' reputation is for blue bloods and well-heeled types (an image bolstered by the presence of the Bush clan in an eye-catching compound on Ocean Avenue), it's not that much more expensive than destinations farther north along the coast. Ways to get on the water here include helming a sailboat, searching for whales on the offshore banks, and paddling into knee-high rollers on a surfboard. Streets are lined with old-fashioned colonial and federal homes, the whitewashed facades and bright shutters of which are classic New England. Even travelers blazing a path for Down East islands could while away an afternoon in Kennebunkport's Dock Square, with its nautical boutiques, galleries, and riverside cafés, or spend some time in Cape Porpoise, a village within Kennebunkport just a few miles up the coast from the city center.

Sights

You won't find the usual local historic paraphernalia at the **Brick Store Museum** (117 Main St., Kennebunk, 207/985-4802, www.brickstoremuseum.org, Tues.-Fri. 10am-5pm, Sat. 10am-4pm, Sun. noon-4pm, $5 adults, free youth under 17).

The Kennebunks

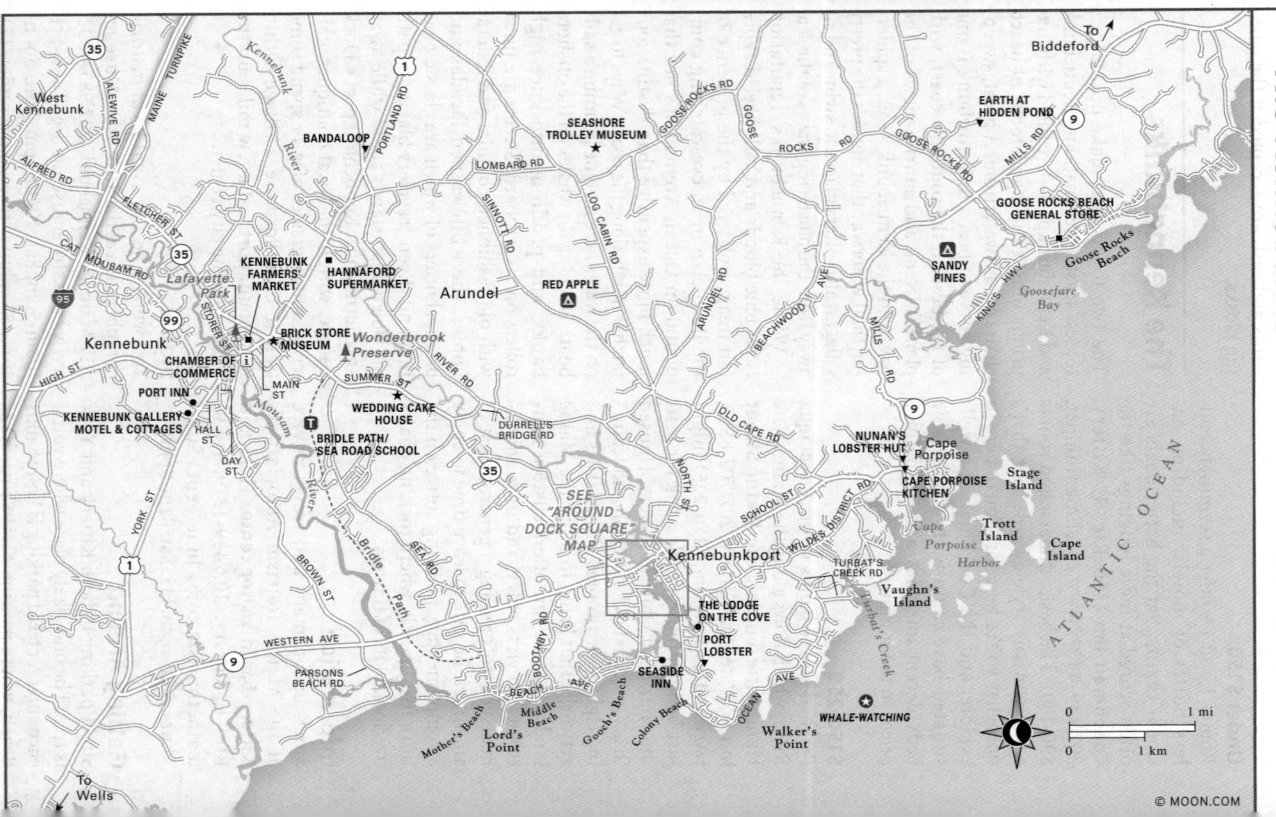

Instead, the staff gets creative with frequently rotated themed displays such as *The Kennebunks During the Civil War* and *Kennebunks A-Z*. The museum also runs a one-hour walking tour of the historic district every Saturday at noon and Thursday at 10:30am throughout the summer. Maps of the sites are also available if you'd prefer to explore the areas on your own (guided tours $5, maps $5).

Step back into the golden days of narrow-gauge rail at the **Seashore Trolley Museum** (195 Log Cabin Rd., Kennebunkport, 207/967-2800, www.trolleymuseum.org, June-Oct. Wed.-Sun. 9:30am-4:30pm, open weekends in May and first two weeks of Dec., $13 adults, $11 seniors and children 6-16, $6 children 3-5, free under 3). With a collection of more than 250 trolleys (some of which you can ride through nearby woods from the museum), plus a gift shop dedicated entirely to streetcars, the museum is well suited to enthusiastic kids and train aficionados alike.

The 1825 **Wedding Cake House** (104 Summer St., Kennebunkport) has become an essential sight for many visitors, who stop along the road to peer through the fence (the house is no longer open to the public). On a street with trim and tidy colonial gems, the overwrought Carpenter Gothic exterior *is* eye-catching, though the building sinks deeper into disrepair with each passing winter.

Entertainment and Events

Nightlife

While there's plenty of nightlife in the Kennebunks to go around, the main event is sunset, when boat drinks and microbrews flow at packed waterside bars. For a local vibe, flotsam-inspired decor, and Geary's beer on draft, the **Pilot House** (4 Western Ave., Kennebunk, 207/967-9961, Mon.-Fri. noon-9pm, Sat. noon-midnight) is right by a marina and often has live music on weekend afternoons. The cavernous **Federal Jack's** (8 Western Ave., Kennebunk, 207/967-4322, www.federaljacks.com, daily 11:30am-10pm) is less atmospheric but has plenty of seating on deep balconies overlooking the water. A little farther into Kennebunk, **Old Vines Wine Bar** (173 Port Rd., Kennebunk, 207/967-2310, www.oldvineswinebar.com, Sun.-Thurs. 4pm-10pm, Fri.-Sat. 4pm-11pm) makes up for an inland location with a rooftop patio, gorgeously crafted cocktails, and the best wine list in town. On the other end of the spectrum, the **Arundel Wharf** (43 Ocean Ave., Kennebunkport, 207/967-3444, daily 11:30am-9pm) is more rum-and-coke than riesling, but you'll be served on a floating dock in the Arundel River.

Festivals and Events

Free **Concerts in the Park** (Lafayette Park, Kennebunk, mid-June-mid-Aug. Wed. 6:30pm-7:30pm) feature classic rock and jazz bands; bring a picnic blanket to spread out on the grass. In early June, the **Kennebunk Festival** (www.facebook.com/thekennebunkportfestival) gathers local celebrity chefs and winemakers for a series of tastings and themed dinners. Later that month, **Launch! Maritime Festival** (www.gokennebunks.com) celebrates the Kennebunks' nautical heritage with seafood cook-offs, boat parties, and the annual Blessing of the Fleet.

Shopping

Packed with adorable gift shops and maritime galleries, Kennebunkport's **Dock Square** easily offers a day's worth of window-shopping. Equal parts hip and classic, **Daytrip Society** (4 Dock Sq., Kennebunkport, 207/967-4440, www.daytripsociety.com, daily 9am-10pm) is full of sweet treasures, nautical doodads, and stylish little books. Among the galleries scattered around downtown, **Landmark Gallery** (31 Ocean Ave., Kennebunkport, 207/967-0020, www.landmarkgallery.net, mid-May-mid-Oct. daily 10am-5pm) has one of the finest collections of maritime art, mostly paintings by regional artists. Find whimsical crafts and gifts at **Abacus** (2 Ocean Ave., Kennebunkport, 207/967-0111, www.abacusgallery.com, Sun.-Thurs. 10am-6pm, Fri.-Sat. 10am-8pm), a sprawling store ideal for aimless browsing.

Sports and Recreation

★ Whale-Watching

Humpback, finback, and minke whales congregate and feed at offshore banks, where they luxuriate in a whale's dream buffet of tiny sea creatures. Try to catch a glimpse aboard ***Nick's Chance*** (4 Western Ave., Kennebunk, 207/967-5507, www.firstchancewhalewatch.com, 4.5-hr trip $59 adults, $39 children and infants), an 87-foot (26.5-m) vessel that makes daily trips mid-June-September and weekend trips in the shoulder season. The boat goes up to 20 miles (32 km) offshore, so even if the weather on the beach is balmy, bring plenty of warm clothing (and your favorite seasickness remedy). No refunds are given for trips when no whales are spotted, but passengers get a free pass for a second outing. The same company also runs 1.5-hour cruises on a **lobster boat** that's a fun, inexpensive way to explore the coast and see what's on the other end of all those colorful lobster buoys ($30 adults, $20 children).

Beaches

The 1.5-mile (2.4-km) stretch of coastline known as **Kennebunk Beach,** located where the Kennebunk River reaches the ocean and about 1.2 miles (2 km) away from Dock Square, is actually a series of three beaches, scalloped curves neatly separated by small, rocky outcroppings. Farthest east and easily the most popular of the three, **Gooch's Beach** is long and easy to access (if you've already secured a parking place downtown, it's easy to reach Gooch's Beach by bicycle or on foot: Leave Dock Square heading west on Western Ave., then turn left onto Beach Ave.) but dwindles to a thin strip of sand at high tide. Next in line is **Middle Beach,** a quieter portion where the sand

Nick's Chance in Kennebunkport, ready for a whale-watching trip

gives way to smooth stones that keep away sunbathers and sandcastle builders. **Mother's Beach** is small and sandy, with a good playground that makes it a hit with young families. A $25 parking fee for Kennebunk Beach is charged from mid-June to mid-September. The local Intown Trolley also makes stops at the three beaches.

On busy summer weekends, it's often worth making the trip to **Goose Rocks Beach** in Cape Porpoise. Wide and scenic, the beach is rimmed with dune grass and perfect for strolling or taking a dip into the bracingly cold water. Parking at the beach is limited, and passes are required 8am-6pm, late May-early September; buy a sticker from the kiosk at **Goose Rocks Beach General Store** (3 Dyke Rd., Kennebunkport, 207/967-2289, June-Aug. 10am-2:30pm, $30). A pass doesn't guarantee you'll find a spot, and the store advises showing up before 8:30am for the best chance at parking.

Biking

Back roads and trails around the Kennebunks invite endless exploration on two wheels. Though the way is narrow, winding, and sometimes clogged with sightseers, the eight-mile (13-km) one-way ride down Ocean Avenue from Kennebunkport to **Cape Porpoise** via Wildes District Road is among the most scenic in town; the jewelbox seaside village has a few good seafood restaurants and an ice cream shop for mid-ride recovery. A gentler option is the flat, dirt **Bridle Path** that runs two miles (3.2 km) along the Mousam River; the main access point and parking is at **Sea Road School** (29 Sea Rd., Kennebunk).

The 65-mile (104-km) **Eastern Trail** (www.easterntrail.org) stretches along the coast from Kittery to South Portland, including 22 miles (35 km) of smooth, off-road trail between Kennebunk and Bug Light in South Portland (parking available at Kennebunk Town Hall). Rent an e-bike, road, or mountain bike at **Coastal Maine Kayak + Bike** (8 Western Ave., Kennebunkport, 207/967-6065, daily 9am-5pm, bikes from $19 half day, $39 full day), which also offers guided tours of coastal roads and trails.

Boating

All eyes are on 55-foot (17-m) schooner *Eleanor* when she cruises down the coast with gaff-rigged sails flying, and a trip with Captain Rich feels like stepping back into the grand old days of New England sailing. ***Eleanor*** (43 Ocean Ave., Kennebunkport, 207/967-8809, www.schoonereleanor.com, $75 day cruise, $85 sunset sail) makes two-hour outings daily May-September, and passengers are welcome to bring snacks and drinks aboard.

Hiking

Kennebunk Beach makes a great place to start the day with a sunrise walk. Just outside of downtown Kennebunk, **Wonder Brook Reserve** (www.kennebunklandtrust.org, parking on

Plummer Lane) has 2.5 miles (4 km) of footpaths through shady upland forest and banks of rustling ferns.

Old, sandy roads-turned-walking-trails run through pine barrens and grassland at **Kennebunk Plains** (Rte. 99, www.nature.org), which the Nature Conservancy bought in order to protect the endangered Morefield's leather flower, threatened northern blazing star plants, and endangered grasshopper sparrows. The reserve also has a treasure trove of **wild blueberries,** and late summer brings a luxurious crop of the tiny, intensely flavored fruit. (It's essential to stay on the trail when picking, however, as some of the plains' most vulnerable birds make their nests on the ground Apr.-Sept.)

Paddling

Paddle the Kennebunk River or follow the shoreline to **Goat Island Light** on a guided kayak outing with **Coastal Maine Kayak & Bike** (8 Western Ave., Kennebunk, 207/967-6065, www.coastalmainekayak.com, three-hour tours $94, kayak rentals from $64 half day and $94 full day), which also has a fleet of stand-up paddleboards. The Arundel River winds through scenic forest as it leaves the coast and is the most popular place for independent kayak trips, but outings must be timed to the tides (some paddlers have found themselves stuck in the mud). For information about local waterways and launch zones, stop by the **Chamber of Commerce** (16 Water St., Kennebunk, 207/967-0857, www.gokennebunks.com, Mon.-Fri. 10am-4pm).

Surfing

Unless there's a hurricane sending giant swells to shore (and sending expert surfers to the beach), the Kennebunks' waves are relatively gentle and beginner-friendly. Learn your way around the break at Gooch's Beach with one of the instructors from **Aquaholics Surf Shop** (166 Port Rd., Kennebunk, 207/967-8650, www.aquaholicsurf.com, 1.5-hr private lesson $110 1 person, $180 for 2, $250 for 3, rental boards from $25 half day and $35 full day), which also rents soft and hard-top boards.

Food

Kennebunk

The main contender for best lobster roll in town is ★ **The Clam Shack** (2 Western Ave., 207/967-3321, www.theclamshack.net, May-Oct. daily 11am-8pm, $15-28), which has gotten top scores from a who's who of food magazines and television shows. The riverside spot charges a premium for its version, but stuffs the toasted hamburger buns with a pound of lobster in large, meaty chunks dressed with your choice of mayonnaise or butter.

It's a travel truism that nothing says "tourist trap" like a giant board screaming: "Locals eat here!" The thing about the **Pilot House** (4 Western Ave., Mon.-Fri. noon-9pm, Sat. noon-11pm, $13-25), though, is that locals really do spend their time on the riverside patio or bellied up to the inside bar outfitted with outboard motors and fishing gear. Geary's beer on tap, a convivial atmosphere, and a decent menu of fried grub (which many regulars like to cap off with a Jell-O shot, or three) make this a fine place to nurse a pint at the end of the day, listening to conversations about tourist foibles and fishing.

Grab a few basic foods, along with deli sandwiches and some prepared items, at **H. B. Provisions** (15 Western Ave., 207/967-5762, www.hbprovisions.com, daily 6am-9pm). For a more extensive selection, a **Hannaford Supermarket** (65 Portland Rd., 207/985-9135, Mon.-Sat. 7am-10pm, Sun. 7am-9pm) is on Route 1. Meet local bakers, farmers, and artisans at the **Kennebunk Farmers' Market** (1 Garden St., www.mainefarmersmarkets.org, May-Nov. Sat. 8am-12:30pm), rain or shine.

Kennebunkport

There's nowhere to sit at **Port Lobster**

(122 Ocean Ave., 207/967-2081, www.portlobster.com, daily 9am-6pm, $15-30), but you can bring your takeout lunch across the street to the edge of the Arundel River and find park benches and views of the local fishing fleet. This seafood shop buys lobster and fish straight from the boat, and its lobster roll is simple and to-the-point: toasted white hot dog bun and tender meat just kissed with mayonnaise. The short menu also includes crab rolls, seafood salads, and chowder that come highly recommended.

A long-standing fine dining destination, **The White Barn Inn** (37 Beach Ave., 207/967-2321, www.whitebarninn.com, daily 5:30pm-9pm, four-course prix fixe $165, nine-course tasting menu $275, wine pairing $90) has won seemingly every award and honor a restaurant can earn in the United States. It has impeccable service, and the 19th-century barn setting makes a luxurious backdrop for the food, which balances classic and creative flavors.

With offbeat offerings ranging from Lemon Pink Peppercorn to Malbec & Berries, **Rococo Artisan Ice Cream** (6 Spring St., 207/251-6866, www.rococoicecream.com, daily noon-10pm, $5-7) is the sweetest game in town. Lucky for wafflers, the shop serves ice cream in "flights," including four small scoops of different flavors.

Just outside Kennebunkport is funky and offhandedly cool **Bandaloop** (1200 Portland Rd., Arundel, 207/967-4994, www.bandalooprestaurant.com, Tues.-Sat. 4:30pm-9pm, $22-35). This is an airy, energetic place to enjoy dinner made from organic, all-natural, and local foods served by a young, hip waitstaff. The menu changes frequently but includes creative dishes like pepita-crusted grilled haddock and Samoan sweet onion and poblano pepper stew. Bandaloop also has beautifully prepared vegetarian and vegan options.

Cape Porpoise

Though it's only three miles (5 km) down the road from the center of Kennebunkport, the village of Cape Porpoise is a place apart, with salt marshes and just a few places to eat in between the vacation homes lining the waterfront.

Cape Porpoise Kitchen (1 Mills Rd., Kennebunkport, 207/967-1150, www.capeporpoisekitchen.com, Mon.-Sat. 7am-7pm, Sun. 7am-6pm, $9-18) is your best bet for breakfast and lunch noshes that you can bring to your preferred beach or outdoor venue. Liberally loaded sandwiches and salads, hearty seafood chowders, and a rich roster of pastries are cornerstones of the menu. The cheese and wine selection here is also impressive, and potentially useful for anyone planning a more romantic oceanside picnic.

Like many Maine entrepreneurs, the late Captain George Nunan went into business in his front yard, selling kettle-cooked lobsters for barely a buck apiece. Word spread, things escalated, and in 1953 the retired fishing boat captain opened **Nunan's Lobster Hut** (9 Mills Rd., Kennebunkport, 207/967-4362, www.nunanslobsterhut.com, daily 5pm-8pm, $19-36). Today the wooden rafters of the hut are still festooned with lobster buoys and other maritime artifacts that speak to the timeless allure of the joint, as does the relatively straightforward Classic Maine menu. For hot-boiled local lobsters, followed by blueberry pie and ice cream, this is the place. Out a bit farther, **Earth at Hidden Pond** (354 Goose Rocks Rd., Kennebunkport, 207/967-6550, www.earthathiddenpond.com, daily 5pm-9pm, $75-100) is a top contender for a night of splashing out with its exquisite food and modern-design-meets rustic chic decor. Its menu of contemporary cuisine is rooted in local products and flavors, and while any spot in the restaurant makes a lovely place to spend the evening, two private screened-in shacks (first-come,

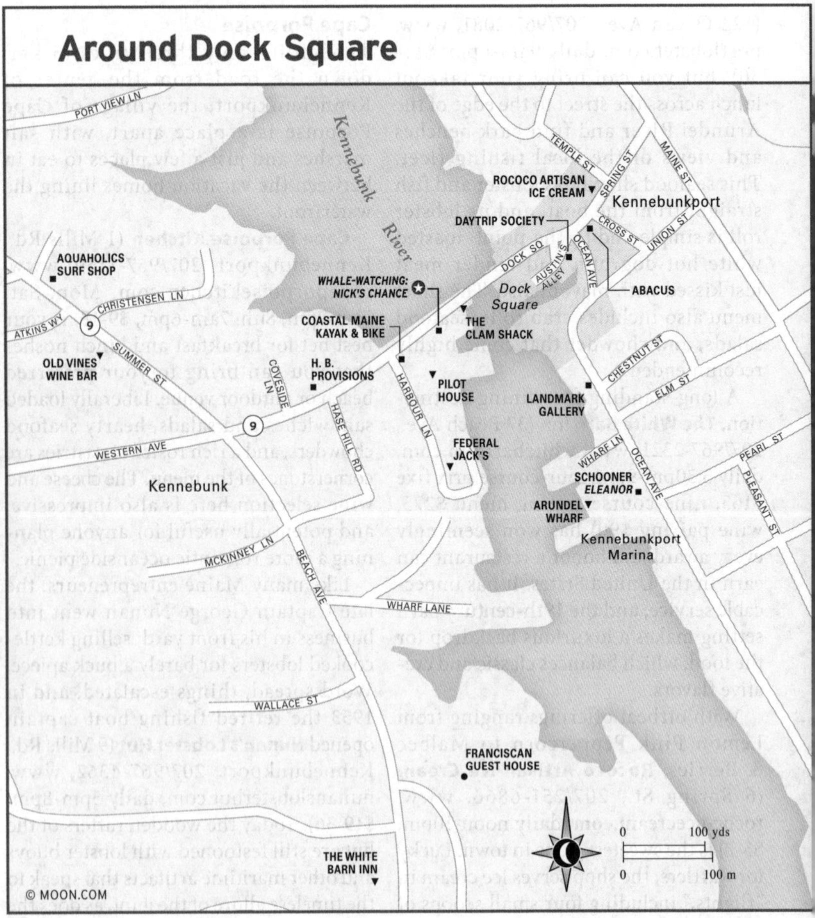

Around Dock Square

PORT VIEW LN
Kennebunk River
TEMPLE ST
MAINE ST
SPRING ST
ROCOCO ARTISAN ICE CREAM
Kennebunkport
DAYTRIP SOCIETY
CROSS ST
UNION ST
DOCK SQ
OCEAN AVE
AUSTIN'S ALLEY
AQUAHOLICS SURF SHOP
WHALE-WATCHING: NICK'S CHANCE
Dock Square
ABACUS
CHRISTENSEN LN
ATKINS WY
9
COASTAL MAINE KAYAK & BIKE
THE CLAM SHACK
OLD VINES WINE BAR
SUMMER ST
COVESIDE LN
H. B. PROVISIONS
CHESTNUT ST
PILOT HOUSE
HARBOUR LN
LANDMARK GALLERY
ELM ST
HASE HILL RD
9
FEDERAL JACK'S
WHARF LN
PEARL ST
WESTERN AVE
SCHOONER *ELEANOR*
Kennebunk
ARUNDEL WHARF
PLEASANT ST
Kennebunkport Marina
MCKINNEY LN
BEACH AVE
WHARF LANE
WALLACE ST
FRANCISCAN GUEST HOUSE
0 100 yds
0 100 m
THE WHITE BARN INN

first-served) are the most stunning places to enjoy a meal.

Accommodations and Camping

Camping

The hospitable **Red Apple Campground** (111 Sinnott Rd., Kennebunkport, 207/967-4927, www.redapplecampground.com, May-Oct., $61 tent, $70 RV, $75 full-service) has neat and tidy campsites set on a grassy clearing in the forest, as well as comfortable **cabins** ranging from four-person units with air-conditioning, cable TV, and a refrigerator to six-person options with a small kitchen, barbecue area, and outdoor fire pit ($150 cabins, 3-day minimum). A heated pool, camp store, and rec room give this spot a convivial feel, and if you order in the morning, the friendly owners will bring a fresh-cooked lobster dinner to your site at far-below Kennebunkport prices.

There's an inherent creativity to setting up a campsite in the middle of an otherwise rustic place, and the folks at ★ **Sandy Pines Campground** (277 Mills Rd., Kennebunkport, 207/967-2483, www.sandypinescamping.com, $149 huts, $259 trailers and wagons) have embraced this and cooked up a tempting menu of "unique retreat" glamping options. Choose from an A-frame hideaway hut, a spruced-up antique camper van, or an Oregon Trail-style Conestoga wagon outfitted with air-conditioning and a plush bed, all perched on the edge of a salt marsh. The on-site general store offers plenty of supplies such as s'mores kits, and the heated saltwater pool is particularly inviting at sundown.

$100-150

There's nothing fancy about **Kennebunk Gallery Motel & Cottages** (65 York St., Kennebunk, 207/985-4543, www.kennebunkcottages.com, May-Oct., $114-189), but the friendly staff and location just outside town make it an excellent find. Larger cottages have small, simple kitchens, and a volleyball court and pool keep things cheery.

$150-250

Set on the serene grounds of a Lithuanian Franciscan monastery, the nonprofit **Franciscan Guest House** (26 Beach Ave., Kennebunk, 207/967-4865, www.franciscanguesthouse.com, $149-299) is a converted boardinghouse that hosts retreats and a regular crowd of Lithuanian summer people. The dated, very simple rooms are not for everybody—same goes for faux wood paneling and flaxen-haired figurines—but it's a half-mile (0.8-km) walk to town or to Kennebunk Beach, and the guesthouse is a good deal for the location, with prices that fall to $129 in the shoulder season. Coffee and tea are available in the lobby each morning; all rooms have a fridge, cable television, and in-room bathrooms; and there's an unheated saltwater pool that's a treat for lounging.

Perfectly tidy and well-maintained, the **Port Inn** (55 York St., Kennebunk, 207/985-6100, www.portinnkennebunk.com, $145-210) has flourishes of contemporary style and color that keep it from feeling generic. A tasty grab-and-go breakfast is offered each morning and, given the location, this spot feels a bit more luxurious than the price would suggest.

Common spaces at the ★ **Seaside Inn** (80 Beach Ave., Kennebunk, 207/967-4461, www.kennebunkbeachmaine.com, $175-400) are somewhere between dated and homey, but rooms are comfortable and bright, and oceanfront rooms have big sliding doors that let in the sound of rolling waves and scent of the sea. For access to the beach, this spot is unmatched, with a private, sandy path that leads straight to the water. The breakfast buffet is essential, old-fashioned Maine: whole grain oatmeal, French toast with blueberries and syrup, and bowls of fresh fruit in a convivial dining room.

$250-350

Tucked in the woods above a secluded cove near Dock Square, **The Lodge on the Cove** (29 S Main St., Kennebunkport, 800/549-1248, www.lodgeonthecove.com, $249-389) takes a classic motor lodge and gives it a second life with dreamy pastel colors, contemporary furnishings, and complimentary beach and kayak rentals. The lineup of on-site amenities, which include a heated pool, bonfires, and a clubhouse with movie screenings, makes this place a good choice for families with kids. A light continental breakfast is served each morning at the hotel's central lodge building, where the friendly staff can help you nab dinner reservations for nearby restaurants.

Information

All the usual pamphlets, along with maps and good advice, are available at the **Chamber of Commerce** (16 Water St., Kennebunk, 207/967-0857, www.gokennebunks.com, Mon.-Fri. 10am-4pm).

Getting Around

A handful of municipal lots near Dock Square (including an especially large one off of Church Street) offer timed parking and easy access to local restaurants and shops, with the first 30 minutes on the house. Visitors seeking a break from driving can climb aboard the **Intown Trolley** (207/967-3638, www.intowntrolley.com, June-Oct., $54 double seat for two, free children under 2) follows a fixed route through town that takes in Kennebunk and Kennebunkport's main sights and beaches, with narration.

Portland

Perched at the aft end of Casco Bay, Portland's the last bit of solidly built earth before the coastline splinters into the bays, inlets, and islands of Midcoast Maine. Look closer, though, and the city itself seems all shoreline: heads, breakwaters, and lighthouses wrap in on themselves, pinching Portland's peninsular center between Back Cove and the Fore River. Downtown bristles with schooner masts and wharves that give way to a rugged, working waterfront.

That blend of picturesque charm and real-world maritime culture infuses the city, and wherever you go in the Old Port and peninsula, the sea is not far away. Cobblestone streets are lined with galleries, a museum, and boutiques celebrating Maine's seafaring traditions, and many of the city's chic bars and restaurants have a boat-to-table philosophy boasting chefs on a first-name basis with fishers, long-liners, and sea captains. The "locally sourced" boom that electrified New England's broader restaurant scene *really* got crackling in Portland during the 2010s, and today, the proof is in the abundance of Portland restaurants turning out the kind of creative and decadent fare that prompts visitors to contemplate relocating. When the weather is fine and Casco Bay sparkling, and the air smells of salt and fresh seafood and braised vegetables, many visitors find themselves brainstorming ways to start a new life in Portland.

Sights

To orient yourself in Portland, find its two major thoroughfares: Commercial Street runs between the Old Port and the working waterfront, which anchor the heart of Portland's peninsula. The Arts District centers on Congress Street, with a collection of fine art galleries, studios, and the excellent Portland Museum of Art. Meanwhile, to the west, up-and-coming areas Munjoy Hill and West Bayside are primarily residential, with a handful of art galleries and cafés. Cape Elizabeth is part of the greater Portland area, about a 20-minute drive south of the city down Route 77.

Lighthouses

With a craggy shoreline that's often wrapped in thick fog, it's no wonder the Portland area needs half a dozen lighthouses to keep boats off the rocks. Even with their blinking beacons, the city's seen centuries of dramatic and often tragic wrecks: the *Annie C. Maguire* ran aground right at the base of Portland Head Light on Christmas Eve 1886, and **Cape Elizabeth**'s two lights didn't save the RMS *Bohemian*, which struck an underwater ledge just off the coast. Set on pretty capes and outcroppings, lighthouses are part of the Maine landscape at its most picturesque, but even on sunny days, their powerful lenses and stout architecture serve as reminders that sailing Maine's waters has always been a dangerous undertaking.

★ Lighthouse Bagging

The most iconic among Portland's lighthouses is the **Portland Head Light** (1000 Shore Rd., Cape Elizabeth, www.portlandheadlight.com, museum and gift shop Mon.-Fri. 10am-2pm, Sat.-Sun. 10am-4pm, park daily sunrise-sunset);

Greater Portland

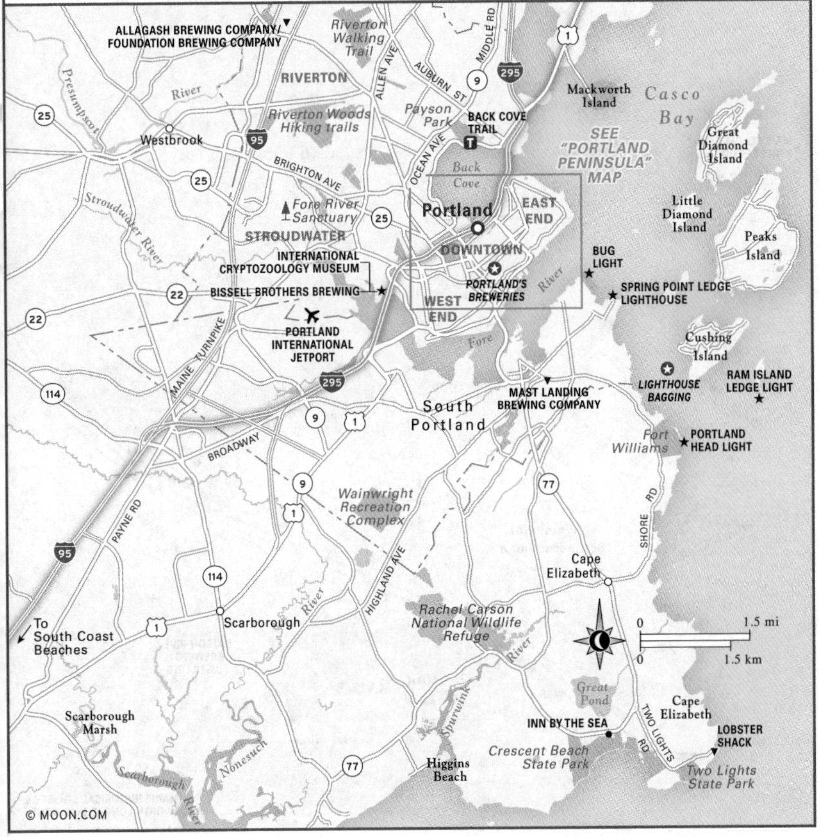

its slender proportions and red-roofed keeper's house are perfectly offset by jagged outcroppings and crashing waves. It was the first lighthouse completed by the U.S. government and has been guiding ships on Casco Bay since 1791; the rocky head is rich with history, including shipwrecks and daring, stormy rescues, and some believe it's haunted by the benevolent ghost of a former lighthouse keeper. One frequent visitor was hometown poet Henry Wadsworth Longfellow, who liked to drink with the lighthouse keeper.

Another favorite spot for lighthouse bagging is **Two Lights** (Two Lights Rd., Cape Elizabeth), a pretty pair of private lighthouses with a small beach and rocks perfect for hopping around and scouting for sea creatures. Confusingly, neither of the two lights is visible from Two Lights State Park, so just keep on down the road until it ends in a small parking lot. Since neither lighthouse is open to the public, the views (and photo opportunities) aren't quite as good as elsewhere, but this shortcoming is easily made up for nearby with a visit to **The Lobster Shack** (225 Cape Lights Rd., Cape Elizabeth, 207/799-1677, www.lobstershacktwolights.com, Mar.-Oct.

Portland Peninsula

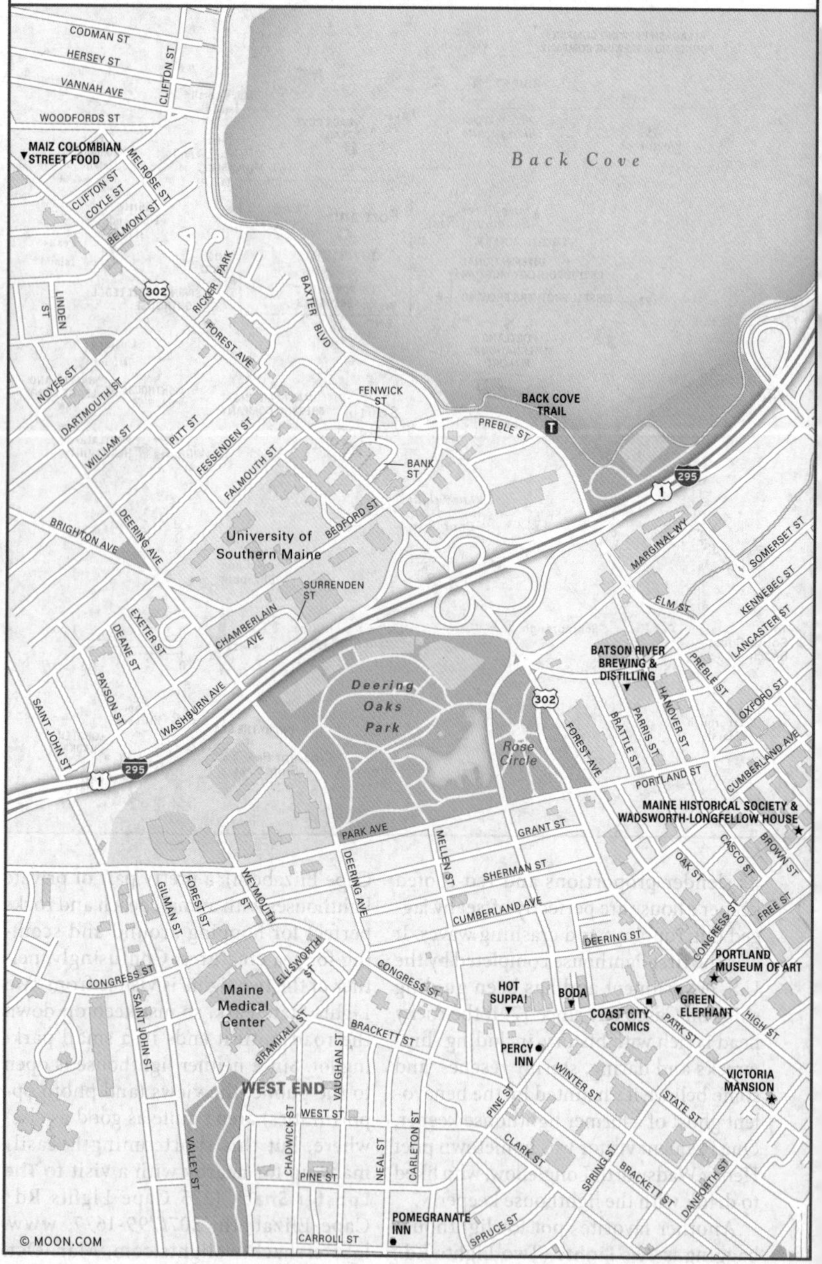
Back Cove
CODMAN ST
HERSEY ST
VANNAH AVE
CLIFTON ST
WOODFORDS ST
MAIZ COLOMBIAN STREET FOOD
CLIFTON ST
COYLE ST
MELROSE ST
BELMONT ST
302
RICKER PARK
BAXTER BLVD
FOREST AVE
LINDEN ST
NOYES ST
DARTMOUTH ST
WILLIAM ST
PITT ST
FESSENDEN ST
FALMOUTH ST
FENWICK ST
BANK ST
PREBLE ST
BACK COVE TRAIL
295
1
BRIGHTON AVE
DEERING AVE
University of Southern Maine
BEDFORD ST
SURRENDEN ST
CHAMBERLAIN AVE
EXETER ST
DEANE ST
PAYSON ST
SAINT JOHN ST
WASHBURN AVE
MARGINAL WY
SOMERSET ST
ELM ST
KENNEBEC ST
LANCASTER ST
BATSON RIVER BREWING & DISTILLING
PREBLE ST
HANOVER ST
PARRIS ST
BRATTLE ST
OXFORD ST
Deering Oaks Park
Rose Circle
FOREST AVE
CUMBERLAND AVE
PORTLAND ST
MAINE HISTORICAL SOCIETY & WADSWORTH-LONGFELLOW HOUSE
PARK AVE
GRANT ST
MELLEN ST
DEERING AVE
WEYMOUTH ST
FOREST ST
GILMAN ST
SHERMAN ST
CUMBERLAND AVE
OAK ST
CASCO ST
BROWN ST
FREE ST
CONGRESS ST
DEERING ST
ELLSWORTH ST
CONGRESS ST
CONGRESS ST
PORTLAND MUSEUM OF ART
Maine Medical Center
HOT SUPPA!
BODA
COAST CITY COMICS
GREEN ELEPHANT
HIGH ST
PARK ST
BRACKETT ST
BRAMHALL ST
SAINT JOHN ST
PERCY INN
WINTER ST
STATE ST
VICTORIA MANSION
WEST END
VAUGHAN ST
WEST ST
CHADWICK ST
PINE ST
NEAL ST
CARLETON ST
PINE ST
CLARK ST
SPRING ST
BRACKETT ST
DANFORTH ST
VALLEY ST
POMEGRANATE INN
CARROLL ST
SPRUCE ST
© MOON.COM

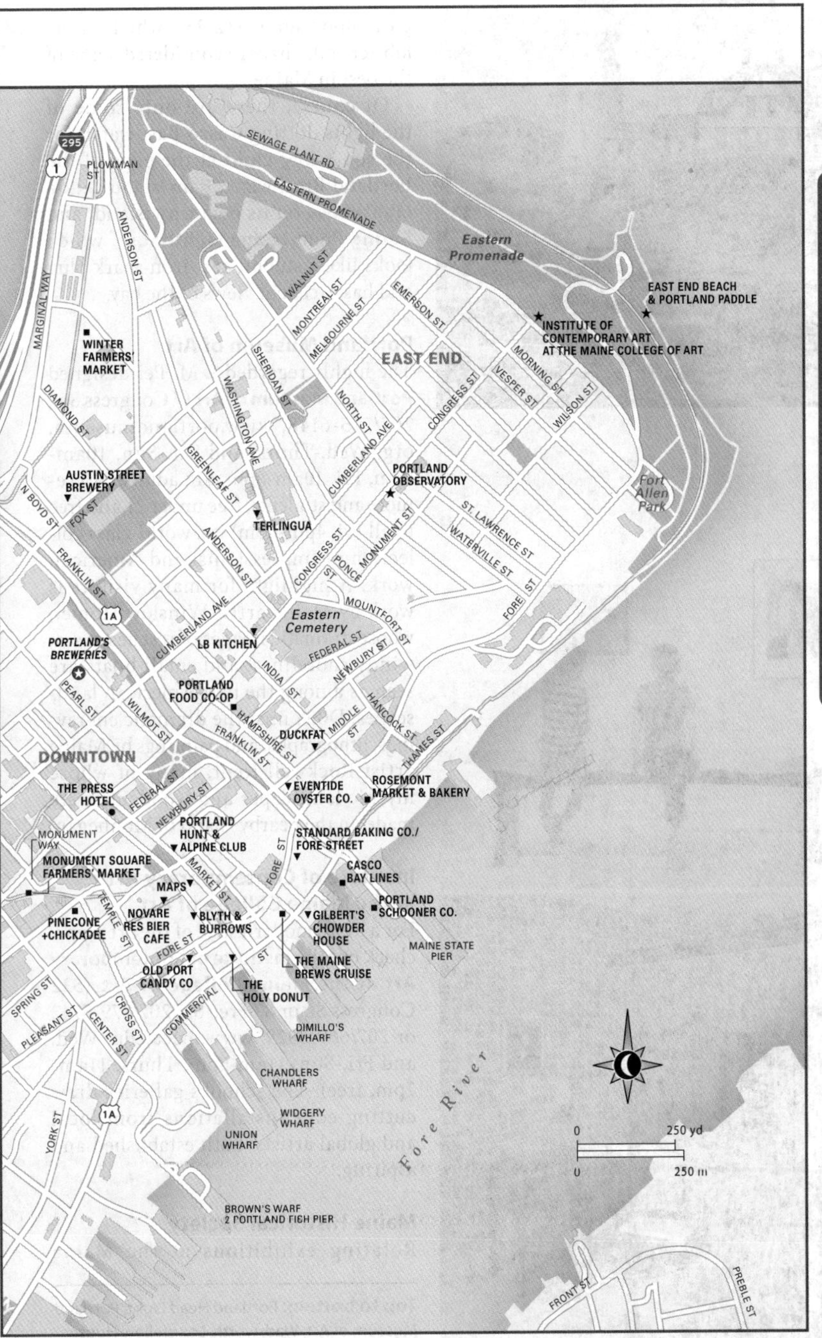

SEWAGE PLANT RD
EASTERN PROMENADE
Eastern Promenade
PLOWMAN ST
ANDERSON ST
MARGINAL WAY
WALNUT ST
MONTREAL ST
MELBOURNE ST
EMERSON ST
EAST END BEACH & PORTLAND PADDLE
INSTITUTE OF CONTEMPORARY ART AT THE MAINE COLLEGE OF ART
WINTER FARMERS' MARKET
EAST END
SHERIDAN ST
WASHINGTON AVE
NORTH ST
CONGRESS ST
VESPER ST
MORNING ST
WILSON ST
DIAMOND ST
GREENLEAF ST
CUMBERLAND AVE
PORTLAND OBSERVATORY
AUSTIN STREET BREWERY
N BOYD ST
FOX ST
TERLINGUA
Fort Allen Park
ST. LAWRENCE ST
WATERVILLE ST
MONUMENT ST
FRANKLIN ST
PONCE ST
FORE ST
MOUNTFORT ST
Eastern Cemetery
LB KITCHEN
PORTLAND'S BREWERIES
FEDERAL ST
NEWBURY ST
INDIA ST
PEARL ST
PORTLAND FOOD CO-OP
WILMOT ST
HAMPSHIRE ST
MIDDLE ST
HANCOCK ST
THAMES ST
DOWNTOWN
DUCKFAT
EVENTIDE OYSTER CO.
ROSEMONT MARKET & BAKERY
THE PRESS HOTEL
PORTLAND HUNT & ALPINE CLUB
MONUMENT WAY
STANDARD BAKING CO./ FORE STREET
MONUMENT SQUARE FARMERS' MARKET
MARKET ST
CASCO BAY LINES
MAPS
PORTLAND SCHOONER CO.
TEMPLE ST
PINECONE +CHICKADEE
NOVARE RES BIER CAFE
BLYTH & BURROWS
GILBERT'S CHOWDER HOUSE
MAINE STATE PIER
OLD PORT CANDY CO
THE MAINE BREWS CRUISE
THE HOLY DONUT
SPRING ST
PLEASANT ST
CENTER ST
CROSS ST
COMMERCIAL ST
DIMILLO'S WHARF
CHANDLERS WHARF
WIDGERY WHARF
UNION WHARF
YORK ST
Fore River
0
250 yd
250 m
BROWN'S WARF
2 PORTLAND FISH PIER
FRONT ST
PREBLE ST

daily noon-8pm, $12-25), which offers lobster rolls that are considered some of the best in Maine.

Of course, these are only some of the lights dotting Casco Bay; watch for the squat **Bug Light** at the edge of the Portland Breakwater, **Ram Island Ledge Lighthouse** on its own tiny island, and **Spring Point Ledge Lighthouse**, which looks like a stubby, cast-iron spark plug and has excellent views of the bay.

Portland Museum of Art

The highly regarded I. M. Pei-designed **Portland Museum of Art** (7 Congress Sq., 207/775-6148, www.portlandmuseum.org, Wed.-Thurs. and Sat.-Sun. 10am-6pm, Fri. 10am-8pm, $18 adults, $15 seniors and students, free under 21 and free to all Fri. 4pm-8pm) is a world-class collection of Impressionist and American work. A highlight for many visitors is work by Maine artist Winslow Homer, whose dramatic images of rescues at sea, windy shorelines, and small boats are seen as among the best American landscapes. Don't miss the dramatic engravings, lithographs, and paintings by Maine artist Rockwell Kent, many of whose mythic landscapes and woodcuts were made on the nearby island of Monhegan.

Institute of Contemporary Art at the Maine College of Art

For a more modern slice of the art scene, check out the **Institute of Contemporary Art at the Maine College of Art** (522 Congress St. or 87 Free St., 207/879-5742 or 207/669-5029, www.meca.edu, Wed. and Fri.-Sun. 11am-5pm, Thurs. 11am-7pm, free). The school's galleries draw cutting-edge installations from local and global artists, both established and aspiring.

Maine Historical Society

Rotating exhibitions at the **Maine**

Top to bottom: Portland Head Light; Portland Museum of Art; Wadsworth-Longfellow House

Historical Society (489 Congress St., 207/774-1822, www.mainehistory.org, Tues.-Sat. 10am-5pm, $10 adults, $5 children 6-17, free under 6) illustrate the state's past through collections, exhibits, and lectures. Particularly riveting are the exhibits pertaining to the shelling that Portland received at the hands of the British during the Revolutionary War, when the port, then known as Falmouth, was burned to the ground in October 1775. The British captain offered mercy if the townspeople would swear allegiance to King George. No oath came, and the city was destroyed—only to be rebuilt over the next two decades.

Wadsworth-Longfellow House

The **Wadsworth-Longfellow House** (487 Congress St., 207/774-1822, www.mainehistory.org, Tues.-Sat. 10am-5pm, guided 45-minute tours at 1pm and 2pm weekdays, $15 adults, $5 children 6-17, free under 7) was built in 1786 and achieved fame as the childhood home of poet Henry Wadsworth Longfellow. It's been restored to the time of the early 1800s, when Longfellow lived there. Guided tours chronicle the life of the poet, as well as other members of the Longfellow family, such as Revolutionary War general Peleg Wadsworth.

Portland Observatory

Tired of waiting for boats to round Spring Point Ledge and come into view, Captain Lemuel Moody built the **Portland Observatory** (138 Congress St., 207/774-5561, www.portlandlandmarks.org, May-Oct. 45-minute tours Thurs.-Mon. 10am-4pm, self-guided tours Tues.-Wed. 5pm-8pm, $10 adults, $8 seniors and students, $5 children 6-16) in 1807 so he could see harbor arrivals—and pass along the news to other shipowners for a tidy $5 annual fee. Climb the cheery red tower for Cap'n Moody's coveted lines of sight across Casco Bay and beyond, a vantage point especially sublime at sunset, when the waterfront and islands seem to glow on the sparkling water.

Victoria Mansion

Fans of Italianate architecture (or anyone who likes a pretty building) can swing by the **Victoria Mansion** (109 Danforth St., 207/772-4841, www.victoriamansion.org, tours May-Oct. daily 10am-4pm, late Nov.-early Jan. check website for off-season hours, $19 adults, $17 seniors, $6 students 6-17, free children under 6, $42 family). Built by a hotel magnate between 1858 and 1860, the mansion is considered one of the greatest surviving examples of pre-Civil War architecture in the country. Ahead of its time, it employed central heating, running water, and gas lighting in an era when such efficiencies were virtually unknown luxuries. These days the house is particularly impressive at Christmastime, when it's decorated from baseboards to ceilings with ornaments and wreaths.

International Cryptozoology Museum

The **International Cryptozoology Museum** (4 Thompson's Point Rd., www.cryptozoologymuseum.com, daily 10am-4pm, $10 adults, $5 children under 13, infants free) is paradise for any visitor who has willingly traded a night of insomnia to finish reading tales about Bigfoot, the Loch Ness Monster, or West Virginia's Mothman. The world's only museum dedicated to creatures that may or may not exist, this little gallery is full of eye-popping exhibits on specimens like the fur-bearing trout and a hybrid monkey-fish mermaid called the "Feejee." Plus, the place is usually busy with Mulder and Scully types who've spent their lives studying the cryptozoological kingdom, which makes for a bonus anthropological exhibit. You'll laugh, you'll gawk, and you might just walk away with that odd sensation that you've just seen something that you're not supposed to see. The museum's irreverent atmosphere makes it a fun stop for both adults and families with kids.

Entertainment and Events

Nightlife

Even if it weren't for all its breweries, Portland would have an amazing bar scene. Some of the most popular places to grab a drink are also restaurants, like **Eventide Oyster Co., Duckfat,** and **Terlingua,** but there are a few that go right to the point.

Nordic chic and Scandinavian-themed small bites prevail at the stylish **Portland Hunt & Alpine Club** (75 Market St., 207/747-4754, www.huntandalpineclub.com, Mon. 5pm-10pm, Tues.-Thurs. 2pm-11pm, Fri.-Sat. noon-1am, Sun. noon-11pm), where the low-ABV cocktails and Finnish meatballs earn rave reviews. Unless you're really looking, you'll walk right by **Novare Res Bier Café** (4 Canal Plaza, 207/761-2437, https://novareresbiercafe.com, Mon.-Thurs. 3pm-11pm, Fri. 3pm-1am, Sat. noon-1am, Sun. noon-11pm), which is tucked down an alley between Union and Exchange Streets. Between the shady beer garden and cave-like interior, it works in any weather, and has an enormous list of beers from around the world.

Drinkers who like their music on vinyl and decor eclectic will *love* **Maps** (64 Market St., 207/272-9263, Tues.-Sat. 4pm-midnight, Sun. 3pm-10pm), which feels like a basement apartment owned by a fashionable friend, but with drinks, cake, and grilled cheese sandwiches. And if you fancy bar-hopping without putting in the street mileage, Old Port-based **Blyth & Burrows** (26 Exchange St., 207/613-9070, www.blythandburrows.com, Mon.-Thurs. 4pm-11pm, Fri. 4pm-midnight, Sat. noon-midnight, Sun. noon-11pm) has you covered with two in-house watering holes and a subterranean speakeasy, all of which boast creative cocktails and briny nautical decor. (The joint is named after two captains who died during the taking of the HMS *Boxer* during the War of 1812, right on the Maine coast.)

Festivals and Events

With such a deluge of art venues, it's no surprise Portland offers a slew of performances, concerts, openings, and other events over the course of every year. One of the most regular—and festive—is the **First Friday Art Walk** (www.creativeportland.com/first-friday-art-walk, 5pm-8pm on the first Fri. of every month). In early June, artists from the Maine Academy of Modern Music collaborate with Old Port businesses to transform the waterfront and nearby parks into a sea-breezy concert ground for the **Resurgam Music and Arts Festival** (www.maineacademyofmodernmusic.org/resurgam). Another favorite is Mast Landing Brewing Company's **Wavy Days Festival** (www.mainebrewersfestival.com) in early August, which brings exceptional brewers from Portland and beyond to Thompson's Point for three days

of sharing their handiwork with the admiring, thirsty public.

Shopping

Pretty shops line the cobblestone streets of Portland's Old Port. For the most efficient browsing, make your way along Exchange and Congress Streets. One local favorite is the sweetly hipster **Pinecone + Chickadee** (6 Free St., 207/772-9280, www.pineconeandchickadee.com, daily 10am-6pm), which stocks unique clothing, vintage finds, and doohickeys that make perfect gifts. Comic book lovers from around the East come to **Coast City Comics** (634 Congress St., 207/899-1505, www.coastcitycomics.com, Mon.-Sat. 11am-8pm, Sun. noon-5pm) for its collection not only of comics but pinball and arcade games and vintage toys so fun the store could charge admission. And since no trip to Maine is complete without lingering by an old-school candy counter, save time for a stop at **Old Port Candy Co.** (422 Fore St., 207/772-0600, www.oldportcandyco.com, daily 11am-6pm), a family-owned emporium of confectionary delights such as gourmet chocolates and fudge, nostalgic gummies, and of course, classic saltwater taffy.

Sports and Recreation

Beaches

With great sunset views and a skinny strip of sand, **East End Beach** is pleasant for walking and kayaking, and more to the point, it's Portland's only public beach. It's set on the southern end of the **Eastern Promenade,** where monuments, cliffs, and smooth trails make for a haven from the city.

For the real Maine beach experience, it's worth heading out of town. Eight miles (13 km) south of Portland, **Crescent Beach** (66 Two Lights Rd., Cape Elizabeth, 207/767-3625, www.maine.gov, \$8 adults, \$2 seniors, \$1 children 5-11) is all dune grass and soft sand, a gorgeous place to watch the fishing fleet cross the horizon.

Congress Street

Boating

Take a turn hoisting the gaff-rigged sails—or let someone else do the work—on a two-hour cruise aboard the *Bagheera* or *Wendameen,* the 72- and 88-foot (22- and 27-m) schooners operated by **Portland Schooner Co.** (Maine State Pier, 56 Commercial St., Portland, 207/766-2500, www.portlandschooner.com, $53-63 adults, $37-63 children 12 and under).

An affordable way to get some water views is with a ticket for one of the ferries connecting Portland with the islands speckling Casco Bay. **Casco Bay Lines** (56 Commercial St., 207/774-7871, www.cascobaylines.com, passenger ferries $10-15, mailboat run $17 adults, $15 seniors, $9 children) runs trips to seven islands, from a quick hop to Peaks Island to the longer trip to Chebeague. The ferry service still delivers the mail to offshore communities, and you can tag along on the **mailboat run,** which lasts 2.5-3.5 hours; while the boat doesn't linger long enough for you to explore the islands, you'll get great views, and the crew narrates the whole experience on a loudspeaker (bring your own food and drinks).

Hiking and Biking

Walking and biking paths wind through Portland's streets, and much of the scenic waterfront is pedestrian-accessible. One of the finest places to walk or bike is **Back Cove Trail,** a 3.6-mile (5.8-km) paved trail that circles a small estuary just north of downtown. Hop on (and leave your car) at Payson Park, the northern access point, or Preble Street. If you're headed from north to south, the Back Cove Trail connects to the **Eastern Promenade,** a slender, waterfront park that caps Portland's East End neighborhood; 2.1 miles (3.4 km) end-to-end, the park has walking trails, a popular swimming beach, and showstopping sunrise views. **Portland Trails** (207/775-2411, www.trails.org) maintains a website with maps and directions to many of the city's best offerings, such as **Jewell Falls,** the only naturally occurring waterfall in Portland and a beauty of a cascade to behold during late spring and early summer as the flowers open up. The waterfall can be found at the northern edge of the **Fore River Sanctuary,** which is part of the vast and well-blazed Portland Trails network.

Paddling

Rent a kayak (or stand-up paddleboard) from **Portland Paddle** (Cutter St. and Eastern Promenade, 207/370-9730, www.portlandpaddle.net, kayaks $30 2 hrs, $40 half day, $55 full day, SUP $25 1 hr or $40 5 hrs) to explore Casco Bay on your own. Paddlers with basic skills can poke along the coast and beaches, while more experienced kayakers can visit uninhabited islands, the historic Fort Gorges, and offshore communities. The company also offers guided tours: Family paddles, moonlight outings, and sunset trips are just a hair more expensive than renting the equipment alone (tours from $40 adults, $35 children 10-17).

Food

From old-school seafood joints to achingly hip bistros, Portland punches far above its weight in the restaurant department, and deciding where to apportion your limited meals in the city can be challenging. Malaysian-style noodles with smoked pork and crab? Super-fresh salads packed with ingredients from local farms? How about cocktails and oysters within earshot of the waterfront's clanging masts and foghorns?

Seafood

A refreshing throwback to Portland's pre-hipster, rough-hewn days, **Gilbert's Chowder House** (92 Commercial St., 207/871-5636, www.gilbertschowderhouse.com, daily 11am-10pm, $8-23) slings fresh corn and clam chowders in a thoroughly unpretentious space. The crisp, flaky haddock sandwiches are another treat, as is the open terrace behind the restaurant; when the restaurant is packed, order a cup of soup to go and find a spot on the nearby wharves for a very Maine picnic.

The interior of the **Eventide Oyster Co.** (86 Middle St., 207/774-8538, www.eventideoysterco.com, daily 11am-11pm, $15-32) is almost too gorgeous: bright teal walls setting off a mammoth chunk of granite filled with crushed ice and sea creatures. The oysters—which mostly come from Maine, with a few out-of-state additions—are the obvious choice and centerpiece, and come with anything from kimchi ice to classic mignonette and cocktail sauce. Other options include small plates like house pastrami buns and halibut ceviche, but Eventide is famed for its lobster roll, a luscious combination of sweet lobster meat, brown butter, and chives in a soft Chinese-style steamed bun.

If you'd prefer a mini road trip with your seafood, **The Lobster Shack** (225 Cape Lights Rd., Cape Elizabeth, 207/799-1677, www.lobstershacktwolights.com, daily noon-8pm, $12-25) is a worthy goal. Nine miles (14 km) south of Portland, this teeny restaurant is located by a pair of lighthouses and has some of Maine's most beloved lobster rolls. The interior is decked out in marine bric-a-brac, and the outdoor picnic tables overlook crashing waves and the lighthouses—but be vigilant about seagulls to avoid losing bits of your meal. While the lobster roll is the main attraction here, The Lobster Shack also serves the standard lineup of market-price seafood, and a homemade strawberry rhubarb pie that gets rave reviews.

Bakeries

From dark chocolate with sea salt to maple bacon, the flavors of the soft, crisp-crusted treats at **The Holy Donut** (177 Commercial St., 207/331-5655, www.theholydonut.com, Mon.-Thurs. 7am-4pm, Fri.-Sat. 7am-6pm, $3-7) are some of the best around—for doughnut lovers, this shop is a pilgrimage place. Arrive early to get the best selection, and avoid coming at the end of the day, as the doors close when the last doughnut sells.

A rustic French aesthetic means great piles of croissants and fruit galettes at **Standard Baking Co.** (75 Commercial St., 207/773-2112, www.standardbakingco.com, daily 8am-5pm, $4-13), a beloved local institution walking distance from the Old Port. Breads and pastries are made with organic wheat flour from regional growers, and all the delightfully crusty loaves are naturally leavened.

Casual Fare

The farm-to-table food revolution that transformed Portland's restaurant circuit inspired people to look at vegetables and grains with a new sense of possibility. **LB Kitchen** (255 Congress St., 207/775-2695, www.lbkitchenportlandme.com, daily 8am-3pm, $10-16) embraces that spirit with a mouthwatering breakfast and lunch menu that feels plucked straight from the garden. Standouts include overnight oats with chia, banana, berry compote, and bee pollen, and the local tofu sandwich with carrot bacon, cashew cheese, and vegan sriracha mayo. The vibe is casual, and yet the soft-lit, cream-white interior makes this "kitchen" feel almost like a gallery for the culinary craft that's happening here.

Cheerful and welcoming, **Hot Suppa!** (703 Congress St., 207/871-5005, www.hotsuppa.com, daily 8am-2pm, breakfast $10-22, lunch $11-20) serves an eclectic selection of comfort food with Southern flair, like jambalaya scrambled eggs, shrimp and grits, fried green tomato BLTs, and some of the best corned beef hash in New England. Waits can get long, so aim to come early.

Named for a map-dot Texas town that hosts a yearly chili cook-off, **Terlingua** (52 Washington Ave., 207/808-8502, www.terlingua.me, Wed.-Mon. noon-9:30pm, $15-26) is a warm, vivid antidote to all that seafood. The barbecue fare at this laid-back restaurant is executed with a reverence for smoke and meat and

TOP EXPERIENCE

★ Portland's Breweries

In recent years, Portland has established itself as one of the best U.S. cities for beer, with microbreweries and tasting rooms cropping up on the margins of downtown and clustered around an industrial complex north of the peninsula. With so many artisan ales and lagers to choose from, navigating such a bountiful brewing circuit in just a day or two can feel overwhelming to first-time visitors.

Rather than try to experience the entire craft brewing scene on your visit, try planning your beer voyage with a more singular, tangible goal in mind: whether it's a type of beer you've been craving, a beer style you're curious about, or a beer venue where you can hang out and chew the scenery.

tasting room pour with lobster rolls at Allagash Brewing Company

♦ **For New England IPAs: Bissell Brothers Brewing** (38 Resurgam Pl., 207/808-8258, www.bissellbrothers.com, Mon.-Sat. 11am-9pm, Sun. 11am-7pm) is right next door to Portland's bus and rail station, reliably cranking out some of the haziest and hoppiest IPAs in Maine, such as their flagship ale, The Substance. If you're lucky, you might just end up here on a day when they're releasing Swish, a deliriously strong and unfiltered double IPA that's the stuff of legend among brew-hounds.

♦ **For Experimental Beers: Foundation Brewing Company** (1 Industrial Way, 207/370-8187, https://foundationbrew.com, Wed.-Sat. and Mon. noon-8pm, Sun. noon-6pm) has won raves for a rotating roster of inventive beers that are imbued with everything from imported Australian hops to seasonal Maine ingredients. Don't sleep on the

Tex-Mex flair, from street corn succotash to smothered brisket burritos. The lunch and dinner "barbecue boards" pair the tender house meats with fixins like pickles and honey butter cornbread, and regulars wash it all down with the killer house margaritas and solid beer choices.

Just down the road is another local favorite: ★ **Duckfat** (43 Middle St., 207/774-8080, www.duckfat.com, daily 11am-10pm, $12-21) serves a casual lineup of paninis, salads, and golden french fries redolent of—you guessed it—duck fat. Decor is exposed brick and magnetic poetry tiles, and the poutine topped with cheese curds, gravy, and a fried egg would fortify you for a week of lighthouse bagging. If at all possible, save room for one of the shop's luxurious milk shakes, and come prepared to wait most nights.

International

Cast-iron-cooked quail eggs with soy sauce and scallions is an appetizer that you won't encounter on many Thai restaurant menus in New England. But Portland favorite **Boda** (671 Congress St., 207/347-7557, www.bodamaine.com, Tues.-Thurs. 5pm-9:30pm, Fri.-Sat. 5pm-11:30pm, $15-26) invites diners to reach beyond staples like pad Thai and tom yum. Co-owner Dan Sripasert makes regular pilgrimages back to his native country to find new dishes to bring to Boda's beautiful wood dining

Bumbleberry Jam, a refreshing tart ale made with blueberries, strawberries, and raspberries, and if you're still acquiring a taste for beer (or ready for a change of suds), go rogue and try the "Zesty" spiked lemonade.

- **For Brewery Bites: Batson River Brewing & Distilling** (82 Hanover St., 207/800-4680, www.batsonriver.com, Tues.-Thurs. 4pm-9pm, Fri. 4pm-10pm, Sat. 11am-10pm, Sun. 11am-7pm) is renowned for malty pilsners and old-fashioned pot still vodka, and the dinner and brunch menus escalate the brewery experience with savory flair. Whether you're leaning toward ancho-braised short rib tacos or the strawberry rhubarb salad with scallops, you're pretty much guaranteed to walk away sated.
- **For Atmosphere: Austin Street Brewery** (1 Industrial Way, 207/200-1994, www.austinstreetbrewery.com, Thurs.-Sat. noon-7pm, Sun. noon-5pm) takes the shell of an old gas station and rejuvenates the space with bright colors, potted plants, and vines of twinkling lights. With indoor and outdoor seating, Austin Street is routinely buzzing with locals and visitors alike, comparing notes on signature offerings such as the citrusy, piney Patina Pale and the sweet-and-toasty, dark-as-espresso Milk Stout.
- **For Classic Beers: Allagash Brewing Company** (50 Industrial Way, 207/878-5385, www.allagash.com, Sun.-Mon. and Thurs. 11am-6pm, Fri.-Sat. 11am-7pm) is one of the hallowed grounds where Portland's craft beer scene began. Their Belgian white ale and trippel are Maine chestnuts that you'll find on tap lines and inside household refrigerators all over New England. But at the Allagash tasting room, you'll also encounter rarer brews like their "From Maine With Love" dark ale.

An excellent way to soak up the Maine brewing scene is on a tour, so you can sip flights to your heart's content without worrying about taking a cab or bus. **The Maine Brews Cruise** (79 Commercial St., 207/200-9111, www.brewscruise.com, tours from $95) runs fun, highly regarded bus tours and walking tours to the best taprooms in town, with food and drinks included.

room, from which diners can watch the bustle of Congress Street at dusk.

Arepas—ground maize dough pockets stuffed with juicy cuts of roasted meat, veggies, cheese, and more—are a Colombian classic that can sometimes get lost amid the broad spectrum of Latin American cuisine in the United States. Not so in Portland, thanks to **MAIZ Colombian Street Food** (621 Forest Ave., 207/400-2881, www.maizportland.com, Tues.-Sat. 11am-9pm, Sun. 11am-5pm, $8-15). This family-run eatery offers both specialty and build-your-own arepas, along with protein-heavy rice bowls and Colombian street eats like chorizo skewers and cheesy corn fritters.

Fine Dining

Vegetarians weary of meat-heavy Yankee fare shouldn't miss **Green Elephant** (608 Congress St., 207/347-3111, www.greenelephantmaine.com, lunch Thurs.-Sat. 11:30am-2:30pm, dinner Tues.-Sun. 5pm-9:30pm, $15-20), a top-notch Asian bistro with stenciled green walls and chandeliers. The spicy ginger noodles are a favorite with regulars, as are the tofu tikka masala and the citrusy vegetable "spare ribs."

Often credited with putting Portland on the international foodie map, ★ **Fore Street Restaurant** (288 Fore St., 207/775-2717, www.forestreet.biz, Sun.-Thurs. 5pm-10pm, Fri.-Sat. 5pm-10:30pm,

$35-53) could rest on its locally sourced, hand-crafted laurels for a decade. That makes it all the more refreshing that the kitchen continues to turn out such high-quality fare. An open kitchen keeps the industrial chic space from seeming too hushed as diners tuck into seafood roasted in a wood-fired oven or house-made charcuterie paired with a serious wine list.

Markets

Located on Munjoy Hill, **Rosemont Market & Bakery** (88 Congress St., 207/773-7888, www.rosemontmarket.com, Mon.-Sat. 8am-7pm, Sun. 8am-6pm) is "human sized" and stocked with regional vegetables, cheese, meat, and house-made baked goods as well as pre-made meals and sandwiches. The **Portland Food Co-op** (290 Congress St., 207/805-1599, www.portlandfood.coop, daily 8am-9pm) has aisles stuffed with local and organic products plus healthy, premade food.

Portland has three farmers markets overflowing with everything from local veggies to goat yogurt and kimchi. A carnival atmosphere commands at the downtown **Monument Square market** (456 Congress St., late Apr.-late Nov. Wed. 7am-1pm), while the market at **Deering Oaks Park** (late Apr.-late Nov. Sat. 7am-1pm) is a bit more relaxed. The **Winter Farmers' Market** (631 Stevens Ave., Dec.-Apr. Sat. 9am-1pm) also has live music and food trucks.

Accommodations

Though Portland has some wonderful top-end offerings, a lack of reasonably priced accommodations in the city makes sites like Airbnb and VRBO good options for travelers on a budget.

$150-250

Set on a quiet side street in the West End, the **Percy Inn** (15 Pine St., 207/871-7638, www.percyinn.com, $129-239) is in a renovated 1830s federal-style brick house that feels like pure, old-fashioned Portland. The house has some quirks and could use a bit of updating, but the overall effect is lovely; rooms are named for famous writers, and the firelit library and spacious common room are welcoming.

$250-350

Somewhere between bohemian whimsy and design-chic, **Pomegranate Inn** (49 Neal St., 207/772-1006, www.pomegranateinn.com, $250-370) is settled on a pretty corner in a historic neighborhood and full of visual treasures. Every room has unique hand-painted walls, and antiques are displayed alongside modern art. A 3rd-floor lounge is stocked with games, and a quiet back patio makes an ideal spot for enjoying the daily cookies, tea, and coffee. "The Pom" is operated by Lark Hotels, and serves the group's characteristic small-plate breakfast that will charm your socks off (and leave some hungry travelers looking for a bit more).

Flying typewriters and wordy art are reminders that **The Press Hotel** (119 Exchange St., 207/808-8800, www.thepresshotel.com, $265-460) was once the home of the *Portland Press Herald*, and the journo-chic theme runs throughout the property. Excellent service gives the large property a boutique feel, and the Inkwell coffee and wine bar feels like just the place to type up some hotel poetry of your own—local touches are everywhere and, all in all, Press offers some of the coolest digs in New England.

Over $350

Twenty minutes south of town (and a world away), ★ **Inn by the Sea** (40 Bowery Beach Rd., 207/799-3134, www.innbythesea.com, $526-2,350) has a perfect location set back from Crescent Beach, the finest stretch of sand in the greater Portland area. The luxurious resort has family-friendly bungalows and cottages as well as beautiful rooms in the main inn and perks like outdoor pools, a fireplace stocked with s'mores, and

That's Weird. . .

During the late 18th century, a family of Maine potato farmers—the Tuttles—purchased a plot of land near the town of Freeport for agricultural use. At first, the land proved splendid for growing potatoes and raising sheep. But for years, the Tuttles neglected to rotate their potato crops or keep their sheep from overgrazing, which caused the nutrient-rich topsoil to erode, exposing a layer of fine sand beneath the soil. (This sand is the byproduct of ancient glaciers moving and grinding rocks into sand particles.) As the Tuttles' soil broke down, more sand was exposed—eventually creating a desert-like expanse surrounded by Maine forest.

entering the Desert of Maine

But the Tuttles' loss was a gain for Henry Goldrup, a businessman who bought the land in 1919 and opened it to the public as the **Desert of Maine** (95 Desert Rd., Freeport, 207/850-3025, www.desertofmaine.com, May-Oct. daily 9am-5pm, $10 adults, children under 6 free). Strolling around the desert dunes is one of the strangest experiences to be had in Maine, and a sobering reminder of how land management can impact the natural world. But, promisingly, the pine trees and vegetation that flank the desert are gradually starting to overtake the sand, inch by inch. The self-guided desert tour is peculiar and unique, but there's also a built labyrinth to explore, which features gemstones, wishing bridges, and a hobbit house. Kids can also try their hands at paleontology and dig for fossils at select sites in the desert sands. And then there's the 19th century-style electric train, which offers scenic rides around the desert grounds 10am-3pm daily (weather dependent).

From Portland, head north on I-295 N toward Freeport. Take Exit 20, make a left at the bottom of the off-ramp, and follow the aptly named Desert Road to these strange sands.

complimentary beach cruiser bicycles for exploring the Cape. What sets the inn apart from other top-notch properties, though, is a remarkable focus on conservation; the on-site wetlands and meadows were overhauled to create habitat for the endangered New England cottontail rabbit, the inn runs environmental science education programs, and the chef works with local fishers to source from underutilized fish populations. It's also easy to leave the inn with an unusual memento of your stay—the staff fosters friendly dogs from the local humane society that can be adopted by guests; hundreds find new homes each year.

Information

The remarkably helpful and informative **Visitors Bureau** (207/772-5800, www.visitportland.com) has a website full of information and links, and runs an information center on the waterfront at 14 Ocean Gateway Pier (207/772-5800, Mon.-Sat. 9am-4pm, Sun. 10am-3pm, winter hours vary). You can also find three racks of brochures and visitor guides in the Jetport Terminal next to baggage claim.

Getting Around

Portland's local bus company is **METRO** (114 Valley St., 207/774-0351, www.gpmetro.org, $2 adults, $1 seniors, free children under 6, $6 all-day pass), which offers efficient connections from downtown to more suburban destinations, including the airport. Compared to most cities, Portland has a decent amount of metered street parking, which doesn't guarantee you'll find any right away (particularly in the summer), but the odds are good. That said, the city has pay lots and garages set up every few blocks. Local taxis to call include **Portland Taxi Service** (207/807-9079).

Bath and Brunswick

The scattershot coast that spreads south from Route 1 is anchored by a pair of solid brick towns, and they're a study in contrasts. Brunswick is home to Bowdoin College, which rambles outward from a picturesque campus filled with elite undergraduates and grand buildings named for famous alums. Nine miles (14.5 km) west, Bath is all union halls, shipyards, and hulking ironworks, an industrial town that once launched the world's grandest schooners.

Look closer, however, and the distinction blurs. Until it closed in 2011, the local naval air station meant that downtown pubs and cafés were likely to have as many service members as students, keeping Brunswick from feeling too precious. And while Bath's riverfront still rings with the sound of shipbuilding and workers, the pretty center is full of cafés, shops, and bookstores run by the liberal-leaning, creative community.

On a state-sized map of Maine, both towns seem to be a breath away from the sea, but it would be easy to pass through Bath and Brunswick with nothing but river views. To experience the best parts of this scenic stretch of coast, drive south, looping into the long peninsulas; the tangled coastlines are classic Maine, with fishing villages, lobster shacks, and sheltered bays that appear around every bend in the road, making for idyllic driving at a leisurely pace.

Brunswick

Sights

Bowdoin College

The pretty campus of **Bowdoin College** (255 Maine St., 207/725-3000, www.bowdoin.edu) is all soaring oaks and grassy quads, and would be a worthwhile place to stroll even without the college's two fascinating museums. The tiny **Peary-MacMillan Arctic Museum** (9500 College Station, 207/725-3416, www.bowdoin.edu/arctic-museum, Tues.-Sat. 10am-5pm, Sun. 1pm-5pm, free) traces the Arctic adventures of two Bowdoin graduates and explorers, Donald MacMillan and Robert Peary. In addition to stuffed Arctic animals and one of the original dog sledges from the Peary expedition, a display honors Matthew Henson, an African American explorer who was the first known person to set foot at the north pole and whose contributions to exploration went unrecognized until late in his life, when he was accepted to the New York Explorers Club at age 70. The other highlight on campus is the **Bowdoin College Museum of Art** (9400 College Station, 207/725-3275, www.bowdoin.edu/art-museum, Tues.-Wed. and Fri.-Sat. 10am-5pm, Thurs. 10am-8:30pm, Sun. 1pm-5pm, free), where an eclectic—and sometimes exquisite—permanent collection is on display alongside exhibits encompassing everything from Renaissance painting to edgy critiques of contemporary culture.

Androscoggin Swinging Bridge and Riverwalk

Maine boasts some of the coolest bridges in New England, as visitors will experience when driving Route 1 north along the coast. One of them is steps away from downtown Brunswick. Take a break from the road and stretch your legs on the **Androscoggin Swinging Bridge** (www.saveourbridge.org), a 332-foot-long

Bath and Brunswick

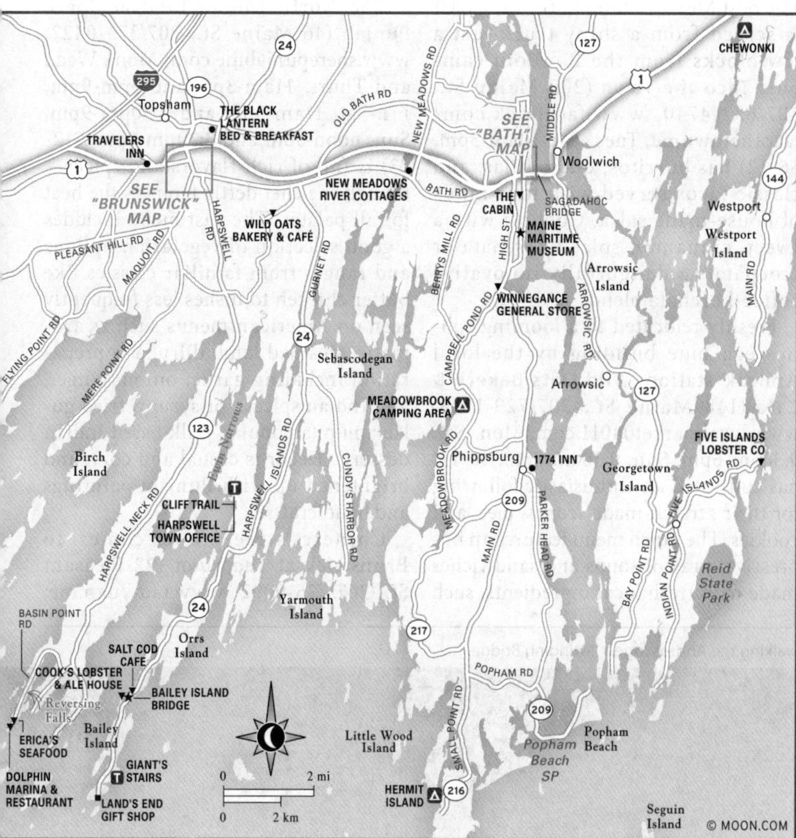

(101-m) suspension bridge that crosses the mighty Androscoggin River, swaying gently in the wind or under heavy foot traffic.

Originally constructed in 1892, the bridge was conceived as a commuter pathway for workers in nearby Topsham, who would cross the river into Brunswick each day to toil at the Cabot textile mill. Much of the bridge was rebuilt after a devastating flood destroyed part of the structure in 1936, but in the decades that followed, Brunswick and Topsham successfully lobbied for funds to perform repairs on the bridge. Their effort was boosted in 2004 when the bridge was added to the National Register of Historic Places for its engineering feat, and by 2006, the bridge was repaired, restored, and reopened to foot travelers once again. If you fancy a longer stroll, try the **Androscoggin Riverwalk,** a path that extends on both sides of the swinging bridge and ambles northeast along the river, eventually crossing the Frank J. Woods Bridge to form a loop. The parking lot for the bridge (on the Brunswick side) is located off Mill Street/Route 1, between its intersections with Swett Street and Cushing Street.

Food

Brunswick

The best Mexican food in the Midcoast is served from a shiny truck just a few blocks from the Bowdoin campus. **Taco the Town** (205 Maine St., 207/632-4740, www.facebook.com/tacothetownme, Tues.-Sat. 10am-3pm, $6-12) has burritos, quesadillas, and classic tacos served with four kinds of house-made salsa. Cool off with a sweet, cinnamon-spiced horchata or "cochata," a delightfully innovative coffee-horchata blend.

Freshly relocated to a looming robin's egg blue building by the local Amtrak station, **Wild Oats Bakery & Cafe** (148 Maine St., 207/729-1328, www.localmarket04011.com, Mon.-Sat. 9:30am-6pm, Sun. 9:30am-5pm, $6-12) has cultivated an enthusiastic following for their scratch-made scones, pies, and cookies. The lunch menu features an impressive array of soups and sandwiches made with fresh local ingredients, such as the vegan-friendly sriracha oat-and-nut burger.

The North Indian food at **Shere Punjab** (46 Maine St., 207/373-0422, www.sherepunjabme.com, Mon., Wed., and Thurs. 11am-3pm and 5pm-9pm, Fri.-Sat. 11am-3pm and 3:30pm-9pm, Sun. noon-3pm and 3:30pm-9pm, $12-23) is full of rich flavors and spices—though the chef deftly tempers the heat for all palates. The vast menu includes a good selection of vegetarian options and ranges from familiar classics like butter chicken to dishes less frequently seen on American menus such as aromatic, steamed lamb dilruba (a preparation including garlic, onion, ginger, and Indian spices), or syrupy, fried gulabjamun (a popular, milk-based Indian dessert). Decor is casual and cozy, and brightened up with Punjabi paintings and handicrafts.

Chinese street food comes to Brunswick at **Tao Yuan** (22 Pleasant St., 207/725-9002, www.tao-yuan.me,

walking the Androscoggin Swinging Bridge

Wed.-Sun. 10am-7pm, $20-35), where Maine-raised meats, seafood, and produce yield colorful creations like tea-smoked chicken with red cabbage kraut and miso mayo. Chef and owner Cara Stadler brings years of experience running a dining club in Beijing to her Brunswick HQ, and visitors passing through the area can also avail themselves of treats like roast pork buns and Asian slaw kits by stopping by satellite outpost **ZaoZe Café & Market** (5 Abbey Rd., 207/725-9012, www.zaoze.cafe, lunch Wed.-Sat. 11:30am-2:30pm, dim sum Sun. 11am-3pm, market Wed.-Fri. 10am-6pm, Sat.-Sun. 10am-4:30pm, $8-21), which Stadler opened when the pandemic began and many restaurants were forced to close.

Little **Morning Glory Natural Foods** (60 Main St., 207/729-0546, www.moglonf.com, Mon.-Sat. 9am-7pm, Sun. 10am-5pm) is stocked with local and organic options, as well as a good selection of picnic-ready items; also nearby is a **Hannaford Supermarket** (35 Elm St., 207/725-6683, Mon.-Sat. 7am-10pm, Sun. 7am-9pm). Find cheese, lobsters, and locally baked bread at the **Brunswick Farmers' Market** (Maine St., May-Nov. Tues. and Fri. 8am-2pm).

South of Brunswick

A pair of seafood stops anchors each side of the cribstone bridge to Bailey Island. The **Salt Cod Café** (1894 Harpswell Island Rd., Orr's Island, 207/833-6210, late May-early Oct. daily 8am-3pm, hours vary at the beginning and end of season) has blueberry pie and quick bites that can be eaten by the shore. Across the bridge, on a pencil-thin peninsula, is **Cook's Lobster & Ale House** (68 Garrison Cove Rd., Bailey Island, 207/833-2818, Wed.-Sat. 11:30am-8pm, Sun. 11:30am-4pm, $12-30), whose dining room has perfect views back toward the water. Cook's serves the usual seafood fare, plus "twin" lobster dinners for ambitious eaters.

With views to Bailey Island and beyond, **Dolphin Marina and Restaurant** (515 Basin Point Rd., Harpswell, 207/833-6000, daily 11am-8pm, $15-36) is also south of Brunswick in Harpswell, and would be a sublime place to dine on a plate of rocks, so the nice quality of the international seafood menu is an added bonus. Nothing is too flashy or creative, but it's solid, and many entrées come with a mystifying (but welcome) blueberry muffin on the side.

If you'd prefer your eats from a take-out window, the nearby **Erica's Seafood** (6 Malcolm Dr., Harpswell, 207/833-7354, www.ericasseafood.com, May-Oct. Thurs.-Tues. 11am-7pm, $8-20) is a popular shack with haddock sandwiches, lobster rolls, and crisp, slender fries. The outdoor picnic tables are right by a working wharf, so you can watch the day's catch arrive on local fishing boats.

Accommodations

The **Travelers Inn** (130 Pleasant St., 207/729-3364, www.travelersinnme.com,

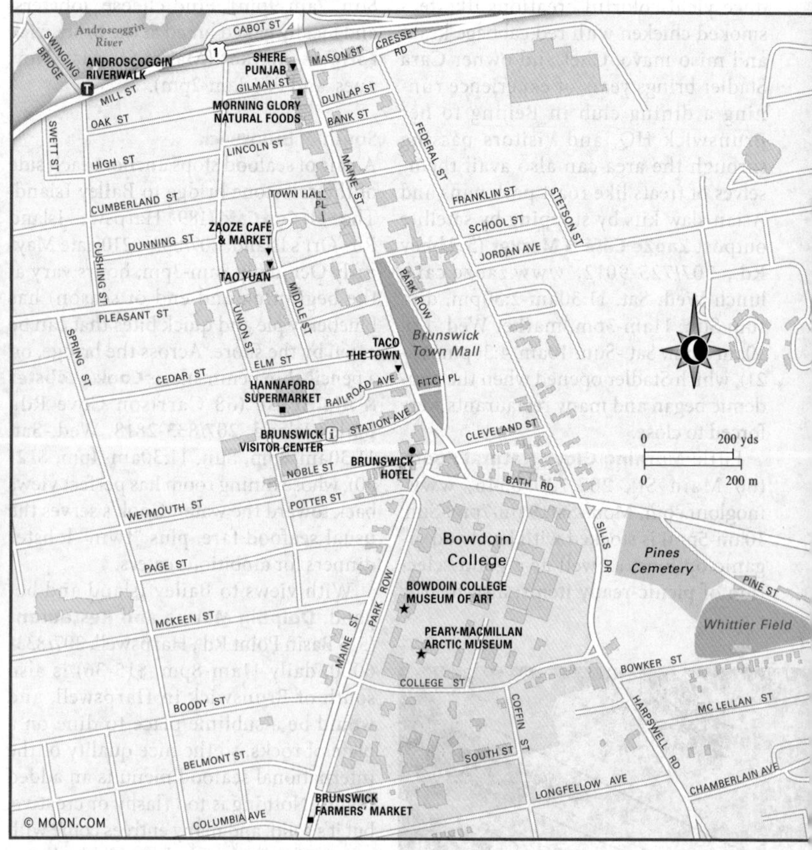

$112-155) is an old-fashioned motel with well-kept rooms. This is an especially good option for families, as some rooms have two beds, with cribs or roll-away cots available. The helpful staff is knowledgeable about the area, and a basic continental breakfast of bagels, fruit, coffee, and juice is served in the lobby.

Just across the Androscoggin River from downtown Brunswick, the **Black Lantern Bed and Breakfast** (57 Elm St., Topsham, 207/725-4165, www.blacklanternbandb.com, $145-200) is walking distance from a scenic bit of riverbank and a gracious, welcoming place to stay. Comfortable beds, en suite baths, hearty breakfasts, and old-fashioned charm are highlights, as are Judy and Tom, the super-friendly innkeepers. (If you're into quilting and knitting, bring your latest project along and talk with Judy about it.)

With a location in the heart of downtown, the **Brunswick Hotel** (4 Noble St., 207/837-6565, www.thebrunswickhotelandtavern.com, $225-350) is often filled with families visiting the nearby college, and it's a comfortable place to enjoy the town. A gracious porch has rocking chairs and plenty of shade,

Scenic Drive: To Land's End and Back

Finding the best bits of the Maine coast means getting off Route 1 and following the curving, narrow roads that stretch into the sea, skipping from peninsulas to islands and back again. For aimless driving and views of tattered coast, nothing beats **Route 24** and **Route 123,** which flank **Harpswell Sound,** south of Brunswick. Following these two country highways, you can make an H-shaped journey using the connecting Mountain Road for a 48-mile (77-km), 1.5-hour trip to both Bailey Island and Harpswell.

Route 24

Route 24 is particularly lovely, passing deep bays rimmed with evergreen trees and rocky beaches as it passes from **Sebascodegan Island** to **Orr's Island** and, finally, **Bailey Island,** the prettiest and smallest of the three.

Just before you reach the **Bailey Island Bridge,** the charming **Salt Cod Cafe** (1894 Harpswell Island Rd., Orr's Island, 207/833-6210, late May-early Oct. daily 8am-3pm, hours vary at beginning and end of season) sells some of the finest slices of blueberry pie along the coast, and the other side of the bridge is flanked by **Cook's Lobster & Ale House** (68 Garrison Cove Rd., Bailey Island, 207/833-2818, Wed.-Sat. 11:30am-8pm, Sun. 11:30am-4pm, $12-30), a beloved spot with views of the water.

Even if you're not hungry, it's worth pausing to take a gander at the 1,150-foot (350-m) bridge itself, which is a Historic Civil Engineering Landmark. In order to withstand the waves and powerful tides, it was built with 10,000 tons of locally quarried granite; the large slabs, known as cribstones, are laid without mortar or cement in a cross-hatched pattern that allows the water to flow freely through, and it's thought to be the only granite cribstone bridge in the world.

Keep going straight to reach the **Land's End Gift Shop** (2391 Harpswell Island Rd., Bailey Island, 207/833-2313, Apr.-Oct. Thurs.-Tues. 9am-5pm, limited hours off-season) at the tip of the island, or turn left on Washington Street (1.5 mi/2.4 km south of the bridge) to reach the **Giant's Stairs,** a 0.25-mile (0.4-km) seaside trail across jutting rocks.

Mountain Road Connector

Head back up Route 24 to Mountain Road, which connects the two lobes of land; this stretch of road crosses **Strawberry Creek** and the **Ewin Narrows,** and it's worth stopping for the excellent 2.3-mile (2.7-km) **Cliff Trail,** which has views of Long Reach to the west. This trail is a great place to witness or build Maine fairy houses—miniature house-like woodland dwellings constructed with moss, sticks, and stones. (Fairy houses are a fixture of Maine's coastal woodlands, though no one knows exactly who started building them, or how the trend caught on.) The trailhead and parking lot are located behind the **Harpswell Town Office** (263 Mountain Rd., 207/833-5771).

Route 123

Continue on Mountain Road to Neck Road, or Route 123, and follow it south into map-dot **West Harpswell,** where the land splits into a Poseidon's trident of Basin Point, Pott's Point, and Ash Point, three smaller promontories that jut into the ocean.

At the tip of the westernmost point is **Dolphin Marina and Restaurant** (515 Basin Point Rd., Harpswell, 207/833-6000, daily 11am-8pm, $15-36), an upscale spot for seafood with showstopping views. A stone's throw up the peninsula is **Erica's Seafood** (6 Malcolm Dr., Harpswell, 207/833-7354, www.ericasseafood.com, May-Oct. Thurs.-Tues. 11am-7pm, $8-20), a casual spot with fried food and views of the working marina.

There's not much on the next point east, but the narrow channel between the two creates an unusual **reversing falls** or **tidal waterfall** at the narrows, visible from the parking lot of the commercial Interstate Lobster Pound (Ash Point Rd., Harpswell).

well-appointed rooms are on the luxurious side of comfortable, and the train station is easy walking distance away. In early February, the hotel bar is transformed into a pop-up winter wonderland with ice sculptures, live music, and special cocktails served in ice luges.

Information

The **Brunswick Visitor Center** (16 Station Ave., 207/721-0999, daily 9:45am-4pm) is adjacent to the Amtrak station.

Bath

Bath offers numerous diversions for visitors, as well as grants access to other coastal pleasures. South of town, the land splits into two squiggly peninsulas, named for their largest towns, each about 15 minutes from Bath: Phippsburg, down Route 209, and Georgetown, down Route 127.

Sights

Maine Maritime Museum

Wide, deep, and sheltered from the raging sea, the Kennebec River is the perfect place for building and launching ships; indeed, the first ocean-going ship built by English shipwrights in the Americas—the *Virginia of Sagadahoc*—was constructed here, a 30-ton pinnace measuring less than 50 feet (15 m) from stem to stern. That ship was just the beginning, and in the mid-18th century, shipbuilding was a roaring industry, with a couple dozen shipyards launching merchant, naval, and pleasure vessels connecting this clattering town in rural Maine with every corner of the globe.

One of those shipyards, Percy & Small, has been transformed into the wonderful **Maine Maritime Museum** (243 Washington St., 207/443-1316, www.mainemaritimemuseum.org, daily 9:30am-5pm, $20 adults, $18 seniors, $11 youth 6-12, free children under 6), a sprawling 20-acre (8-ha) site with exhibits on the state's seafaring traditions.

The yard is dominated by a soaring metal skeleton that evokes the Percy and Small-built *Wyoming*, the largest schooner ever made. (Most of the sculpture's proportions are true-to-size, but the masts stop short of *Wyoming*'s 177 feet/54 m, as the full-sized version would require warning lights for passing aircraft.) Other highlights include reproductions of a shipyard's various workstations, in-depth explorations of lobstering on the Maine coast, and exhibits illustrating the many sides of New England's maritime traditions. The museum also operates scenic cruises to nearby lighthouses and rivers.

Maine's First Ship

In a tiny shipyard in downtown Bath, a quixotic, creative group of volunteers are reconstructing the *Virginia of Sagadahoc* based on the (very) sketchy descriptions that have survived from colonial times. In keeping with the lighthearted, ad hoc attitude of the group, some building materials are recycled, and bits of the ship's framework retain printing from former lives. But the wooden-pegged skeleton is smart as can be, and it's a treat to stop by during construction. Meet the building crew of **Maine's First Ship** (27 Commercial St., 207/433-4242, www.mfship.org, Wed.-Sun. 10am-3pm) on open build days, or visit anytime to peek through the fence as the pinnace takes shape.

Entertainment and Events

Most of the year, **Bath Iron Works** (700 Washington St., 207/443-3311, www.gdbiw.com) is off-limits to the public. That changes during one of its infrequent but spectacular ship launchings. Then the whole town comes out for the celebration, with flags, food, and local dignitaries filling the waterfront to break champagne on the hull.

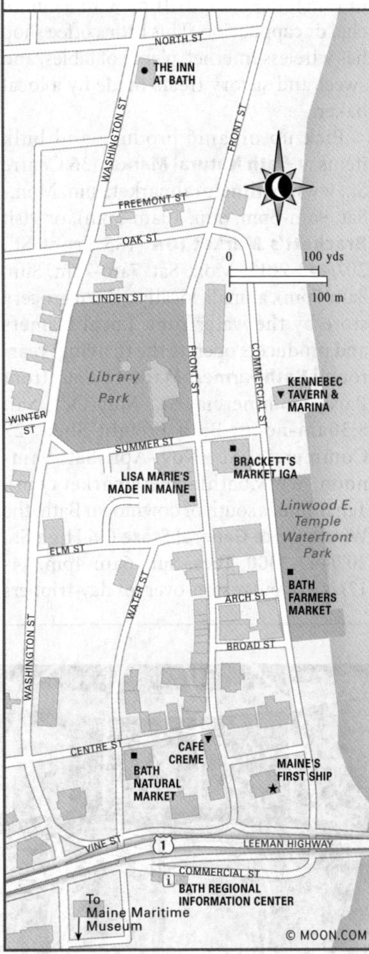

Shopping

Downtown Bath is perfect for browsing and gallery carousing. Search for souvenirs at **Lisa Marie's Made in Maine** (170 Front St., 207/443-2225, www.lisamariesmadeinmaine.com, Jan.-May Mon.-Sat. 9am-6pm, Sun. 11am-4pm, June-Dec. Mon.-Sat. 9am-6pm, Sun. 10am-5pm), which stocks work from a vast range of local artisans, crafters, and artists.

Sports and Recreation

Beaches

South of Bath, the Phippsburg and Georgetown Peninsulas each end in a charming beach. The larger of the two, **Popham Beach** (10 Perkins Farm Ln., Phippsburg, 207/389-1335, $8 adults, $2 seniors, $1 children 5-11, under 5 free), is more Miami than Midcoast, the kind of broad, sandy swath most Mainers can only dream of. Tiny **Fox Island** is just off the beach, and it's possible to walk to it at low tide (beware of getting stranded, which would mean a long wait for the water to drop once again). Popham's charms mean it can be jam-packed on busy days, so arrive early, or head to **Reid State Park** (375 Seguinland Rd., Georgetown, 207/371-2303, 9am-sunset, $8 adults, $2 seniors, $1 children 5-11, under 5 free), where you'll find two sandy beaches framed by rocky outcroppings, a headland with great views to Seguin Island lighthouse, and breaking waves for some of the best surfing in Maine.

Boating

Get an up-close look at the hulking naval ships in Bath's floating dry docks on one of Maine Maritime Museum's hour-long **Shipyards & Lighthouses Cruises** (243 Washington St., 207/443-1316, www.mainemaritimemuseum.org, mid-June-mid-Oct. daily noon and 2pm, $40 adults, $21 youth 6-12, $6 children under 6, ticket prices include museum admission), which also passes by the Doubling Point Lighthouse and Kennebec Range Lights. Check the website; longer tours that go farther afield are available more sporadically.

Food

Bath

While the menu of pub classics and seafood is pretty ordinary (and reportedly inconsistent), that's not really the point at **Kennebec Tavern & Marina** (119 Commercial St., 207/442-9636, www.kennebectavern.com, Sun.-Thurs.

11am-8pm, Fri.-Sat. 11am-8:30pm, $14-33), which boasts a fabulous outdoor seating area that juts out into the current of the Kennebec River offering great views of passing boats. On cool days, there's not much to tempt diners into the bland dining room, but summer afternoons are the perfect time to relax in the shade with a cold beer and a pile of fried scallops.

As the name suggests, stepping into **The Cabin** (552 Washington St., 207/443-6224, www.cabinpizza.com, Wed.-Fri. 11am-9pm, Sat. 2pm-9pm, Sun. 2pm-8pm, $8-25) feels like ducking below the deck of an old ship. Nautical bric-a-brac and dark wood complete the effect, and while the pizza might not live up to its claims of "Best in Maine," it's pretty darn good all the same. Chewy crusts, generous toppings, and addictive, bready garlic knots keep this a favorite with locals and visitors. No credit cards.

With views of the action in the heart of historic Bath, **Café Crème** (56 Front St., 207/443-6454, Mon.-Sat. 7:30am-5:30pm, Sun. 8:30am-3:30pm, $4-13) is the place to watch the town drift by with a cup of chai or cappuccino. This little coffee shop has wireless Internet, plenty of tables, and sweet and savory treats made by a local baker.

Pick up organic produce and bulk items at **Bath Natural Market** (36 Centre St., www.bathnaturalmarket.com, Mon.-Sat. 9am-6pm, Sun. 10am-5pm), or visit **Brackett's Market IGA** (185 Front St., 207/443-2012, Mon.-Sat. 7am-7pm, Sun. 8am-7pm), a small, locally owned grocery store by the waterfront. Local farmers and producers operate the thriving, year-round **Bath Farmers Market** (Waterfront Park, Commercial St., May-Oct. Sat. 8:30am-noon; Bath Freight Shed, 27 Commercial St., Nov.-Apr. Sat. 9am-noon, www.bathfarmersmarket.com). Ten minutes south of downtown Bath, the **Winnegance General Store** (36 High St., 207/443-3300, Tues.-Sun. 6am-4pm, $4-12) is a popular stop-over for day-trippers

Maine Maritime Museum

on their way to Popham Beach. Scones and muffins are baked fresh in the back of the old-fashioned shop, and a few small tables are available for enjoying breakfasts of pancakes or eggs and bacon or homemade soup and sandwiches.

South of Bath

South of Bath in Georgetown, ★ **Five Islands Lobster Co.** (1447 Five Islands Rd., Georgetown, 207/371-2990, check website or call for hours before visiting, $14-30) regularly makes "best of" lists for lobster rolls, steamers, and fried oysters, and it's right on the way to Reid State Park. This is a classic waterside joint with picnic tables and views of a picture-perfect bay dotted with tiny forested islands.

Accommodations and Camping

While bunking up in Bath is the most convenient way to explore the region, a few wonderful campgrounds and a historic inn are tucked down the peninsula by the water, away from the bustle of Route 1.

Camping

Splash out for an oceanfront spot at ★ **Hermit Island Campground** (6 Hermit Island Rd., Phippsburg, 207/443-2101, www.hermitisland.com, $47-77) and you'll get prime views of sandy beaches and coastline. This is a 25-minute drive from Bath, and snagging a site means planning ahead (the reservation rules are byzantine), but even the "value" sites are within easy strolling distance of the shore.

A little bit closer to Route 1, **Meadowbrook Camping Area** (33 Meadowbrook Rd., Phippsburg, 207/443-4967, www.meadowbrookme.com, tent sites $38-40, hookups $42-54, cabins $110-185) has smallish sites that are a tad too closely set in woods and an open meadow, with many campers who come for the whole season, but you can sign up for daily lobster dinners and have a feast at your site or the communal outdoor seating area. The on-site cabins offer a slightly more spruced-up experience with amenities like showers and refrigerators.

Camping is permitted on **Seguin Island,** accessible by ferry from Phippsburg's Popham Beach, mid-May-early October (207/443-4808, www.seguinisland.org, suggested minimum donation of $10 per person per night). There's no running water, but composting toilet facilities are provided. Reservations are required.

Under $150

Simple, sweet, and neat as a pin, **New Meadows River Cottages** (4 Armstrong Way, West Bath, 207/442-9299, www.newmeadowsrivercottages.com, $95-109) are nothing fancy, but the stand-alone rooms have a double bed or double and single as well as air-conditioning, coffeemakers, fridges, and little sitting areas; higher rates are for cottages with little kitchenettes.

$150-250

Gardens surrounding **The Inn at Bath** (969 Washington St., Bath, 207/808-7904, www.innatbath.com, $175-245) are overflowing with blooming rhododendrons and wild mountain laurel, and the interior of the Greek Revival-style building is full of art and unfussy antiques. The quiet neighborhood is about a 15-minute walk from downtown Bath, and breakfasts are an appealing spread of fresh fruit, granola, and one hot option. All rooms have private baths and air-conditioning, but they differ widely in style and decor, and one room opens onto the kitchen.

$250-350

Historic and beautiful, the **1774 Inn** (44 Parker Head Rd., Phippsburg, 207/389-1774, www.1774inn.com, $215-300) is among the most romantic places to stay along the coast, with chairs tucked around its sprawling grounds that abut the Kennebec River. Though the inn is just 7.5 miles (12 km) south of Bath, the experience is serene and secluded. Many of the rooms, which vary widely in style, are exquisite, and guests rave about the thoughtful breakfasts. For an ultra-private experience, book the more rustic Woodshed Suite, a self-contained suite near the river with a private veranda and stunning views.

Information

The **Bath Regional Information Center** (15 Commercial St., 207/443-1513, www.visitbath.com, mid-May-Oct. daily 9am-7pm, check website for off-season hours) has great resources and advice for the entire Midcoast area, and its website is frequently updated with tours and events in town.

Getting Around

Parking in Bath is free for up to two hours on the street or in municipal lots on Commercial, School, and Water Streets. The **town website** (www.cityofbath.com) has a helpful parking map for the downtown area. A convenient way to see Bath car-free is the **Bath Trolley** (207/443-8363, www.cityofbath.com, check website for seasonal schedules, $1), which runs on a fixed loop that connects the Bath Iron Works with the Maine Maritime Museum and downtown.

Boothbay and Pemaquid

Ask a native Mainer for directions on the Midcoast, and you're likely to hear the classic refrain: "You can't get there from here!" The Boothbay and Pemaquid Peninsulas, accessible from Route 1 via Wiscasset and Damariscotta, respectively, are separated by a river that opens onto jagged bays, which means the lobster shacks, gardens, and lighthouses that rim the sea are much farther apart then they appear on a map.

Boothbay is by far the more popular of the two, a scenic stretch of bays that culminates in the town of Boothbay Harbor, the pinnacle of Maine's fudge and T-shirt shop kitsch. It's beyond hectic during school vacation months, but with dozens of ways to get out on the water, it's easy to see why the spot is so beloved. By contrast, Pemaquid is decidedly laid-back, and most visitors head straight down the forested peninsula for Pemaquid Point Light, a classic lighthouse and the stuff of Yankee pinups with its white-washed tower, picket fence, and snapping American flag.

These two peninsulas are also the primary access points for boat tours to Eastern Egg Rock, a seven-acre (2.8-ha) island whose granite shoreline offers a unique habitat for puffins, guillemots, and dozens of other nesting and migratory birds. It's the first of its kind, a restored colony, the success of which inspired dozens of imitators worldwide, as scientists work to protect the dwindling seabird population.

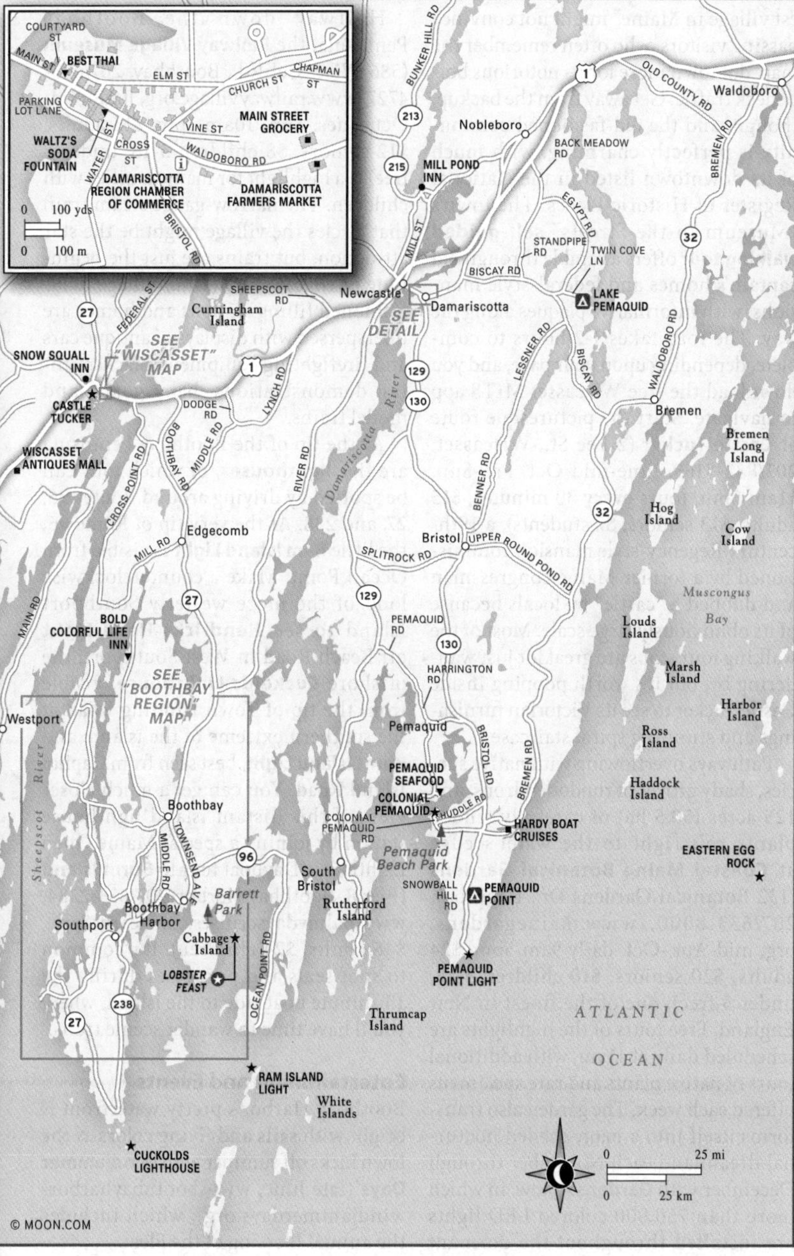
Boothbay and Pemaquid
COURTYARD ST
MAIN ST
BEST THAI
CHAPMAN ST
ELM ST
CHURCH ST
PARKING LOT LANE
MAIN STREET GROCERY
VINE ST
WALTZ'S SODA FOUNTAIN
WATER ST
CROSS ST
WALDOBORO RD
DAMARISCOTTA REGION CHAMBER OF COMMERCE
DAMARISCOTTA FARMERS MARKET
BRISTOL RD
0 100 yds
0 100 m
BUNKER HILL RD
OLD COUNTY RD
Waldoboro
Nobleboro
BACK MEADOW RD
MILL POND INN
BREMEN RD
EGYPT RD
MILL ST
STANDPIPE RD
TWIN COVE LN
BISCAY RD
SHEEPSCOT RD
Newcastle
Damariscotta
LAKE PEMAQUID
Cunningham Island
SEE DETAIL
FEDERAL ST
SEE "WISCASSET" MAP
SNOW SQUALL INN
LESSNER RD
WALDOBORO RD
CASTLE TUCKER
DODGE RD
LYNCH RD
Damariscotta River
Bremen
Bremen Long Island
WISCASSET ANTIQUES MALL
BOOTHBAY RD
MIDDLE RD
RIVER RD
BENNER RD
CROSS POINT RD
Hog Island
Cow Island
Edgecomb
MILL RD
Bristol
UPPER ROUND POND RD
SPLITROCK RD
Muscongus Bay
MAIN RD
PEMAQUID RD
Louds Island
BOLD COLORFUL LIFE INN
HARRINGTON RD
Marsh Island
SEE "BOOTHBAY REGION" MAP
Harbor Island
Westport
Pemaquid
Ross Island
BRISTOL RD
BREMEN RD
PEMAQUID SEAFOOD
Haddock Island
COLONIAL PEMAQUID
Boothbay
HUDDLE RD
COLONIAL PEMAQUID RD
HARDY BOAT CRUISES
TOWNSEND AVE
Sheepscot River
Pemaquid Beach Park
EASTERN EGG ROCK
South Bristol
Barrett Park
SNOWBALL HILL RD
PEMAQUID POINT
Boothbay Harbor
Rutherford Island
Southport
Cabbage Island
LOBSTER FEAST
OCEAN POINT RD
PEMAQUID POINT LIGHT
ATLANTIC
Thrumcap Island
OCEAN
RAM ISLAND LIGHT
White Islands
CUCKOLDS LIGHTHOUSE
0 25 mi
0 25 km
© MOON.COM

Boothbay Region

Sights

Wiscasset's self-branding as the "prettiest village in Maine" might not convince passing visitors, who often remember the map-dot town more for its notorious bottleneck traffic. Get away from the backup, though, and the old-fashioned community is perfectly charming, with much of its downtown listed in the National Register of Historic Places. The town's "Museum in the Streets" **self-guided walking tour** offers a ramble through old captain's homes and federal-style mansions, with informative plaques along the way. The tour takes 1-2 hours to complete, depending upon your pace, and you download the free Wiscasset MITS app to navigate. Start the picturesque route at **Castle Tucker** (2 Lee St., Wiscasset, 207/882-7169, June-mid-Oct. Fri.-Sun. 11am-3pm, tours every 30 minutes, $15 adults, $13 seniors, $7 students), a 19th-century Regency-style mansion commissioned by a former Maine congressman and dubbed a "castle" by locals because of its obnoxiously large scale. Most of the walking tour stops are great for just wandering by, but it's worth popping inside Castle Tucker to see its Victorian furnishings and stunning spiral staircase.

Pathways overflowing with native species, shady groves of rhododendrons, and 125 acres (50.5 ha) of carefully tended plants roll right to the water's edge at **Coastal Maine Botanical Gardens** (132 Botanical Gardens Dr., Boothbay, 207/633-8000, www.mainegardens.org, mid-Apr.-Oct. daily 9am-5pm, $24 adults, $20 seniors, $10 children 3-18, under 3 free), one of the finest in New England. Free tours of the highlights are scheduled daily at 11am, with additional tours of native plants and rare specimens offered each week. The garden also transforms itself into a neon-shaded nocturnal dreamland each November through December with **Gardens Aglow,** in which more than 750,000 colored LED lights are installed throughout the dormant gardens to give them an otherworldly sheen. Advance tickets are required for this event.

Halfway down the Boothbay Peninsula, the **Railway Village Museum** (586 Wiscasset Rd., Boothbay, 207/633-4727, www.railwayvillage.org, June-mid-Oct. Tues.-Sun. 10am-5pm, $15 adults, $12 seniors, $8 children 3-18, under 3 free) is a highlight for many families with children. The narrow-gauge steam train that circles the village might be the star attraction, but trains are just the beginning of this 10-acre (4-ha) village. Old-fashioned filling stations and homes are interspersed with displays of antique cars and firefighting equipment, blacksmithing demonstrations, baby goats, and model trains.

At the tip of the Boothbay Peninsula are five **lighthouses,** of which four can be spotted by driving around Routes 96, 27, and 238. At the very tip of Route 96, the little **Ram Island Light** is visible from Ocean Point. Make a counterclockwise loop of the more westerly Southport Island to see **Hendricks Head Light** off Beach Road in West Southport; the offshore **Cuckolds Lighthouse,** visible from the tip of Town Landing Road at the southern extreme of the island; and **Burnt Island Light,** best seen from Capitol Island Road. You can get a much closer view of this distant island lighthouse station by joining a special Maine Open Lighthouse Dayboat tour to **Burnt Island** (Pier 8, Boothbay Harbor, 207/633-2284, www.balmydayscruises.com, early Sept., $46 adults, $24 children). It's common to spot seals and porpoises during the 15-minute boat ride to the island, where you'll have time to wander scenic trails.

Entertainment and Events

Boothbay Harbor's pretty waterfront is bright with sails and flying colors as the town kicks off summer with **Windjammer Days** (late June, www.boothbayharbor-windjammerdays.org), which includes the annual Blessing of the Fleet.

Boothbay Region

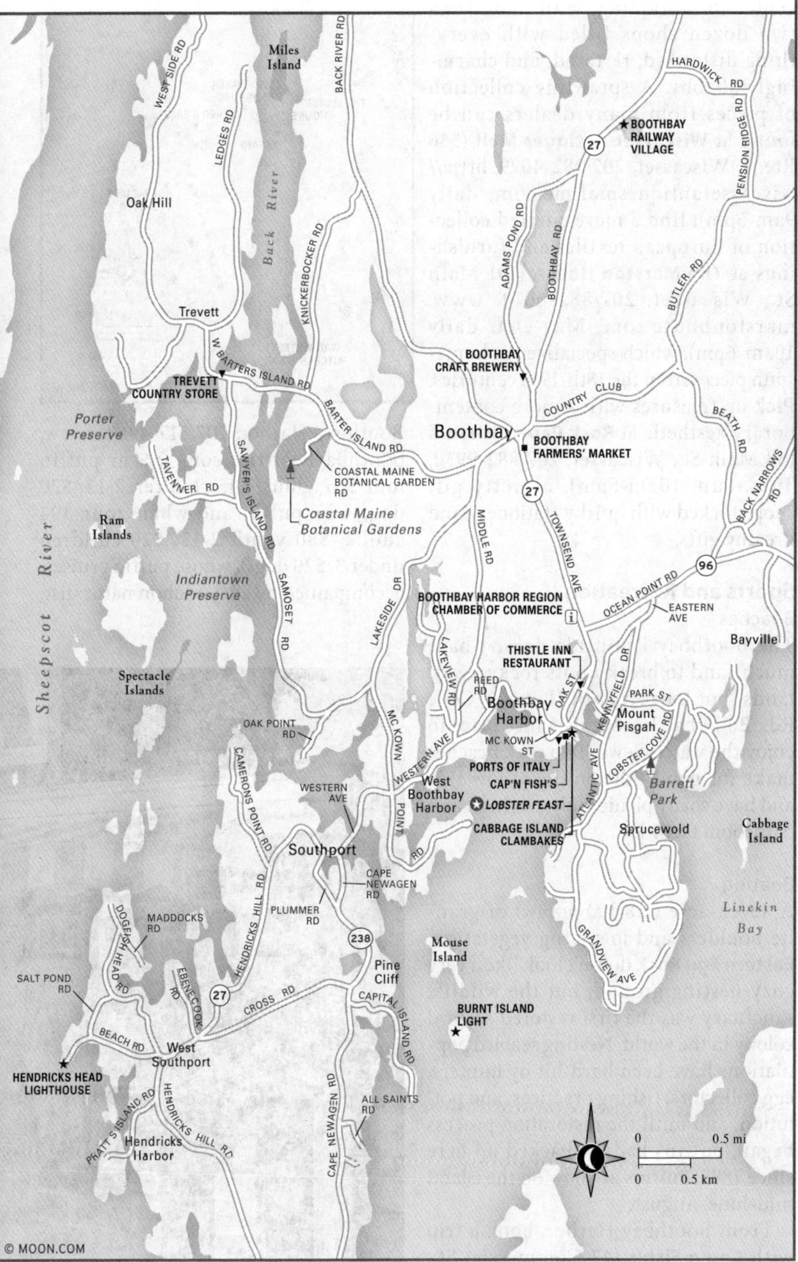

Shopping

Unsurprisingly, Wiscasset is a major center for antiquing, with more than two dozen shops filled with everything distressed, restored, and charmingly shabby. A sprawling collection of pieces from many dealers can be found at **Wiscasset Antiques Mall** (536 Rte. 1, Wiscasset, 207/882-4029, http://wiscassetantiquesmallme.com, daily 9am-5pm); find a more curated collection of European textiles and furnishings at **The Marston House** (101 Main St., Wiscasset, 207/882-6010, www.marstonhouse.com, May-Oct. daily 10am-6pm), which specializes in homespun pieces from the 18th-19th centuries. Pick up treasures with a more contemporary aesthetic at **Rock Paper Scissors** (68 Main St., Wiscasset, 207/882-9930, Tues.-Sun. 10am-5pm), a pretty gift shop stocked with quirky stationery and dreamy gifts.

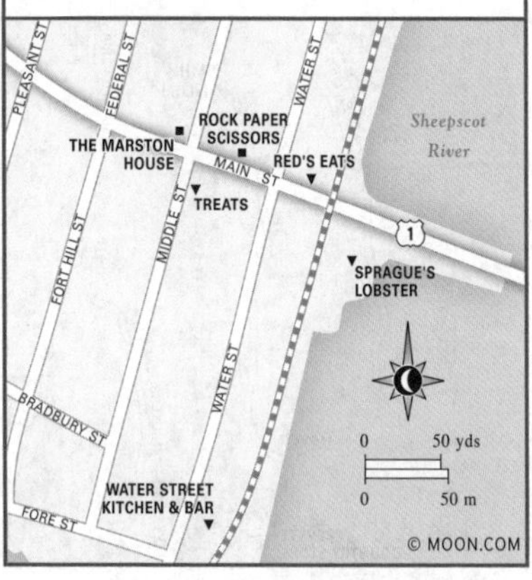

Sports and Recreation

Beaches

The Boothbay Peninsula doesn't have much sand to break up its rocky headlands, but **Barrett Park** (Lobster Cove Rd., Boothbay Harbor) is a nice place to enjoy the water views. Two rock beaches make for good tidepooling at low tide and have shady picnic tables, swings, and bathroom facilities.

Boating

A seven-acre (2.8-ha) sprawl of granite boulders and low-lying vegetation, **Eastern Egg Rock** doesn't look like a very cozy nesting ground, but the wildlife sanctuary was the first restored seabird colony in the world. Nesting seabird populations have been hard-hit by hunters, egg collectors, fishing practices, and pollution, and until the restoration process began, puffins hadn't shacked up here since 1885. **Puffins** are now on the island mid-June-August.

From Boothbay Harbor, book a trip with **Cap'n Fish's** (42 Commercial St., Boothbay Harbor, 207/517-4964, www.boothbayboattrips.com, 2.5-hr puffin tour $55 adults, $45 children 2-12, $20 dog, 4-hr puffin and whale tour $94 adults, $80 youth 2-12, $20 children under 3, $20 dogs), whose puffin cruises, accompanied by an Audubon naturalist,

pass three lighthouses and scattered islands on the way out to Eastern Egg Rock. The company's combination puffin and whale cruises commonly spot finback and minke whales, as well as the humpback whales that arrive on the coast in July.

Food

Another top contender on annual "best lobster roll" lists, **Red's Eats** (41 Water St., Wiscasset, 207/882-6128, www.redseatsmaine.com, Tues.-Sun. 11:30am-5pm, $9-27, cash only) is a James Beard Award-winning shack that fills its buns with a pound of drawn (not chopped) meat, served with a little cup of clarified butter on the side. Picnic tables and umbrellas with views of the water are available on-site, but note two drawbacks to eating at Red's: The line can stretch upward of an hour at busy times, and it's right beside the idling cars stuck in Wiscasset traffic. Just across the street is **Sprague's Lobster** (22 Main St., Wiscasset, 207/882-1236, daily 11am-5pm, $7-24); it hasn't racked up the same list of awards as Red's, but sells a similar style of lobster roll at a lower price (albeit with somewhat less meat).

Half country bakery, half gourmet store, **Treats** (80 Main St., Wiscasset, 207/882-6192, www.treatsofmaine.com, Tues.-Sat. 7:30am-3pm, Sun. 8am-1pm, $3-12) serves pastries ranging from down-home to gourmet, with hefty chocolate babkas, fruit scones, muffins, and layered French confections. The long counter is a welcome place to enjoy a sweet and cup of coffee, and this place also excels at takeout feasts of quiche, wine, cheese, and dessert.

The sea has always been a portal to distant places and palates, and at **Water Street Kitchen and Bar** (15 Water St., Wiscasset, 207/687-8076, www.waterstreetmaine.com, Tues.-Sun. lunch noon-3pm, dinner 4:30pm-9pm, $16-40) chef and owner Ed Colburn mixes Maine ingredients with Spanish,

the lunch line at Red's Eats

French, and Italian culinary tradition. The poached lobster ziti, littleneck clam paella, and creole shrimp all pair nicely with the romantic dining room view of the Sheepscot River.

With a mid-peninsula location just past the Boothbay botanical gardens, **Trevett Country Store** (381 W. Barter's Island Rd., Trevett, 207/633-1140, Mon.-Sat. 7am-5:30pm, $6-18) might seem like a back-road convenience store, but it's a local favorite for sandwiches, simple breakfasts, and fresh seafood. In warm months, the outdoor sundeck is a charming place to eat with water views and a cool breeze.

All cedar shake and dark wood, the **Boothbay Craft Brewery** (301 Adams Pond Rd., Boothbay, 207/633-3411, www.boothbaycraftbrewery.com, Wed.-Sun. 3pm-8pm, $14-32) has the kind of cave-like interior best enjoyed when the weather turns blustery. The food includes a fairly standard pub lineup of burgers, salads, and wood-fired pizzas, but with meat from local farms and appealing house-made additions. Naturally, the brewery's seasonal craft beers are on tap, ranging from super-drinkable session ales to vanilla porters and red lagers.

A destination for sophisticated, traditional food, **Ports of Italy** (47 Commercial St., Boothbay Harbor, 207/633-1011, www.portsofitaly.com, May-Dec. daily 4:30pm-9pm, $25-48) stands head and shoulders above the crowded Boothbay Harbor restaurant scene. Thoughtful service and consistently high-quality food, an excellent wine list, and pleasant seating on an outdoor patio make this a good choice for a romantic evening or celebration. Reservations are essential.

Tucked within one of Boothbay's more elegant B&Bs, the **Thistle Inn Restaurant** (55 Oak St., Boothbay Harbor, 877/579-6004, www.thistleinnrestaurant.com, Thurs.-Tues. 4pm-10pm, $18-34) serves a creative surf-and-turf menu on an open-air patio. But there's more inside. Cozy up to the bar—made from an old dory boat—for burgers, crab cakes, or piles of Maine mussels steamed in white wine. Great cocktails and an extensive beer and wine list make this a nice first stop of the evening for drinks and snacks.

Vendors from around the region set up stalls at **Boothbay Farmers' Market** (1 Common Dr., Boothbay, www.boothbayfarmersmarket.me, mid-May-early Oct., Thurs. 9am-noon).

★ Lobster Feast

Like a Polynesian imu or Maya p'ib, the classic method of cooking up a New England lobster is using a pit oven lined with rocks and heated with a blazing fire. The pit is then filled with seaweed, lobster, clams, and corn on the cob, covered with more seaweed (along with some sand or tarps), and left to cook for hours, infusing everything inside with a briny tang. Aside from swapping out the sand pit for some giant, wood-fired steamers, **Cabbage Island Clambakes** (Pier 6, Boothbay Harbor, 207/633-7200, www.cabbageislandclambake.com, mid-June-early Sept., 4-hour boat tour and clambake $88) does them in classic Maine style. The family-run operation takes a slow cruise to **Cabbage Island,** where you'll sit down to two steamed lobsters, white clams, fish chowder, new potatoes, and corn, followed by blueberry cake. The experience is simply one of the finest ways to get a taste of this traditional feast in Maine. Reservations at least a few days in advance are strongly encouraged, as most days sell out.

Accommodations and Camping

Camping

Drift off amid gentle sea breezes and rustling evergreens at **Chewonki Campground** (235 Chewonki Neck Rd., Wiscasset, 207/882-7426, www.chewonkicampground.com, mid-June-mid-Oct., $65 tent sites, $98 RV sites) which is five miles (8 km) southwest of Wiscasset and situated on 50 acres (20 ha) overlooking the Back River. On-site canoe and kayak rentals make it easy to explore the local coves and marshes, and the weekly ice cream social that happens each Saturday night gives the place a pleasant summer camp atmosphere.

$150-250

Walking distance from Wiscasset's historic downtown, the **Snow Squall Inn** (5 Bradford Rd., Wiscasset, 207/882-6892, https://snowsquallin.com, $140-250) is all comfort and relaxation. Rooms are bright and uncluttered, with soft linens and simple furnishings, and the well-traveled, gracious owners prepare a fabulous breakfast each morning, with hot and cold options. The property includes a barn that's been converted into an airy yoga studio, and classes are offered throughout the day (www.wickedgoodyoga.com, $16).

Gorgeous lawns roll from a rambling farmhouse to the water's edge at the **Bold Colorful Life Inn** (802 Back River Rd., Boothbay, 207/633-6566, www.boldcolorlifeinn.com, $169-239), a laid-back estate that's halfway down the Boothbay Peninsula. Enjoy the quiet spot in a hammock, or wander the trails and gardens. Common spaces include a great room with a piano and bookshelves, and the unsurprisingly bright and colorful rooms each have private baths. The inn is run by a welcoming psychotherapist and life coach.

Information

The **Boothbay Harbor Region Chamber of Commerce** (192 Townsend Ave., Boothbay Harbor, 207/633-2353, www.boothbayharbor.com, May-Oct. daily 9am-5pm) runs a visitor center at its office.

Getting Around

The only place in this region where parking is an issue is in Boothbay Harbor, where your choices are leaving your car on the street ($2/hr) or parking in one of the town's metered lots—the largest is adjacent to the town office (11 Harbor St., Boothbay Harbor, $2/hr). That town also has the only noteworthy in-town transit, the **Boothbay Trolley,** a free sightseeing trolley that makes a limited loop through downtown starting from the **Flagship Inn** (200 Townsend Ave., Boothbay Harbor).

Pemaquid Region

Sights

Pemaquid Point Light

Crashing waves and jagged rocks are the perfect setting for **Pemaquid Point Light** (3115 Bristol Rd., New Harbor, 207/677-2492, www.visitmaine.com, early May-late Oct. daily 9am-5pm, $4). Classic calendar material, it was commissioned by John Quincy Adams and is considered by many the loveliest of New England's lights—by popular vote, its image landed on the Maine state quarter. Climb a wrought-iron spiral staircase to the top of the tower for a seagull's-eye view of the craggy headland, and get an up-close look at the fourth-order Fresnel lens, one of just six in the state. After exploring the tower and clambering around the rocks, it's worth stopping in to the adjoining keeper's house, where the **Fishermen's Museum** (207/677-2494, mid-May-mid-Oct. daily 9am-5pm, free) displays mementos of the lobstering life. Also on-site is the **Pemaquid Art Gallery** (207/677-2752, early June-late Oct. daily 10am-5pm), which displays juried work from local artists.

Colonial Pemaquid

Three forts were raised and destroyed at the gaping mouth of the Pemaquid River as fur traders, pirates, the English, Native Americans, the French, and early settlers scrapped for control of the strategic stronghold. **Colonial Pemaquid** (2 Colonial Pemaquid Dr., New Harbor, 207/677-2423, www.friendsofcolonialpemaquid.org, late May-late Aug. daily 9am-5pm, $4 adults, $1 seniors, children under 12 free) offers a look at those tumultuous times, with

historic reenactments, demonstrations, and nicely preserved structures. **Fort William Henry** is the centerpiece of the site (and a reconstruction of the second fort built here), where a trio of flags flies above a stone tower; the fort's permanent exhibit explores the intersection of fur trading and politics in the early years of European settlement. The sprawling grounds offer plenty to explore, including a visitor center museum, an 18th-century cemetery, and an herb garden stocked with plants that 17th-century settlers used for food and medicine, and the seaside site is a pleasant place to bring a picnic.

Sports and Recreation

Beaches

Just south of Colonial Pemaquid is the appealing **Pemaquid Beach Park** (Snowball Hill Rd., Bristol, 207/677-2754, daily 8am-5pm, $5, children 5-12 $1, under 5 free), a quarter-mile (0.4 km) of pristine white sands with a concession stand, boogie board rentals, and nice views along the coast.

Boating

Hardy Boat Cruises (132 Rte. 32, New Harbor, 207/677-2026, www.hardyboat.com, 1.5-hr puffin tour $51 adults, $42 children 2-12, under 2 free) is just five miles (8 km) from Eastern Egg Rock and runs its trips in the early evening, with an Audubon naturalist aboard, to catch the puffins rafting together in the water and lounging on the rocks. Hardy operates a somewhat smaller boat, meaning fewer people and a slightly rougher ride when waves are choppy.

Food

The old-timey treats at **Waltz's Soda Fountain** (167 Main St., Damariscotta, 207/563-7632, Mon. and Thurs.-Sat.

Top to bottom: Pemaquid Point Light; Farnsworth Art Museum in Rockland; Rockland Harbor

11am-4pm, Tues. 11am-3pm, $2-9) are right at home in Damariscotta's brick-and-window-glass downtown. Twirl on the red leather stools, sip an egg cream or ice cream soda, or go all-out with a sundae under gobs of hot fudge sauce. A simple menu of sandwiches and snacks is also available, albeit overshadowed by the creamier options.

An outlier among Midcoast lobster shacks and bistros, **Best Thai** (74 Main St., Damariscotta, 207/5633-1440, www.bestthaimaine.com, Tues.-Sun. noon-2:30pm and 4pm-8:30pm, lunch $10-16, dinner $18-25) really does serve the best Thai food in the region (until you hit its sister restaurant in Bath). Panang curry and noodle dishes are consistently good, and the tom kha (chicken soup) gets rave reviews.

Pemaquid's take on lobster "in the rough," **Pemaquid Seafood** (32 Co-op Rd., Pemaquid, 207/677-2642, www.pemaquidseafood.com, daily noon-7pm, $9-30) has the seafood, and you can supply the fixings. Bring beer or wine—some regulars even bring their own side salads—to go with whole lobsters swabbed in melted butter, steamers, and crabs. Outside seating offers great views of the Pemaquid River.

Find all the basics at **Main Street Grocery** (1 Coastal Market Dr., Damariscotta, 207/563-3507, Mon.-Sat. 7am-8pm, Sun. 8am-7pm), or visit **Rising Tide Co-Op** (323 Main St., Damariscotta, 207/563-5556, www.risingtide.coop, daily 7am-8pm), a cooperatively owned natural food store that also has a deli and café.

The **Damariscotta Farmers Market** (www.damariscottafarmersmarket.org) is a reliable pop-up destination for locally grown produce and homemade treats. On Fridays mid-May-late October, farmers set up at **Round Top Farm** (3 Round Top Rd., Fri. 9am-noon).

Accommodations and Camping

Quiet and filled with shade trees, **Pemaquid Point Campground** (9 Pemaquid Point Campground Rd., New Harbor, 207/677-2267, www.pemaquidpointcampground.com, tent sites $35, RV sites $48) has hot showers, a playground, horseshoe pits, and easy access to the beach, Colonial Pemaquid, and the lighthouse, so you can beat the crowds coming from Boothbay. If you're just passing through and don't want to make the 20-minute trek down the peninsula, book a site at **Lake Pemaquid Campground** (100 Twin Cove Rd., Damariscotta, 207/563-5202, www.lakepemaquid.com, $31-59), whose 200 sites surround a pleasant, freshwater lake.

Leave the crowds (and any hope of cell service) behind at **Mill Pond Inn** (50 Main St., Nobleboro, 207/563-8014, www.millpondinn.com, $150-210), which has five guest rooms on the shore of Damariscotta Lake. Fresh flowers in each room and a wonderfully peaceful setting make this feel like a retreat from the world. The full country-style breakfast often includes blueberry pancakes or French toast, bacon, and eggs, and the friendly innkeepers have a great collection of books, games, and music to enjoy during your stay. The house was built in 1780 and retains a wonderfully historic feel.

Information

Information on the area is available through the **Damariscotta Region Chamber of Commerce** (15 Courtyard St., Damariscotta, 207/563-8340, www.damariscottaregion.com, Mon., Wed., Fri. 9am-5pm).

Penobscot Bay

Down East begins where the Penobscot River opens onto a scenic bay filled with low-lying rocky islands. This is classic sailing territory, though submerged shoals and the maze-like geography make navigation difficult. Lobster boat captains work hundreds of traplines passed down through generations. Much of the bay's edge is thoroughly rural, with forest broken only by the occasional village, but at the southern end is a trio of beautiful communities—Rockland, Rockport, and Camden—each with a scenic harbor and plenty to explore.

Rockland

A thriving commercial fishing fleet has long been the heart of this working harbor, and at first glance the sturdy brick Main Street has a staid, old-fashioned look. It's got a deep history with the sea: The Abenaki name for the harbor is Catawamtek, "great landing place," and in the 19th century, the waterfront was alive with shipbuilding and lime production as fishing boats arrived laden with cod and lobster.

Rockland's charms have long been overshadowed by picture-perfect Camden and Rockport, but in recent years the storefronts have filled up with destination restaurants and cozy bistros, and it has begun to feel unexpectedly chic. It's a good home base for exploring Penobscot Bay, and remains fairly low-key. Even if you're making tracks for Acadia or other parts of Down East Maine, it's worth stopping to see the fabulous collection of Andrew Wyeth paintings at the Farnsworth Art Museum and walk the breakwater to the harbor lighthouse.

Sights

Farnsworth Art Museum

The main draw may be the unparalleled collection of works by the artists of the Wyeth family, but the wonderful **Farnsworth Art Museum** (16 Museum St., 207/596-6457, www.farnsworthmuseum.org, daily 10am-5pm, $20 adults, $18 seniors, $10 students 17 and older, 16 and under free) encompasses far more. Explore beautifully curated works depicting Maine's landscape and people, including pieces by Robert Bellows, Eastman Johnson, Georgia O'Keeffe, and George Inness.

The **Wyeth Center at the Farnsworth Art Museum** highlights the very different works of Andrew Wyeth's father, N. C., and his son Jamie. Andrew Wyeth's best-known work, *Christina's World*, isn't here (it's at MoMA in New York City), but the next best thing is—the house that inspired the arresting and melancholy character study. Docents can give you directions to the museum-operated **Olson House** (Hathorn Pt. Rd., Cushing, $5), a half-hour drive away, where on-site guides tell the story of the painting. From June-September, admission to the museum is free on Wednesdays 5pm-8pm.

Owls Head Transportation Museum

The little town of Owls Head, a 10-minute drive south from Rockland, seems an unlikely place for the sprawling **Owls Head Transportation Museum** (117 Museum St., Owls Head, 207/594-4418, www.shead.org, daily 10am-4pm, $15 adults, $12 seniors, free youth under 18), whose remarkable collection of pre-1940s vehicles celebrates everything that whirs, sputters, rolls, and glides. Aircraft, automobiles, and motorcycles are all fully functional, and the bicycle exhibit covers everything from an 1868 velocipede "boneshaker" to a turn-of-the-20th-century dual propulsion tricycle. Ask upon arrival about riding in a Ford Model T; if a staff member is available, he or she will take you for a turn around the grounds. Aircraft—including 19th-century gliders, a Wright flyer, biplanes, and a "Red Baron"-style triplane—get off the ground during outdoor events that take place frequently during the summer months.

Other Sights

Almost 700,000 tons of granite were sunk off Jameson Point to create the **Rockland Breakwater** (207/785-4609, www.rocklandharborlights.org), a 4,346-foot (1,325-m) pile of rocks with a pretty

Penobscot Bay

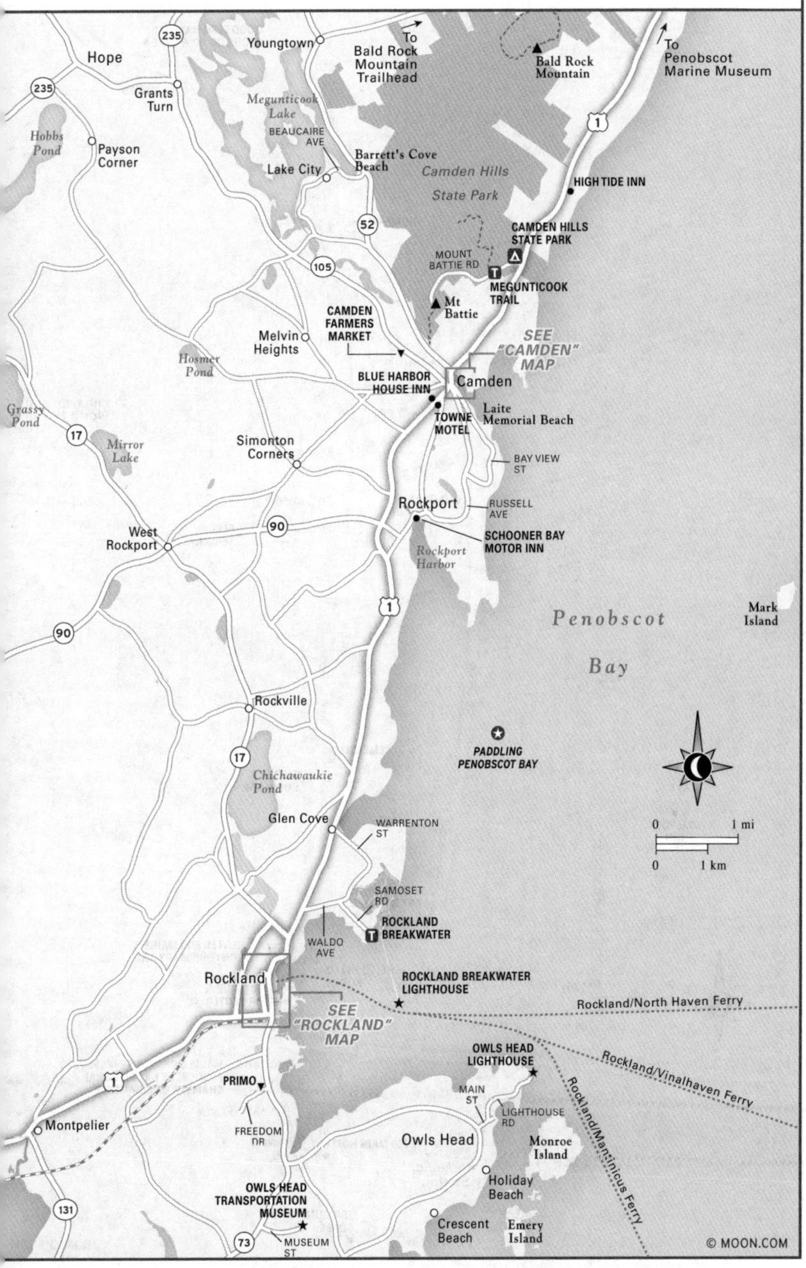

Rockland

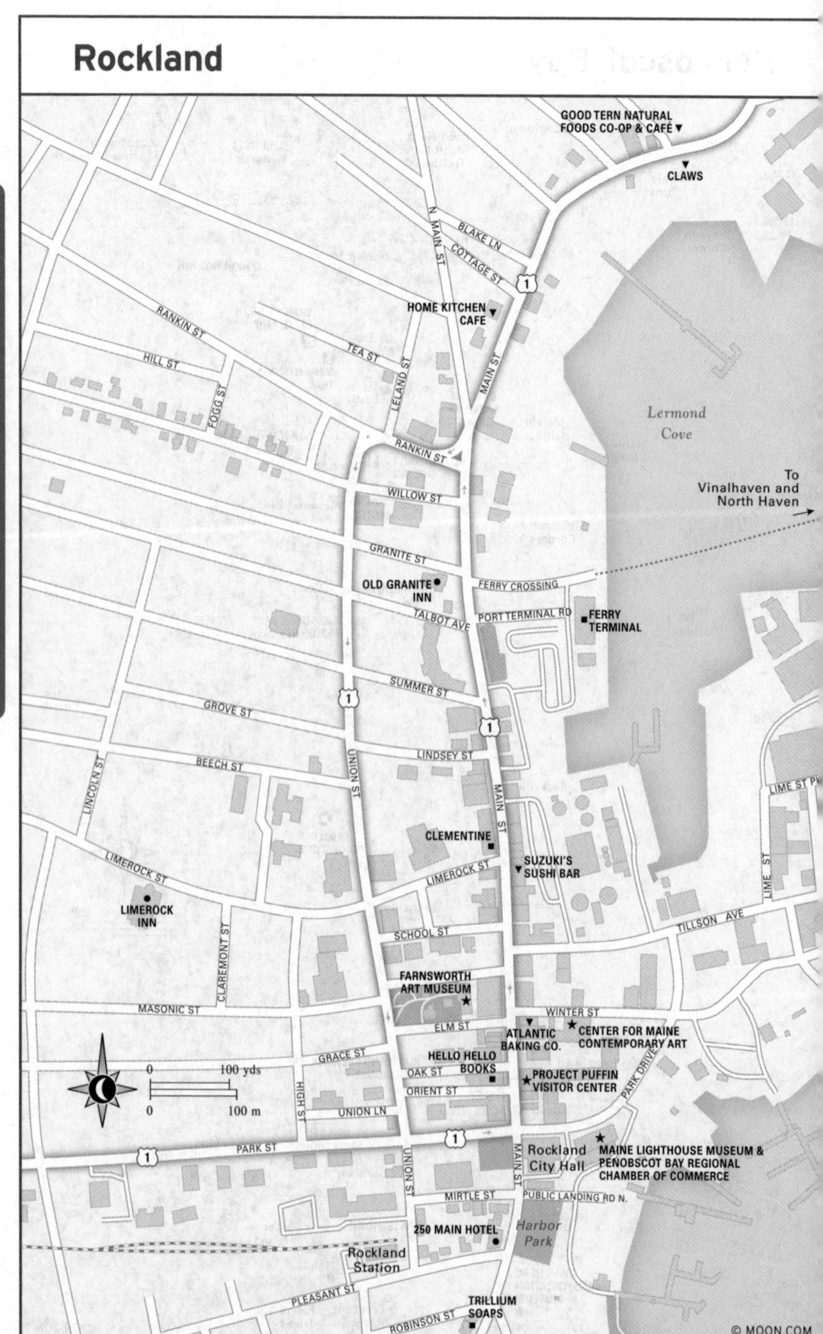
GOOD TERN NATURAL FOODS CO-OP & CAFÉ
CLAWS
BLAKE LN
COTTAGE ST
N MAIN ST
1
HOME KITCHEN CAFE
RANKIN ST
HILL ST
TEA ST
LELAND ST
FOGG ST
MAIN ST
Lermond Cove
RANKIN ST
WILLOW ST
To Vinalhaven and North Haven
GRANITE ST
OLD GRANITE INN
FERRY CROSSING
PORT TERMINAL RD
TALBOT AVE
FERRY TERMINAL
SUMMER ST
GROVE ST
1
1
LINDSEY ST
BEECH ST
UNION ST
LINCOLN ST
MAIN ST
LIME ST
CLEMENTINE
SUZUKI'S SUSHI BAR
LIMEROCK ST
LIMEROCK ST
LIMEROCK INN
CLAREMONT ST
SCHOOL ST
TILLSON AVE
FARNSWORTH ART MUSEUM
MASONIC ST
WINTER ST
ELM ST
ATLANTIC BAKING CO.
CENTER FOR MAINE CONTEMPORARY ART
GRACE ST
HELLO HELLO BOOKS
0
100 yds
0
100 m
OAK ST
ORIENT ST
PROJECT PUFFIN VISITOR CENTER
PARK DRIVE
HIGH ST
UNION LN
1
PARK ST
1
UNION ST
MAIN ST
Rockland City Hall
MAINE LIGHTHOUSE MUSEUM & PENOBSCOT BAY REGIONAL CHAMBER OF COMMERCE
MIRTLE ST
PUBLIC LANDING RD N.
250 MAIN HOTEL
Harbor Park
Rockland Station
PLEASANT ST
TRILLIUM SOAPS
ROBINSON ST
© MOON.COM

brick lighthouse at the end. The scale of the building project, which was completed in 1900, is staggering, and the bulk of the structure is underwater—a cross section of the breakwater would be trapezoidal, with the base measuring 175 feet (53 m) across. Walking the breakwater is an experience in itself, as sailboats, seabirds, and seals add to the scenery, and the **Rockland Breakwater Lighthouse** is fun to visit when open (if the flag is flying, the lighthouse is open—sharp-eyed visitors can spot the flag from Jameson Point, or check out the oddly hypnotizing live webcam feed on the breakwater website). Don't set out down the breakwater during storms, though, as heavy waves can wash over the rocks.

Short and pert, the **Owls Head Lighthouse** (Lighthouse Rd., Owl's Head, free) commands beautiful views of the rocky coastline, and is accessible via a short, gentle walk through coastal forest. Over the years, the lighthouse has collected a remarkable list of legends and ghost stories. The light is said to be haunted by two ghosts (one helpful spirit left one-way tracks in the snow when he visited to polish the brass and clean the lens), and the lighthouse has been the site of some remarkable rescues. In a December 1850 storm, a small schooner smashed up on the rocks near Owls Head, and two survivors huddled on the rocks while a third sought help. By the time a search party arrived, the two are said to have been fully encased in a block of frozen sea spray; the rescuers chipped off the ice and dunked the victims in cold water to revive them. According to legend, the two survivors later married and had four children.

While it might not thrill the casual visitor, lighthouse aficionados shouldn't miss the **Maine Lighthouse Museum** (1 Park Dr., 207/594-3301, www.mainelighthousemuseum.com, daily 10am-4pm, $10 adults, $8 seniors, free children under 12), which bills itself as the country's most significant collection of lenses and artifacts. The attached chamber of commerce has brochures and maps for lighthouse hopping up the coast. If puffins are more your thing, stop by the **Project Puffin Visitor Center** (311 Main St., 207/596-5566, https://seabirdinstitute.audubon.org, May-Oct. Wed.-Sun. 10am-5pm, June-Oct. daily 10am-5pm, free), which has a small but interesting exhibit on the birds and their habitat on Eastern Egg Rock.

Featuring Maine's best artists, the **Center for Maine Contemporary Art** (21 Winter St., Rockland, 207/701-5005, www.cmcanow.org, June-Oct. Mon.-Sat. 10am-5pm, Sun. noon-5pm, closed Mon.-Tues. in winter, $10 adults, $8 students and seniors, free children) is worth a look for its dozens of summer art shows held in a converted firehouse.

Entertainment and Events

Lobster lovers arrive from all over for the five days of cook-offs and contents at the **Maine Lobster Festival** (800/596-0376, www.mainelobsterfestival.com, early Aug.), which has been held in Rockland since 1947. The event doesn't really get going until King Neptune crowns the Maine Sea Goddess on Wednesday night, and then it's a frenzy of pancake breakfasts, music, and 20,000 pounds of lobster that goes straight from the boats into the world's largest lobster pot. It ends on Sunday with the "International Great Crate Race," where fleet-footed contestants run across lobster crates suspended in the harbor, overseen—and sometimes fished out—by umpires in rowboats. Admission to the fest is free (once inside, you'll pay for what you eat) but a queue can sometimes form at the gate, so budget an extra half hour or so for waiting in line.

Shopping

If you're looking for a place to browse or buy, **Main Street** around the Farnsworth Art Museum has a profusion of little boutiques and shops interspersed with small galleries. Find summer reads and literature at the adorable **Hello Hello books** (316 Main St., 207/593-7780, www.hellohellobooks.com, Mon.-Thurs. 10am-5pm, Fri.-Sat. 9am-6pm, Sun. 9am-4pm), an indie shop with a good selection of new and used titles. Quilters and DIY fashionistas will love **Clementine** (428 Main St., 207/596-3905, www.clementineme.com, Tues.-Sat. 10am-4pm), a boutique fabric shop that overflows with color, and you can find pretty handmade beauty products at **Trillium Soaps** (216 Main St., 207/593-9019, www.trilliumsoaps.com, Wed.-Sat. 10am-5pm).

Sports and Recreation

Unlike more cumbersome square-rigged ships, Maine's "windjammer" schooners can sail close-hauled to the wind, making them remarkably nimble and fast for their size. Five of the nine ships that make up the **Maine Windjammer Association** (207/374-2993, www.sailmainecoast.com) are National Historic Landmarks, and they're overhauled each spring with fresh paint, polished brass, and gleaming wood. Without a steady stream of tourists, it's hard to imagine these ships staying afloat; even a small wooden sailboat is a labor of love, and a grand, historic schooner even more so.

Cruises are 3-6 days in length, poking around rocky islands, sailing into coves in search of seals, and providing evening deck views under brilliant stars. Accommodations are snug but atmospheric, with plenty of varnished wood and portholes. And throughout the cruise, the galley crew prepares a hearty menu of surf-and-turf, salads, and fresh-baked breads. Guests can lend a hand in hoisting sails and anchors, or just lie back and watch the show.

The ***J. & E. Riggin*** (207/594-1875, www.mainewindjammer.com, 3-day trips from $795) leaves from Rockland and is known for the best schooner food on the coast, and the 1922 ***Ladona*** (207/594-4723, www.schoonerladona.com, 3-day trips from $1,398) has cornered the upper end of the market after a full-boat overhaul, with wonderfully pristine deck chairs, luxurious beds, elegant tiled showers, and cabins with plenty of natural light.

Food

A huge menu of hearty breakfasts and lunch plates is the draw at **Home Kitchen Café** (650 Main St., 207/596-2449, www.homekitchencafe.com, Mon. and Wed.-Sat. 8am-2:30pm, Sun. 8am-2pm, $8-17), a bright, friendly spot with a sunny rooftop patio. The recurring lobster tacos special is legendary, but the café's homemade sticky buns and corned beef hash also have passionate fans.

The busy bakers at **Atlantic Baking Co.** (351 Main St., 207/596-0505, www.atlanticbakingco.com, Mon.-Sat. 7am-5pm, $3-14) turn out an impressive display of sweets, breads, and savory pastries. This centrally located spot is a favorite for quick, simple lunches of soups, salads, or sandwiches on house-made bread, and it's good for picnic supplies if you're headed out to Owls Head Lighthouse or the Rockland Breakwater.

In a region renowned for some of the freshest seafood in New England, **Suzuki's Sushi Bar** (419 Main St., 207/596-7447, www.suzukisushi.com, Wed.-Sat. 5pm-close, $25-50) imbues local fish and mollusks with Japanese flavors. Served under balloon-like paper lanterns in a colorful dining room, the menu includes a rich assortment of sashimi, sushi rolls, and noodle dishes. But for the ultimate trip through umami-rich territory, try chef Keiko Suzuki Steinberger's rotating omakase tasting menu.

Superb, farm-to-table cuisine is beautifully presented at ★ **Primo** (2 South Main St., 207/596-0770, www.primorestaurant.com, May-June and Sept.-Oct. Wed.-Sat. 5pm-9:30pm, July-Aug. Wed.-Mon. 5pm-10pm, Nov.-Jan. Thurs.-Sun. 5pm-9pm, $39-64), an Italian restaurant on a four-acre (1.6-ha) farm. James Beard Award-winning chef Melissa Kelly creates a

Local Legends

Leah and Leslie Ranquist got their first taste of **lobstering** as children when their grandfather took them out in his skiff to bait traps and band lobsters. After completing a strenuous apprentice program, the two sisters, who both prefer the traditional term "lobsterman," began carrying on the family tradition from their home on Swan's Island, where each captains a lobster boat. Following a long day of hauling some of her 600 traps, Leah shared a bit about the lobstering life:

What's a typical day like for you?

It's pretty repetitive—at 5 or 5:30 I'll head out and haul through 180-250 traps, depending on the day, then I head back in. My sternman is there to bait the pockets and band the lobsters, and I fish singles, pairs, and triples. A triple is three traps on one buoy, so when that first trap comes up, I'll have him grab the first trap, and I'll grab the second trap.

What do you like about lobstering?

I like a lot about lobstering! I mostly like that I'm my own boss, and I can make my own schedule. It's pretty relaxed, and I like being out on the water. The beautiful days are really worth the not-so-good ones. I'll be fishing five or six days a week for six months a year, then I haul my traps out in November, and I pick away at them and fix them through the winter. I do have to work in the winter, but that's my version of taking a break.

What are some challenging things facing the Maine lobster industry in coming years?

We're trying to prepare for uncertainly. Lobsters have been doing very good the last few years, and not knowing if it's going to keep up, or if they'll disappear like other fisheries have, we have to plan for disaster just to keep in mind that it might not be there forever.

What's your favorite way to eat a lobster?

Steam it in a pot, then eat it hot with hot butter! I also enjoy a lobster roll here and there.

Try it Yourself

Just-caught Maine lobsters find their way to tanks and tables well beyond Midcoast Maine, but for the freshest catch, Rockland and Camden offer several choices.

- For a big, buttery lobster roll, positively heaped with meat, roll up to the takeout window at **CLAWS** (743 Main St., Rockland, 207/596-5600, www.clawsrocklandmaine.com, $11-27).
- If you'd prefer the classic, minimalist Maine lobster dinner experience, nab a harborside table at **Peter Ott's on the Water** (16 Bayview Landing, Camden, 207/236-4032, www.peterotts.com, Tues.-Sun. 11:30am-9pm, $18-38), order the steamed Maine lobster with lemon and hand-drawn butter, and have a cracking good time.

menu that changes with the season, and plates are a heady blend of classic flavors and Maine ingredients, like seared scallops with morel mushrooms and fiddleheads, or a branzino fillet with local whelks, shrimp, and clams. Reservations are recommended: Book the downstairs dining room for a romantic, more formal feel, or dine in the upstairs lounge, full of colorful nooks, bar seating, and a convivial atmosphere. Cocktails are as garden-fresh as the food.

Tiny **Good Tern Natural Foods Co-op and Café** (750 Main St., 207/594-8822, www.goodtern.com, Mon.-Sat. 8am-7pm, Sun. 9am-5pm) has a good selection of organic, GMO-free foods, a deli, and a small café with a sitting area.

Accommodations

Rockland has few accommodations compared to Rockport and Camden, making Airbnb a good option here.

$150-250

Modern touches and eclectic, original art keep the ★ **Old Granite Inn** (546 Main St., 207/594-9036, www.oldgraniteinn.com, $95-225) from feeling fusty, but the common spaces of the granite colonial house retain a historical feel. Rooms range from a compact queen with detached private bath to four-person suites that are an excellent value for families; some have electric fireplaces and whirlpool tubs, while two rooms on the 2nd floor boast views of the Rockland Harbor Lighthouse. The hearty breakfasts served in the communal dining room get raves from guests.

$250-350

The elegant Queen Anne architecture of **LimeRock Inn** (96 Limerock St., 800/546-3762, www.limerockinn.com, $180-320) is brightened up with an eye-popping coat of teal paint and garden full of blooming plants. Welcoming owners and a location that's walking distance from downtown restaurants and the Farnsworth Art Museum make this a good choice for exploring Rockland, but the gracious wraparound porch, living room, and comfortable rooms are tempting reasons to stay in as well. All rooms have a private bath and fun, varied decor that ranges from a somewhat princess-y pink suite to staid Yankee plaid.

Luxurious and ultramodern, **250 Main Hotel** (250 Main St., 207/594-5994, www.250mainhotel.com, $299-449) offers stunning views of the harbor from many rooms, some of which feature floor-to-ceiling glass. Clever nautical touches and original art are everywhere in the hotel's 26 rooms and common spaces. Don't miss the wonderful rooftop patio.

Information

The **Penobscot Bay Regional Chamber of Commerce** (1 Park Dr., 207/596-0376, www.therealmaine.com, Mon.-Fri. 10am-4pm) runs a large and well-stocked information center in a new building by the harbor.

Rockport and Camden

Forested, sloping hills running straight to the water are the perfect frame for Camden's sheltered harbor and picturesque downtown; the elegant little community is one of New England's most beautiful. Schooners and sleek yachts stand to attention at mooring buoys and floating docks, and on quiet mornings you can hear the slapping of halyard ropes against masts and outboard motors from all over town. There's no finer place on the coast to see Maine's windjammer fleet, breathtaking wooden vessels crowned with acres of flying sails and trim lines.

All that beauty has made Camden a tourist destination since the mid-19th century, and downtown can be a madhouse in the heat of summer. When the ice cream shop has a line out the door and there's nowhere to park within a mile (1.6 km) of the water, it's worth taking in your harbor views from the relative quiet of Camden Hills State Park, where Mount Megunticook and Mount Battie look out on Penobscot Bay.

Just down the coast, tiny Rockport feels like Camden in dollhouse scale: Turn away at the wrong moment, and you'd totally miss the perfect little harbor and downtown. There are just a few restaurants on the little Main Street, and

Camden

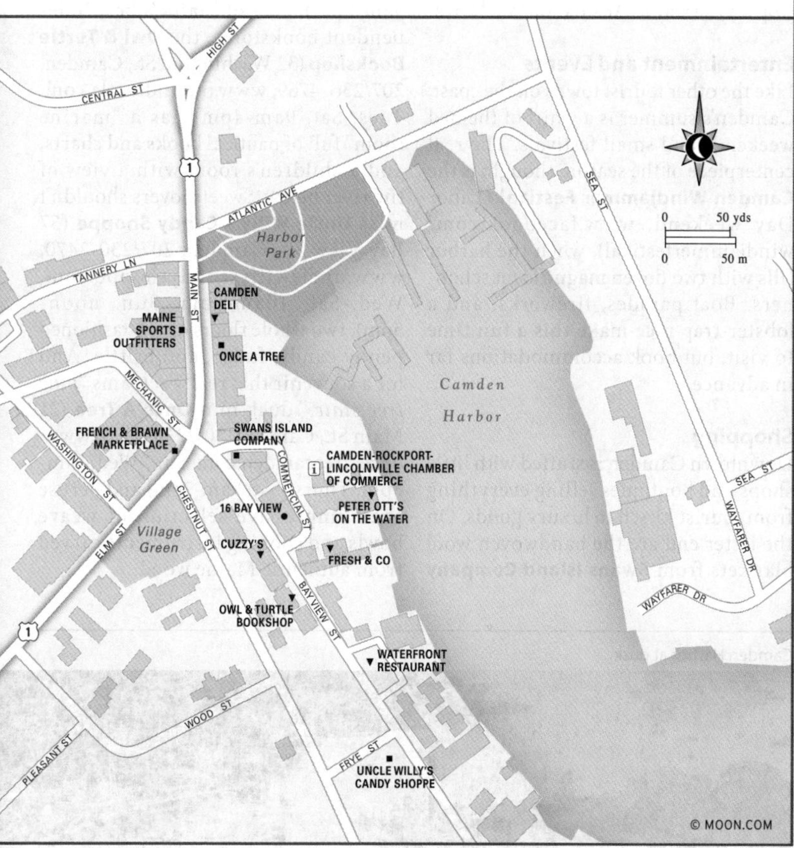

no sights to speak of, but the waterfront park is ideal for watching lobster boats and sailors.

Sights

Starting in the 18th century, Mainers produced lime by burning locally quarried limestone in wood- and coal-fired kilns. At the time, lime was an essential part of almost any construction project, and, at the industry's peak in 1892, millions of casks of lime left the Maine coast. Keep an eye out and you'll see traces of the lime business everywhere, including a ruined **lime kiln** by the river in the Rockport Harbor.

While it's not quite as extensive as the maritime museum in Bath, the collection of nautical treasures, art, and artifacts at the **Penobscot Marine Museum** (2 Church St., Searsport, 207/548-0334, www.penobscotmarinemuseum.org, late May-mid-Oct. Mon.-Sat. 10am-5pm, Sun. noon-5pm, $15 adults, $12 seniors and students, $10 children 8-15, $40 family, free children under 8) is fascinating. You'll find a trove of model ships and scrimshaw here, along with practical tools and navigation equipment. The museum is about 30 minutes up the coast from Camden in Searsport, so make a stop on the way to Acadia National Park.

Entertainment and Events

Like the other tourist towns on the coast, Camden's summer is a whirl of themed weekends and small festivals. The real centerpiece of the season, though, is the **Camden Windjammer Festival** (Labor Day weekend, www.facebook.com/windjammerfestival), when the harbor fills with two dozen magnificent schooners. Boat parades, fireworks, and a lobster-trap race make this a fun time to visit, but book accommodations far in advance.

Shopping

Downtown Camden is stuffed with little shops and boutiques selling everything from tourist kitsch to luxury goods. On the latter end are the handwoven wool blankets from **Swans Island Company** (2 Bay View St., Camden, 207/706-7926, www.swansislandcompany.com, daily 9am-9pm). One of Maine's best independent bookstores, the **Owl & Turtle Bookshop** (32 Washington St., Camden, 207/236-4769, www.owlandturtle.com, Tues.-Sat. 9am-4pm) has a "marine room" full of nautical books and charts, and a children's room with a view of the river below. Sweets lovers shouldn't miss **Uncle Willy's Candy Shoppe** (57 Bay View St., Camden, 207/230-2470, www.unclewillyscandyshoppe.com, Wed.-Sat. 10am-5pm, Sun. noon-5pm), two whole floors of old-fashioned penny candy, fudge, and brittle. And for a souvenir that really screams "*pine tree state,*" duck into **Once A Tree** (31 Main St., Camden, 207/236-3995, www.onceatreecamden.com, Sun.-Wed. 9am-6pm, Thurs.-Sat. 9am-7pm) and peruse their impressive selection of weave bowls and cooking instruments carved from authentic Maine wood.

Camden Harbor at dusk

Sports and Recreation

★ Paddling Penobscot Bay

As beautiful as Rockport and Camden are, getting out on a boat is the only way to really take in Penobscot Bay. Tiny forested isles and town-sized islands are dreamlike on sunny days, when the sparkling water lights up the coast. But the bay is a sprawl of rocky shoals and hazards, and a thick layer of fog can turn even familiar harbors into a dangerous maze. Would-be adventurers shouldn't be deterred—local captains and kayak guides are well versed in keeping people safe.

The lacy, rocky edges of Penobscot Bay are perfectly suited to kayaks, which can nose in and out of coves too small for bigger boats. **Maine Sports Outfitters** (24 Main St., Camden, 207/236-8797, www.mainesport.com, kayak trips $60-120 adults, $50-110 children 10-15) runs trips ranging from two hours to a full day. A two-hour Camden Harbor Tour is a good way to see the schooners and yachts from the water as you work your way to a small island at the mouth of the harbor, but the half-day Harbor-to-Harbor paddle goes farther afield, starting in Rockport Harbor and going to Camden Harbor, with a picnic lunch on Curtis Island.

Experienced kayakers can rent from the same company (full-day sea kayak rental $65/single, $75/tandem), which is full of good advice on day trips and overnight paddles from Camden Harbor.

Beaches

The Camden area isn't known for great beaches, but there are some fine places to cool off on a hot day: At the eastern end of Megunticook Lake, **Barrett's Cove Beach** (Beauclaire Ave. off Route 52) has a bit of sand and picnic tables. By midsummer, the water here is far warmer than the bay, making it a good choice for families. A one-mile (1.6-km) walk from downtown Camden, **Laite Memorial Beach** (south side of Camden Harbor, off Bay View St.) is a pleasant, grassy park with a sandy beach that narrows to a sliver at high tide.

Boating

Sailing out of Camden, the 1871 ***Lewis R. French*** (270/230-8320, www.schoonerfrench.com, three-night trips from $725) is the oldest windjammer in the United States, and still has no inboard engine; with all sails set, she flies a remarkable 3,000 square feet (279 square m) of canvas. Another Camden favorite is the ***Angelique*** (800/282-9989, www.sailangelique.com, three-night trips from $875), a modern vessel that's particularly dramatic under deep red, gaff-rigged sails.

Hiking

Aside from Mount Desert Island, **Camden Hills State Park** (280 Rte. 1, Camden, 207/236-3109, www.maine.gov, 9am-sunset, $6 adults, $2 seniors and children) is the only place in Maine where the mountains hew so closely to

The Places in Between: Vinalhaven

the verdant preserve at Lane's Island

No pilgrimage to Maine is complete without a ferry ride to one of the seemingly countless islands that speckle the coastline.

When it comes to these island communities, Vinalhaven is special. An hour from Rockland by boat, Vinalhaven is the home of Maine's largest lobstering fleet and countless swimming holes, woodland trails, and coastal vistas. It's also a more "lived-in" Maine island than nearby North Haven, where the wealthier out-of-staters summer in palatial estates and rental homes. Vinalhaven's central waterfront town of Carver's Harbor is a proudly working-class enclave that's been hauling lobsters from Penobscot Bay for generations. Between the boats anchored in the harbor and the pre-sunrise crowd of fishers fueling up on pancakes and coffee at the **Surfside** (35 W. Main St., 207/863-2767, daily 4am-10:30am, $7-12), Maine doesn't get more real than this.

the coast, and the views of Penobscot Bay are unmatched. You'll earn your views on the steep 2.6-mile (4-km) round-trip **Megunticook Trail** as you climb almost 1,000 feet (305 m) in elevation on your way to the top. (Pro tip: The best view is actually found at the "Ocean Lookout" overlook, just below the summit.) Another good choice for views of the bay is the 3-mile (4.8-km) loop trail up the 1,200-foot (366-m) **Bald Rock Mountain,** where two rustic Adirondack shelters are set just below the bare crest. Unless you're a very brisk walker, set aside two hours for either hike, and be sure to pick up a free hiking map at the entrance to the park.

Of course, you also don't have to walk anywhere for views in this park. An auto road to the summit of **Mount Battie** climbs from just inside the state park entrance.

Food

Camden

Find great coffee and something to read at **Owl & Turtle Bookshop** (33 Bay View St., 207/230-7335, www.owlandturtle.com, Tues.-Sat. 9am-4pm, $5-8), which also has a small selection of fresh pastries. Friendly staff and a good crowd of locals make this a nice place to linger with a crossword puzzle.

No one goes to **Cuzzy's** (21 Bay View St., 207/236-3272, www.cuzzysrestaurant.com, daily 11am-1am, $10-25) for a

Getting There

The ferry to Vinalhaven leaves from the **Rockland Ferry Terminal** (517A Main St., www.maine.gov/mdot, Mar.-Nov., walk-ons $17.50 adults, $11.25 ages 6-17, under 6 free, add $5/ticket if bringing a bicycle; cars $38.50), with the first ride departing at 7am and the last ride back to Rockland leaving Vinalhaven at 4:30pm. If you'd prefer to leave your vehicle in Rockland, the terminal offers parking for $12 per day.

Sights, Food, and Accommodations

Once you debark the ferry, walk, bike, or drive down Main Street into Carver's Harbor. Indulge your sweet tooth with some penny candy at **Go Fish** (56 Main St., 207/863-4193, Tues.-Sat. 10am-5pm) or wolf down one of the *Downeast Magazine* award-wining lobster rolls at **Greet's Eats** (11 W. Main St., Thurs.-Sat. 11am-2pm, $5-22), a tiny red food truck that overlooks the harbor and its lobstering fleet.

From there, consider a stroll through beach roses, seaweed-festooned rocks, and hidden coves at **Lane's Island Preserve** (a gentle 0.8-mile (1.3-km) walk from Carver's Harbor by foot, maps at www.townofvinalhaven.org), or plunge into the waters of **Booth Quarry** (Booth Quarry Rd.), where you'll have your choice of ledges to leap from.

For a sunset dinner, head to **Dot & Millie's** (49 E Main St., 207/863-2300, www.dotandmilliesvh.com, check website for seasonal hours, $15-28). A local favorite among Vinalhaven's constantly changing restaurant offerings, Dot & Millie's offers a decadent roster of local seafood, salads, wines, and Maine craft beer, steps away from a primo harbor view.

If you fancy an overnight stay on the island, plump for a waterfront room at **The Tidewater** (15 W. Main St., 207/863-4618, www.thetidewatervh.com, $140-220), which perches right over the harbor. The co-founder, Phil Crossman, is also an author and local historian, and if he happens to be around (his daughter is the current manager) he might just regale you with some stories about the island's more irreverent and elegiac qualities.

Whether you spend a foggy morning, a sun-soaked afternoon, or even a weekend on Vinalhaven, you'll return to the mainland with a better understanding of what "Maine living" actually looks like for the people who call the state's islands home. Vinalhaven is one of the last places in Midcoast Maine where you can escape the thrum of summer tourism and immerse yourself in a Maine community.

gourmet meal, but that's somewhat beside the point. There's a huge menu of affordable pub food, very decent chowder, and all kinds of fried seafood to eat at the bar, where fishers and schooner crews come to relax in a cave-like interior or on the sunny back patio. Happy hour specials on cheap beer and pizza are available daily 3pm-6pm.

With a solid menu of seafood standards and patio seating that juts over the harbor, **Waterfront Restaurant** (40 Bay View St., 207/236-3747, www.waterfrontcamden.com, daily 11:30am 4pm and 5pm-8pm, $17-32) is a perennial favorite. No individual dish seems to blow anyone away, but watching the boats roll in and out of the harbor over a glass of local beer and plate of oysters is a true Camden experience. On busy nights, waits can get very long, and since the interior seating is a bit lackluster, it's often worth going elsewhere.

Reasonably priced sandwiches, soups, and salads at **Camden Deli** (37 Main St., 207/236-8343, www.camdendeli.com, daily 7am-6pm, $9-15) are a simple option right downtown. Limited seating is available inside (window seats have great views of the harbor), but this is a nice place to pick up sandwiches to take around the corner to the small park where paths and benches face the water.

In a cheerfully decorated, historic brick building, the chef-owned ★ **Fresh & Co** (1 Bay View Landing,

207/236-7005, www.freshcamden.com, Tues.-Sat. 4pm-9pm, $23-37) is just that, with an eye-opening menu of international food that seems to bounce from one continent to another, depending on the season. The citrusy Brazilian moqueca stew with whitefish, shrimp, and mussels is a favorite here, as are the lamb tzatziki "lollipops" and the Maine lobster toast with pimento and green tomato relish. Despite the upscale food (and prices), this restaurant has a casual atmosphere, with outdoor seating and the occasional live act.

Find high-quality baked goods, meat, cheese, and drinks at **French & Brawn Marketplace** (1 Elm St., 207/236-3361, www.frenchandbrawn.com, Mon.-Sat. 6am-8pm, Sun. 8am-8pm), which is the only market in downtown Camden. Small but vibrant, the **Camden Farmers Market** (116 Washington St., www.camdenfarmersmarket.org, May-Oct. Sat. market 9am-noon; mid-June-Sept. Wed. market 3:30pm-6pm) has local breads, cheeses, vegetables, and fruit.

Rockport

Tiny Rockport doesn't have much of a dining scene, but **Nina June** (24 Central St., 207/236-8880, www.ninajunerestaurant.com, Tues.-Sat. 5:30pm-9pm, brunch $6-18, lunch/dinner $20-30) is a noteworthy exception. A deck overlooking the Rockport Harbor makes a sublime setting for a Mediterranean menu that changes with the season. On a recent July evening, the menu included wild-foraged dandelion greens with bacon and bleu cheese dressing, and spinach spaghetti with buffalo ricotta and saffron. During the summer, visiting guest chefs add their own spin to the menu, with flavors from Iran, Peru, and more. Reservations for dinner sometimes sell out as soon as one month in advance, so if you're interested in dining at Nina June, treat this meal like a ticketed event.

Accommodations and Camping

Camping

Set in the rolling forest along the coast, **Camden Hills State Park** (280 Rte. 1, 207/236-3109, www.maine.gov, $35-45) has amazing views of Penobscot Bay, trails to explore, and level campsites that range from simple tent pads to extra-large options with water, electric, and space for a 35-foot (10-m) camper. The campground is divided into reservable sites that must be booked 48 hours in advance (though it's worth planning ahead for peak season), and a smaller number of sites that are set aside on a first-come, first-served basis.

$150-250

A quiet, 15-minute walk from Rockport's gem of a harbor, **Schooner Bay Motor Inn** (337 Commercial St., Rockport, 888/308-8855, www.sbaymotorinn.com, $110-230) has trim furnishings and a thoughtful, local character that sets it apart from the other motels along Route 1. Light sleepers should request a room at the forested back of the property, where there's a small, shady creek. A breakfast of homemade muffins, fruit, and quiche is served May-December.

If you're looking for a lower-budget place to stay in downtown Camden, the **Towne Motel** (68 Elm St., Camden, 207/236-3377, www.camdenmotel.com, $139-199) is hard to beat. The super-clean, motel-style rooms are nothing fancy, but the friendly owners have renovated the space in recent years. All of the colorful rooms have coffeemakers, cable televisions, air-conditioning, wireless Internet, and small fridges, and an appealing breakfast with staples like pecan coffee cake is served during summer months; in the off-season, the owners deliver a little breakfast packet to each room that includes their killer homemade granola.

Find Maine country style with a few nautical touches at the **Blue Harbor House Inn** (67 Elm St., Camden, 207/236-3196, www.blueharborhouse.com, $175-255), a homey spot that's a short walk from downtown. Rooms are stocked with coffeemakers and comfortable beds, and afternoon tea and the innkeeper's two-course breakfast are served in a welcoming common room. All rooms have en suite bathrooms, and more expensive options have steam showers or claw-foot soaking tubs.

An expansive lawn rolls all the way to a private beach, a wonderful perk that makes the **High Tide Inn** (505 Rte. 1, Camden, 207/236-3724, www.hightideinn.com, $140-200, deck house $250-330) feel like a retreat just a few minutes' drive from downtown Camden. A handful of options are available on this property: the somewhat lackluster Oceanview Motel (where you can just spy a bit of blue); the sweet, compact rooms in the old-fashioned inn; a collection of oceanfront rooms a stone's throw from the water; and six little cottages, nostalgic and rustic. A homemade continental breakfast is served on a glass-enclosed porch with views to the water.

Over $350

Find all the top-end perks at ★ **16 Bay View** (16 Bay View St., Camden, 207/706-7990, www.16bayview.com, $350-525), a 21-room boutique hotel in a 100-year-old industrial brick building with perfect views of the harbor from ocean-side rooms and the rooftop bar. Great piles of silky pillows, gas fireplaces, spa bathrooms, and balconies are luxurious, and the hotel, which opened in early 2016, is beautifully decorated. A continental breakfast is served in the Prohibition-themed Vintage Room.

Information

The **Camden-Rockport-Lincolnville Chamber of Commerce** (2 Public Landing, 207/236-4404, www.camdenrockland.com, Mon.-Fri. 10am-4pm) runs a helpful information center on the Camden waterfront.

Getting Around

No real in-town public transit is available in any of the Penobscot Bay locales, but they're small enough to explore on foot. In Camden, free parking is available at two public lots (Washington Street, turn north when Route 1 passes the Camden Village Green). In Rockland, there's free, two-hour parking on Main Street, and a larger lot at **Oceanside High School** (400 Broadway, Rockland, July and Aug. only).

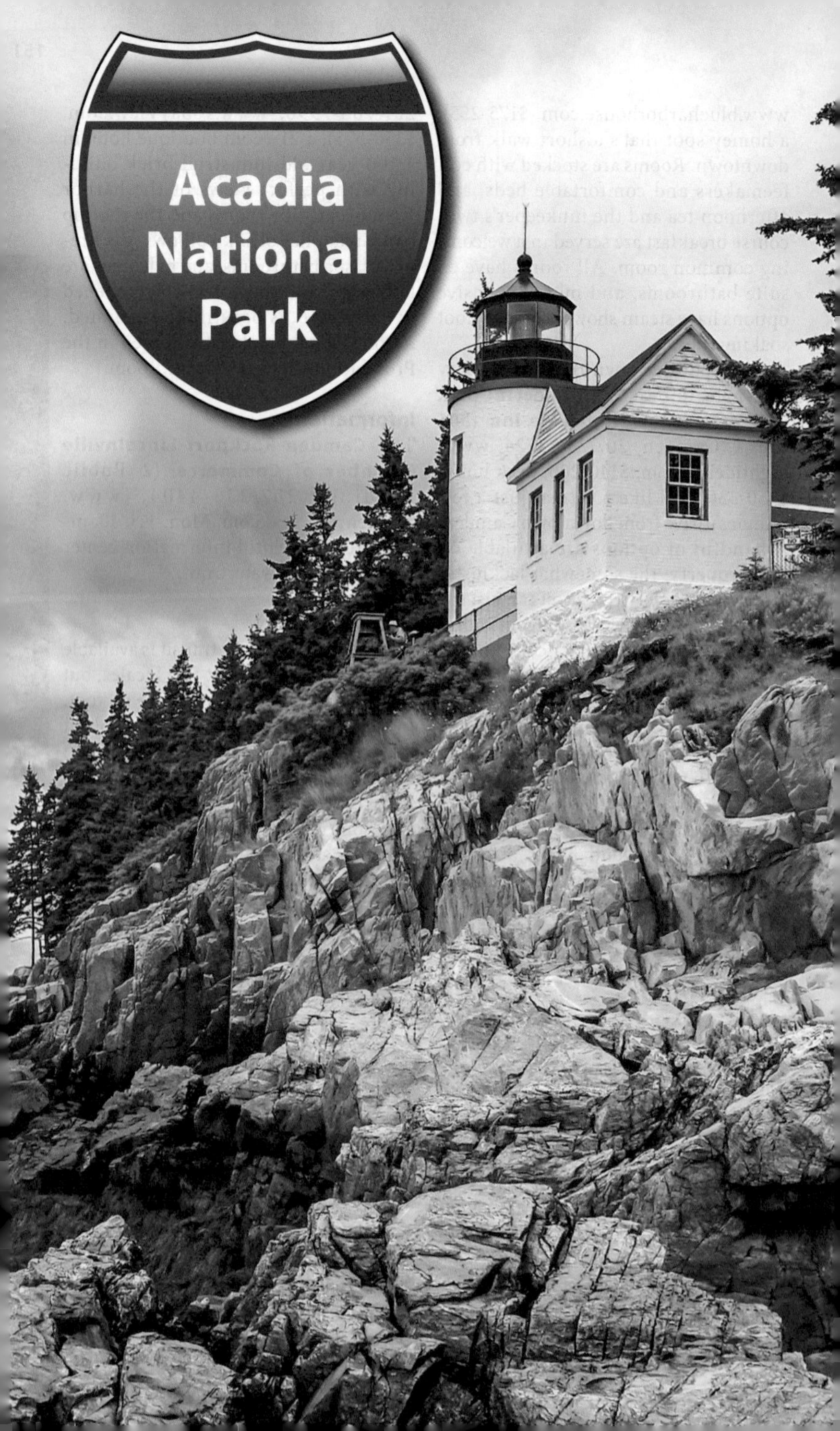
Acadia
National
Park

Highlights

★ **Driving the Park Loop Road:** Find ocean views and sheer cliffs around every corner of this 27-mile (43-km) drive, which loops through the heart of Acadia National Park (page 162).

★ **Sunrise at Cadillac Mountain:** Catch first light from the tallest peak on the Eastern Seaboard (page 164).

★ **Carriage Roads:** Walk or bike this extraordinary network of car-free roads—or hop a horse-drawn carriage to a rocky summit (page 165).

★ **Tidepooling:** The sandbars and rocky inlets around Mount Desert Island trap diverse sea creatures every time the tide goes out (page 168).

★ **Bar Harbor's Ice Cream Shops:** Line up for cones and cups in this classic Vacationland town, where a pair of beloved ice cream shops serve everything from Moose Tracks to lobster ice cream (page 175).

Acadia National Park

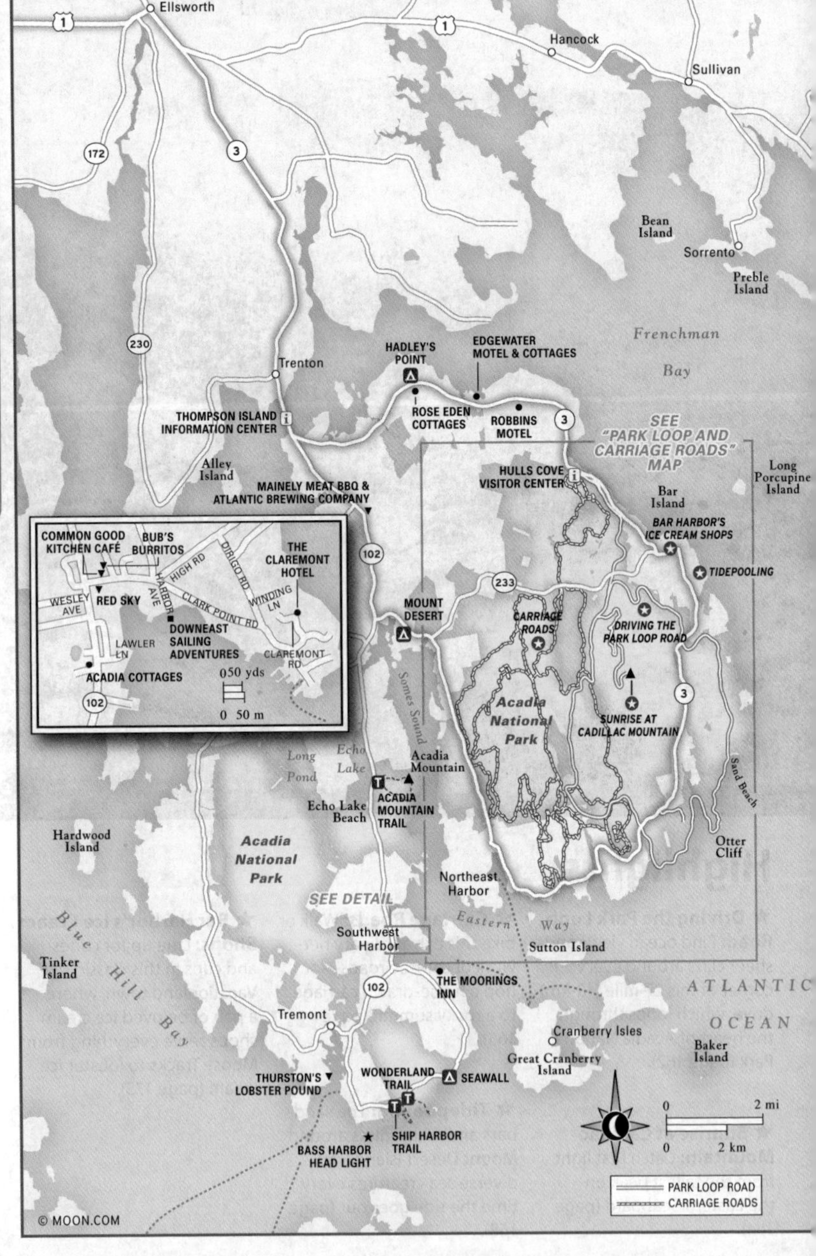

Best Restaurants

★ **Jordan Pond House:** Buttery popovers with strawberry jam and a view are a long-standing tradition at Acadia National Park's only restaurant (page 169).

★ **Common Good Kitchen Café:** Nestled amid the shops and gardens of quiet Southwest Harbor, this nonprofit café wins raves for its popovers and housemade spreads (page 169).

★ **Thurston's Lobster Pound:** Get all the fixings and a million-dollar view at this longtime favorite near a sheltered harbor (page 170).

★ **2 Cats:** Find a spot on the shady porch to enjoy the best breakfast on the island (page 173).

★ **Terrace Grille at the Bar Harbor Inn:** Tuck into a lobster dinner on a sunny patio, then nibble blueberry pie as the sun sets (page 174).

Maine's scenic drama comes to a head in Acadia National Park, a 47,000-acre (19,020-ha) preserve that spills across Mount Desert Island to the surrounding islets and shoreline.

Twenty-four mountain peaks display the island's dramatic history in sparkling granite. Geologic clues are everywhere here, from odd-looking rocks left perched on mountaintops to ice-carved U-shaped valleys and deep gouges in bare granite. A deep, fjord-like bay nearly splits the island in two. For ocean-view hiking, rocky trail exploration, and tidepooling, New England's only national park is incomparable. Acadia is a miracle of ecology and geology, and the trail construction might just be the finest in the northeast. No wonder people flock here to scrabble along the pink rocks of Ship Harbor or ascend the "iron rung" trails up mountains such as The Beehive. It's a thrill, but above all, an inspiration.

The Wabanaki people have inhabited this stretch of coast for thousands of years, hunting and fishing in year-round settlements and trading widely with other regional groups. In 1604, French explorer Samuel de Champlain stopped by long enough to record a name—*Isles des Monts Déserts,* or islands of bare peaks—and was followed by waves of Jesuit missionaries, French and British soldiers, and European settlers eager to fish and farm. By the mid-18th century, though, the dramatic scenery was the main draw, as a generation of "rusticators," city people seeking simpler country pleasures, came by steamship for entire summers of hiking, sailing, and painting by the sea. Those early lodges were replaced by grander hotels and Gilded Age homes, and Bar Harbor became a favorite retreat of the East Coast elite. By the turn of the 20th century, some of those landowners began to set aside large tracts of land for public use, then finally turned the land over to the federal government for the 1919 creation of the first national park east of the Mississippi River.

It remains an extraordinary place, with rugged mountains, beaches, and headlands so tightly packed they can be explored in a single day. Acadia is glorious in the summer sunshine, but it's equally entrancing when thick fog creeps across the water, isolating the island into a world of its own. One vibrant town and a handful of scattered communities are interwoven with the park land, so your experience in Acadia can be as luxurious, or remote, as you choose.

Best Accommodations

★ **Mount Desert Campground:** Start your day with a chilly dip in Somes Sound at a campground that's perfectly placed at the center of the island (page 170).

★ **Acadia Cottages:** Sweet cottages scattered through the woods make this a true "quiet side" destination (page 171).

★ **The Claremont Hotel:** One of two surviving hotels from the elegant years of Gilded Age getaways, this old-fashioned gem is a gentle time machine by the sea (page 171).

★ **Acacia House Inn:** Fabulous breakfasts, welcoming hosts, and comfortable rooms are a find in downtown Bar Harbor (page 175).

★ **Edgewater Motel and Cottages:** Strike a balance between town and country with a sweet cottage on a private beach (page 176).

Planning Your Time

Mount Desert Island is 108 square miles (280 square km), and accounting for winding roads and slow-moving traffic, it can take quite a while to drive from one side to the other. It's worth choosing one of the two sides as a home base: Opt for Bar Harbor for great access to kid-friendly activities, shops, and restaurants, or sleep on the western "quiet side" to escape the crowds. From spring to fall, the free Island Explorer shuttle makes frequent loops of the island following eight different routes; if you'd like to explore car-free (highly recommended), choose accommodations on a shuttle route. As in other destinations on coastal Maine, the true high season is during the school vacation months of July, August, and early September. Many prices drop substantially in June and October, whose mild weather and sunshine also make them some of the prettiest months on the island. The leaves begin to change color in late September, reaching a brilliant peak just a few weeks later in mid-October. While the Park Loop Road is open year-round, many restaurants and hotels close their doors between November and May.

Orientation

For many people, Acadia National Park and Mount Desert Island are synonymous, but the national park is a patchwork that covers much of the island and a bit of mainland coast. The bulk of the park territory is on the eastern side of Mount Desert Island, where the Park Loop Road circles some of the most dramatic scenery and best-known hiking trails. On the other side of Somes Sound is the "quiet side," good for less-frequented hikes. The remaining parkland is on the harder-to-reach Isle au Haut, and the Schoodic Peninsula, which is linked by passenger ferry to Bar Harbor.

Getting to Acadia National Park

Driving from Coastal Maine

175 mi/282 km, 3 hr

Coastal Maine's **Route 1,** which you can take almost the entire way up to Acadia National Park, passes through pretty villages and forests, occasionally breaking out into shoreline views. Sections of this road, especially from **Rockland** to **Lincolnville** and at the **Penobscot**

Narrows Bridge, are very scenic, and there are plenty of places to stop along the way for window-shopping and walks along the ocean. For this drive, take Route 1 all the way to Ellsworth, turning right onto High Street in town to stay on Route 1, then continue straight for **Route 3,** which crosses the **Trenton Bridge** onto Mount Desert Island and into **Bar Harbor** (190 mi/306 km, 4.25 hrs).

While Route 1 is undeniably lovely, it's also notoriously congested and may be worth avoiding on crowded weekends. Without accounting for traffic, using the inland interstate highway saves about an hour. When traffic is at its worst, it would be easy to spend an additional two hours sitting in Route 1 traffic jams in **Wiscasset** and **Camden.** If you're headed straight to Acadia from destinations between the Kennebunks and Bath, you can avoid frequent congestion by following the quicker, less-trafficked I-95 (and I-295). This route passes mostly through thick forest, missing the towns and harbors along Route 1, but it's worth considering on busy weekends and during high season when traffic slows to a crawl.

To follow this inland route from **Portland** (175 mi/282 km, 3 hrs) or **Kennebunkport** (205 mi/330 km, 3.5 hrs), travel north on **I-295** until it merges with **I-95 North** in **Gardiner** ($5 toll, cash only). Stay on I-95 for 79 miles (127 km), then take Exit 182A in Bangor to merge onto **I-395 East.** After 4.7 miles (7.5 km), merge onto **Route 1A East** at Exit 6A. Follow **Route 1A** as it changes into **Route 3** in Ellsworth, then crosses the **Trenton Bridge** onto Mount Desert Island and into **Bar Harbor.**

Driving from New Hampshire's White Mountains

215 mi/346 km, 4 hr

Several routes link **Conway, New Hampshire,** with Mount Desert Island, on roads that wind through Maine's **deep inland forest.** The most straightforward way to reach the coast is to take **Route 113 East** from Conway, and turn right in Fryeburg, Maine, for **Route 113 South.** In Brownfield, you'll turn left on **Route 160 North,** which merges into **Route 117 North** in Denmark. Follow signs and turn right to stay on Route 117, then make another right onto **Route 302 East.** You'll next turn left onto **Route 11 North** (watch closely for signs, as the route zigzags for the 10 mi/16 km you'll be on it) before turning right onto **North Raymond Road,** then left onto Cleve Tripp Road after 1.7 miles (2.7 km), then right onto Range Hill Road after 1.3 miles (2 km). Next, turn left onto **Carpenter Road/Route 122,** then right at Poland Spring Road to stay on Route 122. Make a left onto Washington Street, then merge onto **I-95 North** (toll $1.75).

Stay on I-95 for about **106 miles** (170 km), then take Exit 182A in Bangor to merge onto **I-395 East.** After 4.7 miles (7.5 km), merge onto **Route 1A East** at Exit 6A. Follow **Route 1A** as it changes into **Route 3** in Ellsworth, then crosses the **Trenton Bridge** onto Mount Desert Island and into **Bar Harbor.**

Driving from Boston

Interstate 95 is by far the most efficient way to cover the considerable distance from Boston to Mount Desert Island. Leave Boston heading northeast on **Storrow Drive.** Use the left two lanes to take the **Route 1 North** exit, and after merging onto **Route 1 North** cross the **Tobin Bridge** ($3) and continue through Revere and Saugus for 14.2 miles (23 km) before mering onto **I-95 North** ($8), which you'll follow through the New Hampshire seacoast into Maine. After 215 miles (346 km), take Exit 182A, merge onto **I-395 East,** and continue for 4.7 miles (7.5 km) to Exit 6A for **Route 1A.** Follow this local expressway through Ellsworth as the route changes to **Route 3** and continue over the **Trenton Bridge** to Mount Desert Island.

One Day in Acadia National Park

cliffs along Park Loop Road

Morning

Ambitious visitors can rise in the dark for a predawn pilgrimage to **Cadillac Mountain,** where sunrise reveals thick forests, remote islands, and granite peaks. Wait out the crowds for a quiet walk around the short **Summit Loop** before descending into Bar Harbor for a well-deserved stack of Maine blueberry pancakes and coffee at the quirky **2 Cats.**

Afternoon

Take a stroll around town to shop for a picnic lunch for a day in the park, then get your bearings with a scenic drive around **Park Loop Road,** stopping for views and time on the beach. Leave your vehicle behind in the afternoon and explore the **carriage roads,** 47 miles (75 km) of car-free bliss: Walk, bike, or ride a horse-drawn carriage to sweeping views of the mountainous interior, hulking granite bridges, and hidden streams.

Evening

Head to the quiet side of the island for an early dinner at **Thurston's Lobster Pound,** then take in sunset on the water at the nearby **Bass Harbor Head Light.**

Driving from New York City

Head north from New York City on **FDR Drive.** Use the left lane to access Exit 17 to the **Robert F. Kennedy Bridge** ($10.17 toll), then stay left to merge onto **I-278 East.** After 4.5 miles (7.2 km), I-278 East merges with **I-95 North** ($1.75 toll). Follow I-95 North 46 miles (74 km) to Exit 27A in Bridgeport, Connecticut; exit right onto **Route 8 North,** which you'll follow 5.5 miles (8.8 km) to Exit 9 and **Route 15 North.**

Take Exit 68 NE to merge onto **I-91 North** toward Hartford/Middletown, then stay right for Exit 29 and merge onto **Route 15 North** toward **I-84 East.** Use the left two lanes to continue onto I-84 East toward Boston. North of Sturbridge, I-84 East merges with **I-90** ($7.25 toll, no cash); stay right at the split for **I-90 East.** Take Exit 11A and merge onto **I-495 North,** which you'll follow into New Hampshire to its terminus. Merge onto **I-95 North,** drive north through Maine for 193 miles

(310 km), and take Exit 182A for **I-395 East.** Follow the highway to Exit 6A and continue to Mount Desert Island by way of **Route 1A,** which becomes **Route 3** shortly before reaching the island.

Getting There by Air, Train, or Bus

Air

It's relatively easy to reach Bar Harbor without wheels of your own. **Cape Air** (a JetBlue affiliate) offers direct flights from Boston to **Bar Harbor-Hancock County Airport** (www.bhbairport.com); during its months of operation between June and mid-October, the **Island Explorer** (www.exploreacadia.com) shuttle has free service from the airport to Bar Harbor. Hertz and Enterprise both offer car rentals at the airport.

Train

Amtrak's **Downeaster line** (800/872-7245, www.amtrakdowneaster.com) runs from Boston along the coast as far as Brunswick, where it's possible to rent a car or connect with a twice daily bus service to Bangor on **Concord Coach Lines** (800/639-3317, www.concordcoachlines.com).

Bus

Greyhound (800/231-2222, www.greyhound.com) offers bus service to Bangor from Portland, as does **Concord Coach Lines** (800/639-3317, www.concordcoachlines.com). From Bangor, you can reach Bar Harbor by taking the **Bar Harbor-Bangor Shuttle** van service (207/479-5911, www.barharborshuttle.net, $70, advance reservation required).

Visiting the Park

Entrances

Because of the patchwork way Acadia National Park was stitched together, driving around Mount Desert Island means passing in and out of park territory, often without notice. The only real gateways to the park are the kiosks at the on-ramps to Park Loop Road, where you'll be asked to present your pass; otherwise, leave it displayed in your car (park rangers suggest that cyclists and motorcyclists carry their pass with them on hikes).

Park Passes and Fees

From May to October, the entrance fee for a private vehicle seating 15 people or fewer is $35. Motorcycles with one or two passengers pay $30, cyclists and pedestrians pay $20 each, and individuals 15 years old and younger are admitted free of charge. Most passes are valid for seven days; annual passes to Acadia National Park are $70, while an Interagency Annual Pass is $80 and covers all National Park Service and Forest Service entrance fees. Active military, people with disabilities, and U.S. fourth-grade students are eligible for a free Interagency Annual Pass; an annual interagency pass is available to seniors for $20. Passes are sold at all park visitor centers, campgrounds, and information booths, but for trips during peak season, it's worth purchasing online to avoid lines (www.nps.gov/acad/planyourvisit).

Visitor Centers

As Route 3 crosses the Mount Desert Narrows, the small **Thompson Island Information Center** (mid-May-mid-Oct. daily 8:30am-5:30pm) is a useful stop for passes and maps if you're making a beeline to a trail or campground on the west side of the island. Otherwise, keep going to **Hulls Cove Visitor Center** (Rte. 3, 207/288-3338, mid-June-Oct. daily 8:30am-4:30pm), which has several exhibits orienting visitors to Acadia's natural and cultural history, including a 15-minute film about the park. It's also possible to sign up for guided naturalist and history programs here; multiple ranger-led programs are held each day throughout the summer in Acadia National Park, from walks and

Local Legend

Search-and-rescue missions. Parking violations. Helping hikers find their way through the woods. This could be a standard day's work for **Thérèse Picard.** As Acadia National Park's former **Chief Ranger**—a position she earned through 17 years of experience with the National Park Service—Picard has pretty much seen it all. Keeping Acadia's communities, visitors, and wildlife safe can be a rigorous task—and a downright daunting one for someone unused to getting their boots muddy. But for Picard, knowing virtually every root and rock across Mount Desert Island's premier park is a timeless thrill, just like the park's oceanside landscapes, its winding carriage roads, and its epic hand-built trails.

Thérèse Picard

You've been a ranger at not just Acadia but also Zion National Park. Having been around the block, what do you think makes Acadia's trails unique?

For me, it's the way that they're carefully woven into the landscape. This isn't a western park with huge and groomed switchbacks. Many of the trails are built on navigation routes that go all the way back to Maine's Indigenous peoples. In the 1800s, all the stonework that was done basically led to one of the biggest Stairmasters you'll ever

demonstrations to outdoor art lessons. Many of these are free; for more information, visit the events webpage (www.nps.gov/acad/planyourvisit).

Reservations

Reservations are essential for the two campgrounds—Blackwoods and Seawall—inside the national park, which can be made through the **National Recreation Reservation Service** (877/444-6777, www.recreation.gov). A small number of sites in each campground is set aside for day-of arrivals with no reservations; call each location first thing in the morning to inquire about openings, though sites don't become available every day. When visiting the island during school vacations, it's important to reserve in advance almost everywhere, but there are many rooms on the island, and it's generally possible to find something during shoulder seasons.

Information and Services

While there are no markets, banks, or other services within Acadia National Park itself, they can be found in nearby **Bar Harbor,** or in **Southwest Harbor** on the western side of the island. Southwest Harbor has two **banks,** a small **market,** and a **public library** (338 Main St., Southwest Harbor, 207/244-7065, www.swhplibrary.org, Mon.-Tues. and Thurs.-Fri. 9am-5pm, Wed. 9am-8pm, Sat. 9am-1pm) with free **Internet access.**

Getting Around

While a car is convenient for reaching less-frequented trailheads, and for early morning trips up Cadillac Mountain, limited parking and congestion during busy months make it worth parking your

find—trails that just go straight up through the rocks and trees via these carved granite steps. In general, the trails in the park are very closely tied to the natural features, whether it's a gentler path surrounded by lots of moss and ferns in the valley forest, or one of the iron rung trails like **The Beehive,** [which runs] along a sunny exposed rock face.

Having logged some serious miles in Acadia, what are some of your favorite places to walk off a day's work?
Honestly, it depends on the day, my energy level, and what I want to deal with. I've hiked all of the trails in the park and there are ones that I revisit more often. Sometimes I'll stroll on the **carriage roads** early in the morning or at dusk, particularly in the fall for the foliage colors. Then there's the new **bog walk around Jordan Pond,** which is a phenomenal experience, thanks to the work of all the trail construction volunteers who spent years building the bridges along the pond. Walking that trail has kind of a personal connection for me, knowing the people who created it and all the time they spent. I mean, they had to float the logs across the pond to build all the bridges!

What's something that visitors to Acadia should do if they want to avoid meeting a ranger in the context of getting lost or banged up?
Look at a map [laughs]. Technology is awesome. Believe me, I'm addicted to my smartphone, too. Websites like AllTrails.com can be helpful. But taking something at its word and not double-checking a map beforehand... We have this one trail, the West Face Trail on Cadillac Mountain, and people will often take it downhill thinking, "Oh, it's only 0.4 mile [0.6 km] to Bubble Pond. This is great!" And what they don't realize is that it's one of the steepest graded trails in the park. If people fall, they fall hard. The most common refrain we'll get on search-and-rescues on trails like that is, "It was short. I thought it would be easy." It's easy to underestimate the topography in Acadia.

vehicle and exploring on public transport. Late June-early October, the free, convenient **Island Explorer** (207/667-5796, www.exploreacadia.com) makes it easy to get around Acadia without a car. The fleet of propane-powered buses follows 11 fixed routes all over the island and on the Schoodic Peninsula, and covers most of Park Loop Road and all the villages, hotels, campgrounds, and trailheads. While there are automatic stops at many of the most notable destinations, drivers will stop to let you out whenever it's safe. Likewise, many hotels can recommend spots to flag down passing buses, even if there's not an official stop nearby.

To see the only part of Acadia National Park that's on the mainland, take the **Bar Harbor Ferry** (Bar Harbor Inn Pier, 7 Newport Dr., 207/288-4585, www.barharborferry.com, June-early Oct., one-way tickets $18 adults, $14 children under 12) to the tiny town of **Winter Harbor** on the **Schoodic Peninsula.**

Even more so than other destinations in New England, this is an excellent place to have a bicycle, as the slow-moving traffic on Park Loop Road and extensive network of car-free carriage roads are ideal for riders of all skill levels. If you'd like to combine shuttling with bicycling, note the Island Explorer buses have racks that accommodate up to six bikes, but popular routes (particularly afternoon return trips from Jordan Pond) can fill up quickly. For a better chance of catching a ride with your bike, look up the schedule for the **Island Explorer Bicycle Express** bus, which has a trailer that fits 12 bikes.

To take in the main sites in 2.5 hours, **Acadia National Park Tours** (207/288-0300, www.acadiatours.com, $55 adults, $30 children 12 and under) runs a bus

contracted with the NPS to give sightseeing tours of Park Loop Road. The narrated trip includes three 15-minute stops to stretch your legs and snap photos, and tickets can be purchased online.

Sights and Recreation

Park Loop Road

Passing headlands, trailheads, beaches, and stunning views of Penobscot Bay, the 27-mile (43-km) Park Loop Road winds through some of Acadia's finest scenery. Traffic moves one way—clockwise—from the main entrance near Hulls Cove Visitor Center to Jordan Pond, then two-way traffic completes the loop and heads all the way up to the summit of Cadillac Mountain. Alternate entrances, where passes are also checked, are at Sieur des Monts, south of Bar Harbor; Sand Beach; Stanley Brook, by Seal Harbor; and off Route 233, just north of Cadillac Mountain Road. For much of the one-way section, parking is allowed in the right-hand lane, which makes it easy to spot a view and pull over for a closer look. It also means the road is often full of unexpected parked cars, pedestrians, and cyclists (along with the occasional moose), so it's important to take the Park Loop Road at a careful pace. There are also several low bridges that may be a problem for some RVs—the lowest of these is the 10-foot-4-inch (3.1-m) span across the Stanley Brook Entrance.

★ Driving the Park Loop Road

Driving the whole road at once is a nice way to get an overview of the park, but allow plenty of time to stop for picture-taking, tidepooling, walking, and otherwise exploring. From the main entrance at Hulls Cove, the road rises steeply to **Sieur de Monts,** where the small **Wild Gardens of Acadia** re-creates typical

Top to bottom: view from Park Loop Road; Thunder Hole; bridge at Jordan Pond

Park Loop and Carriage Roads

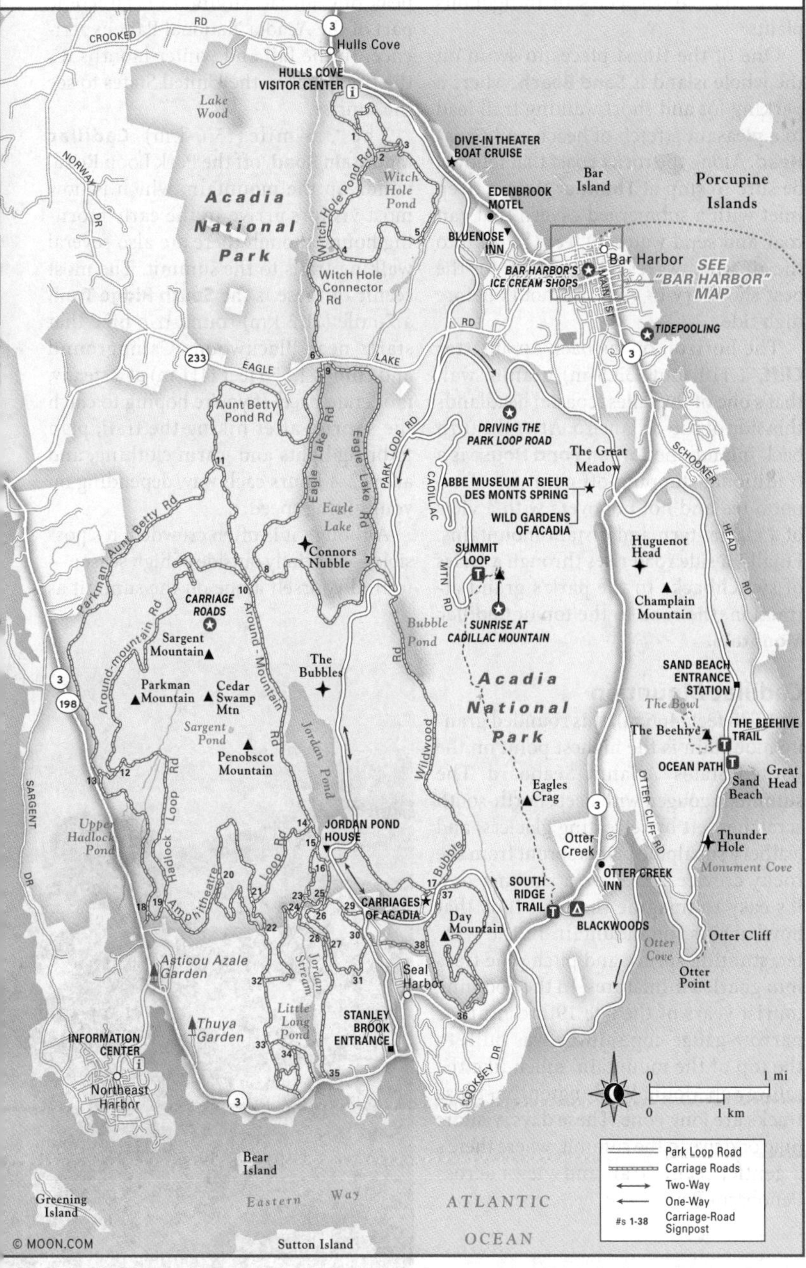

habitats found on Mount Desert Island from heath to coniferous forest, with more than 400 species of indigenous plants.

One of the finest places to swim on the whole island is **Sand Beach,** where a parking lot and short walking trail lead to a pleasant stretch of beach and **Great Head.** Along the rocky coast that follows, be sure to stop at **Thunder Hole,** a deep inlet with a submerged cavern that can roar and send water 40 feet (12 m) into the air when waves hit just right; for the best show, try to visit two hours before high tide.

The horizon opens back up at **Otter Cliff,** a 110-foot (33.5-m) granite wall that's one of the tallest coastal headlands this side of Rio de Janeiro. After the turn back inland, the **Jordan Pond House** is a traditional stopping-off point for afternoon tea and hot popovers with a view of a glacial tarn and distant mountains. Finally, a side road rises through a series of switchbacks to the park's grand attraction, the road to the top of **Cadillac Mountain.**

Cadillac Mountain

At 1,528 feet (466 m), this rounded granite mountain is the highest point on the United States' Atlantic Seaboard. The summit is gouged with deep, north-south scratches left by retreating glaciers, and leathery subalpine plants sprout from the rocky crevices. Even on a summer day, it's easy to imagine the icy winds that howl across the mountain in the winter, stunting spruce and pitch pine trees into gnarled miniatures. In the booming tourist years of the late 19th century, a narrow-gauge cog railway was built to the top of the mountain, much like the railway up Mount Washington, but those tracks are long gone. These days, visitors hike or drive to the summit, where there's a gentle, scenic trail and views across Penobscot Bay.

★ Sunrise at Cadillac Mountain

Watching the sun come up from the peak of Cadillac Mountain is an iconic part of the Acadia National Park experience. In the fall and winter months it's the first place in the United States to see the sunrise.

The 3.5-mile (5.6-km) **Cadillac Mountain Road,** off the Park Loop Road, winds up the mountain, which is how most visitors arrive in the early morning hours, though there are also several walking trails to the summit. The most scenic of these is the **South Ridge Trail,** a 7-mile (11.2-km) round-trip hike that starts near Blackwoods Campground and climbs 1,350 feet (411 m) at a steady, moderate pace. If you're hoping to catch the sunrise after hiking the trail, plan to bring lights and warm clothing, and allow 2-4 hours each way, depending on your hiking speed.

Although it is often crowded, it's possible—especially outside of high season—to find yourself alone on the summit as

dawn breaks over Penobscot Bay, lighting up islands and deep forests. A more likely scenario involves clusters of chatting families and several sleepy hikers who started up the peak in the middle of the night. Inevitably, though, the crowd begins to thin as soon as the sky lights up, and one of the nicest times to enjoy the short 0.3-mile (0.5-km) **Summit Loop** is when everyone else heads to Bar Harbor for breakfast.

★ Carriage Roads

Concerned that Mount Desert Island would be destroyed with the introduction of automobiles, John D. Rockefeller Jr. started building a vast network of roads in 1913, determined they would remain closed to motorized traffic. Today, the 47 miles (76 km) of crushed-stone roads are perfect for walking and biking as well as a favorite destination of cross-country skiers in the winter. The roads curve gently through a forest of birch, beech, and maple trees, over beautifully crafted granite bridges, and through tunnels and arches, perfect for exploration by bicycle. Numbered wooden signposts at each intersection make it easy to find your way around. A park map, available at the visitor center, is essential for exploring the carriage roads, which continually intersect with the Park Loop Road and other roads on the island. Two of the most popular **parking areas** for accessing the carriage roads are at Sieur de Monts and the Jordan Pond House.

To really immerse yourself in Rockefeller's vision of Acadia, though, take an actual carriage ride: **Carriages of Acadia** (Wildwood Stables, Park Loop Rd., 207/276-5721, tours from $65 adults, $55 children 2-12, free 2 and under) offers a range of jaunts in horse-drawn carriages, including tours of stone bridges, trips to Jordan Pond for popovers, and a climb to the top of Day Mountain.

view from Cadillac Mountain

Thuya Garden and Asticou Azalea Garden

This pair of tranquil gardens is a must-see for plant lovers and a convenient side trip from the Park Loop Road.

Thuya Garden (Rte. 3, Northeast Harbor, www.gardenpreserve.org, mid-June-early Oct. daily during daylight hours, trails and garden accessible during the off-season weather permitting, $5 requested donation) is in the semi-formal English style, with butterfly gardens, pavilions, and a pretty reflecting pool. To approach the gardens from Park Loop Road, head southwest and continue on Stanley Brook Road, turning right onto Route 3. A sign on the harbor side of Route 3 marks a small parking area opposite the Asticou Terrace Trail, whose great, granite switchbacks climb 0.25 mile (0.4 km) to the Thuya Garden gates, passing a trailside shelter and lookout.

For Asticou Azalea Garden parking, head north on Route 3 and turn right on Route 198. Beginning in late May, the **Asticou Azalea Garden** (Rte. 3 and Rte. 198, Northeast Harbor, www.gardenpreserve.org, May-Oct. daily during daylight hours, free) is a riot of bright blooming rhododendrons and azaleas that give way to irises and water lilies in July and August. Its design celebrates attributes of Japanese gardens—circular paths, garden rooms, and carefully tended views—and it was built in 1956 using plants from the Bar Harbor garden of Beatrix Farrand, a groundbreaking gardener who was a founding member of the American Society of Landscape Architects.

To visit the gardens on the Island Explorer shuttle, ask the driver on Route #6 to drop you at either location, and flag a passing bus to continue onward. It is possible to connect the two gardens on foot by taking the sidewalk on Route 3 from the Asticou Azalea Garden to the Asticou Terrace Trail.

Bass Harbor Head Light

Set on the edge of a rocky sea cliff, the scenic **Bass Harbor Head Light** (Bass Harbor Head Rd., off 102A) is at the southern extreme of Mount Desert Island. The lighthouse itself is a private residence, but it's a scenic spot to catch the morning light. For the classic photograph of the lighthouse above the rocks, take the staircase at the eastern end of the parking lot and shoot back toward the cliffs.

Hiking

There is a lifetime of hiking available in Acadia National Park, and the park rangers are experts at helping you find just the right one. The following are a few favorites on Mount Desert Island; for all of these hikes, it's essential to bring an **Acadia National Park map** (available for free at all information centers). While most of the trails are easy to follow, the many trails that intersect within the park would be impossible to navigate without a map.

Sure-footed walkers can head up one of the island's "iron rung" trails, where the narrow cliffside paths are supplemented by metal bars set directly in the granite. The strenuous **Beehive Trail** is one of these, with exposed, stony sections along the south face of the 520-foot (158-m) peak that make the hike seem longer than its 1.6 miles (2.6 km) round-trip. To reach the trailhead, leave your car in the Sand Beach parking lot (which is also a stop on the Island Explorer shuttle bus), and cross the Park Loop Road.

One of the easiest trails to hop on for a leisurely walk is **Ocean Path,** which follows the Park Loop Road for about two miles (3.2 km) between the Sand Beach parking lot and Otter Cliff, with lots of ocean views and rocks for scrambling.

Jordan Pond is famous for its waterside dining patio and popovers, but the pond itself makes for a sublime hike. From the pond house, follow the **Jordan Pond Path** around the west side of the pond and enjoy clomping over an astounding number of recently built wooden bog bridges that traverse the pond's wooded wetlands. After a bit of rock hopping, the path smoothens into a graded route, from which rugged spur trails offer access to nearby **South Bubble Mountain.**

The "quiet side" of Mount Desert Island has plenty of hikes as well, and these are often less busy than the eastern trails. On the southwestern edge of the island, the 1.3-mile (2-km) round-trip **Ship Harbor Trail** is a good place to walk through scenic coastal forest offering views along a deep inlet, and the 1.5-mile (2.4-km) round-trip **Wonderland Trail** is just up the road, with great tidepools on a rocky beach, and a jumble of granite boulders. For the trailheads, drive south from Southwest Harbor, and turn left onto Route 102A to follow the coast. The clearly marked Wonderland Trailhead is 4.1 miles (6.6 km) past the turnoff onto Route 102A, and the Ship Harbor Trailhead is a short distance farther. Both have parking lots.

For fabulous views to Somes Sound and the ocean, the 1.8-mile (2.9-km) round-trip walk up **Acadia Mountain** is a favorite; with 500 feet (152 km) of elevation gain, it's an easier peak to hike than Cadillac Mountain. And if you scramble down the east side of the mountain toward Somes Sound, you can steal a peek at **Man O'War Brook Falls,** one of Mount Desert Island's hidden cascades. The clearly marked parking lot for the Acadia Mountain trail is on Route 102, 3.1 miles (5 km) north of Southwest Harbor.

Biking

By far the best place to ride a bike in Acadia is on the network of **carriage trails**—the crushed stone surface is well suited to mountain bike tires and medium-width road bike tires, and it's a joy to explore the island away from car

Top to bottom: the oasis of Sand Beach; an elegant stone bridge on the carriage roads; Bass Harbor Head Light

traffic. A *Carriage Road User's Map* is available from the Park Service, and bicycles can be rented in Bar Harbor from **Acadia Bike** (48 Cottage St., 800/526-8615, www.acadiabike.com, May-Oct. $36-39 full day, $32 half day).

One favorite activity on the **Schoodic Peninsula** is cycling the scenic roads, which tend to be less trafficked than those on Mount Desert Island. Options are endless, but a pair of loops covering 12 or 24 miles (19 or 39 km) is a good starting point (www.exploremaine.org/bike/downeast).

★ Tidepooling

Fluctuating water levels strand sea creatures in rocky pools all along the Mount Desert Island coast, but finding them involves careful planning. Pick up a copy of the *Acadia Weekly* or stop by any of the ranger stations for information on the tides, which range between 10 and 15 feet (3 and 4.5 m) around the island. The best time to spot wildlife is 1.5 hours before and after extreme low tide.

When searching for tidepools, bring a pair of shoes with good traction that you don't mind getting wet and sandy, and pay close attention to water levels, as some rocky outcroppings can be stranded by rising water.

One favorite way to explore is by walking to **Bar Island** from downtown Bar Harbor (follow Bridge St.); for 1.5 hours before and after low tide, a 0.8-mile (1.3-km) gravel bar that leads from the end of Bridge Street is exposed. There are walking trails on the tiny island, and the outgoing tide usually leaves some sea stars and crabs in sandy tidepools along the bar.

On the southwest side of the island, the **Ship Harbor** and **Wonderland Trails** are also good choices, with plenty of nooks and crannies to trap interesting things in the intertidal zone. **Ranger-led tidepool programs** (www.nps.gov/acad/planyourvisit/calendar.htm) are held at Ship Harbor and Sand Beach in July and August. Drive south from Southwest Harbor and turn left onto Route 102A to find the well-marked Wonderland Trailhead 4.1 miles (6.6 km) past the turnoff onto Route 102A, and the Ship Harbor Trailhead a short distance farther. Both have parking lots.

Paddling

Get a harbor seal's view of the island's rugged coast by touring in a sea kayak. A handful of well-regarded operators lead trips open to paddlers of all skill levels. Visit the remoter western side of the island with **Maine State Sea Kayak** (39 Cottage St., Bar Harbor, 207/244-9500, www.mainestatekayak.com, $79), which plans its trips through Western Bay and Blue Hill Bay so you head downwind. Tours last four hours. **Coastal Kayaking Tours** (48 Cottage Street, Bar Harbor, 800/526-8615, www.acadiafun.com, $64-79) launches right in downtown Bar Harbor and schedules gorgeous sunset tours. Tours run 2.5-4 hours.

Swimming

There are two beaches in Acadia with summer lifeguards. The water at **Sand Beach,** just off the Park Loop Road, stays in the high 50s throughout the summer, but that's warm enough for plenty of visitors; come here for saltwater, views, and a beach vacation atmosphere. Find (somewhat) warmer water at **Echo Lake Beach,** on the west side of Route 102 between Somesville and Southwest Harbor. The lake floor drops gradually from the shoreline, making this a good choice for families with children.

Boating

Lobster boats are synonymous with the Maine seascape, and one of the easiest and most entertaining ways to climb about one of these mythic vessels is taking the ***Lulu* Lobster Boat Ride** (55 West St., Bar Harbor, 207/288-3136, www.lululobsterboat.com, 2-hr tour $41 adults, $38 seniors, $31 children 6-12). Each boat trip includes a live lobster harvest and great running patter about the lobstering life (and the life of a lobster). Come early May-early June to spot adorable baby seals lolling around near Egg Rock Lighthouse.

By far one of the best things to do on the island with nature-loving kids is head out on a **Dive-In Theater Boat Cruise** (105 Eden St., Bar Harbor, 207/288-3483, www.divered.com, $60 adults, $40 children 6-12, $25 children under 6) with "Diver Ed." Ed (and his sidekick "mini Ed") suit up in scuba gear equipped with underwater microphones and cameras. The crowd on deck can follow along, then Ed reappears with underwater creatures that kids can touch before sending them back to the ocean floor. The boat departs from the College of the Atlantic campus. Park and meet Ed in the North Lot by the Dorr Museum of Natural History.

A classic style of sailboat along the East Coast is the Friendship sloop, a graceful, gaff-rigged boat that originated in Friendship, Maine, in the late 19th century. Friendship sloop *Surprise,* operated by **Downeast Sailing Adventures** (Cranberry Island Dock, Southwest Harbor, 207/288-2216, www.downeastsail.com, 2-hr sail $120 pp, private sail for two people, $350), has been sailing the Maine coast since 1964 and offers an intimate, beautiful way to experience it.

Food

Enjoying popovers and tea on the lawn at ★ **Jordan Pond House** (2928 Park Loop Rd., Seal Harbor, 207/813-4342, https://jordanpondhouse.com, daily 11am-9pm, $9-25) is a classic Acadia experience: The warm, oversized pastries are perfect with melting butter and house made strawberry jam, and the restaurant has stunning views of the glacial tarn with the granite "bubbles" in the background. The restaurant itself was rebuilt in 1979 and the interior is fairly charmless, but the afternoon tea experience is delightful and should not be missed. Reservations are recommended from summer to early fall and can be made online.

But Jordan Pond House doesn't completely own the popover world on Mount Desert Island. While it has no views to speak of, everyone agrees ★ **Common Good Kitchen Café** (19 Clark Point Rd., Southwest Harbor, 207/266-2733, www.commongoodsoupkitchen.org, May-Oct. daily 7:30am-11am, by donation) would win hands down in a popover-to-popover showdown. A simple menu of oatmeal, coffee, and popovers with house-made butters and jams is served by volunteers on a sunny patio, with all proceeds going to a meal delivery service for disadvantaged islanders during the winter months.

With a location between Route 102 and Route 3, **Mainely Meat BBQ** (15 Knox Rd., Bar Harbor, 207/288-9200, www.atlanticbrewing.com, May-Oct. daily 11:30am-7pm, $15-29) is the convenient and casual on-site restaurant of **Atlantic Brewing Company** (May.-Oct. daily 11am-7pm, free tastings). Large portions of barbecue basics come with coleslaw, potato salad, and baked beans; ribs are a favorite for many visitors. Tours of the brewery are at 3pm on Fridays, Saturdays, and Sundays during peak season, and are capped at 25 people.

Reservations and robust appetites are strongly advised at **Red Sky** (14 Clark Point Rd., Southwest Harbor, 207/244-0476, www.redskyrestaurant.com, Wed.-Sat. 5pm-8pm, $19-45), Southwest Harbor's softly lit bistro where French-inspired dishes such as pan-roasted duck with port demi-glace and cantaloupe puree are thoughtfully paired with one of the most expansive wine lists on the island. Be sure to leave room for at least one appetizer—perhaps the local mussels prepared Montreal-style in white wine with Dijon mustard and fennel.

The southwestern flavored menu

at **Bub's Burritos** (19 Clark Point Rd., Southwest Harbor, 207/244-8300, www.facebook.com/bubsburritos, Mon.-Sat. 10:30am-4:30pm, $11-18) might appear fairly boilerplate at a glance, but what makes the adobo chicken, chorizo, and shrimp burritos soar are the freshness of the ingredients and the gargantuan size of each burrito. Plan on ending up with leftovers, and leave some room for the tortilla chips with house salsa or guacamole.

If this lobster-loving author had to choose just one of the many lobster places to eat in Maine, it would be ★ **Thurston's Lobster Pound** (9 Thurston Rd., Bernard, 207/244-7600, www.thurstonforlobster.com, late May-mid.-Oct. Tues.-Sat. noon-9pm, $12-38), just outside the park off Route 102 in Bernard. Consider arriving early or late to avoid the line, which can stretch far out the door, but it's worth making an evening trip to the quiet side for a traditional lobster dinner or an overstuffed lobster roll (perhaps followed by sunset at the Bass Harbor Head Light). The restaurant has two sides: Line up on the right to order a whole lobster dinner or sit in the main dining area, or head to the left to sit in the bar, where the rest of the menu is available. You can also sit in the bar with a lobster dinner—it just needs to be ordered in that long line. It's not an unpleasant wait, though, as it's fascinating to watch the servers run in and out with great bags of clams and lobsters to drop in the industrial-size boiler outside. A casual atmosphere, local beers on tap, and views of the pretty harbor make this a true gem.

Accommodations and Camping

A couple of campgrounds are within Acadia National Park's boundaries, but there are no hotels or inns within the park itself; lodging listings below cover places to stay on the "quiet side" that are still convenient to park activities and sights.

Camping

Only two of the campgrounds on Mount Desert Island are inside the park proper, set on the southernmost part of the island on opposite sides of Somes Sound. It's worth reserving either of these far in advance for busy times, but each sets aside a small number of non-reservable sites. Call first thing in the morning to check availability. **Blackwoods Campground** is right on Park Loop Road (Rte. 3, 207/288-3274, www.nps.gov/acad, May-mid-Oct., $30), adjacent to an Island Explorer shuttle stop and convenient to Bar Harbor and Cadillac Mountain. The 281 forested sites often fill up; the campground can feel busy and noisy during peak season. No hookups or showers, but free firewood is provided, and a spot just outside the entrance offers hot, coin-operated showers. Or set up your tent on the "quiet side" at **Seawall Campground** (Rte. 102A, 207/244-3600, www.nps.gov/acad, late May-mid-Oct., $22-30), 18 miles (29 km) from Bar Harbor, and a prime location for beautiful sunsets on the shore as well as access to less-trafficked hikes and Bass Harbor Head Light. Like Blackwoods, Seawall has no hookups or showers, but there are coin-operated showers and a general store five minutes away. Many cell phones get no reception on this side of the island.

The privately owned ★ **Mount Desert Campground** (516 Sound Dr., off Rte. 2, 207/244-3710, www.mountdesertcampground.com, late May-mid-Oct., $43-94) splits the difference, with a superb location at the head of Somes Sound that's the perfect jumping-off point for exploring all of the island. Tent sites roll right up to the water (pricing varies depending on the season and proximity of the site to the water), hookups are available, and the campground rents all kinds of boards and boats for getting in the sound, as well as a launching ramp for private boats. Bathhouses have free hot showers, and the small, convivial "gathering place" offers wireless Internet, snacks, coffee, and ice cream.

There's a summer camp atmosphere at **Hadley's Point Campground** (33 Hadley Point Rd., off Rte. 3, 207/288-4808, www.hadleyspoint.com, mid-May-mid-Oct., tents $32-39, hookups $45-65, cabins $85-110), making it a good choice for families, though tent sites are set close together and don't provide much privacy. A heated swimming pool, coin-operated showers, laundry facilities, a playground, and wireless Internet are available. The campground is on the Island Explorer shuttle bus route for easy access to Bar Harbor, and there's a public beach within easy walking distance. The rustic, tidy cabins have private bathrooms, three beds, and a fire pit (bring your own linens).

Under $150

Completely surrounded by national park land, the **Otter Creek Inn** (47 Otter Creek Dr., 207/288-5151, www.ottercreekinnmaine.com, May-Oct., $135-200) is a perfect place (almost) for non-campers to stay in Acadia. The rooms and cabins are simple but sufficient, and a continental breakfast is served in the attached market. Some guests have noted the rooms' thin walls, though the price, which drops closer to $100 outside of peak season, is hard to beat.

$150-250

The self-contained units at ★ **Acadia Cottages** (410 Main St., Southwest Harbor, 207/244-5388, www.acadiacottages.com, $160-230) are simple and old-fashioned, but well-appointed kitchens, outdoor fire pits, and comfortable mattresses are a cut above other cabins on the island. Wooded grounds make these feel relatively private, and the cottages are walking distance from Southwest Harbor.

Ocean and mountain vistas and a friendly, hospitable atmosphere are the draws at **The Moorings Inn** (133 Shore Rd., Southwest Harbor, 207/244-5523, www.mooringsinn.com, $135-275), which has cozy waterside rooms that range from a budget studio to more expansive suites decked out with maritime artwork and, in some cases, miniature ship models. Wine and cheese nights offered throughout the summer pair nicely with the views of Somes Sound.

$250-350

Perched on the end of Somes Sound, ★ **The Claremont Hotel** (22 Claremont Rd., Southwest Harbor, 207/244-5036, www.theclaremonthotel.com, inn $199-349, cottages $259-699) is an 1884 grande dame that rambles across a 6-acre (2.4-ha) waterfront property. The 24 rooms in the main house have been recently renovated, but are full of historical charm, their old-fashioned quirks left intact (which is not necessarily to everyone's taste). This feels like a glimpse of old Maine, and for afternoons on the porch, games of croquet on the perfectly trimmed lawn, and sunset drinks at a dockside bar, it remains a wonderful destination.

Bar Harbor

Times have changed since the first 19th-century "rusticators" came to Bar Harbor for society parties with wilderness views. The stunning landscape of forested islands is still there, but the town itself can feel overstuffed and kitschy, an ice cream-fueled frenzy of T-shirt shops and minigolf. Still, Bar Harbor is the "town" for Mount Desert Island, with restaurants, museums, services, and loads of places to stay. This is the jumping-off point for many boat cruises and activities, and it's a perfect foil to the quiet trails and mountaintops inside Acadia National Park.

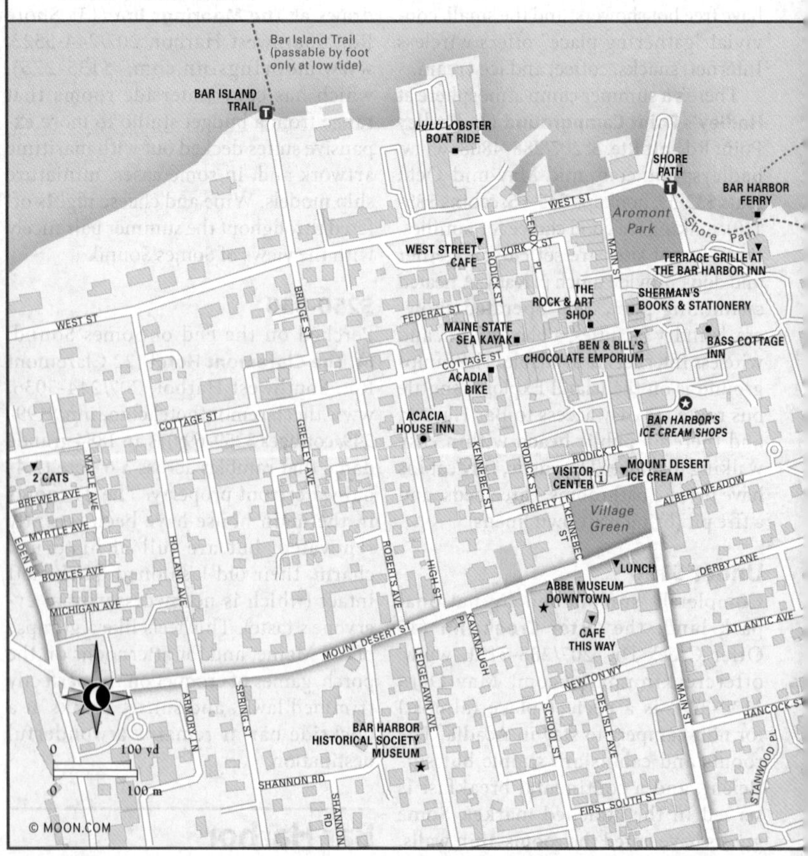

Sights

Step into the world of Mount Desert Island's earliest locals at the **Abbe Museum,** which has two campuses focusing on modern-day and bygone Wabanaki lives. Visit the **Abbe Museum downtown location** (26 Mount Desert St., 207/388-2519, www.abbemuseum.org, May-Oct. Mon.-Fri. 10am-5pm, call for off-season hours, $10 adults, $7 seniors, $5 children 11-17, free 10 and under and visitors with tribal or military ID) for a stronger focus on today's Wabanaki, along with stories from the past and a few artifacts. Located inside Acadia National Park, the **Abbe Museum at Sieur des Monts Spring** (Sieur des Monts, Park Loop Road and Route 3, June-Sept. daily 10am-5pm, $3 adults, $1 children 11-17, free 10 and under and visitors with tribal or military ID) is much smaller, but has fascinating artifacts and depictions of archaeological digs in the area. A ticket to Abbe Downtown also includes admission to the Sieur des Monts Spring venue, and the cost of the Abbe Museum at Sieur de Monts Spring ticket is deducted from the admission price if you visit the downtown location as well.

Small but interesting, the **Bar Harbor**

Historical Society Museum (127 West St., 207/288-0000, www.barharborhistorical.org, June-Oct. Mon.-Sat. 10am-2pm, guided tours 10am Fridays, $15 adults, $13 seniors and students, $7 children 7-12, free children 6 and under) has a remarkable collection of images from the town's Gilded Age heyday—think lots of full-length tennis skirts and boating parties. The 1903 building, known as the La Rochelle Mansion, was originally built by wealthy French Protestants fleeing religious persecution in their home country, and after the glitz and glamour of the Roaring Twenties burned off, the lavish 41-room fortress was acquired by the heirs of the Campbell Soup Company. La Rochelle was also the first brick building on Mount Desert Island (an expensive undertaking, given the lack of brick factories on Mount Desert Island) and the interior contains dishware from opulent hotels that used to speckle the region, before things came crashing down in the 1930s.

Watch the ships come in and out of the harbor from Bar Harbor's gentle **Shore Path,** a paved walking trail that stretches 0.75 mile (1.2 km) from the town pier to Wayman Lane. It's especially nice as a morning walk, when the harbor begins to flood with early sunshine.

Entertainment and Events

From the end of June through mid-August, the **Bar Harbor Band** (www.barharborband.org) plays hour-long concerts on the Village Green; shows are on Mondays and Thursdays at 7:30pm. Another summer tradition is heading to the **Great Room** lounge at the **Bluenose Inn** (90 Eden St., 800/445-4077, www.barharborhotel.com), where pianist Bill Trowell plays laid-back favorites Monday through Saturday at 7pm from late May to October.

A unique way to see the communities of Mount Desert Island at their most jubilant is by attending (or running) the annual **Mount Desert Island Marathon** (www.runmdi.org, mid-Oct.). Featuring marathon and half-marathon events, the two routes converge for a breathtaking meander along Somes Sound, where ships will toot their horns at the runners in solidarity. Along the whole course, you'll encounter locals playing music and banging pots and pans as belabored runners wheeze by. The race concludes in Southwest Harbor, where food vendors are ready with lobster rolls, chowder, and taps of Maine craft beer. The marathon is one of the most scenic distance races in America. Better yet, it's a chance to witness islanders enjoying each other after the summer hordes have returned home.

Shopping

Many of the shops in Bar Harbor sell variations on a theme—lobster and moose stuffed animals, T-shirts, Christmas ornaments. Find these along Main Street. Before you go on a wildlife expedition, stop by **Sherman's Books & Stationery** (56 Main St., 207/288-3161, www.shermans.com, daily 9am-9pm), which carries an exceptional selection of bird-watching and wildlife guides and trail maps in addition to a full stock of books and cards. Another fun stop is **The Rock & Art Shop** (13 Cottage St., 207/288-4800, www.therockandartshop.com, daily 10am-6pm, hours vary seasonally), which does have both rocks and art, but also stuffed fish, skulls, and other fascinating, odd treasures.

Food

In a bright, rambling home on the edge of downtown, ★ **2 Cats** (130 Cottage St., 207/288-2808, Mon.-Thurs. 6:30am-1pm, Fri.-Sun. 6am-1pm, $6-15) is a funky gem and the best place for breakfast on the island. Simple breakfast classics like eggs Benedict and blueberry pancakes are done nicely, and the café's fresh, flaky biscuits come with a dreamy side of homemade strawberry butter. Come early to snag a spot on the deep wraparound porch.

A menu of classic seafood options, salads, and pasta is surprisingly reasonable at this waterside spot, given that the ★ **Terrace Grille at the Bar Harbor Inn** (7 Newport Dr., 207/288-3351, https://barharborinn.com, daily 11:30am-dark, $18-36) has the best outdoor seating in town. Tables on the lawn and patio overlook the harbor and Bar Island, making this a great place to catch a sunset over a bowl of chowder or lobster stew. At $42, the steamed lobster—served with corn on the cob, roasted Yukon gold potatoes, and grilled asparagus—is an excellent deal for downtown Bar Harbor.

Simple, sunny, and laid-back, **West Street Café** (76 West St., 207/288-5242, www.weststreetcafe.com, daily 11:30am-9pm, $14-33) has a big menu of beef and chicken dinners, pastas, and seafood. The menu of early bird specials, served from 4pm to 6pm, is an excellent value for an early dinner, especially the $17 broiled Gulf of Maine salmon and the "downeast special" lobster served with chowder, fries, coleslaw, and blueberry pie.

It would be easy to miss **Café This Way** (14 Mt. Desert St., 207/288-4483, www.cafethisway.com, daily 6:30am-1pm, breakfast $6-12, dinner $19-28), a restaurant with art nouveau flair that's tucked down an alley between School and Main Streets. The breakfast omelets, burritos, and blueberry pancakes in particular get raves.

Good old deli sandwiches and salads get a Maine ingredient upgrade at the appropriately named **Lunch** (8 Mt. Desert St., 207/901-0018, www.lunchbarharbor.com, Tues.-Sun. 10am-4pm, $9-15), where chefs Meghan Bishop and Aaron Porter regularly cook up intriguing specials like wild forest mushroom and kale soup, and a grilled nectarine panini with arugula, brie, and honey drizzle.

Farmers and artisans from around Penobscot Bay attend the **Eden Farmers Market** (YMCA, 21 Park St., May-Oct. Sun. 9am-noon), which is a great place

Bar Harbor

to find farm-fresh Maine blueberries in season.

★ Ice Cream Shops

There are two ice cream greats in downtown Bar Harbor: The granddaddy is **Ben & Bill's Chocolate Emporium** (66 Main St., 207/288-3281, www.benandbills.com, Mon.-Thurs. 9am-10:30pm, Fri.-Sat. 9am-11pm, Sun. 10am-10:30pm, $3-9), a candy store with a zillion flavors (including Maine lobster), big servings, and a landmark lobster sculpture out front that's a classic Bar Harbor selfie spot. The scoop-wielding young gladiators of the waffle cone scene are at **Mount Desert Ice Cream** (7 Firefly Ln., 207/801-4001, www.mdiic.com, daily 11am-10:30pm, $5-9), where flavors range from Maine Sea Salt Caramel to Blueberry Sour Cream and Vietnamese Cinnamon. Not all the flavors are quite so offbeat—President Obama ordered a scoop of plain ol' coconut while visiting with his family in 2010.

Accommodations

Under $150

Seriously no-frills, **Robbins Motel** (Rte. 3, 207/288-4659, www.robbinsmotel.com, May-mid-Oct., $59-79) features the rates of yesteryear and rooms to match. Amenities include cable TV, a pool, and wireless Internet, but the overall experience is pretty bare-bones.

The smallest cottages at **Rose Eden Cottages** (864 Rte. 3, 207/288-3038, www.roseeden.com, $83-230) are like nautical dollhouses, with just enough room for a double bed, coffeemaker, and compact bathroom. Each of the 11 cottages is different, some with kitchenettes, second bedrooms, and sitting areas; the largest has a full kitchen. A location on the main road 7.5 miles (12 km) outside of Bar Harbor means that the sounds of traffic are an issue for some guests, but the owners provide white noise machines, and some units are set farther back on the grassy property, which has a gas grill and laundry facilities for guests.

One of the best values among the generic digs that line Route 3 is **Edenbrook Motel** (96 Rte. 3, 207/288-4975, www.edenbrookmotel.com, $99-159), which is adjacent to the College of the Atlantic and 1.5 miles (2.4 km) outside of Bar Harbor. The simple, super clean rooms have air-conditioning, a television, and a coffeemaker, and the Island Explorer shuttle stops right in front, making it a breeze to head into town or the park.

$150-250

With a location right in downtown Bar Harbor, the ★ **Acacia House Inn** (6 High St., 207/288-8122, www.acaciahouseinn.com, $160-225) is a wonderful value, with sweet, simple decor and great breakfasts cooked with lots of local and organic ingredients, including create-your-own omelets made with local eggs. All rooms have private bathrooms, organic cotton sheets, and cable TV. The quiet side street the inn sits on lends a surprisingly

The Places in Between: Bangor

Orono Bog boardwalk

Maine's northern city, once a lumber town and often seen as a gateway to Acadia, can be an enigma even to New Englanders. But just like Portland before it became *Portland,* modern Bangor boasts the striking creativity and rugged beauty that can often be found in overlooked cities.

Start at the edge of the city and stretch your legs by traversing the bobbing boardwalks at the **Orono Bog Walk** (trailhead at the end of Tripp Dr., Orono, www.umaine.edu/oronobogwalk, June-early-Sept. daily 7am-6:30pm, mid-Sept.-late Sept. daily 7:30am-5:30pm, Oct. daily 8am-4:30pm). You'll loop one mile (1.6 km) through forested wetlands and a spectacular peat moss bog that will make you feel like you've teleported into Scotland.

From there, head into town and take a photo outside horror wunderkind **Stephen King's House** (47 W. Broadway), where even the wrought iron gates bear macabre shapes of spiders and webs. Dazzle the kids and relive your childhood at the **Maine Discovery Museum** (74 Main St., Bangor, 207/262-7200, www.mainediscoverymuseum.org, Tues.-Sat. 10am-5pm, $10 adults and children, $9 seniors, free 18 months and under), whose exhibits include hands-on fossil digging and a journey through a human digestive tract.

Take a stroll through Bangor's reanimated downtown along **Main Street,** where boutique shops and savory aromas are springing up like mushrooms. Consider popping into the **Zillman Art Museum** (40 Harlow St., 207/581-3300, www.zam.umaine.edu, Tues.-Sat. 10am-5pm, free), which is located in a former department store and is home to one of Maine's largest collections of modern pop art.

Afterward, you'll have your pick of comfort foods and internationally inspired fare downtown, but if you feel like splurging, the Maine-sourced, Mediterranean-accented cuisine at **11 Central** (11 Central St., 207/922-5115, www.11centralbangor.com, Wed.-Sat. 4pm-9:30pm, $17-35) is as fresh, colorful, and beautifully composed as the paintings from local artists that adorn the restaurant's exposed brick walls. The joint is illustrative of Bangor's vivacious new chapter.

laid-back atmosphere given the downtown location.

Smart whitewashed cottages and tidy motel-style rooms look out on Frenchman's Bay at ★ **Edgewater Motel and Cottages** (137 Old Bar Harbor Rd., 207/288-3941, www.edgewaterbarharbor.com, cottages $150-249, motel $152-219), where a broad lawn dotted with Adirondack chairs gives a resort feel to this five-acre (2-ha) property that's 6.5 miles (10 km) from Bar Harbor. The cottage kitchens are stocked with cooking equipment and coffeemakers, and you can spot harbor seals and porpoises from the outdoor decks.

$250-350

Stylish and luxurious, the **Bass Cottage Inn** (14 The Field, 207/288-9552, www.basscottage.com, $309-489) strikes a balance between the personal experience of a bed-and-breakfast and thoughtful service of a top-end hotel. The inn is tucked down a private lane a few minutes' walk from the waterfront, so it feels like a retreat in downtown Bar Harbor. The 1885 building has been carefully restored with a clean, airy design and comfortable common spaces. Breakfast is prepared to order and evening wine and snacks create a convivial atmosphere.

Information and Services

The **city's informative website** (www.barharborinfo.com) has useful walking maps of the town, and there's a **visitor center** (19 Firefly Ln., 207/288-3338, June-Oct. daily 8am-5pm) on the Bar Harbor Green. There are several **banks** and **ATMs** located along Main Street and Cottage Street in downtown, and free wireless Internet is available at **Jesup Memorial Library** (34 Mt. Desert St., 207/288-4245, www.jesuplibrary.org, Wed.-Thurs. 10am-8pm, Fri.-Sat. and Tues. 10am-5pm).

Getting Around

As in the national park, the **Island Explorer** (207/667-5796, www.exploreacadia.com) is the best way to get around Bar Harbor. The **Eden Street route (#2)** connects major hotels along Route 3 with the Bar Harbor Green. For the most part, though, the town is easy to walk on foot. Metered parking is available throughout downtown, but the only RV parking is on Main Street south of Park Street on the way out of town.

New Hampshire's White Mountains

Highlights

★ **Mount Washington Cog Railway:** Chug to the top of the highest peak in the East in colorful carriages pushed by coal and biodiesel engines (page 187).

★ **Mount Washington Summit:** Explore wind-whipped ridges, learn about Mount Washington's extreme weather, and take in views across three states (page 188).

★ **Hiking the Presidentials:** Take a stroll along a mountain ridge, or tackle all ten peaks in a 23-mile (37-km) trek (page 191).

★ **Kancamagus Highway:** This winding road offers a cross section of the White Mountains' rugged terrain and is one of the best places in New England to see the colorful display of autumn foliage (page 199).

★ **Flume Gorge:** Walk to dramatic waterfalls and covered bridges on an easygoing, family-friendly trail (page 202).

New Hampshire's White Mountains

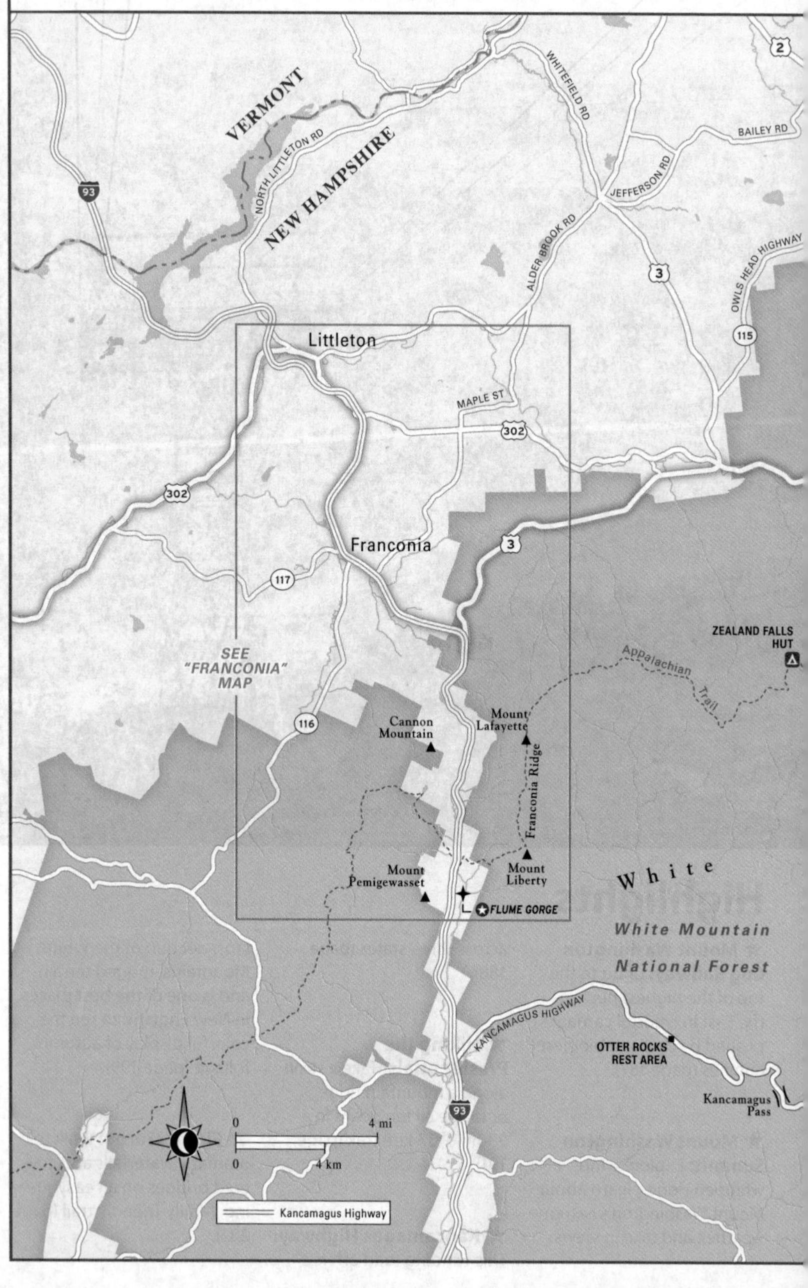

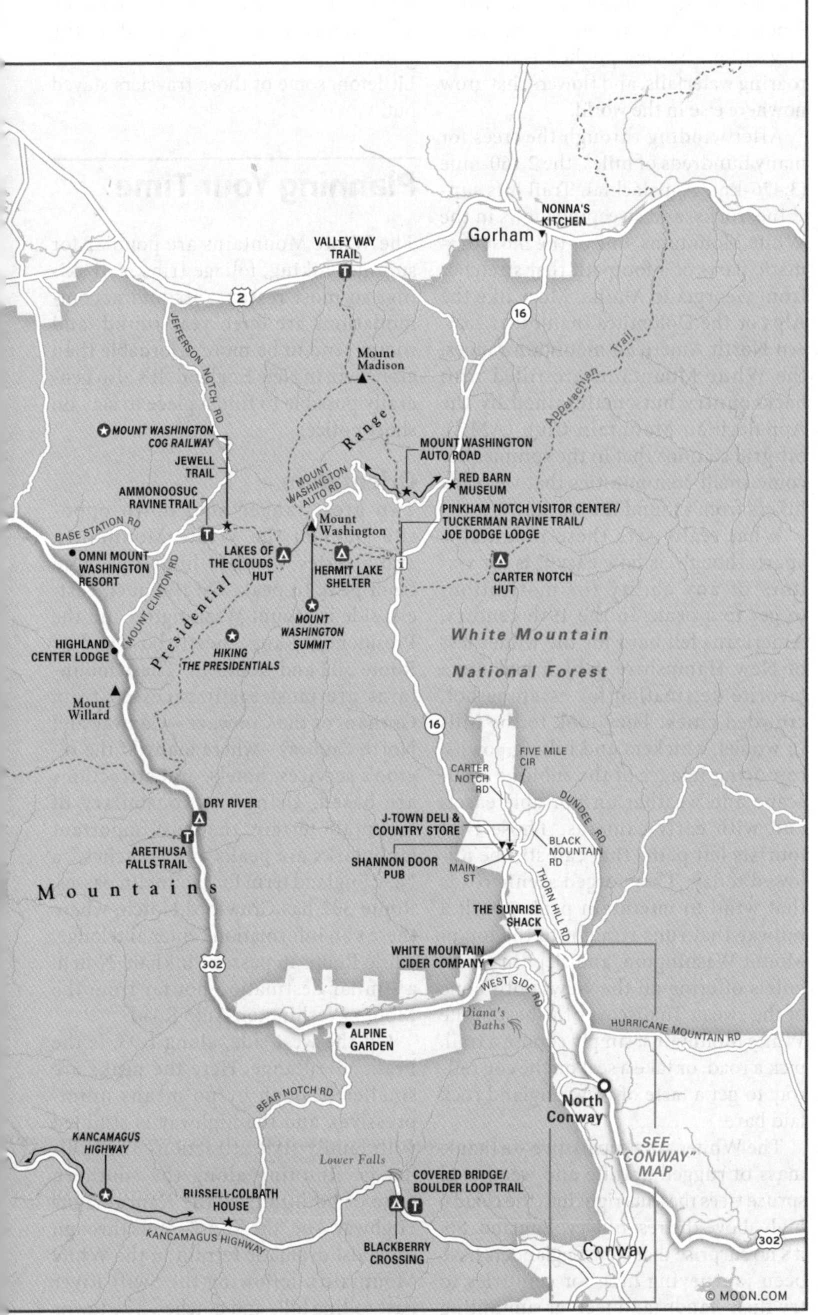
NONNA'S KITCHEN
Gorham
VALLEY WAY TRAIL
2
16
JEFFERSON NOTCH RD
Mount Madison
Appalachian Trail
MOUNT WASHINGTON COG RAILWAY
JEWELL TRAIL
Range
MOUNT WASHINGTON AUTO ROAD
MOUNT WASHINGTON AUTO RD
RED BARN MUSEUM
AMMONOOSUC RAVINE TRAIL
Mount Washington
PINKHAM NOTCH VISITOR CENTER/ TUCKERMAN RAVINE TRAIL/ JOE DODGE LODGE
BASE STATION RD
OMNI MOUNT WASHINGTON RESORT
LAKES OF THE CLOUDS HUT
HERMIT LAKE SHELTER
CARTER NOTCH HUT
MOUNT CLINTON RD
Presidential
MOUNT WASHINGTON SUMMIT
White Mountain
National Forest
HIGHLAND CENTER LODGE
HIKING THE PRESIDENTIALS
Mount Willard
16
FIVE MILE CIR
CARTER NOTCH RD
DUNDEE RD
DRY RIVER
J-TOWN DELI & COUNTRY STORE
BLACK MOUNTAIN RD
ARETHUSA FALLS TRAIL
SHANNON DOOR PUB
MAIN ST
THORN HILL RD
Mountains
THE SUNRISE SHACK
WHITE MOUNTAIN CIDER COMPANY
302
WEST SIDE RD
Diana's Baths
ALPINE GARDEN
HURRICANE MOUNTAIN RD
BEAR NOTCH RD
North Conway
KANCAMAGUS HIGHWAY
SEE "CONWAY" MAP
Lower Falls
COVERED BRIDGE/ BOULDER LOOP TRAIL
RUSSELL-COLBATH HOUSE
KANCAMAGUS HIGHWAY
BLACKBERRY CROSSING
Conway
302
© MOON.COM

In this unique mountain environment you'll find staggering extremes of weather, fiercely pitched trails, rip-roaring waterfalls, and flowers that grow nowhere else in the world.

After winding through the trees for many hundreds of miles, the 2,160-mile (3,476-km) Appalachian Trail hits sunshine, rocks, and sweeping views in the White Mountains, one of the most dramatic parts of a footpath that stretches from Georgia to Maine. More like the Alps or the Dolomites than other eastern North American mountain ranges, the White Mountains are filled with backcountry huts maintained by the Appalachian Mountain Club (AMC), off-grid stations that in the summer become small communities that welcome hikers from around the world.

What really sets these mountains apart, though, is how easy it is for visitors of any ability (or motivation) to get to a peak. In the 19th century, Americans fell hard for the wilderness of New Hampshire, which became a favorite destination for escaping hot, crowded cities. They took to the hills in woolen knickers and hiking gowns, capturing images of the sublime landscape and weather on portable easels and with early cameras. Those first tourists left paths that can still be followed today: They forged scenic roads that wind to mountain peaks, built a railway that runs straight to the top of Mount Washington, and slept in grand hotels offering all the views with none of the sweat. To discover the best of the White Mountains, simply choose a trail, pick a road, or take a seat on the cog railway to get a taste of New England rock laid bare.

The Whites are a superlative—a titanic mass of rugged granite and weathered spruce trees that juts right into the clouds, high above the rest of New England. So, it's no surprise that New Englanders have been journeying here for centuries to try their hands (and feet) at summiting behemoths like Washington, Lafayette, and Adams. And as evidenced by the growth of towns like North Conway and Littleton, some of those travelers stayed put.

Planning Your Time

The White Mountains are popular for summer hiking, foliage trips, and skiing, so most restaurants and accommodations are open year-round, and rooms tend to be more affordable than elsewhere in New England. It's also generally possible to find a place to stay on short notice.

Orientation

Two great ranges hold down opposite sides of the White Mountains, and a series of valley highways wind from peak to peak. On the northeastern side is Mount Washington and the Presidential Range, neatly bordered by Route 302 and Route 16. These mountains are most easily accessed from Gorham or the Conways—Conway and North Conway—where many of the region's services, hotels, and attractions are based. Using the vocabulary of mountain terrain, the most important landmarks are peaks and "notches," a New England term for mountain passes. Route 302 has Crawford Notch, where there's an information center and lodge, while Route 16 passes Pinkham Notch, a similar destination not far from the Mount Washington Auto Road.

On the west side, along I-93, is the Franconia Range. Here the peaks are smaller (though by no means unimpressive), and the highway is studded with family-style attractions and trailheads. Running along the southern edge of both ranges, the Kancamagus Highway—or "the Kanc"—cuts through the most dramatic terrain in the White Mountains, following the Swift River past rolling hills and notches. The towns

Best Restaurants

★ **May Kelly's Cottage:** Hearty plates of Irish food and pub fare go perfectly with live music sessions and a deck with mountain views (page 193).

★ **Nonna's Kitchen:** An Italian oasis in the White Mountains, this elegant gem pairs decadent pastas with views of the Presidential Range (page 196).

★ **White Mountain Cider Company:** Taste the best of regional farms alongside house-made ciders (page 196).

★ **Polly's Pancake Parlor:** Legendary pancakes made from flour ground on-site collide with rivers of maple syrup from the on-site sugarhouse (page 205).

★ **Taste The Thai & Sushi House:** Perched on the edge of the Ammonoosuc River, this cozy family restaurant offers mouthwatering Thai cuisine that ventures beyond standard noodles and curries (page 206).

of Franconia and Littleton are the principal gateways to the Franconia Range, with trailheads, campgrounds, and accommodations. South of Franconia, the road passes through Franconia Notch State Park, a valley with high mountains that rise on both sides.

Getting to the White Mountains

Driving from Coastal Maine

60 mi/97 km, 1.5 hr

Conway is the entry point to the White Mountains when driving from **Portland,** Maine. Leave downtown Portland on **I-295 South,** then take Exit 5B onto **Route 22 West,** Congress Street, which becomes County Road. Turn right onto **Route 114 North,** which you'll follow to a traffic circle; take the second exit onto **Route 112 South.** At the next traffic circle, stay straight to continue on 112. At the following traffic circle, you'll take the second exit onto **Route 25 West.** Next, turn right onto **Route 113 North.** In Fryeburg, turn left on Main Street to stay on Route 113, which here merges with **US-302** and takes you into downtown Conway after about 8 miles (13 km).

Driving from Boston

135 mi/217 km, 2.5 hr

From Boston, the White Mountains are easily accessible via the interstate. To reach **Conway,** take **I-93 North** out of the city, then use Exit 37A to merge onto **I-95 North.** Stay on I-95 North for 48.5 miles (78 km), ($2.00 toll, cash, E-ZPass, or pay by plate), then merge left at Exit 4 onto **Route 16 North,** which brings you to Conway (135 mi/217 km, 2.5 hrs). For **Franconia** (150 mi/241 km, 2.5 hrs), take **I-93 North** from the city to **Exit 38** ($1 toll, cash, E-ZPass, or pay by plate).

Driving from Southern Vermont

65 mi/105 km, 1.25 hr

From the southern Vermont hub of **White River Junction,** about 14 miles (22.5 km) northeast of **Woodstock** via **Route 4,** leave town on **I-91 North.** For **Franconia,** follow **I-91 North** for about 38 miles (61 km). Take Exit 17 to **Route 302 East;** in Wells River, turn right onto Main Street North and left onto Railroad Street to stay on Route 302, then turn left at the next juncture in Woodsville to stay on the route. Next, turn right onto **Route 117 East** and, after about 8 miles (13 km), right onto **Route 116** to reach downtown Franconia (65 mi/105 km, 1.25 hrs).

Best Accommodations

★ **CoHo Hostel:** Bunk down in a friendly hostel popular with through-hikers on the Appalachian Trail, then try to keep up with them at breakfast (page 197).

★ **Red Elephant Inn Bed & Breakfast:** Find all the modern comforts in this cozy inn stocked with gourmet treats (page 198).

★ **Alpine Garden:** Set up base camp in a gorgeous forest cabin beside a stream, and be sure to make use of the record player and vinyl LPs that each dwelling includes (page 199).

★ **Kinsman Lodge:** Settle onto the porch of this rustic, rambling spot and you may never want to leave (page 206).

For **Conway,** take **I-91 North** to Exit 15. In Fairlee, turn right onto Lake Morey Road, then left onto Main Street for half a mile (0.8 km) before turning right onto **Route 25A East.** Turn right for a brief bout on **Route 10/Route 25A** before turning left to continue on **Route 25A.** In Wentworth, turn left onto **Route 118 North,** merging with **Route 112** just outside of Lincoln. Continue on Route 112 for about 38 miles (61 km), then turn left onto **Route 113,** Main Street, for downtown Conway (95 mi/153 km, 2.25 hrs).

Driving from the Berkshires

185 mi/298km, 3.25 hr

To reach **Franconia** from **North Adams,** leave the city on **Route 2 East,** the scenic Mohawk Trail, for 34 miles (55 km). At the traffic circle, use the third exit to merge onto **I-91 North,** following the interstate for 122 miles (196 km). Take Exit 17 to **Route 302 East,** in Wells River, turning right onto Main Street North and left onto Railroad Street to stay on Route 302, then turn left at the next juncture in Woodsville to stay on the route. Next, turn right onto **Route 117 East** and, after about 8 miles (13 km), right onto **Route 116** to reach downtown Franconia (185 mi/298 km, 3.25 hrs).

To reach **Conway** from **North Adams,** follow **Route 8 North** out of town, and turn right when it intersects with **Route 9.** After about 25 miles (40 km), turn left to enter **I-91 North** for 2.7 miles (4 km), then take Exit 3 for **Route 9 East,** making a sharp left after about 15 miles (24 km), in Keene, to remain on the route. In Hopkinton, merge onto **I-89 South** for 8 miles (13 km), then exit onto **I-93 North,** which you'll follow for 33 miles (53 km). Take Exit 23 to **Route 104 East/Route 132 North,** then turn left onto **Route 3 North** for 1 mile (1.6 km), and make a right onto **Route 25 East,** which you'll continue on for about 19 miles (30.5 km). Turn left onto **Route 113,** turning left again on Tamworth Road then right on Chocorua Road, which becomes Page Hill Road, to remain on Route 113. Turn left onto **Route 16 North,** which continues into downtown Conway (190 mi/306 km, 4 hrs).

Driving from New York City

330 mi/531 km, 6.5 hr

From New York City to **Franconia,** leave the city heading north on **FDR Drive.** Use the left lane to access Exit 17 to the **Robert F. Kennedy Bridge** ($10.17 toll), then stay left to merge onto **I-278 East.** After 4.5 miles (7 km), I-278 East merges with **I-95 North** ($1.75 toll). Follow I-95 North 46 miles (74 km) to Exit 27A in Bridgeport, Connecticut. Keep right for **Route 8 North,** which you'll follow 5.5 miles (9 km) to Exit 9, merging onto **Route 15 North.** Take Exit 68 NE to merge onto **I-91 North,** and stay on

Two Days in the White Mountains

Mount Washington

Day 1

With two days in the Whites, head straight for the highest point—**Mount Washington.** The summit of this commanding peak combines history and a rugged alpine landscape and is easily accessible by car or the cog-driven train to the top. If you're feeling ambitious, though, make a day of it by walking up the **Jewell Trail** that pitches straight up the rocky mountain slopes. Either way, by the time the sun gets low you'll be ready for a snack at the **Omni Mount Washington Resort,** where you can take an elegant afternoon tea in the **Princess Room** or settle into the gracious veranda for a cocktail with perfect views of the peak. Then take a scenic drive through the mountain pass of Crawford Notch State Park to the doorstep of **May Kelly's Cottage.** Savor authentic Irish fare, and then backtrack to **Alpine Garden** for a campfire under the stars and a cozy night's rest in your own "Hobbit Home."

Day 2

On day two, rise early for a beautifully backlit drive along the **Kancamagus Highway,** leaving plenty of time to stop at the river swimming holes that pock the cool Swift River. Grab a late breakfast of loaded flapjacks from **Polly's Pancake Parlor** and turn south for the **Franconia Notch,** where you can shed a tear for the Old Man of the Mountain, slip into **Flume Gorge,** and take an afternoon tram ride to the top of **Cannon Mountain** before heading north to **Schilling Beer Company** for a round of Germanic ales and lovingly made pub grub beside the roaring Ammonoosuc River at sundown.

I-91 North for about 200 miles (322 km). Take Exit 17 to **Route 302 East,** in Wells River turning right onto Main Street North and left onto Railroad Street to stay on Route 302, then turning left at the next juncture in Woodsville to stay on the route. Next, turn right onto **Route 117 East** and, after about 8 miles (13 km), right onto **Route 116** to reach downtown Franconia (330 mi/531 km, 6.5 hrs).

For **Conway** from New York City, you'll stay on **I-91 North** for about **105 miles** (169 km) before taking Exit 3 for **Route 9 East.** Make a sharp left after about 15 miles (24 km), in Keene, to remain on Route 9. In Hopkinton, merge onto **I-89 South** for 8 miles (13 km), then exit onto **I-93 North,** which you'll follow for 33 miles (53 km). Take Exit 23 to **Route 104 East/Route 132 North,** then turn left onto **Route 3 North** for 1 mile (1.6 km), and make a right onto **Route 25 East,** which you'll continue on for about 19 miles (30.5 km). Turn left onto **Route 113,** turning left again on Tamworth Road and then right on Chocorua Road, which becomes Page Hill Road, to remain on Route 113. Turn left onto **Route 16 North,** which continues into downtown Conway (350 mi/563 km, 6 hrs).

Getting There by Air, Train, or Bus

Air

The White Mountains' closest commercial airport is **Portsmouth International Airport at Pease** (PSM, https://flypsmairport.com), which is primarily served by Allegiant Air, but for convenience and price, flying into **Boston Logan International Airport** (www.massport.com) is a much better option, with direct flights from around the world and across the United States. The drive from Pease Airport to the nearest White Mountain town (North Conway) takes just under 2 hours without traffic, while driving from Logan Airport to Franconia is usually a 2.5-hour drive.

Train

There's no train service to New Hampshire; the closest station is White River Junction in Vermont, which is served by **Amtrak** (800/872-7245, www.amtrak.com) on its Vermonter route. **Enterprise** rental car branches are available in White River Junction (60 Jasmin Lane, 802/280-9953) and in nearby West Lebanon, New Hampshire (1 Glen Road, 603/298-0218), and you can call each branch to schedule a pickup from the train station. From White River Junction, it's generally a 1.5-hour drive to Franconia and a 2.5-hour drive to North Conway.

Bus

Concord Coach Lines (800/639-3317, www.concordcoachlines.com) runs a daily bus from Boston through the White Mountains, stopping at Conway (First Stop Market & Deli, 13 W. Main St.), North Conway (Eastern Slope Inn, 2760 Main St./Rte. 16), and Gorham (Irving Oil, 350 Main St.). A more westerly route heads to Franconia (Franconia Market and Deli, 347 Main St.). **Greyhound** (800/231-2222, www.greyhound.com) also runs buses to Conway (First Stop Market & Deli, 13 W. Main St.).

Mount Washington and the Presidential Range

TOP EXPERIENCE

A series of bare peaks pushing high above the tree line, the Presidential Range is the heart of White Mountain National Forest (WMNF), a rugged spine that culminates in Mount Washington, the highest summit in the northeastern United States. While the area isn't vast—the entire Presidential Range can be hiked in one punishing 23-mile (37-km) day—it has the feel of true wilderness. Trails tackle slopes head-on or hop from one rock to another without a scrap of flat, even ground. Visitors used to hiking the higher-elevation Rockies, Sierras, and Cascades are often surprised by how challenging the White Mountains can be; though they're less than half the size of the Western peaks, the Presidential summits are serious climbs.

Even in summer, the temperature difference between the peak of Mount Washington and neighboring valleys averages around 30 degrees. The weather observatory on that peak has recorded some of the world's most extreme weather, including the highest wind speeds on record, and the Presidentials get hammered by winter storms that coat them in thick layers of rime ice, snow, and frost.

The White Mountains have a fascinating legacy of travel. By the mid-19th century, the area was a favorite destination for U.S. artists and tourists eager to explore the wilderness. Dozens of trains came to the Whites from Boston each day, stopping at a series of elegant hotels, nearly self-contained cities with their own train stations and hundreds of staff.

Anyone with time and strong legs can find lonely trails and solitude in the White Mountains, and it can be a sublime experience. But for all the carnival atmosphere atop Mount Washington, it's pure, giddy fun to enjoy the Presidential Range in 19th-century style, chugging upslope in "The Cog," bagging a few stony summits, and then taking high tea in the Princess Room at the Omni Mount Washington Resort.

Sights

★ Mount Washington Cog Railway

When Chicago meatpacking baron Sylvester Marsh first presented his idea for a railway to the top of Mount Washington, the state legislature told him he might as well "build a railway to the moon." In the spirit of the times, he was undeterred and began work on the world's first mountain-climbing train using materials hauled through thick forest by oxen teams. When the railway first opened in 1869, it was the first in the world to employ toothed gears, or cogs, that meshed with a pinion on the track to prevent the train from slipping backward. In those early years, the railway was powered with staggering quantities of wood, which gave way to coal in 1908.

These days the historic coal-fired trains alternate with more ecofriendly biodiesel engines, and though the railway is slower (and more expensive) than the auto road, it's wonderfully fun to chug your way up Mount Washington as the steam whistle echoes off the surrounding peaks. The trains of the **Mount Washington Cog Railway** (Base Rd., off Rte. 302, Bretton Woods, 603/278-5404, www.thecog.com, 3-hr round-trip on steam/biodiesel, $89 adults, $59 children 4-12, free under 4, one-way $60) run late May-mid-October. After climbing Mount Washington's exposed upper slopes at a surprisingly steep angle and reaching the summit, it's worth asking the engineer for a peek inside the engine to see the coal bin, brakes, levers, and gauges. Trips allow for one hour on the summit, so if you'd like to spend the day hiking, you'll have to book a standby return ticket—though you're guaranteed to get down by the end of the day, it's not possible to reserve a spot on any given train.

Mount Washington Auto Road

You'll see the bumper stickers as soon as you start driving around New England: "This Car Climbed Mount Washington." It doesn't seem like much to brag about until you're white-knuckling the steering wheel around the zigzag highway to the summit, earning breathtaking views with every turn of the **Mount Washington Auto Road** (Rte. 16, Pinkham Notch, 603/466-3988, https://mt-washington.com, mid-May-early Nov. variable hours, $45 car and driver, $20 each adult, $10 each child, children under 5 free, $30 motorcycle and driver, no bicycles). The 7.6-mile (12.2-km) trip, off Route 16, goes by at a snail's pace, taking about 30 minutes on the way up, 40 on the way down, and it's not for everyone—both drivers and passengers who are unnerved by heights may be better off in one of the guided van tours (from $55 adults, $50 seniors, $35 children 5-12, $10 under 5). The driver shares stories and anecdotes on the way up the mountain, and groups have one hour on the summit before heading back downslope.

For hikers who'd like to make a one-way trip up or down Mount Washington, there's an irritatingly expensive one-way shuttle ($55 adults and children, $30 dogs); hitchhiking is prohibited and shuttle availability is not guaranteed, so if you're climbing to the top of Mount Washington, be prepared to hike back out.

At the bottom of the road, the **Red Barn Museum** (1 Mount Washington Auto Rd., 603/466-3988, late May-early Oct., Fri.-Mon. 10am-4pm, free) displays objects relating to the auto road's past, including antique cars and a carriage that used to climb the mountain.

★ Mount Washington Summit

With views stretching from the Adirondacks to Maine, the Mount Washington summit is unlike any mountain peak in the United States: It's the high point of the 2,160-mile (3,476-km) Appalachian Trail in New England, a day-trippers' destination complete with gaily painted steam engines, and the site of an extraordinary weather station that records storms that can howl in on any day of the year. When going to the summit, it's worth bringing more clothing than seems necessary, as temperatures can be bone-chilling when the valley is balmy. For all the train tracks, crowds, and postcard racks, this is a mountain that commands respect, and seasoned hikers and climbers die here every year, usually from hypothermia.

Learn about Mount Washington's infamously gnarly weather and scientists who live and work at the top at the **Sherman Adams Visitor Center** (summit building, daily 10am-5pm), which has displays explaining the mountain's meteorological hazards and telling the story of the day in 1934 when a record-breaking 231 mile-per-hour (372 kph) wind was recorded at the summit. There's also a rather sobering memorial for all of hikers who have perished on Mount Washington—often amid punishing subzero temperatures, rain, or snow. Those willing to join the observatory's membership program can register for a tour of the **Mount Washington Observatory**

Mount Washington Cog Railway

Weather Station (603/356-2137, ext. 211, https://mountwashington.org/donate/membership, membership $60 individual). A small cafeteria by the weather station entrance offers basic bites like hot dogs and pizza, all of which can taste like heaven after wheezing your way to the top of Mount Washington via any of the local trails.

The oldest surviving building on the summit is the **Tip Top House,** a rustic stone lodge built in 1853 as a hotel, which then became the office for *Among the Clouds,* a mountain newspaper that chronicled social events, train schedules, weather, and gossip 1888-1915. Tiny bunks, communal tables, and a few dusty reproductions of the newspaper are on display.

Other Sights

In many ways, the White Mountains were easier to reach a century ago than today—frequent trains made the trip from Boston a breeze, with whistle stops at lodges and hotels. The small, volunteer-run **Gorham Historical Society & Railroad Museum** (25 Railroad St., Gorham, 603/466-5338, www.gorhamnewhampshire.com, May-Oct. Tues.-Sat. 10am-3pm, free) preserves artifacts from that era in Gorham's 1907 railway station. Call before visiting, as hours can vary with volunteer availability.

Entertainment and Events

What nightlife there is in this corner of the mountains is firmly based in the Conways, the cultural hub of the Whites. You can try local beers well into the early evening at **Tuckerman Brewing Company** (66 Hobbs St., Conway, 603/447-5400, www.tuckermanbrewing.com, Mon.-Thurs. 2pm-7pm, Fri. 2pm-8pm, Sat. noon-8pm, Sun. noon-7pm), where you taste your way through a lineup of stouts, ales, and IPAs. A good way to meet some locals is at the Sunday afternoon Irish music session at **May Kelly's Cottage** (3002 Rte. 302, North Conway, 603/356-7005, www.maykellys.com, Thurs. 4pm-9pm, Fri.-Sat. noon-9pm, Sun. noon-8pm), which has a pleasant porch for afternoon beers and a convivial feel. A more upscale watering hole is the **Library Lounge at Stonehurst Manor** (3351 Rte. 302, North Conway, 603/356-3113, www.thewildroserestaurant.com, 4:30pm-11pm daily), whose leather furniture and elaborately carved fireplace mantle bring to mind a summer retreat for Bruce Wayne. Up the road in the little village of Jackson, the **Shannon Door Pub** (Rte. 16, Jackson, 603/383-4211, www.shannondoor.com, Thurs.-Fri. and Sun. 6pm-9pm, Sat. 7pm-10pm) has live music nightly Thursday-Saturday, and a fun, country Irish atmosphere.

If you're visiting the Whites in early October, as the foliage peaks, consider crossing the state line into nearby Fryeburg, Maine, for a unique slice of North Country life at the **Fryeburg Fair**

Local Legend

As an Appalachian Mountain Club (AMC) hut "croo" member, **James Wrigley** used to spend his summers hauling 60-plus-pound loads of food up some of the most punishing White Mountain trails on an old-school wooden packboard. Today, Wrigley is the director of AMC's White Mountain lodging facilities. Raised in Massachusetts, Wrigley found himself under the White Mountains' spell as a teenager, and the rest is history.

James Wrigley with his daughter, in their element

What was the moment that made you realize, "You know, I've gotta spend some more time exploring the Whites"?

I was hiking with my dad during high school, up over the moon-like landscape of Mount Adams and Madison, looking out at the valley all day, and as soon as we set up our tent in the boreal forest for the night, the clouds opened up and just started pouring down rain. We laid there, listening to the rain pelting down on the tent fly and the woods. It was like nothing I'd experienced before.

Suppose you're showing a friend around the Whites for the first time. Where would you take them hiking?

The Zealand Trail through the woods and beaver bogs of Zealand Valley is one of my favorite hikes. It's a flat path that goes through a gorgeous space where you have the opportunity to see wildlife and waterfalls in a six-mile (9.6-km) round trip. For a higher-altitude hike, the Caps Ridge Trail is the shortest, most direct route to the alpine zone of the Presidential ridgeline. You can see the fragile wildflowers and tundra up there.

Where do you like to unwind and refuel after a long, grueling day of hiking in the White Mountains?

I personally love **The Shannon Door,** which is a great little Irish bar on a hilltop in Jackson. The **Moat Mountain Brewery & Smokehouse** is a classic standby in the Mount Washington Valley for a hearty dinner, but if you're over in the Franconia Notch area, **Schilling Beer Co.** is a really great spot for beer and food, and you can have it right on their deck overlooking the Ammonoosuc River.

(207/935-3268, www.fryeburgfair.org, early Oct., $15 daily admission adults, free for children under 12). This weeklong event is a smorgasbord of festivities that showcase rural life. It began in 1851, when a group of local farmers and merchants met up to show off their finest cattle. Today, the fair offerings have expanded to include ax-throwing contests with local lumberjacks and firehose assembly (and blasting) races in which firefighters compare their skills. But the livestock contests remain the premier events here, and during a given year, you'll encounter everything from oxen to llamas, rabbits, and draft horses at the fair. There are also enough carnival rides and midway games to keep the kids entertained if admiring the corpulent blue-ribbon pigs just isn't doing it for them.

Shopping

While there are plenty of shops for poking around in the Conways, the most useful stores in the White Mountains are gear shops stocked with everything you need to walk, ride, or climb your way into the hills. The Conways have a plethora: **International Mountain Equipment** (2733 Rte. 302, North Conway, 603/356-7013, www.ime-usa.com, daily 10am-6pm) is a well-stocked outdoor gear shop (with a bounteous bargain basement) run by the International Mountain Climbing School, which also rents hiking and camping equipment. **Stan & Dan Sports** (2936 Rte. 302, North Conway, 603/356-6997, www.stananddansports.com, daily 9am-5pm) is a go-to for bike and ski gear. If you're heading north of the Conways, take a brief detour to Intervale to experience the hiking boot-making workshop of **Peter Limmer & Sons** (9 Limmer Ln., Intervale, 603/356-5378, www.limmercustomboot.com, Tues.-Sat. 8am-5pm), which has outfitted some of the world's top mountaineers with incredibly sturdy leather boots, said to last as long as 50 years. In Gorham, stop by **Gorham Hardware & Sport Center** (96 Main St., Gorham, 603/466-2312, www.nhhockeyshop.com, Tues.-Fri. 8am-4pm, Sat. 9am-3pm, hours may vary seasonally) for hiking, climbing, skiing, and camping setups.

Hiking

There are endless ways to enjoy these mountains, but before setting out it's worth stopping by one of the ranger stations or visitor centers for maps and updated advice; some trails are closed seasonally to protect wildlife, and it's especially important to learn mountain weather forecasts before setting out above the tree line. In Conway, the White Mountain National Forest **Saco Ranger Station** (33 Rte. 112, Conway, 603/447-5448, late May-mid-Oct. Tues.-Sun. 8am-4:30pm, Mon. 9am-4:30pm) has maps, advice, and updated weather reports, as does Gorham's White Mountain National Forest **Androscoggin Ranger Station** (300 Glen Rd., Gorham, 603/446-2713, May-Oct. daily 8am-4:30pm). On Route 16, the Appalachian Mountain Club's **Pinkham Notch Visitor Center** (361 Rte. 16, 603/466-8116, www.outdoors.org, daily 6:30am-9pm) has plenty of the same, along with a small trading post for supplies, and the **AMC Highland Center** (3575 Rte. 302, Crawford Notch, 603/466-2727, 9am-4pm, closes earlier in off-season) is a popular trailhead and hiker information spot. The Highland Center also has a trail information and weather hotline (603/466-2721).

For hikers who want to do longer, one-way hikes, it's worth looking into the **AMC Hiker Shuttle** (www.outdoors.org, early June-Oct., $24), which has a fixed route that accesses many popular trailheads in the area, especially those that lead to the AMC's mountain huts.

★ Hiking the Presidentials

Mount Washington

Bar none, the most iconic hike in the White Mountains is the **Tuckerman Ravine Trail,** a 4.2-mile (6.75-km) route to the summit of Mount Washington, which leaves from the **Pinkham Notch Visitor Center** (361 Rte. 16). Doing this hike as a round-trip is a full-day outing of at least six hours, and it's especially important to bring extra clothes, water, and a headlamp for this strenuous trail. After some initial switchbacks through thick forest, the trail rises fairly gradually, following the route of the Cutler River for 2.4 miles (3.8 km) and reaching the **Hermit Lake Shelter,** which has lean-tos, tent platforms, and potable water from a hand-operated pump. This scenic spot is the jumping-off point for many of the backcountry skiers who tackle the famous headwall of Tuckerman Ravine each spring. After the lake, the trail begins to climb in earnest, then aims straight up the western edge of Tuckerman Ravine, earning elevation and views with every

step. Upon cresting the valley headwall, the trail reaches a junction that's clearly signed for the Mount Washington summit (0.6 mi) and Lakes of the Clouds (0.8 mi), the most spectacular of the White Mountains' AMC huts, and a pleasant spot to stop for hot drinks (and sometimes freshly baked treats from the hut staff). For a return trip to Pinkham Notch that's easier on the knees, it's possible to descend via the more moderate **Boott Spur** or **Lion Head Trail.**

It's also possible to ascend Mount Washington by a pair of trails on the **Crawford Notch** side, accessible from Route 302; parking for these routes is at the Cog Railway station, and you should allow a full day for a round-trip hike up either trail. The most direct route is the 4.4-mile (7-km) **Ammonoosuc Ravine Trail,** which climbs *very* steeply to Lakes of the Clouds, then continues up a rocky path to the summit; in addition to passing scenic ponds and the AMC hut, this trail has gorgeous views as it works its way up the southwest face of the mountain. Somewhat longer and more gradual, the 5.1-mile (8.2-km) **Jewell Trail** ascends the western slope of Mount Clay, then skirts the summit to join a ridge trail to the top of Mount Washington. This is another stunner on clear days; it's delightful to hike parallel to the Cog Railway for views of the brightly colored trains with an endless backdrop.

The Presidential Traverse

Strictly for extremely fit, experienced hikers, the **Presidential Traverse** is a remarkable 23-mile (37-km) hike that goes up and over every peak in the range—tellingly, this hike is often referred to as the **Death March,** and many hikers begin and end in the dark (although the classic Death March is a long day hike, it's possible to break it up with a night in

Top to bottom: the glacial bowl of Tuckerman Ravine; the Presidential Range near Mount Washington; Arethusa Falls

the **Lakes of the Clouds** hut). Most hikers go north to south, taking the **Valley Way Trail** from the Appalachia parking lot (Rte. 2, 5 mi/8 km west of the intersection with Rte. 16) up Mount Madison before ticking off a who's who of American presidents, ending with Mount Jackson, then descending into Crawford Notch. The one-way hike requires a car on either end, or you can use the **AMC Hiker Shuttle** (603/466-2727, www.outdoors.org, $24). More information can be obtained at the **Pinkham Notch Visitor Center** (361 Rte. 16, 603/466-8116, www.outdoors.org, daily 6:30am-10pm).

Mount Jefferson

Another option is the full-day, 10-mile (16-km) round-trip hike to Mount Jefferson, which is equal parts challenging and rewarding, following a rocky ridge that looks out across the White Mountains. The **Castle Trail** takes off from Route 2, 9.2 miles (14.8 km) west of the junction between Route 2 and Route 16 in Gorham; a brown sign on the south side of the road marks the entrance, and a parking area is at the end of the road. Mount Jefferson is also accessible by way of the shorter **Caps Ridge Trail,** which departs from Jefferson Notch Road, off of Route 2, and still manages to pack a whopping 2,690 feet (820 m) of vertical elevation gain into a 5.3-mile (8.5-km) round-trip.

Family-Friendly Hikes

Not all the hikes in the White Mountains are quite so strenuous. One favorite option for families is the 3.2-mile round-trip hike up **Mount Willard,** which earns fabulous views of Crawford Notch with more gradual slopes (for that reason, this hike tends to be crowded on busy days in the Whites, so don't expect solitude). Park at the railroad depot information center adjacent to the **AMC Highland Center** on Route 302.

Another good choice for hiking with kids is the gentle, 0.6-mile (0.9-km) walk to **Diana's Baths** between North Conway and Bartlett, which has an enchanting series of waterfalls ideal for cooling off in wading pools (the baths vary greatly with water level, though, and by late summer the waterfalls can be mere trickles). To reach the parking area from North Conway, take Route 302 north out of town, then turn left on River Road (which becomes West Side Rd. after 1 mi/1.6 km) for 2.5 miles (4 km). A large parking lot is on the left with a self-service, cash-only parking fee station ($5). Get here as early as you can in the summer, as cars will often queue up along the road, waiting for parking spaces to become available.

Find the highest single-drop waterfall in New Hampshire at the end of the **Arethusa Falls** trail, a 2.6-mile (4.2-km) round-trip hike along Bemis Brook. Park on the west side of Route 302 about a mile (1.6 km) south of Dry River Campground in Crawford Notch State Park. The hike is moderately steep but well suited for families with older kids, and it's possible to extend it into a more challenging 4.7-mile (7.5-km) loop by returning via **Frankenstein Cliff Trail,** which has lovely views of the valley. The falls' musical name is said to be taken from a poem by Percy Bysshe Shelley about a Greek nymph who was transformed into a flowing spring.

Food

The Conways

A year-round favorite is ★ **May Kelly's Cottage** (3002 Rte. 302, 603/356-7005, www.maykellys.com, Thurs. 4pm-9pm, Fri.-Sat. noon-9pm, Sun. noon-8pm, $15-25), which serves hearty Irish classics and American pub fare in a relaxed, old-world setting. With fabulous mountain views and shaded tables, the outdoor patio is perfect for an early evening meal, while the interior is decked with a pleasant jumble of Americana and Irish bric-a-brac. Shepherd's pie, soups, and hearty salads all come with homemade, grainy bread, and regulars love the fried

The Appalachian Mountain Club's White Mountain Huts

The Appalachian Mountain Club has maintained a system of eight backcountry huts in the White Mountains since 1888, making the wilderness accessible for hikers without the gear and experience to rough it on their own. Spending a night at one of the AMC huts feels like alpine summer camp, with bunk beds, communal meals, and a convivial atmosphere among the tired hikers. While rates can seem high (especially given the rustic experience), you're paying for meals hiked in by hardy college students in a wild, scenic place, and staying in the backcountry is an unforgettable experience.

Lakes of the Clouds hut

Favorite Huts

- The most famous—and perhaps most spectacular—among the AMC huts is **Lakes of the Clouds,** set by a cluster of alpine ponds just a ridgeline away from the top of Mount Washington.
- The trail to pretty **Zealand Falls Hut** is far less challenging, a relatively gradual 2.8-mile (4.5-km) hike that ends at a perfect river swimming spot.
- Less popular (and crowded) than those two all-stars, **Carter Notch Hut** is the easternmost hut in the AMC system, a 1914 stone structure set between Wildcat Dome and Carter Mountain.
- One of the Appalachian Mountain Club's most easily accessible huts from the Franconia Range side is **Lonesome Lake Hut,** which is a 1.6-mile (2.6-km) hike from the trailhead in Lafayette Campground and has fabulous views of the mountains, naturalist programs, and rustic co-ed bunkrooms.
- Another favorite in the Franconia area is **Greenleaf Hut,** which is at the end of a moderate 2.7-mile (4.3-km) walk and offers an equally spectacular perspective on the rugged terrain.

Practicalities

Rates include dinner the night of arrival and breakfast the morning after, and **reservations** (www.outdoors.org, 603/466-2727, $95-150) can be made online or by phone.

Visitors must bring their own sleeping bags and pillowcases, and guests share simple, often solar-powered bathrooms with cold running water.

The most popular huts, and especially Lakes of the Clouds, are often booked months in advance, but there's usually last-minute space if you're traveling in a small party and are flexible about where you stay.

potato cakes with spinach and horseradish sauce. On Sunday afternoons, a fun group of Irish musicians holds a relaxed live session, playing around a table over beers.

For heaping mounds of meat and locally brewed craft beers (two cornerstones of North Country decadence), there's nothing in town quite like **Moat Mountain Smokehouse & Brewing Company** (3378 Rte. 302, North Conway, 603/356-6381, www.moatmountain.com, Sun.-Tues. 11:30am-9pm, Fri.-Sat. 11:30am-10pm, $13-27). Staples like the Czech pilsner, the brisket-laden Longhorn nachos, and the Thai chicken flatbread pizza are worth the stopover, but what really makes the Moat special is how the place can feel like the hub of the universe. On most nights, the bar is packed with everyone from town officials to Mount Washington weather observatory scientists. Go in with a growling stomach and a gregarious spirit. Or take your food and beer (available in cans and growlers) to a more bucolic spot.

Fresh, simple breakfasts and hearty lunches at **Stairway Café** (2649 Rte. 302, North Conway, 603/356-5200, www.facebook.com/stairwaycafe, Fri.-Wed. 8am-2pm, $10-21) are the main draws, but the atmosphere is pretty great too—the decor strikes a curious balance between country kitchen and rock and roll (imagine a bacon and egg skull on a floral print menu). Both the breakfast and lunch menus are served all day and include plenty of basic egg plates, burgers, and sandwiches, along with offbeat additions like wild game sausage and Maine lobster Benedict.

Part of a small chain of earthy pizza joints with a focus on natural, organic ingredients, **Flatbread Company** (2760 Rte. 302, North Conway, 603/356-4470, www.flatbreadcompany.com, daily 11:30am-9pm, $15-23) pulls thin-crust pies from a wood-fired oven, topped with homemade pepperoni and sausage, piles of fresh vegetables, and tomato sauce that

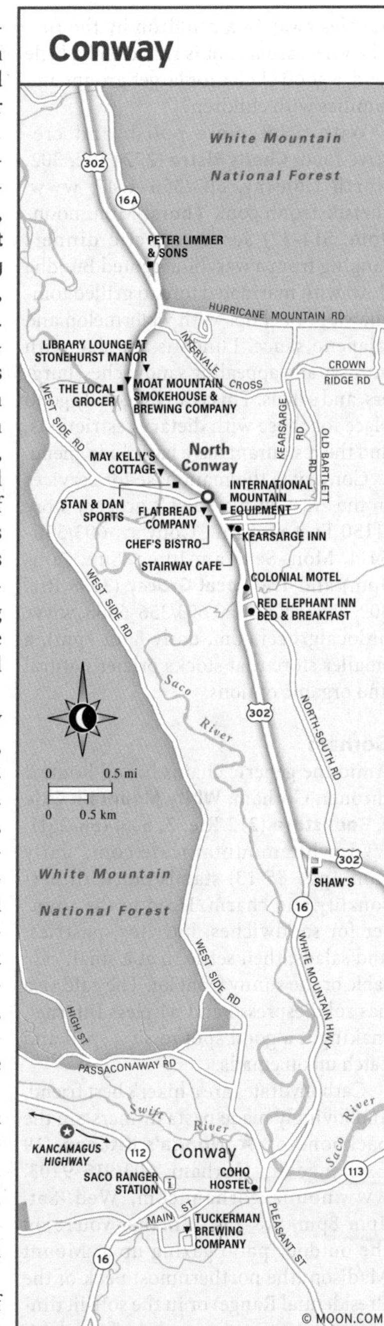

bubbles away in a cauldron by the fire. The very casual spot is rustic and a little loud, a good choice for larger groups and families with children.

With a bit more polish and creative food, **Chef's Bistro** (2724 Rte. 302, North Conway, 603/356-4747, www.chefsbistronh.com, Thurs.-Mon. noon-9pm, $14-32) serves eclectic dinners ranging from a wasabi-accented Buddha Bowl with marinated tofu to grilled tomahawk pork chops with watermelon and jalapeno sauce. Lunch is simpler, with unfussy and appealing sandwiches, burgers, and salads. This is an especially good place for those with dietary restrictions, and the restaurant has a basic kids' menu.

Conway is the main base for services in the area, with a **Shaw's** grocery store (1150 Eastman Rd., Conway, 603/356-5471, Mon.-Sat. 7am-10pm, Sun. 7am-9pm) and **The Local Grocer** (3358 Rte. 302, North Conway, 603/356-6068, www.nhlocalgrocer.com, daily 8am-7pm), a smaller store that stocks pricier natural and organic options.

Gorham

Amid the generic chains lining Route 2 through Gorham, **White Mountain Café & Bookstore** (212 Rte. 2, 603/466-2511, www.whitemountaincafe.com, daily 7am-4pm, $5-13) stands out with personality and charm. Head to the counter for sandwiches, burritos, pastries, and salads, then settle in at a small café table or the sunny front lot. The café also has solid espresso and wireless Internet, making it a good spot to sit a spell and catch up on emails.

Carbohydrates are a hiker's best friend, and lovingly made pasta dinners are the backbone of ★ **Nonna's Kitchen** (19 Exchange St., Gorham, 603/915-9203, www.nonnasgorham.com, Wed.-Sat. 4pm-8pm, $18-25). Whether you're on the outdoor patio gazing up at Mount Madison (the northernmost peak of the Presidential Range) or in the soft-lit dining room tucking into a plate of spaghetti salsiccia or haddock puttanesca, a meal at Nonna's brings the convivial energy of a Sunday Italian dinner to the Whites. The chefs and owners, Ellen and Mike Conley, are almost always on-site, and the eclectic range of diners who congregate here for hearty scratch cooking lend the place a gregarious vibe that can be hard to find in mountain towns.

Off Routes 16 and 302

Between the Conways and Gorham are a cluster of shops and restaurants in Jackson, on Route 16, that make a good stopping point. Among the most convenient is **J-Town Deli & Country Store** (174 Main St., Jackson, 603/383-8064, www.jtowndeli.com, daily 8am-6pm, $7-12), where you can pick up breakfast and lunch to eat at on-site picnic tables or take with you—breakfast sandwiches, subs, and wraps include gluten-free and vegetarian-friendly options, and the store also prepares dinners to go, which are a good value if your accommodation has a kitchen.

Another nearby favorite for breakfast among locals and visitors alike is **The Sunrise Shack** (644 Rte. 302, Glen, 603/383-7169, www.sunriseshack.com, daily 7am-2pm, $10-15), which pairs the interior design of an old-school country diner with innovative, hearty scrambles, wraps, and bowls, smothered with fixings like crisp bacon, roasted poblano peppers, and tomato onion jam. There's often a wait, but free coffee at the door makes it bearable.

If you visit the ★ **White Mountain Cider Company** (207 Rte. 302, Bartlett, 603/383-9061, www.ciderconh.com, deli Wed.-Sun. 8am-4pm, restaurant Wed.-Sun. 4pm-9pm, $23-45) mid-September-early winter, you'll find it pressing apple cider with an old-fashioned mill and serving the unbeatable pairing of fresh juice and apple cider doughnuts. The deli side of the operation offers doughnuts, cider, sandwiches, and coffee, and by night the restaurant serves gourmet bistro fare in a charmingly rustic setting. Menu items change frequently, but the house ribeye with black garlic and roasted shishito peppers is a favorite, as is the ricotta basil gnocchi. A full menu of beer, wine, and cocktails makes this a good spot for a night out as well.

Thirty-four miles (55 km) up Route 302 from Conway, the **Omni Mount Washington Resort** (Rte. 302, Bretton Woods, 603/278-1000, www.mountwashingtonresort.com) would be out of the way if it weren't such a worthwhile destination of its own. The giant hotel has a small city's worth of restaurants, but two stand out as destination-worthy. For alpine elegance, you can't beat high tea in the **Princess Room** (Mon.-Fri. 7am-10:30am, Sat.-Sun. 7am-11am, $20 adults, $12 children 10 and under): Grown-ups sip their brews along with ceviche, savory tartlets, scones, and sweets, while kids get mini marshmallows in their hot chocolate, and a menu of tiny sandwiches, savory muffins, macarons, and strawberry tarts. The elegant room is named for Princess Caroline, the eccentric, glamorous wife of the hotel's original owner. As charming as those princess-worthy tea parties can be, though, the finest seats in the hotel are on the broad back veranda, where comfortable wicker chairs are pointed straight at the southern slope of Mount Washington. Sunsets are spectacular here, and sharp-eyed visitors can spot the glint and smoke of the Cog Railway as it chugs up the slope. Guests on the veranda can order from the **Rosebrook Bar** (noon-9pm, $10-16), and sip wine, beer, and cocktails along with savory nibbles that would seem overpriced in a different venue.

Accommodations and Camping

Camping

In the White Mountain National Forest, backcountry camping is allowed below the tree line, as long as tents are more than 200 feet (61 m) from trails and water. WMNF also operates a number of excellent campgrounds: Six miles (9.6 km) south of Gorham, **Dolly Copp Campground** (Rte. 16, 603/536-6100, mid-May-mid-Oct., reservations accepted with some sites first-come, first-served, $25) is one the largest in the forest, with vault toilets, campfire rings, and ranger-run programs. There are no showers on-site, but coin-operated showers are available five miles (8 km) south at the AMC's **Pinkham Notch Visitor Center** (361 Rte. 16, 603/466-2721, www.outdoors.org, daily 6:30am-9pm, $1 for 3 minutes, quarters only).

For good access to the Cog Railway and hikes on the Crawford Notch side of Mount Washington, Crawford Notch State Park's **Dry River Campground** (2057 Rte. 302, Bartlett, 603/374-2272, www.nhstateparks.org, May-Oct., $25) is a good option, with 36 primitive sites, good bathroom facilities, and showers.

Under $150

Compare blisters with fellow travelers at the ★ **CoHo Hostel** (36 Washington St., Conway, 866/902-2521, www.cohohostel.com, dorms $42, private rooms $109), a super-friendly spot with a communal kitchen, comfortable common areas, and very clean (if rather plain) quarters. The six-bed dorms include female-only, male-only, and co-ed options, and the private rooms are an excellent choice for families; each has a full bed, and some have an additional twin or bunk bed.

Ten minutes from the center of North Conway by foot, the **Colonial Motel** (2431 Rte. 302, North Conway, 603/356-5178, www.thecolonialmotel.com, $59-99) offers simple but comfortable rooms in a two-story motor lodge alongside Route 302. The outdoor pool and some of the rooms offer surprising views of nearby Middle Mountain, and the seasonally variable rates are improbably reasonable for a motel that's steps away from NoCo's main commercial district. Don't count on any fancy amenities but do expect a reliable, affordable base camp for local exploration.

In addition to remote backcountry huts, the AMC runs a pair of front country lodges that are fun and convenient to trailheads—it's something of a hostel experience, but an especially good fit for families. The older of the two is **Joe Dodge Lodge** (Rte. 16, Pinkham Notch, 603/466-2727, www.outdoors.org, room with dinner and breakfast from $110 pp), where both private rooms and bunk rooms share bathrooms, and there's often a blazing fire in the living room and library. Meals are served family-style at big tables, and knowledgeable staff lead guided hikes and give talks on the natural world.

On the other side of Mount Washington is the newer **Highland Center Lodge** (Rte. 302, Crawford Notch, 603/466-2727, www.outdoors.org, room with dinner and breakfast from $125 pp), which has all the communal joys of Joe Dodge (fireplaces, friendly cafeteria), but with a few private bathrooms for those who prefer not to share sinks. If you're staying at the Highland Center, you get free access to the gear room, which has all the warm layers and hiking boots you need for tackling some peaks.

$150-250

With a central location in North Conway, the ★ **Red Elephant Inn Bed & Breakfast** (28 Locust Ln., North Conway, 603/356-3548, www.redelephantinn.com, $140-220) combines the best of a classic bed-and-breakfast—giant breakfast spread, a friendly atmosphere, and cozy common spaces—with the amenities and style of a more luxurious inn. Complementary afternoon wine and snacks are just the thing after a day spent on the trails, and the big library is stocked with local maps and books to read by the unheated outdoor pool. A hot drink and snack bar is available throughout the day for guests to help themselves, and rooms balance a warm wood-and-plaid White Mountains aesthetic with bits of art deco flair that keep things fresh and contemporary.

Elegant four-poster beds, colorful quilts, and fireplaces make the **Kearsarge Inn** (42 Seavey St., North Conway, 603/356-8700, www.kearsargeinn.com, $152-319) one of the more charming places to stay in the White Mountains. The inn is a restoration of one of the very first hotels in the White Mountains, which first opened its doors to travelers in the 1800s. Savor a cup of coffee or glass of wine from a lounge chair on the front porch, or stroll right into town for breakfast or dinner, as the inn is located in North Conway's most walkable district.

$250-350

Of the dozens of grand hotels that dotted the mountains at the turn of the 20th century, the red-roofed 1902 **Omni Mount Washington Resort** (Rte. 302, Bretton Woods, 800/843-6664 or 603/278-1000, www.mountwashingtonresort.com, $199-604) is the most perfectly preserved, and discovering the gorgeous historic touches throughout the building could easily occupy a rainy afternoon. The most desirable rooms are those facing the mountains, which get stunning sunrise views, but for trips during fall foliage season, book the front of the hotel, which looks across the valley at a slope crowded with flaming maple trees. Next door, the ski village of Bretton Woods offers recreational diversions like a zip line, golf courses, and riding stables. Even if you're not staying here, stopping by for a drink on the deck—or an utterly charming high tea in the Princess Room—is a wonderful experience, and a posh counterbalance to the White Mountains' rugged scenery. And if you do set up base camp here, be sure to venture outside to watch the stars from the outdoor fire pit or heated pool.

For a more rustic White Mountain lodging experience that still offers high comfort and style, make for the eastern edge of Crawford Notch State Park and spring for a woodland cabin at ★ **Alpine Garden** (1255 Rte. 302, Bartlett, 603/374-5154, www.alpinegardenglamping.com, $215-450). The menu of dwellings at this family-run "glampsite" includes not just cabins, but also an enormous treehouse and more compact, pod-like "Hobbit Homes." All of the structures include showers, mini-fridges, and fire pits, as well as a complimentary record player with a handful of thoughtfully selected vinyl LPs. (If you've never listened to *Led Zeppelin IV* in the middle of the White Mountain National Forest, you're in for a treat.) Steps away from the glamping area, there's a heated pool and an on-site winery, where the owners' son offers homemade wines and ciders under twinkling lights in the evenings.

Information

For everything in the White Mountain National Forest, the **Saco Ranger Station** (33 Rte. 112, Conway, 603/447-5448, Tues.-Sun. 8am-5pm, Mon. 9am-4:30pm) is the place to start. Brochures and maps of regional attractions can be found in many restaurants, hotels, and gas station stores throughout town.

Getting Around

While it's only really useful for longer, point-to-point hikes, the **AMC Hiker Shuttle** (www.outdoors.org, early June-Oct., $24) stops at trailheads throughout the mountains.

★ Kancamagus Highway

Between Conway and Lincoln, 35 miles (56 km) of tightly inscribed switchbacks, swooping valleys, and perfect mountain views make the Kancamagus Highway among the most iconic drives

Top to bottom: Alpine Garden accommodations; the Kancamagus Highway in early fall; Flume Gorge

in New England. Route 112, affectionately known as "the Kanc," rolls through the heart of White Mountain National Forest, following the twists and curves of the Swift River and climbing to almost 3,000 feet (914 m); at 2,855 feet (870 m), the Kancamagus Pass has fabulous views, especially when autumn turns the surrounding forest into a riot of color. A traverse of the Kanc can be anything from an hour-long scenic ride to a full day of exploring the waterfalls, overlooks, and trails that you'll find alongside the sidewinding, roly-poly highway.

Sights and Recreation

There are plenty of places to stop along the way on the Kancamagus Highway—look for clusters of cars along the side of the road, which often signals a favorite local swimming spot—including a series of scenic overlooks, hiking trails, and historic sites.

Driving from Conway to Lincoln, mile zero is at the White Mountain National Forest ranger station, making it easy to find landmarks along the way. Six miles (9.6 km) after leaving Conway, the **Boulder Loop Trail** is a moderate, three-mile (5.8-km) hike that takes 2-3 hours and has good views of rocky ledges and forest. A series of interpretive signs illustrates the geologic history, flora, and fauna of the White Mountains. At 7.0 miles (11.3 km), **Lower Falls** is a popular spot for swimming in the Swift River and has bathrooms and a picnic area near a small, scenic falls. You can peer into daily life in 19th-century New Hampshire at 12.7 miles (20.4 km) in the volunteer-run **Russell-Colbath House,** which is open when staff are available. It's small but free, and docents are happy to share the mysterious story of Thomas Colbath's years-long disappearance and possible reappearance.

Keep winding up to the **Kancamagus Pass,** which at 2,855 feet (870 m) is the highest point on the road, then you'll find the **Otter Rocks Rest Area** at 26 miles (42 km), with restrooms and a short trail to another lovely swimming area on the Swift River.

Camping

Six miles (9.6 km) west of Conway on the Kancamagus Highway are a pair of appealing campgrounds, the 49-site **Covered Bridge** (Rte. 112, 877/444-6777, mid-May-mid-Oct., reservations accepted, $25), as well as the smaller, walk-up only **Blackberry Crossing** (Rte. 112, 877/444-6777, mid-May-mid-Oct., $25).

The Franconia Range

An alpine backbone runs along this compact range from Mount Lafayette to Mount Flume, a 2.5-mile (4-km) sprint of rock with fabulous views. While the Presidential Range outdoes the highest of these by a cool 1,000 feet (305 km), the Franconia Range is just as rugged; there's no way to drive to the top of these mountains, so if you sweat to the top of Mount Lafayette, you won't need to share the view with crowds in flip-flops. Set dramatically between the Franconia Range and the Cannon Cliffs, Franconia Notch State Park runs along the Pemigewasset River, with easily accessible hiking trails to waterfalls, lakes, and a deep natural gorge.

The towns of Littleton and Franconia are the main bases for visiting Franconia Notch, and the road into the park is an especially dramatic one, twisting between high peaks. Franconia Notch itself is a bustling vacation spot, with an enormous campground, a lake with a swimming beach, a mountain tram, and trailhead after trailhead heading up into the hills.

Sights

Frost Place

From 1915-1920, Robert Frost lived in a small house with views of the mountains,

Franconia

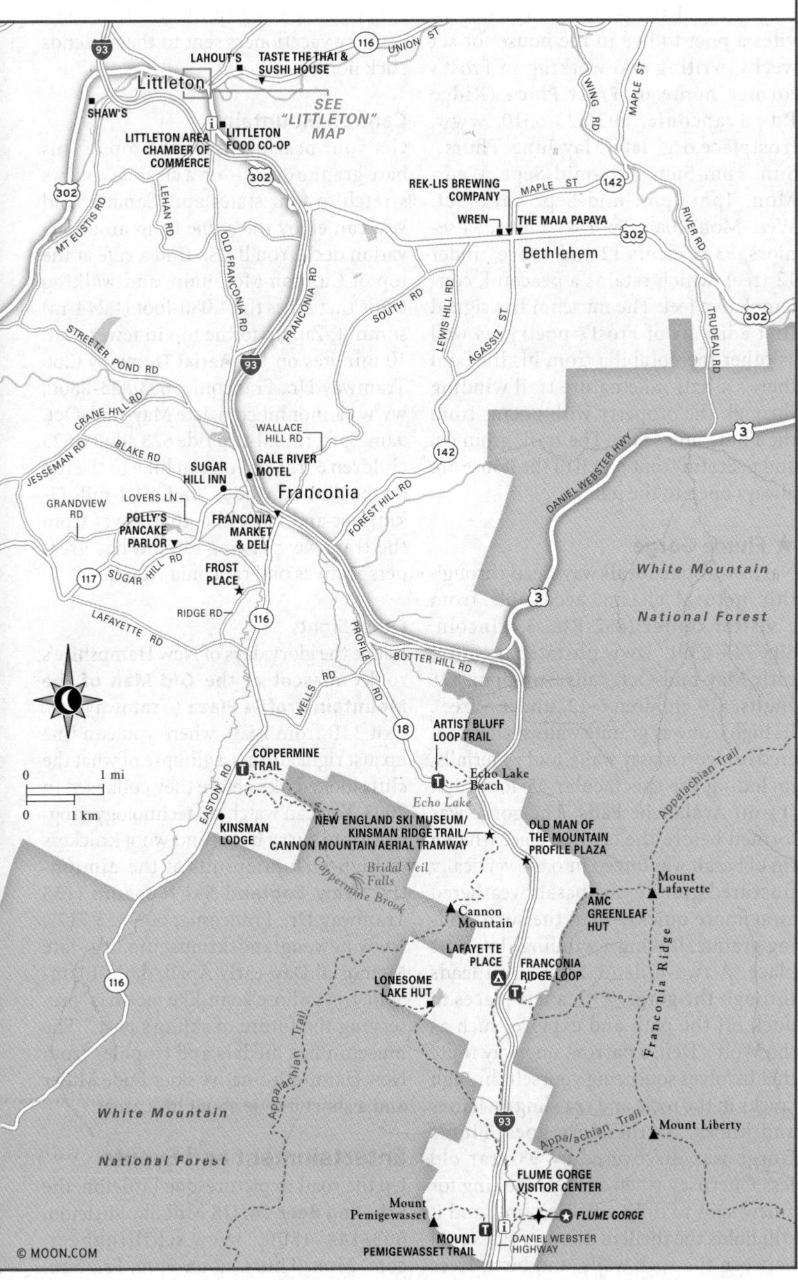
Littleton
LAHOUT'S
TASTE THE THAI & SUSHI HOUSE
SEE "LITTLETON" MAP
SHAW'S
LITTLETON AREA CHAMBER OF COMMERCE
LITTLETON FOOD CO-OP
UNION ST
MT EUSTIS RD
LEHAN RD
OLD FRANCONIA RD
FRANCONIA RD
SOUTH RD
LEWIS HILL RD
AGASSIZ ST
WING RD
MAPLE ST
RIVER RD
TRUDEAU RD
REK-LIS BREWING COMPANY
WREN
THE MAIA PAPAYA
Bethlehem
STREETER POND RD
CRANE HILL RD
JESSEMAN RD
BLAKE RD
WALLACE HILL RD
SUGAR HILL INN
GALE RIVER MOTEL
Franconia
FOREST HILL RD
DANIEL WEBSTER HWY
LOVERS LN
GRANDVIEW RD
POLLY'S PANCAKE PARLOR
FRANCONIA MARKET & DELI
SUGAR HILL RD
FROST PLACE
RIDGE RD
LAFAYETTE RD
PROFILE RD
BUTTER HILL RD
WELLS RD
White Mountain National Forest
ARTIST BLUFF LOOP TRAIL
COPPERMINE TRAIL
Echo Lake Beach
Echo Lake
EASTON RD
KINSMAN LODGE
NEW ENGLAND SKI MUSEUM/ KINSMAN RIDGE TRAIL/ CANNON MOUNTAIN AERIAL TRAMWAY
OLD MAN OF THE MOUNTAIN PROFILE PLAZA
Appalachian Trail
Bridal Veil Falls
Coppermine Brook
Cannon Mountain
Mount Lafayette
AMC GREENLEAF HUT
LAFAYETTE PLACE
FRANCONIA RIDGE LOOP
LONESOME LAKE HUT
Franconia Ridge
Mount Liberty
FLUME GORGE VISITOR CENTER
FLUME GORGE
Mount Pemigewasset
MOUNT PEMIGEWASSET TRAIL
DANIEL WEBSTER HIGHWAY
0 1 mi
0 1 km
© MOON.COM

and his spirit lives on at the secluded farmstead, now a museum and poetry center. Each year, the museum invites a poet to live in the house for six weeks, writing and working in Frost's former home of **Frost Place** (Ridge Rd., Franconia, 603/823-5510, www.frostplace.org, late May-June Thurs.-Sun. 1pm-5pm, July-mid-Sept. Wed.-Mon. 1pm-5pm, mid-Sept.-mid-Oct. Wed.-Mon. 10am-5pm, $5 adults, $4 seniors, $3 students 12 and above, under 12 free), which retains a peaceful, contemplative feel. The museum has signed first editions of Frost's poetry, as well as other memorabilia from his life, and there's a half-mile nature trail winding through the property with poems from the Franconia years. The trail, grounds, and peaceful front porch of the house are always open to the public.

★ Flume Gorge

Narrow wooden walkways lead through this natural chasm, accessible from a **visitor center** (852 Rte. 3, Lincoln, 603/745-8391, www.nhstateparks.org, early May-mid-Oct. daily 9am-5pm, $21 adults, $19 children 6-12, under 6 free). Its high Conway granite walls shelter covered bridges, mossy walls, and waterfalls, including the spectacular 45-foot-high (14-m) Avalanche Falls. The gorge was formed before the last Ice Age, when a fin of basalt was forced into the vertically fractured granite; the basalt weathered away more quickly than the surrounding granite, leaving a winding slot in its place. A two-mile (3.2-km) trail leads through the gorge, with a few places to duck off the path and explore, such as the Wolf's Den, a narrow, one-way route that involves squeezing yourself through cracks in the rock, and crawling on hands and knees. As the story goes, Flume Gorge was discovered by 93-year-old Jess Guernsey when she was looking for a new spot to drop a fishing line, and it still holds the thrill of discovery: It's cool between the rock walls, and birch trees worm out of stony cracks. Don't miss the visitor center's display case full of old-timey Flume Gorge postcards that 19th-century vacationers sent to their friends back home.

Cannon Mountain

Get your bearings from the top of this bare granite dome—on a clear day, views stretch to four states and Canada, and you can enjoy the scene from an observation deck. You'll also find a café at the top of Cannon Mountain, and walking trails that cross the 4,080-foot (1,244-m) summit. Zip up to the top in fewer than 10 minutes on the **Aerial Tramway** (260 Tramway Dr., Franconia, 603/823-8800, www.cannonmt.com, late May-mid-Oct. 9am-5pm, round-trip ride $28 adults, $23 children 6-12), or you can hike to the top on the **Kinsman Ridge Trail,** a 4.4-mile (7-km) out-and-back hike that leaves from the tramway parking lot and has great perspectives on Franconia Notch.

Other Sights

Relive the glory days of New Hampshire's rocky mascot at the **Old Man of the Mountain Profile Plaza** (Tramway Dr., Exit 34B from I-93), where you can line up just right and get a glimpse of what the cliffs looked like before they collapsed in 2003. You can watch ski technology progress from furry boots and wool knickers to high-tech jumpsuits at the diminutive **New England Ski Museum** (135 Tramway Dr., Franconia, 603/823-7177, www.newenglandskimuseum.org, late Memorial Day-early April, daily 10am-5pm, free) whose koan-like motto is "preserving the future of skiing's past." The museum has medals and trophies from New Hampshire-native skier Bode Miller and a short movie about his career.

Entertainment and Events

Up the road in picturesque Littleton, the **Schilling Beer Co.** (18 Mill St., Littleton, 603/444-4800, www.schillingbeer.com, Mon.-Thurs. noon-9pm, Fri.-Sun.

That's Weird. . .

The rocks of Coppermine Brook hide a mysterious relic.

The Coppermine Trail to Bridal Veil Falls, a gorgeous cascade just outside of Franconia, follows the Coppermine Brook up the haunches of Cannon Mountain. But the waterfall isn't the only star here. Affixed to a boulder along the brook is a **bronze plaque** that reads, "In Memory of Arthur Farnsworth, the Keeper of Stray Ladies." Farnsworth was an innkeeper from the area and the late husband of Hollywood icon Bette Davis, who met "Farny" while vacationing in New Hampshire. Rumor has it that Davis had the plaque installed on the boulder after Farnsworth suddenly died from a bad fall down some stairs at Butternut, the cottage that Davis kept in nearby Sugar Hill.

Today, the enigmatic plaque is a classic New England mystery that hikers will often hunt for on their way to the falls. (Look for it when the **Coppermine Trail** reaches the brook.) It speaks to the many characters and curious stories that have taken root around the White Mountains, and the trail itself is a wonderful day hike for families. From the trailhead, it's about one mile (1.6 km) to Coppermine Brook and 2.2 miles (3.5 km) to Bridal Veil Falls. The trail is steadily rocky and root-filled, but never steep, and the route includes wooden footbridges and even an old lean-to shelter where experienced hikers will sometimes bunk down for a night of mosquito swatting. Bridal Veil Falls also features one of the most pleasant swimming holes in the Whites: a shallow ovular pool at the foot of the 80-foot-tall (24-m) cascade. Dogs must be leashed, and the trail is not wheelchair accessible.

11am-9pm) brews small-barrel batches of European-style beers that range from more familiar Hefeweizens and pilsners to experimental IPAs and sours; on a recent summer afternoon, the family-owned brewery was pouring a toasty jet-black Schwarzbier, tart blackberry and currant gose, and crisp Japanese rice lager in a historic riverside barn.

The mountain meadows north of the notch are filled with violet blossoms every year in time for the **Lupine Festival** (603/823-8000, www.franconianotch.org, mid-June), a street festival and art show with events throughout the region. By governor's decree, each year in early July, Frost Place holds **Frost Day** (603/823-5510, www.frostplace.org), with readings of poetry by the poet-in-residence and musical performances at the farmstead. Littleton author Eleanor H. Porter created the super-chipper Pollyanna in a pair of children's novels, and the town has adopted the character as a kind of local mascot. The official **Pollyanna Glad Day** (https://gladdaynh.com, early June) celebrates her optimistic legacy with readings, awards, and festivities.

Shopping

Shopping in this area usually means picking up an extra layer for a hike, so stores lean more toward gear than souvenirs. But there are exceptions. In Littleton, stop by one of America's oldest ski and outdoor gear shops at **Lahout's** (245 Union St., Littleton, 603/444-5838, Mon.-Fri. 10am-5:30pm, Sat. 9:30am-5:30pm, Sun. 10am-4:30pm). Bethlehem, a cute little town five miles (8 km) down Route 302 from Littleton, has a supercool shop stocked with work by local artists and artisans, a worthwhile exception to the mostly gear rule; visit **WREN** (2011 Main St., Bethlehem, 603/869-9736, www.wrenworks.org, Mon.-Sat. 10am-5pm, Sun. 11am-4pm) to pick up truly local gifts, which are otherwise hard to find in the area.

Sports and Recreation

Beaches

Set just at the base of Cannon Mountain, **Echo Lake Beach** (Exit 34C, Franconia Notch State Park, 603/823-8800, $4 adults, $2 children 6-11, under 6 free) is sandy and scenic, with a lifeguard on duty during the day; it's possible to rent canoes, kayaks, and pedal boats here for $20/hour.

Hiking

For hikes in the area, stop by the hiker cabin at **Lafayette Place Campground** (Franconia Notch State Park, 603/823-9513, www.nhstateparks.org, daily 8am-3pm) for updated trail conditions, maps, and alpine weather reports—even when valley weather is blissful, the exposed alpine trail can get howling wind and whiteout fog. For the ultimate Franconia hike, plan for at least 6 hours on the 8.2-mile (13.1-km) **Franconia Ridge Loop,** a rugged New Hampshire classic that goes up and over three peaks: Little Haystack Mountain, Mount Lincoln, and Mount Lafayette. The trail starts on the east side of I-93, opposite Lafayette Place Campground, and starts straight up the fall line, climbing 3,480 feet (1,061 m) in around four miles (6.4 km), passing a series of scenic waterfalls on the way up Little Haystack. The ridgeline trail between Mount Lincoln and Mount Lafayette is a highlight, a knife-edge ridge that's all exposed rock and perfect views.

Earn your views with (somewhat) less work on the **Mount Pemigewasset Trail,** a moderate, 3.3-mile (5.3-km) out-and-back that takes roughly 2-3 hours to complete from the Flume Gorge Visitor Center parking lot. Much of the way is wooded and shady, and the trail crosses a series of pretty brooks, but the summit is bare rock, and though the mountain tops out at 2,557 feet (779 m), it feels like a real adventure. For more information on this hike, ask at the on-site visitor center.

Easy enough for younger children, the 1.5-mile (2.4-km) **Artist Bluff Loop Trail** looks out toward Cannon Mountain and Franconia Notch from the valley floor. To access the trailhead from Littleton or Franconia, take Exit 34C from I-93, then take Route 18 west for 0.5 mile (0.8 km), and park in the large lot on the right. This trail is particularly nice in early spring, when wildflowers bloom along the edge of Echo Lake, and hikers seeking a bit more of a challenge should be sure to scramble up to the summit of **Bald Mountain,** which is accessible via a short, steep spur path along the loop hike.

Food

Franconia

The elegant dining room at the **Sugar Hill Inn** (116 Rte. 117, Sugar Hill, 603/838-3229, www.sugarhillinn.com, reservations recommended, $20-34) has a refined menu that changes with the season, using plenty of fresh, local ingredients, some of which come from regional farms. A recent menu included duck confit with gingered cauliflower, horseradish-crusted beef tenderloin, and Idaho trout with morel mushrooms. On clear evenings, you can gaze out the window and see the nearby mountain summits bathed in a hazy reddish light—a naturally occurring optical phenomenon known as "alpenglow."

Two miles (3.2 km) west of Franconia, ★ **Polly's Pancake Parlor** (672 Rte. 117, Sugar Hill, 603/823-5575, www.pollyspancakeparlor.com, daily 7am-3pm, $10-15) serves legendary stacks of three-inch (2.5-cm) cakes with housemade maple syrup ("the fake stuff" is available on request, but it's sure to come with a tart helping of side eye). Buckwheat, cornmeal, and whole wheat flours are stone-ground on-site, and while some nostalgic visitors note that the newly renovated building doesn't have the down-home charm of the original, it has loads of seating, which reduces the impressive lines on weekend mornings.

Find basic groceries in Franconia at **Franconia Market and Deli** (347 Main St., Franconia, 603/823-2064, Mon.-Thurs. 6:30am-7pm, Fri.-Sun. 6:30am-8pm), which is small, but has beer, wine, and deli products.

Bethlehem

Housed in a colonial abode, right on the main drag in Bethlehem, **Rek-Lis Brewing Company** (2085 Main St., Bethlehem, 603/991-2357, www.reklisbrewing.com, Sun.-Tues. and Thurs. noon-9pm, Fri.-Sat. noon-10pm, $13-25) boasts a reliably diverse roster of craft brews. You can enjoy your juicy IPA or malty red ale in an Adirondack chair in their outdoor beer garden or on one of the benches nestled among the greenery and flowers around the building. The gastropub menu covers a wide spectrum of comfort food, from the buttermilk fried chicken sandwich with slaw and a fried dill pickle, to the seared scallops with cider buerre blanc.

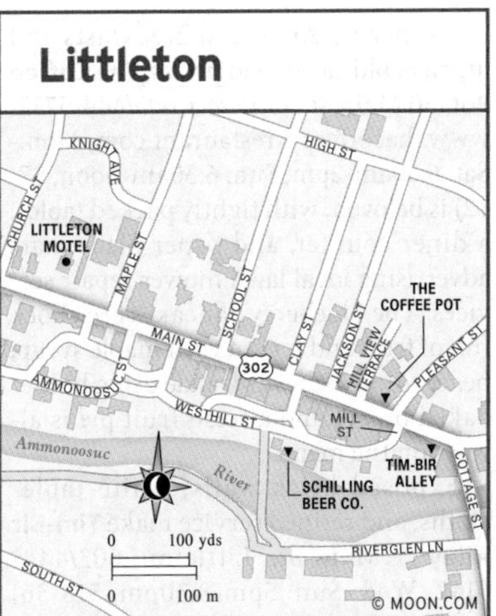

A favorite among locals for its potent coffee, fluffy pastries, and hearty vegetarian wraps and quiches is **The Maia Papaya** (2161 Main St./Rte. 302, Bethlehem, www.themaiapapaya.com, Thurs.-Mon. 8am-3pm, $6-15). The warm interior colors, leather seats, and in-house Wi-Fi also make this joint an inviting place to settle in for an hour or so and get some work done. You'll often find trail crews and AMC hut staff hunkered here, nursing lattes and checking their email before clomping back into the woods for another days-long shift in the backcountry.

Littleton

In addition to its brews, the **Schilling Beer Co.** (18 Mill St., Littleton, 603/444-4800, www.schillingbeer.com, Sun.-Thurs. noon-8pm, Fri.-Sat. noon-9pm, $7-22) serves Neapolitan-style pizza from a wood-fired oven, and when the riverside patio is open, it's easily the most scenic, relaxing place to eat in town. The patio also features an on-site food truck with juicy smash burgers and kraut-festooned bratwurst that would pass muster in Munich.

For hearty American breakfasts and lunch at old-fashioned prices, **The Coffee Pot** (30 Main St., Littleton, 603/444-5722, www.thecoffeepotrestaurant.com, Mon.-Sat. 6:30am-2pm, Sun. 6:30am-noon, $7-12) is beloved, with tightly packed tables, a diner counter, and paper place mats advertising local lawn mower repair services. The blueberry pancakes are chock full of fruit and served with maple syrup, hearty sandwiches are made using house-baked bread, and a fresh fruit pie is always on the menu.

Exposed brick walls, white tablecloths, and refined service make **Tim-Bir Alley** (7 Main St., Littleton, 603/444-6142, Wed.-Sun. 5pm-8:30pm, $18-36) easily the most romantic place to eat in Littleton, and the small, handwritten menu changes frequently to reflect the season. Skillet-roasted sirloin steak, grilled salmon burgers with kimchi, and shrimp and pea risotto were included on a recent summertime menu, and it's a genuine challenge not to fill up on the breadbasket full of fresh-baked biscuits and butter.

It takes serious culinary prowess to make classics like pad thai and green curry taste new again, imbued with a tantalizing spectrum of flavors, and that's the secret of ★ **Taste The Thai & Sushi House** (406 Union St., Littleton, 603/575-5488, www.tastethethaiandsushihouse.com, Thurs.-Tues. noon-9pm, $12-25). This humble-looking family restaurant whips up seriously tasty noodles, stir-fries, and chef specialties like crispy basil duck. The sushi menu is equally impressive, with a tempting selection of nigiri, sashimi, and hand rolls, and the weekday lunch specials served from noon to 2:30pm are great deals.

Stock up on groceries at **Shaw's** (625 Meadow St., Littleton, 603/444-1017, Mon.-Sat. 7am-10pm, Sun. 7am-9pm) or the **Littleton Food Co-op** (43 Bethlehem Rd., Littleton, 603/444-2800, https://littletoncoop.com, daily 7am-9pm), which has a very good selection of local and organic products, a bulk department, and prepared foods.

Accommodations and Camping

Camping

The sites at **Lafayette Place Campground** (1 Franconia Notch State Park, Franconia, 603/823-9513, www.nhstateparks.org, $25) are right in the heart of the action, with quick access to the trails and destinations within Franconia Notch State Park and hiker information on-site. The location also means the campground has quite a bit of road noise, contained by the high valley walls, but the 97 sites have showers, a camp store, and fire rings, and are ideal for an early start up the Franconia Ridge.

Under $150

Claiming the title of "oldest motel in New Hampshire," the **Littleton Motel** (166 Main St., Littleton, 603/444-5780, www.littletonmotel.com, May-Oct., $88-148, 2-bedroom suites $188-298) does have time-warp pine walls and floral bedspreads, but the friendly management has added welcome updates like in-room coffeemakers and fridges, Wi-Fi and cable television. There's a grill and fire pit on the grounds, and it's walking distance from downtown shops and restaurants—all in all, this clean, well-run place is an excellent value.

Find country hospitality at the ★ **Kinsman Lodge** (2165 Easton Rd., Franconia, 603/823-5686, www.kinsmanlodge.com, $70 s, $120 d), which Chet and Sue Thompson run with a minimum of fuss in a rambling historic building. Guest rooms share superclean bathrooms in the hallway, and the accommodations are simple but comfortable. After a hot day of hiking it's hard to beat a rocking chair on the broad, shady porch, or a seat in the library, which is stocked with books and games. A big "country style" breakfast is served in the sunny dining room.

Simple motel rooms and cottages have

The Places in Between: Evans Notch

ambling around The Basin in Evans Notch

The White Mountains are thought of as a New Hampshire destination, but they spill eastward into Maine. Right along the Maine-New Hampshire border, intrepid visitors will encounter Evans Notch. Located at the northeastern edge of the Whites, a 15-minute drive from Gorham (45 minutes from North Conway), this eerily quiet, craggy, and verdant valley that divides the Androscoggin and Saco Rivers is a lost world for outdoorsy folks who want to escape the crowds.

Whether it's paddling around the rippling waters of **The Basin** (Basin Rd., Chatham, 28.2 mi/45.4 km from North Conway, 22.2 mi/35.7 km from Gorham), braving the root-filled and rugged rim trail alongside the **Bickford Slides waterfalls** (Brickett Place, Stow, ME, 28.3 mi/45.5 km from North Conway, 21.9 mi/35.2 km from Gorham, $5 fee at the trailhead for day use), or huffing your way to the top of **Caribou Mountain** (Caribou/Mud Brook trailhead, 29.4 mi/47.3 km from North Conway, 16.1 mi/26 km from Gorham) for a panoramic view of three mountain ranges, serene outdoor recreation is what draws locals here each summer and fall.

Even the drive north on Route 113, up through the notch from North Conway, is worth a detour. It peaks at **Evans Notch Overlook,** one of the most dramatic vistas in the Whites. Picture the conclusion of *The Land Before Time,* when Littlefoot and his friends lay their eyes on the Great Valley, and you'll have a sense of how it feels to gaze into Evans Notch from the windy ledge: true wonder that this place somehow exists.

views of Mount Lafayette and Franconia Notch at **Gale River Motel** (1 Main St., Franconia, 603/823-5655, www.galerivermotel.com, rooms $95-200, cottages $180-250), where fairly basic accommodations are set on a six-acre (2.4-ha) property with a shuffleboard, pool, and barbecue area. Rooms have coffeemakers, fridges, wireless Internet, and televisions; the lobby always has fresh baked cookies, cocoa, and tea; and the friendly owner is happy to lend out a DVD player and board games. This motel attracts many guests with pets and kids.

$150-250

As in the wonderful restaurant on-site, lodgings at the **Sugar Hill Inn** (116 Rte. 117, Sugar Hill, 603/838-3229, www.sugarhillinn.com, $160-320) are full of well-polished rustic charm. Hardwood floors, luxurious iron frame beds, whirlpool tubs, fireplaces, and a private porch adjoined to several rooms are right in keeping with the inn's nostalgic, lodge-like feel. Chocolates, champagne, and flower arrangements are available for romantic getaways, hot stone massages are offered at the in-house spa, and breakfast in the dining room each morning includes house-made muffins, fresh fruit, and a rotating selection of entrees such as stuffed French toast or omelets with local cheddar and herbs.

Information and Services

The **Franconia Notch Chamber of Commerce** (603/823-2000, www.franconianotch.org), on I-93 just north of the notch, runs an unstaffed **information center** stocked with brochures, open 24 hours a day. The booth is right next door to the **Abbie Greenleaf Library** (439 Main St., Franconia, 603/823-8424, Mon. and Wed. 1pm-5:30pm, Tues., Thurs., and Sat. 10am-1pm, Fri. noon-3pm). In downtown Littleton, information is available at the **Littleton Area Chamber of Commerce** (260 Cottage St., Littleton, 603/444-6561, www.littletonareachamber.com, Tues.-Fri. 9am-4pm). Another good source of outdoors info is the hiker cabin at **Lafayette Place Campground** (Franconia Notch State Park, 603/823-9513, www.nhstateparks.org, daily 8am-3pm).

Getting Around

It's generally easy to find street parking in both Littleton and Franconia; neither town has public transit.

Southern
Vermont
1852
CLEARANCE
10' 6"

Highlights

★ **Billings Farm & Museum:** Experience Vermont's agricultural heritage with wagon rides, award-winning cheddar, and a picture-perfect herd of Jersey cows (page 216).

★ **President Calvin Coolidge State Historic Site:** Explore "Silent Cal's" rural roots at the president's boyhood home, then snack your way through the nearby cheesemaking factory (page 226).

★ **Following the Cheese Trail:** Sample award-winning cheddar and creamy chèvre along the Vermont Cheese Council's Cheese Trail (page 229).

★ **Apple Picking at Scott Farm Orchard:** Fill up on heirloom fruit and literary history at this stunning property, where Rudyard Kipling's Vermont home presides over rolling lanes of apple trees (page 232).

★ **Brattleboro's Gallery Walk:** Mingle with world-class artists, hippie farmers, and circus students at this monthly event, when Brattleboro throws open its doors to celebrate local art (page 234).

★ **Bennington Museum:** An excellent collection of work by folk artist Grandma Moses is just the beginning at this fascinating museum, whose exhibits trace the history of Bennington's Gilded Age industrialists and modernist movement (page 243).

Southern Vermont

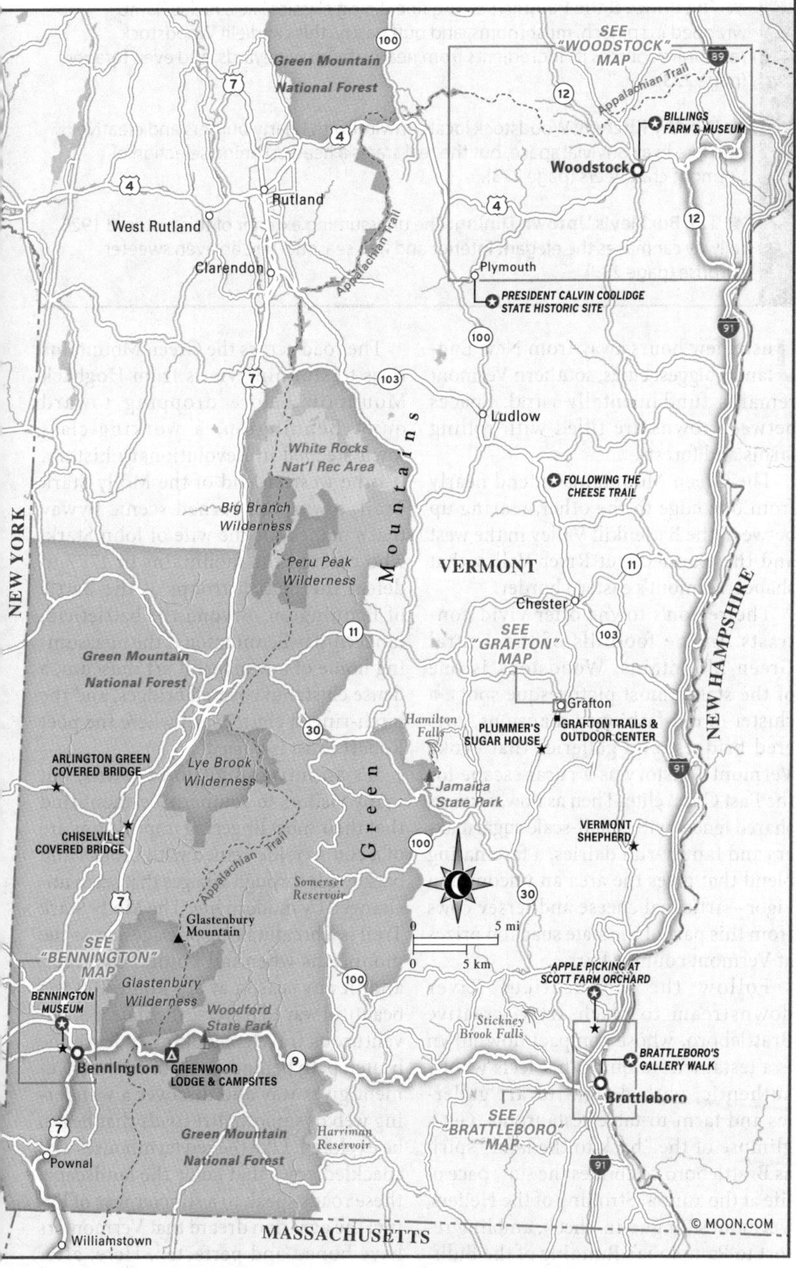

Best Restaurants

★ **The Prince & the Pauper:** Serving fine dining classics like a rack of lamb wrapped in spinach, mushrooms, and puff pastry, this candlelit Woodstock restaurant sources its ingredients from nearby farms, vineyards, and even foragers (page 223).

★ **Worthy Kitchen:** Woodstock locals unwind with hearty burgers and creative pub fare in a convivial space, but the real star is a head-spinning selection of Vermont craft beers (page 223).

★ **T. J. Buckley's Uptown Dining:** The unassuming exterior of this restored 1925 railway car makes the elegant interior and fine seasonal fare an even sweeter surprise (page 239).

Just a few hours away from New England's biggest cities, southern Vermont remains fundamentally rural. Spaces between towns are filled with rolling farms and forests.

The Green Mountains extend nearly from one edge to the other, rearing up between the Battenkill Valley in the west and the Connecticut River Valley that shapes Vermont's eastern border.

The region's towns offer vivid contrasts. In the foothills of the central Green Mountains, Woodstock is one of the state's most picturesque spots: a cluster of old-fashioned mansions, covered bridges, and galleries that evoke Vermont's history as a rural escape for the East Coast elite. Then as now, farmers shared fences with small-scale sugarmakers and family-run dairies, a fascinating blend that gives the area an uncommon vigor—artisanal cheese and Jersey cows from this part of the state snag top prizes at Vermont country fairs.

Follow the Connecticut River downstream to reach artsy, creative Brattleboro, whose compact downtown is a testament to quirk that feels wholly authentic, with delightful art galleries and farm-to-table restaurants. Get a glimpse of the "back to the land" spirit as Brattleboro celebrates the slow pace of life at the annual Strolling of the Heifers, Vermont's tongue-in-cheek, ambling retort to Pamplona's Running of the Bulls.

The road across the Green Mountains rises to stunning views from Hogback Mountain before dropping toward quiet Bennington, a working-class town steeped in Revolutionary history. It's the western end of the Molly Stark Trail, a warpath turned scenic byway that's named for the wife of John Stark, who crossed the mountains in 1777 to defeat the British troops at the Battle of Bennington. Beyond the battlefield, modern-day Bennington is the unassuming home of a wonderful art museum, a dense cluster of covered bridges, and the birch-ringed churchyard where the poet Robert Frost is buried.

It's an intriguing trio of towns, but many visitors to southern Vermont find that their most lingering impressions are of a countryside veined with brooks and back roads through villages that seem unchanged by modern life. The Molly Stark Trail is a breathtaking passage across the mountains when fall kindles the trees, and in any season at all, Route 100 is a beautiful way to traverse the state. For adventurous travelers looking to leave the beaten path behind, drive until the pavement gives way and discover a wandering web of smooth dirt roads that beg to be explored. Like the red farmhouses and speckled cows that color the landscape, these roads speak to a simpler way of living: the agrarian dream that Vermonters have honed and perfected. Here, after

Best Accommodations

★ **Jackson House Inn:** Start your day with a hearty, homemade breakfast made with locally sourced ingredients at this charming and historic bed-and-breakfast (page 225).

★ **Woodstock Inn & Resort:** Channel Vermont's county gentry at this elegant property on the village green, and unwind with afternoon teas, luxurious rooms, and an intriguing roster of posh activities (page 226).

★ **Greenwood Lodge & Campsites:** The fresh mountain air and hiking trails that surround southern Vermont's only hostel make this Green Mountain whistle-stop an appealing place to linger (page 247).

★ **Harwood Hill Motel:** A roadside motel meets local art and million-dollar views (page 247).

★ **Eddington House Inn:** After a day exploring Revolutionary battle sites and Robert Frost's Vermont digs, history buffs can relax in comfortable suites furnished with plush linens and beautifully curated antiques (page 249).

enjoying some lovingly made blue cheese or India pale ale, the natural thing to do is take a wildflowery stroll and contemplate the wonders of nature *and* human craftsmanship.

Planning Your Time

You could breeze through the slender southern end of Vermont in a day, but travelers who slow down to the pace of this area will discover back roads to explore, a fascinating rural culture, and endless spots to linger.

Orientation

Logical bases are Woodstock—a jewel-box village at the edge of the Green Mountains—and funky Brattleboro, Vermont's beguiling, pint-sized cultural mecca. They offer intriguing contrasts, and since they're just over an hour apart, it's easy to explore one or the other as a day trip, with a dozen ways to go from one to the other on scenic back roads. History-rich Bennington is right on the way for travelers continuing to the Berkshires from southern Vermont. It's also an easy day trip from Brattleboro across a classic mountain road lined with tempting lakes and sweeping views.

Getting to Southern Vermont

Driving from New Hampshire's White Mountains

80 mi/129 km, 1.5 hr

To get to **Woodstock** from **Franconia** (80 mi/129 km, 1.5 hrs), head out of town on **Route 18 North,** and take **Route 117 West** to **Route 302.** Turn left to merge onto **I-91 South,** and remain on it for about 40 miles (64 km). Exit to **I-89 North,** taking Exit 1 to **Route 4 West** into the center of town. For **Brattleboro,** remain on **I-91 South** for 101 miles (162.5 km), then take Exit 2 for **Route 9 East** into town (130 mi/209 km, 2.25 hrs).

For **Woodstock** from **Conway** (115 mi/185 km, 2.5 hrs), take the **Kancamagus Highway** (Rte. 112) west and remain on it for about 48 miles (77 km) before turning left onto **Route 116 West,** staying on it for 10 miles (16 km). Turn left onto **Route**

Two Days in Southern Vermont

With a couple of days to explore the area, stick to the eastern side of the Green Mountains and discover art, farms, and historic villages, with plenty of time to take the long way home.

Day 1

Enjoy a leisurely, maple syrup-drenched breakfast at one of Woodstock's gracious B&Bs, then head to **Billings Farm & Museum** to meet a beauty queen herd of Jersey cows, ride a hay wagon, and learn to churn your own butter. History buffs can continue next door to the well-preserved mansion at **Marsh-Billings-Rockefeller National Historical Park,** but if you're primed for more agricultural excitement, opt for a quick trip to **Sugarbush Farm** to learn about the sugarmaking process, and sample farm-made cheese and syrup.

Pick up some picnic supplies at the **Woodstock Farmers' Market** (a great place to sample local sugarmakers' syrups) store as you head back through town to **President Calvin Coolidge State Historic Site,** where outdoor tables have an idyllic view of "Silent Cal's" childhood home. Trace his path from the rural family homestead to the White House, then graze award-winning cheddar at nearby **Plymouth Artisan Cheese.**

Turn back up Route 100A toward Bridgewater Corners, where you'll toast Vermont's thriving beer scene at **Long Trail Brewing Company,** then spend the rest of the afternoon strolling Woodstock's art galleries and shops, or cooling off in an Ottauquechee River swimming hole. If you're feeling romantic, cozy up over regional Italian fare at itsy-bitsy **The Prince & the Pauper;** if not, join a friendly crowd of locals for craft beer and burgers at **Worthy Kitchen,** Woodstock's unofficial living room.

Day 2

Wake up early for a sunrise hike up **Mount Tom,** then hit the road to explore some of Vermont's most scenic byways. If you've already visited Plymouth Notch, the best way to Grafton is south on Route 106 to Route 10 and Route 35 South. Stroll through the perfectly preserved village center, and eat enough of the excellent aged cheddar at **Grafton Village Cheese Company** to keep you going to **Brattleboro,** where **Superfresh! Organic Café** is the perfect place to meet the locals over vegan grain bowls, "mylk," and hearty salads.

Use the café Wi-Fi to download a map of Brattleboro's latest **art gallery** exhibits, then visit the remarkable collections of fine arts, crafts, and photography in the walkable downtown. If it's apple-picking season (mid-Aug.-Oct.), trace the Connecticut River Valley north to Dummerston, where **Scott Farm Orchard** is a sublime place to fill your suitcase with a funky variety of apples, quince, and medlar.

Take I-91 all the way to Route 4 west so you can visit the tiny town of **Quechee.** Hike into Vermont's deepest gorge at **Quechee State Park,** then head to **Simon Pearce** to watch a team of expert glassblowers shape the elegant wineglasses for sale upstairs in the gallery showroom. Stay in Quechee for dinner—Simon Pearce has a beautiful on-site restaurant—or head back to Woodstock for a meal at **Richardson's Tavern,** an informal pub inside the elegant Woodstock Inn.

10 South, then right onto Newbury Road and left onto **Route 5 South.** You'll next turn right on South Main Street, left onto Mill Street, left again onto Old Creamery Road, and then right onto **Route 25 North.** Merge onto **I-91 South** and stay on it for about 28 miles (45 km). Exit to **I-89 North,** taking Exit 1 to **Route 4 West** into the center of town. For **Brattleboro,** remain on **I-91 South** for 88 miles (142 km), then take Exit 2 for **Route 9 East** into town (160 mi/257 km, 3 hrs).

Driving from Boston

115 mi/185 km, 2.25 hr

To get to **Brattleboro** from Boston (115 mi/185 km, 2.25 hrs), head out of town on **I-93 North,** then take Exit 31 for **Route 16 West,** using the second exit at the traffic circle for Alewife Brook Parkway before merging onto **Route 2 West.** Continue on Route 2 to **Greenfield,** then follow signs to merge onto **I-91 North.** Take Exit 1, and follow Canal Street into town.

To get to **Woodstock** from Boston, head out of town on **I-93 North** and stay on it for about 62 miles (100 km, $1 toll). Exit onto **I-89 North** for 65 miles (105 km), then take Exit 1 for **Route 4 West** (150 mi/241 km, 2.75 hrs).

Driving from the Berkshires

40 mi/64 km, 1 hr

Coming from the Berkshires, **Bennington** is a short and scenic drive north on **Route 7** from **Lenox** (40 mi/64 km, 1 hr), on a sweetly curving road across the Housatonic floodplain. Just north of Pittsfield, the road passes Pontoosuc Lake; turn left on **Hancock Road** for a pleasant sandy swimming beach.

To get to **Brattleboro** from **Stockbridge** (95 mi/153 km, 1.5 hrs), take **Route 102 East** to **I-90 East,** staying on it for 34.5 miles (55.5 km) ($2.75 toll). Take Exit 4 for **I-91 North,** remaining on it for about 52 miles (84 km) until **Exit 1,** and then follow Canal Street into town. Add 30 minutes and some appealing countryside views by taking the scenic route (80 mi/129 km, 2 hrs): Take **Route 7 North,** and continue on to **Route 8** to Searsburg, then turn onto **Route 9** for a rolling descent into the Connecticut River Valley.

For **Woodstock,** continue on **I-91 North** for **105 miles** (169 km) to **Exit 9,** turning left onto **Route 5 North** and continuing onto **Route 12 North.** Turn left onto **Route 4 West** into town (160 mi/257 km, 2.75 hrs).

It's worth leaving the highway for the stretch between Brattleboro and Woodstock; see *Getting to Woodstock* (page 226) and *Getting to Brattleboro* (page 242) for routes that trace some of the state's prettiest roads.

Driving from New York City

For travelers setting off from New York, the closest gateway to southern Vermont is Bennington. (Driving from New York to Brattleboro is not only farther but also much more congested with commuter traffic!) Leave New York City heading north on **FDR Drive.** Use the second from the right lane to continue north along **Harlem River Drive,** and take Exit 18 to cross the **Willis Avenue Bridge.** From here, use the left lane to take the ramp for **I-87 North** to Albany. Continue to Exit 5, where you'll merge onto **Route 100 North.** Drive for 1 mile (1.6 km) and then make a left to merge onto **Sprain Brook Parkway,** which you'll follow through the suburbs north of the city. The highway eventually becomes the **Taconic State Parkway,** which you'll continue following for another 100 miles (160 km).

Take Exit 102 in Chatham, turn left onto **Birge Hill Road,** and then make a right onto **Route 295 East,** which you'll follow for 6.8 miles (11 km) before making a slight left onto **Post Road** and then a hard left onto **Route 5.** Drive north along this road, turn right on **Route 20 East,** and after 2 miles (3.2 km), make another left onto **Route 22 North.** Continue through the countryside for 29 miles (47 km), turn right onto **Route 7,** and follow this final road east over the Vermont state line, where it becomes **Route 9** and continues into Bennington.

Getting There by Air, Train, or Bus

Air

It's easy to fly *near* to southern Vermont, but unless you packed your pilot's license, the region's postage-stamp airports won't be of much use. The largest selection of flights connects to Boston's **Logan International Airport** (BOS, www.massport.com/logan-airport), which is served by every major airline (3 hrs, 147 mi/236 km to Brattleboro, 2.5 hrs, 142 mi/228 km to Woodstock). Get a little bit closer by booking to **Bradley International Airport** (BDL, www.bradleyairport.com) in Hartford, Connecticut, which has nonstop flights to locations within the United States and Canada (1.25 hrs, 78 mi/125 km to Brattleboro; 2.25 hrs, 142 mi/228 km to Woodstock), or **Albany International Airport** (ALB, www.albanyairport.com, 1.75 hrs, 80 mi/129 km to Brattleboro; 2.5 hrs, 128 mi/206 km to Woodstock).

Train

Amtrak (800/872-7245, www.amtrak.com) offers service to Vermont from Washington DC that also passes through New York City and New Haven, Connecticut, on its way to Brattleboro, White River Junction, and the Burlington area. The aptly named **Vermonter** isn't the quickest (or cheapest) way to get into the Green Mountain State, but the trains have space for bicycles and excellent views (book bicycle spots in advance).

Bus

Greyhound (www.greyhound.com) has daily bus service between Brattleboro and Bennington, and all over New England.

Woodstock

With a bit of starch and a lot of history, this picture-book village is among the prettiest in New England. Rolling hills and farms are the perfect backdrop for Woodstock's covered bridges, elegant homes, and tiny town center. That "country gentleman" feel is no accident—this part of Vermont was a rural escape for some of the 19th-century's most affluent U.S. families, and names like Rockefeller, Billings, and Marsh continue to define today's landscape of historic inns, parks, and farms.

In part due to its carefully maintained past, Woodstock attracts transplants from urban areas around the East. This blend of new and old lends an unusual vitality to the small town, where upscale restaurants, art galleries, and boutiques cheerfully coexist with farm stores and a quirky "town crier," a community blackboard listing contra dances and church suppers. Nestled at the foot of the Green Mountains, Woodstock's surrounded by farms and breweries to visit, and endless back roads invite lazy drives with no destination. It's an alluring base for explorers who like to finish a day of adventure with white tablecloth dining and a well-curated wine list.

Sights

★ Billings Farm & Museum

One of Woodstock's most successful native sons was Frederick Billings, who made his money as a San Francisco lawyer in the heat of the gold rush. In the 1870s he returned to Woodstock and bought the old Charles Marsh Farm, which he transformed into a model dairy farm complete with imported Jersey cows. Today visitors to the grounds of the **Billings Farm & Museum** (53 Elm St., 802/457-2355, www.billingsfarm.org, late May-Oct. daily 10am-5pm, Nov.-Feb. Sat.-Sun. 10am-4pm, $17 adults, $15 seniors, $10 children 5-15, $4 children 3-4, under 3 free) can tour the property in wagons drawn by Percheron draft horses, meet the well-groomed herd of milking cows, and churn fresh cream into butter. The farm produces two varieties of cheddar from a herd of all Jersey cows: full-flavored and creamy sweet cheddar and butter cheddar that is slightly salty with a rich, melty texture.

Next door, **Marsh-Billings-Rockefeller National Historical Park** (54 Elm St., 802/457-3368, www.nps.gov/mabi, Memorial Day-Oct. daily 10am-5pm, free) is home to the mansion built by natural philosopher Charles Marsh during 1805-1807 and bought by Billings in 1861. The mansion, open for tours by advance reservation, has a Tiffany stained-glass window and an extensive collection of American landscape paintings. In 1934, Billings's granddaughter married Laurance Rockefeller, and they donated the land to the National Park Service in 1992. The main visitor center is the former Carriage Barn, which houses a permanent exhibit about conservation history, a reading library, and a bookstore.

Sugarbush Farm

Cows and other farm animals can be found at **Sugarbush Farm** (591 Sugarbush Farm Rd., 802/457-1757, www.sugarbushfarm.com, daily 9am-5pm), which produces excellent cheddar cheese and keeps their maple sugar shack open all year (though syrup is made between February and April). Set atop a scenic hill, the farm also produces maple syrup, mustards, and jams—all of which are free to sample. To get here, take a right across the covered bridge at the small village of Taftsville and follow the signs to the farm. Call ahead for road conditions in winter and early spring.

Dana House Museum

For a glimpse into Woodstock's nonagricultural past, visit the **Woodstock History Center** (26 Elm St., 802/457-1822, www.woodstockhistorycenter.org, June-mid-Oct. Mon.-Fri. 9am-4:30pm, free) and experience the Dana House, a federal-style home once owned by a prosperous local dry goods merchant. Now a museum run by the Woodstock Historical Society, it contains period rooms full of fine china, antique furniture, kitchen instruments, and children's toys.

Woodstock's Art Galleries

It's easy to visit the town's vibrant art galleries on foot, as they're in a compact cluster at the center of town, on Elm and Center Streets. Walk in the direction of the town green to reach **The Woodstock Gallery** (6 Elm St., 802/457-2012, www.woodstockgalleryvt.com, Mon.-Sat. 10am-5pm, Sun. 11am-4:30pm), where the imagery is closer to home. Fine and folk artists offer their takes on the New England landscape and other themes, and the gallery stocks a good selection of work by **Victoria Blewer,** a prolific Vermont artist who hand colors her own black-and-white photography to give the Vermont landscape an otherworldly sheen.

Turn left on Center Street for a short stroll to **Collective—the art of craft** (46 Central St., 802/457-1298, www.collective-theartofcraft.com, Mon.-Sat. 10am-5pm, Sun. 11am-4pm), where a small group of local artists and artisans display their work in an old stone mill. Handwoven fabrics, blown glass, pottery, woodwork and metal work are of a remarkably high quality.

Make a U-turn (or, as they say in these parts, bang a uey) and head back up the street to **Gallery on the Green** (1 The Green, 802/457-4956, www.galleryonthegreen.com, Tues.-Wed. and Fri.-Sat. 10am-5pm, Sun. 11am-3pm), which has an extensive collection of sweetly pastoral paintings by Chip Evans, as well as other fine examples of the New England "red barns and Holsteins" genre.

Woodstock Town Crier

Vermont, with its gregarious yet tranquil small towns, can feel like an escape from the digital cacophony of today. But nothing quite exemplifies this like the **Woodstock Town Crier** (6 Elm St.). Erected on a grassy plot near the center of town, this message board dates back to the colonial New England era, when locals would use chalk to scrawl anything they wanted to amplify on the Crier, from upcoming church worship services to missing livestock notices and alchemy class advertisements. And just as Vermont embraces its historic ways, the Woodstock Town Crier remains an active community board today, festooned with writings and offerings from those

Woodstock

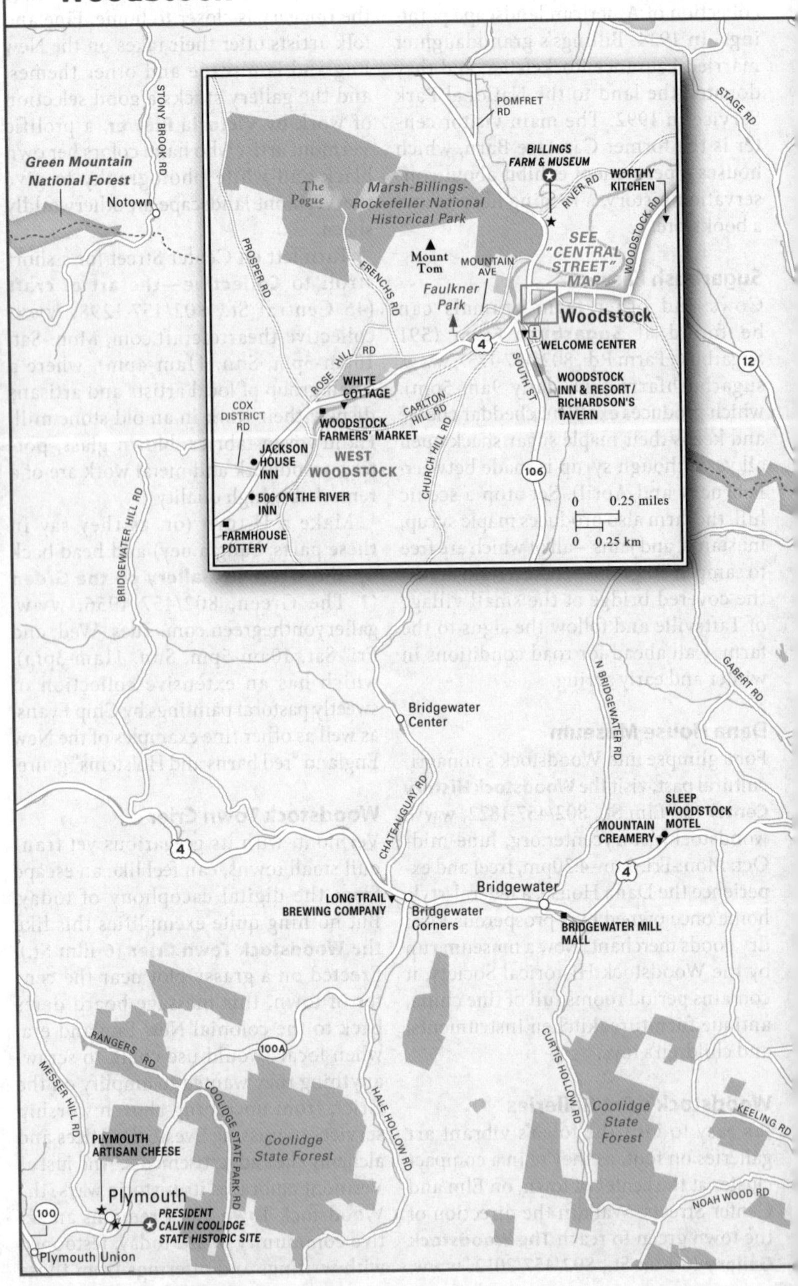

Green Mountain
National Forest
Notown
STONY BROOK RD
The Pogue
Marsh-Billings-
Rockefeller National
Historical Park
Mount
Tom
MOUNTAIN
AVE
Faulkner
Park
POMFRET
RD
BILLINGS
FARM & MUSEUM
RIVER RD
WORTHY
KITCHEN
STAGE RD
WOODSTOCK RD
SEE
"CENTRAL
STREET"
MAP
Woodstock
WELCOME CENTER
PROSPER RD
FRENCHS RD
ROSE HILL RD
4
SOUTH ST
12
WHITE
COTTAGE
COX
DISTRICT
RD
WOODSTOCK
FARMERS' MARKET
CARLTON
HILL RD
WOODSTOCK
INN & RESORT/
RICHARDSON'S
TAVERN
JACKSON
HOUSE
INN
WEST
WOODSTOCK
CHURCH HILL RD
106
506 ON THE RIVER
INN
FARMHOUSE
POTTERY
0 0.25 miles
0 0.25 km
BRIDGEWATER HILL RD
N BRIDGEWATER RD
GABERT RD
Bridgewater
Center
CHATEAUGUAY RD
SLEEP
WOODSTOCK
MOTEL
MOUNTAIN
CREAMERY
Bridgewater
LONG TRAIL
BREWING COMPANY
Bridgewater
Corners
BRIDGEWATER MILL
MALL
RANGERS RD
100A
MESSER HILL RD
COOLIDGE STATE PARK RD
HALE HOLLOW RD
CURTIS HOLLOW RD
Coolidge
State
Forest
KEELING RD
PLYMOUTH
ARTISAN CHEESE
Coolidge
State Forest
NOAH WOOD RD
Plymouth
100
PRESIDENT
CALVIN COOLIDGE
STATE HISTORIC SITE
Plymouth Union

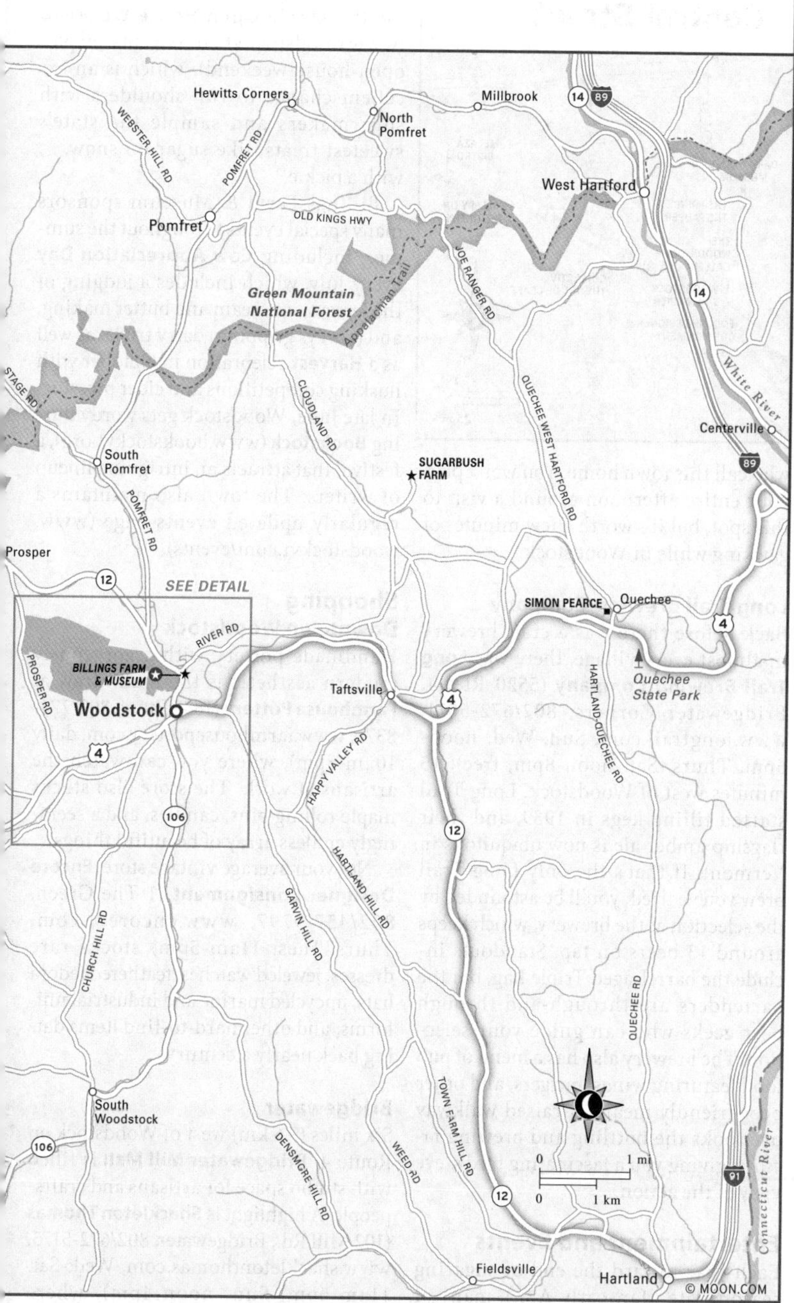
Hewitts Corners
Millbrook
North Pomfret
WEBSTER HILL RD
POMFRET RD
West Hartford
Pomfret
OLD KINGS HWY
JOE RANGER RD
Green Mountain National Forest
Appalachian Trail
STAGE RD
CLOUDLAND RD
QUECHEE WEST HARTFORD RD
White River
Centerville
South Pomfret
SUGARBUSH FARM
POMFRET RD
Prosper
SEE DETAIL
SIMON PEARCE
Quechee
RIVER RD
BILLINGS FARM & MUSEUM
Quechee State Park
PROSPER RD
Taftsville
Woodstock
HAPPY VALLEY RD
HARTLAND-QUECHEE RD
HARTLAND HILL RD
GARVIN HILL RD
CHURCH HILL RD
QUECHEE RD
TOWN FARM HILL RD
South Woodstock
DENSMORE HILL RD
WEED RD
0
1 mi
0
1 km
Connecticut River
Fieldsville
Hartland
© MOON.COM

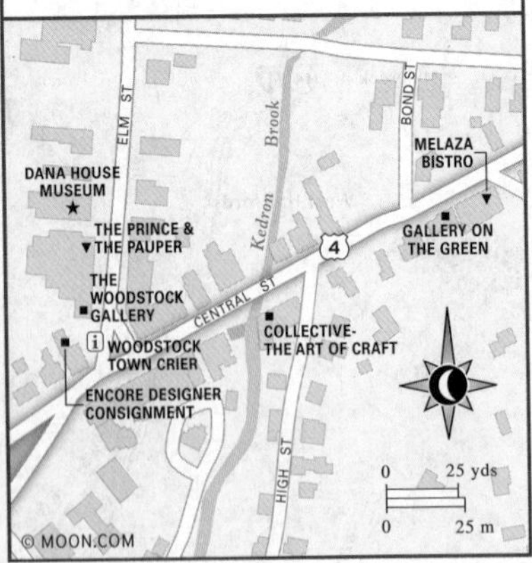

who call this town home. You won't plan your entire afternoon around a visit to this spot, but it's worth a few minutes of gawking while in Woodstock.

Long Trail Brewing Company

Back before there was a craft brewery in almost every village, there was **Long Trail Brewing Company** (5520 Rte. 4, Bridgewater Corners, 802/672-5011, www.longtrail.com, Sun.-Wed. noon-6pm, Thurs.-Sat. noon-8pm, free), 15 minutes west of Woodstock. Long Trail started filling kegs in 1989, and their flagship amber ale is now ubiquitous in Vermont. If that's the only Long Trail brew you've tried, you'll be astounded by the selection at the brewery, which keeps around 13 beers on tap. Standouts include the barrel-aged Triple Bag, but the bartenders are through-and-through beer geeks who can guide your selection. The brewery also has a menu of pub food featuring wings, burgers, and other beer-friendly meals. A raised walkway overlooks the bottling and brewing facility, giving you a fascinating bird's-eye view of the action.

Entertainment and Events

Each year toward the end of sugaring season (late Mar.-early Apr.), many of Vermont's sugarhouses open their doors for the **Maple Open House Weekend** (www.woodstockvt.com/events/maple-open-house-weekend), which is an excellent chance to rub shoulders with sugarmakers and sample the state's sweetest treats, like sugar on snow. . . with a pickle.

Billings Farm & Museum sponsors many special events throughout the summer, including **Cow Appreciation Day** every July, which includes a judging of the Jerseys, ice cream and butter making, and (always gripping) dairy trivia, as well as a **Harvest** celebration in October with husking competitions and cider pressing. In late June, Woodstock gets wordy during **Bookstock** (www.bookstockvt.org), a festival that attracts an intriguing lineup of writers. The town also maintains a regularly updated events page (www.woodstockvt.com/events).

Shopping

Downtown Woodstock

Handmade pottery with a gorgeously modern aesthetic is the main draw at **Farmhouse Pottery** (1837 Rte. 4, 802/774-8373, www.farmhousepottery.com, daily 10am-5pm), where you can watch the artisans at work. The store also stocks maple rolling pins, candles, and a seemingly endless array of beautiful things.

Not your average vintage store, **Encore Designer Consignment** (1 The Green, 802/457-9797, www.encorevt.com, Thurs.-Tues. 11am-5pm) stocks rare dresses, jeweled watches, feathered fedora hats, upcycled marine and industrial uniforms, and other hard-to-find items dating back nearly a century.

Bridgewater

Six miles (9.6 km) west of Woodstock on Route 4, **Bridgewater Mill Mall** is filled with studio space for artisans and craftspeople. A highlight is **Shackleton Thomas** (102 Mill Rd., Bridgewater, 802/672-5175, www.shackletonthomas.com, Wed.-Sat. 11am-5pm, Sun. noon-4pm), where

Charles Shackleton—a distant relation of Antarctic explorer Ernest Shackleton—crafts simple but elegant Shaker and modern-style furniture. It's fascinating to watch the woodcarvers, who train for years, and the display room is stocked with eclectic gifts with unusual charm.

Quechee

Even if you're not in the market for their high-end glassware, **Simon Pearce** (1760 Main St., the Mill at Quechee, 802/295-1470, www.simonpearce.com, Mon.-Tues. 10am-4pm, Wed.-Sat. 10am-5pm) is a fascinating stop that's seven miles (11 km) east of Woodstock in the village of Quechee. Located in an old mill building run entirely by hydroelectric power, the studio is open to the public, who can watch glassblowers blow bubbles into glowing orange balls of 2,400-degree silica. It's an extraordinary sight, especially the way multiple craftspeople coordinate individual components of a delicate wineglass with precise timing and handiwork. If they slip up, of course, that's one more glass for the shelf of perfect-seeming "seconds," which are available for purchase at somewhat lower prices.

Sports and Recreation

Hiking

In addition to the exhibits at **Marsh-Billings-Rockefeller National Historical Park** (54 Elm St., 802/457-3368, www.nps.gov/mabi, Memorial Day-Oct. daily 10am-5pm, free), the preserve has 20 miles (32 km) of walking trails, which are accessible from the park entrance on Route 12 and a parking lot on Prosper Road. The roads circle around the slopes of Mount Tom, which is forested with old-growth hemlock, beech, and sugar maples. Popular hikes include the 0.7-mile (1.1-km) loop around the mountain pond called **The Pogue** and the gentle,

Top to bottom: Billings Farm & Museum; feeding the cows at Billings Farm & Museum; downtown Woodstock

1-mile (1.6-km) climb up to the **South Summit** of Mount Tom, which lords over Woodstock and the river below. No mountain bicycles are allowed on the trails; in the winter, they are groomed for cross-country skiing.

It's also possible to walk 2.75 miles (4.4 km) round-trip to the summit of **Mount Tom** starting at the centrally located **Middle Covered Bridge** on Mountain Avenue. Cross the bridge and follow Mountain Avenue as it curves around to the left along a rock wall. An opening in the rock wall leads to the **Faulkner Trail** at Faulkner Park, where it begins to switchback up the gentle south flank of the peak. The last 300 feet (91 m) of the trail get a bit steeper, giving wide views of the Green Mountains. Allow an hour for the hike.

East of Woodstock's town green 7.7 miles (12.4 km), **Quechee State Park** (5800 Woodstock Rd., Hartford, 802/295-2990, www.vtstateparks.com/quechee.html, May 14-Oct. 17, $5) has a pleasant 2.2-mile (3.5-km) round-trip trail into Vermont's deepest gorge, starting at the informative visitor center. The **Quechee Gorge Trail** hike takes about an hour.

Swimming

There's an actual swimming pool inside the **Woodstock Recreation Center** (54 River St., 802/457-1502, https://woodstockvt.myrec.com, Mon.-Fri. 6am-8pm, Sat. 8am-1pm, Sun. 9am-noon), but the real treat is a dip in the **Ottauquechee River.** There's a short path that leaves from right behind the Rec Department, descending to a gentle swimming area that's suitable for families.

Food

Dining on mostly fried, salty fare at a "snack bar" is a quintessential summer experience in Vermont, and **White Cottage** (863 W. Woodstock Rd., 802/457-3455, May-Oct. daily 11am-10pm, $4-25, cash only) is a fine place to get your fix. Golden mounds of fried

Quechee Gorge

clams come with tartar sauce and lemon, maple creemees are piled high on sugar cones, and hamburgers are simple and to-the-point. Snack bar food doesn't vary much from place to place, but White Cottage's outdoor tables, riverside location, and friendly staff make it a favorite—and you can wade in the river while you wait for your order.

Pick up supplies at the confusingly named **Woodstock Farmers' Market** (979 W. Woodstock Rd., 802/457-3658, www.woodstockfarmersmarket.com, Tues.-Sun. 9am-6pm), which turns out to be a specialty food shop that stocks plenty of locally made treats, cheese, beer, wine, and everything else you might need for a showstopping picnic on the road.

Great piles of pancakes and home fries make **Mountain Creamery** (33 Central St., 802/457-1715, www.mountaincreameryvt.com, Thurs.-Tues. 7am-3pm, $7-15) a breakfast favorite in downtown Woodstock, and many of the ingredients come from the owners' Killington farm. When local fruit is ripe, don't miss the "Mile High Apple Pie."

Sedate and sophisticated, ★ **The Prince & The Pauper** (24 Elm St., 802/457-1818, www.princeandpauper.com, Tues.-Sat. 5pm-8pm, $38-75) serves fine dining classics—don't miss the restaurant's signature carré d'agneau royale, a tender dish of lamb, spinach, and mushrooms wrapped in puff pastry—in a candlelit country setting. Think high-backed wooden booths, exposed beams, and local art for sale on the wall. It's an ideal date setting, though families and groups are also welcome. The menu pairs fine dining classics like magret of duck with cardamom currant sauce with bistro-style comfort foods such as creamy cheddar ale onion soup.

If you've had enough of Woodstock's white tablecloth scene, you may be ready for a meal at the relaxed and convivial ★ **Worthy Kitchen** (442 E. Woodstock Rd., 802/457-7281, www.worthyvermont.com, Thurs.-Fri. 4pm-9pm, Sat.-Sun. 11:30am-9pm, $16-25), a "farm diner" that has a hearty selection of pub food with flair, from loaded burgers to poutine. Steak frites, mac and cheese, and maple bacon wings are other favorites, and there's an excellent beer selection.

Scope out the elegant digs at the Woodstock Inn & Resort on your way into **Richardson's Tavern** (14 The Green, 888/338-2745, www.woodstockinn.com, Fri.-Mon. 5pm-9pm, $17-31), which offers an appealing blend of pub fare and hearty, grown-up options. Tuck into seafood stew with sourdough crostini, a lamb flatbread, or smashed papas bravas with lemon aioli in a cozy, dimly lit booth; on chilly fall evenings, arrive early to snag a prime table by the open fireplace.

For a vivacious escape from traditional North Country cooking, step into the softly lit dining room at **Melaza Bistro** (71 Central St., 802/457-7110, www.

Local Legend

Vermont is the largest producer of maple syrup in the country—roughly 2.2 million gallons (8.3 million liters) in 2019 alone! But the flavors and applications of Vermont maple go well beyond the breakfast table. Just ask **Allison Hope,** executive director of the Vermont Maple Sugar Makers' Association, founded in 1893. The state of Vermont employs a grading system to classify maple syrups based on flavor and hue, and Hope is more than happy to give newcomers a crash course in her state's sweetest export.

Allison Hope

Let's talk about the grading system for Vermont maple syrup. What should first-time Vermont visitors know about this?

We have four grades. They start with the lightest in color and taste, and they move down to darker colors and deeper flavors. Of course, these things vary slightly, season to season—sometimes Mother Nature does what she wants—but the system goes like this:

- Grade A Golden Color maple is the most delicately flavored, almost like vanilla. This used to be considered the fanciest type of syrup. If you had waffles or even ice cream that you wanted to add syrup to, this used to be the go-to grade. It's usually made toward the beginning of syrup season, in March.

- Grade A Amber Color, which a lot of folks prefer these days, has a more noticeable maple flavor. You'll notice this with syrup grades: As they darken, they'll taste more

melazabistro.com, Fri.-Tues. 5:30pm-8:30pm, $15-29) and tuck into an inspired menu of amply portioned Caribbean-inspired fare like Jamaican jerk chicken with sweet plantains and Spanish rice, or the guava-glazed roast pork shank. The meats and produce might be Vermont-sourced, but the flavors here are downright tropical—especially the house mojitos and rum punch.

Accommodations and Camping

Woodstock has some of the most appealing accommodations in the state. Prices tend to be higher than elsewhere and rise dramatically during peak foliage season, while off-season prices may be significantly lower than those listed.

Camping

Quechee State Park (5800 Woodstock Rd., Hartford, 802/295-2990, www.vtstateparks.com/htm/quechee.html, May 14-Oct. 16, $5) has some excellent spots for river **swimming** near a bustling, friendly **campground,** with lean-tos and 45 RV and tent sites along a forested loop (tents $28-30, lean-tos $38-40).

Under $150

There's nothing fancy about **Sleep Woodstock Motel** (4324 West Woodstock Rd., 802/332-6336, www.sleepwoodstock.com, $118-208), but it's friendly, the rooms are clean and comfortable, and you can use the extra cash for cheddar cheese. This is Woodstock's only budget

maple-y. If you're making frosting and the recipe calls for artificial maple flavoring, don't do it! Instead, try using amber syrup. You could even boil it down to bring out the maple flavor even more.

- Grade A Dark Color will have a significantly more robust sweetness. This is what I'll sometimes use if I'm baking something that needs to have a stronger heft of maple flavoring.

- Grade A Very Dark Color is on the verge of being like molasses. Commercial cooks who are making food on a large scale will often use this. It's not what I'd choose to put on my pancakes.

Then, you've got Vermont sugarmakers who are doing things that are outside the grade system. Infused syrups, with everything from mint to food-grade glitter, are being made across the state. Some sugarmakers will buy wooden barrels that were used to store bourbon and they'll put the syrup in there and let it sit and absorb the bourbon flavors.

What are some of your favorite outside-the-box ways to utilize maple syrup?

I put it in my pizza dough. When you want your yeast to eat a little sugar to froth up and proof, a tablespoon of maple syrup is perfect for that. Or, if you want a nice appetizer, you can take some maple syrup and mix it with some goat cheese until it's nice and creamy enough to spread on a piece of baguette or a cracker. Vermont maple is a wonderful sweetener for Vietnamese-style peanut sauce. My favorite salad dressing is equal parts Dijon mustard, balsamic vinegar, and maple syrup. You put that in a mason jar—no oil necessary—and just shake it up. And I would be remiss if I didn't mention all the ways Vermont maple is used in Vermont craft beer! One of my favorites is the "breakfast stout" from 14th Star Brewing. It has the most subtle hint of syrup. You can find it in stores all over the state.

You can find a robust selection of Vermont maple syrups at weekly farmers markets like the **Brattleboro Farmers' Market** (page 240).

offering, and the roadside motel evokes another era of travel: It was built in 1959, and as the owners renovate, they're adding flourishes with retro style. The motel is a short drive west of the center.

$150-250

Elegant, well-appointed rooms at the ★ **Jackson House Inn** (43 Senior Ln., 802/457-2065, www.jacksonhouse.com, $196-285) manage to avoid fussiness. Quarters in the main house are somewhat more in keeping with the old-fashioned style of the place, but new additions come with perks like massage tubs. Each one is different, so peek into a few before making your choice. The crackling fire is an appealing place to thaw, but in summer months the broad porch entices. The congenial owners, Rick and Kathy, are devoted to local food, and Rick prepares sumptuous breakfasts with ingredients from area farms.

The **506 on the River Inn** (1653 Rte. 4, 802/457-5000, www.ontheriverwoodstock.com, $219-389) was renovated in 2014 and has an appealingly chic take on Woodstock's genteel country style. Throw pillows are emblazoned with folksy Vermont expressions, antiques are used with restraint, and welcome extras include a game room, library, and toddler playroom. Breakfast is well prepared and lavish, served in a dining room and bar that open to the public at night. The inn's bistro menu covers classed-up pub food and child-friendly diner standbys like mac and cheese.

Over $350

You can't miss the elegant ★ **Woodstock Inn & Resort** (14 The Green, 888/338-2745, www.woodstockinn.com, $350-725), which dominates the green in the heart of the village. The rooms and facilities are some of the prettiest in Vermont, full of thoughtful touches and design. This location has been a tourist destination since a tavern with accommodations was established in 1793, but Laurance Rockefeller built the current structure in the 1970s. There are seemingly endless facilities: spa, fitness center, cruiser bikes for exploring the town, organic gardens, and a celebrated 18-hole golf course. You can take courses on farming and falconry, or just watch the weather from the glassed-in conservatory.

Information and Services

The **Woodstock Area Chamber of Commerce** (802/457-3555, www.woodstockvt.com) runs a **welcome center** (3 Mechanic St., Mon.-Fri. 9am-5pm) and an information booth (on the green). ATM machines are conveniently located in town at **M&T Bank** (2 The Green, 802/457-2660, Mon.-Thurs. 8:30am-5pm, Fri. 8:30am-5:30pm) and **Citizens Bank** (431 Woodstock Rd., open 24 hours). In an emergency, contact the **Woodstock Police** (454 Rte. 4, 802/457-1420).

Getting Around

Getting to Woodstock

To get to Woodstock from **Brattleboro** (70 mi/113 km, 1.25 hrs) head up I-91 North to Exit 9 to Route 12 North, then turn left onto Route 4 East. **Scenic versions** of this route are almost endless; one option follows Route 30 North to Route 35 North into **Grafton,** then traces Route 103 North to Route 100 to **Plymouth** and continues onto Route 100A North and Route 4 East (75 mi/120 km, 2 hrs). Alternately, leave town heading west on the winding Route 9 to **Wilmington,** and take Route 100 North all the way through the mountains to Plymouth, before continuing onto Route 100A North and Route 4 East (100 mi/160 km, 2.5 hrs).

Getting Around Woodstock

Most of Woodstock's main attractions are clustered in the small town center, but a number of inns are on Route 4 (also known as W. Woodstock Rd.), which winds west from the Town Green along the Ottauquechee River.

Parking in the village is metered Monday-Saturday 10am-4pm, but it's often possible to find free parking on the west side of town. Woodstock also has an unusual parking validation policy—if you get a ticket in a metered spot, you can bring it to any merchant or restaurant, who can validate it (cancel it) for free.

Plymouth Notch

Tucked into a lush, intimate valley, Plymouth Notch doesn't seem to have changed much since President Calvin Coolidge took office in 1923. The family homestead has been scrupulously maintained, and the nearby state park has miles of hiking trails. Despite being near to one of the state's most important historic sites, Coolidge State Park tends to be overlooked by summer crowds, making it an excellent place to find a trail to yourself. There are only limited services—and no restaurants, so plan on eating in nearby Woodstock.

★ President Calvin Coolidge State Historic Site

One of the best presidential historic sites in the country, the **President Calvin Coolidge State Historic Site** (3780 Rte. 100A, 802/672-3773, www.historicsites.vermont.gov/calvin-coolidge, late May-mid-Oct. Tues.-Sun. 10am-5pm, office exhibits only Mon.-Fri., $12 adults, $4 children 6-14, under 6 free, $30 family pass) is situated on the grounds of the 30th president's boyhood home, a sprawling collection of houses, barns, and factories in a mountain-ringed valley. The exhibits inside give a rare intimate look into the upbringing of the president who was known as "Silent Cal" for his lack of emotion, but who restored the dignity of the office during a time of widespread scandal. The family parlor preserves the spot where Coolidge was sworn into office—by his father, a notary public. Even in 1924, when Calvin Coolidge ran for reelection, the homestead swearing-in must have seemed like a scene from a simple, earlier time—one radio campaign ad described it in heavily nostalgic terms, pitching Cal as a rustic counterpoint to Washington DC's modernity and urban sophistication.

Nearby **Plymouth Artisan Cheese** (106 Messer Hill Rd., 802/672-3650, www.plymouthcheese.com, daily 11am-4pm) was founded in 1890 by John Coolidge, Calvin Coolidge's father. Their granular curd cheeses were once relatively common in the United States, but are now rare. Learn about the cheesemaking process at the on-site museum, then sample everything from squeaky-fresh cheese curds to granular aged cheeses that have been hand-dipped in wax.

Sports and Recreation

Travelers who packed their gold panning kits can prospect for nuggets in **Coolidge State Park** (855 Coolidge State Park Rd., 802/672-3612, www.vtstateparks.com/coolidge.html, Memorial Day weekend-early Oct., $5), which was at the epicenter of the (very) short-lived Vermont gold rush. No one got rich then and you probably won't either, but locals still find bits of precious metal in the area streams. The park's hiking trails are a safer bet—the 3.6-mile (5.8 km) round-trip up **Shrewsbury Peak Trail** takes about two hours and is an appealing way into the forest; the trail gains elevation slowly as it climbs through the trees, and there are views to the south and east from the mostly wooded summit at 3,681 feet (1,122 m). If you're tempted to spend the night in the park, the **campground** has 26 tent sites and 32 lean-to shelters that are among the most appealing in the Vermont state park system (tent sites $28-30, lean-tos $38-40).

Getting Around

To get to Plymouth Notch from **Woodstock,** take Route 4 west to Route 100A South. Turn right on Route 100 to reach the **President Calvin Coolidge State Historic Site.**

Grafton

Once a country crossroads, the village of Grafton hosted presidents and poets as they traveled through 19th-century Vermont. Theodore Roosevelt, Ralph Waldo Emerson, Woodrow Wilson, and Oliver Wendell Holmes all stayed here, but by the 1960s the town's population had dwindled and the village was lapsing into dereliction.

It's a familiar story in rural communities across the state, but Grafton's decline was reversed by Dean Mathey, a New Jersey investment banker with family ties to the region. In 1963 he established the Windham Foundation that essentially bought and restored the entire place to a high shine, including the elegant Grafton Inn, which has been in business since 1801.

The result is a company town with undeniable charm, an extraordinary cheesemaking company, and a 2,000-acre (809-ha) recreation area: the Grafton Trails & Outdoor Center, with cross-country skiing, hiking, mountain biking, and paddling. It's the perfect excuse to avoid the interstate while traveling between Woodstock and Brattleboro.

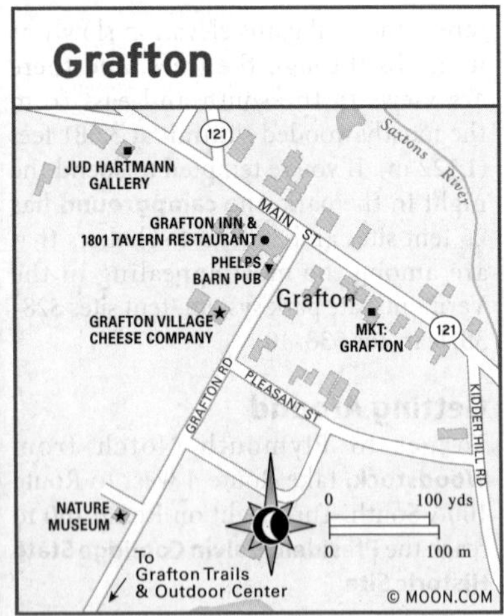

Sights

Grafton Village Cheese Company

The **Grafton Village Cheese Company** (56 Townshend Rd., 802/843-1062, www.graftonvillagecheese.com, daily 10am-6pm) singlehandedly revived the Grafton cheesemaking tradition. The original, farmer-founded cooperative burned down in 1912, but the Windham Foundation rebuilt it in the 1960s, with a vision of making cheese in the rural tradition, with raw milk from family farms. Graze samples of all their cheeses—don't miss the four-year cheddar—and peer down at workers that are making the stuff. You may wish to dive in the vat when you see the cheesemakers "cheddaring," or turning, blocks of soft curd.

Plummer's Sugar House

There's not much overlap between road-tripping season and sugarmaking season, when the early spring thaw turns Vermont's back roads into churning mud. Any time of the year, though, you can get a glimpse of Vermont's sweetest crop at **Plummer's Sugar House** (2866 Townshend Rd., 802/843-2207, daily 10am-4pm), where the owners will walk you through the process with a purchase from the maple store.

Nature Museum

Grafton is home to a small **Nature Museum** (186 Townshend Rd., 802/843-2111, www.nature-museum.org, museum Fri-.Sun. 10am-4pm, playscape daily dawn-dusk, free), which is filled with dioramas and stuffed examples of the local fauna. Though some of the exhibits are a bit mangy, the museum is worth a look for its impressive catamount. According to scientists, Vermont's only mountain lion has been extinct for 50 years, despite the dozens of locals that claim to see them each year—those sightings are likely western mountain lions, whose population has been expanding eastward. The museum hours are somewhat limited but the onsite "Magic Forest Playscape," an interactive woodland trail with suspension bridges, balance beams, and other kid-friendly elements, is open during all daylight hours.

Hamilton Falls

Standing at the misting base of a gargantuan, tumbling Vermont waterfall is a hallmark of hiking here, and **Hamilton Falls** offers one of the most dramatic cascades in the entire region. The falls slice their way through an immense wall of rock, forming a horsetail cascade that spills 125 feet (38 m) into a stony pool that's especially inviting on a broiling summer afternoon. Located half an hour from Grafton near **Jamaica State Park** (40 Salmon Hole Ln., Jamaica, 802/874-4600, www.vtstateparks.com/jamaica.html, Apr. 30-mid-Oct., $4) the falls can be reached directly by taking Windham Road and Hamilton Falls Road to a very small parking area near the falls. But for a more sumptuous countryside journey, enter the park and hike to the cascade via the **West River Trail** and **Hamilton Falls Trail,** a 5.6-mile (9-km) out-and-back route that meanders along the flowering banks of the West River at a flat grade before making the final climb to the falls.

TOP EXPERIENCE

★ The Vermont Cheese Trail

It's only fitting that a place speckled with dairy cows should have cheesemakers to match, and Vermont's got more of them per capita than any other state. Cheddar has marquee appeal, but local artisans are producing everything from richly veined blues to creamy chèvres, and racking up international awards that have put Green Mountain cheese on the world stage. The Vermont Cheese Council maintains a **Cheese Trail map** (www.vtcheese.com) of the cheesemakers that welcome visitors, and the truly dedicated can hopscotch across the state filling their luggage with tangy wedges. Here are some of the highlights along the route:

Grafton Village Cheese Company

The Grafton Village Cheese Company

A delightful place to start, you can graze samples at the retail store (page 228), and the factory is just a short walk down the road, with a viewing window to watch the action most weekdays 7am-2pm. While you're there, don't miss the **Shepsog,** a blended sheep's and cow's milk cheese that's cave-aged for five months. The firm, earthy cheese has brought home a shelf full of trophies and awards for its standout flavor.

Plymouth Artisan Cheese

There's nothing but beautiful back roads to the next stop at Plymouth Artisan Cheese (page 227), which has been operating continuously since John Coolidge (father to President Calvin Coolidge) founded it in 1890. Their distinctive granular curd cheeses are made with raw cow's milk, which you can learn about and sample in the on-site museum and store. Try the **Plymouth Original** or the sharp **Plymouth Hunter.** They don't make cheese every day, so call ahead to find out when they're producing.

Vermont Shepherd

Cows might be Vermont's marquee attraction, but even die-hard cheddar lovers should consider the options at Vermont Shepherd (281 Patch Farm Rd., Putney, 802/387-4473, www.vermontshepherd.com, farm store daily 9am-5pm). The family-owned business makes aged and fresh sheep's milk cheeses that have racked up national accolades. Their flavors are inspired by Spanish-style cheeses from the Pyrenees, and the aged versions have a richly flavored, nutty quality. A highlight is the aged **Invierno,** a natural rind cheese that's heavenly with a pint of cider or beer. The shop is self-service, but visitors are welcome to bring a picnic to enjoy the picturesque spot.

Shopping

Many of the sculptures at the **Jud Hartmann Gallery** (6 Main St., 802/843-2018, https://judhartmanngallery.com, mid-Sept.-early Nov. daily 10am-5pm) are vivid renderings of Native Americans from northeastern tribes. They're full of life and exquisite details; particularly dynamic are those that depict Iroquois lacrosse players. The hours can vary, so

call ahead to confirm that the gallery is open.

Sports and Recreation

A sprawling expanse of fields and forest, **Grafton Trails & Outdoor Center** (783 Townshend Rd., 802/843-2350, www.graftoninnvermont.com, May-Oct. daily 9am-4pm, $20 adults, $10 children, canoe rental $15 for two hours, bike rental $30) has nine miles (14.5 km) of hiking and mountain biking trails, and a mountain bike terrain park. On warm days, the pond is tempting and cool, with a floating dock for basking.

Food

The Windham Foundation-owned **Grafton Inn** (92 Main St., 802/843-2248, www.graftoninnvermont.com) dominates the dining scene in Grafton, but fortunately for hungry visitors, they serve commendable food in both of their establishments. The more casual of the two is the **Phelps Barn Pub** (92 Main St., 802/843-2263, Tues.-Sat. 5pm-8pm, $16-27), serving comfort food that is remarkably refined for something dubbed "pub grub." Burgers and mac and cheese line up alongside options like pesto-seared salmon over smoky tomato risotto and lemony arugula. The pub is in the inn's one-time carriage barn and retains an appealingly rustic ambience.

The inn's fine dining option is the **1801 Tavern Restaurant** (92 Main St., Fri.-Sat. 5pm-8pm, $20-36), whose menu overlaps with the Phelps Barn Pub, but offers a wider range of plated entrées in a beautiful dining room in keeping with the inn's historic feel.

Grab some delicious made-to-order sandwiches and salads at **MKT: Grafton** (162 Main St., 802/843-2255, Mon.-Tues. and Thurs.-Fri. 9am-7pm, Wed. and Sat. 7:30am-7pm, Sun. 9am-6pm, $10-23).

Top to bottom: barn at President Calvin Coolidge State Historic Site; Hamilton Falls; pond at Grafton Trails

Sweet Inheritance: Heirloom Apples

heirloom apples: an essential Brattleboro product

The wax-shined, blemish-free apples that gleam in grocery store coolers are a far cry from the fruits that early New Englanders baked into pies and pressed into cider. Nineteenth-century farmers grew hundreds of varieties of apples chosen for their unique flavor profiles and uses, but over time those diverse varieties have been passed over for fruit that's easy to grow and can withstand months of shipment and cold storage. In recent years, a new crop of growers is putting heirloom varieties back on the shelf, growing old cultivars kept alive by generations of farmers.

These heirloom apples can seem homely in contrast with widely distributed Red Delicious and Granny Smith varieties, but many Vermonters have learned to love the nubbly, colorful, russeted fruits for their extravagantly varied flavor and appearance. Because apples are grown from cuttings, rather than seed, every single apple represents an unbroken chain of cultivation—one generation of fruit trees lost to disease or frost means the end of that particular variety.

It doesn't get better than **Scott Farm Orchard** in Dummerston, a shrine to eclectic fruit that's worthy of a pilgrimage. Orchardist Zeke Goodband grows over 100 varieties with intriguing names like Lamb Abbey Pearmain and Zabergau Reinette along with other offbeat tree fruits like quince and medlar. The farm is open for pick-your-own, and during harvest season Scott Farm distributes to stores around Vermont.

Don't miss these favorite heirloom varieties:

- **Ananas Reinette:** Fine fleshed and crisp, this small, yellow apple is named for the faint pineapple flavor that some tasters can detect—it's a zesty, bright-tasting fruit that's wonderful eaten out of hand.
- **Blue Pearmain:** With sweet-tart, dry flesh and a beautifully deep color, this apple was a favorite of the writer Henry David Thoreau, who loved to gather them from a tree near his home, saying: "I fill my pockets on each side, and... I eat one first from this side, and then from that, to keep my balance."
- **Esopus Spitzenberg:** Thomas Jefferson grew this aromatic, faintly spicy apple in his orchard at Monticello.
- **Hubbardston Nonesuch:** Red-gold skin dappled with freckles and russet make this dessert apple as pretty as it is sweet, but it's notoriously hard to grow, making it a rare find.

The atmospheric general store also sells excellent cheeses, wines, and sweets—along with any other fixings you might need for a country picnic.

Accommodations

If you like Grafton enough to stick around, the **Grafton Inn** (92 Main St., 802/843-2248, www.graftoninnvermont.com, $220-400) is just as sweetly historic as the village, with period antiques and tasteful country style. Rooms have been updated with luxurious beds and modern bathrooms. Rates include a hearty breakfast with freshly baked pastries and plenty of maple syrup.

Getting Around

If you're looking for a scenic route between **Woodstock** and **Brattleboro**, Plymouth and Grafton are perfect destinations (75 mi/121 km, 2 hrs). From the north, head west on Route 4 to VT 100A South, which passes through **Plymouth** before turning into Route 100. Take Route 103 South to Route 35 South and Route 35 South into **Grafton.**

Brattleboro

Brattleboro's brick-lined center is rimmed by gentle mountains that lend the town a dreamy, insular feel. The Connecticut River drifts right through the heart of downtown, where locals linger in cozy cafés, farm-to-table restaurants, and a remarkable collection of galleries with work by local artists. A heady blend of art and ideas infuse life in this famously progressive community, partly driven by students that come to study everything from international development to circus skills. Maybe there's just something in that fresh Green Mountain air, because even the prolific author Rudyard Kipling came here to be inspired and penned some of his best-loved work from a desk at Naulakha, his home just outside of town.

For the visitor, Brattleboro is the perfect place to experience Vermont's free-spirited, intellectual side by rubbing elbows with unreconstructed hippies, professors, and aspiring clowns at one of the town's frequent community events. Strap on dancing shoes, join the lineup and do-si-do in a traditional contra dance, browse organic apples at the vibrant farmers' market, or time your visit to attend the monthly gallery walk, when dozens of local venues unveil exhibits that they'll display throughout the month.

And if you'd like to explore the serious work of the good life in Brattleboro, plan to attend the annual Slow Living Summit, when academics, artists, and activists hash out a game plan for a better world. If that sounds too serious, you can just fall in line behind the cows that lead the Strolling of the Heifers parade, a slo-mo, Green Mountain take on a bull run.

Sights

★ Apple Picking at Scott Farm Orchard

Just north of Brattleboro is the magnificent **Scott Farm Orchard** (707 Kipling Rd., Dummerston, 802/254-6868, www.scottfarmvermont.com, weekends in Aug. 10am-6pm, Labor Day-Nov. daily 10am-6pm), a rolling expanse of apple trees, forest, and fields dotted with fascinating historic structures. It's a memorable experience to pick your own fruit from the trees that march up and down the hills in parallel lines, and the on-site Farm Market sells jugs of unpasteurized cider made from the farm's dozens of heirloom varieties (unlike most ciders, which are made from easier-to-grow Macintosh apples). Pick-your-own season usually extends from Labor Day through mid-October, but call ahead for apple updates.

The rambling property is also home to **Naulakha,** where author Rudyard Kipling lived from 1893 through 1896. He built the vaguely ship-shaped building on a

Brattleboro

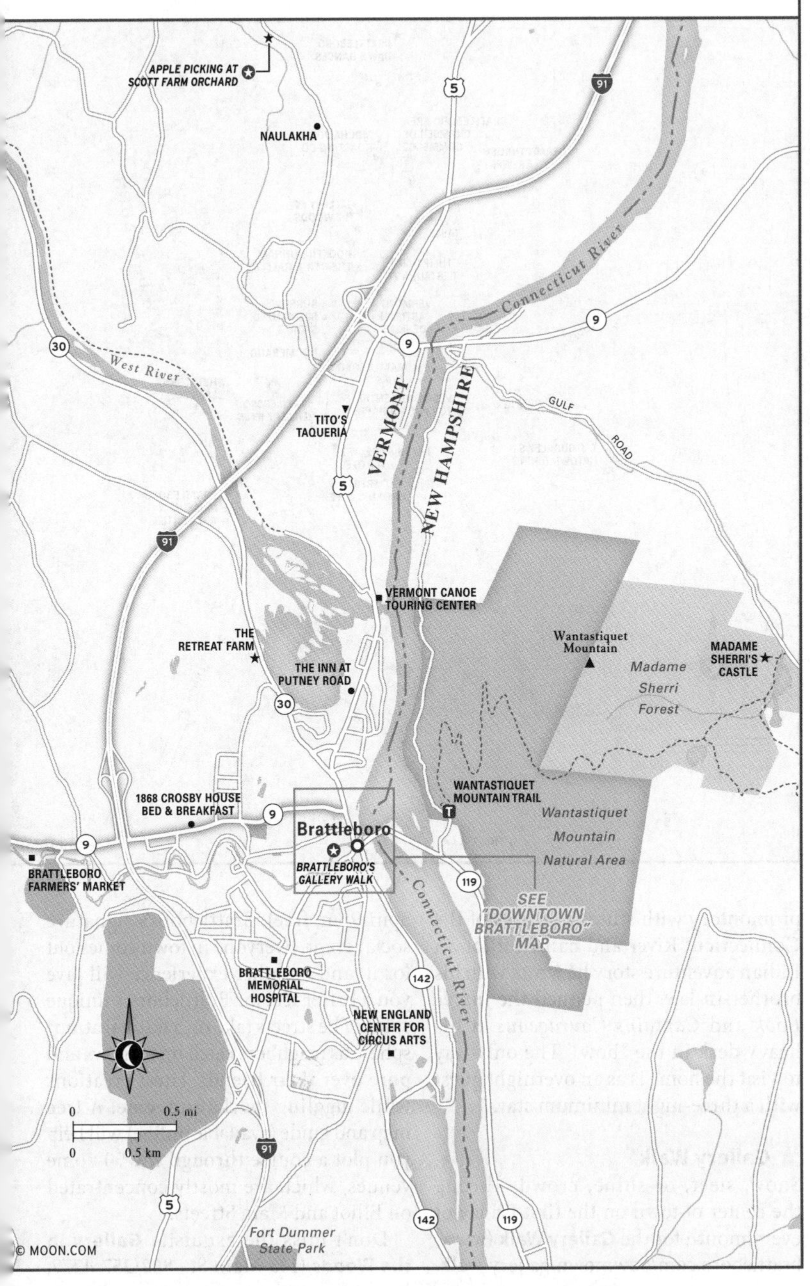

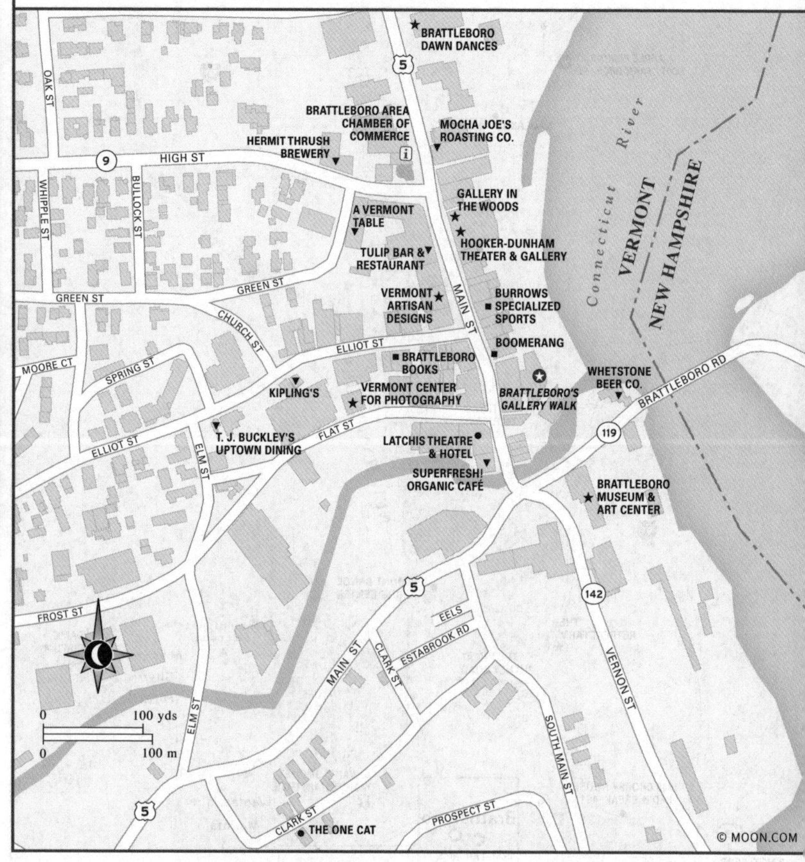

promontory with stunning views of the Connecticut River and named it for an Indian adventure story he wrote with his brother-in-law, then penned the *Jungle Book* and *Captains Courageous* at his heavy desk in the "bow." The only way to visit the home is as an overnight guest with a three-night minimum stay.

★ Gallery Walk

Snow, sleet, or shine, crowds throng the center of town on the first Friday of every month for the **Gallery Walk** (www.brattleboro.com/downtown/gallery-walk, 5pm-9pm, free), Brattleboro's signature social event. Everyone in town comes out for it, and no other experience will give you a better feel for Brattleboro's unique spirit. The streets take on a festival atmosphere as neighbors catch up on news and pore over their friends' latest creations while juggling snacks and wine. A free map and guide (available online) will help you plot a course through the 50-some venues, which are mostly concentrated on Elliot and Main Streets.

Don't miss the exquisite **Gallery in the Woods** (145 Main St., 802/257-4777, www.galleryinthewoods.com, Mon.-Sat. 11am-5:30pm, Sun. noon-5pm), whose focus on the "Visionary, Surreal, Fantastic and Sacred" results in surprisingly grounded and relatable exhibits that range from folk traditions to fine art. Another gem is the **Vermont Center for Photography** (49 Flat St., 802/251-6051, www.vcphoto.org, Wed.-Sun. 11am-5pm), which hosts work by some of the region's most skilled and creative photographers. There's a broad range of media on display at **Vermont Artisan Designs** (106 Main St., 802/246-7245, www.vtart.com, daily 10am-5pm), and it's an ideal place to browse for unique handmade gifts.

Brattleboro Museum & Art Center

Recent exhibits at the eclectic **Brattleboro Museum & Art Center** (10 Vernon St., 802/257-0124, www.brattleboromuseum.org, Wed.-Sun. 10am-4pm, free) have included Bahamian ceramic dolls and sculptures, and a "human nature walk" where plastic debris stands in for the trees and understory. The museum's climate change residency program pretty much guarantees at least one exhibit that invites viewers to engage with the present and future climate crisis. And this museum's unusual location in a renovated railway station is a draw, as are the one-off events, like yo-yo tutorials, poetry readings, and lectures.

Hermit Thrush Brewery

The diminutive brewhouse at **Hermit Thrush Brewery** (29 High St., 802/257-2337, www.hermitthrushbrewery.com, daily 11am-6pm, taproom hours Mon. and Thurs.-Sat. 11am-7pm, Sun. 11am-6pm) makes highly acclaimed sour beers with mixed culture Brattleboro brewers' yeast, in a tiny, rustic space downtown. Try their adventurous seasonal options, but don't miss the BrattleBerry, a tart golden ale aged in oak barrels for 18 months with local raspberries and apples. The finished elixir has the hue of rosé and the crisp taste of a champagne.

The Retreat Farm

On the outskirts of town, **The Retreat Farm** (45 Farmhouse Sq., 802/490-2270, www.retreatfarm.org, daily sunrise-sundown, free) has a family-friendly "petting farm" with dozens of animals that range from familiar to exotic. The 500-acre (202.3-ha) property is still a working farm owned by the Windham Foundation, a private foundation dedicated to preserving Vermont's rural traditions. In the spirit of being a "gateway farm," the Retreat offers plenty of ways to interact with the resident critters, so you can scratch a pig's belly, go eye-to-eye with a one-ton ox, and snag a selfie with an impossibly adorable dwarf goat.

All year round, the **Retreat Trails** are accessible from the main visitor center or from several other entry points. The network includes about nine miles (14.5 km) of trails. One popular walk travels 1.15 miles (1.85 km) from the farm to scenic **Ice Pond** via **Morningside Trail.** A recent addition is the **Woodlands Interpretive Trail,** a 1-mile (1.6-km) loop that is accessed at the Solar Hill trailhead off Western Avenue; the trail has a folksy, 30-minute audio guide that can be downloaded from the farm website, with idiosyncratic stories from locals.

Madame Sherri's Castle

Just across the Vermont state line, one of the most beguiling sights in the Brattleboro area is **Madame Sherri's Castle** (Chesterfield, New Hampshire, www.chesterfieldoutdoors.com/madame-sherri-forest). Enter the forest of Chesterfield and take a short, pleasant stroll along a boggy pond to reach the crumbling ruins and preserved spiral staircase of a castle-esque mansion that belonged to Antoinette Sherri, a Broadway costume designer and New England's real-life Jay Gatsby. A social hedonist, Sherri would use the mansion to host parties for her friends from the New York theater circuit during the 1940s and '50s.

A fire destroyed Sherri's castle in 1962, but the Chesterfield Conservation Commission preserved the ruins and built networks of trails through the surrounding forest. Most visitors never tread beyond the castle, which is a shame: The two-mile (3.2-km) **Daniels Mountain Loop** offers a fun ascent to **Moon Ledge,** where hikers can gaze toward the Pioneer Valley in Massachusetts. To reach this trail, take the gentle **Ann Stokes Trail** southeast from the castle ruins for one mile (1.6 km), alongside a boggy area. When visiting the castle itself, bear in mind that the arched staircase is fragile and pieces of it have fallen off in recent years. Visitors should refrain from climbing on or beneath the structure.

Entertainment and Events

Nightlife

There's always a friendly crowd at **Whetstone Beer Co.** (36 Bridge St., 802/490-2354, www.whetstonebeer.com, Sun.-Thurs. noon-9pm, Fri.-Sat. noon-10pm), which serves its own beers alongside a hearty roster of pub grub to help soak it all up. The open-air 2nd-floor dining area offers marvelous views of the Connecticut River and Wantastiquet Mountain Natural Area in nearby New Hampshire.

There are bars named for Rudyard Kipling in places from Michigan to Mumbai, but **Kipling's Tavern** (78 Elliot St., 802/490-2904, Mon.-Thurs. 4pm-9pm, Fri.-Sat. 4pm-10pm) has a distinctively Brattleboro feel. Maybe it's the unexpected mashup of Irish bar, fish-and-chips joint, local hangout, and literary mecca (try Emerson's Chili Cheddar Burger). This is the sort of bar where regulars bang out tunes on the piano.

The Arts

The landmark art deco building that houses the **Latchis Theatre** (50 Main

Madame Sherri's Castle

St., 802/246-2020, www.latchis.com, $10 adults, $8 children under 12 and seniors, $8 matinees) is as much a part of the show as anything on the screen. Its 750-seat main theater has an iridescent mural of the zodiac on the ceiling and frolicking Greeks along the walls. Three movie theaters show a mix of first-run and independent films. The 1938 building is also a hotel.

On the other end of the spectrum, patrons of the **Hooker-Dunham Theater & Gallery** (139 Main St., 802/281-3232, www.hookerdunhamtheater.org, events $15-25, gallery admission free) enjoy its funky subterranean feel. This venue showcases art-house films, folk and chamber music, and avant-garde theater.

Jugglers, acrobats and trapeze artists take center stage at the **New England Center for Circus Arts** (10 Town Crier Dr., 802/254-9780, www.necenterforcircusarts.org, $5-25), a serious training camp for performers both silly and spectacular. Shows are held at the end of school sessions, or when a visiting circus troupe is in town, with one or two performances a month through the summer.

Festivals and Events

Follow step-by-step instructions from the caller, and you'll be twirling and swinging along with a crowd at the **Brattleboro Dawn Dances** (207 Main St., 802/451-0822, www.dawndance.org, Sun. 8pm-7am Mon., $10), a biannual contra dance marathon hosted at the Gibson-Aiken Center for recreation. With three bands scoring the revelry, the communal dance stretches from dusk till dawn, and it takes place on Memorial Day and Labor Day. Dancers should bring a pair of clean, soft-soled shoes to change into.

Vermont might be the most prolific state in New England when it comes to crafting prize-winning beers and ciders, and a great way to sample the fruits of the entire state is to swing through town in early summer when the **Brattleboro Brewer's Festival** (40 University Way, www.brattleborobrewersfestival.com, late May) brings dozens of suds wizards to town to showcase their handiwork. Recent lineups of brewers have included northern Vermont legends like The Alchemist (makers of the world-famous Heady Topper Double IPA) and the Von Trapp Brewery, which is part of the Trapp Family Lodge, founded by the real-life Trapp family who fled World War II-era Austria for Vermont, as dramatized in *The Sound of Music*. With more than 100 drafts to choose from, savory bites from food trucks, and a competitive keg toss, there's a palpable taste of exuberance to the fest.

Taking place shortly thereafter in early June is the **Slow Living Summit** (www.slowlivingsummit.org), where issues like sustainability, mindfulness, and the good life get serious attention, and keynote speakers come from around the world.

That's Weird...

a salamander venturing across the road

It might look like a practical joke, but if you see a **"Salamander Crossing"** sign, don't laugh—just ease off the gas pedal and watch for slow-moving amphibians. Every spring, salamanders—including the strikingly spotted red eft—trek to vernal pools to lay their eggs after a sleepy winter below the frost line. When warming weather gets them moving, they start to walk to their pool of choice over the course of several rainy nights in April. But if the migration route crosses a road, entire populations risk being wiped out by passing cars.

To protect the amphibious creatures, volunteers around the state post signs to alert cars of their presence, and on the "Big Nights" when they start to migrate, an ad hoc platoon of crossing guards slows traffic and runs a salamander shuttle service. The poky salamanders get scooped up one at a time and carried to the opposite side of the road, where they can continue to mosey through forests and fields to lay their eggs. If you're in southern Vermont in salamander season, you can sign up to receive updates on all things salamander from the **Bonnyvale Environmental Education Center** (www.beec.org) and even volunteer to help the adorable amphibians get where they're going.

Shopping

Downtown Brattleboro has an eclectic mix of shops that invites leisurely browsing, like **Boomerang** (12 Elliot St., 802/257-6911, www.boomerangvermont.com, Mon.-Sat. 10am-6pm, Sun. 11am-5pm), which stocks new, used, and vintage clothing for men and women, including many picks with flair.

Books tower from floor to ceiling at **Brattleboro Books** (36 Elliot St., 802/257-7777, www.brattleborobooks.com, Tues.-Sat. 10:30am-5:30pm, Sun.-Mon. 11am-4pm), an independent store with the best selection in town, including many used and out-of-print copies.

You can find one-of-a-kind gifts at **Vermont Artisan Designs** (106 Main St., 802/246-7245, www.vtart.com, daily 10am-5pm), which features pottery, furniture, and other crafts made by artisans from across the state.

Sports and Recreation

Biking

With easygoing traffic and loads of scenic country roads, Brattleboro is the perfect place to ditch four wheels for two. If you've got your own bike, the Windham Regional Commission has a useful pdf bicycle suitability map (www.windhamregional.org/bikemap), and 21-speed hybrid bikes are available to rent at **Burrows Specialized Sports** (105 Main St., 802/254-9430, $25/day). The friendly staff is happy to suggest rides, which are either flat out-and-backs in the Connecticut River Valley, or hilly climbs into the Green Mountains. As is the case throughout Vermont, some of the finest riding is on unpaved dirt roads, which outnumber the nearby asphalt options three to one, and these offer an ideal way to escape into quiet country hollows.

Boating

Canoes, kayaks, and SUP paddleboards can be rented on a first-come, first-served basis from the **Vermont Canoe Touring Center** (451 Putney Rd., 802/257-5008, www.vermontcanoetouringcenter.com, kayak $30 for 2 hrs, $40 4 hrs, $50 full day, canoe $40 2 hrs, $50 4 hrs, $60 full day, paddleboards $30 2 hrs, $40 4 hrs, $50 full day) at the confluence of the Connecticut and West Rivers. The stretch of the Connecticut above Vernon Dam is wide and pleasant, with some small islands along the way for paddlers to get out and explore; the West River is smaller but similarly peaceful, though it can also offer some great Class II and III whitewater in the early spring when the snow melts, or on one of a few release dates from the upstream dam each year.

Hiking

Three short, gentle nature trails leave from the Fort Dummer State Park Campground; the 1-mile-long (1.6-km) **Sunrise Trail,** the 0.5-mile (0.8-km) **Sunset Trail** loop through the forest, and the 0.5-mile (0.8-km) **Broad Brook Trail,** which leads from the southern edge of the campground loop to a river swimming hole that's a pleasantly shady haven on a hot summer day.

Brattleboro's rolling skyline is dominated by **Wantastiquet Mountain,** but the trail to the top of the 1,368-foot (417-m) peak starts in New Hampshire, just across the Connecticut River. To reach the trailhead take Rte. 119 across the river from downtown Brattleboro, and turn left onto Mountain Road just after the second bridge. The trailhead is 0.9 miles (1.4 km) from downtown Brattleboro at a small parking area on the right side of the road. The 1.5 miles (2.4 km) of switchbacks earn you sweeping views of the Connecticut River Valley from the summit, where an exposed granite slab makes an excellent picnic spot.

Swimming

The Connecticut River looks temptingly cool as it burbles past town, but there are cleaner, more peaceful options a short drive outside of city limits. Though the river is generally too shallow for swimming, just flopping into a pool at **Stickney Brook Falls** is a delightful way to spend a hot afternoon. The series of gentle falls is on the left-hand side of Stickney Brook Road; from downtown Brattleboro, drive north on Route 30, and continue 3.7 miles (6 km) past the I-91 underpass. Turn left on Stickney Brook Road, and watch for cars parked along the road.

Stickney Brook is a tributary of the **West River,** which runs parallel to Route 30 north of Brattleboro. There are excellent swimming holes all along the waterway, notably just under the West Dummerston covered bridge (7.3 mi/11.7 km north of Brattleboro, with a sometimes strong current).

Half an hour west of Brattleboro, the sinuous **Harrington Reservoir** is pocked with pleasant spots to slip into the water. To reach the reservoir, drive west on Route 9 to the intersection with Route 100 in Wilmington. Access points and swimming beaches are located on the right side of Route 100, several with picnic areas and grills. The reservoir's most famous swim spot is **The Ledges,** a pristine, clothing-optional crook in the shoreline that's back in the buff after losing its nudist privileges in a hotly contested town vote. Thanks to support from groups like A.A.N.R.—that's the American Association for Nude Recreation—the vote was eventually overturned.

Food

Fine Dining

The contrast between the thoughtful menus and the offbeat setting—a 1925 Worcester diner car—only heighten the experience at ★ **T. J. Buckley's Uptown Dining** (132 Elliot St., 802/257-4922, www.tjbuckleysuptowndining.com, Thurs.-Sun. 5:30pm-9pm, $45-58), a long-standing Brattleboro favorite. There are just eight tables, so chef-owner Michael Fuller gives personal attention to each dish and offers a handful of options nightly. All of them feature bold flavor combinations, such as scallops on stone-ground polenta cake with local greens, or the braised rabbit with double smoked bacon.

Hanging plants and colorful floral paintings set the stage for homegrown dining at **A Vermont Table** (22-26 High St., 802/387-0151, www.avermonttable.com, Mon. 4pm-8pm, Thurs.-Sat. 5pm-9pm, Sun. 10am-2pm, $16-28). Originally a catering service fueled by regional farms and gardens, this relatively new addition to Brattleboro's culinary circuit opened its doors in 2022, embracing the seasonality of Vermont-raised ingredients and offering a rotating menu of inspired plates like beef bourguignon with autumnal root vegetables, or the summery roasted bean curd with miso-ginger slaw. The Sunday brunch menu leans into old-school countryside traditions, including pillowy maple-glazed donuts. It's almost too Vermont. Almost.

International

With its sepia-toned walls, complete with illustrations of leafy trees, **Tulip Bar and Restaurant** (126 Main St., 802/254-2327, www.tulipbrattleboro.com, Mon.-Tues. and Fri. 11am-8pm, Sat.-Sun. 9am-4pm, $12-24) beckons on gray afternoons. The menu has global versions of meat on bread, with Turkish flair: kofte and kebabs alongside steak and cheese wraps, and lighter bites such as watermelon and feta salad.

Like more and more contemporary brick-and-mortar eateries, **Tito's Taqueria** (898 Putney Rd., 802/490-2748, www.titostaqueria.com, Mon.-Sat. 11am-8pm, $5-14) began life as a mobile operation, with its namesake founder standing on the side of the road with a cooler full of loaded breakfast tacos. The scale of the venture has expanded considerably, with two restaurants in Brattleboro and Greenfield, Massachusetts, and the menu includes not only hearty tacos with chipotle lime pork and grilled steak, but also burritos, rice bowls, and salads topped with Grafton cheddar and farm-sourced pickled onions. The portions are generous, so consider Tito's a suitable destination after a day of hiking or boating.

Cafés and Bakeries

Tucked into a cozy basement nook, **Mocha Joe's Roasting Co.** (82 Main St., 802/257-7794, www.mochajoes.com, daily 8am-4pm) roasts coffee sourced from around the world, with direct trade programs in Cameroon and Nicaragua. The café serves pastries and snacks but the brews are the real focus, and the friendly space may tempt you to while away the morning.

Vegetable lovers who've tired of Vermont's typically meat-heavy menus should head to **Superfresh! Organic Café** (30 Main St., 802/579-1751, Fri.-Mon. noon-6pm, $6-16), which fills plates with vibrant salads, filling sandwiches and wraps, and ample gluten-free options. You'll find plenty of smoothies, vegan "mylks," and elixirs for what ails you. The laid-back, artsy style is right at home in downtown Brattleboro, attracting a colorful crowd of locals.

Markets

The **Brattleboro Farmers' Market** (570 Western Ave., www.brattleborofarmersmarket.com, May-Oct. Sat. 9am-2pm) is the best in southern Vermont, with piles of local produce, cheese, and meat from over 50 local farms, crafters, and producers. Snap up artisanal kimchi, gelato, and pasta, among many other things. The market is on Route 9 near the covered bridge.

Accommodations and Camping

Camping

A 1908 dam on the Connecticut River flooded Fort Dummer—Vermont's first permanent European settlement—but the area around it has been preserved as **Fort Dummer State Park** (517 Old Guilford Rd., 802/254-2610, www.vtstateparks.com/fortdummer.html, June 26-Columbus Day, campsites and lean-tos $28-40). The 217-acre (87.8-ha) forest is just south of downtown, with a pleasant mix of oak, beech, and birch trees that shelter wild turkey and ruffed grouse. The campground's 50 wooded tent sites are comfortable, if not particularly private, or you can spend the night in one of 10 more secluded lean-tos. Hot showers and a dumping station are available, but no hookups.

Under $150

Diminutive and homey, **The One Cat** (34 Clark St., 802/579-1905, www.theonecatvermont.com, $130-250) is as funky as Brattleboro itself. The two guest rooms—New England and Brighton—are named for the Anglo-American couple's homes, and come with appropriate decorative flourishes. The tiny library is full of intriguing books and calls out for intimate wintertime reading. A full English breakfast is served, and a 20 percent discount is available for guests that arrive without cars.

$150-250

The Inn on Putney Road (192 Putney Rd., 802/254-6268, https://vermontbandbinn.com, $200-280), a pristine white house surrounded by specimen trees and meticulous gardens, is filled with serenely decorated rooms evocative of Provence or the English countryside. A full gourmet breakfast is included.

The lobby at the **Latchis Hotel** (50 Main St., 802/254-6300, www.latchishotel.com, $149-269) retains art deco flourishes from its heyday in the 1930s, and for some, it doesn't get any better than a room at a downtown movie theater. Period details like terrazzo floors and chrome fixtures maintain historical cool, recent renovations have spruced up the down-at-the-heel rooms, and suites with small sitting rooms are available.

Sweet old-fashioned rooms have romantic appeal at the **1868 Crosby House Bed & Breakfast** (175 Western Ave., 802/490-3560, www.crosbyhouse.com, $175-245). Each of the two individual suites has a queen-size bed and fireplace; the larger one has a double-whirlpool bath. Fans of forest-bathing will be happy to learn that behind the on-site Victorian gardens is a trailhead where visitors can directly access more than 9 miles (14.4 km) of wandering paths through Vermont Land Trust woodlands. These trails are perfect for morning or sunset walks. During peak weeks of summer and fall, the Crosby House may have minimum stay requirements.

Over $350

Slow down for a few days on the property that surrounds **Scott Farm Orchard** (707 Kipling Rd., Dummerston, 802/254-6868, www.scottfarmvermont.com), and you'll be rewarded with a sublimely peaceful retreat into scattered apple orchards and shady forests. The **Landmark Trust USA** (www.landmarktrustusa.org) maintains five historic buildings that are destinations worth planning a trip around, especially the exquisite **Naulakha** (sleeps 8, 3-night minimum stay, $635/night), Rudyard Kipling's scrupulously maintained home. The property favors historical preservation over modern-day comforts, but the grounds offer sweeping views of Wantastiquet Range, where Kipling loved to watch Mount Monadnack break the clouds "like a giant thumbnail pointing heavenwards." The other on-site rentals include the Kiplings' charming **Carriage House** (sleeps 4, 3-night minimum stay, $385/night), a renovated sugarhouse, and two historic farmhouses. All properties must be booked in advance, and have minimum stay requirements.

Information and Services

The **Brattleboro Area Chamber of Commerce** (180 Main St., 802/254-4565, www.brattleborochamber.org, Mon.-Fri.-9am-5pm) runs a visitor center downtown.

The area's premier hospital is **Brattleboro Memorial Hospital** (17 Belmont Ave., 802/257-0341, www.bmhvt.org). For nonmedical emergencies, contact the **Brattleboro Police** (230 Main St., 802/257-7946).

Banks are found all over the downtown area, particularly on Main Street. ATMs are plentiful around retail stores, in and around hotels, and in convenience stores. Most cafés have **wireless Internet.** Computers are available for public use at **Brooks Memorial Library** (224 Main St., 802/254-5290, Mon.-Wed. 10am-9pm, Thurs.-Fri. 10am-6pm, Sat. 10am-5pm).

Getting Around

Getting to Brattleboro

To get to Brattleboro from **Bennington** (40 mi/64 km, 1 hr), drive east on Route 9, the **scenic Molly Stark Byway,** which links both towns' downtown areas. The most direct route from **Woodstock** (65 mi/105 km, 1.25 hrs) is to follow Route 4 East to Route 12 South, then cruise south along I-91. With a bit of extra time, however, it's worth taking the **scenic route** through the mountains. Take Route 4 West to the 100A through bucolic Plymouth, then turn onto Route 100 South. There are two excellent options for reaching Brattleboro: stay on Route 100 South through Weston and catch up to Route 9 in **Wilmington** (100 mi/160 km, 2.5 hrs), or take Route 103 to Route 35 and Route 30, which passes through the cheesemaking village of **Grafton** (75 mi/121 km, 2 hrs).

Getting Around Brattleboro

Metered parking is available all over downtown Brattleboro, and the town's small downtown is compact and easy to navigate. Four fare-free city bus lines connect at the Flat Street Transportation Center in downtown; buses operate Monday-Saturday, and a service map is available at www.moover.com.

Bennington

Bennington has a long and rich history, but the town is best known for a battle that took place 12 miles (19 km) to the west, just over the New York border. The Battle of Bennington was a defining moment for the American Revolutionary cause, a fascinating clash between the pro-British forces—a mixed group of German dragoons, Native Americans, Canadians, and loyalists—and a rebel force led by General John Stark and reinforced by Ethan Allen's Green Mountain Boys.

Tensions have simmered down since 1777, and modern-day Bennington is a tranquil former mill town with a liberal arts college and a number of attractions worth a visit, including an excellent art and history museum, Robert Frost's gravesite and nearby home, and a towering monument that commemorates the famous battle.

Sights

Bennington Battle Monument

It's hard to miss the **Bennington Battle Monument** (15 Monument Cir., 802/447-0550, www.benningtonbattlemonument.com, late May-Oct. daily 10am-5pm, $5 adults, $1 children 6-14), a 306-foot-tall (93-m) limestone obelisk that's the tallest structure in the state. Inside is a diorama of the second engagement of the Battle of Bennington, along with an elevator that takes visitors two-thirds of the way up for a knockout view of the Green Mountains, Berkshires, and Taconic Range (in Vermont, Massachusetts, and New York, respectively). Statues of the battle's heroes, General John Stark and Colonel Seth Warner, strike dashing poses on the monument grounds, and a

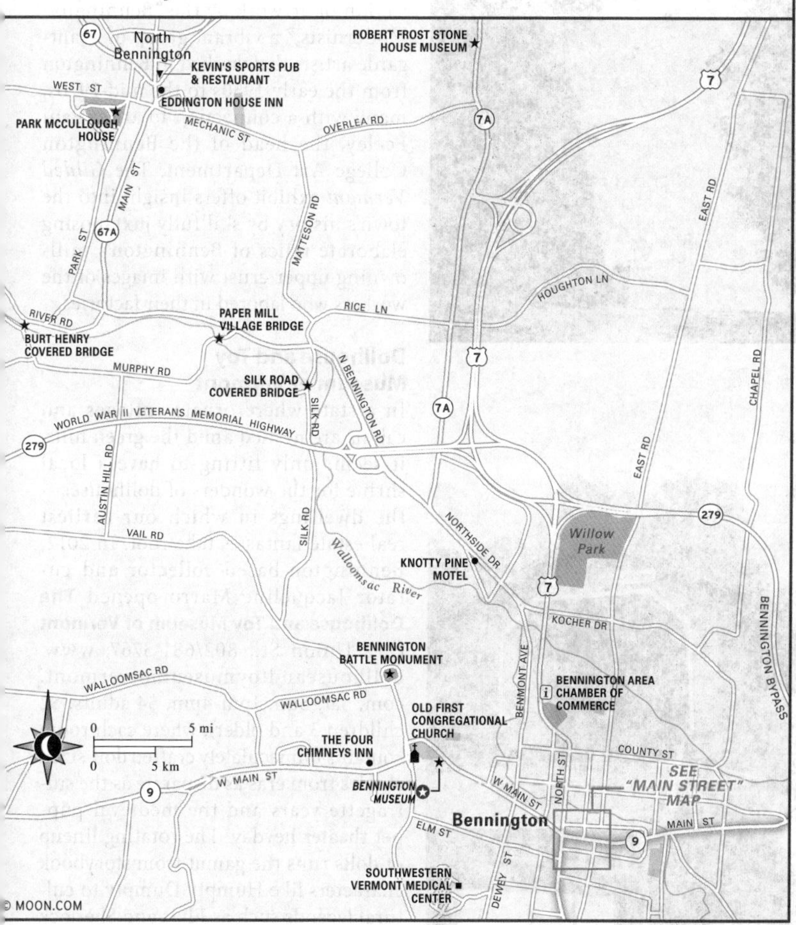

kitschy gift shop occupies the site of the storehouse the British had hoped to capture in the skirmish.

★ Bennington Museum

The art-filled **Bennington Museum** (75 Main St., 802/447-1571, www.benningtonmuseum.org, Apr.-May and Nov.-Dec. Thurs.-Mon. 10am-4pm, June-Oct. Thurs.-Tues. 10am-4pm, $15 adults, $12 students and seniors, under 18 free) is a detour-worthy destination. The museum has the largest public collection of work by folk artist Grandma Moses, along with her sweetly decorated painting desk and chair. Anna Mary Robertson Moses lived in Bennington for eight years, from 1927 to 1935, and developed a simple (some might say simplistic) style that celebrated America's rural roots—harvests, mills, sleigh rides, and ice skating—during a time when the United States was undergoing rapid industrialization.

The museum's scope extends beyond folk art and includes a permanent selection of artwork by the "Bennington Modernists," a vibrant group of avant-garde artists that worked in Bennington from the early 1950s to the mid-1970s, many with a connection to artist Paul Feeley, the head of the Bennington College Art Department. The *Gilded Vermont* exhibit offers insight into the town's history by skillfully juxtaposing elaborate relics of Bennington's mill-owning upper crust with images of the workers who labored in their factories.

Dollhouse and Toy Museum of Vermont

In a state where ornate cottages and cabins are nestled amid the green hills, it seems only fitting to have a local shrine for the wonders of dollhouses—the dwellings in which our earliest real estate fantasies take root. In 2012, Bennington-based collector and curator Jacqueline Marro opened **The Dollhouse and Toy Museum of Vermont** (212 Union St., 802/681-3767, www.dollhouseandtoymuseumofvermont.com, Sat.-Sun. 1pm-4pm, $4 adults, $2 children 3 and older), where each room contains immaculately crafted doll-sized abodes from eras as disparate as the suffragette years and the medieval puppet theater heyday. The rotating lineup of dolls runs the gamut from storybook characters like Humpty Dumpty to cultural legends such as Elvis and Sherlock Holmes.

Old First Congregational Church

Robert Frost once wrote, "One could do worse than be a swinger of birches," and his beloved trees keep watch above his gravesite, where he was buried alongside his wife, Elinor, behind the **Old First Congregational Church**

Top to bottom: Bennington Battle Monument; Burt Henry Covered Bridge; local pottery

(1 Monument Cir., 802/447-1223, www.oldfirstchurchbenn.org, Sun. worship service Sept.-June 11am, July-Aug. 10am, donations welcome). In addition to Frost's grave, the cemetery also contains those of American, British, and Hessian soldiers killed at the Battle of Bennington.

Park-McCullough House

One of the most impressive Victorians in New England is the **Park-McCullough House** (1 Park St., 802/442-5441, www.parkmccullough.org, May-Dec. Fri.-Sun. 10am-2pm, $15 adults, $12 seniors, $8 students and youth 8-17, under 8 free), a Second Empire mansion filled with lavish antiques and period furniture. The grounds and gardens are open year-round and can be accessed free of charge, as can the neighboring **Mile-Around Woods,** a forested idyll looped with a carriage path that is precisely one mile (1.6 km) around.

Covered Bridges

The country roads around Bennington are the perfect place to explore Vermont's distinctive wooden covered bridges, icons of the New England landscape that were built to withstand harsh winter weather. Start at the elegantly trussed **Silk Road Covered Bridge** across the Walloomsac River, a single-lane "town lattice truss" that dates to 1840; follow Route 7 north from downtown Bennington to Route 67A, and turn left onto Silk Road (3.9 mi/6.3 km from the intersection of Route 7 and Route 9). Continue northeast on Route 67A to a left turn on Murphy Road, where the **Paper Mill Village Bridge** stretches over the river (0.2 mi/0.3 km). The original bridge construction was in 1889, but the existing structure was rebuilt in 2000.

Drive across the Paper Mill Village Bridge, and continue south on Murphy Road, which loops around to **Burt Henry Covered Bridge,** another 1840 structure with town lattice trussing (1.3 mi/2 km). Keep an eye out for **Henry House,** to the left of the road just south of the bridge; built in 1769, it is one of the oldest surviving houses in Vermont.

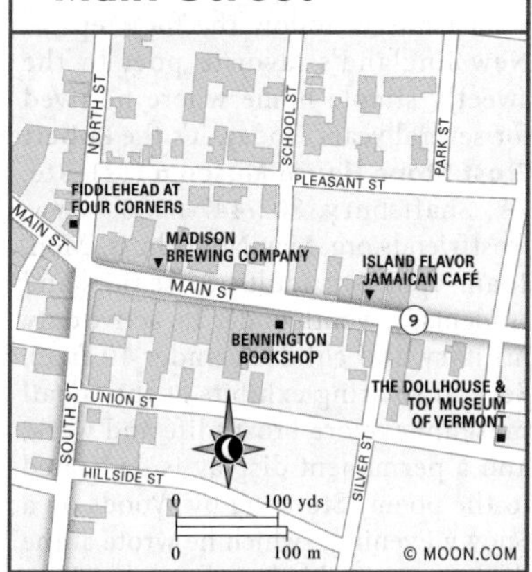

The area's other two covered bridges are 15 miles (24 km) north, in the village of Arlington. Cross the Burt Henry Bridge and turn right on River Road, then follow Route 67A to Route 67 and 7A North. Just before the Stewart's Shop in Arlington, turn right on East Arlington Road, which turns into Sunderland Road before reaching the **Chiselville Covered Bridge** across Roaring Branch Brook (15.3 mi/25 km). Set over a steep embankment, this 1870 bridge features a threatening one-dollar fine for crossing above a walking pace.

Retrace your path back to Route 7A, and go north for 0.2 mile (0.3 km) before turning left on Route 313. Take a left onto the aptly named Covered Bridge Road after 4.2 miles (6.75 km), and you'll find the **Arlington Green Covered Bridge** (6.3 mi/10.1 km). With a bucolic view of West Arlington's town green and forested hills, this bridge is among Vermont's most photogenic, especially when fall colors highlight its iconic rust-red color. The bridge is a stone's throw from the home where artist Norman Rockwell lived and painted for 15 years, now the Inn on Covered Bridge Green.

Robert Frost Stone House Museum

After visiting his gravesite at the Old First Church, follow the footsteps of New England's favorite poet to the sweetly simple home where he lived for several years. Today, it's the **Robert Frost Stone House Museum** (121 Rte. 7A, Shaftsbury, 802/447-6200, www.frostfriends.org, May-Nov. Thurs.-Mon. 10am-4pm, $10 adults, $6 seniors and students, $5 youth under 18, active duty military and children under 10 free). Several rotating exhibits at this small museum explore Frost's life and work, and a permanent display is dedicated to the poem "Stopping by Woods on a Snowy Evening," which he wrote at the dining room table here "on a hot June morning in 1922." Some of Frost's own apple trees remain on the slightly ramshackle grounds, along with crumbling stone walls and groves of birch.

Entertainment and Events

On August 16 of every year, Vermont celebrates its very own holiday, **Bennington Battle Day** (802/442-1037, www.benningtonvt.org), during which the town holds an annual parade along with battle reenactments on the monument grounds.

A few weeks later, bring your breath mints to **Garlic Town USA** (www.garlictownusa.com), an annual Labor Day weekend celebration that offers up plenty of piquant samples of garlic spreads, garlic jellies, garlic salsas, and even garlic ice cream (don't miss the tent with garlic margaritas) at a fairground off Route 9 west of town. In between eating and not kissing, fairgoers can take in musical performances, face painting, and a hay maze.

Set in a nondescript brick building in workaday downtown Bennington, it's hard not to love that **Oldcastle Theatre Company** (331 Main St., 802/447-0564, www.oldcastletheatre.org) has been putting on professional caliber performances since 1972. Catch shows that range from Shakespeare to show tunes and slapstick.

Shopping

The shelves at **Bennington Bookshop** (109 South St., 802/442-5059, www.benningtonbookshop.com, Mon.-Sat. 10am-6pm, Sun. 10am-4pm) are built for browsing, with an ample selection of children's books, beach reads, and serious literature, along with plenty of local subject matter.

Browse a fun collection of jewelry, art, and crafts at **Fiddlehead at Four Corners** (338 Main St., 802/447-1000, daily 9am-6pm), a friendly store set into an old bank with a slate-lined vault where visitors can scrawl messages in chalk. The friendly, knowledgeable owner makes this shop a local favorite, and he's an excellent source of local lore and attractions.

Hiking

The Appalachian Trail becomes the **Long Trail** when it passes into Vermont. The closest access point to Bennington is where the trail crosses Route 9—drive 5.2 miles (8.4 km) east of the intersection of Route 9 and Route 7, and park in the small roadside lot. To follow a bit of the famous trail, you could head north or south, though the Long Trail mostly winds through thick forest on either side of the road.

Northbound, the Long Trail climbs to **Glastenbury Mountain,** where hikers earn panoramic views of the Green Mountain National Forest from a rickety fire tower. The dense, rustling Glastenbury Wilderness through which the trail runs has also inspired eerie legends involving UFOs, sasquatch-like creatures, and giant man-eating rocks. The hike is 7.3 miles (11.7 km) one-way, and should only be attempted as a full-day walk.

Southbound, the Long Trail climbs more steeply, pitching up **Harmon Hill.** The round-trip hike from Route 9 is 3.7 miles (6 km) round-trip; plan for 2.5-3 hours. The trail switchbacks and steps its way up 1,200 feet (366 m) of elevation gain to an open meadow that peers down on the town of Bennington, where the Bennington Battle Monument pokes high above the trees.

For maps and hiking information, contact the **Manchester Ranger District** (2538 Depot St., Manchester Center, 802/362-2307, www.fs.usda.gov).

Food

Casual Fare

Six miles (9.6 km) from downtown Bennington, **Kevin's Sports Pub & Restaurant** (27 Main St., North Bennington, 802/442-0122, www.kevinssportspubandrestaurant.com, Mon.-Thurs. 11am-9pm, Fri. 11am-10pm, Sat. 8am-10pm, Sun. 8am-9pm, $10-23) is a neighborhood bar and restaurant that's fiercely beloved by locals. They come for burgers, fried chicken, and steak or just to lean an elbow on the bar and watch the whole town come and go. There's often live music on Friday and Saturday nights, and the game is always on.

International

The authentic Caribbean cooking at **Island Flavor Jamaican Café** (512 Main St., 516/884-9130, Sun.-Fri. 11am-7pm, $13-21) sometimes has lines of hungry visitors running out the door of this aromatic little family-owned eatery. The curried goat, jerk chicken, and braised oxtail are the real deal, and portions are offered in "regular" and "large" sizes, so come here prepared for leftovers or a digestive siesta.

The convivial **Madison Brewing Company** (428 Main St., 802/442-7397, www.madisonbrewingco.com, Mon.-Sat. 11:30am-9pm, Sun. 11:30am-4pm, $11-24) serves handcrafted beers along with pub grub from around the world: cottage pie, mezze platters, Irish lounge fries, and pork schnitzel are among the democratic offerings. The malty, smooth, and potent Old 76 Strong Ale is a standout among their brews, many of which change with the season.

Bakeries

A veritable smorgasbord of Vermont-made munchies, the **Apple Barn Country Bake Shop** (604 Rte. 7, 802/447-7780, www.theapplebarn.com, Sun.-Thurs. 8:30am-4pm, Fri.-Sat. 8:30am-6pm, $4-11) doubles as a bakery and an edible marketplace. Each morning's roster of pastries includes temptations like apple cinnamon muffins, blueberry scones, and rocky road brownies, while the aisles are liberally stocked with bounty such as colorful squash, local honey and preserves, and during early fall, crates of heirloom apples.

Accommodations and Camping

Camping

Eleven miles (18 km) east of the town of Bennington on Route 9, the solitude and integrity of **Woodford State Park** (142 State Park Rd., 802/447-7169, www.vtstateparks.com/woodford.html, Memorial Day-mid-Oct.) are magnified by its location at the heart of the 400,000-acre (161,874-ha) Green Mountain National Forest. The park maintains a wooded, 103-site **campground** (tent sites $28-30, lean-tos $38-40), which has an RV dump station, but no hookups. Rowboats, canoes, and kayaks are available to rent at the park ($10/hr, $40/full day), and there's a family-friendly swimming beach and picnic area.

You can plug in your rig a few miles west at ★ **Greenwood Lodge & Campsites** (311 Greenwood Dr., Woodford, 802/442-2546, www.campvermont.com/greenwood, mid-May-late Oct., tent sites $28-33, 20- to 30-amp sites $36-40, 50-amp sites $42-45 for one/two people, no credit cards), where the 40 wooded campsites have full hookups with 20, 30, and 50 amps.

Under $150

The owners at the ★ **Harwood Hill Motel**

The Places in Between: The Northeast Kingdom

Hill Farmstead brewery

If you're driving from southern Vermont to the White Mountains, or vice versa, take a dreamy detour through the tuft-like green hills of northeastern Vermont, aka the **Northeast Kingdom**—a quieter, less tourist-oriented agrarian realm. Here, dairy farms are flanked by craggy mountains and boreal spruce forests give the region a more Nordic vibe.

For an arresting vista of the Kingdom, clamber up to the summit of **Mount Pisgah** on the challenging four-mile (6.4-km) **Mount Pisgah Trail** (VT-5A, Orleans). Take an invigorating swim at **Caspian Lake Beach** (125 Beach Rd., Greensboro), then sample hoppy pale ales at award-winning **Hill Farmstead** (403 Hill Rd., Greensboro Bend, 802/533-7450, www.hillfarmstead.com, Wed.-Sat. 11:30am-5pm), or wolf down a parmesan-crusted pizza at **The Parker Pie Company** (161 County Rd., Glover, 802/525-3366, www.parkerpie.com, Tues.-Sun. 11am-9pm, $15-26), a cozy general store where you can also stock up on local goods like the world-renowned Harbison and Bayley Hazen blue cheeses.

If you fancy a taste of the Kingdom's funkier side, pop into **The Museum of Everyday Life** (3482 Dry Pond Rd., Glover, www.museumofeverydaylife.org, daily 8am-8pm, free), a ramshackle roadside barn whose collection of beautiful and junky household items are an ode to the weirdness of life.

For a cultural experience like none other in Vermont (or anywhere), take in an outdoor circus show in the amphitheater-esque field at **Bread and Puppet Theater** (753 Heights Rd., Glover, 802/525-3031, www.breadandpuppet.org, June-Aug. Fri.-Sat., check website for performance times and ticket prices). Puppets range from human-size to gigantic puppets that have to be carried around on sticks by multiple puppeteers. The "circus" part of the show, which is the first half and what most people come for, is funny, exciting, and warm-hearted. It's family friendly and full of political satire and commentary (from a leftist/humanist angle). But the circus is followed by a more hymnal "pageant" with large puppets in the nearby woods, which is moving and even a little chilling, in a beautiful way. The only risk for families with this segment of the show is that some kids might get bored and very young kids might get a little spooked by the huge puppets in the woods, compared to the circus part. Fresh bread with fiery garlic aioli is served after the pageant.

(864 Harwood Hill Rd., 802/442-6278, www.harwoodhillmotel.com, $110-150, two-bedroom suite $180) have put together spruced-up rooms with paintings by local artists and added appealing splashes of color to the simple roadside motel, which has a sweeping view over the town. All rooms have coffeemakers and refrigerators, and rollaway beds are provided for no extra charge. The two-bedroom farmhouse suite includes a full kitchen and living room. If you're staying for two nights and plan to take in the sights, the Arts Package is an amazing deal: $295 covers both evenings as well as admission and discounts at a laundry list of local attractions, and the date-dependent $345 option includes a pair of tickets to a show at Oldcastle Theatre.

Just down the hill from the Bennington Battle Monument, the **Knotty Pine Motel** (130 Northside Dr., 802/442-5487, www.knottypinemotel.com, $109-159) offers good value and spotless rooms, including queens, doubles, and efficiencies with kitchenettes.

$150-250

The sweetly restored ★ **Eddington House Inn** (21 Main St., North Bennington, 802/681-7636, www.eddingtonhouseinn.com, $159-229) is full of thoughtful touches: handmade truffles, afternoon snacks, and delicious breakfasts make it a welcoming place, as do the friendly owners. The rooms are decorated with beautiful taste, antiques are atmospheric but uncluttered, and each room includes a sitting area that's perfect for curling up with a book. The Eddington House is in North Bennington, a village that's about six miles (9.6 km) north of downtown Bennington.

Four chimneys really do project from the roof of **The Four Chimneys Inn** (21 West Rd./Rte. 9, 802/447-3500, www.fourchimneys.com, $220-400), a sprawling Revolutionary-era parsonage that has been converted to an upscale bed-and-breakfast. As might be expected, many of the rooms have fireplaces, including one with a real wood-burning hearth. The white-tablecloth dining room has French doors looking out on the grounds and serves a menu of refined New England cuisine, with specialties such as seared octopus with white bean ragout and nine-hour crispy pork belly.

Information and Services

The **Bennington Area Chamber of Commerce** (100 Veterans Memorial Dr., 802/447-3311, www.bennington.com) runs a visitor center in town. Emergency medical services are handled by **Southwestern Vermont Medical Center** (100 Hospital Dr., East Bennington, 802/442-6361, www.svhealthcare.org). For medications, **Extended Care Pharmacy** (207 North St., 802/442-4600) is located in the center of town. For nonmedical emergencies, contact the **Bennington Police Department** (118 South St., 802/442-1030).

Several banks with ATMs are located at the corner of Route 7 and Route 9, including **M&T Bank** (37 Bennington Sq.), **Citizens Bank** (310 Main St.), and **TD Bank** (500 Main St.). Free Internet use is offered at the **Bennington Free Library** (101 Silver St., 802/442-9051, www.benningtonfreelibrary.org, Mon. 10am-7pm, Tues.-Wed. 10am-5pm, Thurs. 1pm-7pm, Fri. 1pm-5pm, Sat. 10am-1pm).

Getting Around

To get to Bennington from **Brattleboro** (40 mi/64 km, 1 hr), drive east on **Route 9,** the **scenic Molly Stark Byway,** which links both towns' downtown areas. Precisely halfway between the two, the diminutive town of **Wilmington** is the perfect place to pause for a swim or take in views to the south from the Hogback Mountain overlook.

The
Berkshires

Highlights

★ **Massachusetts Museum of Contemporary Art (MASS MoCA):** Explore a sprawling complex of former mill buildings filled with modern art, installations, and performances (page 262).

★ **Mount Greylock:** Tackle a steep trail to the top of the highest point in Massachusetts (or take a leisurely drive to the same place), and earn views that stretch to Vermont and New York (page 266).

★ **The Mount:** Tour the gorgeously understated country home that Edith Wharton designed herself, where she gathered a who's who of intellectuals and artists (page 268).

★ **Tanglewood Music Festival:** Spread your blanket and pour the wine for the summer's most glamorous picnic at the warm-weather home of the Boston Symphony Orchestra (page 270).

★ **Norman Rockwell Museum:** Learn about the art and life of an artist enchanted by small-town living and the New England landscape (page 275).

The Berkshires

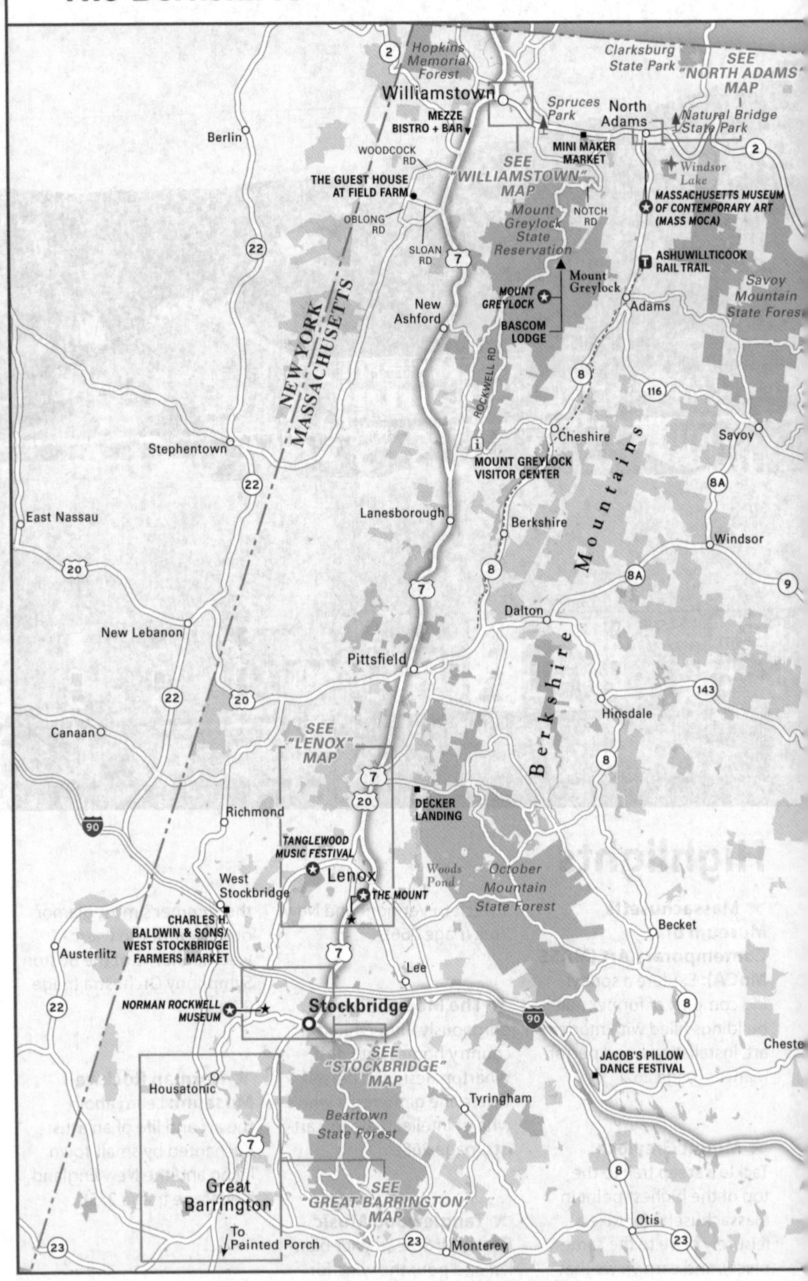

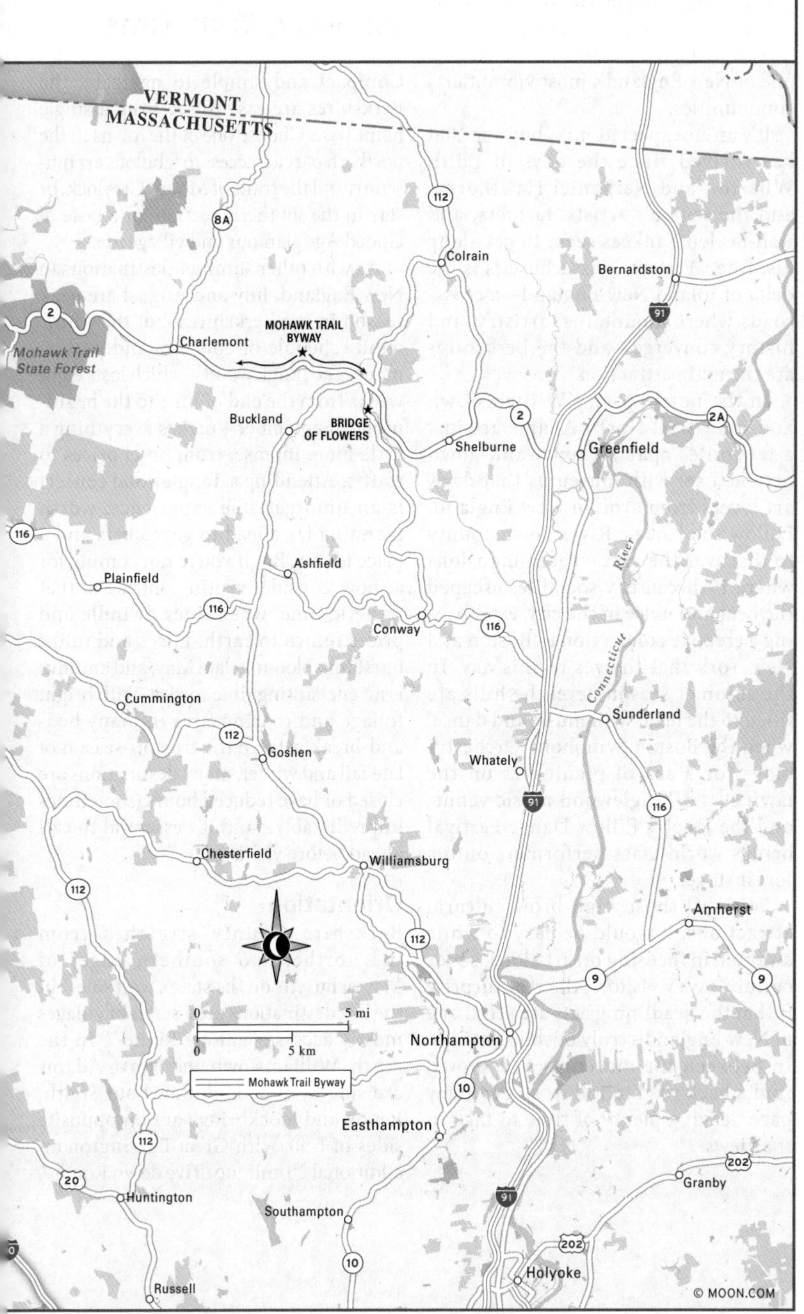
VERMONT
MASSACHUSETTS
Colrain
Bernardston
Charlemont
Mohawk Trail State Forest
MOHAWK TRAIL BYWAY
BRIDGE OF FLOWERS
Buckland
Shelburne
Greenfield
Ashfield
Plainfield
Conway
Connecticut River
Cummington
Sunderland
Goshen
Whately
Chesterfield
Williamsburg
Amherst
Northampton
Easthampton
Granby
Huntington
Southampton
Holyoke
Russell
0 5 mi
0 5 km
Mohawk Trail Byway
© MOON.COM

All rolling hills and twisting rivers, the Berkshires' gentle landscape shelters quaint villages, grand mansions, and one of New England's most vibrant arts communities.

It's an unexpected mix, but one that has thrived since the days of Edith Wharton and Nathaniel Hawthorne, and the region's artists, farmers, and well-heeled Yankees seem to get along just fine. Western Massachusetts is the delta of inland New England—a crossroads where mountains, artistry, and history converge—and the Berkshires are the main attraction.

In the north, pretty Williamstown and industrial North Adams are just a few miles apart, a town-and-gown matched set with museums that draw art lovers from around New England. Follow the Hoosic River down county to discover the extravagant mansions where 19th-century socialites escaped the heat and noise of the city, establishing a creative connection to Boston and New York that thrives to this day. In the summer season here, the hills are filled to the brim with music and dance, when the Boston Symphony Orchestra plays for a sea of picnickers on the lawn at the Tanglewood music venue, and the Jacob's Pillow Dance Festival brings world-class performers onto a forest stage.

With all those high-brow cultural attractions, it would be easy to while away a trip focusing on art alone, so for culture-savvy visitors, the real surprise is that the headlining acts are set in one of New England's truly bucolic settings. In between the museums and shows, find a back road to follow at a country pace, leaving plenty of time to take in the views.

Planning Your Time

Compact and simple to navigate, the Berkshires are easy to see from a single home base: Choose one of the towns in the northern part for access to fabulous art museums and the trails of Mount Greylock, or stay in the southerly section for a taste of Gilded Age glamour and village life.

As with other summer destinations in New England, July and August are peak season in the Berkshires, but the whirlwind schedule of concerts and performances at Tanglewood—which lasts eight weeks from the end of June to the beginning of September—makes everything a little more intense, from hotel prices to traffic. Attending a Tanglewood concert is an unforgettable experience, worth planning far ahead to get tickets and a place to stay. But if you're not coming for a show, consider visiting outside of that frenetic time, when lines dwindle and prices return to earth. Lilacs and tulips burst into bloom in late May, and autumn is an enchanting time to visit, with bright foliage and roaring fires in many bed-and-breakfasts. In the true off-season of late fall and winter, many destinations are closed or have reduced hours (sometimes unpredictably), and it's essential to call ahead before visiting.

Orientation

Berkshire County stretches from the northern to southern edges of Massachusetts on the state's west side, but the key destinations are a series of villages mostly accessible along Route 7. In the north, Williamstown and North Adams are side by side; about an hour south, Lenox and Stockbridge are on opposite sides of I-90, with Great Barrington an additional 20-minute drive down Route 7.

Best Restaurants

★ **Public Eat + Drink:** Industrial cool meets farm to table, just down the street from MASS MoCA (page 266).

★ **Brava:** Score a patio table, order a bottle of wine and a round of small plates, and cross paths with visiting musicians in search of a late-night bite (page 273).

★ **Haven Café and Bakery:** Watch the whole town come and go at this relaxed, centrally located hangout (page 273).

★ **Once Upon a Table:** Tucked into a sweet, sunny alley, this friendly bistro is a longtime favorite for locals and visitors alike (page 277).

★ **The Bistro Box:** The casual fare at this roadside stand is a Berkshires take on the New England snack bar done right (page 282).

Getting to the Berkshires

Driving from Southern Vermont

15 mi/24.1 km, 0.5 hr

Williamstown is just across the border from **Bennington** (15 mi/24 km, 0.5 hr), a short drive south on **Route 7.** From **Brattleboro,** drive about 23 miles (37 km) west on **Route 9** to Searsburg, then turn left on **Route 8.** After about 5 miles (8 km), turn right to remain on Route 8. After 8.5 miles (13.7 km) and crossing the state line, turn right onto Middle Road, which becomes Franklin Street, then Eagle Street, and leads into downtown **North Adams** (45 mi/72 km, 1.25 hrs).

Driving from New York City

140 mi/225.3 km, 2.5 hr

From New York City to **Great Barrington,** leave the city heading north on **FDR Drive.** Use the left lane to access Exit 17 to the **Robert F. Kennedy Bridge** ($10.17 toll), then stay left to merge onto **I-278 East.** Take Exit 52 to merge onto the **Bronx River Parkway** for 8.4 miles (13.5 km), continuing onto **Sprain Brook Parkway** north for 12.5 miles (20 km). Proceed onto the **Taconic Parkway North**—among New York state's most scenic drives, passing through Hudson Valley farms and forest—for 85 miles (137 km), then exit right for **Route 23 East** toward Claverack/Hillsdale. Continue on Route 23 though South Egremont, where it merges with **Route 41,** following it until turning left onto Main Street in Great Barrington.

Driving from Boston

135 mi/217.3 km, 2 hr

Leave Boston on **I-90 West,** following the highway for approximately 125 miles (201 km, $12.95 toll). For **Stockbridge,** take Exit 10 for **Route 20 East,** then keep right to merge onto **Route 102 West** into downtown Stockbridge. For **Lenox,** take Exit 10 for **Route 20 West.** In Lee, turn right onto Main Street, following it slightly left to Center Street to remain on Route 20. After about 3 miles (5 km), turn left onto Walker Street, which leads into Lenox. It's about the same amount of driving time and distance from Boston to either Stockbridge or Lenox.

Driving from Newport

160 mi/257.5 km, 2.5 hr

From Newport, take Farewell Street north from downtown and follow it as it becomes **Route 238 North,** then merge onto **Route 138 West,** which leads across the **Newport Bridge** ($6 toll). Exit onto

Best Accommodations

★ **Clover Hill Farm:** Make friends with horses, ducks, and a surly goat at this wonderfully friendly family farm (page 261).

★ **The Porches Inn:** Thoughtful design and bits of Americana make this the Berkshires' most exciting hotel, just steps away from MASS MoCA (page 268).

★ **Bascom Lodge:** Watch the sun set over the Catskills from a rustic stone lodge built by the Civilian Conservation Corps in the 1930s (page 268).

★ **Yankee Inn:** Colorful and spacious rooms, bargain prices, and a stunning backyard with a pond and mountain views make this roadside inn a surprise winner (page 274).

★ **Brook Farm Inn:** A classic country inn with modern comforts and historic charm, Brook Farm overflows with poetry books perfect for reading over the afternoon tea service (page 274).

Route 1 North toward Provincetown, then use the left two lanes to turn onto **Route 4 North.** After 10 miles (16 km), merge onto **I-95 North** for 2.8 miles (4.5 km), staying left to continue on **I-295 North** for 18.6 miles (30 km). Take Exit 9B and keep left for **Route 146 North,** which you'll follow for about 25 miles (40 km), crossing into Massachusetts.

Exit toward Route 20/I-90, then use the left two lanes to enter **I-90 West** ($4.75 toll), on which you'll remain for approximately 83 miles (133 km). For **Stockbridge,** take Exit 10 for **Route 20 East,** then keep right to merge onto **Route 102 West** into downtown Stockbridge. For **Lenox,** take Exit 10 for **Route 20 West.** In Lee, turn right onto Main Street, following it slightly left to Center Street to remain on Route 20. After about 3 miles (4.8 km), turn left onto Walker Street, which leads into Lenox. It's about the same amount of driving time and distance from Newport to either Stockbridge or Lenox.

Getting There by Air, Train, or Bus

Air

The closest airport to the region is **Albany International Airport** (737 Albany Shaker Rd., Albany NY, 518/242-2200, www.albanyairport.com). Taxi service from the airport is available from a variety of car services including **Capital City Taxi** (518/488-2273, www.albanynycapitalcitytaxi.com), which charges $110 to Williamstown and $90 to Lenox.

Train

Amtrak (800/872-7245, www.amtrak.com) offers service from Boston to Pittsfield, the westernmost city in Massachusetts on Route 7, 17 miles (27 km) north of Lenox (4 hrs, from $9), and from New York City to Hudson, New York (2 hrs, from $31), 32 miles (51 km) east of Stockbridge. New York's **Metropolitan Transit Authority** runs trains from the city to Wassaic (2.5 hrs, from $26), 50 miles (80 km) south of Lenox.

Williamstown

A sign at the crossroads of Williamstown's center designates the town "the village beautiful," and few would dispute the claim. Completely ringed by mountains, it's dominated by

Two Days in the Berkshires

The Mount

Day 1

Work your way from north to south—or reverse the trip—and experience the best of the Berkshires' art, nature, and culture. Modern art lovers should head straight for North Adams's **MASS MoCA** for a morning of wild installations and contemporary masterpieces, while those more interested in the classics can go up the Hoosic River to **The Clark Art Institute** in Williamstown.

In the afternoon, drive to the summit of **Mount Greylock** for sweeping views of the mountains and lunch at a communal dining table in **Bascom Lodge,** then strike out along the **Appalachian Trail** to tick off a few of its 2,160 miles (3,476 km); keep an eye on the time, and head back to the peak in time for its showstopping sunsets. Dine in town, then perk up with a cup of after-dinner coffee—the grounds at The Clark Art Institute are open all night for **stargazing** by the reflecting pools.

Day 2

Continue south for a taste of classed-up country life, starting with **The Mount,** Edith Wharton's gorgeous estate and grounds, and followed by truffle fries and nourishing sandwiches at **The Bistro Box.** From there, if you're ready for more art, don't miss the collection at the **Norman Rockwell Museum,** or join a canoe trip down the Hoosic River, whose gentle curves and oxbows offer unmatched perspectives on the mountains, waterside forests, and fields.

Finish the day with a slow-moving procession of small plates and wine at **Brava,** or catch some tunes in the lair-like basement bar of the historic **Red Lion Inn.**

Williams College, and the green lawns, old-fashioned architecture, and student-filled cafés conjure pure New England college nostalgia. The school is one of the oldest in the country, founded in 1791 through the will of Colonel Ephraim Williams, who was killed during the French and Indian War but left his money for the establishment of a "free school" in the town of West Hoosac—provided it changed its name to Williamstown. Just 30 years after its founding, the president and half the student body left to found Amherst College to the southeast, thus ensuring a rivalry that continues through sports to the present day. Today, the town is well known for its art museums and theater

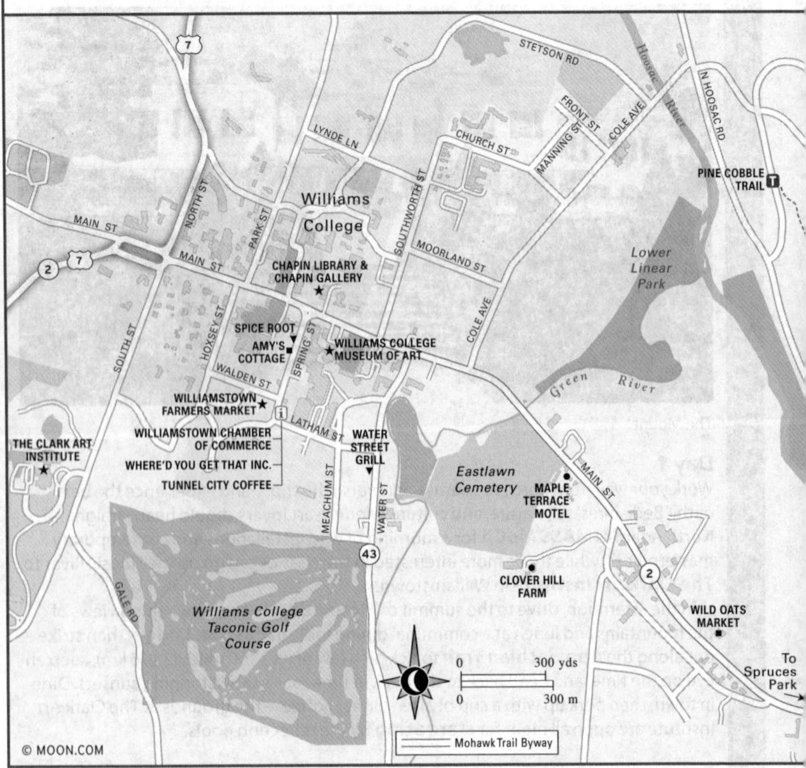

festival, which brings theatergoers from New York and Boston every summer.

Sights

The Clark Art Institute

The extensive collection of high-quality art at **The Clark Art Institute** (225 South St., 413/458-2303, www.clarkart.edu, Sept.-June Tues.-Sun. 10am-5pm, July-Aug. daily 10am-5pm, $20 adults, free students and youth under 22) is remarkable, as is the institute's parklike setting. The Clark is simply one of the best small museums in the country, with a collection full of gems by Renoir, Monet, Degas, Copley, Remington, and other well-known artists that seem handpicked for their individual beauty or interest. Beyond the gallery walls are 140 acres (56.6 ha) of walking trails, meadows, and forest, free to access at any time; one of the most romantic ways to enjoy the campus is to make a late-night trip to the Clark's reflecting ponds, where comfortable Adirondack chairs invite all comers for an evening of stargazing.

Williams College

Historic buildings and a picture-perfect backdrop make the **Williams College campus** (880 Main St., 413/597-3131, www.williams.edu) an excellent place to explore on your own, with a few highlights not to be missed. Rounding out the town's reputation as a showstopping arts destination is the **Williams College**

Museum of Art (15 Lawrence Hall Dr., 413/597-2429, https://artmuseum.williams.edu, Tues.-Sun. 10am-5pm, free). The museum has a focus on modern and contemporary art, American art, and the art of world cultures, and houses a noteworthy collection of works by Edward Hopper and Maurice Prendergast. Housed in the thoroughly modern-looking Sawyer Library, Williams's **Chapin Library** is the only institution outside the National Archives to have an original copy of each of the four founding documents of the United States: The Declaration of Independence, Constitution, Bill of Rights, and Articles of Confederation are on permanent display in the **Chapin Gallery** (Sawyer Library, Rm. 406, Williams College Campus, Mon.-Fri. 8am-5pm, free).

Spruces Park

Hidden in plain sight on the road from Williamstown to North Adams, **Spruces Park** (60 Main St., Williamstown, 413/458-3500) is a sprawling plot of wildflower meadows where trees such as Japanese red maples, cypresses, and oaks take root. You may notice that these trees are something of an odd combination, and that the dirt road traversing the park has a grid-like pattern. In fact, the park used to be a mobile home community called The Spruces. In 2011, Tropical Storm Irene caused the nearby Hoosic River to swamp the neighborhood and it was condemned by the town. While the resultant exodus may have ceded the land back to nature, many of the trees that grow here were actually planted by the former residents. To walk among these arbors today is a truly eerie experience—serene, haunting, and humbling.

Entertainment and Events

For more than 60 years, some of the biggest Hollywood names have descended upon the **Williamstown Theatre Festival** (413/458-3253, www.wtfestival.org, July-Aug.) to try out their acting chops on the stage. The festival runs a range of productions, from gala premieres to intimate play readings, allowing theatergoers a chance to see a different side of well-known and up-and-coming stars.

Shopping

The main drag of **Spring Street** is full of college-themed shops geared to alumni and stocked with gear in Williams College's single color: purple. Unfortunately, the school's traditional rivals at Amherst College opted for purple and white, so the "Ephs" (that's short for Ephraim Williams, the college founder) tend to spruce up their gear with some yellow to underscore the difference. For gifts in other hues, **Where'd You Get That Inc.** (100 Spring St., 413/458-2206, www.wygt.com, Mon.-Sat. 10am-6pm, Sun. 10am-5pm) carries a carefully curated selection of puzzles and games, science kits, home decor, and doodads from indie makers, while **Amy's Cottage** (39 Spring St., 413/458-4305, www.amyscottage.com, Mon. and Wed.-Sat. 10am-6pm, Tues. and Sun. 10am-5pm) combines eclectic earrings and necklaces with luxury bath and body goods in a boutique setting.

Sports and Recreation

Mount Greylock dominates the landscape here, but there are many ways to get into the woods from Williamstown. One favorite outing is the trail up **Pine Cobble,** a quartzite outcropping with views of the Hoosic River Valley. To reach the trailhead, take Cole Avenue from Route 7 and turn right onto North Hoosic Road. Turn left on Pine Cobble Road and park 0.2 mile (0.3 km) up on the left, opposite the trailhead. The 1.6-mile (2.6-km) trail to Pine Cobble is moderately steep and takes at least an hour; the trail is maintained by the **Williams Outing Club,** which has a detailed trail description on its website (woc.williams.edu/pine-cobble-trail-2).

Find a more extensive trail system in **Hopkins Memorial Forest** (entrance on Northwest Hill Rd., 109 yards north of Bulkley St., https://hmf.williams.edu/?dts=1), where 15 miles (24 km) of paths wind through forests and fields. A good place to start is the 1.5-mile (2.4-km) **Lower Loop,** which takes roughly one hour, and the hike can be extended by connecting to the 2.6-mile (4.2-km) **Upper Loop,** which takes an additional two hours; together, the two loop trails form a figure-eight shape.

Food

The floor-to-ceiling windows at **Tunnel City Coffee** (100 Spring St., 413/458-5010, Tues.-Thurs. 6am-2pm, Fri.-Mon. 6am-5pm, $4-10) are flung wide open on warm days, and students kick back in comfortable couches and armchairs. Aside from the people-watching, locally roasted coffee is the draw, along with pastries and snacks.

King-size chili and cheese nachos, Vermont-raised pulled pork sandwiches, and hearty salads with ample fixin's make the **Water Street Grill** (123 Water St., 413/458-2175, www.waterstgrill.com, daily 11:30am-9pm, $14-22) a local favorite for nourishing and thoughtfully prepared pub grub. With 21 draft beers on tap, this is also a reliable outpost for sampling the work of regional brewers. And on crisp fall nights, the crackling fireplace is a welcome atmospheric touch.

The village's culinary jewel is **Mezze Bistro + Bar** (777 Rte. 7, 413/458-0123, www.mezzerestaurant.com, Wed.-Sun. 5pm-8:30pm, $28-55), a sophisticated restaurant in a beautifully renovated 19th-century home just south of town. Local ingredients are transformed on an international menu with an Italian emphasis; small plates, mains, and pasta dishes star alongside an extensive (and very reasonable) wine list.

In the persistently quaint Berkshires, the colorful decor and bold Indian flavors at **Spice Root** (23 Spring St., 413/458-5200, www.spiceroot.com, Tues.-Sat. lunch 11:30am-2:30pm, Sun. lunch

The Clark Art Institute

noon-3pm, Tues.-Sun. dinner 5pm-10pm, $12-25) are a tonic. The ample vegetarian and vegan choices are popular here, and the weekday lunch buffet is a fabulous deal.

Grab provisions at **Wild Oats Market** (320 Main St., 413/458-8060, www.wildoats.coop, daily 8am-8pm), where some produce, prepared foods, and other groceries are sourced locally. Shop for bread, crafts, honey, produce, local arts, and crafts at the **Williamstown Farmers Market** (125 Spring St., https://williamstownfarmersmarket.com, May-Oct. Sat. 9am-1pm), which also has prepared foods.

Accommodations and Camping

Camping

Shady and quiet, the campground at **Clarksburg State Park** (1199 Middle Rd., Clarksburg, 413/664-8345, www.mass.gov, late May-early Sept., $54) has 45 sites, five miles (8 km) northeast of Williamstown's center. The park also has extensive hiking trails and a tempting pond (where swimming is not allowed).

Under $150

Simple rooms are clean and well appointed at **Maple Terrace Motel** (555 Main St., 413/458-9677, www.mapleterrace.com, $95-215), whose convenient Main Street location is walking distance to the Williams College campus. The continental breakfast of good coffee and fresh bread is an unexpected treat, but the real treasure is behind the motel, where a swimming pool and lawn abut a rolling horse pasture that feels like a bit of country in the middle of town.

$150-250

While scores of "farms" to stay at abound in the Berkshires, you'll find the real thing at ★ **Clover Hill Farm** (249 Adams Rd., 413/458-3376, www.cloverhillfarm.net, $150-250), home to horses, chickens, ducks, and an adorably grouchy goat named Suzie (after she took on a few too many cars, her horns were wrapped in soft cloth—bottles labeled "Goat H2O" are stashed all over the farm to rebuff her mostly harmless butts). The wonderful owners have two single rooms, a five-person suite, and a guesthouse that are casual, comfortable, and dog-friendly. This is a great choice for families, and riding lessons can be arranged in advance.

$250-350

A tiered, cubist exterior, painted in hues of teal and mauve, is your first sign that **The Guest House at Field Farm** (554 Sloan Rd., 413/458-3135, www.fieldfarm.org, $269-359) is not your ordinary bed-and-breakfast. A Bauhaus-inspired modernist masterpiece, the home is full of modern art and design-conscious period furniture. A heated outdoor pool, private decks, and terry-cloth robes create a sense of peaceful refuge, combined with the natural setting—300 protected acres (121.4 ha) surround the house.

Information

The **Williamstown Chamber of Commerce** (84 Spring St., 413/458-9077, www.williamstownchamber.com) runs a small information booth that is seasonal and volunteer-staffed.

Another helpful resource, not just for Williamstown but also for the entire Berkshires region, is **1Berkshire,** a countywide economic development organization whose visitor website (www.berkshires.org) offers lots of information about destinations, seasonal events, and more.

Getting Around

Buses throughout the region are run by the **Berkshire Regional Transit Authority** (413/499-2782 or 800/292-2782, www.berkshirerta.com). Williamstown itself is easily walkable, and metered parking is available on Spring Street.

North Adams

With hulking factory buildings and a gritty, rustbelt mood, North Adams isn't a place where you'd expect to find the largest collection of modern art in the United States, and the Massachusetts Museum of Contemporary Art can seem like a colonial outpost of some hip, faraway community. But if you take the time to explore the town, you'll find art entwined with the old brick structures, vibrant murals brightening up highway bridges, and studios tucked above Main Street shops. MASS MoCA brought energy, visitors, and an infusion of much-needed cash after the town's leading employer, Sprague Electric, shut its doors in the 1980s, ending North Adams's long history as a mill and manufacturing town. Faded Victorian homes and an elegant public library are legacies of those prosperous years, when whirring woolen mills, shoe factories, sawmills, and ironworks were powered by the twin branches of the Hoosic River.

Sights

★ Massachusetts Museum of Contemporary Art (MASS MoCA)

Built on the sprawling campus of Sprague Electric, the size of the **Massachusetts Museum of Contemporary Art** (1040 MASS MoCA Way, 413/662-2111, www.massmoca.org, Wed.-Mon. 10am-6pm, $20 adults, $18 seniors and veterans, $12 students, $8 children 6-16, free for children under 6) is stunning. Composed of 27 redbrick former factory buildings and connected by an interlocking network of bridges, walkways, and courtyards, it has vast gallery spaces that allow for artwork of an unusually epic scale—from enormous installations to expansive performance art. The scale of the museum also affords more inclusiveness than many institutions, and MASS MoCA has a lack of pretension and takes an infectious delight in the creative process: small, unexpected touches abound, like the sidewalk cracks that employees fill in with gleaming gold paint.

Other Sights

The Barbara and Eric Rudd Art Foundation transformed a historic church into the **Berkshire Art Museum** (159 E. Main St., 413/664-9550, www.bamuseum.org, June-Aug. Wed.-Sun. noon-5pm, Sept.-Oct. Sat.-Sun. noon-5pm, $5 adults, $3 seniors, students, and children 6-12, free for children under 6), a home for local contemporary work. Eric Rudd's own work is on display in a moving, spiritually focused space at the same site, in the **Chapel for Humanity** annex.

Housed in the grand former home of local factory owner Sanford Blackinton, the **North Adams Public Library** (74 Church St., 413/662-3133, https://naplibrary.libguides.com, Mon.-Tues. and Thurs. 10am-5pm, Wed. 10am-8pm, Fri.-Sat. 10am-1pm) is a beautiful old building worth a look. Free wireless Internet and cozy reading chairs make this a comfortable place to wait out a rainy day.

North Adams

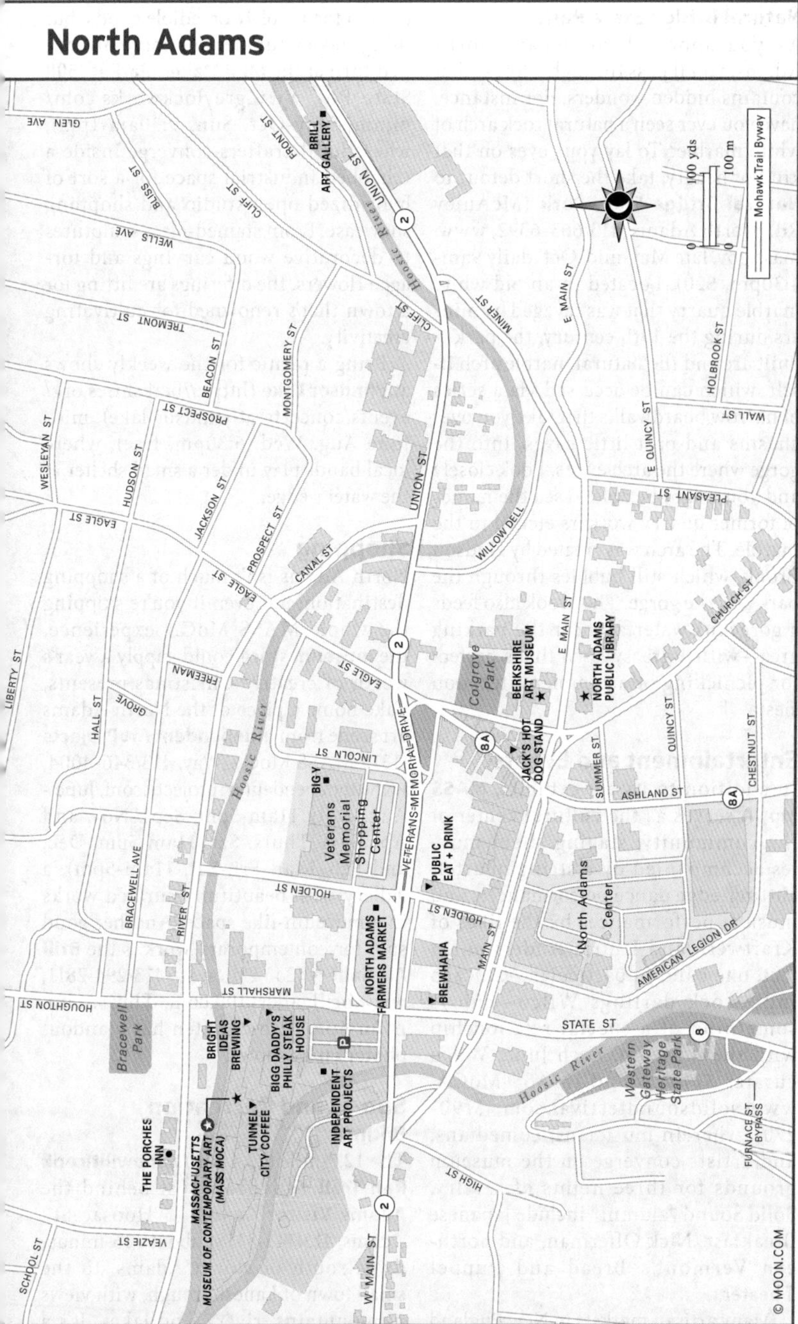
GLEN AVE
BLISS ST
WELLS AVE
CLIFF ST
FRONT ST
BRILL ART GALLERY
UNION ST
Hoosic River
TREMONT ST
BEACON ST
MONTGOMERY ST
CLIFF ST
MINER ST
E MAIN ST
100 yds
100 m
Mohawk Trail Byway
HOLBROOK ST
WALL ST
PROSPECT ST
WESLEYAN ST
HUDSON ST
JACKSON ST
E QUINCY ST
PLEASANT ST
EAGLE ST
PROSPECT ST
CANAL ST
WILLOW DELL
EAGLE ST
CHURCH ST
LIBERTY ST
FREEMAN
EAGLE ST
Colgrove Park
BERKSHIRE ART MUSEUM
E MAIN ST
NORTH ADAMS PUBLIC LIBRARY
HALL ST
GROVE
VETERANS MEMORIAL DRIVE
JACK'S HOT DOG STAND
8A
QUINCY ST
CHESTNUT ST
SUMMER ST
LINCOLN ST
BIG Y
Veterans Memorial Shopping Center
ASHLAND ST
PUBLIC EAT + DRINK
BRACEWELL AVE
RIVER ST
HOLDEN ST
HOLDEN ST
NORTH ADAMS FARMERS MARKET
MAIN ST
North Adams Center
AMERICAN LEGION DR
BREWHAHA
MARSHALL ST
HOUGHTON ST
Bracewell Park
BRIGHT IDEAS BREWING
BIGG DADDY'S PHILLY STEAK HOUSE
STATE ST
8
Western Gateway Heritage State Park
INDEPENDENT ART PROJECTS
P
THE PORCHES INN
MASSACHUSETTS MUSEUM OF CONTEMPORARY ART (MASS MOCA)
TUNNEL CITY COFFEE
FURNACE ST BYPASS
HIGH ST
2
VEAZIE ST
SCHOOL ST
W MAIN ST
© MOON.COM

Natural Bridge State Park

As you approach or depart North Adams, you'll pass through a forest that contains hidden wonders. For instance, have you ever seen a natural rock arch of white marble? To lay your eyes on that kind of beauty, take the short detour to **Natural Bridge State Park** (McAuley Rd., North Adams, 413/663-6392, www.mass.gov, late May-mid-Oct. daily 9am-4:30pm, $20). Located in an old white marble quarry that was ravaged by miners during the 19th century, the park is built around the natural marble arch itself, which can be accessed via a series of narrow boardwalks that take you over chasms and past little caves, into the gorge where the arch exists. Look closely and you might be able to see the names of former quarry workers etched in the marble. The arch was created by Hudson Brook, which still bubbles through the park and the gorge. The brook also feeds a gorgeous waterfall near the parking area—with a grassy lawn that's perfect for picnicking or a summer afternoon siesta.

Entertainment and Events

In addition to its art exhibits, **MASS MoCA** serves as the cultural center of the community, staging silent movies accompanied by a string quartet, cutting-edge dance performances, and musical performances by the likes of Kraftwerk and Laurie Anderson. In fact, one band in particular—Chicago indie rock darlings Wilco—enjoys something of a special relationship with the museum. Each June, Wilco curates **Solid Sound** (MASS MoCA, www.solidsoundfestival.com, $190-270), wherein musicians, comedians, and artists converge on the museum grounds for three nights of revelry. Solid Sound "alumni" include Japanese Breakfast, Nick Offerman, and northern Vermont's Bread and Puppet Theater.

Many artisan markets in New England tend to focus solely on edible goods, but things take a funkier and more diversified turn at the **Mini Maker Market** (508 State Rd., www.greylockworks.com/mmm, May-Oct. Sun. 9:30am-1pm), where local crafters converge inside a rehabbed industrial space for a sort of hybridized open studio and shopping showcase. From stained-glass sculptures to decorative wood carvings and foraged flowers, the offerings are fitting for a town that's renowned for cultivating creativity.

Bring a picnic for the weekly shows at **Windsor Lake** (https://berkshires.org/events/concerts-at-windsor-lake), mid-June-Aug. Wed. 6:30pm, free), where local bands play under a small shelter at the water's edge.

Shopping

North Adams isn't much of a shopping destination, but even if you're skipping the whole MASS MoCA experience, the **museum store** could supply a year's worth of creative Christmas presents. Take home a piece of the North Adams art scene from **Independent Art Projects** (1315 MASS MoCA Way, 413/346-4004, www.independentartprojects.com, June.-Aug. daily 11am-5pm, Sept.-Nov. and Apr.-May Thurs.-Sat. 11am-5pm, Dec. and Feb.-Mar. Fri.-Sat. 11am-5pm), a gallery with beautifully curated works in a museum-like space. Another good spot for contemporary work is the **Brill Art Gallery** (243 Union St., 413/294-2811, www.brillgallery109.com, Thurs.-Sun. noon-6pm), which often has standout photography shows.

Sports and Recreation

Biking

The 12.7-mile (20.4-km) **Ashuwillticook Rail Trail** runs from just behind the **Adams Visitor Center** (3 Hoosac St., Adams, 413/743-8358), about a 15-minute drive south of North Adams, to the small town of Lanesborough, with views of mountains, rivers, and lakes. It's a

Scenic Byway: Driving the Mohawk Trail

the winding Mohawk Trail byway

The soul of travel may be in the journey rather than the destination, but it's not always easy to keep that in mind when flying past the off-ramps and strip malls lining the Massachusetts Turnpike. For drivers coming from the east, the Mohawk Trail is a scenic alternative that evokes the golden age of road-tripping, winding through 63 miles (101 km) of rolling hills, villages, and gorgeous scenery on its way from Athol, a small town in north-central Massachusetts, to North Adams. The route alternates between Route 2 and Route 2A, following a traditional Native American path through the mountains, and was one of the first auto-tourism roads in the United States when it opened in 1914. In contrast to the Berkshires, the Mohawk Trail still has a retro feel, with motor lodges, trading posts, and scenic overlooks lining the roller-coaster ride through the mountains. If you're driving the trail as an out-and-back, the finest portion is the eight-mile (13-km) stretch from North Adams to the trail's highest point, Whitcomb Summit, which is marked with a bronze statue of an elk. It's a lovely route for some Sunday driving, or easy to incorporate if you're coming from Boston. Here are some of the trail's highlights:

- **Mohawk Trail State Forest:** Old-growth forest, mountains, and streams are shot through with five miles (8 km) of hiking trails that connect to a much larger system in Savoy Mountain State Forest. A favorite hike is the Mahican-Mohawk Trail, which offers access to meadows buzzing with life and a path to the top of Todd Mountain; there are also hiking trails and family-friendly places to swim (Rte. 2, Charlemont, 413/339-5504).
- **Shelburne Falls:** Pretty and old-fashioned, this village has a creative, castaway feel, and the picturesque downtown is lined with art galleries and workshops. The main attraction, though, is the **Bridge of Flowers,** a disused trolley bridge that overflows with blooms April-October. Travelers visiting the region in 2024 should take note that a closure and restoration are under way, with a reopening slated for the following spring.

pleasant, easy trail, and you can rent a bike just off it at **Berkshire Outfitters** (169 Grove St., Adams, 413/743-5900, www.berkshireoutfitters.com, Tues.-Sat. 10am-5pm, Sun. 11am-3pm, hybrid bikes $33 for 3 hrs, $55 for 24 hrs).

Hiking

★ Mount Greylock

The 3,491-foot (1,064-m) summit of **Mount Greylock** (Rockwell Rd., Lanesborough, 413/499-4262, www.mass.gov, access free, summit parking $20), the highest peak in Massachusetts, is both accessible and wild. The 92-foot (28-m) **Massachusetts Veterans War Memorial Tower** looms over the summit and draws hikers and road trippers alike, and the surrounding peaks are favorites for overnight hikes or leisurely afternoon drives. Several trails lead up into the mountains from both North Adams and Williamstown: Trace some of Henry David Thoreau's 1844 hike to the peak on a challenging 9.6-mile (15.4-km) loop, which takes about 6-8 hours, from Notch Road in North Adams—follow **Bellows Pipe Trail** to the **Appalachian Trail** (AT), and return via the AT and **Bernard Farm Trail.**

Or try the slightly easier, 6.2-mile (10-km) round-trip summit hike that takes 4-5 hours from the Mount Greylock Campground. This route starts off signed as the **Campground Trail,** then follows **Hopper Trail** for 1.4 miles (2.25 km), and links up with the Appalachian Trail for the final 1.1 miles (1.8 km).

As there are many trails in the area, it's essential to have a detailed map, available at the **Mount Greylock Visitor Center** (30 Rockwell Rd., 413/499-4262, May-Sept. daily 10am-5pm, Oct.-May Thurs.-Mon. 10am-4pm).

If all that sounds a bit strained, you can take a scenic, winding road straight to the top of Mount Greylock, savoring the partial roadside views before taking in the grand vista from the top of the mountain.

Food

Locals have been sidling up to the counter at **Jack's Hot Dog Stand** (12 Eagle St., 413/664-9006, www.jackshotdogstand.com, Mon.-Sat. 10am-7pm, $3-7) since 1917 for a simple menu of hot dogs, burgers, and fries. If the microwave now figures more visibly into kitchen prep than is conducive to misty-eyed nostalgia, Jack's is right at home in gritty North Adams, and the friendly service and vintage pricing are unbeatable.

Like its sister café in Williamstown, North Adams's **Tunnel City Coffee** (87 Marshall St., 413/398-5304, Mon.-Fri. 7am-6pm, Sat.-Sun. 9am-6pm, $4-10) serves pastries, snacks, and locally roasted coffee. This one, however, is inside the MASS MoCA complex (though the café can be accessed without buying a museum ticket), which means your cappuccino comes with a side of world-class people-watching, as the museum employees and visitors come and go.

Also in the MASS MoCA complex, **Bright Ideas Brewing** (111 MASS MoCA Way, 413/346-4460, www.brightideasbrewing.com, Sun.-Mon. and Wed. 11am-9pm, Thurs. 11am-10pm, Fri.-Sat. 11am-11pm, $6-9) is full of references to North Adams's industrial past, with gorgeous brick walls and a 40-foot (12-m) bar made by local workers. Its diverse lineup of beers manages to bridge the divide between the town's art lovers and townies. And if you like your beer paired with a cheesesteak or golden onion rings, the MASS MoCA complex is also home to **Bigg Daddy's Philly Steak House** (2601 MASS MoCA Way, 413/346-4431, www.biggdaddys.net, Wed.-Mon. 11am-9pm, $12-17), where you order from a window and choose a noshing spot on the immense museum grounds.

Modern, industrial decor and a gastropub menu make ★ **Public Eat + Drink** (34 Holden St., 413/664-4444, www.publiceatanddrink.com, Tues.-Thurs. 4pm-9pm, Fri.-Sat. 4pm-10pm, $15-30) the most stylish place to eat in town, and regulars love the fish-and-chips, burgers, and great drink menu, which includes beers from around New England.

Popular with the locals, the casual **Brewhaha** (20 Marshall St., 413/664-2020, Fri.-Mon. 7am-2pm, $3-10) serves coffee, sandwiches, salads, and excellent soups in a small café. Music, friendly staff, and bright posters on the wall make this a welcoming spot.

Pick up the essentials at **Big Y** (45 Veterans Memorial Dr., 413/663-6549, daily 7am-9pm), a basic grocery store in the center of town. Or if you're in town on a Saturday in season, head to the **North Adams Farmers Market** (43 Veterans Memorial Dr., June-Oct. Sat. 9am-1pm), a producers-only market, which also has live music 10am-noon.

Dine on top of Mount Greylock at **Bascom Lodge** (3 Summit Rd., Adams, 413/743-1591, www.bascomlodge.net, June-Oct. breakfast Wed.-Mon. 8am-10:30am, lunch Wed.-Sun. 11am-4:30pm, sunset drinks Wed.-Sun. 4pm-7pm, dinner Wed.-Sun. seating 7pm, breakfast/lunch $6-12, prix fixe dinner $40-45), an Arts and Crafts-style mountain hut with an unbeatable location. The simple breakfast and lunch menus include basic sandwiches, egg dishes, hot dogs, and hamburgers, and the fixed price dinner includes a salad and dessert. While the food gets mixed reviews, dining at heavy communal tables in a mountaintop dining room is the real experience, and the "sunset beverage hour" commands some of the finest views in the Berkshires.

Accommodations and Camping

There aren't many places to stay in North Adams, so unless you're splashing out at The Porches Inn, it's worth booking a room in Williamstown. Alternatively, there are quite a few places listed on Airbnb and other private rental sites for

Top to bottom: inside MASS MoCA; Massachusetts Veterans War Memorial Tower at Mount Greylock; Kennedy Park, Lenox

significantly less than the local hotels, and if you're prepared to drive to the summit of Mount Greylock, you'll find a historic Arts and Crafts-style lodge with unforgettable views.

With a focus on design and impeccable comfort, ★ **The Porches Inn** (231 River St., 413/664-0400, www.porches.com, rates vary daily from $270-800, call for date-specific prices) stands out for channeling the spirit of North Adams—both old and new. Workers' row houses from the 1890s have been transformed into luxury guest rooms with ultrasoft sheets and lighthearted touches. Each room is different, with vintage decor and thoughtfully chosen color schemes (and just about everything that's not bolted to the floor is for sale). Rates include a fresh, appealing continental breakfast, and coffee and baked goods are available in-room by request.

If you've come prepared with backpacking gear, the remote tent sites at **Mount Greylock Campground** (park 413/499-4262 or reservations 877/422-6762, www.mass.gov, mid-May-early Sept., $20, free off-season) are blissfully backcountry, and a series of five **lean-to shelters** within the park are open year-round (register at 413/499-4262, free).

One remarkable way to experience the Mount Greylock State Reservation is by spending the night at ★ **Bascom Lodge** (3 Summit Rd., Adams, 413/743-1591, www.bascomlodge.net, late May-late Oct., bunks $45, private rooms $140), on the mountain's summit, which also serves meals in the on-site dining room. The Arts and Crafts-style lodge has shared bathrooms, and staying in it provides a hostel-like experience, a chance to rub shoulders with Appalachian Trail through-hikers, and the best views in the county. The lodge is a 25-minute drive from downtown North Adams.

Information

The **Adams Visitors Center** (3 Hoosac St., Adams, 413/743-8358, www.town.adams.ma.us, Mon.-Fri. 9am-4pm) runs a mammoth visitor center providing information on the entire Berkshires region, open seasonally.

Getting Around

Bus services for the region are provided by **Berkshire Regional Transit Authority** (413/449-2782 or 800/292-2782, www.berkshirerta.com).

Lenox

In the midst of the glamourous Gilded Age excess of the late 19th century, Boston's barons of industry erected palatial homes in the Berkshires, which became their carefully sculpted havens from city life. For that very small, exclusive society, it was one of a few summertime escapes—along with places like Newport, Rhode Island, and Bar Harbor, Maine—where the wealthy made extended visits surrounded by small armies of servants. More than any other town in the area, Lenox retains that sheen of upscale country living, and when the Boston Symphony Orchestra takes up its annual summertime residence at Tanglewood, the town is packed to the gills. Lenox also has the greatest concentration of places to stay in the area, along with a thriving arts scene, dance festival, and celebrated yoga retreat.

Sights

★ The Mount

Edith Wharton's incisive, prolific writing is among the best in American literature, but she once contended that she was "a better landscape gardener than novelist." Judge for yourself at **The Mount** (2 Plunkett St., 413/551-5100, www.edithwharton.org, daily 10am-5pm, $20 adults, $18 seniors, $13 students, $10 military, youth under 18 free), the gorgeously restored estate she designed from the ground up. With the exception of the library, most of the author's personal

Lenox

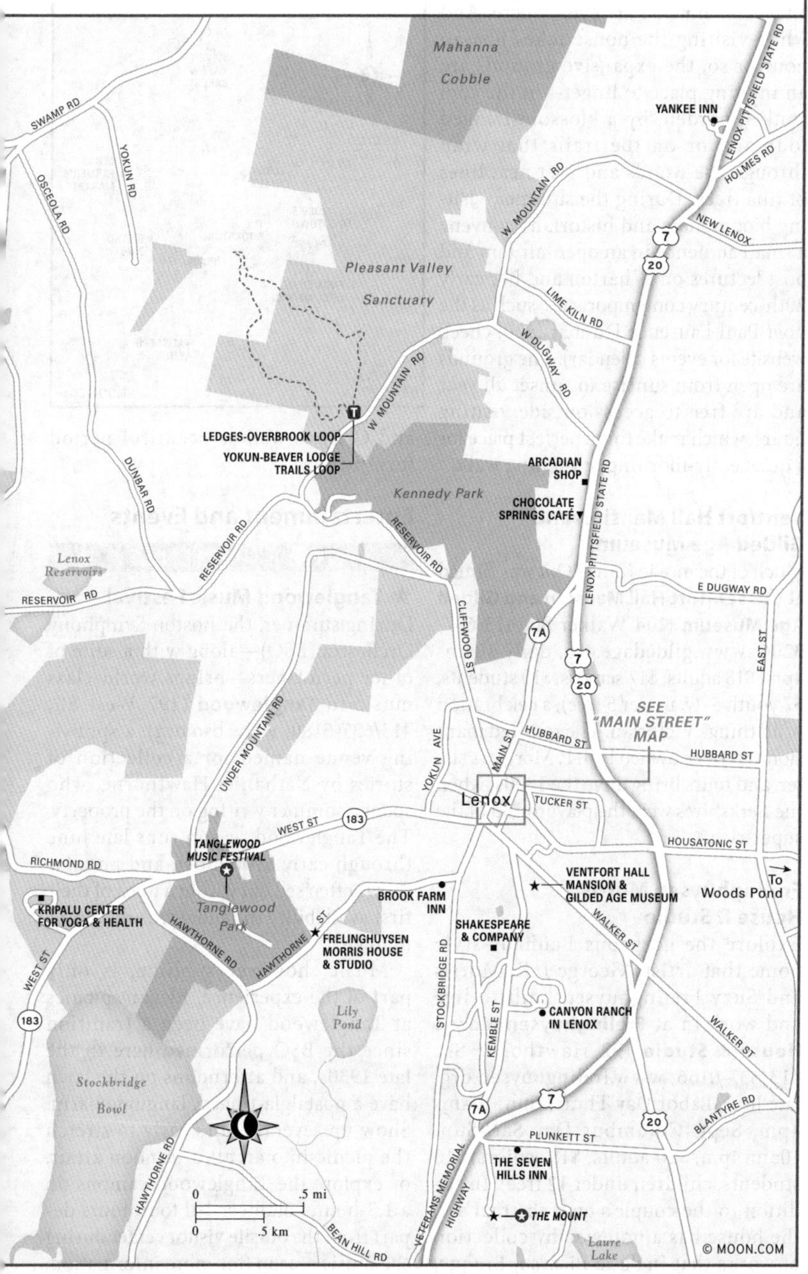
Mahanna
Cobble
YANKEE INN
LENOX PITTSFIELD STATE RD
HOLMES RD
NEW LENOX
SWAMP RD
YOKUN RD
OSCEOLA RD
W MOUNTAIN RD
Pleasant Valley
Sanctuary
LIME KILN RD
W DUGWAY RD
LEDGES-OVERBROOK LOOP
YOKUN-BEAVER LODGE
TRAILS LOOP
DUNBAR RD
ARCADIAN
SHOP
Kennedy Park
CHOCOLATE
SPRINGS CAFÉ
RESERVOIR RD
Lenox
Reservoirs
E DUGWAY RD
CLIFFWOOD ST
EAST ST
UNDER MOUNTAIN RD
SEE
"MAIN STREET"
MAP
HUBBARD ST
YOKUN AVE
MAIN ST
Lenox
TUCKER ST
WEST ST
HOUSATONIC ST
TANGLEWOOD
MUSIC FESTIVAL
RICHMOND RD
VENTFORT HALL
MANSION &
GILDED AGE MUSEUM
To
Woods Pond
BROOK FARM
INN
KRIPALU CENTER
FOR YOGA & HEALTH
Tanglewood
Park
HAWTHORNE RD
HAWTHORNE ST
FRELINGHUYSEN
MORRIS HOUSE
& STUDIO
SHAKESPEARE
& COMPANY
WALKER ST
STOCKBRIDGE RD
KEMBLE ST
CANYON RANCH
IN LENOX
Lily
Pond
Stockbridge
Bowl
BLANTYRE RD
PLUNKETT ST
THE SEVEN
HILLS INN
VETERANS MEMORIAL HIGHWAY
HAWTHORNE RD
0 .5 mi
0 .5 km
BEAN HILL RD
THE MOUNT
Laure
Lake
© MOON.COM

belongings and furniture are long gone, but Wharton's taste for symmetry, balance, and allusion are everywhere. And while visiting the house takes just an hour or so, the expansive grounds are an inviting place to linger—in the cool sunken garden, by a blossom-fringed fountain, or on the trails that wrap through the woods and past neat lines of tilia trees. During the summer, visiting biographers and historians convene a small audience in an open-air tent and host lectures on Wharton and her early 20th-century contemporaries, such as the poet Paul Laurence Dunbar ($20, check website for events calendar). The grounds are open from sunrise to sunset all year and are free to access outside visiting hours, which make this a perfect place for a quiet early-morning or evening walk.

Ventfort Hall Mansion and Gilded Age Museum

Much of the movie *Knives Out* was filmed at the **Ventfort Hall Mansion and Gilded Age Museum** (104 Walker St., 413/637-3206, www.gildedage.org, daily 10am-4pm, $18 adults, $17 seniors, $10 students, $7 youth 5-17, under 5 free), a celebration of all things Victorian. The restored mansion was once owned by J. P. Morgan's sister, and tours bring alive the 1890s, when the Berkshires were the playground of the super-rich.

Frelinghuysen Morris House & Studio

Explore the gorgeous Bauhaus-style home that artists George L.K. Morris and Suzy Frelinghuysen built to live and work in at **Frelinghuysen Morris House & Studio** (92 Hawthorne St., 413/637-0166, www.frelinghuysen.org, late June-Labor Day Thurs.-Sun. 10am-4pm, Sept.-Columbus Day Sat.-Sun. 10am-4pm, $20 adults, $18 seniors, $10 students, children under 12 free). In addition to the couple's own abstract art, the house has a noteworthy collection of works that include Picasso, Braque, and Gris, as well as beautiful period furniture.

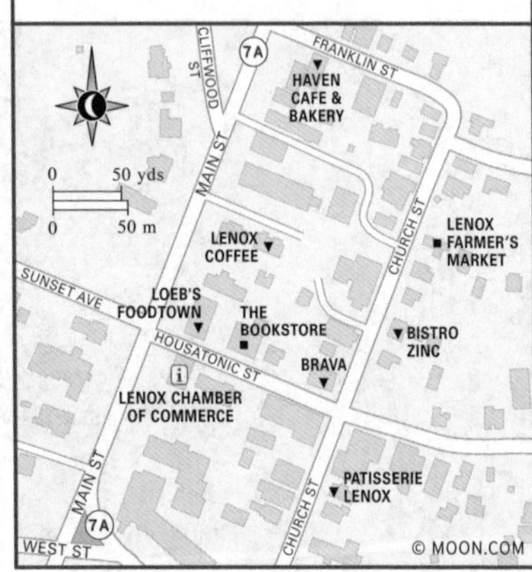

Entertainment and Events

TOP EXPERIENCE

★ Tanglewood Music Festival

During summer, the Boston Symphony Orchestra (BSO)—along with a suite of other performers—brings world-class music to **Tanglewood** (297 West St., 413/637-5180, www.bso.org), a sprawling venue named for a collection of stories by Nathaniel Hawthorne, who spent a summer writing on the property. The Tanglewood season runs late June through early September, and popular shows often sell out within a week of their first availability in January, as do rooms in town.

Music, however sublime, is only part of the experience. Elegant picnics at Tanglewood have been a tradition since the BSO performed here in the late 1930s, and afternoons on the lawn have a nostalgia-tinged, languid charm. Show up several hours early to stretch the picnic into an all-afternoon affair, or explore the Tanglewood campus on a 1.5-hour, volunteer-led tour; tours depart from the on-site visitor center during the music season (for more information, call 617/266-1200). Part of the thrill of Tanglewood is heading out on the town in Lenox to rub shoulders with the musicians (the local wine bar, Brava, is said to be especially popular with the musical set).

Other Festivals

Stars of the dance world invigorate the tiny nearby town of Becket every summer with the internationally renowned **Jacob's Pillow Dance Festival** (358 George Carter Rd., Becket, 413/243-9919, www.jacobspillow.org, mid-June-Aug., free-$100), founded by modern-dance pioneer Ted Shawn. Every style from hip-hop to ballet gets its time in the spotlight during the two-month celebration, which includes dozens of free performances and gallery talks. The main draw, however, is the showcases of artists from around the world, featuring established companies such as Mark Morris and Alvin Ailey alongside emerging choreographers.

Some of the best summer Shakespeare in the country is performed by **Shakespeare & Company** (70 Kemble St., 413/637-3353, www.shakespeare.org, free-$60) in five unique theaters, including a Roman style garden and a 540-seat open-air amphitheater flanked by towering spruce trees. In addition to plays by the Bard, the company also stages premieres by area playwrights and special events, such as one-acts by Edith Wharton, reimaginings of contemporary classics such as August Wilson's *Fences*, or interpretations of Edgar Allan Poe stories by actor F. Murray Abraham.

Shopping

The main street of Lenox is packed with little boutiques that invite browsing, mostly clustered along **Church Street** and **Housatonic Street.** Only at **The Bookstore** (11 Housatonic St., 413/637-3390, www.bookstoreinlenox.com, daily 10am-6pm), though, can you browse the shelves with a glass of wine in your hand from the house wine bar.

Sports and Recreation

Biking

Right in the center of town, **Kennedy Park** (275 Main St., https://lenox.org/kennedy-park) has over 10 miles (16 km) of old carriage roads, multiuse trails, and singletracks popular for mountain biking. The trails, which connect to more extensive singletracks outside the park's boundaries, aren't particularly well marked, but it's hard to get lost for too long without crossing a road. The closest option for rental bikes is the Adams-based **Berkshire Outfitters** (169 Grove St., Adams, 413/743-5900, www.berkshireoutfitters.com, Tues.-Sat. 10am-5pm, Sun. 11am-3pm, hybrid bikes $33 for 3 hrs, $55 for 24 hrs). Right next door to the vast park, you'll find maps and friendly advice about where to ride at the **Arcadian Shop** (91 Pittsfield Rd., 413/637-3010, www.arcadian.com).

Boating

The gentle Housatonic River is scenic and approachable for boaters of all skill levels, and one of the prettiest stretches is the meandering section between **Decker Landing,** between Lenox and Pittsfield, and **Wood's Pond** in Lenox, a 4.6-mile (7.4-km) trip that takes 2-3 hours and has great views of the mountains. **Arcadian Shop** (91 Pittsfield Rd., 413/637-3010, www.arcadian.com, $45 single or $75 tandem kayak) rents boats, and will drop your boat at Decker Landing and pick it up at Wood's Pond for $20. Another good option is to join a group from **Berkshire Canoe Tours** (413/442-2789, www.berkshirecanoetours.org, $75 adults, $50 children 8-17, $40 under 8), which makes a 2-hour trip from Decker Landing multiple times daily during summer months in canoes and kayaks.

Hiking

Just a few miles north of town, Massachusetts Audubon's **Pleasant Valley Sanctuary** (472 West Mountain Rd., 413/637-0320, www.massaudubon.

Local Legend

Anthony Fogg

The bucolic magic of the Berkshires draws visitors from places far beyond the New York and Boston metro areas. Take **Anthony Fogg.** Born, raised, and trained as a pianist in Australia, Fogg eventually found his way to the **Boston Symphony Orchestra,** where he now serves as the artistic administrator and director of Tanglewood. Happily rooted on three acres (1.2 ha) in the Berkshires, Fogg still finds himself humbled and inspired by the land and its histories.

How familiar were you with the Berkshires prior to taking the Tanglewood job?

I knew a little bit about Tanglewood; one has associations with Bernstein and Copland. There's also a piece by Charles Ives called "The Housatonic at Stockbridge," which I was very fond of. But I'd never been to the Berkshires. I came for a week in 1994 when I started working for the BSO, and the breadth of the land was beyond what I envisioned. The topography of the Tanglewood grounds itself means you look down on the Stockbridge Bowl, also called Lake Mahkeenac. There's just something very centering and very calming about it, that leaves someone with a sense of awe.

Do you ever feel overwhelmed by the scale of creativity that's happened here?

Of course! You go back to the 19th century when the great writers made the Berkshires their home in the summer. Hawthorne, Melville, they did some of their most important work here. Then, in the early 1930s, we see Ted Shawn starting up Jacob's Pillow dance festival. So there's been this constant ferment of creation and performance here. I did a project where we recorded a series of video recitals at Tanglewood's Linde Center for Music and Learning, which is built around a giant red oak tree. You can look out the windows and see it. And just watching the changing patterns of the foliage during the recording sessions... this direct melding of music and the natural world... it was quite startling.

Suppose you're introducing someone to the Berkshires for the first time. Where do you take them?

I'd probably take them for a walk up to **Kennedy Park,** right in the heart of Lenox. There's a hiking trail to an observation area where you get a breathtaking view of the south side of Berkshire County. Then, we'd go to the **Norman Rockwell Museum,** which touches on American identity in a powerful way, or perhaps up to MASS MoCA. Because the scale of the museum is so incredibly vast, it changes your biological clock. You have to take things at a slower pace. The pieces and the spaces are huge, and it just makes you go at a different rate.

org, visitor center and restrooms open daily 9am-4pm, trails open sunrise-sunset, $5 adults, $3 seniors and youth 2-12) has over 1,000 acres (404.6 ha) of wetlands, forests, and meadows with seven miles (11.2 km) of trails for exploring the eastern slope of Lenox Mountain. The strenuous, three-mile (4.8-km) **Ledges-Overbrook Loop** climbs at a steep grade through groves of mountain laurel to the 2,126-foot (648-m) summit for views of Mount Greylock, the Taconic Range, and the Catskills, while the gentler 1.5-mile (2.4-km) **Yokun-Beaver Lodge Trails Loop** is popular for birding.

Spas and Yoga

East meets western Massachusetts at the **Kripalu Center for Yoga & Health** (297 West St., 413/448-3500, www.kripalu.org, day-pass $125-150), one of the foremost yoga training centers in the country. The sprawling campus has fabulous views and lots of places to lounge on the grass between workshops on yoga, meditation, and mindfulness, and offers healthy meals in the dining room as well as dormitories and private rooms for those who want to stay over.

At the other end of the spectrum, the ultra-luxe **Canyon Ranch Lenox** (165 Kemble St., 413/637-4100, www.canyonranch.com/lenox/massachusetts-resort, day-pass $350) opens its elegant spa to the public for daytime access including classes, use of spa pools and gyms, lunch in the Canyon Ranch restaurant, and treatments like massages and facials.

Food

In a strip mall just north of town, **Chocolate Springs Café** (55 Pittsfield Rd., 413/637-9820, www.chocolatesprings.com, daily 9am-7pm, $6-12) is a cozy little space devoted to all things chocolaty, from rich gelato to truffles with whisper-thin shells. A comfortable seating area makes this a nice place to read, and the café often hosts local musicians at night.

Picture-perfect French pastries are the highlights of **Patisserie Lenox** (30 Church St., 413/551-9050, www.patisserielenox.com, Mon.-Thurs. 8:30am-6pm, Fri.-Sun. 8:30am-6:30pm, $4-15), whose brioche, macarons (French meringue-based confections), and éclairs will leave you dreaming of Paris. The shop also has prepared salads and light lunch items, though the intimate tables for two fill up quickly.

For a multicourse feast that mirrors the scenic grandeur of the Berkshires, **Bistro Zinc** (56 Church St., 413/637-8800, www.bistrozinc.com, daily lunch 11am-3pm, dinner 5pm-9pm, $21-38) beefs up the culinary foundations of a Parisian bistro with locally sourced ingredients and an impressive collection of photographs and paintings, displayed steps away from the literal zinc bar (where a tempting cocktail list awaits). The menu is heavy on modernized classics like sweet corn vichyssoise and chili-glazed duck confit rolls, and reservations are strongly recommended for dinner.

Appealing small plates and a show-stopping wine list make ★ **Brava** (27 Housatonic St., 413/637-9171, www.bravalenox.com, Tues.-Wed. 5pm-10pm, Thurs.-Sat. 5pm-1am, $17-27) a treat for a slow dinner, and the tiny spot keeps the lights on far later than anyone in town; many Tanglewood musicians make this their hangout while summering in the Berkshires, so it's a good place to rub shoulders with the performers at the casual bar.

For an easy, fresh breakfast or lunch, ★ **Haven Café and Bakery** (8 Franklin St., 413/637-8948, www.havencafebakery.com, Thurs.-Mon. 8am-2pm, $5-16) is the hands-down locals' favorite. It has laid-back counter service, plenty of seating, and a menu of burgers, salads, and sandwiches, as well as a pleasant outdoor patio for warm afternoons.

Tucked back from the main drag in a shingled house, **Lenox Coffee** (52 Main St., 413/637-1606, Mon.-Sat. 7am-5pm,

Sun. 8am-5pm, $3-7) has a good selection of pastries and the best espresso in town, made from locally roasted coffee, in addition to seats on a shady porch, wireless Internet, and fun local art on the walls.

Friendly and locally owned, **Loeb's Foodtown** (42 Main St., 413/637-0270, https://loebsfoodtown.com, Mon.-Sat. 7am-7pm, Sun. 7am-4pm) has all the usual groceries along with deli foods and snacks. Local farmers and other artisans ply their wares each week at the **Lenox Farmer's Market** (80 Church St., late May-mid-Sept. Fri. 11am-3pm), a good place for an outdoor lunch.

Accommodations and Camping

The region's travel department estimates the Berkshires offer 4,500 hotel rooms, and that 30,000 people descend on the area during busy summer weekends. Lenox is the heart of the action, and prices spike during Tanglewood season. Many locals list their guest bedrooms on Airbnb, which can be a convenient alternative to commercial options.

Camping

October Mountain State Forest (317 Woodland Rd., Lee, 413/243-1778, www.mass.gov, May-Oct., yurts $120-140, tent and RV sites $54) is just seven miles (11 km) west of town, with hiking trails, a scenic gorge, and a secluded campground with 44 sites, rustic yurts, and bathrooms with hot showers. Book yurts well in advance, and bring your own sleeping bags or bedding.

Under $150

The motor lodge exterior of the ★ **Yankee Inn** (461 Pittsfield Rd., 413/499-3700, www.yankeeinn.com, $115-155) might look like any roadside motel, but the 92 guest rooms within are comfortably furnished and spacious, and the inn's unremarkable façade conceals a scenic gem of a backyard. The inn offers direct access to the grassy banks of a beaver pond, where guests can sit in Adirondack chairs and gaze up at the roly-poly Yokun Ridge, which runs between Lenox and Pittsfield.

$150-250

Elegant and historic, the manor house at **The Seven Hills Inn** (40 Plunkett St., 413/637-0060, www.sevenhillsinn.com, $159-310) is full of antiques and old-world charm, and surrounded by perfectly manicured grounds. When booking a room in the manor house, review the online gallery, as decor varies from charmingly restrained to somewhat lurid boudoir plush. In addition to rooms in the manor house are motel and carriage house options. The least expensive rooms are in the on-site **Terrace House,** and though they're somewhat dated and dingy, the high-rent setting makes this spot a good choice if you're not planning to linger in your room. A third option is the **Carriage House,** where prices fall in between the inn and motel, and furnishings are light, pretty, and modern (and a suite with a kitchenette is also available).

It's possible to spend the night at the **Kripalu Center for Yoga & Health** (297 West St., 413/448-3500, www.kripalu.org), which has somewhat charmless dormitories and more appealing private rooms. All-inclusive retreats start at $195 Monday-Thursday and $225 Friday-Saturday; note that one-night stays are only available Monday through Thursday.

$250-350

The comfortable, welcoming rooms at ★ **Brook Farm Inn** (15 Hawthorne St., 413/637-3013, www.brookfarm.com, $199-379) are full of country charm, ruffles, and floral wallpaper. The house has a few barrier-free rooms that are fully accessible, and the appealing breakfasts incorporate food from local farms and artisans. The inn has a long literary tradition dating back to the art-loving original owners, and one highlight for many guests is the wonderful collection of poetry and history books in the on-site library, where classical music is often reverberating.

Information

The **Lenox Chamber of Commerce** (4 Housatonic St., 413/637-3646, www.lenox.org, Mon.-Sat. 10am-4pm) runs a visitor center in town.

Getting Around

Berkshire Regional Transit Authority (413/449-2782 or 800/292-2782, www.berkshirerta.com) provides bus services throughout the region.

Stockbridge

On quiet summer mornings before the tour buses arrive, the quaint town of Stockbridge looks unchanged by the half-century that's passed since Norman Rockwell captured its postage-stamp downtown in *Main Street, Stockbridge,* and you could easily use the painting to find your way around the historic center. Rockwell painted here for the last 25 years of his life in a 19th-century carriage-barn-turned-studio behind Stockbridge center, and the museum dedicated to his work is one of the region's most popular attractions. The town has gone to great lengths to preserve its Rockwellian character, with white picket fences and a general store packed with nostalgic bits and bobs. You could walk the strip in a few minutes flat, and there isn't much in the way of nightlife or events in town, but it's a nice place to linger; from the shady porch at the Red Lion to the alleyway cafés, time in Stockbridge is all about watching life drift by.

Sights

★ Norman Rockwell Museum

With his sweet depictions of soda

Top to bottom: Norman Rockwell's barn studio; Naumkeag; Berkshire Botanical Garden

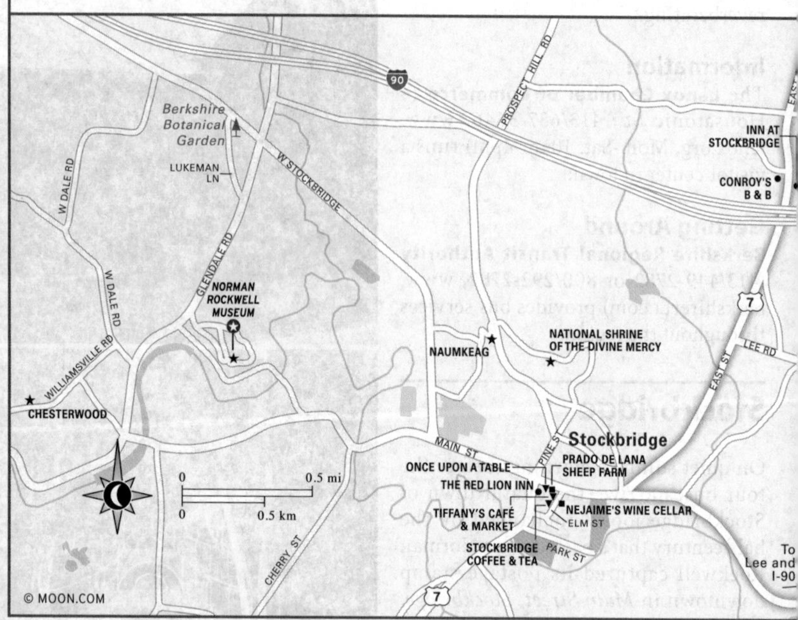

fountains, small towns, and kids goofing around, Norman Rockwell can elicit strong reactions, from nostalgic sighs to eye rolls. With the world's largest collection of the artist's original work, the **Norman Rockwell Museum** (9 Rte. 183, 413/298-4100, www.nrm.org, Thurs.-Tues. 10am-5pm, $20 adults, $18 seniors, $10 students, 18 and under free) may surprise viewers who know the artist from his *Life* magazine covers alone. Among the paintings on exhibit is the series Rockwell did on civil rights, including a haunting depiction of the three civil rights workers killed in Mississippi; the artist emerges as someone who cared deeply about social justice, even as he looked toward the past.

Behind the museum is the artist's barn studio (open May-mid-Nov.), preserved almost identically to when Rockwell painted here, with lovely views of rolling forest and lawns. The grounds are speckled with sculptures by his son, Peter Rockwell, whose work shows a refreshing taste for the weird.

Nearby Sights

Even if you've never heard of sculptor Daniel Chester French, you've likely seen images of his work, from the Lincoln Memorial in Washington DC to *Minute Man* in Concord, Massachusetts. His country home and "heaven" was **Chesterwood** (4 Williamsville Rd., 413/298-3579, www.chesterwood.org, mid-May-mid-Oct. Wed.-Mon. 10am-5pm, $20 adults, $18 seniors, $15 veterans, $10 youth 13-17, under 13 free). Tours take visitors through his elegantly appointed house, intimate studio, and 122 acres (49 ha) of grounds designed by the artist.

Another of the Berkshire's Gilded Age "cottages," **Naumkeag** (5 Prospect Hill Rd., 413/298-8138, www.thetrustees.org, late May-early Oct. Thurs.-Mon. 10am-3pm, adults $20, seniors and students $15, children under 12 free) stands out for being preserved in its entirety, with gorgeous original furnishings that make visiting the house a transporting experience. For many visitors, though, the grounds are the real draw, with deep pools, rustling groves of birch trees, and great mounds of blooming flowers that are perfectly manicured and maintained. Advance timed admission tickets are strongly recommended and can be purchased online.

The flowers at the **Berkshire Botanical Garden** (5 West Stockbridge Rd., 413/298-3926, www.berkshirebotanical.org, May-Oct. daily 9am-5pm, $18 general admission, $16 seniors, under 12 free, pay-what-you-want admission on Tues.) are carefully chosen so that each week brings fresh blooms, and the 15-acre (6-ha) grounds are a pleasure for plant lovers. Tables and benches invite afternoon picnics, and many of the trails are wheelchair accessible.

While the **National Shrine of the Divine Mercy** (Eden Hill, 413/298-3931, www.thedivinemercy.org, free) might not be well known outside the Catholic Church, it's an important pilgrimage place for American Roman Catholics. Thousands flock to the shrine's Easter Services, and during the 2015-2016 Extraordinary Jubilee of Mercy, the church offered plenary indulgences that used to be available only at the four papal basilicas in Rome. Non-pilgrims can enjoy the beautiful main church and large, peaceful grounds.

Shopping

Stock up on penny candy, gadgets, and old-fashioned knickknacks at **Charles H. Baldwin & Sons** (1 Center St., West Stockbridge, 413/232-7785, www.baldwinextracts.com, daily 10am-5pm), a family-owned country store that also dispenses homemade syrups and extracts that Berkshire bakers swear by. Or take a piece of the agrarian countryside home with you by stocking up on heavenly soft colorful yarn at **Prado de Lana Sheep Farm** (44 Main St., 610/233-8105, www.pradodelana.com, Wed.-Sun. noon-6pm). For a monthly fee, you can even follow one of the resident sheep digitally, learn about its personality traits, and receive shipments of yarn from your new fluffy friend.

Food

Just off Main Street, **Stockbridge Coffee & Tea** (6 Elm St., 413/931-7044, www.stockbridgecoffeeandtea.com, daily 7am-3pm, $4-10) serves espresso drinks and Harney & Sons tea in a cozy bookshop, where the small collection of volumes is unusually well chosen and organized. Locally made pastries and quiche of the day are available.

Bright yellow walls and vintage French posters give ★ **Once Upon a Table** (36 Main St., 413/298-3870, www.onceuponatablestockbridge.com, Mon., Wed.-Thurs., and Sun. 4pm-8:30pm, Fri.-Sat. 4pm-9pm, $19-38) the cheerful feel of a country bistro, with food that veers on the international side, such as summer gazpacho with sweet piquillo peppers, and wild mushroom polenta with pepita pesto. A good selection of wines by the glass makes this an especially appealing alleyway spot, with its outdoor seating on fine days.

A menu of short-order favorites like grilled cheese and hearty egg breakfasts makes the counter at **Tiffany's Café & Market** (4 Elm St., 413/298-7007, www.elmstreetmkt.com, daily 6am-8pm, $7-15) a convenient option for a simple breakfast or lunch, and the stools at the counter have a pleasantly Rockwellian feel to them. It also sells basic groceries.

It's easy to imagine any of the five American presidents that have stayed at **The Red Lion Inn** (30 Main St., 413/298-5545, www.redlion.com, Sun.-Thurs.

That's Weird...

Sheffield's covered bridge

One night in 1969, Sheffield resident Thom Reed was driving over the town's covered bridge when something unthinkable happened: A craft with bright lights emerged from the river. In seconds, Reed and his fellow passengers were spirited away to an airplane hangar-esque structure where insectoid creatures roamed, before suddenly being transported back to their car. Residents from nearby towns reported seeing the same craft that night, and Reed's story was chronicled in Netflix's *Unsolved Mysteries* series.

The covered bridge remains, but it's no longer open to vehicles. Instead, the bridge is now something of a shrine to Reed's encounter—considered the most famous UFO encounter in the Berkshires' history. The grassy lawn by the bridge once featured a concrete monument with a plaque that read "Our nation's first off-world/UFO incident," which the town of Sheffield removed, citing legalities over its placement beside the bridge. (It's also likely that the town wasn't exactly thrilled about this particular claim to fame.) But you can still walk through the **Thom Reed UFO Monument Park** (Covered Bridge Ln., Sheffield). Just ... maybe don't go there after dark.

5:30pm-8:30pm, Fri.-Sat. 5:30pm-9pm, $23-50) tucking into the dining room menu of meat and potatoes, which combines with dark wood, old china, and white tablecloths to thoroughly old-fashioned effect. If that's not your scene, you can head down the hall to the casual and atmospheric **Widow Bingham's Tavern** (lunch Mon.-Fri. noon-2:30pm, Sat.-Sun. noon-3pm, dinner daily 5:30pm-9pm, $18-40) for burgers, sandwiches, and charcuterie under a ceiling that clinks with beer steins.

Nejaime's Wine Cellar (3 Elm St., 413/298-3454, www.nejaimeswine.com, Mon.-Sat. 9am-7pm, Sun. 11am-6pm) has a great selection of wine, spirits, and beer, including some local varieties. A few miles outside of downtown Stockbridge, the **West Stockbridge Farmers Market** (Foundry Green, Harris St., West Stockbridge, late May-early Oct. Thurs. 3pm-6pm) brings in vendors, crafters, and farmers from around the Berkshires.

Accommodations

$150-250

Somewhat homier than other rooms in Stockbridge, **Conroy's B & B** (11 East St.,

413/298-4990, $170-240) is full of laid-back country charm. The helpful owner cooks breakfast each morning and is an excellent resource for things to do, and there are gardens full of blooming perennials and an outdoor pool in the summer.

$250-350

The wraparound veranda at **The Red Lion Inn** (30 Main St., 413/-5545, www.redlioninn.com, $195-415) is a relaxing place to sink into a rocking chair and watch the passersby, and the warren-like inn is a fascinating place to explore. Rooms in the main building are furnished with appealing antiques, and the bowed floors and crackled portraits give the hotel a deliciously "olde New England" feel. Stockbridge is something of a company town, and the Red Lion owns much of the block it occupies, with annexes, guesthouses, and a wonderful turn-of-the-20th-century firehouse that was the subject of a Rockwell painting.

On the road from Stockbridge to Lenox, the **Inn at Stockbridge** (30 East St., 413/298-3337, www.stockbridgeinn.com, $200-420) is another plush find, with inviting common spaces and treasures from the owners' travels around the world. Home-cooked breakfasts, a heated pool, all-day snacks, and an exercise room are appealing perks, but the inn's location by the highway means more noise than elsewhere.

Information

The **Stockbridge Chamber of Commerce** (413/298-5200, www.stockbridgechamber.org) has a small, unstaffed visitors booth on Main Street with information.

Getting Around

Regional buses are run by the **Berkshire Regional Transit Authority** (413/449-2782 or 800/292-2782, www.berkshirerta.com).

Great Barrington

Trees and picket fences give way to faded mill buildings along the Housatonic River when you cross the border into Great Barrington, an appealing blend of tourist town and rural hub that offers a real glimpse of life in the Berkshires. With restored brick buildings and a mix of old-fashioned hardware stores, boutiques, and restaurants, downtown Great Barrington is a refreshing change of scene from the curated centers of Lenox and Stockbridge, and a good base for exploring if you need a break from all the quaintness. Just up the road, the village of Housatonic is an unexpected gem, a tiny satellite of Great Barrington where disused railway depots and crumbling factory buildings keep watch over a tiny downtown with a celebrated bakery and a hip café. Not much remains beside a few signs and markers, but Great Barrington was the childhood home of the great African American writer and academic W.E.B. DuBois, who attended an integrated public school in the late 19th century and left for college with the support of the local church.

Sights

The tiny spire and whitewashed facade of the old Trinity Lutheran Church seem an unlikely place to celebrate a raucous, rebellious folk singer—but peace sign windows offer a hint of what's inside **The Guthrie Center** (2 Van Deusenville Rd., 413/528-1955, www.guthriecenter.org, Tues.-Fri. 10am-3pm, free). Arlo Guthrie's album covers and posters decorate every surface of the church's small welcome center, which hosts interfaith services on Sundays 11am-noon (services are "BYOG," or "bring your own god"). Free lunch is served to all comers each Wednesday at noon, and local musicians gather for an informal hootenanny on select Thursday nights (doors 7pm, show 8pm, $5, performers free). Back when

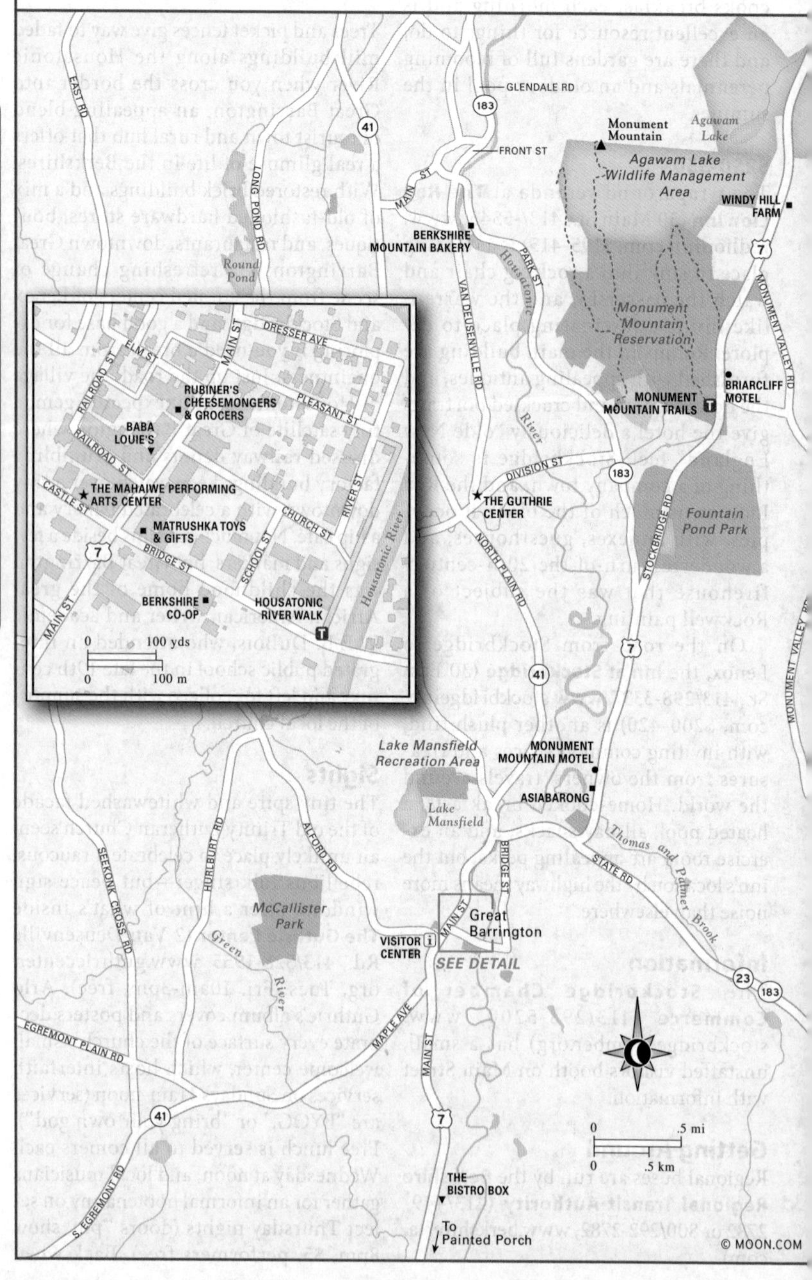
Great Barrington
GLENDALE RD
FRONT ST
Monument Mountain
Agawam Lake
Agawam Lake Wildlife Management Area
WINDY HILL FARM
BERKSHIRE MOUNTAIN BAKERY
MAIN ST
PARK ST
LONG POND RD
EAST RD
VAN DEUSENVILLE RD
Housatonic River
Round Pond
Monument Mountain Reservation
MONUMENT VALLEY RD
BRIARCLIFF MOTEL
MONUMENT MOUNTAIN TRAILS
DIVISION ST
THE GUTHRIE CENTER
NORTH PLAIN RD
STOCKBRIDGE RD
Fountain Pond Park
DRESSER AVE
ELM ST
RAILROAD ST
RUBINER'S CHEESEMONGERS & GROCERS
PLEASANT ST
BABA LOUIE'S
THE MAHAIWE PERFORMING ARTS CENTER
CASTLE ST
RIVER ST
CHURCH ST
MATRUSHKA TOYS & GIFTS
BRIDGE ST
SCHOOL ST
Housatonic River
BERKSHIRE CO-OP
HOUSATONIC RIVER WALK
0 100 yds
0 100 m
Lake Mansfield Recreation Area
MONUMENT MOUNTAIN MOTEL
ASIABARONG
Lake Mansfield
BRIDGE ST
Thomas and Palmer Brook
STATE RD
SEEKONK CROSS RD
HURLBURT RD
ALFORD RD
McCallister Park
Green River
VISITOR CENTER
SEE DETAIL
EGREMONT PLAIN RD
MAPLE AVE
S. EGREMONT RD
THE BISTRO BOX
To Painted Porch
0 .5 mi
0 .5 km
© MOON.COM

Arlo Guthrie was a student at a progressive boarding school in Stockbridge, the church was home to Alice and Ray Brock, and was immortalized in the rambling, shaggy-dog antiwar song "Alice's Restaurant."

Fill your bags with blueberries and crisp fall apples at **Windy Hill Farm** (686 Stockbridge Rd., 413/398-3217, www.windyhillfarminc.com, Apr.-Dec. daily 9am-5pm), where pretty rows of Paula Red and Gingergold apples give way to stunning views of nearby Monument Mountain and rolling berry fields. Blueberry season opens around the beginning of July, and apples are ripe from September until late autumn.

Entertainment and Events

Pronounced muh-HAY-wee, **The Mahaiwe Performing Arts Center** (14 Castle St., 413/528-0100, www.mahaiwe.org) is located in a restored 100-year-old theater and presents a first-rate, if eclectic, lineup of music, spoken-word, and theater performances. The 2023 season included Béla Fleck, Samantha Bee, and a cabaret-style storytelling set by Alan Cumming and Ari Shapiro. What Tanglewood is to symphony music, the **Aston Magna Festival** (Daniel Arts Center, Alford Rd., 413/528-3595, www.astonmagna.org, $20-60 per concert) is to chamber music. During weekends in July and early August, both vocal and instrumental masters of the genre perform at Saint James Place.

Shopping

There are plenty of places to browse for antiques in town, but one of the most intriguing is **AsiaBarong** (199 Stockbridge Rd., 413/528-5091, Thurs.-Mon. 11am-5pm), an enormous multilevel collection of art from all over Asia that encompasses everything from treasures to trinkets. For more antiques, outside of Great Barrington, the stretch of Route 7 down to Sheffield is known as **antiques alley** for its many fine such stores (maps of the antiques stores are available at most destinations). One particularly worthy stop is the **Painted Porch** (102 S. Main St., Sheffield, 413/229-2700, www.paintedporch.com, Fri.-Sun. 10am-4:30pm, Mon.-Thurs. by appointment), whose owners scour the English and French countrysides for rare furniture.

Founded by supporters of the progressive Rudolph Steiner school, Great Barrington's **Matrushka Toys & Gifts** (309 Main St., 413/528-6911, www.berkshiretoys.com, Mon. and Wed.-Sat. noon-5pm) is strictly electronics-free, instead filled with hand-crafted toys made from natural materials, as well as children's costumes, clothes, and books.

Sports and Recreation

Biking

The plentiful back roads around Great Barrington offer endless opportunities for riding, though it's hard to avoid stretches of highway that can be heavily trafficked and narrow (and often full of meandering sightseers). An excellent resource for finding a route is **Great Barrington Trails & Greenways** (www.gbtrails.org), whose online map designates the roads best suited for cycling; among the best is the 15-mile (24-km) ride down the Housatonic River Valley to Sheffield and back. Before hitting the trails, plan to pick up a rental bike north of town at **Berkshire Outfitters** (169 Grove St., Adams, 413/743-5900, www.berkshireoutfitters.com, Tues.-Sat. 10am-5pm, Sun. 11am-3pm, hybrid bikes $33 for 3 hrs, $55 for 24 hrs).

Hiking

Right in the center of Great Barrington, the **Housatonic River Walk** (www.gbriverwalk.org) runs a half-mile (0.8 km) along the riverbed. The shady trail has plenty of comfortable benches and places to enjoy the view and is divided into two sections. The **upstream** portion can be accessed behind 195 Main Street, or the church parking lot at 15 Dresser

Avenue, and the **downstream** segment continues to Bridge Street.

Find a clear day to ascend **Monument Mountain,** and you'll get views from Mount Greylock on the Vermont border to the New York Catskill Mountains, with plenty of Housatonic River Valley scenery in between. Two trails leave from a small parking lot on Route 7 (parking $6, just north of Briarcliff Motel): Turn left onto the 1.5-mile (2.4-km) **Mohican Monument Trail,** which traces a relatively gentle path past crumbling stone walls and carriage roads, or head right on the 0.8-mile (1.3-km) **Hickey Trail,** and pick a line straight up the slope. The two trails join at 0.6 mile (about 1 km) beneath the summit, where the **Peeskawso Peak Trail** reaches the finest views of the hike. Regardless of the route, plan on two hours for a return trip to the summit.

The **Appalachian Trail** passes just south of Great Barrington as it winds from Georgia to Maine, and you can get a taste of the 2,160-mile (3,476-km) trail in **Beartown State Forest** (69 Bluehill Rd., Monterey, 413/528-0904, $30), which has miles of hiking and multiuse trails. Walking on the Appalachian is generally an out-and-back that can be as long, or short, as you like, but the forest's most popular trail is the gorgeous **Benedict Pond Loop Trail,** an easy hike that wraps 1.5 miles (2.4 km) around a tree-fringed lake.

Food

Great Barrington's answer to the New England snack bar is ★ **The Bistro Box** (937 S. Main St., 413/717-5958, www.thebistrobox.rocks, May-Nov. Thurs.-Tues. 11am-4pm, $8-14), run by a pair of married chefs with serious kitchen chops. Hand-cut truffle fries are luxurious alongside grass-fed burgers topped with tomato jam and garlic aioli, and the chefs incorporate fresh and foraged foods into specials like wild ramp pesto and blueberry lemonade. Lawn seating and picnic tables are available.

The thin and crusty sourdough pizza at **Baba Louie's** (286 Main St., 413/528-8100, www.babalouiespizza.com, lunch Thurs.-Mon. noon-3pm, dinner Sun.-Mon. and Thurs. 5pm-8pm, Fri.-Sat. 5pm-9pm, $15-24) is a strong contender for the best in the Berkshires, and the cozy, hole-in-the-wall restaurant is impressively laid-back for the quality of its pies. Gluten-free crusts get raves, and the fig, gorgonzola, and prosciutto pizza is an outrageously flavorful blend of sweet and savory.

Pack the picnic hamper of your dreams at **Rubiner's Cheesemongers & Grocers** (246 Main St., 413/528-0488, www.rubiners.com, Mon.-Sat. 10am-6pm, Sun. 11am-5pm), which stocks cheese from farms in the Berkshires, Vermont, and beyond, along with a charcuterie case stocked with rich pâtés, dried sausages, and duck confit. Then find award-winning wholesome loaves in Housatonic's **Berkshire Mountain Bakery** (367 Rte. 136, Housatonic, 413/274-1313, www.berkshiremountainbakery.com, Mon.-Sat. 8am-7pm, Sun. 8am-6pm), where baker Richard Bourdon has been making artisanal bread since long before it was cool. Many grains are sprouted and ground on-site, and breads are naturally fermented. Cooperatively owned and stocked with piles of local food, **Berkshire Co-op** (42 Bridge St., 413/528-9697, www.berkshire.coop, daily 8am-7pm) also has a good deli with smoothies, sandwiches, and salads.

Accommodations and Camping

Beartown State Forest (69 Bluehill Rd., Monterey, 413/528-0904, $40) has just 12 sites (and no showers), but the 10,000-acre (4,047-ha) preserve is a wonderfully quiet place to spend the night about 30 minutes outside of Great Barrington, especially if you can snag site #11, which occupies an idyllic, private spot on the edge of a lake.

Bright white bedspreads and fresh renovations set **Monument Mountain**

The Places in Between: Pittsfield

Berkshire Museum

The Berkshires may be where the New York crowd retreats from the day-in, day-out of city life, but in the heart of the mountains, the streets and alleyways of **Pittsfield** offer hidden beauty and cosmopolitan treats. The westernmost city in Massachusetts is in the midst of a cultural and culinary revival after several years of economic tribulations, and yet the vibe of Pittsfield remains affable and accessible.

Given Pittsfield's centralized location between Great Barrington (30 minutes to the south) and Williamstown (35 minutes to the north), many Berkshire visitors motor through the city along Route 7 without exploring its tempting restaurants, artisan shops, and historic sites. Whether you're looking for a memorable bite or an escape from the more mainstream Berkshire haunts, Pittsfield is worth the stopover.

Kick things off with a cheddar scallion scone or a Cinnamon Toast Crunch latte at **Dottie's Coffee Lounge** (444 North St., 413/443-1792, www.dottiescoffeelounge.com, Mon.-Fri. 7am-2pm, Sat.-Sun. 8am-2pm, $4-12). Then, saunter down North Street, enjoying the mountain views along the way, and check out the wildlife dioramas and the basement aquarium at the funky, Wes Anderson-esque **Berkshire Museum** (39 South St., 413/443-7171, www.berkshiremuseum.org, Mon.-Sat. 10am-5pm, Sun. noon-5pm, $15 adults, $8 children 4-17, free under 4).

Flirt with witchcraft and metaphysics by perusing the aisles of **Witch Slapped** (78 North St., 413/464-9597, www.witch-slapped.com, Sun. and Wed. 11am-4pm, Thurs.-Sat. 11am-7pm), and then bring it back home with custom decked-out pies at **Crust Pizza** (505 East St., 413/464-7977, www.crustpz.com, Tues.-Thurs. 11am-8pm, Fri. 11am-8:30pm, Sat. 11:30am-8:30pm, Sun. 11:30am-8pm, $12-20) or a pint of local honey-infused blonde ale at **Hot Plate Brewing Co.** (1 School St., www.hotplatebeer.com, Sun.-Mon. noon-9pm, Tues.-Wed. noon-10pm, Thurs.-Sat. noon-11pm), which is one of the few Latina-owned breweries in the United States.

Once you've had your fill of downtown, continue to the more rural south side of Pittsfield and step into the former home of Herman Melville, known today as **Arrowhead** (780 Holmes Rd., 413/442-1793, www.berkshirehistory.org, late May-Oct. guided tours Thurs.-Mon. 10am-3pm, $20 adults, $10 students, free under 13). From Melville's preserved writing desk or the porch of the old farmhouse, you can gaze out at a nearby ridgeline that resembles the expanse of a giant whale. Sort of. Kind of.

Motel (247 Stockbridge Rd., 413/528-3272, www.monumentmountainmotel.com, $150-225) apart from the other motels that line Route 7 on the outskirts of Great Barrington. Rooms are a bit dated, but neat as a pin, and the in-ground pool, play area, and basketball court make it a nice choice for families, or for anyone seeking a comfortable, budget-friendly base camp for jaunting around the southern Berkshires.

The standard roadside exterior of the **Briarcliff Motel** (506 Stockbridge Rd., 413/528-3000, www.thebriarcliffmotel.com, $160-250) offers few clues to the attractive rooms, which are decorated with modern flair and a great sense of style. Each is unique, with artwork on the walls and small sitting areas, as well as several barrier-free accessible bathrooms, a rarity in the Berkshires. Great coffee and homemade granola are served along with pastries, organic yogurt, and hard-boiled eggs for the continental breakfast; DVD players, a fire pit, and a pleasant wooded location outside of town make this a nice place to relax.

Information

The **Southern Berkshires Chamber of Commerce** runs a **visitor center** (326 Main St., 413/528-1510, www.southernberkshirechamber.com, daily 10am-4pm) with information on the town as well as the rest of the region. The hours at this small office can vary somewhat unpredictably, especially during off-season months, so call before visiting.

Getting Around

The **Berkshire Regional Transit Authority** (413/449-2782 or 800/292-2782, www.berkshirerta.com) runs buses throughout the region.

Rhode
Island

Highlights

★ **Newport's Mansions:** Channel the 19th-century elite while visiting their sprawling summer homes that combine Gilded Age glamour, exquisite art, and monumentally bad taste (page 294).

★ **Cliff Walk:** Stroll between the mansions and the sea on this seven-mile (11-km) walking path (page 294).

★ **Touro Synagogue:** Discover Newport's Jewish heritage in an elegant historic synagogue (page 298).

★ **Newport's Music Festivals:** Watch musicians from around the world at the legendary festivals where performers like Miles Davis and Bob Dylan have made musical history (page 300).

★ **RISD Museum:** The immense art collection here spans from ancient Chinese sculptures to French Impressionist paintings to the creations of present day RISD students themselves (page 307).

★ **Federal Hill:** Experience the Italian-American influence of this historic Providence neighborhood with an outdoor dinner, a trip to a bustling market, or a conversation with any of the shopkeepers who've called this place home for decades (page 310).

★ **WaterFire:** Stroll along the Providence River at dusk with a beer or glass of wine as boats of torchbearers light pyres staged in the middle of the river in this one-of-a-kind ritual (page 313).

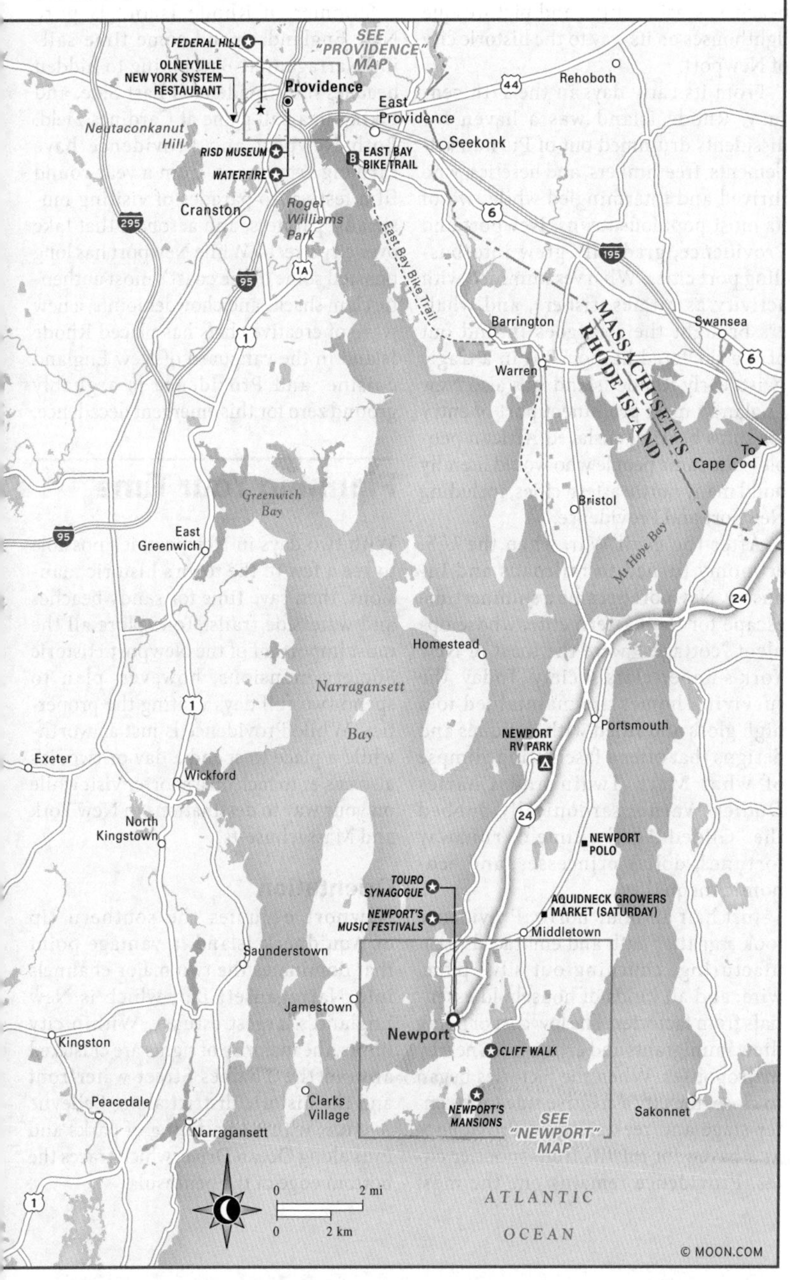

Rhode Island
FEDERAL HILL
SEE "PROVIDENCE" MAP
OLNEYVILLE NEW YORK SYSTEM RESTAURANT
Providence
Rehoboth
East Providence
Neutaconkanut Hill
Seekonk
RISD MUSEUM
EAST BAY BIKE TRAIL
WATERFIRE
Roger Williams Park
Cranston
East Bay Bike Trail
Barrington
Swansea
MASSACHUSETTS
RHODE ISLAND
Warren
Exeter
To Cape Cod
Greenwich Bay
Bristol
East Greenwich
Mt Hope Bay
Homestead
Narragansett
Bay
Portsmouth
NEWPORT RV PARK
Exeter
Wickford
North Kingstown
NEWPORT POLO
TOURO SYNAGOGUE
AQUIDNECK GROWERS MARKET (SATURDAY)
NEWPORT'S MUSIC FESTIVALS
Middletown
Saunderstown
Jamestown
Newport
Kingston
CLIFF WALK
Peacedale
Clarks Village
NEWPORT'S MANSIONS
Sakonnet
SEE "NEWPORT" MAP
Narragansett
0 2 mi
0 2 km
ATLANTIC
OCEAN
© MOON.COM

Rhode Island's 400-mile (644-km) coastline curves around sandy beaches, seaside cliffs, and picturesque lighthouses on its way to the historic city of Newport.

From its early days in the 17th century, Rhode Island was a haven for dissidents drummed out of Puritan settlements, freethinkers, and heretics, who thrived and intermingled while two of its most populous towns, Newport and Providence, gradually grew into bustling port cities. Wharves hummed with activity as pirates, fishers, and whalers brought their cargoes in and out of the sheltered harbor. But in a tragic twist, early Rhode Island was also New England's most prominent port of entry for ships bearing enslaved African people—the same people who would literally build many northeastern cities, including Newport and Providence.

After the Civil War, when the U.S. economy turned to railroads and industry, Newport became a summertime escape for the Eastern elite, whose opulent "cottages" were the toast of New York's upper-class society. Today, the surviving homes are maintained to a high gloss and filled with antiques and designs that offer a fascinating glimpse of what Mark Twain and Charles Dudley Warner sardonically dubbed the "Gilded Age," a time of runaway fortunes, dollar princesses, and economic inequality.

Just half an hour north, Providence took a grittier path and embraced manufacturing, churning out silverplate, wire, and all kinds of household essentials from factories. The low cost of living drew immigrants and artists from nearby metropolises. When the factories began to close, the city's creative side took center stage and reestablished Providence as a haven for misfits from snootier cities. Providence remains one the most eccentric cities in New England and residents are damn proud of it.

Summer in Rhode Island is pure New England: Spend some time sailing Narragansett Bay, biking to hidden beaches on Providence's East Side, and taking in a ball game at Cardines Field. Both Newport and Providence have thriving arts scenes, from a year-round film festival to parades of visiting musicians, painters, and acrobats that take over city streets. While Newport has long boasted some of the coast's most authentic clam shacks and chowder joints, a new wave of creative chefs has placed Rhode Island in the vanguard of New England cuisine, and Providence is arguably ground zero for this emergent decadence.

Planning Your Time

With two days in Newport, it's possible to see a few of the town's historic mansions, then save time for sandy beaches and waterside trails. To explore all the most important of the Newport Historic Society mansions, however, plan to spend two full days visiting the properties. While Providence is just as worthwhile a place to spend a day or two, it's also easier to tack on a shorter visit while on your way to destinations in New York and Massachusetts.

Orientation

Newport occupies the southern tip of Aquidneck Island, a vantage point that dominates the two major channels into Narragansett Bay, which is New England's largest estuary. Within city limits, the majority of sights are clustered around the Thames Street waterfront and the historic district along Bellevue Avenue, with a smattering of parks and inns along Ocean Drive, which traces the bottom edge of the peninsula.

Best Restaurants

★ **Midtown Oyster Bar:** Nab a seat on the sun-splashed outdoor deck here and wolf down fresh-caught, creatively prepared seafood (page 303).

★ **Flo's Clam Shack:** Join the summer pilgrimage across Easton Bay to indulge in piles of crisply fried seafood, served amid 80 years of buoys, awards, and maritime kitsch (page 305).

★ **Los Andes:** Come for the hefty Peruvian-style steaks and locally sourced ceviche, and linger in this restaurant's beautiful "backyard" garden (page 318).

★ **Al Forno:** Experience the original Rhode Island "grilled pizza" and high-end Italian fare at this waterside dining room (page 318).

★ **Aleppo Sweets:** The sweet Syrian baklava and the za'atar flatbreads here are the epitome of nourishing homestyle cooking (page 319).

Getting to Rhode Island

Driving from Boston

75 mi/121 km, 1.5 hr

Newport is an easy drive from Boston. From downtown, follow **I-93 South** for 12 miles (19 km) to **Route 24 South.** Stay on Route 24 for about 38 miles (61 km) before exiting onto **I-195 West** toward Fall River and then, after another 0.9 mile (1.4 km), taking Exit 8A to remain on Route 24, which merges with **Route 114 South** when you reach Aquidneck Island heading into town.

Boston to Providence is an even simpler jaunt. From downtown, take **I-93 South** for 13 miles (21 km) to its terminus at I-95. Use the right two lanes to merge onto **I-95 South** and continue for 32 miles (51.5 km) into Providence. Take Exit 37A for **Atwells Avenue,** and at the end of the ramp, make a left for downtown or a right for Federal Hill.

Driving from New York City

185 mi/298 km, 3 hr

Coming from New York City, Newport is a half-day drive up the coast. Head north on **FDR Drive,** using the left lane to access Exit 17 to the **Robert F. Kennedy Bridge** ($10.17 toll), then stay left to merge onto **I-278 East.** After 4.5 miles (7.2 km), I-278 East merges into **I-95 North** ($1.75 toll). Follow I-95 North for 137.5 miles (221 km). Take Exit 4 for **Route 3** and, after about 4 miles (6.4 km), turn right onto **Route 102 North,** then merge onto **Route 4 South,** continuing on as it becomes **Route 1 South.** Shortly after, turn onto **Route 138 East** to cross the **Newport Bridge** ($4 toll), then turn right onto **Route 238 South** into downtown Newport.

To drive from New York to Providence, follow the same configuration of roads to **I-95 North** and continue for 180 miles (290 km) as the highway veers away from the coast and crosses into southwest Rhode Island. As you enter downtown Providence, take the **Route 6 West** exit ramp on the right and then take Exit 37B, which connects to **Francis Street** in the heart of the city.

Driving from Cape Cod

55 mi/89 km, 1 hr

To reach Newport from Cape Cod, make your way to the **Bourne Bridge,** which connects Cape Cod and the mainland across the southerly side of the Cape Cod Canal. From there, continue onto **Route 25 West** for 9.1 miles (14.6 km), then use Exit 1 to merge onto **I-195 West**

Best Accommodations

★ **Crow's Nest at the Seamen's Church Institute:** Browse a sailor's library and dream of the ocean in this historic, nonprofit hotel that also offers services to the "men and women of the sea" (page 306).

★ **Forty 1° North:** Boats pull right up to the waterside lounge at this modern hotel filled with iridescent touches and design books (page 306).

★ **The Dean Hotel:** Elegantly minimalist rooms, thoughtful decor, and a fabulous in-house restaurant lend character to this budget-friendly hotel that was once a church mission and a brothel (page 319).

★ **Graduate Providence:** Upscale elegance meets quirky Rhode Island-rooted artwork and memorabilia (including a life-sized *Dumb and Dumber* shaggin' wagon) at this reimagined historic hotel in Downtown Providence (page 320).

toward New Bedford/Providence. After 26 miles (42 km), use Exit 8A for **Route 24 South** toward Tiverton, which merges onto **Route 114 South** and continues into downtown Newport.

Driving from the Berkshires

160 mi/257 km, 2.5 hr

To reach Newport from **Stockbridge,** follow **Route 102 East** 5.3 miles (8.5 km) before merging onto **I-90 East** for 83 miles (133.5 km, $4.75 toll). Use exit 10A to turn onto **Route 146 South.** Follow Route 146 South for 25 miles (40 km), crossing the state line into Rhode Island, then exit onto **I-295 South** toward Warwick. After 18.6 miles (30 km), merge onto **I-95 South** for 3 miles (4.8 km), then stay left to continue onto **Route 4 South.** Route 4 merges with **Route 1 South.** Shortly after, turn onto **Route 138 East** to cross the **Newport Bridge** ($4 toll), then turn right onto **Route 238 South** into downtown Newport.

Getting There by Air, Train, or Bus

Air

United, JetBlue, Delta, American and Southwest Airlines offer service to **T.F. Green Airport** (2000 Post Rd., Warwick, 888/268-7222, www.pvdairport.com), though fares tend to be higher than flying into Boston.

Train

Amtrak (800/872-7245, www.amtrak.com) connects Providence with **New York City** (frequent trains, 3-3.5 hrs, $50-170) and **Boston** (frequent trains, 1 hr, $7-12). The Providence train station is a short walk from Kennedy Plaza, where frequent buses depart for Newport.

Bus

Peter Pan Bus Lines (800/343-9999, www.peterpanbus.com) has buses between **New York City** and **Providence** (five times daily, 4 hrs, $35). And from Providence, the same carrier runs buses to **Boston** (three daily, 1.5 hrs, $20) and **Cape Cod** (once daily, Provincetown: 4.5 hrs, $30).

Rhode Island Transportation Authority (RIPTA, 401/781-9400, www.ripta.com) #60 connects Providence and Newport (frequent buses, 1 hr, $2) leaving from the centrally located Kennedy Plaza in Providence and arriving at the Gateway Center adjacent to the Newport Visitors Center.

Two Days in Rhode Island

Day 1

Start your day early with a morning stroll on **Cliff Walk,** and watch the sun light up the mansions along this scenic coastal path. Once you've worked up an appetite for breakfast, head to friendly **Annie's Restaurant** for a quiche or a stack of "hotcakes," then pick a pair of **Newport mansions** to explore. Start with The Breakers, Newport's ne plus ultra of historic ostentation, then continue to Marble House, The Elms, or the intriguing Gothic Revival Kingscote.

WaterPlace Park along the Providence Riverwalk

Watch for surfers as you cross the bay toward **Flo's Clam Shack** for great piles of clam cakes, lobster rolls, and stuffed quahogs before heading to the beach to while away the day in the sand. Join the action by signing up for surf lessons at **Sachuest Beach,** or opt for **Easton's Beach** and alternate rides on a vintage carousel with time in the water.

Join the crowds on Thames Street to browse souvenir shops and watch the yachties try to dock their powerboats, then climb to the 3rd floor at **The Mooring Seafood Kitchen & Bar** for sunset cocktails and an oyster dinner.

Day 2

After making the breezy drive to Providence and parking near downtown, get your gears whirring with a stroll along the **Providence RiverWalk.** Then, amble over to **PVDonuts** for some of the most creative and mind-numbingly sweet baked goods in New England. Take a digestive foray over to the leafy campus of **Brown University** on College Hill and you'll be perfectly situated to get lost in the 19th-century bookshelves of **The Providence Athenaeum** or the student galleries of the **RISD Museum.**

Refuel with an artfully assembled vegetarian lunch at **Plant City** and cross the river into downtown. Shop for alternative fashions at **Queen of Hearts,** or step back into the history of African American life in Providence with a visit to **Stages of Freedom** bookstore and museum. As the heat of the day burns off, drive west and tone those calves with a hike to the top **Neutaconkanut Hill** for a view of the city that would make Roger Williams weep.

Change your duds and begin your evening in **Federal Hill.** Take in the scenery at **DePasquale Square,** where live Italian love songs, a bubbling fountain, and outdoor dining are par for the course. Wander down the north side of the hill and cut into Peruvian-style prime rib in the luxe garden dining area of **Los Andes.** Be sure to get to the waterside bar at **The Hot Club** by 8:30pm so you can take part in Good Night Lights, a ritual where people flash lights toward Hasbro Children's Hospital across the river as a gesture of Providence solidarity.

Newport

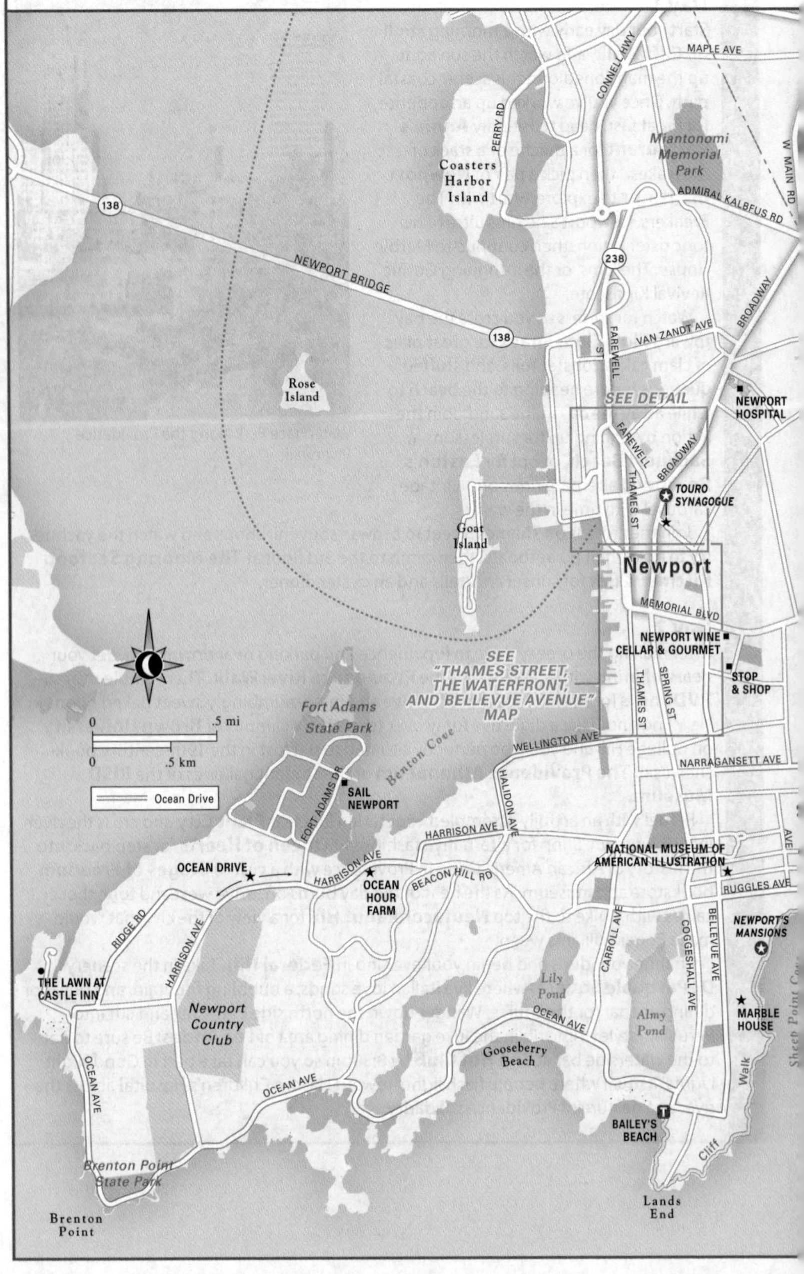
MAPLE AVE
CONNELL HWY
PERRY RD
Miantonomi Memorial Park
W MAIN RD
Coasters Harbor Island
ADMIRAL KALBFUS RD
138
NEWPORT BRIDGE
238
138
BROADWAY
VAN ZANDT AVE
FAREWELL ST
Rose Island
SEE DETAIL
NEWPORT HOSPITAL
FAREWELL
BROADWAY
TOURO SYNAGOGUE
THAMES ST
Goat Island
Newport
MEMORIAL BLVD
NEWPORT WINE CELLAR & GOURMET
SEE "THAMES STREET, THE WATERFRONT, AND BELLEVUE AVENUE" MAP
STOP & SHOP
THAMES ST
SPRING ST
Fort Adams State Park
0 .5 mi
0 .5 km
Benton Cove
WELLINGTON AVE
NARRAGANSETT AVE
Ocean Drive
FORT ADAMS DR
SAIL NEWPORT
HALIDON AVE
HARRISON AVE
NATIONAL MUSEUM OF AMERICAN ILLUSTRATION
OCEAN DRIVE
HARRISON AVE
OCEAN HOUR FARM
BEACON HILL RD
RUGGLES AVE
RIDGE RD
CARROLL AVE
COGGESHALL AVE
BELLEVUE AVE
NEWPORT'S MANSIONS
THE LAWN AT CASTLE INN
HARRISON AVE
Lily Pond
Almy Pond
MARBLE HOUSE
Newport Country Club
OCEAN AVE
Sheep Point Cove
Gooseberry Beach
OCEAN AVE
Walk
OCEAN AVE
BAILEY'S BEACH
Cliff
Brenton Point State Park
Lands End
Brenton Point

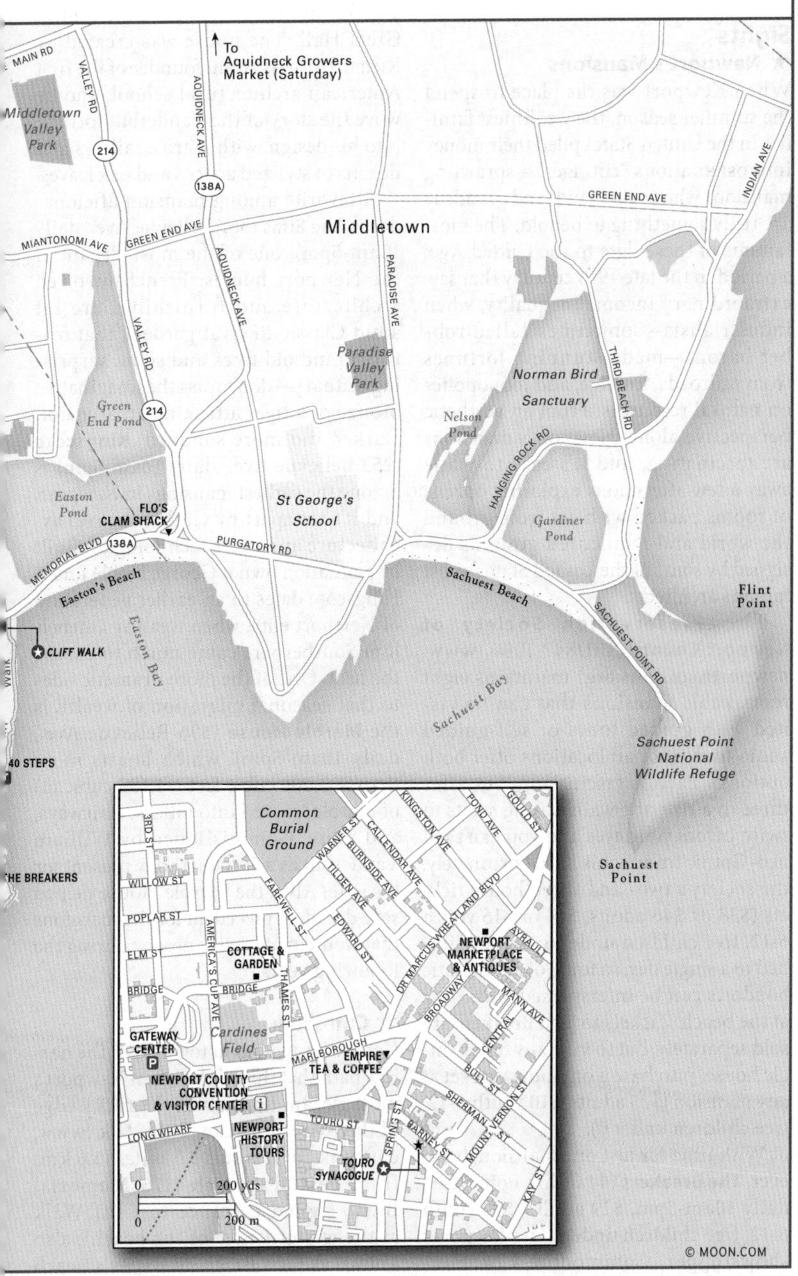
To Aquidneck Growers Market (Saturday)
MAIN RD
VALLEY RD
AQUIDNECK AVE
Middletown Valley Park
214
138A
GREEN END AVE
INDIAN AVE
Middletown
MIANTONOMI AVE
GREEN END AVE
AQUIDNECK AVE
PARADISE AVE
VALLEY RD
Paradise Valley Park
Norman Bird Sanctuary
THIRD BEACH RD
Green End Pond
214
Nelson Pond
HANGING ROCK RD
Easton Pond
FLO'S CLAM SHACK
St George's School
Gardiner Pond
138A
PURGATORY RD
MEMORIAL BLVD
Easton's Beach
Sachuest Beach
Flint Point
SACHUEST POINT RD
Easton Bay
CLIFF WALK
Sachuest Bay
Sachuest Point National Wildlife Refuge
40 STEPS
THE BREAKERS
Sachuest Point
Common Burial Ground
3RD ST
KINGSTON AVE
POND AVE
GOULD ST
WARNER ST
CALLENDAR AVE
BURNSIDE AVE
TILDEN AVE
FAREWELL ST
WILLOW ST
POPLAR ST
EDWARD ST
DR MARCUS WHEATLAND BLVD
AYRAULT
ELM ST
AMERICA'S CUP AVE
COTTAGE & GARDEN
THAMES ST
NEWPORT MARKETPLACE & ANTIQUES
BRIDGE
BRIDGE
BROADWAY
MANN AVE
GATEWAY CENTER
Cardines Field
CENTRAL
MARLBOROUGH
EMPIRE TEA & COFFEE
NEWPORT COUNTY CONVENTION & VISITOR CENTER
BULL ST
SHERMAN ST
MOUNT VERNON ST
TOURO ST
LONG WHARF
NEWPORT HISTORY TOURS
SPRING ST
BARNEY ST
TOURO SYNAGOGUE
KAY ST
0
200 yds
0
200 m
© MOON.COM

Newport

Sights

★ Newport's Mansions

When Newport was *the* place to spend the summer season, the wealthiest families in the United States piled their money into ostentatious "cottages"—sprawling mansions whose gilt, gaud, and grandeur are truly something to behold. The most famous of these date to the Gilded Age, a period in the late 19th century that saw extraordinary income inequality, when industrialists—sometimes called robber barons—made stunning fortunes from railroads, finance, and monopolies on natural resources. From an aesthetic perspective alone, Newport's mansions are fascinating, and it's easy to while away a few afternoons exploring dozens of rooms packed with art from around the world and manicured grounds designed by some of the United States' most famous architects.

The **Preservation Society of Newport County** (401/847-1000, www.newportmansions.org) maintains eight remarkable mansions that can be visited with guided tours or self-guided audio tours (not all locations offer both options). Each is fascinating, but after three in a row, the wainscoting starts to swim before your eyes and you can't tell neo-Gothic from Louis XIV. Fortunately, the society's two- and three-house tickets ($38 or $46 adults, $14 or $16 youth 6-12, free children under 6) are not limited to a single day, so tours of aristocratic boudoirs can be interspersed with time at the beach. Tickets to The Breakers are sold separately, but to visit any other single house, purchase a one-house ticket at any mansion ($25 adults, $10 youth 6-12, free children under 6).

With time for just one mansion, however, **The Breakers** (44 Ochre Point Ave., daily 10am-5pm, $29 adults, $10 youth 6-12, free children under 6) is Newport's showstopper. Commodore Cornelius Vanderbilt II built the Italianate behemoth to resemble an open-air palazzo, and downy clouds arc above the central Great Hall. The house was created by Richard Morris Hunt, founder of the first American architectural school, and he wove the story of the Vanderbilt fortune into his design, with marble railcars and dozens of stylized acorns and oak leaves.

A favorite among mansion aficionados is **The Elms** (367 Bellevue Ave., daily 10am-5pm), one of the most elegant of the Newport homes. French-inspired architecture and furnishings are set amid Classic Revival gardens that feature grand old trees and some surprising statuary—don't miss the imaginative bronze of a tiger attacking an alligator. Darker and more subdued, **Kingscote** (253 Bellevue Ave., daily 10am-5pm) is among the earliest mansions in Newport, and it's set apart by Gothic Revival architecture and older technologies. Built by plantation owner George Noble Jones, Kingscote dates to an earlier generation of Newport elite, when wealthy antebellum Southerners came north to escape the heat. One of the more dramatic odes to that seasonal migration of wealth is the **Marble House** (596 Bellevue Ave., daily 10am-5pm), which boasts more than 500,000 cubic feet (14,158 cubic m) of marble, carved into pillars, stairways, and more. Commissioned by William Vanderbilt as a 39th birthday present for his wife, Alva, the Marble House helped set a decadent precedent for the mansions that would materialize nearby during the following years.

★ Cliff Walk

Get the best views in town from the narrow path that threads between Newport's most elegant homes and the rocky edge of the Atlantic Ocean. **Cliff Walk** (www.cliffwalk.com) winds 3.5 miles (5.6 km) from **Easton's Beach** (175 Memorial Blvd., signed entrance to Cliff Walk at the western edge of the beach), also known as First Beach, to **Bailey's Beach**

Thames Street, the Waterfront, and Bellevue Avenue

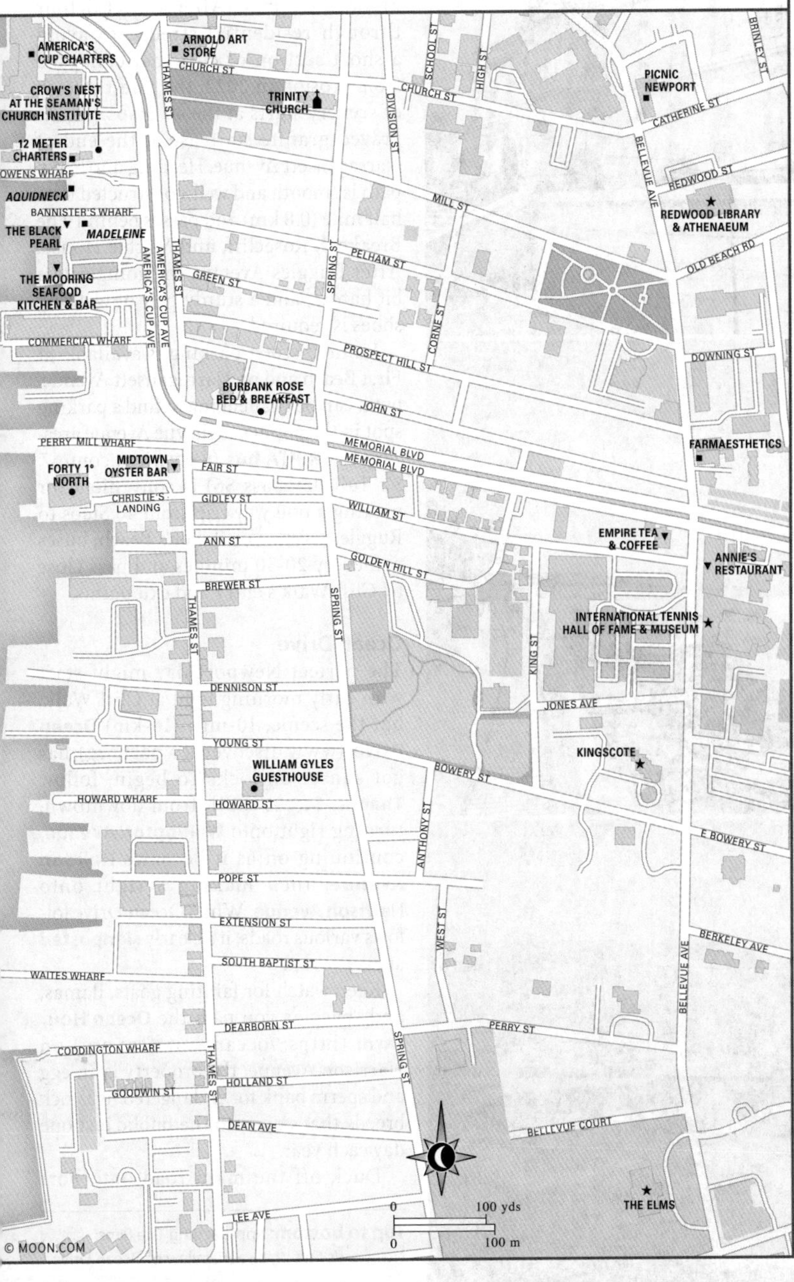

at Bellevue Avenue, known locally as "Reject's Beach" since it's open to, you know, the public. After a brief detour through residential streets, to avoid a short section of cliff that collapsed from erosion in 2022, the finest stretch of scenery starts at the **40 Steps,** an engraved granite staircase at the end of Narragansett Avenue. Heading north, the path is smooth and well-constructed for a half mile (0.8 km) and passes behind The Breakers, Rosecliff, and Marble House. After Ruggles Avenue, the going gets a bit harder, and a sturdy pair of walking shoes is required.

Limited street parking is available at First Beach and on Narragansett Avenue, but it can be challenging to find a parking spot in the popular Bellevue Avenue area. The #67 **RIPTA bus** (www.ripta.com/67, $2, full-day pass $6) is convenient for making a one-way trip from 40 Steps to Ruggles Avenue or Bailey's Beach; buses run every 20-30 minutes and pass close by Cliff Walk's entry and exit points.

Ocean Drive

The perfect Newport day might start with early morning light at Cliff Walk, but the scenic, 10-mile (16-km) **Ocean Drive** (www.discovernewport.org) has got sunset on lock. To begin, follow **Thames Street** south from downtown, turning right onto **Wellington Avenue,** continuing on as it becomes **Halidon Avenue,** then making a right onto **Harrison Avenue.** While Ocean Drive follows various roads, it's clearly **signposted** at every turn.

Keep watch for fainting goats, llamas, and sheep as you pass the **Ocean Hour Farm** (https://oceanhourfarm.org) on Harrison Avenue; the property is an egg and sperm bank for endangered livestock breeds that's open to the public just one day each year.

Duck off the main road onto Fort

Top to bottom: approaching The Elms; Newport's Cliff Walk; aerial view of Ocean Drive

Newport's Legacy of Enslavement

Rhode Island's founders came to Aquidneck Island to find freedom from the strictures of Puritan society. But that foundational ideal wasn't extended to all of the state's inhabitants. The first recorded enslaved African Americans arrived less than 15 years later, and many of them were exchanged for previously enslaved Indigenous people. The colony, founded in 1636, became a leader in the New England slave trade—between 1709 and 1807, local merchants sent 930 slave ships to Africa—and by the mid-18th century, it had the highest percentage of enslaved inhabitants in the North.

While many enslaved people were forced to work in Rhode Island homes and plantations, much of the area's involvement in human trafficking was a part of New England's "triangle trade." Newport rum distilleries imported molasses from Caribbean sugar plantations, which depended on enslaved laborers, and shipped rum to Africa to trade for enslaved people who'd be brought back to the Caribbean to swap for molasses.

That tragic commerce permeates Rhode Island's history; Brown University, Touro Synagogue, and the Redwood Library and Athenaeum were built with money from slave-trading families, and Newport's Brick Market and Old Colony House were constructed in part by enslaved workers.

Even though the famous Newport mansions were largely constructed after the Civil War and the passage of the Emancipation Proclamation, we can't overlook the role that enslavement played in transforming early Newport into a gilded seaside "escape" where America's white ruling class would eventually build their lavish retreats.

Where to Learn More

- Today, one can reflect on Rhode Island's legacy of slavery by visiting the **Common Burial Ground** (Warner St. and Farewell St., www.islandcemeterynewport.com), where many enslaved people in Newport were buried. The cemetery is known by the local Black community as God's Little Acre.

- **Newport History Tours** (127 Thames St., 1.25-hr tours \$20 adults, \$10 children 5-12) offers guided visits to the cemetery, as well as a tour called **Creative Survival,** which provides a thorough look at Newport's history of African American enslavement, and the enterprises and local industry created by Black residents in the wake of slavery's evils.

- The Rhode Island **Black Heritage Society** (www.riblackheritage.org) features a timeline of the state's civil rights history, and spotlights local historic sites.

Adams Drive for a side trip through historic **Fort Adams** (401/847-2400, www.fortadams.org, free), then continue south along Harrison Avenue to Ridge Road. Turn right onto Castle Hill Avenue then right again onto Ocean Avenue to pause for a drink on **The Lawn at Castle Hill Inn** (590 Ocean Dr., 888/466-1355, www.castlehillinn.com), one of the most elegant stretches of grass in Newport. After your break at the inn, turn right on **Ocean Avenue** to stay on the Ocean Drive route to **Brenton Point State Park** (Ocean Ave., 401/849-4562, www.riparks.ri.gov, free), which wraps all the way around the point where Narragansett Bay meets the Atlantic Ocean. Brenton Point's consistent winds make it the best **kite-flying** spot around, so bring your own or pick one up at the park's small shop, then grab a **Del's Lemonade** from one of the trucks that prowl the parking lot.

You'll eventually loop up by way of **Bellevue Avenue.** Ocean Drive can take a brisk 35 minutes or extend through a leisurely afternoon.

National Museum of American Illustration

In 1998, one of Newport's great mansions was transformed into the **National Museum of American Illustration** (492 Bellevue Ave., 401/851-8949, www.americanillustration.org, late May-early Sept. Thurs.-Sun. 11am-5pm, Sept.-late May Fri. 11am-5pm, guided tours year-round Fri. 3pm, $20 adults, $18 seniors, $14 students, $10 children 5-12, under 5 not admitted), the first museum in the country devoted to illustration art. The collection includes work by N.C. Wyeth, Maxfield Parrish, and Norman Rockwell, the most iconic names from the golden age of American illustration, which stretched from the post-Civil War era to the 1950s. It's a fascinating look at the intersection of popular culture, propaganda, and fine art. Don't leave the museum without exploring the grounds of Vernon Court; a romantic rose garden, terraces, and a sunken garden are beautifully maintained in the neoclassical style.

Fort Adams State Park

As the British navy set up floating blockades during the War of 1812, the militia at Fort Adams manned an impressive array of 17 cannons that would give any invading fleet a rough welcome to the Newport Harbor. Join a guided tour at **Fort Adams State Park** (90 Fort Adams Dr., 401/847-2400, www.fortadams.org, May-Oct. daily, tours hourly 10am-4pm, Nov.-Jan. Sat.-Sun., tours at noon and 2pm, late May-late March daily, tours at noon and 2pm, $50 families, $20 adults, $10 youth 6-17, self-guided tours $15 families, $6 adults, $3 youth 6-17, under 6 free) to explore officers' quarters, the ramparts, and fascinating tunnels to the outer defenses, or visit the fort at your own pace (though tunnels aren't accessible on self-guided tours).

The rest of the park is free to explore, and swimming beaches, picnic areas, and rolling grass make it a pleasant spot on warm afternoons. The 2.2-mile (3.5-km) **Bay Walk** loops along the shoreline, up the western side of the park with views of the Narragansett Bay, and back down the eastern edge, where you can see the bristling masts and white sails of Newport Harbor.

★ Touro Synagogue

Rhode Island is thought to be the first civil authority in the world to guarantee religious freedom to all citizens, and it became a haven for Quakers, Jews, and freethinkers that Puritans saw as a threat to their social fabric. Perhaps the most vivid place to hear about this part of Rhode Island's legacy is at the historic **Touro Synagogue** (85 Touro St., 401/847-4794, www.tourosynagogue.org, July-Aug. Sun.-Fri. tours every 45 min. 10am-3:15pm, Sept.-Oct. tours every 45 min. 10am-1:45pm, $14 adults, $12 seniors, $10 students and military, under

13 free), the only surviving colonial-era synagogue in the United States.

Construction on the building began in 1759, and the layout resembles those of synagogues in the Caribbean islands and Amsterdam; Newport's Jewish community was descended from the Sephardic people expelled from Spain by the Inquisition, who continued to more tolerant homes in the Netherlands and the New World. The synagogue itself is a stunning building, with an airy balcony for the formerly gender-divided congregation, a 500-year-old Torah, and a framework of 12 Ionic columns—one for each tribe of Israel.

International Tennis Hall of Fame

Tennis fans won't want to miss the **International Tennis Hall of Fame Museum** (194 Bellevue Ave., 401/849-3990, www.tennisfame.com, daily 10am-5pm, $20 adults, $17 seniors and students, youth under 13 free), a shrine to the history, arcana, and heroes of the game, complete with a life-size talking hologram of Roger Federer. Even the setting is infused with tennis history; the museum grounds once housed the Newport Casino, a social club that hosted the first U.S. National Men's Singles Championship in 1881.

Entertainment and Events

Festivals and Events

From yacht races to film festivals, Newport has one of the busiest event calendars in New England. The season kicks off with the **Newport Oyster & Chowder Festival** (late May, www.bowenswharf.com/events, free admission), a two-day bivalve blowout with oyster farmers from around the state and live music, followed by the **Newport Flower Show** (last weekend in June, www.newportmansions.org/events/newport-flower-show, tickets $30 adults), when the Preservation Society's mansions open their grounds for juried shows, garden parties, and afternoon teas. See the city's salty side at the

Newport Jazz Festival

Newport International Boat Show (mid-Sept., www.newportboatshow.com). All year round, visitors can attend screenings by **Newport Film** (401/649-2784, www.newportfilm.com), often in some of the city's most dramatic settings, from Gilded Age mansions to seaside gardens.

★ Music Festivals

For two weekends each summer, Newport fills to the brim with music lovers, drawn to two of the country's most important—and historic—festivals. **Newport Jazz Festival** (www.newportjazz.org) is the original, a three-day extravaganza that always includes some of the genre's biggest names. Dizzy Gillespie and Billie Holiday played the 1954 festival, and Miles Davis, Duke Ellington, and Ella Fitzgerald each released live albums of their Newport performances. Five years later, **Newport Folk Festival** (www.newportfolk.org) kicked off with a memorable show that included the debut performance of 18-year-old Joan Baez (who invited Bob Dylan to join her on stage in 1963). Dylan came back in 1964 and 1965, when he famously played his first live electric set; after being booed by some members of the audience, he didn't return to the festival for 37 years.

Both festivals remain vital, and artists that range from rock and roll to R&B pack the fields at Fort Adams State Park. To make the festivals a part of your road trip, start planning soon—tickets and many of accommodations in the area sell out the previous winter, and prices skyrocket during both weekends. Visit the festival websites for more information, and be aware of the festivals while planning your trip; if you're not in town *for* the festivals, you'd likely rather be somewhere else entirely.

Shopping

As in all New England tourist towns, there are plenty of fudge shops and kitschy souvenir stores around Newport, but there are also some beautiful places to browse nautical knickknacks, clothing, and gifts.

Downtown

Tempting shops are sprinkled all along the waterfront, but a good place to start would be the cozy and intimate **Newport Marketplace and Antiques** (130 Broadway, 401/848-2398, www.newportmarketplaceandantiques.com, daily 10am-5:30pm), where local antique vendors pile up everything from ships in bottles to leather-bound books and fine china.

From lithographs of J-class sloops to oil paintings of Newport beaches, **Arnold Art Store** (210 Thames St., 800/352-2234, www.arnoldart.com, Mon.-Sat. 10am-4pm) brings together marine artists like Keith Reynolds and Helena Sturtevant—some of the area's most recognizable names.

Bellevue Shopping District

Tony boutiques around Bellevue Avenue sell charming bits of the Newport lifestyle, like the perfectly sweet **Cottage & Garden** (9 Bridge St., 401/848-8477, www.facebook.com/cottageandgarden, Tues.-Sat. 11am-5pm, Sun. noon-5pm), where displays of vintage furnishings, antiques, and garden supplies are arranged just so. Pick out lush, natural gifts at **Farmaesthetics** (144 Bellevue Ave., 401/619-4199, www.farmaesthetics.com, Wed.-Sun. 11am-6pm), a light-filled shop loaded with herbal cosmetics and beauty products.

Sports and Recreation

Beaches

Much of Newport's coastline is rocky and rugged, but those salty points shelter wonderful beaches that are bustling all summer—though some are livelier than others.

Watch surfers catch waves and take a ride on the vintage carousel at **Easton's Beach** (aka First Beach, 175 Memorial Blvd., 401/845-5300, parking $25 weekends, $15 weekdays), a 0.75-mile (1.2-km) stretch of sand that fills up with a friendly crowd of families. With ice cream shops and frozen lemonade trucks, this is a sweetly nostalgic place to enjoy the sun, and the on-site **Rosie's Beach Store** rents out umbrellas, chairs, and boogie boards. It's sometimes possible to find free parking on the side streets off Memorial Boulevard.

A few miles past Easton's Beach is **Sachuest Beach** (aka Second Beach, 474 Sachuest Point Rd., 401/842-6522, parking $30 weekends, $20 weekdays), where there are better waves and sometimes a thinner crowd. This beach is also the home of **Rhody Surf** (401/236-4846, www.rhodysurf.com, private lessons $75 per person), which offers surfboard rentals and surfing lessons with certified instructors. The western edge of the beach catches the biggest swell, while the eastern end is calmer, so toss out your beach blanket accordingly.

A rocky cove shelters **Gooseberry Beach** (123 Ocean Ave., parking $30), making it a good choice for quiet swims and smaller children, and the beach is often less crowded than other places in town. Open-topped kayaks are available for rent, but the nearby beach club is not open to the public so it's worth bringing your own supplies. Avoid the Bellevue Avenue traffic and expensive parking by hopping on public transportation; Gooseberry Beach is just under a mile (1.6 km) from the final stop on the RIPTA #67 bus route.

Boating

Aspiring yachties and ambitious landlubbers can hit the harbor in 12-meter America's Cup sailboats—a class of racing boats designed for the prestigious America's Cup race—with a pair of local charter companies. **America's Cup Charters** (49 America's Cup Ave., 401/846-9886, www.americascupcharters.com, $90 2-hr sail adult or $50 child under 13, $195 3-hr racing experience) has the largest fleet of winning boats in the world, while **12 Meter Charters** (12 Bowens Wharf, 401/851-1216, www.12metercharters.com, $110 2-hr harbor sail, $210 3-hr racing experience) has a slightly smaller but equally impressive quiver of sailing yachts.

Slower moving and breathtakingly beautiful, old-fashioned schooners are among the prettiest sails on Narragansett Bay, and they're notably more comfortable than the sleek and speedy America's Cup boats. The 80-foot (24-m), teak-trimmed ***Aquidneck*** (32 Bowen's Wharf, 401/849-3333, www.sightsailing.com, $47 1.75-hr sightseeing cruise, $60 sunset sail) has gaff-rigged sails and a broad, comfortable deck that's perfect for a glamorous turn around the coast. Two-masted, wooden ***Madeleine*** (22 Bowen's Wharf, 401/847-0000, www.sail-newport.com, $45 1.5-hr sightseeing cruise, $55 sunset sail) is 72 feet (22 m) and impossibly elegant, with a pretty mermaid figurehead to lead the way across the water.

Experienced sailors rent their own boats from **Sail Newport** (60 Fort Adams Dr., 401/846-1983, www.sailnewport.org, from $123 3-hr keelboat, from $222 6-hr keelboat) after being checked out by a staff member, then hit the harbor at the helm of a J22 or a Rhodes 19.

Parks

In addition to the seven-mile (11.25-km) **Cliff Walk** and the trails at **Fort Adams State Park** there are plenty of ways to escape the crowds on scenic trails near the sea. Remember: It's important to be aware of ticks while hiking in this area.

With woodland habitats, streams, and fields, **Norman Bird Sanctuary** (583 Third Beach Rd., Middletown, 401/846-2577, www.normanbirdsanctuary.org, daily 9am-5pm, $7) attracts a diverse range of birds, from bobolinks to black-crowned night herons. Seven miles (11.25 km) of hiking trails thread through 325 acres (131.5 ha); the 1.4-mile (2.25-km)

Nelson Pond Trail traces a ridge covered with cedar and oak trees stunted by the wind and salt air, while the 1.2-mile (1.9-km) **Valley Trail** passes through one the preserve's most diverse areas. Each of the tree species that grows within Norman Bird Sanctuary may be found along the trail, including four species of oak and eastern red cedar, the area's only native conifer.

Borrow a pair of binoculars and a wildlife identification guide from the visitor center at **Sachuest Point National Wildlife Refuge** (Sachuest Point Rd., Middletown, 401/619-2680, www.fws.gov/refuge, daily sunrise-sunset, free), then watch for snowy owls, harlequin ducks, and the incredibly adorable New England cottontail rabbits. The 1.5-mile (2.4-km) **Ocean View Loop** offers lots of water access and can be linked to the 1.2-mile (1.9-km) **Flint Point** trail for a longer walk. Don't miss the explanation of the area's fascinating geological history at the visitor center—the rock record in the refuge retains traces of Rhode Island's 356-million-year-old run-in with present-day Africa.

Spectator Sports

Grab a wiener and some popcorn, then watch the Collegiate League **Newport Gulls** go to bat at **Cardines Field** (W. Marlborough St. and America's Cup Ave., 401/845-6832, www.newportgulls.com, $5 adults, $2 seniors and youth 13-18, $1 under 13), where there's baseball two or three times a week from early June through the August playoffs. The historic field offers an old-fashioned taste of the sport that's largely been lost in the corporatized professional leagues.

On Saturday afternoons from June through September, Newport dons its pearls and polo shirts for the matches at **Newport Polo** (250 Linden Ln., Portsmouth, 401/846-0200, www.nptpolo.com, lawn seating $20 adults, youth under 16 free). It's the perfect place to bring an elegant picnic and enjoy the

sailing Newport Harbor

sunshine as national and international teams hook, bump, and pass their way through a series of chukkas, or periods. Matches begin at 5pm and gates open at 1pm (noon in Sept.), so plan to arrive early for prime picnic spots.

Food

Bustling Thames Street is home to some of Newport's best seafood restaurants. It's the heart of the tourist scene and can get jammed with visitors, but joining the summer crowds by the water is just part of the Newport experience. In recent years, however, a cluster of hip, locals-oriented places have opened on Broadway, and when Thames Street starts looking like an out-of-control yacht party, it's worth heading over there to enjoy a meal away from the din.

Thames Street

Seafood is the star attraction in the refined waterfront comforts of **The Mooring Seafood Kitchen & Bar** (1 Sayers Wharf, 401/846-2260, www.mooringrestaurant.com, Sun.-Thurs. 11:30am-9pm, Fri.-Sat. 11:30am-10pm, $27-50). In the warmer months, visitors clamber onto the mahogany-planked patio for primo views of Newport Harbor and its armada of sailing vessels, which are all the better savored over tempting small plates such as pan-seared prawns in Calabrian chili-lime butter, and heftier offerings like the local fluke (a regular on Rhode Island menus) with fennel puree and beet vinaigrette. The raw bar menu packs a wallop, too. When in Little Rhody, always consider adding some oysters or crudo to the agenda.

Cozy up to the bar at **The Black Pearl** (Bannisters Wharf, 401/846-5264, www.blackpearlnewport.com, daily 11am-9pm, $14-28) for a bowl of award-winning chowder—rumor has it that The Black Pearl won Newport's chowder cook-off so frequently they got barred from entry. The casual tavern is the place to be here, where you can rub elbows with sailors and sightseers in a room that feels like a piece of maritime history.

You can watch all of Newport come and go at ★ **Midtown Oyster Bar** (345 Thames St., 401/619-4100, www.midtownoyster.com, Sun.-Thurs. 11:30am-9:30pm, Fri.-Sat. 11:30am-10pm, lunch $17-29, dinner $22-40), a popular hangout with a raw bar, dining room, and comfortable pub. The outdoor decks are dreamy on hot summer evenings, and you can wander around until you find the perfect place to sit. Mains like peppercorn swordfish with polenta and roasted maitake mushrooms are appealing and super-fresh, but the appetizers tend to be Midtown's most creative options; tuna tartare tacos are a favorite with regulars, and the charred octopus is a highlight.

Broadway, Bellevue, and Beyond

Settle in with a good book and better coffee at the Broadway outpost of **Empire Tea & Coffee** (22 Broadway, 401/619-1388, www.empireteaandcoffee.com, daily

Rhode Island's Iconic Foods

True to its history as an outlier from the institutions and traditions of New England, Little Rhody boasts some of the region's strangest yet improbably delicious dishes, from snail salad to hot wieners.

- **Coffee Milk and Cabinets:** Rhode Island's state drink is the unassuming coffee milk, a sweet blend of cold milk and coffee syrup that's available everywhere (the two major labels are almost identical, but each claims passionate partisans). Order a milk shake here, and you'll get sweetened milk; the frosty, blended ice cream drink is called a cabinet, and the very last word in cabinets is the **Awful Awful** from **Newport Creamery** (page 304). It's "awful big, awful good."

hot wieners with coffee milk

- **Hot Wieners:** Order one of these distinctive sausages "all the way," and it will come in a steamed bun topped with beef sauce, chopped onions, and a bump of celery salt. Try the classic version at the Providence location of **Olneyville New York System Restaurant** (18 Plainfield St., Providence, 401/621-9500, www.olneyvillenewyorksystem.com, Sun.-Thurs. 11am-2am, Fri.-Sat. 11am-3am, $4-10). . . just don't call it a hot dog.

- **Quahogs and Stuffies:** Hard-shelled clams are called quahogs (pronounced koh-hogs) in the Ocean State, and there are dozens of ways to prepare the briny bivalves. Head to **Flo's Clam Shack** (page 305) to try them as stuffies—the chopped clam meat is mixed with bread and spices, then baked in the shell. Some versions are spiced up with chourica sausage, a reminder of Rhode Island's Portuguese heritage.

6am-4pm, $3-11), a rambling café with plenty of spots to work and read. Wireless internet, well-made espresso, and excellent teas make this an appealing place to ride out a rainy day.

A salt-of-the-earth respite from Bellevue glitz is **Annie's Restaurant** (176 Bellevue Ave., 401/849-6731, www.anniesnewport.com, daily 7am-3pm, $7-16). At this cozy "breakfast all day" nook, greasy spoon classics are prepared with care and pride. The hotcakes are big, fluffy, and liberally decorated with syrup and fresh fruit, while the house-made corned beef hash pairs nicely with the quiche lorraine. For good measure, the menu also includes golden-fried seafood platters and prime rib au jus. At Annie's you're just as likely to be seated near Newport residents or visitors who've managed to get the lowdown on this hidden treasure. And the uninitiated should try ordering a "Tim Tam Slam" with their hot drink—it's an Aussie tradition worth globalizing.

An Awful Awful from the **Newport Creamery** (208 West Main Rd., Middletown, 401/846-2767, www.newportcreamery.com, daily 7am-11pm, $5-11) is a summertime tradition in Rhode Island; the name of the thick ice cream shake stands for "awful big, awful good." A somewhat generic selection of sandwiches and burgers rounds out the menu, and the low prices make the Newport Creamery a decent option for families, but this place is all about the ice cream.

Head past the sandy crescent of Easton's Beach for another Rhode Island food pilgrimage: ★ **Flo's Clam Shack** (4 Wave Ave., Middletown, 401/847-8141, www.flosclamshacks.com, daily 11am-9pm, $9-27) has been ruling the old-school seafood scene since 1936. Buoys, lobster traps, fishing nets, and Rhode Island kitsch hang from every surface, and the menu features all the seafood shack classics: Golden fried clams come piled atop french fries and coleslaw, and chowder arrives creamy, clear, or red. Flo's does brisk business in Rhode Island-style clam cakes, a fried, hush puppy–like dumpling speckled with bits of clam meat that can be ordered singly or by the dozen. When coming to Flo's during the summer, be prepared to wait in line; there's a small parking lot out back, otherwise try across the street near the park.

From sandy beaches to polo matches, there are plenty of prime picnic spots in town. Pick up basic supplies at the centrally located **Stop & Shop** (250 Bellevue Ave., 401/848-7200, Mon.-Sat. 6am-10pm, Sun. 6am-9pm), or pack your hamper with more elegant fare at **Picnic Newport** (28 Bellevue Ave., 401/619-1181, www.picnicnewport.com, daily 8am-6pm), which spreads out a tempting array of house pastries, baguette sandwiches, soups, and specialty cheeses.

Another excellent stop is **Newport Wine Cellar & Gourmet** (5 Merton Rd., 401/619-3966, www.newportwinecellar.com, Wed.-Sat. 11am-7pm, Sun. noon-5pm), offering ready-to-eat salads, fresh bread, and cheese that pairs well with an excellent wine selection.

Accommodations and Camping

There's an inn on every corner in Newport's compact downtown, but finding a bed that won't break the bank can be a challenge in peak season. Rooms fill up months in advance for popular festival weekends, and many places maintain a two-night minimum on the weekends. That said, there are some incredible places to stay in town, ranging from homey dorms to aristocratic suites, and off-season prices are considerably lower than those listed.

Camping

Twenty minutes north of downtown, the **Newport RV Park** (181 Bradford Ave., Portsmouth, 401/682-2424, www.melvillepondscampground.com, Apr.-mid-Nov., tent sites $65, RVs $80-140, airstream trailers $169-203) is a friendly place to put down stakes, with hot showers, picnic tables, fire rings, and a pretty stream through the property. While the campground has moved away from tent camping and primarily become a recreational vehicle game, you don't need to own an RV to stay here. Glamping accommodations are available in the form of polished Airstream trailers with fully stocked kitchens, showers, and outdoor fire pits. Consult the map on the campground website before booking, as some sites are a fairly long walk from the bathhouses, and beware of holiday weekends and Newport's festival dates, as sites go up in price and have a two- or three-day minimum.

Under $150

With a central location and a homey atmosphere, **William Gyles Guesthouse** (16 Howard St., 401/369-0243, www.williamgylesguesthouse.com, mid-May-Sept., $70-225) is an increasingly rare budget option for Newport visitors. Tucked in Newport's historic Yachting Village and steps away from the waterfront, the guesthouse offers spacious and thoughtfully decorated rooms, an open-air deck that's perfect for nursing a beer or glass of wine at sundown, and an in-house library packed with travel books.

The compact rooms at ★ **Crow's Nest at the Seamen's Church Institute** (18 Market Sq., 401/847-4260, www.seamensnewport.org, $125-185) are neat as a pin, decorated with sweet quilts and images of the sea. This unique accommodation was designed as a haven for seamen on shore leave, and the Seamen's Church Institute's profits still go to providing services for "the men and women of the sea," as well as other people in need. All rooms share clean communal bathrooms, and visitors have access to the ocean-themed Seamen's Chapel and a library stocked with all the books you need to plan a round-the-world sailing trip. Fishers, military, and mariners should inquire about discounts.

$150-250

Just a short walk from the harbor front, the **Burbank Rose Bed & Breakfast** (111 Memorial Blvd. W., 401/855-9199, www.burbankrose.com, $155-235, parking $19/day) feels like a glimpse into Newport's past—simple rooms are furnished with old-fashioned charm, and the owner prepares freshly baked pastries for the generous continental breakfast. The steep, narrow stairs are as authentic as the hospitality, and 3rd-floor suites may be a challenge for some guests.

Over $350

With an unbeatable location on the Thames Street waterfront, LEED-certified ★ **Forty 1° North** (351 Thames St., 401/846-8018, www.41north.com, $359-1,299) eschews Newport's beachy pastels for a palette of muted grays and iridescent highlights—the result is a kind of mermaid modernism. Artfully placed design books, stunning harbor views, and elegant indoor-outdoor spaces are lightened up with a billiard room and excellent in-room bars. And for travelers arriving in Newport on their own yachts, Forty 1° North has a private, full-service marina—for the rest of us, it's easy to while away an afternoon on the dock, enjoying a cocktail and watching the dock lines fly.

Information and Services

Stock up on brochures, maps, and any other kind of information on the area at the centrally located **Newport County Convention & Visitors Bureau** (21 Long Wharf Mall, 401/845-9130, www.discovernewport.org, daily 10am-5pm).

The area's major hospital is **Newport Hospital** (11 Friendship St., 401/846-6400, www.lifespan.org/newport). Local pharmacies include **CVS** (181 Bellevue Ave., 401/846-7800, www.cvs.com, pharmacy hours Mon.-Fri. 8am-9pm, Sat.-Sun. 9am-6pm) and **Walmart** (199 JT Connell Hwy., 401/848-5861, www.walmart.com, pharmacy hours Mon.-Sat. 9am-7pm, Sun. 10am-6pm). A handful of banks are found on Thames Street, and several ATMs are located on Thames Street and on Bellevue Avenue, as well as at the bus station and in convenience stores. Free **Internet access** is available in several local cafés and at the majority of hotels (offered to guests only) in town. Faxing and shipping services are offered at **The UPS Store** (270 Bellevue Ave., 401/848-7600, www.theupsstore.com).

Getting Around

Newport's Thames Street area and Bellevue Avenue can get clogged with traffic during peak season, and **parking** can also be a challenge during summer months; the largest public lot is at **Gateway Center** (23 America's Cup Ave., $2.50/half hr, $40 all day maximum), and metered parking is available in the center for $2/hour.

For visitors who prefer to leave their cars parked, it's easy to visit the main attractions on Bellevue Avenue on the #67 **RIPTA buses** ($2, www.ripta.com/67), which run frequently every day of the week. Another good way to get around is by **bicycle;** rent one at **Ten Speed Spokes** (18 Elm St., 401/847-5609, www.tenspeedspokes.com, Tues.-Fri.

10am-6pm, Sat.-Sun. 10am-5pm, $10 per hr or $50-85 full day). Taxi service is available from **Orange Cab** (401/841-0030, www.newportcabs.com).

Providence

Sights

Providence River

No matter where you wander in Providence, all roads seem to lead back to the river. A blue ribbon that cuts right through the parks and high-rises of downtown, the **Providence River** is actually a merger of three inland rivers: the Moshassuck, the Seekonk, and the Woonasquatucket. For decades, the Providence River was largely covered by a massive concrete bridge until industrial decline in the 1980s prompted the city government to incorporate the river into a broader urban renewal program. The river was uncovered and rerouted. Today, it's one of the city's top recreation destinations. You can kayak the Providence River, take an architecture tour of the city by boat, or even book a ride in an authentic Venetian gondola for a more romantic river experience.

But you don't have to get on the water to make the most of the Providence River. You can stroll along the water in style by picking up the **Providence RiverWalk,** a mile-long (1.6-km) cobblestone pathway that flanks the river on both sides. The RiverWalk begins at **WaterPlace Park,** a beautiful constructed basin that sits at the foot of the hill where the Rhode Island state capitol building is located. You'll pass flowering parklets, cafés, galleries, and some of the city's most curious public artworks, such as Boris Bally's ***Gun Totem,*** a 12-foot-tall (3.6-m) obelisk made of old handguns procured during a buyback program (the piece has some historical significance for Providence, where warring mafia families dispatched adversaries and infested local politics from the 1960s through the 1980s).

The RiverWalk ultimately connects downtown Providence with the affluent neighborhoods of the East Side. Upon reaching the southern end of the pathway, you'll be rewarded with an epic view of the **Fox Point Hurricane Barrier,** a towering dam-like structure built during the 1960s to prevent storm surges from flooding the city. (The Providence River is a tidal river and thus vulnerable to swells from gnarly coastal weather.) But no matter where you begin or conclude your walk, you'll find yourself in good company. In Providence, there's always something, or someone, on the river.

TOP EXPERIENCE

★ RISD Museum

One of New England's top art schools is rooted right in the heart of Providence. Located on the river, the Rhode Island School of Design is where contemporaries Kara Walker and Shepard Fairey cut their teeth as emerging artists, and you can step into their former stomping grounds by paying a visit to the **RISD Museum** (20 N. Main St., 401/454-6500, www.risdmuseum.org, Tues.-Wed. and Fri.-Sun. 10am-5pm, Thurs. noon-8pm, $20 adults, $15 seniors, $10 students, youth 18 and under free, free admission Thurs. 5pm-8pm and Sun. 10am-5pm). Boasting a collection of more than 100,000 works spanning centuries and continents, the RISD Museum can easily hold its own next to some of the most famous museums in the United States. But what really makes this place special are the RISD student galleries, where you can admire sculptures, paintings, video art, and more from tomorrow's creators. Be sure to leave time for a foray through the RISD Works shop, where you can actually get your mitts on original artwork and gifts, hand-crafted by Rhode Island artists.

The Providence Athenaeum

Cream-white columns, busts of Athena and Cicero, and shelf after shelf of rare

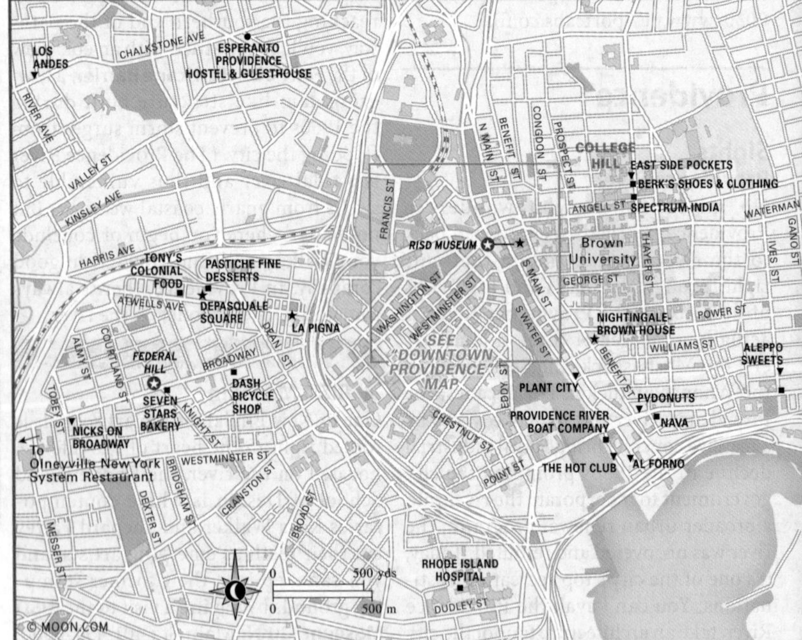

books are just a few of the atmospheric charms of the **Providence Athenaeum** (251 Benefit St., 401/421-6970, www.providenceathenaeum.org, Tues.-Sat. 10am-6pm, Sun. 11am-5pm, $5 suggested donation). Housed in a Greek revival building on the hillside where Brown University's campus is located, the Athenaeum's story began in 1753, when book-starved Providence residents pooled their limited cash together and imported hardcovers from Europe for shared use. It was a predecessor to the city's first public lending library and it drew local authors like moths to candlelight. To this day, the Athenaeum casts spells on anyone who knows what it's like to get sucked into a good novel. The Athenaeum's contemporary offerings have expanded to include concerts, speaker series, and events like cocktail parties and wedding galas. But you can still find treasures like the 1835 edition of Walt Whitman's *Leaves of Grass* nestled in the stacks.

Benefit Street and College Hill

Who says Newport has a monopoly on Rhode Island mansions? On **Benefit Street,** a 1.2-mile-long (1.9-km) corridor of tall trees and colonial and Victorian homes, you'll encounter enough architectural grandeur to fill a coffee table book. This is where the city's merchant class used to live. Intriguingly, opulent dwellings like the towering **Nightingale-Brown House** (357 Benefit St.), one of the largest wood-frame houses in the country, are complemented by more modest Federal-style houses such as the home of poet, spiritualist, and Edgar Allan Poe's former flame, Sarah Helen Whitman. (Some claim to have seen Poe's ghost wandering Benefit Street, looking for Sarah.) You

Downtown Providence

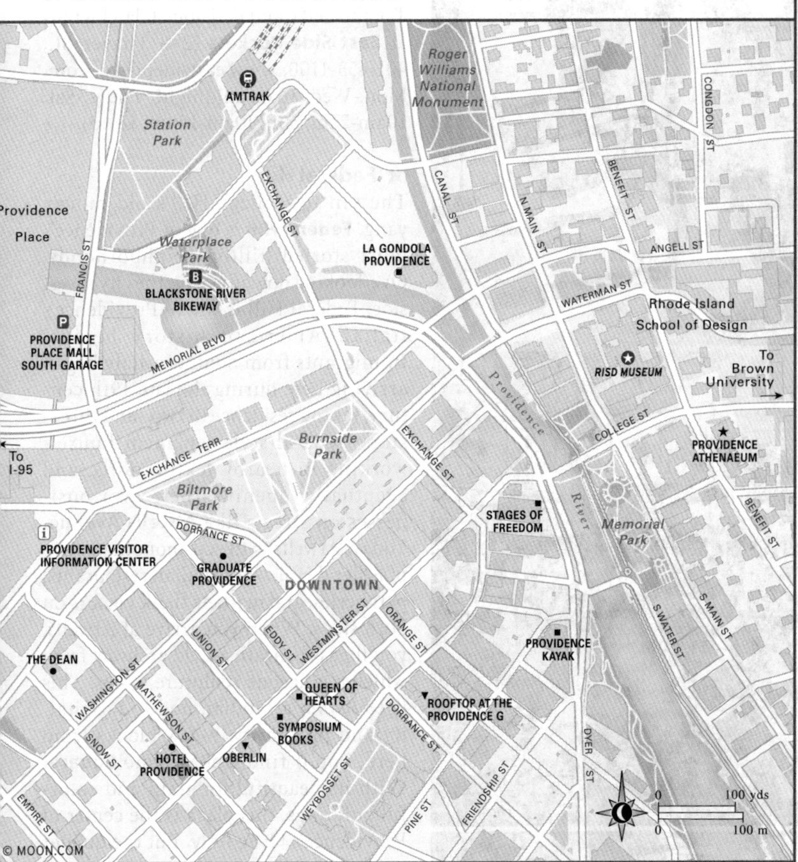

can roam the historic street at your own speed or link up with the **Rhode Island Historical Society** (401/331-8575, www.rihs.org) for one of their 90-minute walking tours of Benefit Street, offered June through October.

The steep hillside along which Benefit Street runs is none other than **College Hill.** This is where the earliest settlements of Providence took root in the mid-1600s, as Roger Williams and a band of families cased the area and plotted their exodus from the Puritan grips of the Massachusetts Bay Colony. It's also where, in 1761, residents of nearby Newport proposed building the "literary institution" that would become **Brown University** (401/863-1000, www.brown.edu). The grassy quads and brick buildings of Brown's campus are the stuff of Ivy League dreams, and simply bumbling around the campus (or lounging in the grass with a good book) is one of the purest pleasures you can have on College Hill. But if you fancy mingling with the university crowd, you'll find students eating and imbibing on nearby **Thayer Street,** where fast-casual international

takeout and thrift shops teeming with forgotten fashion are scenic hallmarks. Try the hefty and delicious falafel wraps at **East Side Pockets** (278 Thayer St., 401/453-1100, www.eastsidepocket.com, Mon.-Wed. 10am-midnight, Thurs.-Sat. 10am-2am, Sun. 10am-10pm, $8-13).

★ Federal Hill

The yin to College Hill's old money yang, **Federal Hill** is one of Providence's most storied hilltop neighborhoods. Overlooking downtown on the city's west side, Federal Hill is where Providence's Italian American history begins. Immigrants from Southern Italy began arriving here during the late 19th century, taking residence in two- and three-story Federal-style tenement houses, working in nearby textile mills, and eventually, opening their own businesses on streets like **Atwells Avenue.** Today, Atwells is the cosmopolitan strip of Federal Hill, where Italian restaurants, patisseries, and markets flank visitors on both sides. When you arrive at Atwells, you'll pass beneath an old archway from which a pinecone sculpture hangs. This is ***La Pigna,*** an Italian nod to hospitality and prosperity. A few blocks from here, you'll find **DePasquale Square.** With its beautiful fountain and colorful buildings, this plaza is the center of Providence's **Little Italy.** But the quieter residential side streets are worth a gander too. Federal Hill has re-emerged as one of Providence's hottest neighborhoods for new residents, especially young people seeking affordable housing, prime access to urban culture, and a welcoming community.

Roger Williams Park

On the southern edge of Providence, a 427-acre (173-ha) expanse of forests, hills, flowers, and lakes awaits anyone thirsting

Top to bottom: gallery-hopping at the RISD Museum; Federal Hill's DePasquale Square; a goat encounter at Roger Williams Park Zoo

Local Legend

Barnaby Evans came to Providence from the West Coast to study biology at Brown and become a scientist. Instead, he created **WaterFire,** the city's most unique and popular arts event. Now a recognized artist who consults with city governments around the world, Evans remains happily planted in Providence and credits the history and spirit of Providence with sparking the idea that bloomed into WaterFire.

Barnaby Evans

How did Providence first cast its spell on you?

When I first arrived here, I noticed a few interesting things about the city. There was a timelessness to it. Providence had the classic effect of a small place where everyone knew each other. There was this sense of communitarian spirit, of building something together. And that goes all the way back to the founding [of the city] by Roger Williams.

So how did you hatch this idea to light the river on fire?

It was inspired by the removal of the bridge that used to cover the rivers in downtown Providence. This was quite literally the *daylighting* of the rivers—an illumination of the water. The idea behind WaterFire is to have people rediscover the beauty of their city, the beauty of their rivers, through another form of illumination. Because with rediscovery comes reimagination.

WaterFire is now 26 years old. What's it like for you, seeing people experience it for the first time?

This one night, I met this guy, a construction worker from the Providence Place Mall project. He had seen me directing some people in the boats and he said, "Are you with WaterFire?" and when I said yes, he went, "I've gotta tell you... I come here with my family, my kids. I was here with my mother-in-law past midnight and we didn't have one fight!" I told him that's great that you had a nice time, and he went, "No, no, no. You don't understand. We don't go *anywhere* without having a fight. We take two cars! But this WaterFire thing... I don't want you to take this wrong, but it's almost like it's art or something."

for a reprieve from city life. The foundations for **Roger Williams Park** were laid in 1638, when two chiefs of the Narragansett people, Canonicus and Miantonomo, bequeathed a parcel of land to Williams. More than two centuries later, in 1872, Betsey Williams (one of Roger's last surviving descendants) ceded 102 acres (41.2 km) of that land to the city. Thus, Roger Williams Park was born. To transform the space into an oasis where people could escape the drudgery of industrial life, the city recruited Horace Cleveland, a landscape architect at the forefront of the 19th-century urban parks movement. Since then, Roger Williams Park has quadrupled in size, daily attendance has surpassed 15,000 visitors, and the attractions have evolved, too.

The biggest draw here is the **Roger**

Williams Park Zoo (1000 Elmwood Ave., 401/785-3510, www.rwpzoo.org, Thurs.-Mon. 9am-4pm, $21 adults, $17 seniors, $15 children under 13), one of the country's first zoos, which has grown considerably since its founding. Back in the 1940s, "Bunny Village" was among the top exhibits at the zoo. Today, more than 150 rare animals such as the red wolf and the West African crowned crane roam the zoo's multi-systemic environments (though the bunnies, including a giant Flemish rabbit, remain enthralling).

Beyond the zoo, flora fans should find plenty to marvel at in the greenhouses of the **Roger Williams Park Botanical Center** (Floral Ave., 401/680-7263, www.providenceri.gov/botanical-center, Tues.-Sun. 10am-4pm, $5 adults, $2 seniors, military, and children 6-12, children under 6 free). At 12,000 square feet (1,115 square m) this is the largest public indoor garden in New England, and with well over 100 flora species rooted here, you can easily make a morning or afternoon of admiring varieties like the carnivorous pitcher plants. But even if you're breezing through Roger Williams Park for an hour, you'll have a robust menu of recreation options, like wandering through a Japanese garden or taking a ride on an old-fashioned swan boat.

Entertainment and Events

Nightlife

The Hot Club (25 Bridge St., 401/861-9007, www.hotclubprov.com, Sun.-Thurs. noon-1am, Fri.-Sat. noon-2am) might be the most iconic waterfront bar in Providence, with its enviable location on the RiverWalk, its expansive deck where you can taste the salty breeze of the water, and its curious clientele of Providence lifers, hipster transplants, and the occasional tourist who saw this bar featured in movies such as *There's Something About Mary*. Keep your libation orders on the simpler side (an ice cold 'Gansett on a broiling summer day is a unique

WaterFire

kind of heaven) and enjoy the panoramic views of the Fox Point Hurricane Barrier and a National Grid building with enormous smokestacks that tower over the river like minarets. But if you want to feel like one of the regulars, head to the Hot Club by 8:30pm to take part in Good Night Lights, a ritual wherein bargoers flash lights across the river at Hasbro Children's Hospital, wishing the families there "good night" and reminding them that in sickness or in health, they're not forgotten.

For a more stimulating look at how the formerly derelict hub of downtown Providence has come roaring back in recent years, follow the river to the city center and take the elevator up to **Rooftop at the Providence G** (100 Dorance St., 401/632-4904, www.rooftopattheg.com, Mon.-Wed. 4pm-10pm, Thurs. 4pm-1am, Fri.-Sat. 3pm-2am, Sun. 2pm-10pm). This open-air cocktail lounge offers enviable views of the city skyline and its waterways, with visiting DJs providing beats and young people throwing down on the dance floor.

Festivals

The convivial atmosphere of Providence makes the city a natural hosting ground for hundreds of festivals. Whether it's sampling insalata and cured meats at the **Federal Hill Summer Festival,** joining the illuminated night parade of **PrideFest,** or introducing your kids to the art of cinema at the **Providence Children's Film Festival,** being in Providence comes with high odds of stumbling into something enlivening. But two city events in particular showcase the city's lived creativity.

TOP EXPERIENCE

★ WaterFire

One of the first things Providence visitors often notice are the strange metal pyres erected in the Providence River. What are they for? The city's most unique and haunting event: **WaterFire** (select Sat., May-Nov., www.waterfire.org). Created by local artist Barnaby Evans, WaterFire is a public art installation, a civic tradition, and a moment of solidarity that can feel elusive in bigger cities. On occasional Saturdays, as the sun goes down, people gather along the river, often with a glass of local wine or beer, and boats carrying torchbearers fill the pyres with wood and light them on fire. The fire-starting moves toward WaterPlace Park, where more torchbearers form a ring around the perimeter of the basin, lighting up the city with shades of orange and red. Each event is themed, paying homage to the labors and sacrifices made by different groups of people (say, veterans or health care workers) and all manner of elements are employed, from costumed performers on boats to new age music that echoes from speakers staged along the RiverWalk.

Often, it feels like the entire city has come out for WaterFire. People arrive with takeout, in a gregarious mood, ready for a long night of gallivanting or zoning out. Street vendors sell wine and beer for imbibing.

Each iteration of WaterFire takes place once or twice a month from May through early November, on Saturday nights, usually concluding by 11pm. You can stake out a good viewing spot near WaterPlace Park to watch the main ceremony in the basin, or you can simply amble along the river as the fires crackle and kick sparks into the night.

PVDFest

PVDFest (Sept., www.pvdfest.com) showcases the wild, colorful spectrum of Providence's creative community with the hedonism and crowds of Mardi Gras. For three days, downtown Providence is transformed into an open studio where artists of innumerable disciplines do their thing for an enthusiastic audience. From metalworkers to rappers to aerial artists and marching bands, the lineup each year is stacked with local and visiting talent, and the whole thing feels like one giant party. You can wander from one live exhibition or performance to another with a libation in one hand and your camera in the other. Sometimes, the art demos and cocktail soirees happening in nearby bars coalesce into events like musical parades so innocent and fun that they can feel spontaneous.

Shopping

Providence's history as an incubator for craftsmanship and creativity touches pretty much all facets of life here, including shopping. Whether you enjoy trying on vintage jackets, inspecting produce and artisan cooking oils, or digging through crates for early Throbbing Gristle records, it's easy to spend an afternoon getting wrapped up in Providence's shopping circuit.

Westminster Street boasts some of downtown's most eclectic retail destinations. One of the most popular boutiques here is **Queen of Hearts** (222 Westminster St., 401/421-1471, www.

aerial dancers at PVDFest

shopqueenofhearts.com, daily 11am-7pm), which features handcrafted jewelry from Providence artists along with brands like Free People and Mink Pink. Mere steps away, **Symposium Books** (240 Westminster St., 401/273-7900, www.symposiumbooks.com, Sun.-Wed. 11am-5pm, Thurs.-Sat. 11am-8pm) features not just towering shelves of paperbacks, but also a generous stock of vinyl records and a listening station with headphones, where you can often glimpse DJs nodding vigorously to what could be early midwestern house music. A more unique reading experience awaits visitors at **Stages of Freedom** (10 Westminster St., 401/421-0606, www.stagesoffreedom.org, Wed.-Fri. 3pm-6pm, Sat.-Sun. noon-4pm), a nonprofit bookshop and museum loaded with donated books that detail the history of African American life in Providence (former Rhode Island Representative Ray Rickman is the store's executive director). On-site sales help fund the organization's mission to provide access to swimming lessons and facilities in Rhode Island's Black communities.

The tonier streets of the East Side offer even more places to lighten your wallet. On **Wickenden Street,** particularly rich with new and vintage clothing retailers, **NAVA** (197 Wickenden St., 401/453-6282, www.shopnava.com, Mon.-Thurs. 11am-6pm, Fri.-Sat. 11am-7pm, Sun. noon-5pm) strikes an interesting balance between carrying well-known brands such as Herbivore and customizing vintage fashion with their own alterations. Next door to Brown, **Thayer Street** is home to a quirkier array of stores, from time-tested footwear purveyor **Berk's Shoes and Clothing** (272 Thayer St., 401/831-0174, www.berkstore.com, Mon. 9am-7pm, Tues.-Wed. 10am-6pm, Thurs.-Sat. 10am-7pm, Sun. 11am-6pm) to **Spectrum-India** (252 Thayer St., 401/421-1010, https://spectrumindiastore.com, daily 9am-9:30pm), a bohemian emporium with unique earrings and bangles, silk and wool shawls, and soy candles in dozens of scents.

On **Federal Hill,** shop life takes a tastier turn. The cannoli and lemon squares at **Pastiche Fine Desserts** (92 Spruce St., 401/861-5190, www.pastichefinedesserts.com, Tues.-Thurs. 9am-10pm, Fri.-Sat. 9am-10:30pm, Sun. 10am-10pm) ensure a steady flow of customers at all times of the day. (Lusting after the colorful contents of the pastry counter here can feel like being in a museum.) For crispy, buttery croissants or a note-perfect loaf of sourdough, saunter over to **Seven Stars Bakery** (342 Broadway, 401/521-2200, www.sevenstarsbakery.com, Mon.-Fri. 6:30am-6pm, Sat.-Sun. 7am-6pm). And if you've got extra room in your luggage, consider stocking up on some of the imported Italian pastas, olive oils, and sweets at **Tony's Colonial Food** (311 Atwells Ave., 401/621-8675, www.tonyscolonial.com, Mon.-Sat. 8:30am-6pm, Sun. 8am-5pm), which has shelf after shelf of edibles that would be right at home in any trattoria.

Sports and Recreation

Biking

Providence can be a surprisingly friendly city for bikes. The traffic is far milder than the rivers of brake lights in Boston, and once you pedal beyond downtown, you'll have a robust network of scenic bike trails at your disposal. Whether you're a hardened cyclist or someone who enjoys going for a spin on a rail trail every so often, you'll find that biking is one of the easiest ways to discover the beauty of the Providence region.

If coasting along the deep blue waters of Narragansett Bay sounds like the epitome of summer, make for the **East Bay Bike Trail.** This 14.5-mile (23-km) bike path begins at India Point Park on Providence's East Side and takes riders for a scenic ride worthy of a Terrence Malick movie. You'll cruise along the Providence River, past briny estuaries and hidden coves until the river empties into the expanse of the bay. The trail leads to Colt State Park, near the town of Bristol, which boasts sunny picnicking greens, excellent views of North Prudence Island, and even an open-air seaside chapel.

Technically a work in progress, the **Blackstone River Bikeway** is a newer bike path beginning at Providence's WaterPlace Park and snaking through the craggy hills and old-growth forests of the Blackstone Valley. The trail follows the Blackstone River, a waterway that connects Providence to the former mill city of Worcester, Massachusetts. During the early 19th century, an adjacent canal was built between the two cities for industrial transportation. Eventually, the Blackstone River Bikeway will echo that history by connecting the two cities once again. Currently, the trail extends 10 miles (16 km) north of Providence, from Valley Falls to Woonsocket. Additional segments of the trail can be found farther north near Uxbridge and Millbury (in Massachusetts). The plan is to eventually have one, long, contiguous trail from Providence to Worcester, only this time, instead of barges, the inter-city traffic will be much friendlier to the Blackstone Valley environment.

Boating

The **Providence River** is one of the city's recreational arteries, guaranteeing enviable views of the architecture, industry, and coastal environments that characterize the region. Finding a serviceable seacraft for some paddling or sightseeing is relatively easy. Rather than schlepping your own boat to the city and dealing with the headache of parking with oversized cargo, consider availing yourself of one of the local outfitters and hitting the water at your leisure.

The **Providence River Boat Company** (15 Bridge St., 401/580-2628, www.providenceriverboat.com, $27 adults, $25 seniors and children ages 0-12) hosts 50-minute narrated boat tours of the cityscape. From the deck of an open-air vessel, you'll get up close to the old infrastructure of the Providence Industrial Harbor and learn about how the hurricane barrier protects the city from coastal flooding. The tour is particularly memorable at dusk, as shades of amber and violet bathe the city in dreamy soft light.

For a more athletic river experience, consider renting a kayak from **Providence Kayak** (101 Dyer St., 401/829-1769, www.providencekayak.com, Thurs.-Sun. 10am-5pm, $20-30 single, $30-50 tandem) and charting your own course along the waterway. One of the perks of kayaking here is the option to paddle into tighter spaces like the WaterPlace Park basin, or through the hurricane barrier. But if you'd rather let someone else do the paddling, a gondola ride might be just the ticket. **La Gondola Providence** (1 Citizens Plaza, 401/421-8877, www.gondolari.com, Mon.-Thurs. 1pm-10pm, Fri. 1pm-11pm, Sat. 10am-11pm, Sun. 10am-10pm,

$89-180 starting at 40 minutes long) offers Venetian-style gondola trips along the river, some of which coincide with events like WaterFire. Best booked for sundown, a Providence gondola ride is a treat you won't find elsewhere in New England.

Parks

Overlooked by many out-of-town visitors, **Neutaconkanut Hill** is a lumbering heap of hardwoods and rock with an impressive network of hiking trails. Located on the western edge of Federal Hill and standing 296 feet (90 m) above sea level, Neutaconkanut Hill is the highest point in Providence, and the most interesting way to reach the "summit" of the hill is the 1.5-mile-long (2.4-km) **Pinnacle Trail,** which traverses boardwalks, glens, and a set of stone stairs built by the Works Progress Administration during the New Deal years. The view of Providence from the top of the hill is spectacular, but the most curious sight along the trail may be the ruins of two red Camaros, which one can observe nestled in tall grass along the Pinnacle Trail. Back in the 1960s, people used Neutaconkanut Hill as an informal garbage dump, and when volunteers finally began a cleanup effort, rusted cars were among the junk hauled away. The old Camaros were left in place as a reminder of what happens when our natural spaces are misused.

Food

Food is a big deal in Providence, and one of the cornerstones of the city's history. The Italian eateries of Federal Hill have been a draw for gourmands for decades, but the dining scene in Providence has diversified dramatically in recent years. Storefronts in downtown that went derelict during the industrial decline are home to some of New England's hottest farm-to-table restaurants, and the East

Top to bottom: riding the East Bay Bike Trail; a Providence gondola ride; Al Forno's grilled pizza

Side has added more dining options to its wealth of bookstores and boutique fashion shops. The quality of Providence food is exceptional and reservations are easy to come by—for now, at least.

Downtown and Federal Hill

Choosing a top Italian restaurant in Providence is a cruel challenge, given the wealth of offerings in Federal Hill alone, but **Camille's Restaurant** (71 Bradford St., 401/751-4812, www.camillesonthehill.com, Tues.-Thurs. 11:30am-10pm, Fri. 11:30am-10:30pm, Sat. 4pm-10pm, $23-38) is an institution. Housed in an old mansion since 1914, with ritzy decor like framed silverware, burgundy drapes, and leatherbound seats, Camille's is the sort of place where you order several dishes to share before staggering out into the night, moaning softly. Classics like gnocchi in pink vodka sauce, chicken marsala, and wagon wheel pasta smothered with Bolognese are suitably decadent. And the restaurant's 2019 Wine Spectator Award of Excellence testifies to its impeccable selection of whites and reds.

If brunch is your preferred meal for indulgence, enter the street-side dining room of **Nicks on Broadway** (500 Broadway, 401/421-0286, www.nicksonbroadway.com, Wed.-Sat. 10am-8pm, Sun. 10am-4pm, $11-26), which offers a rolling menu of locally sourced morsels best consumed slowly as part of a long, luxuriant dining experience. The menu features staples such as eggs Benedict with poached greens and a buttermilk biscuit and internationally inspired fare like sweet corn risotto with roasted local fish. Sometimes the menu reads like a Rolodex of regional farms. That's how much chef Derek Wagner cares about ethical food sourcing.

Just north of Federal Hill and downtown Providence, adventurous eaters with big appetites will find glory at ★ **Los Andes** (903 Chalkstone Ave., 401/649-4911, www.losandesri.com, Wed.-Thurs. 5pm-9pm, Fri. 5pm-10pm, Sat. 3pm-10pm, Sun. 3pm-8pm, $17-35), where brothers Omar and Cesin Curi offer a dizzying menu of Peruvian-style char-grilled steaks, paella, and street food appetizers like fresh ceviche with jumbo Andean corn. If you can, get a table in the "backyard" dining area, which features koi ponds, bridges, and statues that look straight out of ancient Cusco. The seafood here is often sourced from chartered fishing trips on which the Curi brothers will occasionally invite guests.

Local fish is something of an obsession for Providence chefs—sometimes a cut of fluke or black bass is best consumed au naturel. This ethos is exemplified at **Oberlin** (186 Union St., 401/588-8755, www.oberlinrestaurant.com, Sun.-Mon. and Thurs. 5pm-10pm, Fri.-Sat. 5pm-10:30pm, $25-41), where co-owners Heidi and Ben Sukle serve the freshest local catch with a little olive oil and lemon. Pair it with a kohlrabi Caesar salad and handmade cappelletti with shishito peppers and pecorino cheese, and you've got a meal worth traveling for. The soft-lit and small dining room here fills up fast, so don't be afraid to take a high-top seat at the bar.

East Side

As more Americans tiptoe toward plant-based diets, chef Matthew Kenney's **Plant City** (334 S. Water St., 401/429-2029, www.plantcitypvd.com, Sun.-Thurs. 8am-9pm, Fri.-Sat. 8am-10:30pm, $8-16) is the perfect gateway experience. With an outdoor terrace by the Providence RiverWalk and a sleek cafeteria with plenty of natural light and hardwood, Plant City offers a savory smorgasbord of plant-based treats like wild mushroom "carnitas" tacos and heirloom tomato and zucchini lasagna.

Every dining scene has its progenitor, and for Providence, much of that history belongs to ★ **Al Forno** (577 S. Water St., 401/273-9760, www.alforno.com, Tues.-Fri. 5pm-10pm, Sat. 4pm-10pm, $23-38). Launched by Johanne Killeen and George

Germon in 1980, this upscale ristorante on the river's edge took an intrepid approach to traditional Italian cooking, and today it's something of a sacred site for local foodies. The menu is vast but the most famous offering here is the grilled pizza, which involves draping pizza dough across a grill and finishing it on both sides. It's a Providence classic and best devoured at the restaurant where it was born.

Providence has long been something of a sanctuary city for refugees, sometimes literally. Take ★ **Aleppo Sweets** (107 Ives St., 401/533-9019, www.alepposweets.com, Sun. and Wed.-Thurs. 11am-8:30pm, Fri.-Sat. 11am-9:30pm, $6-14). A charming little café with plenty of plants and decorative bronze tea kettles, the joint was launched by the Ahktarini family, who escaped the Syrian civil war, resettled in Providence, and decided to open a bakery similar to the one they used to run back in Aleppo. Flatbreads with za'atar, pepper paste, and lamb, nutty baklava, and steaming hot tea with fresh mint are among the essentials here.

Donut shops are a religion in Providence (an online search reveals at least one Dunkin franchise per square mile) but the holiest of them all is **PVDonuts** (79 Ives St., www.pvdonuts.com, Wed.-Fri. 8am-3pm, Sat.-Sun. 8am-4pm, $4-8). Housed in a little charcoal-gray house on a leafy residential street in the Fox Point neighborhood, the modest exterior belies a stupefyingly sweet array of brioche and cake donuts tricked out with toppings like brookie (brownie/cookie) bits, maple bacon crumbles, marshmallows, and even Dunkaroos! Add a coffee milk, take your order to go, and let the sugar rush fuel your morning.

Accommodations

Hotel bargains are one of Providence's best-kept secrets. While visitors to Boston and Newport can expect to pay top prices for stylish digs during peak travel seasons, Providence accommodations can be booked for relatively lower rates—a testament to the city's reemergence as a travel destination, after years spent in the shadows of neighboring hot spots. While international hotel brands have franchises here, the city's independent hotels offer more local flavor and spirit.

Under $150

Fancy making friends on the road? Consider hanging your hat at the **Esperanto Providence Hostel and Guesthouse** (62 Nolan St., 401/216-8807, www.providencehostel.com, $40-95). Situated north of Federal Hill, a 20-minute walk from downtown, the Esperanto is a seafoam-green house. A flag bearing a purple-bellied owl welcomes visitors to the lodging's mixed dorms and female-only dorms, as well as some private rooms. The bunk beds are spartan and the decorative touches are fairly minimal, but it's a clean, well-designed space with a big living room that gets lots of natural light and serves as the perfect spot for socializing with fellow travelers. There's free coffee in the communal kitchen each morning, and the staff are exceedingly friendly and generous with local sightseeing intel.

Housed in a brick building downtown (formerly a church mission and then a brothel) and featuring 52 rooms with vintage rugs, Edison-style lightbulbs, and reclaimed wood, ★ **The Dean Hotel** (122 Fountain St., 401/455-3326, www.thedeanhotel.com, $125-195) might be the chicest boutique lodging in Providence. Designed for budget-conscious travelers, the rooms are beautiful but compact, the showers don't have doors, and the prices are reasonable for such an elegant place. The halls are decked out with original works from Providence artists, and the hotel's ground floor is also the home of Boombox, a karaoke lounge where you can work up your courage with cocktails and belt out a few verses of "Rock Lobster." (Don't worry: the hotel rooms have sufficient sound insulation.)

$150-250

The former Biltmore Hotel in downtown Providence was the sort of extravagant place where cigar-chewing bankers would drain martinis under chandeliers. But the upscale hotel has been given a renovation and an injection of local irreverence. Rebranded as ★ **Graduate Providence** (11 Dorrance St., 401/421-0700, www.graduatehotels.com, $160-290), the hotel still towers above the city and boasts the same cavernous lobby and spacious rooms. But what makes the place fun are the little touches that pay tribute to city culture. Framed pictures of famous Providence alumni, wallpaper with illustrations of mollusks, and an oil painting of Jeff Daniels' ill-fated parakeet from *Dumb and Dumber* (filmed in Providence) are among the decorative elements here.

For travelers looking to splurge, the **Hotel Providence** (139 Mathewson St., 401/861-8000, www.hotelprovidence.com, $179-329) is the only AAA Four Diamond luxury hotel in the city. The expansive guest rooms and suites here boast pillowtop mattresses, luxury linens, elaborately carved headboards, and ample floor-to-ceiling windows that overlook the theater district. The marble bathrooms and complimentary robes add an extra touch of class, and the attached courtyard, with its globe-shaped central fountain, is a wonderful place to savor your morning coffee and watch Providence come alive.

Information and Services

Before arriving in town, take a gander at the website of the **Providence Warwick Convention & Visitors Bureau** (www.goprovidence.com) to load up with walking maps, restaurant and shopping listings, and neighborhood guides. You can also pick up these items in person at the

the lobby at Graduate Providence

Providence Visitor Information Center (1 Sabin St., 401/751-1177, Mon.-Sat. 9am-5pm).

The primary, centrally located hospital in Providence is the **Rhode Island Hospital** (80 Dudley St., 401/444-4000), which includes the Hasbro Children's Hospital and the Women & Infants Hospital. Downtown Providence and the East Side offer plenty of pharmacies, banks, and ATMs. (Federal Hill is slightly more limited in its offerings.)

Getting Around

While traffic in Providence rarely gets too onerous, **I-95** can become very congested during the summer months, especially during rush hours. **Street parking** downtown can fill up on weekend nights but is generally easy enough to find. The meter rate is $1.25 per hour; meter rates and time limitations are enforced 8am-9pm Monday through Saturday. In Federal Hill and the East Side, free parking on residential streets is widely available. One of the largest **public parking lots** in Providence is the **Providence Place Mall South Garage** (87 Providence Place), located downtown near the train station. The first two hours of parking here are free. From there, it's $2 for 5 hours and $15 for 8 hours, with a daily maximum of $25.

For roving around town without a car, the easiest option is picking up a rental e-bike or scooter from one of the **Veo hubs** around downtown (download the Veo app to get started), or from **Dash Bicycle Shop** (228 Broadway, 401/453-3274, www.dashbicycle.com, daily rentals from $40), which is located right in the heart of Federal Hill.

The **Rhode Island Public Transit Authority (RIPTA)** runs public buses and trolleys on fixed routes throughout the city. The cash fare is $2 for each ride, $6 for a day pass, or $25 for a seven-day pass. You can purchase and use these passes by downloading the RIPTA Wave app. Taxi service is available from **PVD Taxi** (401/225-2050, https://providence-taxi.business.site) and **Providence Taxi LLP** (401/227-0584).

Cape Cod
and the
Islands

Highlights

★ **Cape Cod's Clam Shacks:** Don't leave the Cape without sampling fried fare and hearty soups at a clam shack; forget the Kennedys, these rustic seafood joints are Cape Cod's real democratic powerhouses, attracting celebrities, politicians, and sunburned families (page 338).

★ **Cape Cod Rail Trail:** The going's always easy on this 22-mile, (35-km) mostly flat bicycle path, even when traffic is hopelessly snarled on the Cape's one highway (page 340).

★ **Cape Cod National Seashore:** Stroll miles of sandy beaches with nothing but waves between you and Portugal (page 351).

★ **Provincetown's Drag Shows:** People come to P-town to let it all hang out—and so do the wisecracking, arch performers in the community's legendary drag performances (page 357).

★ **Whale-Watching Tours:** Whales, dolphins, and sharks flock to the nutrient-rich waters at the tip of Cape Cod. In recent years, long-endangered right whales have begun returning to the coast (page 359).

★ **Aquinnah Cliffs:** Learn about Martha's Vineyard's Wampanoag heritage in this stunning setting. Cliffs washed in brilliant hues, a historic lighthouse, and perfect beaches are a highlight of the rural up-island landscape (page 380).

★ **Nantucket Whaling Museum:** Scrimshaw, harpoons, and a giant skeleton bring *Moby-Dick* to life (page 384).

Cape Cod and the Islands

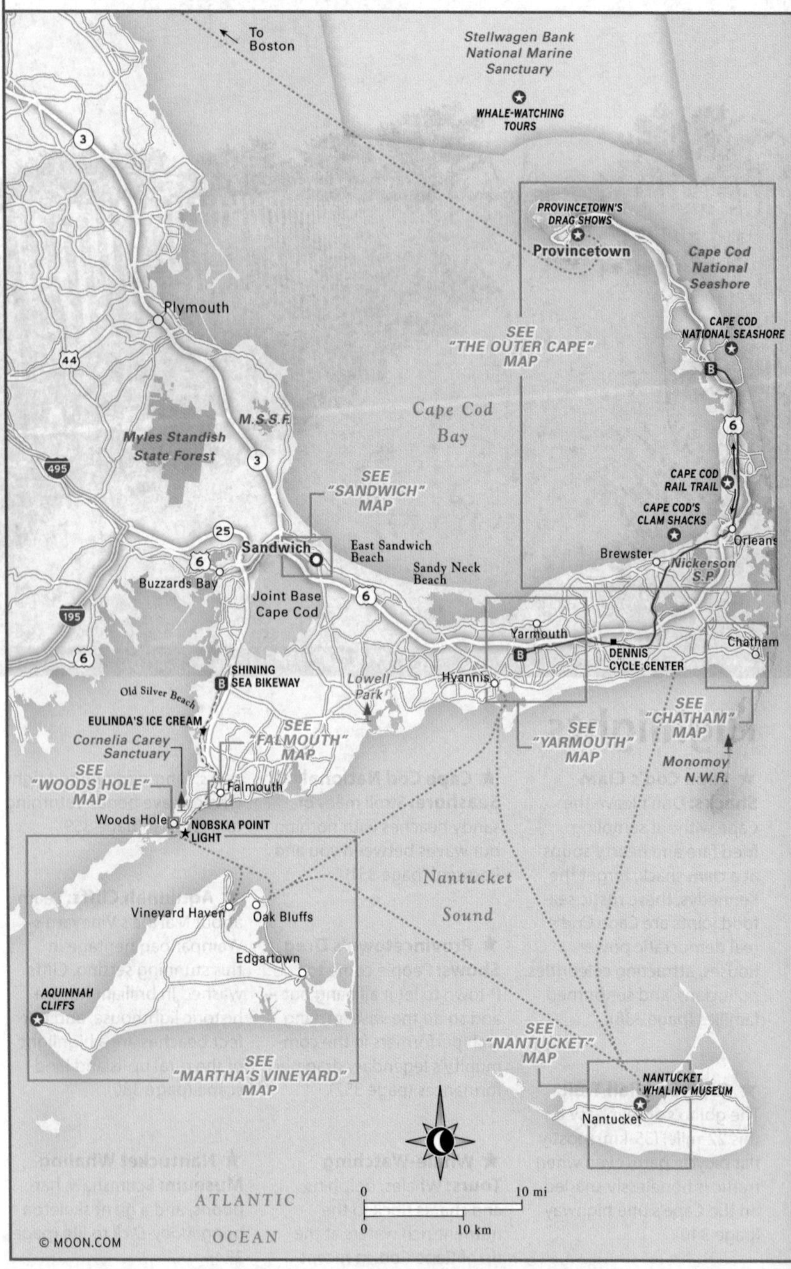

Endless beaches and sandy cliffs line the Cape Cod National Seashore, while the interior is a maze of rustling cranberry bogs and rolling dunes.

Wild and beautiful, the Cape is the traditional home of the Nauset tribe; it was also the first land sighted when the Mayflower Pilgrims touched down in 1620. In the 18th century, it attracted a rugged population of Portuguese fishers and whalers. In the centuries since, generations of travelers, artists, and renegades have flocked to the Cape for its isolation. Many decided to stay.

Humpback whales patrol the coast from April through October, and Provincetown's historic lighthouses command dramatic views of sunrise and sunset above the sea. The sandy coastline shifts with every storm, but the scenery feels timeless, from Chatham's tiny saltbox cottages to the artist shacks scattered in the Provincetown dunes.

Cape Cod's blend of old, new, and wild offers the opportunity to weave between worlds. You can spend the morning wandering world-class galleries in an artists' colony, trace the Cape Cod Rail Trail on two wheels, and then catch an evening performance at one of Provincetown's raucous drag shows. Spot wildlife from a kayak, sailboat, or cruise boat, sample clam chowder at a seaside shack, and dance the night away at a beachfront bar. Whatever your thread—whether it's nature, wildlife, history, or culture—you can follow it from Sagamore Bridge to Land's End, where the sand finally gives way to the sea.

If Maine's coast is the pinnacle of naturalistic seaside living, Cape Cod is a more rambunctious alternative where human commerce and creativity are features of the landscape. You can choose between the gregarious festivals of P-town and sleepier hamlets like Truro, but the mainstay of Cape Cod is the characters who've been living or summered there for generations—characters who might just invite you over for a moonlit swim or supper.

Planning Your Time

It's best to find a single region as a home base for your time in the Cape, as moving around the peninsula can be time-consuming when summer traffic hits. For quick chowder-and-cottage overnight stopovers, the Inner Cape is easy to reach and convenient to the mainland—this is also a good base for visiting Nantucket and Martha's Vineyard, a pair of scenic islands that have personalities all their own. The diverse Mid Cape region bundles all the Cape's charms from kitschy tourist joints to picture-perfect villages into a single, compact corridor, where family-friendly Yarmouth and romantic Chatham are excellent getaways.

When you turn the 90-degree corner at Chatham to the Lower Cape, though, things begin to get wilder (in every sense). Come here to explore the lonely dunes and sprawling beaches of the Cape Cod National Seashore, or sip planter's punch with a crowd of shirtless tea dancers in Provincetown, known locally as "the end of the world." P-town's bustling center is all the more thrilling for being so isolated; it's easy to get away from the hustle and walk to rustic artists' shacks, discover thriving wildlife, and catch stunning sunsets from Pilgrim Point.

Orientation

The writer Henry David Thoreau called Cape Cod the "bared and bended arm of Massachusetts: the shoulder is at Buzzard's Bay. . . and the sandy fist at Provincetown." It's a good description of the Cape's eccentric shape. Severed from the mainland by the Cape Cod Canal, the historic towns of Cape Cod's "shoulder" are part of the Inner Cape, and if you keep driving east, you'll be traveling through the Lower Cape.

Make a 90-degree turn at Chatham, then you'll arrive at the oak forests of

Best Restaurants

★ **The Brown Jug:** The wood-fired pizzas here may just be the best on the Cape, hot, bubbly, and decked out with a colorful palette of veggies and meats (page 332).

★ **Chatham Pier Fish Market:** With super-fresh seafood straight from the dock, this unpretentious waterside market is the perfect place to grab a bite while watching for whales and sharks (page 346).

★ **PB Boulangerie Bistro:** The Cape Cod Rail Trail ends by this sweet French bakery, which is the perfect place to refuel with a chocolatine or tarte au citron (page 354).

★ **Canteen:** Rub shoulders with locals and tourists enjoying seafood classics with creative sides (page 363).

★ **The Port Hunter:** Local seafood and produce give island roots to this hip tavern and restaurant, which adds a contemporary edge to Edgartown's elegant food scene (page 379).

Mid Cape. Thoreau's "sandy fist" is what Codders call the Outer Cape, the slender passage that extends from Truro to Provincetown.

For driving purposes, the Cape is simple; it's accessed by the Sagamore Bridge if approaching from the north, and the Bourne Bridge when driving from the west. Route 6 runs from the Sagamore Bridge to Land's End and is paralleled by two smaller highways on the Mid Cape, Route 6A and Route 28.

Getting to Cape Cod and the Islands

Cape Cod has notorious summer traffic, and on busy weekends Route 6 can be backed up for miles. When planning a drive to Cape Cod, it's best to **avoid Friday and Sunday afternoons** at all costs, as those are the times that Boston weekenders flood to the beach.

Driving from Boston

60 mi/97 km, 1.25 hr

To reach Cape Cod from Boston, leave the city on **I-93 South,** following the interstate for 10 miles (16 km), then use Exit 7 to merge onto **Route 3 South.** Upon reaching the **Sagamore Bridge,** Route 3 continues into **Route 6.** Cross the Sagamore Bridge, then use Exit 1C to merge onto **Route 6A,** turning right at the base of the ramp. Route 6A passes through downtown **Sandwich** (60 mi/96.5 km, 1.25 hrs).

For **Falmouth** and **Woods Hole,** cross the Sagamore Bridge, then use Exit 1C to merge onto Route 6A, turning left at the base of the ramp. At the **Bourne Rotary,** take the exit for **Route 28 South.** For all other Cape Cod destinations, including **Provincetown** (115 mi/185 km, 2.25 hrs), continue straight from the Sagamore Bridge on **Route 6.**

Should you find the Sagamore Bridge under construction, take the nearby **Bourne Bridge** from Route 3; take Exit 1A to merge onto Route 6 West toward Buzzards Bay. As you approach the bridge, turn right onto the ramp to Route 28 South. Merge onto the highway, cross the Bourne Bridge, and at the Bourne Rotary on the Cape side, take the second exit to continue along Route 28 South to Falmouth and Woods Hole. For

Best Accommodations

★ **Inn at the Oaks:** Sleep in this comfortable, historic Victorian where Henry Beston wrote the *The Outermost House* (page 354).

★ **HI Truro Hostel:** A simple, convivial gathering place, steps away from the Cape Cod National Seashore, this hostel is a stellar budget base camp (page 354).

★ **North of Highland Camping Area:** Pitch your tent beneath the pines and walk to some of the Cape's finest beaches (page 354).

★ **Land's End Inn:** Watch the sun rise over P-town's lighthouses from this exquisite inn furnished with art nouveau antiques and contemporary art (page 365).

★ **Duck Inn:** Primo beach access, delicious organic breakfasts, and shiatsu massages make this Nantucket hideaway an extra luxuriant choice (page 382).

Sandwich, take the third exit from the rotary and drive north along Sandwich Road.

Driving from Newport

65 mi/104 km, 1.25 hr

Head north on **Route 114** out of the city, then use the right two lanes to exit onto **Route 24 North.** Two miles (3.2 km) after crossing the Massachusetts border, merge onto **I-195 East** for 25 miles (40 km). Take Exit 22A to merge onto **Route 25 East** toward Cape Cod. Take Exit 3 onto **Route 6 East.** Cross the **Sagamore Bridge,** then use Exit 1C to merge onto **Route 6A,** turning right at the base of the ramp. Route 6A passes through downtown **Sandwich** (65 mi/105 km, 1.25 hrs).

For **Falmouth** and **Woods Hole,** stay on Route 25 to cross the **Bourne Bridge** and, at the **Bourne Rotary,** exit onto **Route 28 South.** For all other Cape Cod destinations, including **Provincetown** (120 mi/193 km, 2.5 hrs), continue straight from the Sagamore Bridge on **Route 6.** If the Sagamore Bridge is closed, cross the Bourne Bridge and take the third exit from the Bourne Rotary onto **Sandwich Road** to reach all other Cape Cod destinations.

Driving from New York City

240 mi/386 km, 4.25 hr

Leave New York City heading north on **FDR Drive.** Use the left lane to access Exit 17 to the **Robert F. Kennedy Bridge** ($10.17), then stay left to merge onto **I-278 East.** After 4.5 miles/7.2 km, I-278 East merges with **I-95 North** ($1.75 toll). Stay on I-95 for approximately 165 miles (265 km) and then, in **Providence, Rhode Island,** take Exit 19 to merge onto **I-195 East.** Take Exit 22A to merge onto **Route 25 East** toward Cape Cod. Take Exit 3 onto **Route 6 East.** Cross the **Sagamore Bridge,** then use Exit 1C to merge onto **Route 6A,** turning right at the base of the ramp. Route 6A passes through downtown **Sandwich** (240 mi/386 km, 4.25 hrs).

For **Falmouth** and **Woods Hole,** stay on Route 25 to cross the **Bourne Bridge** and, at the **Bourne Rotary,** exit onto **Route 28 South.** For all other Cape Cod destinations, including **Provincetown** (300 mi/483 km, 5.25 hrs), continue straight from the Sagamore Bridge on **Route 6.**

Getting There by Ferry, Air, Train, or Bus

Ferry

A pair of passenger ferries makes the trip from Boston to Provincetown several times daily in high season. **Bay State Cruise Company** (World Trade Center, 200 Seaport Blvd., Boston, 617/748-1428, www.baystatecruisecompany.com, mid-May-mid-Oct., $80 one-way/$118 round-trip adults, $75/106 seniors, $53/90 children 3-12, $10/20 bikes). Somewhat newer, slicker, and more comfortable, **Boston Harbor City Cruises** (1 Long Wharf, Boston, 617/748-14505, www.cityexperiences.com/boston, mid-May-mid-Oct., $70 one-way/$100 round-trip adults, $68/97 seniors, $61/85 children 3-11, free children under 3, $9/18 bikes) makes the same trip in a catamaran.

Air

Cape Air (508/771-6944, www.flycapeair.com) runs daily flights from Boston to Provincetown, as well as daily flights from Boston, Providence, and the Islands (Nantucket and Martha's Vineyard) to **Cape Cod Gateway Airport** (480 Barnstable Rd., Hyannis, 508/775-2020, www.flyhya.com).

Train

From Memorial Day to Labor Day (end of May-early Sept.), the **CapeFLYER** (508/775-8504, www.capeflyer.com) has service from Boston's South Station Friday-Sunday to **Buzzards Bay** (1.5 hrs, $20/35 for one-way/round-trip) and **Hyannis** (2.5 hrs, $22/40 for one-way/round-trip), where buses connect to destinations around the Cape.

Bus

Buses by **Plymouth & Brockton** (508/746-0378, www.p-b.com) and **Peter Pan Bus** (800/343-9999, www.peterpanbus.com) leave daily from Logan Airport and South Station, with stops at most Cape Cod towns including **Hyannis** (2.25 hrs, $25-31 one-way) and **Provincetown** (3.5 hrs, $28-39 one-way).

Inner Cape

If the Cape is a place apart, then the Cape Cod Canal is what protects the lifelong residents and weekend trippers from the rest of the world. As soon as you cross the Bourne or Sagamore Bridge, interstate highways sliver into smaller roads that wind past historic towns and fishing villages. From historic **Sandwich** to the bustling villages of **Falmouth and Woods Hole,** the Inner Cape is an easy place to get a quick taste of Cape Cod without driving all the way to Provincetown. These towns also make good stops for travelers heading for the Martha's Vineyard or Nantucket ferries. Route 6 is the main route between towns along the northern edge of the Inner Cape, but with extra time to explore, Route 6A is especially scenic, lined with cranberry bogs and antiques stores.

Sandwich

Refugees from Boston's chaotic traffic are relieved to find this quiet town just a few miles past the Sagamore Bridge. Founded 17 years after the Pilgrims touched down, Cape Cod's oldest town remains quaintly old-fashioned, with saltbox houses, tree-lined streets, and a gray-shingled gristmill at the edge of a swan pond. Sandwich is the place to exhale, slow down, and adapt to the pace of life on the Cape. Spend an afternoon exploring small historic sites, browsing antiques, or pedaling along the seven-mile (11-km) canal that divides Cape Cod from the rest of the world.

Sights

Cape Cod Canal Visitors Center

Sailing around Cape Cod's shifting sands was painfully slow and shockingly dangerous. The early 17th-century colonists were the first to dream of a canal that would provide a shortcut. Despite repeated surveying, the real digging didn't start until 1909, when New York financier

Two Days in Cape Cod

With two days to explore the Cape, it's worth driving all the way out past the elbow to the **Lower Cape,** which offers unmatched access to nature, and **Provincetown,** which provides nightlife and culture and makes a good home base.

the Pilgrim Monument

Day 1

Make your first stop the visitor center at **Cape Cod National Seashore,** to get the background on the area's equally wild geology and history, then spend the rest of the morning walking, swimming, or lounging at one of the park's many fine beaches.

After lunch at **Canteen,** dive into the downtown Provincetown scene, visiting art galleries and boutiques, and taking in unmatched views of "the end of the world" from the **Pilgrim Monument.** Snag a harbor-side window at the **Lobster Pot** for a classic seafood dinner—or perhaps join the shirtless crowd at the **Tea Dance**—then kick off the evening with a drag show by one of the town's resident queens.

Day 2

Stop by the **Portuguese Bakery** for snacks to bring on an early morning **whale-watching** tour, and keep your eyes open for the pilot, humpback, and minke whales that thrive along Provincetown's coast. Spend the afternoon in the sand of your choice: Head to **Race Point Beach** to lounge in the sunshine, or take your walking shoes to the **dunes,** where footpaths lead to the rustic dune shacks that have attracted generations of artists.

If you're headed to Martha's Vineyard or Nantucket, little **Woods Hole** is a good jumping-off place, and it's worth saving time to visit the town's lighthouse and **Jim's Clam Shack of Falmouth** before hopping a boat to the islands.

Cape Cod for Families

Yarmouth or **Brewster** makes a perfect home base for families, both with easy access to the beaches of the **Cape Cod National Seashore** and plenty of kid-friendly ways to keep busy when you're not playing in the sand. Get oriented in the national seashore visitor center, then hit **Coast Guard Beach** for a day of playing in the waves. When you've had enough sun and sand, go to town to play a round of minigolf or explore gleefully macabre art at the **Edward Gorey House.**

On day two, rent a fleet of bicycles to take on the **Cape Cod Rail Trail,** saving time to stop along the way for ice cream cones, French pastries, and jaunts to small beaches. By the time the sun sets, you'll be sufficiently tired out to enjoy both of the double features at the old-fashioned **Wellfleet Drive-In Theatre.**

August Belmont Jr. broke ground on a project that would drag on to 1916. The mammoth undertaking was slowed by the enormous ice age boulders that had to be blown apart by hand-placed underwater dynamite charges. When

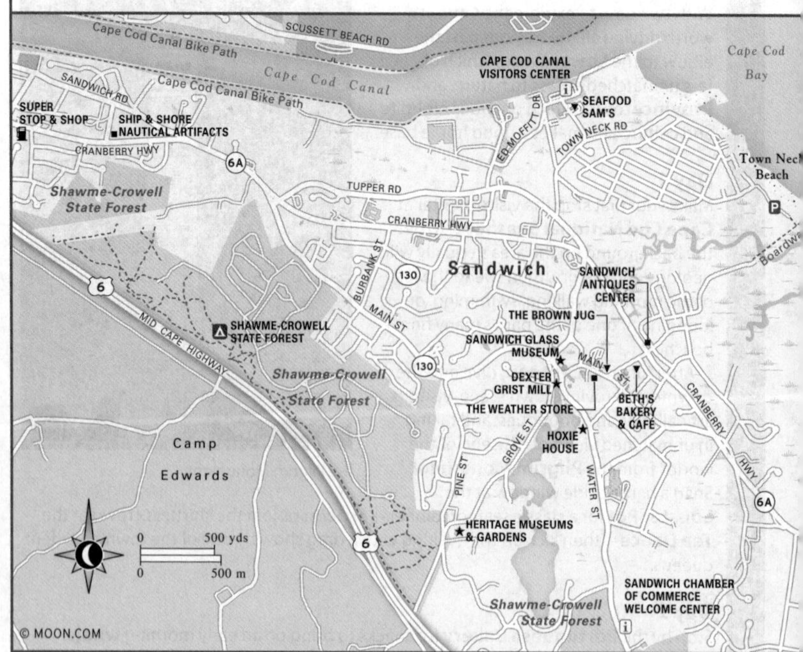

Belmont's toll scheme never became profitable, the canal was turned over to the U.S. Army Corps of Engineers. Learn the whole story at the fascinating **Cape Cod Canal Visitors Center** (60 Ed Moffit Dr., 508/833-9678, www.capecodcanal.us, May-mid-June and late Sept.-mid-Oct., Tues.-Sat. 10am-5pm, mid-June-late-Sept. Tues.-Sun. 10am-5pm, free), where kid-friendly interactive displays bring the canal's construction, shipping, and ecology to life. Take the helm of a 40-foot (12-m) patrol boat, learn to signal using marine flags, and pick up maps of the **bike trail** (www.capecodbikeguide.com/canal.asp) that links the Bourne and Sagamore Bridges and offers unparalleled views of boat traffic.

Heritage Museums & Gardens

Explore pharmaceutical mogul J. K. Lilly's obsessive collections of classic cars, art, and Americana at **Heritage Museums & Gardens** (67 Grove St., 508/888-3300, www.heritagemuseumsandgardens.org, mid-Apr.-mid-Oct. daily 10am-5pm, $22 adults, $12 children 3-11, free children under 3) on his superbly maintained former estate. One hundred acres (40.5 ha) of display gardens wrap around living mazes and labyrinths that bloom with wisteria, honeysuckle, and hyacinth. Inside the museum, browse three sprawling galleries that house a vintage carousel, automobiles, art, and traveling exhibitions, along with a noteworthy collection of Nantucket baskets, scrimshaw, weathervanes, and other New England folk art. The grounds are especially breathtaking in late May during the **rhododendron festival**, which draws flower lovers from around the world.

Other Sights

Get a taste of life in 17th-century Sandwich at a historic saltbox house—the oldest house on Cape Cod. Named for a 19th-century whaling captain, the **Hoxie House** (18 Water St., 508/888-4361, late May-mid-Oct. Mon.-Sat. 11am-4:30pm, Sun. 1pm-4:30pm, $5 adults, $3 children 9-12, free children under 9) is carefully maintained with period antiques, and the enthusiastic docents are full of information about how early Cape Codders worked, played, ate and—occasionally—bathed.

Just down the road from the Hoxie House is the 1654 **Dexter Grist Mill** (2 Water St., 508/888-4361, late May-mid-Oct. Mon.-Sat. 11am-4:30pm, Sun. 1pm-4:30pm, $5 adults, $3 children); with a working water wheel and shingles faded to silver gray, it's a pretty spot for taking photos of the swans that bob around in the adjacent pond. Take a picnic to enjoy by the water's edge, but don't think about abandoning your personal geese and ducks there—a very specific sign warns of a steep fine if you're apprehended.

The Boston Sandwich & Glass Company supplied 19th-century Americans with mold-blown glassware that imitated the cut glass from England and Ireland at much lower prices. See historic pieces and glassblowing demonstrations at the **Sandwich Glass Museum** (129 Main St., 508/888-0251, www.sandwichglassmuseum.org, Feb.-Mar. Wed.-Sun. 9:30am-4pm, Apr.-Dec. 9:30am-5pm, $12 adults, $2 children 6-14, under 6 free), which also has an excellent on-site shop full of traditional and contemporary glass pieces.

Shopping

Boutiques and souvenir shops cluster around Main Street and Jarves Street in downtown Sandwich. It's easy to while away an afternoon browsing art, antiques, and cottage-y home furnishings.

If antique barometers and state-of-the-art weather systems are more your style, however, don't miss **The Weather Store** (146 Main St., 800/646-1203, www.theweatherstore.com, Mon.-Fri. 10am-4pm), where you'll find everything you need to know which way the wind blows. It's a fascinating place stocked with beautiful tide charts, compasses, hygrometers, brass telescopes, and other esoterica, as well as practical tools for modern-day sailors.

The bits and bobs of Cape Cod life sift into the **Sandwich Antiques Center** (131 Route 6A, 508/833-3600, www.sandwichantiquescenter.com, Mon.-Sat. 10am-6pm, Sun. noon-6pm) along with some unique finds and a good selection of Sandwich glass.

Visitors in search of maritime antiques, signal flags, and ship wheels will find their hearts' desire at **Ship & Shore Nautical Artifacts** (165 Cranberry Hwy., Sagamore, 508/888-9545, Mon.-Sat. 10am-6pm, Sun. noon-6pm), a museum-like shop that's two miles (3.2 km) from the center of Sandwich.

Sports and Recreation

If you can find a place to park or leave your car in town, **East Sandwich Beach** (parking at western end of N. Shore Blvd., parking $20) offers grass-covered dunes and soft sand with serene views to the north. To get a closer look at the area's fragile dunes and salt marshes, walk the 1,350-foot (411-m) **boardwalk to Town Neck Beach** (parking at the end of Boardwalk Rd., $10). The walk is especially scenic at sunset, when the dune grass glows a dusky pink, and is a favorite among bird-watchers.

There's more parking (and people) farther east at **Sandy Neck Beach** (425 Sandy Neck Rd., Barnstable, 508/362-8300, Memorial Day-Labor Day $20 weekend parking, $15 weekday parking, off-season parking free), six miles (9.6 km) of pebbly sand rimmed by rolling dunes that extend all the way to Barnstable, where the beach's main access points are located. A network

At Home on the Cape

Cape Cod-style homes

Saltboxes

Cape Cod lent its name to one of America's most ubiquitous architectural styles, but the region's real signature is the wood-framed, asymmetrical home known as the **"saltbox,"** a reference to the wooden boxes once used to store salt under sloping lids. It's easy to spot the distinctive houses around New England; when facing the home head-on, they look just like the simple, English style of houses that the first colonists built, with two rooms on the first floor, two on the second, and a squat brick chimney in the center of the roof. From the side, however, the rooflines extend almost to the ground. When a blustery gale is blowing off the ocean, the houses look like they've hunched their backs against the chilly wind.

Cape Cod's most historic saltbox is the **Hoxie House** in Sandwich (page 331).

Cape Cod Houses

Cape Cod houses are just as storied—though they weren't called Cape Cod houses until the early 19th century. They were also adapted from an English building style, with similarities to cottages in Cornwall and Devon. They're generally a story-and-a-half high, with four rooms on the lower floor, a central chimney and staircase, and a pair of 2nd-floor bedrooms with sloping roofs and windows on the gable ends. Cape Cod houses are endlessly adaptable and can take on a patchwork appearance as years go by. Henry David Thoreau said that it looked like each inhabitant "had punched a hole where his necessities required it... without regard to outside effect. There were windows for the grown folks, and windows for the children—three or four apiece."

To see a historic example of a Cape Cod house (albeit one with a gambrel roof), visit the **Atwood House Museum** (page 342).

of walking trails threads between the dunes, from a 0.5-mile (0.8-km) loop to a 13-mile (21-km) round-trip hike that goes within sight distance of the Sandy Neck lighthouse. Campfires are allowed on Sandy Neck Beach after 7pm, but as a non-resident, you'll need to buy a $10 fire permit from the beach gatehouse when they go on sale at 5pm.

Food

Stock up for an elegant picnic at ★ **The Brown Jug** (155 Main St., 508/888-4669, www.thebrownjug.com, Tues.-Wed.

9am-5pm, Thurs. 9am-8pm, Fri.-Sat. 9am-9pm, Sun.-Mon. 10am-5pm, $9-25), which has an excellent selection of wines, cheeses, and other goodies. The real treat, though, is the wood-fired pizza, which is among the best on the Cape. Toppings are mostly traditional, and they emerge from the oven blistered and bubbling, with a thin crust that is cooked just right. The menu also includes sandwiches, salads, and house-baked pastries, and while seating inside the shop is limited, the outdoor patio is a sunny place to enjoy a slice in fine weather.

The cavernous dining room and counter service at **Seafood Sam's** (6 Coast Guard Rd., 508/888-4629, www.seafoodsams.com, daily 11am-9pm, $12-27) might not win awards for ambience, but that can be just the ticket when your party is caked with sand and looking for lunch. Fried whole belly clams, lobster bisque, and clam chowder are favorites among regulars, and the midweek dinner specials sometimes include non-maritime offerings like fried chicken with biscuits and mac and cheese.

The busy ovens at **Beth's Bakery and Café** (16 Jarves St., 508/888-7716, www.bethsbakery.net, daily 8am-3pm, $6-12) turn out a tempting array of scones, cinnamon rolls, and cookies. Homey decor and comfortable seats make this a pleasant place to linger over tea and a treat, and a simple lunch menu of salads, soups, and sandwiches is freshly prepared and appealing.

Pick up basics at **Super Stop & Shop** (65 Rte. 6A, 508/833-1302, Mon.-Sat. 7am-11pm, Sun. 7am-10pm).

Camping

The pine-shaded campsites at **Shawme-Crowell State Forest** (42 Main St., 508/888-0351, $55 tents, $120-140 yurts) are just outside of Sandwich three miles (4.8 km) past the Sagamore Bridge. It's the perfect base for visiting the Inner Cape, and with more than 285 sites, it tends to have more vacancies than the popular campgrounds near Provincetown. For groups, the yurts are a particularly good deal, through the simple wall tents don't come with linens—bring your own sleeping bag.

Information

Information about Sandwich and surrounding towns is available at the **Sandwich Chamber of Commerce Welcome Center** (520 Rte. 130, 508/681-0918, www.sandwichchamber.com, mid-May-early Oct. Mon.-Fri. 10am-2pm).

Falmouth and Woods Hole

Many travelers pass through Falmouth on their way to the Martha's Vineyard ferry, but a scenic harbor, summery beaches, and a world-renowned oceanographic center in the adjacent village of Woods Hole make this a fine Cape Cod destination of its own. Falmouth loves to boast that it was the childhood home of Katherine Lee Bates, a professor and poet who wrote "America the Beautiful," but visitors may be more impressed with the town's beloved clam shack, a Cape Cod classic at the water's edge that's a pilgrimage spot for anyone looking for great piles of fried seafood.

Sights

Woods Hole Oceanographic Institution

The scientists from the Woods Hole Oceanographic Institution, or WHOI (pronounced "hooey"), spend their time exploring sunken ships, tracking the global climate, and keeping an eye on the critters that live beneath the ocean surface, from whelks to whales. Learn about their work at the small **Ocean Science Exhibit Center** (15 School St., Woods Hole, 508/548-1400, www.whoi.edu, Memorial Day-Labor Day daily 11am-5pm, early Sept.-Oct. Mon.-Sat. 11am-4pm, $5 suggested donation), which has a replica of the Alvin submersible that first explored the wreck of *Titanic,* as well as exhibits and videos on some of the ocean's weird and wonderful life-forms.

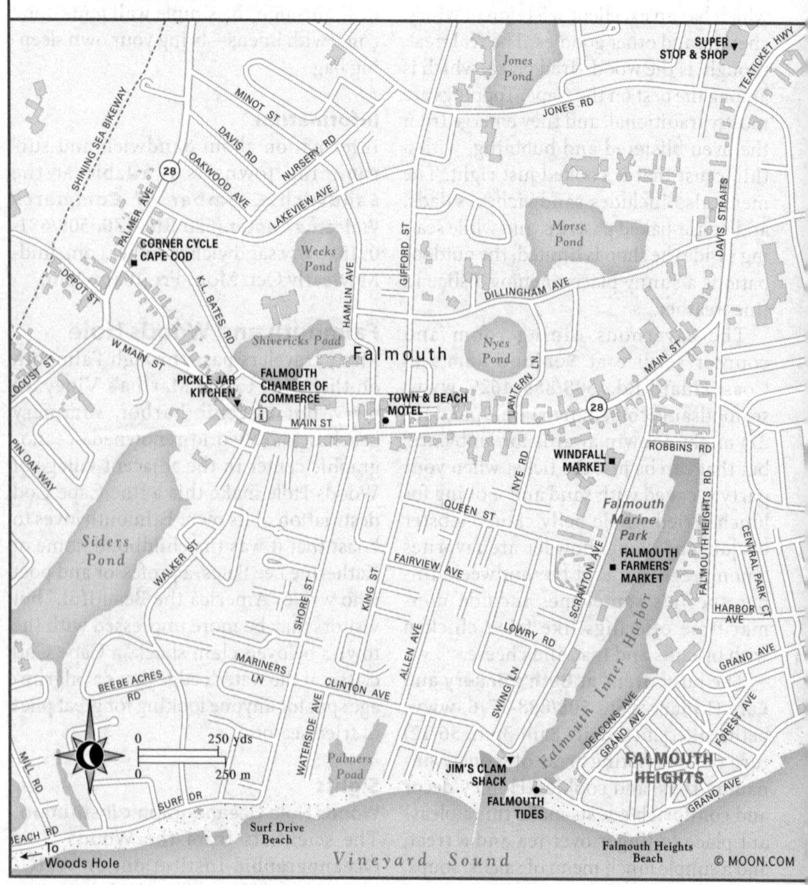

Get an insider's look at WHOI's latest work by joining one of the institute's free, volunteer-led **walking tours** of the dock area and research facilities that aren't regularly open to the public (1 hr, 93 Water St., 508/289-2252, July-Aug. Mon.-Fri. 10:30am and 1pm, reservations required).

Woods Hole Science Aquarium

Do your own research on the adorable—and adorably ugly—things of the deep at the small, kid-friendly **Woods Hole Science Aquarium** (166 Water St., Woods Hole, 508/495-2001, www.fisheries.noaa.gov, Tues.-Sat. 11am-4pm, donations accepted) that's just down the street from WHOI. The aquarium is home to around 140 species of native New England fish and invertebrates, and kid-friendly touch tanks are a fun, hands-on break from all the learning. Time your visit to see the fascinating seal feeding at 11am and 4pm most days; the seals are rescues that can't survive in the wild, including a blind seal named Bumper that survived a shark attack and is living the good life on a hand-fed diet of fresh fish.

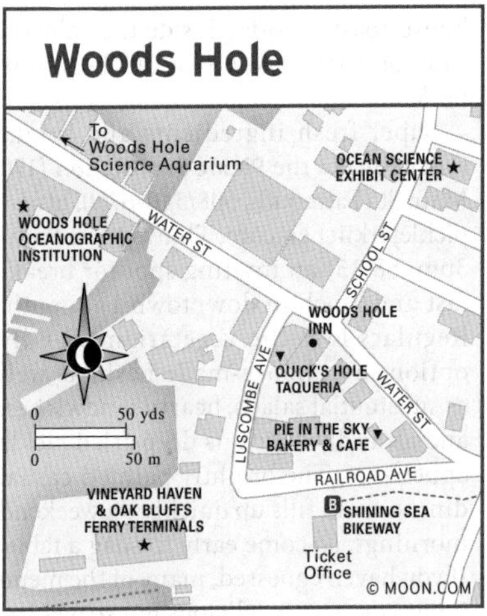

Nobska Point Light

Sailors shooting the narrow channel between Woods Hole and Nonamesset Island don't have much leeway, and the 1828 **Nobska Point Light** (233 Nobska Rd., Woods Hole, www.friendsofnobska.org) helped guide a staggering amount of maritime traffic before the Cape Cod Canal shortened their trip. Through much of the 19th century, lighthouse keepers recorded each passing vessel; in 1829, 10,000 boats were spotted from the Nobska light. Even in the days of sophisticated satellite navigation, the light and foghorn are reassuring presences to passing mariners, and Nobska is a sublime place to watch the sun set over Buzzards Bay, with views that stretch clear to Martha's Vineyard.

Entertainment and Events

June's three-day **Arts Alive** event (www.artsfalmouth.org) brings artists from around the Cape, and in late July, the **Woods Hole Film Festival** (www.woodsholefilmfestival.org) features indie movie screenings at multiple venues across town.

Sports and Recreation

Beaches

Soft sand and the warm water of Buzzards Bay make **Old Silver Beach** (Quaker Rd., Falmouth, May-Sept. parking $20) a favorite among locals and visitors alike, and it's among the best places to throw out your beach blanket on the entire Inner Cape. There are restrooms, showers, and a snack bar on-site, but parking can be an issue during high season.

Biking

Get out of the car and off the road on the 10.7-mile (17.2-km) **Shining Sea Bikeway** (www.capecodbikeguide.com/shiningsea.asp) that runs from North Falmouth to Woods Hole, winding past beaches, cranberry bogs, and salt marshes. Parking is available at the northern terminus, on the north side of Route 151 in North Falmouth, just west of Route 28A. For a shorter trip, start in Falmouth Village, 3.6 miles (5.8 km) north of Woods Hole; park on Depot Avenue, west of the main road. As the bike path arrives in Woods Hole, it's easy to take a short side trip past **Nobska Point Light;** turn on to Fay Road, which curves past the lighthouse and rejoins the bike path (the road portion of this ride is narrow and winding, however, and might not be a good option for riders with children).

Maps of the bike path are available on the **Woods Hole Business Association** (https://woodshole.com/2012/08/11/biking-along-the-shining-sea) website. Find a pair of wheels at **Corner Cycle Cape Cod** (115 Palmer Ave., Falmouth, 508/540-4195, www.cornercycle.com, Mon.-Fri. 10am-6pm, Sat.-Sun. 10am-5pm, $27-37 full-day rentals, child trailer available), which also keeps maps of the path in stock.

Hiking

Walk "the path to the knob" at **Cornelia Carey Sanctuary** (Quissett Harbor Rd., Woods Hole), a 12-acre (4.8-ha) reserve with striking views of Buzzards Bay.

A 1.2-mile (1.9-km) loop trail winds through thick forest on the way to the water's edge, then crosses a narrow causeway to "the knob," a scenic spot for watching birds, boats, and the setting sun.

Food

The harbor-side **Jim's Clam Shack** (227 Clinton Ave., Falmouth, 508/540-7758, late May-early Sept. daily 11:30am-7:45pm, $9-28 cash only) has the fryolator covered. Fried clams and scallops are lightly battered and succulent. Shrimp rolls and lobster rolls are also favorites.

A perennial favorite for whiling away the time before the ferry is the sweet-as-can-be **Pie in the Sky Bakery & Café** (10 Water St., Woods Hole, 508/540-5475, www.piecoffee.com, daily 5am-9pm, $5-13). The freshly baked pastries are the stars here, from fruit pies to bread pudding and brioche, but a lunch menu of salads, soups, and sandwiches (at distinctly un-Cape prices) is satisfying and simple. Grab a cup of organic, house-roasted coffee inside the colorful café, or settle into a seat on the sunny deck.

Super-fresh ingredients and bright flavors make the **Pickle Jar Kitchen** (170 Main St., Falmouth, 508/540-6760, http://picklejarkitchen.com, Thurs.-Mon. 9am-3pm, $8-15) an inviting spot for breakfast and lunch in downtown Falmouth. Regulars love the vegetarian-friendly options and house-made hash, as well as substantial salads, hearty sandwiches, and absurdly delicious deep-fried pickle appetizers. The brightly painted casual dining room fills up quickly on weekend mornings, so come early to snag a table. If you haven't guessed, many of the menu items come with delicious house pickles, which are also available by the pound.

Joining the crowd at **Eulinda's Ice Cream** (634 West Falmouth Hwy., West Falmouth, 508/548-2486, late Apr.-Oct daily noon-10pm, $4-8) is a summertime tradition in Falmouth. The tiny shack serves a long list of ice cream flavors,

riding the Shining Sea Bikeway

sundaes are piled with hot fudge and whipped cream, and frappes are thick and creamy—keep in mind that a New England milk shake is a thin, flavored milk, and frappes are blended drinks made with ice cream.

Get your seafood in taco form and "wicked fresh" at **Quick's Hole Taqueria** (6 Luscombe Ave., Woods Hole, 508/495-0792, www.quicksholewickedfresh.com, Apr.-Sept. 11:30am-8pm, $14-27), an offbeat spot with counter-service Mexican food, local beer, and a sunny deck. The lobster tacos win raves, but there are also plenty of options for landlubbers and vegans, like pulled pork burritos or tacos piled with fire-roasted veggies.

Pick up organic produce and gourmet food at the small **Windfall Market** (77 Scranton Ave., Falmouth, 508/548-0099, www.windfallmarket.com, Mon.-Sat. 8am-8pm, Sun. 8am-7pm) and more standard fare at Falmouth's **Super Stop & Shop** (20 Teakettle Hwy., Falmouth, 508/540-7481, Mon.-Sat. 6am-11pm, Sun. 6am-10pm). Find local pastries, hand-made souvenirs, and produce at the **Falmouth Farmers' Market** (180 Scranton Ave., Falmouth, https://falmouthfarmersmarket.com, late May-early Oct. Thurs. noon-5pm).

Accommodations

Under $150

Good budget options are scanty in this part of the Cape, which makes **Town and Beach Motel** (382 Main St., Falmouth, 508/548-1380, www.townandbeachmotel.com, $95-195) an excellent find. The rooms in the low-rise building are somewhere between outdated and vintage, but the motel is walking distance from the village, and nautical bedspreads and wood-paneled walls feel like an unpretentious taste of a different time.

$150-250

Another pleasantly retro place to land is **Falmouth Tides** (267 Clinton Ave., Falmouth, 508/548-3126, www.falmouthtides.com, $190-225). The Tides has basic, sunny rooms that are spotlessly clean, but what makes this spot a perennial favorite is the motel's private beach; 1st-floor rooms can open a door to the sand, with a pair of beach chairs for watching boats go in and out of Falmouth's narrow harbor.

$250-350

Charmingly decorated rooms, complimentary bikes, and thoughtful amenities make the **Woods Hole Inn** (28 Water St., Woods Hole, 508/508-495-0258, www.woodsholeinn.com, $325-500) feel like a place to escape to, as do the sumptuous breakfasts. In keeping with the town's science and conservation bent, the inn makes an effort to keep it green with local products, biodegradable cleaners, and employees that bike to work.

Information

Info for Falmouth and Woods Hole is available from the **Falmouth Chamber of**

★ Cape Cod's Clam Shacks

typical clam shack fare—fried clams, scallops, and onion rings

The peninsula's got enough starched linen for a year of fine dining, but find Cape Codders far from home, and the meal they're dreaming of is probably served in a shack. The free-standing, seasonal spots are a truly democratic experience, as everyone from fishers to day-tripping families stop by for great mounds of fried clams, onion rings, coleslaw, and lobster rolls.

Just about every clam shack in New England posts a weathered sign claiming to be "famous" for something; here are some Cape Cod favorites that really are:

- **Jim's Clam Shack, Falmouth:** Belly up to a pile of seafood while watching the fishing fleet come and go from a rooftop deck. Shrimp rolls and lobster rolls are also favorites here (page 336).
- **Captain Frosty's Fish & Chips, Dennis:** Just a couple of miles outside downtown Yarmouth, this popular seafood joint and dairy is the place to be for local families. If you can find a place to park, don't miss the chance for crab rolls and golden onion rings, which go beautifully with a thick, frosty frappe—that's a milk shake for you non-Yankees (page 341).
- **Cap't Cass Rock Harbor Seafood, Orleans:** There isn't much to see in little Orleans, but it's a quick detour on the way to or from other Cape Cod destinations. The weathered buoys that deck the outside of this tiny shack are like lures for hungry locals, and this homey spot can still feel like a slice of old New England, with handwritten signs and gingham curtains. The fried scallops have a loyal following, as do the lobster and crab rolls that boast "all meat—no filler" (page 349).
- **Arnold's Lobster & Clam Bar, Eastham:** With kids meals served on Frisbees, minigolf, and a faux "shack" built inside a spotless cafeteria, Arnold's is pure Cape Cod vacationland camp, but the fried seafood, chowder, and lobster rolls keep even the locals coming back. Aficionados love the hot lobster rolls and onion rings, and there's outdoor seating and an excellent raw bar on-site (page 353).

Commerce (20 Academy Ln., Falmouth, 508/548-8500, www.falmouthchamber.com, Mon.-Fri. 10am-4pm).

Getting Around

Route 28 connects Woods Hole and Falmouth with Sandwich (23 mi/37 km, 0.5 hr). The **Cape Cod Regional Transit Authority** (800/352-7155, www.falmouthchamber.com, hourly $2 adults and youth, $1 seniors) runs the **SeaLine** bus from Woods Hole along the coast to Hyannis and Barnstable, while the **Sandwich** line brings riders from the Sagamore Bridge to Hyannis, where there are connecting buses to all over the Cape.

Mid Cape and Lower Cape

This stretch of the Cape is where vacationland hits a fever pitch, with a healthy (and sometimes hilarious) mix of Olde New England meets Moby-Dick-themed minigolf. It's one of the easiest places to settle in with a family; it's easy driving distance from Cape Cod National Seashore, and boasts the refined, old-fashioned town of Chatham, the access point for Monomoy National Wildlife Refuge. The Nantucket ferry departs from the Mid Cape's biggest town, Hyannis; it's not as quaint as other Cape towns, but it has a few excellent budget accommodations.

Yarmouth

A cluster of Yarmouths—West Yarmouth, South Yarmouth, and Yarmouth Port—straddle the Mid Cape. On the northern edge of the Cape, Yarmouth Port is all white-steepled churches and old-fashioned homes, but the south is packed with family-friendly vacation kitsch that visitors tend to love or hate, so choose your Yarmouth accordingly.

Sights

Fans of cheerfully macabre art won't want to miss the **Edward Gorey House** (8 Strawberry Ln., Yarmouth Port, 508/362-3909, www.edwardgoreyhouse.org, early Apr.-early July and early Oct.-Dec. Thurs.-Sat. 11am-4pm, Sun. noon-4pm, early July-early Oct. Wed.-Sat. 11am-4pm, Sun. noon-4pm, $10 adults, $8 students and seniors, $4 children 6-12, free children under 6), now an intimate museum that celebrates his work and devotion to animal welfare. The author, illustrator, and costume designer might be best known for the intro to "Masterpiece Mystery." His drawings and rhymes in the *Gashlycrumb Tinies*—"A is for Amy who fell down the stairs; B is for Basil assaulted by bears"—are as delightful today as they were in 1963. In addition to guided tours, the museum also has a scavenger hunt that's great for kids.

Take aim at Captain Ahab, lighthouses, and an eye-catching pink whale at **Putter's Paradise miniature golf** (119 Rte. 28, West Yarmouth, 508/771-7394, www.puttersparadise.net, Apr.-Oct. Mon.-Thurs. 11am-10pm, Fri. 10am-10pm, Sat.-Sun. 9am-10pm, hours may vary in spring and fall, $12 adults, $11 children under 12). It's a summertime ritual for many visitors, and the friendly staff, Cape-themed courses, and ice cream stand make it a favorite for families. Check the website for coupons.

The Cape Cod Astronomical Society opens doors to **Werner Schmidt Observatory** (210 Station Ave., Dennis-Yarmouth High School, South Yarmouth, 508/398-4765, www.capecodastronomy.org, late-June-Aug. Thurs. 7:30pm lecture, 8:30pm star party, free) on Thursday nights in the summer, and joining a "star party" offers the chance to take in the skies above the Cape through 16- and 18-inch telescopes.

Shopping

Stock up on beach reading at the **Parnassus Book Services** (220 Rte. 6A, Yarmouth Port, 508/362-6420, www.parnassusbooks.com, Mon.-Sat.

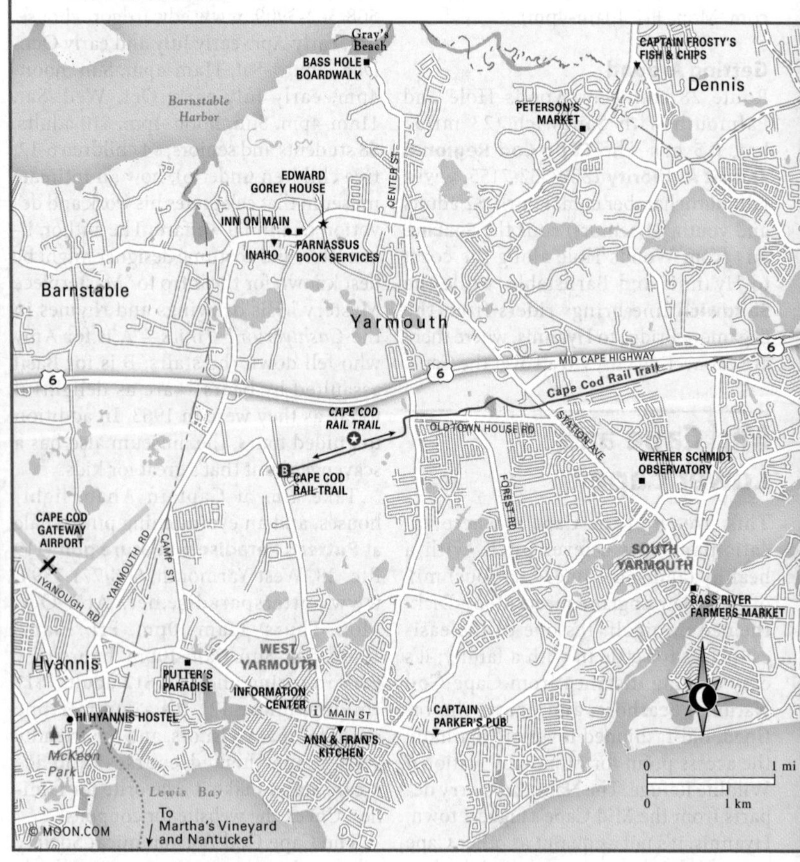

10am-5pm, Sun. 10am-4pm, hours vary in winter), which carries thousands of used volumes along with new books on the Cape and a complete catalog of Edward Gorey. An outdoor extension is open around the clock on the honor system.

Sports and Recreation

Beaches

The **Bass Hole Boardwalk** crosses 900 feet (274 m) of tidal marshes beside **Gray's Beach** (Center Street, Yarmouth Port, free parking), the perfect vantage point for watching scurrying crabs, shorebirds, and tidal sloughs, though the bugs can be daunting on calm days. The beach itself is small, sandy, and sheltered from waves, and the roped-in swimming area is a popular choice for families with small children.

★ Cape Cod Rail Trail

The paved, mostly flat **Cape Cod Rail Trail** (www.mass.gov/locations/cape-cod-rail-trail) follows 25 miles (40 km) of former railroad track between South Dennis and Wellfleet, passing ponds, forests, and short spurs to reach the coast. There is parking at the trailhead in South Dennis

(Rte. 134, 0.5-mi/0.8 km south of Rte. 6 on the left, free), and if you're renting your wheels, there's parking available at **Dennis Cycle Center** (249 Great Western Rd., South Dennis, 508/398-0011, www.denniscyclecenter.com, $17 2 hrs, $27 all day), which is located on the bike path.

Food

Seafood lovers weary of fried food can get their fish fix at **Inaho** (157 Route 6A, Yarmouth Port, 508/362-5522, www.inaho-sushi.com, Tues.-Sat. 5pm-10pm, $23-45), a sushi restaurant in a perky converted Cape Cod house. The intimate dining room is comfortable and casual. Regulars rave about the raw scallops in an avocado shell and ultra-fresh sashimi.

Tucked into an adorable cottage with a striped awning, **Ann & Fran's Kitchen** (471 Main St., West Yarmouth, 508/775-7771, www.annandfrans.com, Fri.-Mon. 7am-2pm, $11-16) serves classic diner-style breakfast and lunch. Pancakes and waffles of all stripes and hearty savory breakfasts bring in summertime crowds, but this is a local favorite year-round. Arrive early or plan to wait for a table.

Thick, creamy chowder is the star of the show at **Captain Parker's Pub** (668 Rte. 28, West Yarmouth, 508/771-4266, www.captainparkers.com, daily 11:30am-10pm, $14-30), a family-friendly pub that also serves hearty American steak-house classics in the laid-back dining room.

A few miles northeast of downtown Yarmouth, **Captain Frosty's Fish & Chips** (219 Rte. 6A, Dennis, 508/385-8548, www.captainfrosty.com, May-Oct. Wed.-Mon. 11:30am-8:30pm, $10-26) is a classic family seafood stop, with thick ice cream frappes that go perfectly with big piles of onion rings and soft crab rolls. The clam chowder is another favorite, packed with a generous helping of clams, and creamy as can be. Stand in line to order at the counter, then wait for your food at outdoor picnic tables.

Stock up on locally grown berries, fresh bread, and all things artisanal at **Bass River Farmers Market** (311 Old Main St., Yarmouth, www.bassriverfarmersmarket.org, mid-June-mid-Sept. Thurs. and Sat. 9am-1pm).

You can find picnic supplies—and just about anything else you need—at locally owned **Peterson's Market** (918 Rte. 6A, Yarmouth Port, 508/362-2147, www.petersonsmarket.com, daily 7am-8pm).

Accommodations

Housed in a restored sea captain's home, the **Inn on Main** (186 Main St., Yarmouth Port, 774/994-8478, www.innonmaincapecod.com, $245-375) is comfortable and friendly with fabulous breakfasts and decorations that feel both charmingly historic and modern. The owners, Sarah Bradburn and Chris Kennedy, are gracious and knowledgeable about the Cape. They also welcome dogs at the inn.

Information

Yarmouth has an **information center** (424 Rte. 28, West Yarmouth, Mon.-Fri. 8am-5pm, 508/778-1008, www.yarmouthcapecod.com).

Chatham

Perfectly placed on the outer edge of Cape Cod's "elbow," Chatham is an elegant spot with sweet boutiques, a compact downtown, and many year-round residents, which is perhaps why it's quieter than other towns on the Mid Cape. There are plenty of family-friendly beaches for sandcastles and sunbathing here, as well as the most convenient access to the shifting sands of the Monomoy National Wildlife Refuge. Its barrier islands are habitat for an extraordinary population of birds, including protected piping plover and the roseate tern.

Sights

It's easy to see why sailing off the Chatham coast would be treacherous work on the clearest day. "Nowhere on the Cape's shorelines has the sea kept

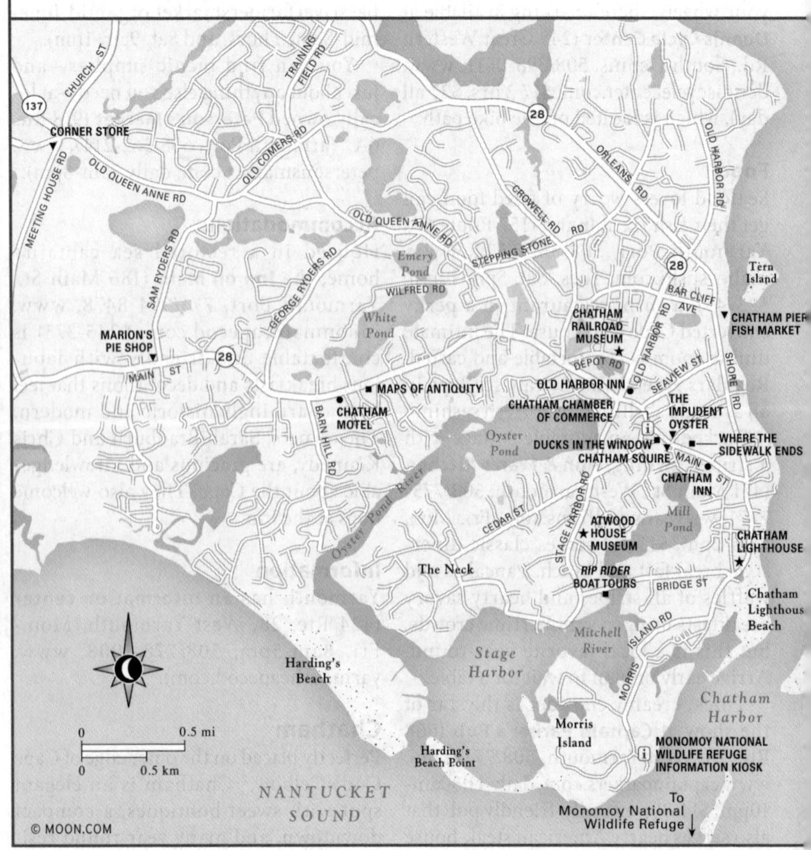

busier than among these storm-bitten sands," wrote Provincetown author Josef Berger in 1937. "Monomoy lies beckoning like the bony finger of death which it has been to countless ships." When twin beams at **Chatham Lighthouse** (37 Main St., tours July-Sept. Wed. 1pm-3:30pm, free) were illuminated in 1808, they must have seemed like a godsend to mariners in a storm; the lighthouse still serves sailors to this day. With a red-roofed Coast Guard station and a snapping flag, it's picture-postcard smart. You may spot seals, whales, and flocks of migratory birds just off the nearby beach.

Learn about life in historic Cape Cod at the small but well-curated **Atwood House Museum** (347 Stage Harbor Rd., 508/945-2493, www.chathamhistoricalsociety.org, June and Sept.-Oct. Tues.-Sat. 1pm-4pm, July-Aug. Tues.-Fri. 10am-4pm and Sat. 1pm-4pm, $10 adults, $5 students 8-18, free for children 7 and under), located in an old Cape Cod house with a gambrel roof. Knowledgeable docents decked in period attire help animate the museum's stories of sea captains, shipwrecks, and day-to-day life.

Brightly painted "railroad Gothic" detailing makes Chatham's 1887

Cape Cod Baseball

summer game in the Cape Cod Baseball League

As the beaches fill and clam shacks open their doors, some of the most talented college baseball players descend on the Cape for a season in the **Cape Cod Baseball League** (www.capecodbaseball.org), one of 11 summer leagues across the country.

Teams like the Brewster Whitecaps, Chatham Anglers, and Hyannis Harbor Hawks have sent over 1,000 players to the Major Leagues, and Cape Cod regulars have seen some big names in their small-town venues, including Hall of Famers Harold "Pie" Traynor, Carlton Fisk, Frank Thomas, and Craig Biggio.

The league is volunteer run, with many of the young players hosted in local homes, and games are free to attend. Attending a game is a fun way to take part in a Cape Cod tradition, and there are games most days of the week from the second week of June through early August.

Check the website for an updated schedule, as well as the whole story behind the Cape Cod Baseball League, and catch games at these popular venues:

- **Lowell Park, Cotuit:** Home field of the Cotuit Kettleers, Lowell Park is the most picturesque baseball diamond on Cape Cod: an old-fashioned field and bleachers surrounded by dense forest that looks like the backdrop for a Norman Rockwell painting (www.kettleers.org).

- **McKeon Park, Hyannis:** You can smell the ocean (along with the peanuts and Cracker Jacks) when you watch the Hyannis Harbor Hawks go to bat in the heart of the Mid Cape. Head to the "Osprey's Nest" on the third-base line for the best views of the action (www.harborhawks.org).

- **Eldredge Park, Orleans:** Bring a blanket or lawn chair to this laid-back park, which has terraced hills along both baselines, but come early—the Orleans Firebirds have a devoted fan base that arrives hours before the first at-bat to stake their claim on prized pieces of grass (www.orleansfirebirds.com).

railway depot an eye-catching home for the **Chatham Railroad Museum** (153 Depot Rd., 508/945-5780, www.chathamrailroadmuseum.com, mid-June-mid-Sept. Tues.-Sat. 10am-4pm, free). It doesn't take long to browse the small collection of model trains, railroad history exhibits, and the fully restored wooden caboose, but it's an interesting glimpse of the golden age of rail.

Shopping

Most of the action in Chatham (shopping and otherwise) is clustered on Main Street. You'll find sweet boutiques, upscale design shops, and souvenir joints on the walkable stretch between Old Harbor Road and Willow Bend. Pick up disco ducks, mad scientist ducks, and "celebriducks" at **Ducks in the Window** (507 Main St., 508/945-0334, www.ducksinthewindow.com, Mon.-Thurs. 10am-6pm, Fri.-Sun. 10am-8pm), the undisputed claimant to the Cape's largest rubber duck collection. Find beach reads and local authors at **Where the Sidewalk Ends** (432 Main St., 508/945-0499, www.booksonthecape.com, July-Sept. 9am-9pm, Oct.-June 10am-5pm), a welcoming bookstore with a small café. A bit beyond the action is the gallery-like **Maps of Antiquity** (1409 Main St., 508/945-1660, www.mapsofantiquity.com, Mon.-Sat. 10am-5pm, Sun. noon-5pm), which has a wonderful collection of historic New England maps as well as maps featuring constellations, cupids, and sea monsters.

Sports and Recreation

Beaches

The most scenic place to hit the sand is at the **Chatham Lighthouse Beach** (Shore Rd., parking $20), which has views of the historic lighthouse and Monomoy National Wildlife Refuge. It's a good place for spotting passing seals (and occasionally the sharks that love them). Because of the often rough water and strong currents, only good swimmers should think about going past the breakers. Find warmer, calmer water at **Harding's Beach** (Harding's Beach Rd., West Chatham, parking $20), which also has lifeguards, a bathhouse, and bigger parking lots.

Boating

One of the coolest ways to see the Monomoy National Wildlife Refuge is to book a **boat tour** of the islands with a private captain. Among the best tours are those aboard the ***Perseverance*** (730 Rte. 28, Harwich Port, 508/430-7772, www.monomoysealcruise.com, 1.5-hr cruises $45 adults, $40 children 4-12, $20 under 4), a 43-foot (13-m) Coast Guard-certified catamaran that visits colonies of gray and harbor seals.

Hiking

The sand that stretches south from Chatham forms a pair of barrier islands that are essential habitat for migrating birds; over 10 species make their nests in the **Monomoy National**

Wildlife Refuge. Many of the refuge's 7,604 acres (3,077 ha) are designated wilderness with limited access, but exploring the rest by boat is a remarkable experience. For a primer on the refuge's most accessible habitats, swing by the on-site **information kiosk** (30 Wikis Way, Morris Island, Chatham, www.fws.gov/refuge/Monomoy, Memorial Day-Labor Day daily 10am-4pm). It's worth keeping in mind that as the visitor center is volunteer-run, the off-season hours are aspirational—if there are no volunteers, the doors stay closed, so call ahead. The 40-acre (16-ha) Morris Island is the only part of the refuge that's accessible by car. A 1.7-mile (2.7-km) **hiking trail** leaves from the information kiosk along the shore and coastal forests.

Paddling

To see the islands under your own power, try renting a kayak for the morning or afternoon from **North Chatham Outfitters** (300 Orleans Rd., North Chatham, 508/348-1638, www.northchathamoutfitters.com, Mon.-Sat. 8am-5:30pm, Sun. 8am-4pm, 24-hr kayak rentals $45/single, $65/tandem). Kayak delivery is available for an additional $10 per vessel. Bear in mind that wind and open water mean that paddling around the refuge is best suited to those with some kayaking experience, but the store staff can point you in the direction of coastal salt marshes and tidal rivers that are better for beginners.

Food

Thick wedges of fruit or savory pie are a summertime tradition for many Chatham visitors. **Marion's Pie Shop** (2022 Main St., 508/432-9439, www.marionspieshopofchatham.com, Tues.-Sat. 8am-6pm, Sun. 8am-4pm, $6-22) started as a home bakery in 1947. The hearty potpies are a comforting option, but don't miss the wild blueberry pie in season.

seal at the Monomoy National Wildlife Refuge

Pick up supplies for a top-notch picnic at **Corner Store** (1403 Old Queen Anne Rd., 508/432-1077, www.chathamcornerstore.com, Wed.-Sun. 8am-2pm, $9-16), whose burrito bar, sandwiches, and homey whoopie pies are super-fresh and simple. Breakfast burritos stuffed with scrambled eggs, home fries, and tomato salsa are a highlight.

Watch the fishing boats come and go as you eat at ★ **Chatham Pier Fish Market** (45 Barcliff Ave., 508/945-3474, www.chathampierfishmkt.com, May-Oct. daily 11am-7pm, $10-28), a simple takeout shack that's right by the docks. Big portions of fish-and-chips, fried clams, and creamy chowder make this spot a perennial favorite; eat at the picnic tables in the parking lot, or head to the second-story observation deck for views of the harbor.

The seafood menu at **The Impudent Oyster** (15 Chatham Bars Ave., 508/945-3545, www.theimpudentoyster.com, Thurs.-Tues. 11:30am-3pm and 5pm-9pm, $16-39) leans toward international classics like pesca fra diavolo and panang red curry, mixed in with substantial salads and sandwiches. In a small, shingled building just off Main Street, dark wood paneling and a cozy dining room make for a warm, welcoming feel—reservations are essential on busy weekends.

In a building that rambles along Main Street, the **Chatham Squire** (487 Main St., 508/945-0945, www.thesquire.com, daily 11:30am-1am, $14-30) is the kind of bar where people bring their kids. Choose a spot in the homey dining room for salads, pastas, and hearty mains alongside fried bar food classics, or head to the pub side to drink local drafts in a room lined with antique license plates and Cape Cod bric-a-brac. A seat at the bar is a friendly place to meet locals and other visitors.

Accommodations

Under $150

Busy and a bit pedestrian, Hyannis is 20 miles (32 km) west of Chatham, but with the only hostel in the Mid Cape area, it's a decent home base for solo budget travelers who want access to Chatham and Monomoy. In a well-maintained home in downtown Hyannis, the **HI Hyannis Hostel** (111 Ocean St., Hyannis, 508/775-7990, www.hiusa.org, mid-May-late Sept., $39-59 dorms, $89-109 private rooms) is the best option for single travelers in the Mid Cape and has decent private rooms as well. Comfortable common spaces make this a good spot to meet other travelers, and the kitchen and free parking are good perks; the hostel can get loud, so bring earplugs.

$150-250

Just outside of town, the **Chatham Motel** (1487 Main St., 508/945-2630, www.chathammotel.com, $175-245) is perfectly tidy, bright, and updated, and it's a solid deal for the area. Refrigerators, coffeemakers, and a swimming pool make this a relaxed place to stay.

Over $350

Old-fashioned and romantic, the **Old Harbor Inn** (22 Old Harbor Rd., 800/942-4434, www.chathamoldharborinn.com, $379-549) is a sweet bed-and-breakfast filled with thoughtful extras. Elegant common spaces are furnished in English country style, and the inn is walking distance to Chatham's lighthouse and beach.

With beautiful design and luxurious touches, **Chatham Inn** (359 Main St., 508/945-9232, www.chathaminn.com, $459-999) feels perfectly beachy and refined. Guests get all the usual amenities plus a gourmet made-to-order breakfast and common spaces that include an outdoor terrace and a cozy room for games and drinks.

Information

The Chatham Chamber of Commerce operates a **seasonal visitors booth** (533 Main St., 508/945-5199, www.chathaminfo.com, July-early Sept. daily 10am-5pm) with information on parking in the area, hotels with current vacancies, and beaches and boat landings. Information is also available year-round at the **main chamber office** (2377 Main St., 508/945-5199, www.chathaminfo.com, Mon.-Fri. 9:30am-3:30pm).

Getting Around

Route 6 and Route 28 run parallel for the length of the Mid Cape, linking up a series of small towns that run together. To reach Chatham from Yarmouth, follow Route 6 east to Old Queen Anne Road, which merges with Route 28 just before entering downtown (16 mi/26 km, 0.5 hr).

Outer Cape

The peaceful forests and salt flats of Brewster mark the transitional zone between the Mid Cape and the Upper Cape. Beyond here, Cape Cod makes a sharp left-hand turn at Orleans and the peninsula narrows to a sandy slip of land that's just under a mile (1.6 km) across in places. But the slender Outer Cape is lined with the stunning beaches and the National Seashore, which make it the finest place to experience the sea at its most beautiful. Locals call the distant tip of Cape Cod "the end of the world." Staying at the end of the Cape offers the chance to move between windblown beaches and the wild waterfront parties of Provincetown.

Brewster and Orleans

This bayside town doesn't have much of a center, but its wealth of natural beauty—from wooded parks to salt marshes and sandy beaches—make it a good jumping-off point for exploring the Cape's wilder, less-developed side. The charming and walkable village center of Orleans does offer easy access to local bites and crafts, but the briny breeze is a reminder that splendorous beaches, wetlands, and dunes are just a short drive away.

Sights

The **Cape Cod Museum of Natural History** (869 Rte. 6A, 508/896-3867, www.ccmnh.org, June-Sept. 30 daily 10am-3pm, Oct.-May Wed.-Sun. 11am-3pm, $15 adults, $12 seniors, $8 children 3-12, free under 3) brings the Cape's geology and natural history to life with wave tanks, interactive exhibits, and art. During summer months, visitors can meet the vivid butterflies in the Pollinator House, and a trail behind the museum leads to salt marshes and a beach that attracts flocks of migratory birds.

Shopping

Brewster's not much of a shopping hot spot, but **The Brewster Store** (1935 Rte. 6A, 508/896-3744, www.brewsterstore.com, daily 7am-10pm) is an old-timey favorite, with penny candy, beach toys, housewares, and antiques. Homesteaders and preppers take note: The Brewster Store is one of New England's premier destinations for oil lamp parts, lamp oil, and hurricane globes.

Sports and Recreation

Beaches

For kid-friendly tidepools and swimming, **Crosby Landing Beach** (Crosby Lane, 508/896-9430, day parking $20) is ideal. If the tide's not too high, walk out to the shallow sandbar to enjoy the warm bay water.

Hiking and Biking

With dense pine forests and freshwater kettle ponds, **Nickerson State Park** (3488 Main St., 508/896-3491, day parking $30) can feel like it's miles away from the coast. **Hiking trails** wrap around the edges of the ponds and **biking trails** wind through the woods, then extend to the Cape Cod Rail Trail. Nickerson does have a bit of very scenic beach, though; plan your visit to the low tide to walk the intertidal **Namskaket Sea Path,** which crosses 1.5 miles (2.4 km) of coastal dunes and tide flats. The state park also

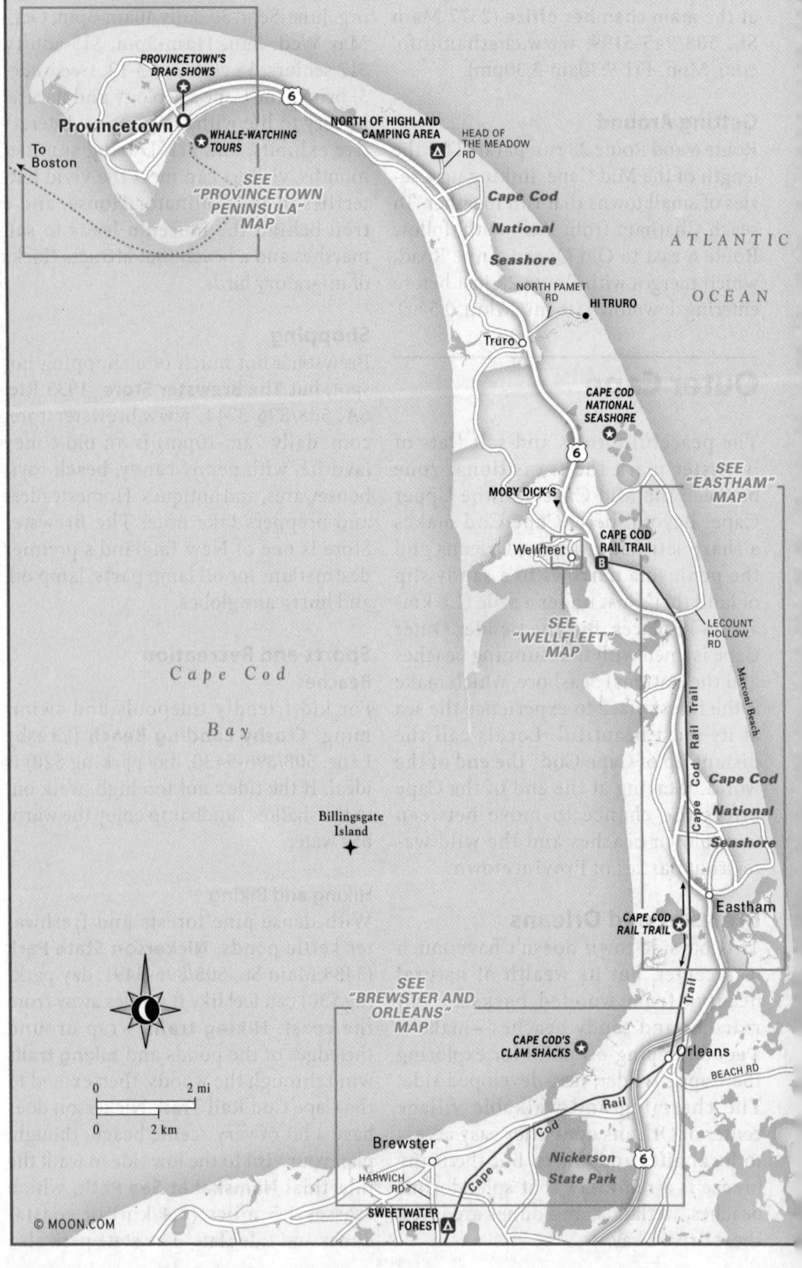
The Outer Cape
PROVINCETOWN'S DRAG SHOWS
Provincetown
WHALE-WATCHING TOURS
To Boston
SEE "PROVINCETOWN PENINSULA" MAP
6
NORTH OF HIGHLAND CAMPING AREA
HEAD OF THE MEADOW RD
Cape Cod National Seashore
ATLANTIC OCEAN
NORTH PAMET RD
HI TRURO
Truro
CAPE COD NATIONAL SEASHORE
SEE "EASTHAM" MAP
MOBY DICK'S
Wellfleet
CAPE COD RAIL TRAIL
LECOUNT HOLLOW RD
SEE "WELLFLEET" MAP
Marconi Beach
Cape Cod Bay
Cape Cod Rail Trail
Billingsgate Island
Eastham
CAPE COD RAIL TRAIL
SEE "BREWSTER AND ORLEANS" MAP
CAPE COD'S CLAM SHACKS
Orleans
BEACH RD
0 2 mi
0 2 km
Brewster
Nickerson State Park
HARWICH RD
SWEETWATER FOREST
© MOON.COM

Brewster and Orleans

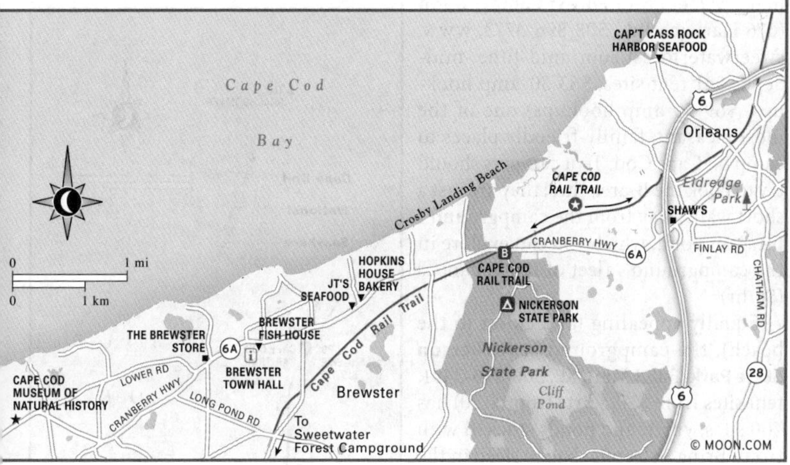

has a 400-site campground (tent sites from $70, yurts from $120). Whether you're here for the day or the night, be sure to perform a tick check after being out in the woods, as their numbers have risen in recent years.

Food

The sunny picnic tables at **JT's Seafood Restaurant** (2689 Rte. 6A, 508/896-3355, www.jt-seafood.com, daily 11am-9pm, $10-25) fill up with families tucking into great piles of beer-battered fish-and-chips, steamers, and lobster rolls that come with little cups of drawn butter. JT's also has a popular ice cream window with hard- and soft-serve ice cream and banana splits.

Fresh-baked muffins and scones are the highlight of **Hopkins House Bakery** (2727 Rte. 6A, 508/896-3450, www.hopkinshousebrewster.com, Thurs.-Sun. 8am-3pm, $4-10), in a rambling Cape Cod that's also home to a country store filled with antiques and folk art. Regulars swear by the hermit cookies, a chewy, spicy New England classic stuffed with dried fruits and nuts.

Built in a former seafood market, the **Brewster Fish House** (2208 Rte. 6A, 508/896-7867, www.brewsterfishhousecapecod.com, Wed.-Sun. noon-3pm and 5pm-9pm, $22-40) serves thoughtful presentations of fish and steak house fare that transcend clam shack offerings. Friendly service, local ingredients, and a cottage filled with nautical decor and fish portraits make this an Outer Cape favorite.

Part fishing shack, part grandma's kitchen, **Cap't Cass Rock Harbor Seafood** (117 Rock Harbor Rd., Orleans, www.captaincass.com, May-Oct. daily 11am-2pm, cash only $8-27) serves piles of seafood with little ado: paper plates slapped onto vinyl tablecloths, an old-fashioned counter, and maritime bric-a-brac on every wall. Generous portions and an "Old Cape" vibe make this little spot worth the six-mile (9.6-km) detour from Brewster—and Cap't Cass' is BYOB, so pick up a bottle of beer or wine on the way.

Stop by **Shaw's** (9 West Rd., Orleans, 508/240-1021, daily 7am-10pm) for picnic supplies and other groceries.

Camping

Wooded sites, fire pits, and playgrounds make **Sweetwater Forest Campground** (676 Harwich Rd., 508/896-3773, www.sweetwaterforest.com, mid-June.-mid-Sept., $41 tent sites, $63 30-amp hookups, $69 50-amp hookups) one of the most pleasant, family-friendly places to camp on Cape Cod. Tent campers should try to book the B-area sites; they are just a short walk away from the campground's pleasant pond, which you can explore in the campground's fleet of rental canoes ($6/hr).

Equally appealing (and closer to the beach), the campground at **Nickerson State Park** (3488 Main St., 508/896-3491, tent sites from $70, yurts from $120) has 400 sites, yurts, and ponds stocked with trout. Bring a sleeping bag to sleep in the yurts, and beware the poison ivy that creeps around many of the campsites.

Information

Brewster no longer has a dedicated information center, but you can still stop by the **Brewster Town Hall** (2198 Rte. 6A, 508/896-3701, www.brewster-ma.gov, Mon.-Thurs. 9am-3pm), where knowledgeable staffers can answer most questions off the tops of their heads.

Eastham, Wellfleet, and Truro

It would be easy to miss Eastham, whose most compelling places are tucked behind a strip of generic storefronts on Route 6A, but the small town is the main gateway to Cape Cod National Seashore. Tiny Wellfleet, though, is a wonderful destination, its small village center filled with galleries and restaurants. Wellfleet's oysters are among the best in the East, and its excellent bird sanctuary makes for a fascinating visit year-round. Continue north along the Cape, and you'll pass through Truro, which has one of the finest places to camp along the Outer Cape. All three laid-back communities are excellent bases for exploring the Cape Cod National Seashore, but

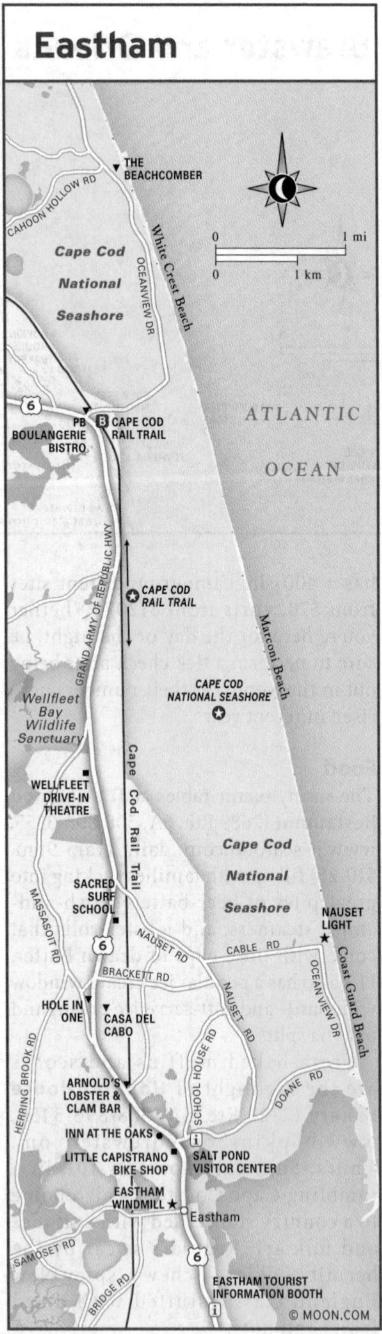

Eastham

THE BEACHCOMBER
CAHOON HOLLOW RD
Cape Cod National Seashore
OCEANVIEW DR
White Crest Beach
0 1 mi
0 1 km
6
PB BOULANGERIE BISTRO
CAPE COD RAIL TRAIL
ATLANTIC OCEAN
GRAND ARMY OF REPUBLIC HWY
CAPE COD RAIL TRAIL
Marconi Beach
CAPE COD NATIONAL SEASHORE
Wellfleet Bay Wildlife Sanctuary
Cape Cod Rail Trail
WELLFLEET DRIVE-IN THEATRE
Cape Cod National Seashore
SACRED SURF SCHOOL
MASSASOIT RD
NAUSET RD
NAUSET LIGHT
CABLE RD
BRACKETT RD
OCEAN VIEW DR
Coast Guard Beach
HOLE IN ONE
CASA DEL CABO
NAUSET RD
SCHOOL HOUSE RD
HERRING BROOK RD
ARNOLD'S LOBSTER & CLAM BAR
DOANE RD
INN AT THE OAKS
LITTLE CAPISTRANO BIKE SHOP
SALT POND VISITOR CENTER
EASTHAM WINDMILL
Eastham
SAMOSET RD
BRIDGE RD
EASTHAM TOURIST INFORMATION BOOTH
© MOON.COM

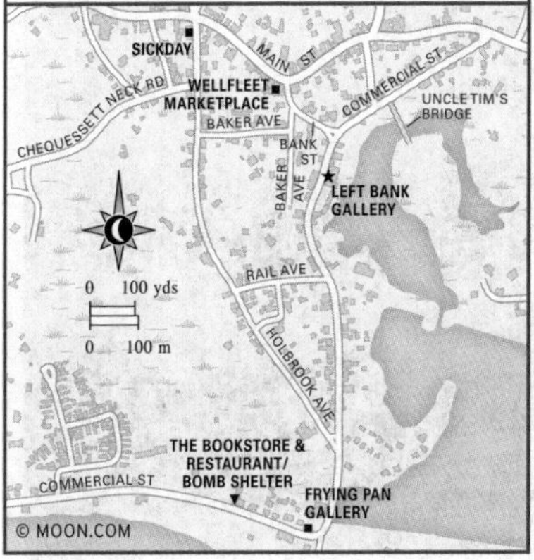

are close enough to Provincetown for a night on the town.

Sights

TOP EXPERIENCE

★ Cape Cod National Seashore

The **Cape Cod National Seashore** is an utterly beautiful swath of coastline. Start your exploration of the park's 43,000 acres (17,401 ha) at the **Salt Pond Visitor Center** (Rte. 6 at Nauset Rd., Eastham, 508/255-3421, www.nps.gov/caco, daily 9am-5pm, extended hours in summer), which stocks maps and information on where to find the best bike trails, lighthouses, and picnic areas. The rangers are deft hands at directing visitors to the finest places to swim, hike, and explore.

For a scenic walk it's hard to beat a stroll down **Coast Guard Beach** to **Nauset Light,** a 1.5-mile (2.4-km) stretch that's among the finest in the Northeast. The stairs to Nauset Light often get washed away in winter storms and may not be accessible in early season. Coast Guard Beach is also a particularly good place to watch wildlife from shore: Keep your eyes peeled for seals and whales, which flock to the food-rich waters of the **Stellwagen Bank National Marine Sanctuary.**

The oldest windmill on Cape Cod is **Eastham Windmill** (Rte. 6 and Samoset Rd., Eastham), built in the mid-17th century in Plymouth, moved to Provincetown in the latter part of that century, and finally moved to Eastham in 1793. Tours are offered in summertime.

Entertainment and Events

Catch a double feature beneath the stars at the **Wellfleet Drive-In Theatre** (51 Rte. 6, Wellfleet, 508/349-7176, www.wellfleetcinemas.com, May-Sept. daily, $15 adults, $12 children 4-11, $10 seniors, under 4 free), which is also the site of a sprawling flea market on Saturdays and Sundays (call 508/349-0541 for updated flea market information).

If life in Wellfleet seems suspiciously quiet for a beach town, it's just because the party's at **The Beachcomber** (1120 Cahoon Hollow Rd., Wellfleet, 508/349-6055, www.thebeachcomber.com, Sun.-Thurs. 11:30am-9pm, Fri.-Sat. 11:30am-1am), an insanely popular beach bar and restaurant that's mostly known just as "da coma." Live music, powerful drinks, and an excellent location keep this place packed all summer; a laid-back daytime crowd of families is replaced by a raging crew of 20-somethings as the moon pops out of the ocean.

Learn the basics of opening oysters, or test your skills against the pros in the annual shucking contest at **Wellfleet OysterFest** (mid-Oct., www.wellfleetspat.org), when the whole town turns out to celebrate its fabulous shellfish.

Shopping

Wellfleet's walkable town center is packed with over 20 **art galleries**, mostly concentrated on Commercial Street and Bank Street. The Wellfleet Art Galleries Association maintains an art map that most of the galleries keep in stock; favorites include **Left Bank Gallery** (25 Commercial St., Wellfleet, 508/349-9451, www.leftbankgallery.com, daily 10am-6pm), which has a large selection of works that celebrate coastal

That's Weird. . .

Three Sisters Lighthouse ruins at low tide

Cape Cod is where lofty architectural dreams meet the beauty and power of the sea. Oftentimes that marriage works out, as you can experience by ambling through Cape Cod's dreamy surfside towns. But sometimes, the sea calls the shots, engulfing all and leaving behind nothing but waterlogged ruins that visitors can hunt for today.

For a start, take **Nauset Light Beach.** Part of the Cape Cod National Seashore in Eastham, Nauset Beach draws hordes each summer, but the seasonal swimmers and suntanners tend to overlook one of the beach's most unique features: the crumbled foundation of an ancient lighthouse, which reveals itself as the tide goes out. This lighthouse was one of the Three Sisters lighthouses, which used to tower above the beach through the 19th century, only to be moved as gnarly weather and erosion literally reshaped the Cape Cod shoreline.

Stranger and eerier is **Billingsgate Island,** a former fishing village on an isle near Wellfleet, sometimes dubbed "the Atlantis of Cape Cod." In 1885, life here took a briny nosedive when a monster storm almost sliced the island in half. Erosion gnawed away at what remained, and by 1912, the island was abandoned (some houses were literally floated across the bay) and the ghost town was swallowed by the sea. But something survived—wooden posts and foundation stones from the lost village that once thrived here. These ruins are now part of a sandbar that resurfaces during low tide, and you can visit them by boat. (The GPS coordinates are 41.8717, -70.0694.)

landscapes, including home furnishings, and **Frying Pan Gallery** (250 Commercial St., Wellfleet, 508/349-0011, www.fryingpangallery.com, May-Oct. Sun.-Thurs. 10am-6pm, Fri.-Sat. 10am-8pm), whose contemporary showcases have included marine-inspired steel sculptures by Cape-based artist Steve Swain.

There are art shops and boutiques in between Wellfleet's pretty galleries, and one fabulous bookstore-cum-seafood joint: **The Bookstore & Restaurant** (50 Kendrick Ave., Wellfleet, 508/349-3154, www.wellfleetoyster.com, daily 11:30am-9pm) carries rare and antique books (perhaps infused with a light, briny scent from the neighboring oyster beds).

Sports and Recreation

Beaches

The finest beaches on the Cape are those in Cape Cod National Seashore, which has miles of sand for walking, swimming, and soaking up the sun. And fishers and seals aren't the only thing you'll spot from the Cape's beaches—the Atlantic coast is a destination for surfers. Hardcore riders hit the beaches when hurricanes stir up enormous swells, but relatively gentle waves and sandy bottoms mean that Cape Cod's surf breaks are very beginner-friendly. Wellfleet's **Marconi Beach** and **Whitecrest Beach** are a good place to start; pick up a rental board at **SICKDAY** (361 Main St., Wellfleet, 508/214-4158, www.sickday.cc, Mon.-Sat. 9am-8pm, $30 board, $18 wetsuit). For beginning surfers, **Sacred Surf School** (4900 Rte. 6, Eastham, 508/415-1555, www.sacredsurfschool.com, $100-180) offers very well reviewed private and group lessons.

Hiking and Biking

Spot migratory birds in the salt marshes, barrier beaches, and pine forests of **Wellfleet Bay Wildlife Sanctuary** (291 Rte. 6, Wellfleet, 508/349-2615, www.massaudubon.org, daily 9am-4pm, $8 adults, $5 seniors, $3 children 2-12). Five miles (8 km) of walking trails wind through the property, and it's common to see fiddler crabs, herons, and kingfishers along the way. Inside the sanctuary's small nature center are aquariums and art focused on Cape Cod's coastal ecosystems.

The 22-mile (35.4-km) **Cape Cod Rail Trail** ends in Wellfleet at LeCount Hollow Road (parking $5). If you're renting wheels in town, you can leave your vehicle at **The Little Capistrano Bike Shop** (1446 Rte. 6, Wellfleet, 508/255-6515, www.littlecapistranobikeshop.com, May-Oct. daily 9am-4pm, bikes from $27 8 hrs and $30 24 hrs); this is also a good stop for maps and advice.

Food

Eastham

Arnold's Lobster & Clam Bar (3580 Rte. 6, 508/255-2575, www.arnoldsrestaurant.com, late May-Oct. Sun.-Mon. and Wed.-Thurs. 11:30am-8pm, Fri.-Sat. 11:30am-8:30pm, $11-28) is a Cape Cod clam shack that's spit-shined and streamlined, and it's about as kid-friendly as it gets. Children's meals come on Frisbees, and the "shack" is in a shiny indoor cafeteria. In addition to well-made standards like fried seafood, lobster rolls, and chowder, Arnold's has a raw bar with ultra-fresh seafood and oysters.

Even oyster farmers need a break from chowder sometimes, and the unexpected, vibrant **Casa del Cabo** (3 Main St., 774/801-2743, www.casadelcaboeastham.com, dinner Mon.-Sun. 4pm-9pm, breakfast Sat.-Mon. 8am-1pm, $20-34) delivers with hearty and inventive Pan Latin cuisine like chorizo stew with saffron rice, or the vegan "Incan Bowl" with garlic-chili tofu and a palette of fresh veggies. The gregarious atmosphere makes this a lively place to dine, and the weekend breakfast menu runs the gamut from greasy spoon classics to saucier offerings such as shrimp and polenta.

A staggering array of hand-cut cake doughnuts are the star attraction at **Hole in One** (4295 Rte. 6, 508/255-9446, www.theholecapecod.com, daily 6am-2pm, $4-9); the sweet treats are worth the wait even when the line stretches out of the door. Arrive early to enjoy yours with coffee at a long counter lined with classic diner stools.

Wellfleet

Wellfleet's got its very own spiffed-up clam shack, and **Moby Dick's** (3225 Rte. 6, 508/349-9795, www.mobys.com, late May-Oct. daily 11:30am-8:30pm, $13-28) is a favorite for relaxed, family-friendly seafood. Locals are divided about whose chowder and clams win out, but the BYO drinks policy at this spot might just tip the balance.

Surely the first (and only) of its kind, **The Bookstore & Restaurant** (50 Kendrick Ave., 508/349-3154, www.wellfleetoyster.com, daily 11:30am-9pm,

$18-33) is just what the name suggests—plus an oyster farm. Order a dozen on the half shell here, and you know they came from just across the street at the family's oyster beds; shellfish and fish stews are the stars of the menu, which also has burgers, salads, and pastas for landlubbers. There's nothing fancy about this place, but seating on the deck is the perfect place to watch a Wellfleet sunset, and the downstairs bar—the **Bomb Shelter**—is a pleasantly divey bar with pool, foosball, and a local crowd most nights of the week.

Cyclists riding the length of the Cape Cod Rail Trail train their sights on the Paris-perfect tarts and éclairs at ★ **PB Boulangerie Bistro** (15 Lecount Hollow Rd., 508/349-1600, www.pbboulangeriebistro.com, Wed.-Mon. 7am-6pm, $3-8, bistro Wed.-Sun. 5pm-9pm, $12-45), along with beautiful croissants and oozy croque monsieur sandwiches. The weekend bistro menu features old-school French classics like canard à l'orange and house-made pâté de campagne, as well as American-style brunch with continental flair. You won't miss the bright pink building by the side of the road.

Get beach snacks and drinks at the little **Wellfleet Marketplace** (295 Main St., 508/349-3156, www.wellfleetmarketplace.com, daily 7am-7pm) in the center of town, which also has a deli and a surprisingly bountiful book section with titles from local authors, which you can peruse as your sandwiches are prepared.

Accommodations and Camping

In a cheerfully painted Victorian home, ★ **Inn at the Oaks** (3085 Rte. 6, Eastham, 508/255-1886, www.innattheoaks.com, $240-425) retains a historic feel that's fresh, bright, and accommodating. The inn is full of nautical flourishes and tempting spots to curl up with a book, the generous continental breakfast includes fresh fruit and baked goods, and warm homemade cookies appear like clockwork in the afternoon. Henry Beston stayed at the inn while visiting the Cape and writing his classic book *The Outermost House*, which helped inspire the creation of Cape Cod National Seashore.

Like Hyannis and Martha's Vineyard, the Cape has a hostel affiliated with Hostelling International USA: ★ **HI Truro** (111 N. Pamet Rd., Truro, 508/349-3889, late June-early Sept., dorms from $49, private rooms from $179) has beautiful sea views—the building was originally constructed as a Coast Guard Station—and you can reach the beach by a sandy trail through the dunes. There's a communal kitchen.

You can't beat the location of ★ **North of Highland Camping Area** (52 Head of the Meadow Rd., North Truro, 508/487-1191, www.capecodcamping.com, late May-mid-Oct., $55 campsite, $15 additional vehicle, rates are for two adults, extra people $15 adults and $5 children), which is a short walk from Head of the Meadow Beach, one of the prettiest along the Cape Cod National Seashore. Scattered in a 58-acre (23.5-ha) sandy pine forest are 237 sites with picnic tables, and the campground has laundry facilities, showers, and a recreation hall with games and a fireplace. There are no fires in the camping area, but there's often a stack of free wood available that you can haul to the beach ($10 beach fire permits are available at www.truro-ma.gov).

Information

The **Eastham Tourist Information Booth** (1700 Rte. 6 at Governor Prence Rd., Eastham, 508/255-3444, www.easthamchamber.com, late May-mid-Oct. daily 9am-7pm) doles out information on local businesses, maps, and local tides.

Provincetown

Provincetown's eclectic population of artists, writers, and creative types like to call it "the end of the world." This curling, shifting plot of sand does feel like a place apart. It's easy to imagine how barren it looked when the Mayflower Pilgrims stopped in November 1620 to pen the famous Mayflower Compact on the shore. As the Native American Nauset tribe knew, however, there was a bounty beneath the waves: Provincetown eventually grew into a thriving fishing and whaling village with a strong Portuguese heritage.

By the late 19th century, the village had become a destination for painters, playwrights, and novelists drawn to the spot's scenic isolation. Rustic shacks began to appear amid the rolling sand and wild roses, creating what became the oldest artist colony in the United States. Over the years, luminaries from Eugene O'Neill to Jack Kerouac, Norman Mailer, and Jackson Pollock came to the end of the Cape to work amid the dunes.

Even as the town has acquired a measure of wealth and commercialism, the undeveloped dunes and shacks remain a refuge. Perhaps because of its creative spirit and spontaneity, P-town has been one of America's most popular LGBTQ+ vacation spots for decades. On any summer Saturday evening, Commercial Street is a bustling mix of vacationing families, drag show touts, wedding processions, and revelers kicking off parties that will still be going strong at sunrise.

Sights

Lighthouses

Provincetown's three lighthouses are among the prettiest on the Cape. The most easily accessible is the 45-foot (14-m) cast-iron **Race Point Light** (Race Point Beach, Rte. 6, 855/722-3959, www.racepointlighthouse.org), built in 1876 to replace an existing stone structure. It can be reached by a 30-minute walk over marsh grass and sand to the far edge of the Cape from the parking lot at **Province Lands Visitor Center** (171 Race Point Rd., 508/487-1256, May-Oct. daily 9am-5pm). It's open for tours on the first and third Saturdays from June to October between 10am and 2pm. You can also stay in the adjoining keeper's house during the summer, when it becomes a bed-and-breakfast.

The other two beacons stand sentinel on the bay side of Provincetown's curving claw. You can hike 1.25 miles (2 km) across the **causeway** at the west end of town to reach **Wood End Light.** From there, continue another 1.5 miles (2.4 km) to **Long Point Light.** Most of the walk is along soft sand, so it can take *much* longer than you expect. Another way to reach Long Point Light is on a boat shuttle from **Flyer's Boat Rental** (131A Commercial St., 508/487-0898, www.flyersboats.com, daily half hourly departures 10am-5pm during summer months, $20 one-way, $25 round-trip).

Pilgrim Monument & Provincetown Museum

Before the Pilgrims touched down at Plymouth Rock, they spent five weeks in Provincetown, where they wrote the Mayflower Compact and met the Nauset Indians for the first time. The **Pilgrim Monument** (High Pole Hill Rd., 508/487-1310, www.pilgrim-monument.org, Wed.-Mon. 10am-5pm, $21 adults, $17 seniors and students, $9 children 4-12, free children under 4, free parking with admission) that memorializes their landfall is an Italianate tower dominating the skyline and offering unmatched views. After you make it up (and down) the tower's 60 ramps and 116 steps, visit the small **Provincetown Museum,** whose classically kitschy dioramas depict the story of the Pilgrims in living color. The museum also has an interesting collection of Wampanoag artifacts, Cape Cod furniture, household items, and ephemera.

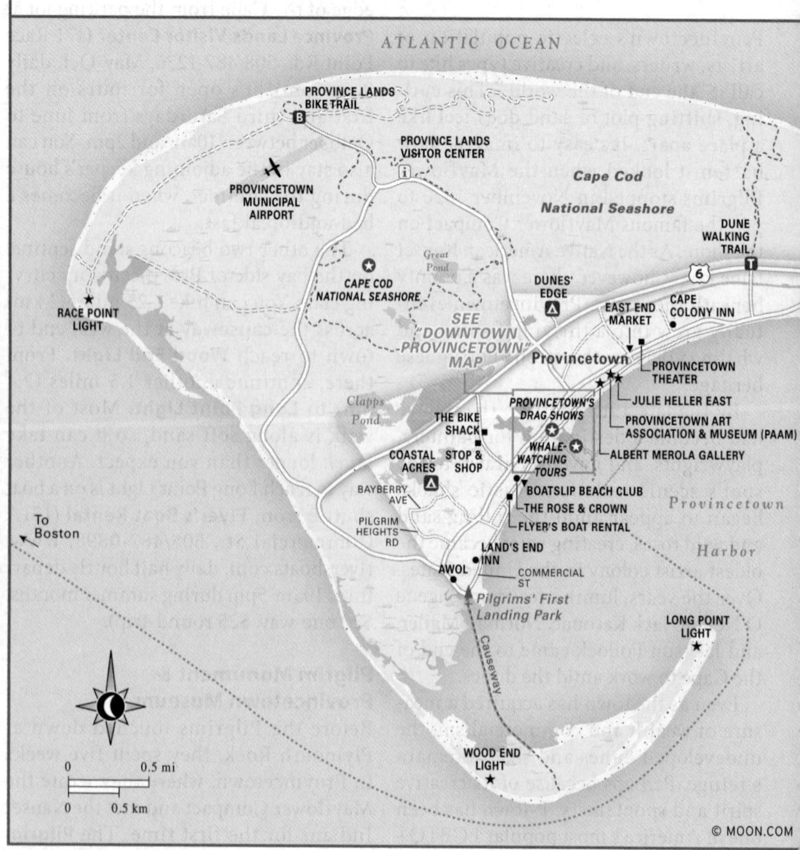

Provincetown Art

Decades of artists that fell for the life and lines of Cape Cod mean a downtown that's packed with galleries, right between the T-shirt shops and drag bars. The majority are on Commercial Street between Montello Street to the west, and Howland Street, at the eastern edge of the strip. From east to west, some not-to-be-missed galleries include **Julie Heller East** (465 Commercial St., 508/487-2166, www.juliehellergallery.com, Mon. and Thurs. 2:30pm-8pm, Tues. and Wed. 10:30am-6pm, Fri. 3pm-8pm, Sat.-Sun. 12:30pm-8pm), where the art historian owner curates a collection of historic and modern Provincetown artists, offering a fascinating look at the Cape's evolving art. The **Albert Merola Gallery** (424 Commercial St., 508/487-4424, www.albertmerolagallery.com) also has a good collection of contemporary and historic work from the Cape. Opening hours are typically 11am-4pm daily in season (June-Sept.) though these times can vary, especially in off-season, so call ahead for information or to make an appointment.

If you were only to make one stop for art in Provincetown, however, the **Provincetown Art Association and**

Downtown Provincetown

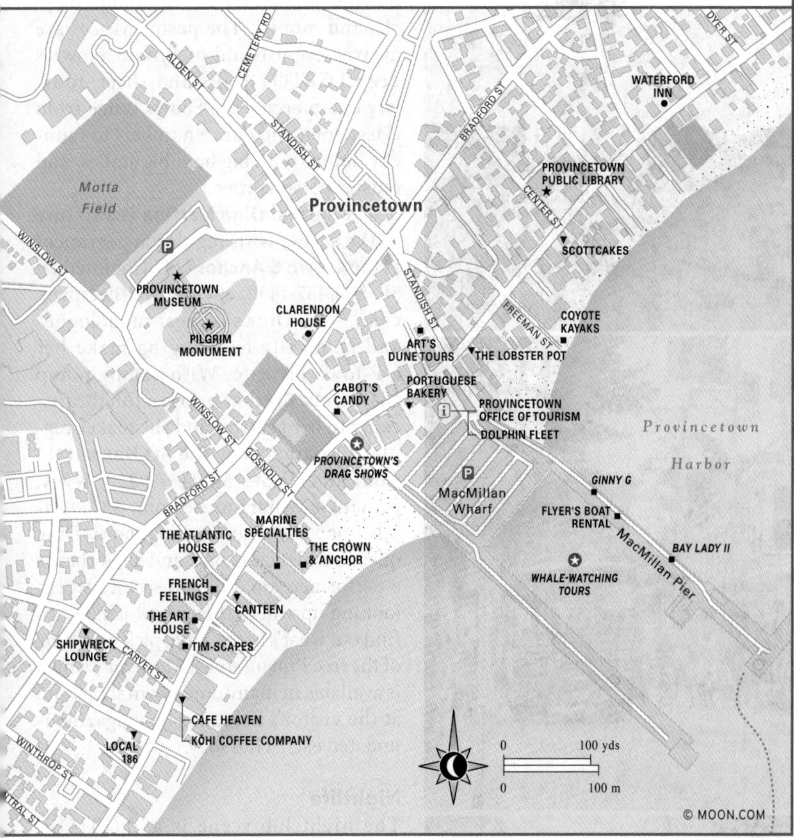

Museum (460 Commercial St., 508/487-1750, www.paam.org, Nov.-Apr. Thurs.-Sun. noon-5pm, May-Oct. Wed.-Thurs. and Sat.-Mon. 11am-5pm, Fri. 11am-8pm, $15) is a treasure trove of Cape Cod and Provincetown art.

Other Sights

Step on the same ground that the Pilgrims did at **Pilgrim's First Landing Park** at the west end of Commercial Street. A plaque there memorializes the Pilgrims' touchdown on November 21, 1620.

It would be easy to read away a rainy day on the coast at the **Provincetown Public Library** (356 Commercial St., 508/487-7094, www.provincetownlibrary.org, Mon. and Fri. 10am-5pm, Tues.-Thurs. 10am-8pm, Sat.-Sun. 1pm-5pm), which has a great collection of books on the area. Stop in to look at the half-size replica of the *Rose Dorothea* fishing schooner, which sails the stacks on the library's 2nd floor.

Entertainment and Events

★ Drag Shows

The drag scene is a classic P-town experience. You don't need to look for a drag show in Provincetown, as one is

likely to find you—watch for flamboyantly dressed performers careening down Commercial Street on foot, bicycle, and moped. The performances are an irreverent blend of Provincetown's deep LGBTQ+ roots and sheer, touristy commercialism. Shows range from classy song and dance numbers to raunchy humor with big hair, big smiles, and outsize personalities.

The surreal **Dina Martina** is a fixture of the scene, with regular appearances at the **Crown & Anchor** (247 Commercial St., 508/487-1430, www.onlyatthecrown.com, $40). Dina's offbeat monologues and comically bad singing make her a P-town favorite. With vampy pinup charm, **Miz Cracker** brings a fun theatricality to her routine, and she makes regular appearances at **The Art House** (214 Commercial St., 508/487-9222, www.provincetownarthouse.com, $43), another popular venue for drag shows. Drag queen residencies come and go; if there's a performer you'd like to see, it's worth looking up where their show is now. To find out what's happening, pick up a copy of the free *Provincetown Magazine,* which is available in many downtown shops and at the visitor's bureau. The magazine is updated each Thursday.

Nightlife

The nightclub scene is as LGBTQ+-friendly as any in New England. Some venues are scene-specific, while others have open-door policies. Festivities kick off early at the late-afternoon **Tea Dance** at the **Boatslip Beach Club** (161 Commercial St., 508/487-1669, www.theboatslip.com, summertime daily 4pm-7pm, spring and fall weekends 4pm-7pm), where revelers sip dangerously powerful planter's punch, which sloughs both inhibitions and clothing.

Predominantly for men, the **Atlantic House** (4-6 Masonic Pl., 508/487-3169,

Top to bottom: Wood End Light; Commercial Street in Provincetown; Carnival street parade

www.ahouse.com) is a classic gay nightclub with underwear-clad bartenders, smoke machines, and an upstairs **Macho Bar** (10pm-1am) that features lots of leather, Levi's, and sexy videos on continuous loop. The Atlantic House also includes the **Little Bar** (noon-1am) and **Big Room bar** (10pm-1am). Most of the patrons stay fully clothed at the **Shipwreck Lounge** (67 Bradford St., 508/487-9005, www.brasskey.com, daily 5pm-1am), which feels like a cozy beach house living room with excellent cocktails.

Theater

Local thespians date the beginning of American drama to 1916, when the first Eugene O'Neill play was performed on P-town's Lewis Wharf. The theater community was reborn in 2001 with the construction of the beautiful 200-seat **Provincetown Theater** (238 Bradford St., 508/487-7487, www.provincetowntheater.org, $25-75), which stages everything from campy musicals to heart-wrenching original dramas.

Festivals and Events

Filmmaker John Waters is a regular at the **Provincetown International Film Festival** (508/487-3456, www.provincetownfilm.org, mid-June), which showcases truly independent films. The town's thriving fishing community celebrates its heritage during the weekend-long **Provincetown Portuguese Festival** (www.provincetownportuguesefestival.com, late June, free), which culminates with the annual "Blessing of the Fleet." The **Fourth of July Celebration** (508/487-3424, www.ptownchamber.com, July 4, free) has the best beachside fireworks on the Cape. Last but not least, **Carnival Week** (508/487-2313, www.ptown.org, late Aug.) is a seven-day Mardi Gras celebration that features a parade, elaborate dance parties, and performances by internationally renowned drag queens.

But during the summer months in Provincetown, it seems like every week is a "week," with a different slice of the scene seizing a piece of the calendar, from bears (stop by in early July to fête large, hairy men with a leather-vest take on masculinity) to whales (come the last week in July to celebrate the marine mammal).

Shopping

Art galleries, penny candy stores, and sex shops line Commercial Street, which is the best place in Cape Cod to browse for souvenirs and unique gifts. A few boutiques stock wonderfully curated collections of clothes and accessories. Browse the latest fashions and fragrances from across the Atlantic at **French Feelings** (220 Commercial St., 774/593-5931, www.facebook.com/frenchfeelings, May-Nov. daily 10am-10pm). At **Tim-Scapes** (208 Commercial St., 917/626-4052, www.tim-scapes.com, late May-early Sept. Sun.-Wed. 11am-7pm, Thurs.-Sat. 11am-8pm, Sept.-May Fri.-Mon. 11am-5pm), artist Tim Convery uses duct tape to create bold graphic designs. Find diving bells, antique life-saving rings, and other intriguing flotsam at **Marine Specialties** (235 Commercial St., 508/487-1730, Mon.-Thurs. 10am-10:30pm, Fri. 9:30am-11pm, Sat.-Sun. 9am-11pm), and stock up on penny candy or saltwater taffy at **Cabot's Candy** (276 Commercial St., 508/487-3550, www.cabotscandy.com, Mon.-Thurs. 10am-9pm, Fri.-Sun. 10am-10pm).

Sports and Recreation

★ Whale-Watching Tours

Just north of Land's End is a shallow, sandy rise in the ocean floor called Stellwagen Bank, where nutrient-rich upwelling and a U.S. National Marine Sanctuary attract a diverse population of dolphins, sea turtles, and whales. From April to October, whales migrate to this coast to feed on schooling fish, and a dozen tour operators offer trips into the sanctuary to spot humpback, finback, minke, sei, and pilot whales. In the winter

Local Legend

Provincetown has long been one of America's most LGBTQ+-friendly locales. For comedian and activist **Kristen Becker,** it was a gateway to another life. After growing up in the Deep South, Becker was introduced to P-town through comedy touring. She dug the scene so much that she not only relocated here but also founded **Summer of Sass** (www.summerofsass.org)—a program that makes it possible for 18- to 20-year-old LGBTQ+ adults from conservative regions of America to spend a summer in P-town, sharing a house together, working for local businesses, exploring the landscape, and experiencing how much better life can get.

Kristen Becker

You came to P-town from a region that's not exactly renowned for social liberalism. How did it feel to arrive here?

Whenever you belong, when you are the Other and you end up in a tribe of Others, you immediately go, "Oh, I'm fine! I was just in the wrong place." There's a default level of comfort for the queer community in P-town, but that also extends to the broader community of Cape Cod. You're surrounded by water and dunes. It can feel like a naturally healing place for anyone.

That seems to foreshadow how you came up with Summer of Sass, but what was the catalyst for this project?

People are always telling queer young people "it gets better," and that's great if you're in San Francisco. But if you're stuck in Tyler, Texas, you probably don't know what "better" looks like yet. In 2016, I was on a comedy tour, and when I visited Shreveport, Louisiana, where I went to high school, I read this article in the paper about a kid named Teddy who had to graduate high school early because he was bullied so much [for his sexual orientation]. This was around the time of the Trump election, and one of the first things Trump did was suspend J1 visas. This created a seasonal worker shortage on the Cape. And Teddy ended up becoming our first "Sasser" that summer.

So, what are some of the places where Cape Cod visitors might encounter Sassers getting a taste of P-town life?

We've had bike shop kids, waiters, retail gallery specialists, and more. I talk with each person at the beginning of the season about what they're interested in, and we try to match them with an ideal job. Some have no work experience just because their presentation makes them unhireable in the places they're coming from, so my goal is to meet them where they are, and help them get toward where they want to be heading. Each Sasser's experience is unique. One thing we do together, though, is a little expedition where we cross the Provincetown breakwater on the rock jetty that goes across the bay to the Wood End lighthouse. It's challenging and just scary enough to be a confidence booster for anyone.

of 2016, a cluster of endangered right whales appeared off the Cape Cod coast, a sign that the struggling population has found a safe, nourishing place to feed; a whale-watching tour is a rare chance to spot one of the known 340-some surviving right whales, many of which visit the Cape each year.

The **Dolphin Fleet** (MacMillan Pier, 800/826-9300, www.whalewatch.com, mid-Apr.-Oct., $57 adults, $32 children 5-12, free children under 5) departs many times a day during the season from downtown Providence, with open decks, enclosed cabins, and free tickets if no whales are sighted. Onboard naturalists help identify any fins and flukes you spot, and, though they're not always operated, some of their boats are equipped with hydrophones for listening for whale vocalizations. A trip with a Dolphin Fleet boat can sometimes feel like hitching ride on a marine research vessel, as the naturalists' efforts to photograph and track the whales is a pillar of conservation efforts. The fleet's operating practices are in accordance with guidelines established by NOAA to minimize impacts on the whales' territory. Tours last 3-4 hours.

Beaches

Stunning **Race Point Beach** is an eight-mile (13-km) stretch of crashing waves and soft sand edged with dune grass. To access the beach, park at the **Province Lands Visitor Center** (171 Race Point Rd., 508/487-1256, May-Oct. daily 9am-5pm), which has observation decks, interpretive displays, and a knowledgeable staff. For sunsets over the surf, it's hard to beat a spot at **Herring Cove Beach,** a peaceful swath that's just a few miles from the center of Provincetown. Turn right at the parking lot to set up at the family-oriented part of the beach, or turn left to reach the more swinging real estate, where visitors tend to self-sort by gender and orientation.

Like other beaches in the Cape Cod National Seashore, parking fees and entrance fees are collected in season ($25 cars, $20 motorcycles, $15 pedestrians). Parking lots get crowded, so it's worthwhile to access the beaches by public transport or bicycle. Shuttles leave Macmillan Wharf for Race Point every 30 minutes 9am-8pm and for Herring Cove every 30 minutes 9am-8pm (visit https://capecodrta.org for more information). To get to Race Point by bike, head down Conwell Street to Race Point Road, where a bike path parallels the roadway. For Herring Cove, cyclists have two options: They can ride right on Route 6, or take the longer but nicer ride along the bike path through the Province Lands. Pick up the trail at the Beech Forest Parking Area off of Race Point Road.

Boating and Fishing

Rent anything from a kayak to a 19-foot (6-m) sloop at **Flyer's Boat Rental** (131A Commercial St., 508/487-0898, www.flyersboats.com, starting at $25). Find a stand-up paddleboard at **Coyote Kayaks** (333R Commercial St., 508/413-9563, www.coyotekayaks.com, $30/hr, $40/4 hrs). The 73-foot (22-m) gaff-rigged schooner ***Bay Lady II*** (20 Berry Ln., 508/487-9308, www.sailcapecod.com, $50-55 adults, $25 children) sails several times daily for the Corn Hill bluffs and Long Point Light. Sportfishing boats lining Macmillan Wharf include the ***Ginny G*** (508/246-3656, www.ginnygcapecodcharters.com), which goes in search of bluefish, bass, cod, and tuna.

Hiking and Biking

Just across from Provincetown's vibrant downtown are the **Province Lands,** a rugged, shifting stretch of dunes that can feel wild and otherworldly, a transporting reminder of why generations of artists came to the Cape to escape the world. The sand is held together with webs of wild, five-petaled roses and grass, sagging fences, and a few spiny scrub pines, and is especially stunning in the fall, when the plants take on a subtle rusty hue. The artists' shacks are the only rustic structures in the dunes, without electricity or running water.

A good place to orient yourself to the dune's natural history, plants, and trails is the **Province Lands Visitor Center** (171 Race Point Rd., 508/487-1256, May-Oct. daily 9am-5pm), which offers ranger-guided hikes and outings.

To see the dune's historic and scenic highlights, though, you can't beat local knowledge, and **Art's Dune Tours** (4 Standish St., 508/487-1950, www.facebook.com/artsdunetours, Apr.-Nov., $40 adults, $21 children 5-8, $15 children under 5) has operated tours of the sand in 4x4 vehicles since 1946. Art's offers every possible variation on the dune tour—add a sunset, clambake, lighthouse, lake, or kayak trip—and has several departures daily.

One of the best **walking trails** into the dunes starts at **Snail Road** off Route 6. Limited parking is available. A sandy road leads to a path that winds past dunes, shacks, and hollows to the shore. It's just a mile or so (about 1.6 km) to the beach, but wandering up and over soft dunes takes much longer than hiking on firm ground. The trail braids and splits at times, so take note of your route throughout the walk and bring shoes and plenty of water—the sand gets surprisingly hot.

Or do as P-town locals do: Park your car and explore on two wheels. An excellent network of bike path and bike-friendly roads makes it easy. The 5.45-mile (8.8-km) **Province Lands Bike Trail** is a dreamy route through dunes with spurs to Race Point Beach and Herring Cove Beach. Pick up a map of the trail at **Province Lands Visitors Center** (Race Point Rd., 508/487-1256, May-Oct. daily 9am-5pm) at a bike shop in town, or online at the National Park Service website (https://nps.gov/caco/planyourvisit/province-lands-bike-trail.htm). The NPS webpage also offers information on natural hazards that can befall certain segments of the trail seasonally,

Lobster Pot

such as flooding and sand drifts. To rent a bike, stop by **The Bike Shack** (63 Shank Painter Rd., 508/487-0232, www.provincetownbikeshack.com, from $10/hr or $17/day), whose fleet includes beach cruisers, road and mountain bikes, and baby trailers.

Food

Provincetown is lined with excellent places to eat, mostly clustered around Commercial Street. Business hours can vary with season and demand; restaurants sometimes close early on slow nights or keep serving as long as the tables are full. It's always worth calling ahead.

It's hard not to love ★ **Canteen** (225 Commercial St., 508/487-3800, www.thecanteenptown.com, Mon.-Thurs. 11am-9pm, Fri.-Sun. 10am-10pm, off-season hours and days vary, $10-23), a tourist joint that's also a local favorite. The nautical theme of this casual lunch spot is bright and hip. The lack of elbow room at large communal tables makes it easy to make friends over plates of excellent fish-and-chips, crispy brussels sprouts, house-made Portuguese sausage, and a good selection of local beers on draft.

The distinctive neon sign at the **Lobster Pot** (321 Commercial St., 508/487-0842, www.ptownlobsterpot.com, late Apr./early May-Nov. daily 11:30am-9pm, $20-34) has been signaling chowder-hungry crowds for years. Among the dozens of places that claim "best chowder" on the Cape, the Lobster Pot is a strong contender. The Portuguese soup is another favorite dish that's steeped in Cape Cod history, and the long menu meanders onto lobster, steaks, tacos, and sushi. The cavernous restaurant has table seating on two levels, and a bar upstairs—the 2nd floor has better views. The raw bar is a good alternative when the wait for a table gets long.

Decked with bright, big art and handwritten menu boards, **Café Heaven** (199 Commercial St., 508/487-1991, www.cafeheavenptown.com, Apr.-Nov. Thurs.-Tues. 8am-2pm and 5:30pm-9pm, $10-22) is a cheerful spot for breakfasting on piles of French toast, home fries, pancakes, and fruit. The compact café stays busy throughout the day, serving sandwiches on homemade bread, as well as hearty soups and salads.

Enjoy a chewy, sugary taste of Cape Cod's heritage at **Portuguese Bakery** (299 Commercial St., 508/487-1803, ww.provincetownportuguesebakery.com, Apr.-Nov. daily 8am-6pm, $3-8), which piles their shelves with fried-dough malasadas, lightly caramelized egg tarts, and cream-filled bolas de berlim.

Burgers made with pasture-raised beef and topped with everything from fried avocado to lobster are the stars of the menu at **Local 186** (186 Commercial St., 508/478-7555, www.local186.com, May-Oct. Thurs.-Tues. 11:30am-10pm, $17-26), a stylish restaurant with butcher charts painted on the walls and a sunny porch for prime people-watching. A solid draft list and creative cocktails round out the menu of clams, oysters, and salads.

When pink-frosted cupcakes are all that will do, head to **ScottCakes** (353 Commercial St., 508/487-7465, www.scottcakes.com, daily 11am-midnight, $2-6), where pink-frosted cupcakes are all that's on the menu. The simple yellow cakes are a P-town icon and the pink hole-in-the-wall bakeshop is just as sweet. Where else can you find a "legalize gay cupcakes" T-shirt?

Find the best coffee in Provincetown at the stylish, diminutive **Kōhi Coffee Company** (199 Commercial St., 774/538-6467, www.kohicoffee.com, daily 7am-7pm, $4-9), which brews organic, single-origin beans into espresso and pour-over drinks. On hot days, the lightly sweet chicory and coffee blend in the New Orleans cold brew is sublime. The tiny shop has a prime spot between the beach and Commercial Street.

Shop for made-to-order deli sandwiches, imported cheeses, and wines at **East End Market** (212 Bradford St., 508/487-2339, www.eastendmarketplace.com, daily 8am-7pm), or pick up supplies at **Stop & Shop** (56 Shank Painter Rd., 508/487-4903, Mon.-Sat. 6am-midnight, Sun. 6am-10pm).

Accommodations and Camping

Camping

Just a 10-minute walk from Provincetown, **Dunes' Edge Campground** (386 Rte. 6, 508/487-9815, www.thetrustees.org, late May-early Oct., basic sites $55, hookups $65-75) has 85 tent sites in a wooded area with coin-operated hot showers and laundry. The sites are small and relatively densely packed, so the campground can get pretty noisy on busy weekends. Sites often fill up weeks in advance, but a handful are released each morning, so it's worth calling on the same day. Slightly slapdash but very friendly, **Coastal Acres Campground** (76R Bayberry Ave., 508/487-1700, www.coastalacresprovincetown.com, Apr.-Nov., basic sites $75-86, hookups $103-115) is a mile (1.6 km) from downtown, with grassy sites and serviceable facilities.

Under $150

A painted figurehead greets guests arriving at the **Rose & Crown Guest House** (158 Commercial St., 508/487-3332, www.roseandcrownptown.com, rooms $95-250, apartments $150-300, parking $20/night), a unique place to stay in the center of town. Rooms are small but imaginatively designed; one is decked out with rose red fabrics and Victorian antiques, another features exposed wood beams, a vaulted ceiling, and oriental rugs. Two less-expensive rooms upstairs share a bath.

Offering something of a localized escape from the cacophony of downtown P-town, the **Cape Colony Inn** (280 Bradford St., 508/487-1755, www.capecolonyinn.com, $99-239) offers compact yet pleasantly decorated rooms with extra-plush mattresses, and convenient amenities such as a heated pool, gas grills, and lawn games. The restaurants and shops are an easy 15-minute walk away, and complimentary parking and continental breakfasts sweeten the deal.

$150-250

There are just six rooms in the **Clarendon House** (118 Bradford St., 508/680-4444, www.theclarendonhouse.com, June-Jan., $215-300, free parking), which was updated in 2016 with furniture that's old-fashioned but thoroughly unstuffy. The friendly owners are a highlight, as are full breakfasts and around-the-clock snacks, coffee, and tea.

Tucked amid Provincetown's art galleries, the **Waterford Inn** (386 Commercial St., 508/413-9892, www.thewaterfordinn.com, $186-338) spruces up cream-colored interiors with beautiful maritime paintings and stained glass, as well as the occasional well-placed 1950s tchotchke. Several of the luxury king bed rooms have balconies with banging views of the harbor, and each night of your stay includes a daily voucher for breakfast at **Far Land Provisions** (150 Bradford St., 508/487-0045, www.farlandprovisions.com), whose buttery pastries and hefty sandwiches earn nods of approval from the early bird crowd.

$250-350

The elegant, secluded ★ **Land's End Inn** (22 Commercial St., 508/487-0706, www.landsendinn.com, $395-725, free parking) commands sweeping views of the ocean, so guests can watch the sun rise—and set—from a glassed-in tower. The owner's exceptional collection of art nouveau antiques fills every conceivable nook of the common areas, while guest rooms feature skylights, interior balconies, and domed ceilings. A breakfast buffet, late afternoon wine reception, and 24-hour tea and coffee make this a soothing place to watch the tide come in.

One of the hotter, newer lodging arrivals to P-town is **AWOL** (59 Province Lands Rd., 508/413-9820, www.larkhotels.com/hotels/awolwww.awolhotel.com, $299-649). Forgoing the usual floral wallpaper and maritime trinkets you'll encounter at other Cape Cod hotels, AWOL offers more modern and minimalist interior design, with svelte rooms and suites that overlook the nearby ocean and estuaries. The complimentary s'mores offered each night (and best enjoyed by the fire pits) are a more grounding, homely touch. Free parking is available on-site.

Information

The **Provincetown Office of Tourism** (330 Commercial St., 508/487-7000, www.ptowntourism.com, Mon.-Thurs. 9am-5pm, Fri. 9am-noon) is conveniently located one block away from the ferry landing.

Getting Around

The Cape Cod Transit Authority runs the **Provincetown shuttle** (800/352-7155, www.capecodrta.org), which provides transport to the airport, beaches, and town center. Or let a strapping cyclist do the driving with **Ptown Pedicabs** (508/487-0660, www.ptownpedicabs.com).

Martha's Vineyard

Celebrity vacation spot, family retreat, rural getaway. . . after more than 200 years of summer people, Martha's Vineyard's diversity still comes as a surprise. It's easy to find your own slice of this wonderfully scenic island, whose quaint villages and tourist traps are interspersed with coastal dunes, pale beaches, and farmland. The Wampanoag tribe has a stronger presence here than elsewhere in the Cape and islands, and families of Vineyard sailors, farmers, and fishers still maintain deep roots.

It's a fun place to explore on a day trip to Oak Bluffs or Edgartown, but really experiencing the Vineyard means taking the time to discover back roads and up-island fishing villages. While the island has a reputation as an expensive retreat, prices aren't far off from those on Cape Cod. A wonderful hostel and campground offer a taste of Vineyard life on a budget.

Residents divide the island into **down-island** (east) and **up-island** (west). The former is home to the island's three main population centers: touristy Vineyard Haven, posh Edgartown, and charming Oak Bluffs. Up-island is more rural, with the cow pastures of West Tisbury and Chilmark sharing space with the scenic fishing village of Menemsha and the cliffs of Aquinnah.

Getting to Martha's Vineyard

Ferries to the Vineyard leave from Cape Cod, Nantucket, and departure points farther afield in New York, Massachusetts, and New Jersey.

From Woods Hole to Vineyard

One Day in Martha's Vineyard

Gay Head Light

Morning

Pack your bathing suit and walking shoes, and catch the first boat of the day to Oak Bluffs, a bustling community whose star attractions are walking distance from the ferry landing. After picking up pastries-to-go at **Back Door Donuts,** take a stroll through the winding streets of **The Campground,** a onetime Methodist revival camp lined with sweet Carpenter Gothic cottages in vibrant colors; then check out the statelier Victorians that surround the town green.

Afternoon

Enjoy the rural up-island scenery by heading north on the island bus to **Aquinnah Cliffs** and **Gay Head Light,** where you can meet members of the Vineyard's Wampanoag at the nearby shops.

Save room for pie after a seafood lunch at **Larsen's Fish Market,** then walk down to the nearby beach to watch for celebrities and soak up the sun before catching a bus back to Oak Bluffs, where a tempting array of souvenir shops, fudge stores, and boutiques stay bustling all summer.

Evening

Make your way back to Oak Bluffs as the sun begins to set and grab an early burger or pizza on the patio at **Offshore Ale Company.** Post-nosh, if you've got a few more minutes before leaving for the mainland, try to snag the brass ring at the **Flying Horses Carousel,** the oldest in the United States.

Haven or Oak Bluffs, take the year-round **Steamship Authority** (508/477-8600, www.steamshipauthority.com, 0.75 hr, round-trip tickets $20 adults, $11 children, $8 bicycles, $128 cars). From Falmouth to Oak Bluffs, take the passenger-only **Island Queen** (508/548-8400, www.islandqueen.com, late May-mid-Oct, 0.5 hr, round-trip tickets $27 adults, $16 children, $8 bicycles). **Hy-Line Cruises** (800/492-8082, www.hylinecruises.com, May-Oct., 1 hr, from Hyannis $70 adults, $43 children, $14 bicycles or from Nantucket $76 adults, $49 children, $14 bicycles) connects Hyannis and Nantucket with Vineyard Haven.

From New Bedford, New York City, Boston, and New Jersey take the

Seastreak (800/262-8743, www.seastreak.com, May-Oct. round-trip tickets from $79 adults, $48 children, $14 bicycles). During the summer, many flights a day are offered by **Cape Air** (508/771-6944, www.flycapeair.com) from Boston, New Bedford, Hyannis, and Nantucket.

Getting Around

Of all the islands off Cape Cod, Martha's Vineyard is on the larger size at 22 miles long and 9 miles wide (35 by 14 km). By car, it takes about 50 minutes to drive from one end of the island to the other, while biking the same route is usually a 3-4 hour endeavor. Meanwhile, a bus ride from the east side of the Vineyard to the west side will clock in just shy of 2 hours.

The **Martha's Vineyard Regional Transit Authority** (508/693-9440, www.vineyardtransit.com) runs buses between all of the towns. A bicycle or e-bike is an excellent way to explore the extensive paths and pretty winding roads. Try **Martha's Bike Rentals** (4 Lagoon Pond Rd., Vineyard Haven, 508/693-6593, www.marthasbikerentals.com, Apr.-Nov., 1-day rental from $29) or **MVeBike** (15 Circuit Avenue Ext., Oak Bluffs, 508/693-0515, www.pedegoelectricbikes.com, 1-day rental from $29).

Unless you are going to be spending a lot of time up-island, having a car is more trouble than it's worth, but **A-A Auto Island** (508/696-5300, www.mvautorental.com) offers convenient pickup locations in Oak Bluffs, Edgartown, and Vineyard Haven, as well as an airport branch.

Vineyard Haven

Ferries arriving in this compact harbor town thread past world-class sailing yachts, tall ships, and fishing boats guarded by an attractive pair of lighthouses. With tourist shops, historic homes, and a pair of public beaches right in town, Vineyard Haven is the first stop for most visitors to the island. Even at its most crowded it's remarkably charming.

Sights

The finest examples of mid-19th-century captain's houses are clustered in the **William Street Historic District** that runs south from Woodlawn Avenue to just past Camp Street. The best way to see the homes is following the self-guided walking tour available at the **Chamber of Commerce** (24 Beach St., 508/693-0085, www.mvy.com, Mon.-Fri. 9am-5pm).

It's an easy, two-mile (3.2-km) jaunt from downtown Vineyard Haven to **West Chop Light** (W. Chop Rd.). While the historic lighthouse isn't open to the public, the low picket fence allows for great views from the road.

Get a glimpse of Vineyard life before the fudge shops and celebrities at the **Martha's Vineyard Museum** (151 Lagoon Pond Rd., 508/627-4441, www.mvmuseum.org, early June-early Oct. Tues.-Sun., $18 adults, $15 seniors, $5 children 7-17, under 7 free). Kid-focused history exhibits make it a pleasant break from the beach. Artifacts from Martha's Vineyard's Wampanoag people, whalers, and early colonists offer a broad perspective on the island's past. The gorgeous Fresnel lens in the central atrium of the museum used to shine from the Gay Head Light.

Shopping

Find beautiful oil paintings of the island by a rotating lineup of local artists at **Louisa Gould Gallery** (54 Main St., 508/693-7373, www.louisagould.com, daily 11am-5pm). The best selection of books by local authors is at **Bunch of Grapes Bookstore** (23 Main St., 508/693-2291, www.bunchofgrapes.com, daily 9am-8pm).

Sports and Recreation

Beaches

Just a thin strip of sand off Main Street, **Owen Park Beach** might not be the island's most scenic, but its location not far from the ferry terminal is a good

Martha's Vineyard

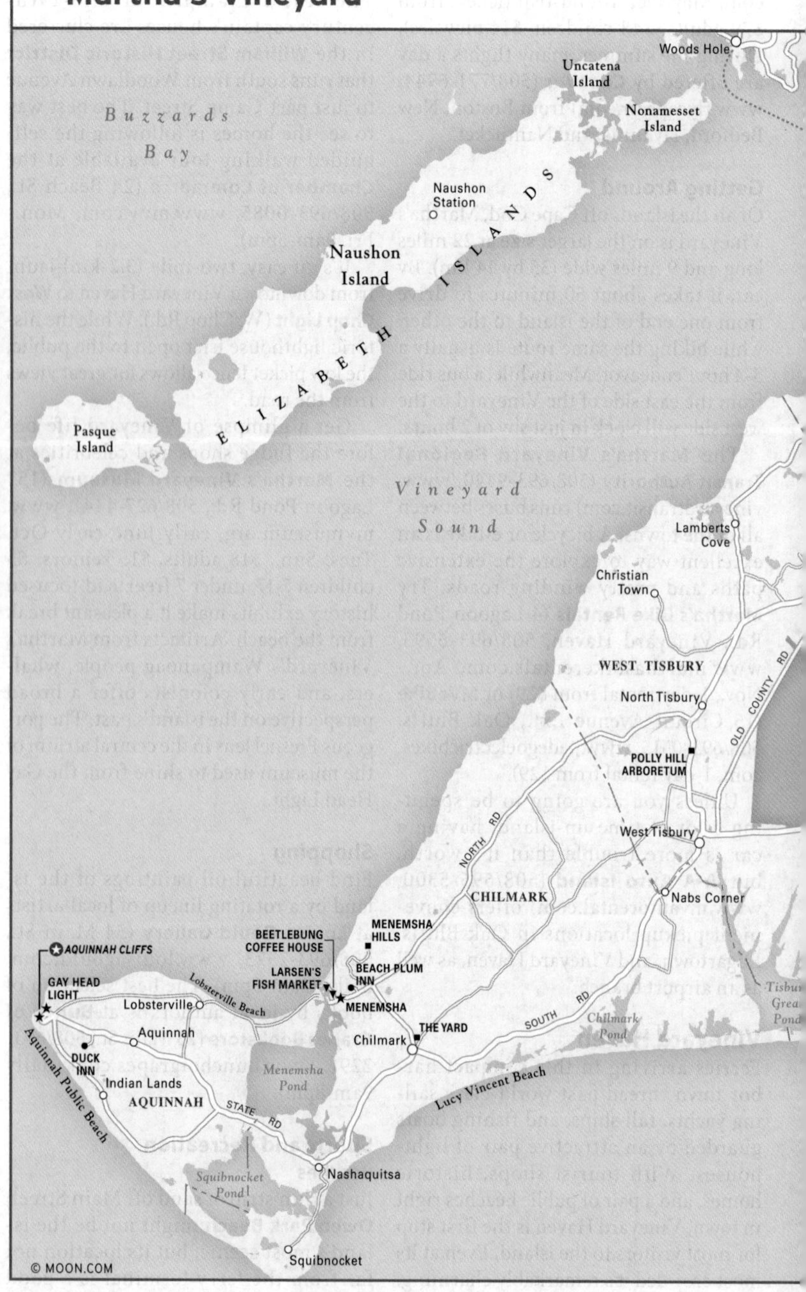

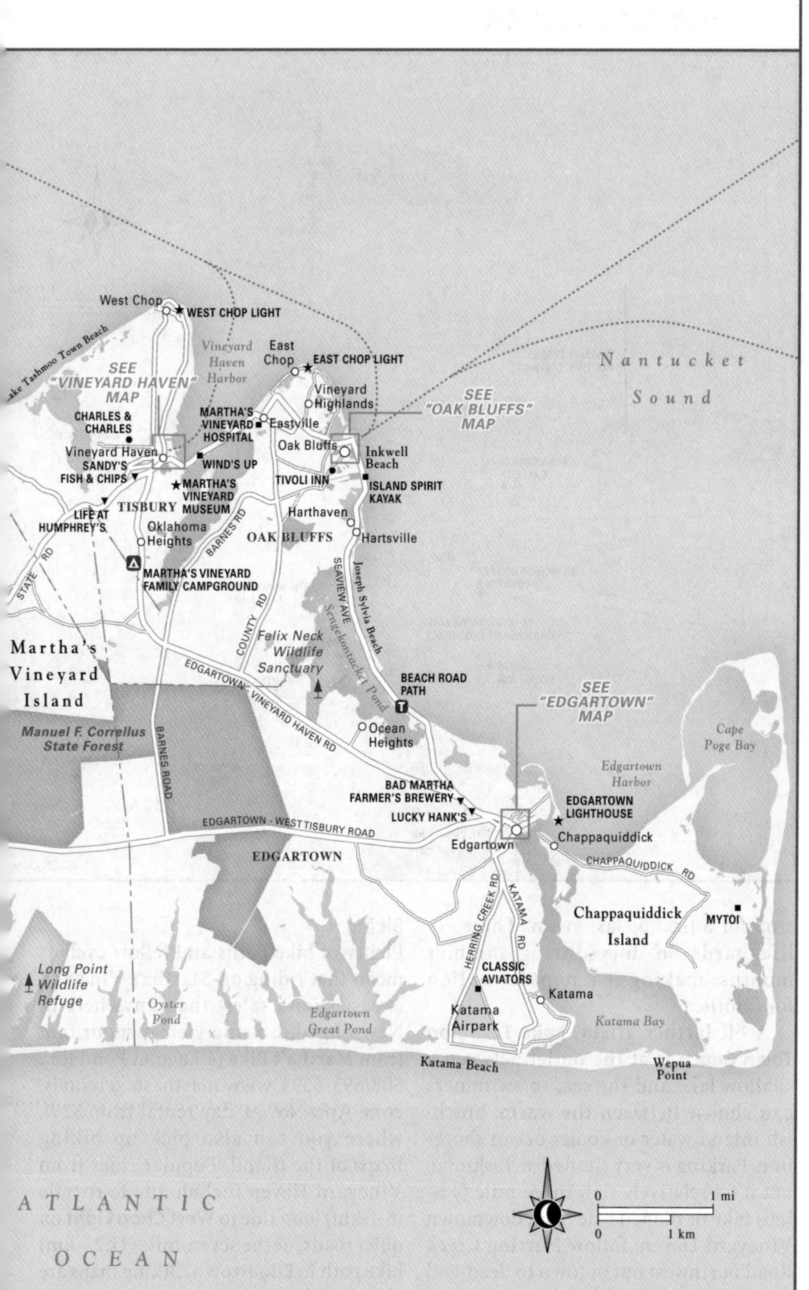
West Chop
WEST CHOP LIGHT
Lake Tashmoo Town Beach
SEE "VINEYARD HAVEN" MAP
Vineyard Haven Harbor
East Chop
EAST CHOP LIGHT
Vineyard Highlands
SEE "OAK BLUFFS" MAP
Nantucket
Sound
CHARLES & CHARLES
MARTHA'S VINEYARD HOSPITAL
Eastville
Oak Bluffs
Inkwell Beach
Vineyard Haven
WIND'S UP
SANDY'S FISH & CHIPS
TIVOLI INN
ISLAND SPIRIT KAYAK
MARTHA'S VINEYARD MUSEUM
LIFE AT HUMPHREY'S
TISBURY
Harthaven
Oklahoma Heights
OAK BLUFFS
Hartsville
BARNES RD
STATE RD
MARTHA'S VINEYARD FAMILY CAMPGROUND
SEAVIEW AVE
Joseph Sylvia Beach
COUNTY RD
Sengekontacket Pond
Felix Neck Wildlife Sanctuary
Martha's Vineyard Island
EDGARTOWN - VINEYARD HAVEN RD
BEACH ROAD PATH
SEE "EDGARTOWN" MAP
Manuel F. Correllus State Forest
BARNES ROAD
Ocean Heights
Cape Poge Bay
Edgartown Harbor
BAD MARTHA FARMER'S BREWERY
LUCKY HANK'S
EDGARTOWN LIGHTHOUSE
EDGARTOWN - WEST TISBURY ROAD
Chappaquiddick
Edgartown
EDGARTOWN
CHAPPAQUIDDICK RD
HERRING CREEK RD
KATAMA RD
Chappaquiddick Island
MYTOI
CLASSIC AVIATORS
Katama
Long Point Wildlife Refuge
Oyster Pond
Edgartown Great Pond
Katama Airpark
Katama Bay
Katama Beach
Wepua Point
ATLANTIC
OCEAN
0
1 mi
0
1 km

Vineyard Haven

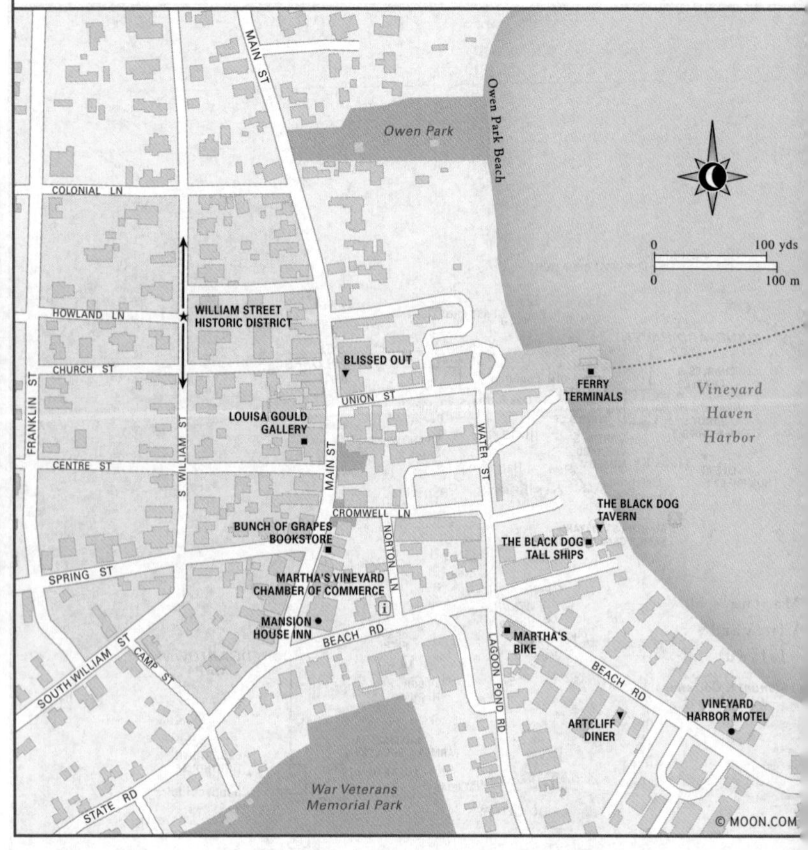

stop for a first or last swim. There are lifeguards on duty during summer months, making it a popular option for families.

A bit farther afield, **Lake Tashmoo Town Beach** is at the outlet between a shallow lake and the sea, so swimmers can choose between the warm, brackish inland water or cooler ocean shoreline. Parking is very limited at Tashmoo, but it's a relatively flat, three-mile (4.8-km) bike or moped ride from downtown Vineyard Haven; follow Herring Creek Road northwest out of town to dead-end at Tashmoo.

Biking

Plenty of bike paths and fellow cyclists mean that riding on Martha's Vineyard is easier (and safer) than anywhere in New England. Bring your own, or rent from **Martha's Bike** (4 Lagoon Pond Rd., 508/693-6593, www.marthasbikerentals.com, Apr.-Nov., 1-day rental from $29), where you can also pick up biking maps of the island. Popular rides from Vineyard Haven include the four-mile (6.4-km) loop ride to **West Chop Light** on quiet roads, or the seven-mile (11.25-km) bike path to **Edgartown.** Biking maps are also available at the town's visitor center.

Boating

All eyes are on the soaring canvas and proud bowsprits of the schooner *Alabama* as it cruises the Vineyard Haven harbor. The majestic seacraft is part of **The Black Dog Tall Ships** (Black Dog Wharf, 20 Beach St., 508/693-1699, www.theblackdogtallships.com, late May-late Sept., 3-hour sail $100 adults, $60 children 4-12). Its fleet makes several daily outings during the summer season. Aspiring sailors can take a turn raising sails or manning the helm.

Paddling

Explore the coast at your own pace with a rental from **Wind's Up** (199 Beach Rd., 508/693-4252, www.windsupmv.com, June-Sept. Mon.-Sat. 10am-5:30pm, Sun. noon-5pm, rentals from $30/2 hrs or $50/day). Find anything with a paddle, from kayaks to canoes to SUPs, or rent a Sunfish or 15-foot (4.5-m) sloop. The shop also offers lessons from $80 per person.

Food

Classic diner fare and friendly service have kept the **Artcliff Diner** (39 Beach Rd., 508/693-1224, www.artcliffdiner.com, daily 8am-3pm, $9-16) a Vineyard favorite for years. It's usually packed all day with fishers and vacationing families. Hearty omelets and the almond-crusted French toast are favorites among regulars, who grab counter seats right by the coffeepot.

The organic smoothies and vegan wraps at **Blissed Out** (13 Union St., 508/338-2938, www.blissedoutmv.com, Mon.-Sat. 9am-4pm, $11-20) come with hefty Vineyard prices, but they're a welcome change from the fried fare that many of the island's casual restaurants serve. The cozy little shop has a friendly, hippie vibe.

Homey cookies, fresh doughnuts, and hearty sandwiches are the draw at **Life at Humphrey's** (455 State Rd., 508/693-6518, www.lifeathumphreys.com, Mon.-Fri. 6:30am-4pm, Sat. 6:30am-2pm, $8-15), a cozy shop with brightly painted chairs and a devoted following. The most beloved sandwich is the Turkey Gobbler, a Thanksgiving-inspired behemoth filled with roasted turkey, stuffing, and house-made cranberry sauce.

Tuck into fried clams, fish cakes, and chowder at **Sandy's Fish & Chips,** inside **John's Fish Market** (5 Martin Rd., 508/693-1220, www.johnsfishmarket.com, Mon.-Sat. 9am-7pm, Sun. 11am-6pm, call for off-season hours, $13-28), one of the best places on the island for clam shack fare. There's nowhere to sit inside the basic market, but in fine weather you can eat at the parking lot tables or order seafood to go.

If you've been rolling your eyes at the sea of Black Dog T-shirts, caps, and bumper stickers, **The Black Dog Tavern** (21 Beach St. Extension, 508/693-9223, www.theblackdog.com, Mon.-Sat. 7am-11am and noon-9pm, Sun. 7am-9pm, $17-38) may come as a pleasant surprise. It's real and rustic, decked with grainy images of old-fashioned schooners and excellent views of the harbor. Island specialties like quahog or codfish chowder are good, as are the hearty breakfasts. The tavern is mobbed from the beginning of summer until the leaves change.

Accommodations and Camping

Oak-shaded sites, playgrounds, and a spot right on the bicycle path make **Martha's Vineyard Family Campground** (569 Edgartown Rd., 508/693-3772, www.campmv.com, mid-May-mid-Oct., tent sites with 2 adults $67-83, additional adult $15, additional child $5, cabins $185-220) an excellent choice for families. Cabins are clean and comfortable with an outside gas grill and picnic tables (no cooking equipment), and the larger two-room cabins sleep six people in double beds and bunks.

The rooms at **Vineyard Harbor Motel** (60 Beach Rd., 508/693-3334, www.vineyardharbormotel.us, $199-389) are somewhat dated and worn, but the waterfront location, private beach, and sunny decks make it an excellent find. Some rooms have full kitchens with cooking supplies. Suites are an excellent choice for families.

Tchotchke-leery travelers will appreciate the **Charles & Charles** (85 Summer St., 508/338-2351, www.charlesandcharlesmv.com, $275-525) guarantee of "no decorative plates on the walls!" The intimate six-room inn delivers a charming blend of modern design and New England style. On sunny days, it's hard to beat their poolside breakfast. Perks like free bicycles, luxurious linens and soaps, and comfy beds make it a wonderful spot to land. The inn is a 10-minute walk from the ferry.

The historic **Mansion House Inn** (9 Main St., 508/693-2200, www.mvmansionhouse.com, $348-574) has an unbeatable location a few minutes' walk from the ferry dock. Bright, comfortable rooms and an on-site health club make it a great getaway. Don't miss the rooftop lounge, which is stocked with cold lemonade in the afternoons and has panoramic views.

Information

The **Martha's Vineyard Chamber of Commerce** (24 Beach St., 508/693-0085, www.mvy.com, Mon.-Fri. 9am-5pm) is stocked with maps and brochures. Its website has a helpful listing of last-minute rooms on the island.

Oak Bluffs

Walking through Oak Bluffs' gingerbread cottages and brightly painted homes feels like a glimpse of a different New England, when charismatic preachers packed enthusiastic crowds into summertime revivals. The town's most distinctive neighborhood is Wesleyan Grove, a cluster of Carpenter Gothic homes surrounding an open-air Tabernacle, the site of popular 19th-century Methodist camp meetings. The elaborate, whimsical style of those cottages spreads throughout the town: the grassy common is lined with hundreds of miniature homes that face an old-fashioned gazebo where bands play weekly concerts.

The historic heart of Martha's Vineyard's African American community, Oak Bluffs was a longtime favorite of intellectuals and luminaries like novelist Dorothy West and Edward Brooke, America's first popularly elected African American senator. It's still a popular vacation spot for Black Americans.

With great access to beaches, atmospheric neighborhoods, and wonderful parks, Oak Bluffs is far and away the best family destination on Martha's Vineyard.

Sights

Don't miss strolling through the adorable cottages in **Wesleyan Grove,** which center on the open-air **Trinity Park Tabernacle** (80 Trinity Park, 508/693-0525, www.mvcma.org), an area known as **The Campground.** It's easy enough to explore on your own, but for a bit of perspective on the neighborhood's history, time your visit to join one of the Martha's Vineyard Campground Meeting Association's **walking tours** (www.mvcma.org, July-Aug. Tues. and Thurs. 11am, 1.5-hr tours $12), which start at the Tabernacle.

A perennial favorite is the **Flying Horses Carousel** (15 Oak Bluffs Ave., 508/693-9481, www.vineyardtrust.org, early June-early Sept. daily 10am-9pm, call for off-season hours, $3.50), a National Historic Landmark and the oldest operating platform carousel in the United States. During summer months, throngs of children wait to ride one of 20 carved wooden horses and take turns grabbing for the brass ring, accompanied by a 1923 Wurlitzer Band Organ that plays the original paper rolls.

With commanding views of the sea, the **East Chop Light** (229 E. Chop Dr., www.mvmuseum.org, June-July Sun. 7pm-9pm, Aug.-Sept. Sun. 6pm-9pm, $5 adults, free children under 13) is a

Oak Bluffs

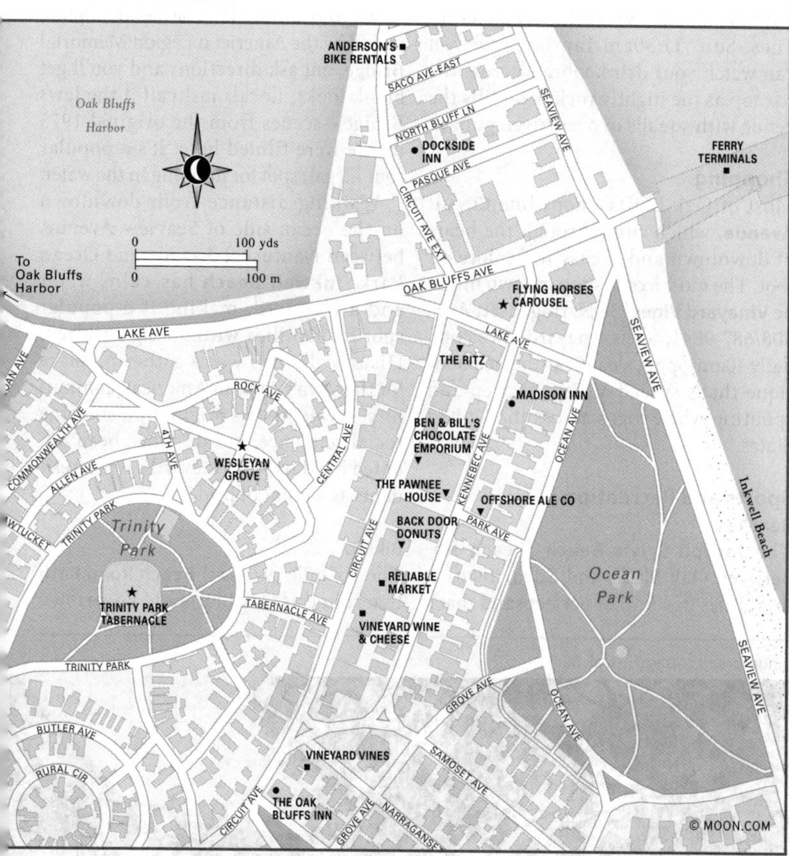

fine place for a picnic. The 1.5-mile (2.4-km) walk or ride from downtown passes through an exclusive neighborhood lined with beautiful homes. The Martha's Vineyard Museum opens the lighthouse to visitors on Sunday evenings in the summer.

Entertainment and Events

Summer on the Vineyard officially kicks off with the **Oak Bluffs Harbor Festival** (www.gomarthasvineyard.com, mid-June), when the waterfront fills with live music, craft vendors, and food booths, and the annual chalk-art contest sees fierce competition. One of the most anticipated nights of the summer is the **Grand Illumination** (Campground, 508/693-0525, www.mvcma.org/grand-illumination, mid-Aug.), when the gingerbread cottages of the Oak Bluffs revival camp are lit up with thousands of paper lanterns. Depending on your frame of mind, the effect can be romantic or intensely spiritual.

Several bars in Oak Bluffs feature live music at night, including craft beer lovers' favorite **Offshore Ale Company** (30 Kennebec Ave., 508/693-2626, www.offshoreale.com, Sun.-Thurs.

11:30am-9:30pm, Fri.-Sat. 11:30am-10pm) and **The Ritz** (4 Circuit Avenue, 508/693-9851, www.theritzmv.com, Tues.-Sun. 11:30am-1am), where you can watch your drink vibrate across the bar top as the nightly rock band fills the venue with squalls of overdriven guitar.

Shopping

Most of Oak Bluffs' shops line **Circuit Avenue,** which runs through the heart of downtown and is easy to explore on foot. The most iconic shop in town might be **Vineyard Vines** (56 Narragansett Ave., 508/687-9841, www.vineyardvines.com, daily 10am-6pm), a nautical-themed boutique that's spread Vineyard-prep and spouting whale logos across the United States.

Sports and Recreation

Beaches

The **Joseph Sylvia Beach** (Beach Rd. between Oak Bluffs and Edgartown) is four miles (6.4 km) of perfect sand that's excellent for swimming and sunbathing. Even on busy days, you can find a spot to stake your umbrella. The slender spit is joined by the American Legion Memorial Bridge, but ask directions and you'll get blank looks. Locals just call it the Jaws Bridge—scenes from the original 1975 movie were filmed here. It's a popular (but illegal) spot for jumping in the water.

Walking distance from downtown on the ocean side of Seaview Avenue, between Nantucket Avenue and Ocean Park, **Inkwell Beach** has calm water and a lifeguard, making it a popular spot for families with young children. Historically this was a gathering place for the town's African American community; the name was originally a sneering racial reference, but it's since been adopted by Martha's Vineyard's Black residents as a point of pride.

Biking

The six-mile (9.6-km) **Beach Road Path** that connects Oak Bluffs and Edgartown

gingerbread cottage in Oak Bluffs

is a wonderful way to see the island, with places to hop off the path and onto the sand all along the way. Rent a bike from **Anderson's Bike Rentals** (23 Circuit Ave. Extension, 508/693-9346, www.andersonsbikerentals.com, May-Oct., 1-day rental from $30).

Boating and Fishing

The tide ponds and lagoons around the island are perfect for maneuvering in and out of by kayak. **Island Spirit Kayak** (Edgartown Oak Bluffs Rd., 508/693-9727, www.islandspiritkayak.com) leads paddling tours that emphasize island geology and wildlife, and rents boats that can be delivered to the shoreline of your choice ($65 half-day and $120 full-day kayak tours, kayak rentals from $40/3 hrs to $60 24 hrs). Island Spirit is located on the outlet from Sengekontacket Pond to the ocean, so paddlers can turn inland to paddle in warm, still water, or explore along the beach.

For anglers, the ***Skipper*** (Oak Bluffs Harbor, 508/693-1238, www.mvskipper.com, half-day trips $90 per person) bills itself as a "party fishing boat," which takes family-friendly trips in search of fluke, flounder, and striped bass.

Food

Crushed peanut shells litter the floor at **Offshore Ale Company** (30 Kennebec Ave., 508/693-2626, www.offshoreale.com, Sun.-Thurs. 11:30am-9:30pm, Fri.-Sat. 11:30am-10pm, $16-29), a warehouse turned brewpub in Oak Bluffs with nautical decor and a friendly atmosphere. Brick-oven pizzas and hamburgers join traditional Vineyard fare like Portuguese fisherman's stew and thick, creamy clam chowder. Offshore Ale Company keeps nine beers on tap and has live music most weeks.

Fine dining can be harder to come by in the Vineyard, but you wouldn't know it reading the menu at **The Pawnee House** (20 Kennebec Ave., 508/338-2770, www.thepawneehousemv.com, Mon. and Thurs. 4:30pm-9:30pm, Fri.-Sat. 4:30pm-10pm, Sun. 3:30pm-9pm, $20-37). Borrowing its name from a Victorian hotel that once occupied the main drag in Oak Bluffs, Debbie and Alex Cohen's restaurant boasts a vegetable-centric menu of artfully prepared comfort foods like warm gruyere and asparagus tarts, and springy farmhouse salads. (Don't worry, carnivores: The chicken pot pie will leave you with gravy-flavored memories.)

Show up at **Back Door Donuts** (1-11 Kennebec Ave., 508/693-3688, www.backdoordonuts.com, Apr.-Oct. Sun.-Wed. 7am-3pm, Fri.-Sat. 7am-5pm, $3-10) as early as possible to pick up sweet, gooey donuts and apple fritters. The joint began as an offshoot of a larger bakery, literally selling its confections from a back alleyway. The ravenous clientele grew and eventually, when the bakehouse mothership shut its doors, the doughnut shop lived on and leveled up to a more visible streetside venue.

Martha's Vineyard has more fudge and

ice cream shops than you could shake a waffle cone at, but **Ben & Bill's Chocolate Emporium** (20 Circuit Ave., 508/696-0008, www.benandbillsmv.com, Apr.-Oct. daily 11am-9pm, extended hours midsummer, $5-14) is one of the best. Drop into the dark-walled interior for a handful of candy from old-fashioned bins of saltwater taffy and brittle, or get a cone of the absurdly rich butter pecan crunch ice cream.

Pick up supplies and snacks at the town's small grocery store, **Reliable Market** (36 Circuit Ave., 508/693-1102, www.thereliablemarket.com, Mon.-Sat. 8:30am-6pm, Sun. 9am-1pm). Gourmet treats, spirits, and wine are available just up the street at **Vineyard Wine & Cheese** (38 Circuit Ave., 508/693-0943, Apr.-Dec. Mon.-Sat. 10am-6pm).

Accommodations

Oak Bluffs' inns are welcoming and comfortable. Prices plummet in the off-season. Some of the privately owned historic cottages in **The Campground** (www.mvcma.org, starting at $2,000/week) are available to rent for visits of a week or more.

$150-250

Country charm and a friendly innkeeper make the **Tivoli Inn** (125 Circuit Ave., 508/693-7928, www.tivoliinn.com, $175-400) a good, relatively lower-budget option. It's a leisurely walk from downtown. Continental breakfast is a full spread of breads, pastries, and cereal served on the gracious porch in fine weather. The flowery latticed porch is a fine venue for enjoying the morning with a fresh cup of coffee.

Brightly painted rooms and pleasant common spaces are the draw at the **Madison Inn** (18 Kennebec Ave., 508/693-2760, www.madisoninnmv.com, $189-319), which also has unexpected amenities for the price. Start the day with coffee and teas, snack on cookies, ice cream, and fruit at will, and use beach towels, toys, chairs, and umbrellas. Rooms also come with white noise machines, which is good, as the walls are a bit thin.

$250-350

With a prime spot on the waterfront, the **Dockside Inn** (9 Circuit Ave. Extension, 508/693-2966, www.vineyardinns.com, $334-515) is simple and immaculate. Bits of modern flair keep the historic building feeling fresh. A comfortable seat on the deep wraparound porch is a dreamy place to watch sails float by. The enclosed garden has a hot tub. Higher-priced rooms accommodate four or five people, an excellent deal for the location.

A pink wedding cake of a house at the top of the main drag, **The Oak Bluffs Inn** (64 Circuit Ave., 508/693-7171, www.oakbluffsinn.com, Apr.-Oct., $315-635) is appointed with a tasteful mix of modern country furniture and old English antiques. The informal, lived-in air and afternoon cookies and lemonade on the porch make it a sweetly hospitable place to stay.

Edgartown

Romantic and old-fashioned, Edgartown is Martha's Vineyard's most elegant destination, with historic homes, narrow lanes, and fine dining. It's also a fine day trip via the Falmouth passenger ferry. The compact center is easy to explore on foot.

Sights

On an island that offers every possible angle of ocean views, the finest place to watch the sunrise may be **Edgartown Lighthouse** (121 North Water St.). Located on a slow strip of sand surrounded by calm bay water, it looks like it was placed by a landscape architect (as opposed to the U.S. Coast Guard). The lighthouse is a 10-minute walk from the ferry landing in downtown Edgartown; follow North Water Street northeast, and when the Harbor View Hotel is on

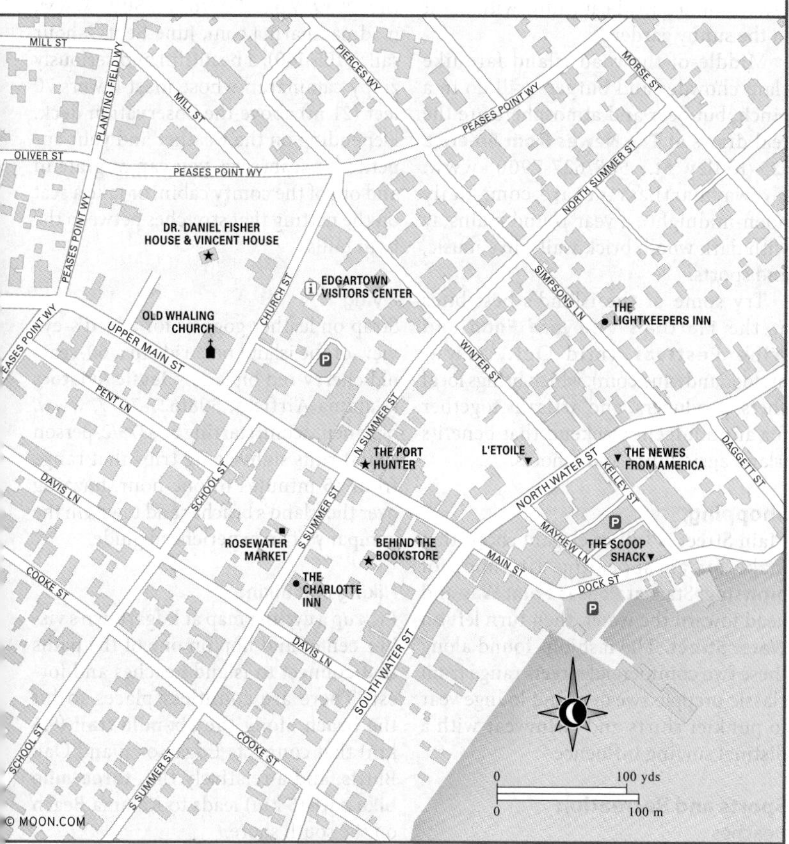

your left, take the short, sandy path to the right that leads toward shore.

Perhaps the best way to soak in Edgartown's historic charm is on foot, and it's easy to see the town's highlights in an hour of walking. A good place to start is the **Edgartown Visitors Center** (29 Church St.), where you can pick up maps of the town; highlights include the nearby **Old Whaling Church** (89 Main St.), an impressive Greek Revival building whose clock tower is visible far out at sea, the **Dr. Daniel Fisher House,** and the **Vincent House** (both 99 Main St.), the oldest unaltered house on Martha's Vineyard. From late May through mid-October, the **Martha's Vineyard Preservation Trust** opens these three properties for 45-minute guided tours (508/627-4440, www.mvpreservation.org, Tues.-Sat. 10am-4pm, Sun. noon-3pm, $25 adults, $10 children 6-17).

Entertainment and Events

Edgartown is pretty sedate by Vineyard standards, but you can catch live shows (and try your hand at the lawn games) at **Bad Martha Farmer's Brewery** (270 Upper Main St., 508/939-4415, www.badmarthabeer.com, daily 11am-9pm). A mason jar full of citra-hopped Vineyard Summer Lager or the toastier Half Shell Oyster Stout pairs beautifully with a seat in the sunny garden.

Middle-of-the-road island fare like clam chowder and burgers will do in a pinch, but beer and atmosphere are the real draws at **The Newes from America** (23 Kelley St., 508/627-7900, www.farawaymarthasvineyard.com, daily noon-midnight), a year-round mainstay with dark wood, brick walls, live music, and sports.

Try some of the island's best bites at the **Martha's Vineyard Food and Wine Festival** (mid-Oct., www.mvfoodandwine.com), which brings local chefs, producers, and artisans together for an indulgent weekend that benefits island agriculture and schools.

Shopping

Main Street is full of elegant shops that make for an appealing afternoon of browsing. Start at **Peases Point Way** and head toward the water, then turn left on **Water Street.** The fashions found along these two commercial streets range from classic preppie sweaters and loungewear to punkier shirts and swimwear with a distinct surfing influence.

Sports and Recreation

Beaches

To access the slender **Joseph Sylvia State Beach** from Edgartown, just hop on the scenic bike path that fronts Beach Road. Don't let the fact that scenes from *Jaws* were filmed here dissuade you; this beach is a good choice for less confident swimmers, as it's fairly sheltered from ocean swells.

A more dramatic landscape is **Katama Beach,** a narrow barrier beach three miles (5 km) south of Edgartown, with surf crashing on one side and a warm saltwater lagoon on the other. Follow South Water Street southeast from downtown, then turn left on Katama Road to find the beach parking area.

Boating

Set sail from Edgartown's harbor on the ***Mad Max*** (508/627-7500, www.madmaxmarina.com, June-Sept. 2-hour sails $105-140), a beautiful and seriously zippy catamaran whose mast towers 70 feet (21 m) above the observation deck. Depending on the weather and your appetite for seabreeze, you can migrate in and out of the comfy cabin, or take a seat on the netting that stretches between the twin hulls.

Flying

Strap on leather goggles for a bird's-eye view of the island on a ride in a 60-year-old cherry-red biplane. **Classic Aviators** (Katama Airfield, 508/627-7677, www.biplanemv.com, starting at $379/2-person tours) runs sightseeing trips that range from 15 minutes to one hour, buzzing over the island's beaches and towns in the company of an experienced guide.

Hiking and Biking

Pick up a cycling map at Edgartown's visitor center and hop on one of the paths that connect to island beaches and forest. There are countless places to hit the beach along the **six-mile trail** (9.6 km) that connects Edgartown and Oak Bluffs, and a relatively flat, **three-mile bike path** (5 km) leads to Katama Beach on the south shore.

To really get away from it all, take your bike to the less-developed **Chappaquiddick Island,** which is connected to Edgartown by a small **passenger ferry** (53 Dock St., vehicle waiting line forms on Daggett St., 508/627-9427, www.chappyferry.com, round-trip tickets $5 passenger, $7 with bike) that runs all day, year-round. A single, four-mile (6-km) paved road leads from Chappaquiddick's ferry dock across the island. Other roads are sandy (and potentially challenging on a bicycle). As you might expect from an island off an island off Cape Cod, Chappaquiddick is wild and scenic; it's a perfect place to escape the crowds. Hop off your bike to visit **Mytoi** (41 Dike Rd., 508/627-7689, www.thetrustees.org, year-round daily sunrise to sunset, $5), a 14-acre (5.6-ha) Japanese garden with beautifully landscaped ponds, forests, and walking trails.

Back in Edgartown, you can spot wood ducks, ospreys, and even nesting barn owls at the **Felix Neck Wildlife Sanctuary** (100 Felix Neck Dr., off Edgartown-Vineyard Haven Rd., 508/627-4850, www.massaudubon.org, Mon.-Fri. 9am-4pm, trails dawn to dusk, $4 adults, $3 seniors and children), a rambling preserve of salt marsh and beach meadow. The sanctuary has four miles (6.4 km) of walking trails (including 1 mi/1.6 km accessible to those in wheelchairs) that take in a diverse range of Vineyard ecosystems.

Paddling

Rent a kayak at **Joseph Sylvia State Beach** from **Island Spirit Kayak** (Edgartown Oak Bluffs Rd., Oak Bluffs, 508/693-9727, www.islandspiritkayak.com, $65 half-day, $120 full-day kayak tours, kayak rentals from $40/3 hrs to $60 24 hrs), which also delivers around the island.

Food

It's easy to miss the tiny café that's tucked behind Edgartown Books, but **Behind the Bookstore** (46 Main St., 774/549-9123, www.btbmv.com, mid-Apr.-Dec. daily 7am-10:30pm, $7-32) is among the most appealing places to eat in town. Seats are available on an enclosed, sunny patio, the espresso is from Intelligentsia Coffee, and the menu's full of fresh, flavorful gems like farro and black rice grain bowls, and gem lettuce and fennel salad. The dinner menu is only served in the middle of the summer, and includes more elaborate (and expensive) seafood plates and mains.

Comfort food made with plenty of local ingredients is the draw at **Lucky Hank's** (218 Upper Main St., 508/939-4082, www.luckyhanksmv.com, Tues.-Sun. 8am-2:30pm and 5pm-8pm, $25-44), a small restaurant in a cozy converted home. Dinner plates like ginger-miso roasted salmon and Waygu sirloin with feta and chive mashed potatoes are hearty and full-flavored. Brunch is very popular (the pancakes get rave reviews).

Romantic and softly lit, **L'Etoile** (22 North Water St., 508/627-5187, www.letoile.net, May-Nov. Sun.-Tues. and Thurs. 5:30pm-9:30pm, Fri.-Sat. 5:30pm-10pm, $36-64) is Edgartown's last word on date night. The French-inspired menu changes frequently, but foie gras, Katama Bay oysters, and beautifully filleted trout are perennial favorites. The dinner menu is also available in the more relaxed bar, which is a fine place for cocktails and snacks.

A little bit hipper than the Edgartown average, ★ **The Port Hunter** (55 Main St., 508/627-7747, www.theporthunter.com, late May-Oct., Mon.-Sat. 5:30pm-12:30am, $26-48) feels like a lively telegram from the next generation of Vineyard chefs. An emphasis on local fish and products is welcome, and the smoked bluefish, oysters, and fish served whole are highlights. As dinnertime winds down, this becomes a happening spot downtown, with live music and powerful drinks.

Old-fashioned candy and offbeat ice cream flavors keep **The Scoop Shack** (22 Dock St., 508/627-7829, daily 10am-11pm, $4-8) bustling all summer. The house-made s'mores ice cream is summer vacation in a cone.

Find prepared foods, gourmet treats, and baked goods at **Rosewater Market** (20 South Summer St., 508/627-1270, www.rosewatermv.com, Thurs.-Tues. 7am-4pm), which stocks many products made on-island. It also has a simple, thoughtful take-away menu.

Accommodations

The quaint, airy suites at **The Lightkeepers Inn** (25 Simpsons Rd., 508/627-4600, www.thelightkeepersinn.

com, 4-person suites $225-450) are just a short walk from the ferry dock. Kitchenettes, coffeemakers, and sitting areas make these comfortable places for a family. The inn's bright blue shutters and shingled exteriors exemplify classic Vineyard style.

The Charlotte Inn (27 S. Summer St., 508/627-4751, www.relaischateaux.com, $325-850) is a romantic old-world retreat. The elegant house is furnished with antiques, oil paintings, and sparkling chandeliers, the perfectly tended English gardens overflow with blooming flowers and hidden sitting areas, and an à la carte menu is available in a glass-walled dining room.

Up-Island

With all of its celebrity sightings and souvenir shops, it's a real surprise that much of Martha's Vineyard remains fundamentally rural. Up-island roads wind past cattle barns, sleepy corner stores, and fishing villages. While it's nice to have a car to really do justice to the area, frequent buses pass by all the major sites. Although up-island roads are quite narrow and often have no shoulder, experienced cyclists can certainly make the trip. The Vineyard buses have racks that accommodate three or four bikes, so it's possible to bike out to Gay Head and return on the bus, but you may find that others had the same idea, and end up waiting some time for a bus with an open rack.

Addresses on Martha's Vineyard can be confusing, and some destinations listed in Vineyard Haven turn out to be right in the center of the island, but Aquinnah and Chilmark stake out the slightly bulbous, left-hand corner of the island, and are the gateway to the teeny Menemsha fishing community.

Sights

★ Aquinnah Cliffs

Striped with wild layers of ochre clay, green sand, and glittering quartz, the **Aquinnah Cliffs** are a stunning and dramatic sight that has drawn mainland tourists for centuries. The cliffs also feature in Wampanoag stories about the island's formation; the legendary supernatural giant Moshup resided in a den beside the cliffs, where he lived off a hearty diet of roasted whales—one per meal. When he would see a whale approach the shore, he'd kill it by heaving it against the cliffs, then cook it over the enormous fire that he tended all day and all night. Streaming red whale blood, black coals, and pale bones stained the cliffs, lodging in each layer, still visible to this day. The walkway to the cliff overlook is lined by shops and information booths maintained by the Wampanoag and is a great place to learn more about their history and culture.

Gay Head Light

In rusty brick that echoes the nearby cliffs, the **Gay Head Light** (9 Aquinnah Cir., Aquinnah, www.gayheadlight.org, July-Aug. daily 10am-4pm, Thurs.-Fri. 6pm-sunset, Labor Day-Indigenous Peoples Day Fri.-Mon. 10am-4pm, $5, under 12 free) is among the most picturesque in New England. A lighthouse was built on this spot in 1799, just on the edge of the cliff—a little too close, as it turned out. The lighthouse was moved back from the erosion-prone cliff in 1844, and a second time in 2015.

Menemsha Harbor

Fishing villages don't get any prettier than old-fashioned **Menemsha Harbor,** where weathered, gray-shingled shacks stand watch over an active fleet of trawlers and lobster boats. Watch the Vineyard's fishers bring in the day's catch while nibbling on clam shack fare. If you're exploring by bike, Menemsha is connected by a convenient but somewhat unpredictable bike ferry, so you don't have to climb back up the big hill that leads in to town. Does the town look familiar? It's the site of the fictional Amity Island in the movie *Jaws.*

Entertainment and Events

The dancing at **The Yard** (1 The Yard, off Middle Rd. near Beetlebung Corner, Chilmark, 508/645-9662, www.dancetheyard.org) ranges from top-notch contemporary and tap performances to joyful themed public dance hall events (registration required).

Every Thursday and Sunday during July, local artists and crafters display their wares at the **Vineyard Artisans Festivals** (Grange Hall, West Tisbury, www.vineyardartisans.com, July Thurs. and Sun. 10am-2pm). There is always a good selection of watercolors and photography of island scenes.

The week following the Grand Illumination is the annual Martha's Vineyard Agricultural Society **Livestock Show and Fair** (West Tisbury, 508/693-4343, www.marthasvineyardagriculturalsociety.org, $15 adults, $10 seniors, veterans, and children 5-12, free under 5), which for over 160 years has celebrated the farming history of the island. Displays include sheep and cow pens, wood-chopping competitions, country bands, fireworks, and, of course, a Ferris wheel.

Shopping

At first glance, the shops that line the path to the Aquinnah Cliffs lookout seem like run-of-the-mill kitsch, but they're worth exploring further. Located on traditional Wampanoag land, many of the shops are operated by tribe members selling handmade gifts among the T-shirts. Wampum jewelry made from shells, hand-thrown pottery, and silver makes an exquisite souvenir.

Sports and Recreation

Beaches

One of the finest up-island beaches is **Lucy Vincent Beach,** which is only open to Chilmark residents and renters in the summer (and is reason enough to make friends with a local). For the rest of us, Aquinnah's **Lobsterville Beach** is a favorite for beachcombing, with plenty of shells and sea glass washing up on the shore. Bring your bike, however, as there is no parking along the road.

The beach at the base of the Aquinnah Cliffs is no longer accessible, but the **Aquinnah Public Beach** is a beautiful, family-friendly spot to spend the afternoon; the beach is a 10-minute walk from the parking lot (summer parking fee $15).

Boating

Cruise around the sweet Menemsha Harbor with a kayak, stand-up paddleboard, powerboat, or sailboat from **Book-A-Boat** (Menemsha waterfront, 508/645-2400, www.bookaboatmv.com, rentals from $42 half day and $60 full day). Fish with Captain Buddy Vanderhoop of **Tomahawk Charters** (W. Basin Rd., 508/645-3201, www.tomahawkcharters.com, half-day charters from $800), a local fishing celebrity and Wampanoag tribal member.

Hiking and Biking

The Vineyard's off-road bike paths don't reach up-island, but experienced cyclists can make the trip from Edgartown (18 mi/29 km) or Vineyard Haven (16.5 mi/26.5 km). A bike ferry crosses the short channel at Menemsha starting in late May, but hours are a bit sporadic.

Three miles (5 km) of hiking trails thread through the **Menemsha Hills** (North Rd., Chilmark) and past wetland, woodland, and coastal plain on the way up **Prospect Hill**—at a towering 308 feet (94 m) above sea level, it's just shy of the tallest point on the Vineyard, Peaked Hill, which has an extra three feet (1 m) of height. In August, the highbush blueberries along the path make for blissful grazing.

Island naturalist Polly Hill gathered nearly 1,000 species of plants at the **Polly Hill Arboretum** (809 State Rd., West Tisbury, 508/693-9426, www.pollyhillarboretum.org, mid-May-mid-Oct. daily 9:30am-4pm, $5, children under 13 free), which has miles of walking paths through wildflower meadows and woodland of dogwood and magnolia.

The 600-acre (243-ha) **Long Point Wildlife Refuge** (Scrubby Neck Rd., West Tisbury, 508/693-7392, www.thetrustees.org, mid-June-mid-Sept. $20-25 car, $5 cyclist or pedestrian, children under 15 free) wraps around the long, narrow Long Cove Pond, and ends in a wildly scenic barrier beach. Two miles (3.2 km) of hiking trails pass through coastal dunes and dry forest, and paddleboards and kayaks are available to rent on-site (from $30/hr). If you plan on visiting the refuge with a car, you'll need to book a timed entry reservation on the website beforehand.

Food

Dinner at the **Outermost Inn** (81 Lighthouse Rd., Aquinnah, 508/645-3511, www.outermostinn.com, early June-Sept. Tues.-Sun. 5pm-10pm, $35-57) feels like eating at the edge of the world, with views of rolling hills that give way to ocean-side cliffs. The prix fixe offerings evolve seasonally to showcase the bounty of regional farms and fisherfolk, with standouts such as chestnut mascarpone lobster dumplings and duck confit with candied collard greens. Call ahead for a reservation and as you case the menu, consider leaving a little extra room for some raw bar morsels.

Dig into Katama Bay oysters, lobster bisque, and steamers at **Larsen's Fish Market** (56 Basin Rd., Chilmark, 508/645-2680, www.larsensfishmarket.com, May-Oct. daily 9am-7pm, $9-25), where you can watch the fishing fleet unload from a seat at the outdoor tables—lobster traps topped with unfinished plywood.

The hip little **Beetlebung Coffee House** (24 Basin Rd., Menemsha, 508/645-9956, late May-Sept. daily 11am-6pm, $5-12) has good alternatives to Menemsha's seafood shack fare. Hearty sandwiches, smoothies, and bagels are fresh and appealing, and the coffee is the best in town.

Accommodations

Of all the picturesque enclaves in New England, up-island Martha's Vineyard is one of the most expensive places to bunk down for the night. When you're competing with movie stars and heads of state for limited lodging amid all that bucolic open space, prices tend to go up. Reservations for up-island hotels should be made *at least* a few months in advance, if not earlier. While there's not much of anywhere "cheap" to stay on the island, relatively more affordable options can be found nearby in Vineyard Haven and Oak Bluffs, either of which is a solid base camp for poking around the up-island territory.

The secluded ★ **Duck Inn** (10 Duck Pond Way, Aquinnah, 508/645-9018, www.duckinnonmv.com, $155-350) is located in an 18th-century home with bohemian furnishings and a knockout ocean view. One room has a bathtub in the middle; another is swept at night with the beam from Gay Head Light. The personable owner, Elise LeBovet, is a decades-long island resident who gives therapeutic massages and makes killer organic breakfasts.

On the other side of the island, the **Beach Plum Inn** (50 Beach Plum Ln., Menemsha, 508/645-9454, www.beachpluminn.com, $260-750) is a secluded retreat, with six acres (2.4 ha) of hilltop property overlooking Vineyard Sound and the Elizabeth Islands. Rates include a full breakfast and a coveted pass to the residents-only Lucy Vincent Beach, one of the most beautiful on the island. Bear in mind that during the summer, two-night minimum stays are often required.

Information and Services

Find all the maps and information you need to get around the island—plus advice on accommodations and dining—at **Martha's Vineyard Chamber of Commerce** (24 Beach Rd., Vineyard

Haven, 508/693-0085, www.mvy.com, Mon.-Fri. 9am-5pm).

The island's full-service hospital is **Martha's Vineyard Hospital** (One Hospital Rd., Oak Bluffs, 508/693-0410, www.mvhospital.org), with emergency services offered 24 hours a day. Fill prescription needs at **Leslie's Pharmacy** (65 Main St., Vineyard Haven, 508/693-1010, Mon.-Fri. 8:30am-4pm, Sat. 8:30am-3pm). The commercial centers of Edgartown and Vineyard Haven are home to several **banks.** Each also has an **ATM**—which are also scattered around the streets of those towns, as well as in Oak Bluffs.

Major cell phone networks function within the main towns, but can be undependable in the island's less-crowded areas. Free **Internet access** and terminals are offered at the **Vineyard Haven Public Library** (200 Main St., Vineyard Haven, 508/696-4211, www.vhlibrary.org, Tues. 10am-7pm, Wed.-Thurs. 10am-6pm, Fri.-Sat. and Mon. 10am-5pm) and **Edgartown Free Public Library** (58 North Water St., Edgartown, 508/627-4221, www.clamsnet.org, Tues.-Wed. 10am-6pm, Thurs.-Sat. 10am-5pm).

Nantucket

With cobblestone streets and misty beaches, pretty Nantucket is a dreamy world unto itself, a tiny curve of sand that points out toward the sea. It's among the most exclusive (and expensive) destinations in New England, but before the blue bloods and boutiques arrived, the island had a salty history of Native Americans, colonial refugees, and whalers. Then, as now, Nantucket seemed like the last place on Earth: Early colonists arrived fleeing restrictive mainland towns and found Wampanoag residents who'd fled the European encroachments on Cape Cod—the island's name means "the faraway place" in their language.

These days, Nantucket is the finest place to see the historic architecture of maritime New England; picture-perfect saltbox houses are crowned with widow's walks and five-petaled roses, and residents still "go laning," strolling the narrow streets that wind through the center. It's impossibly charming on foggy summer mornings when the harbor is smooth as glass, or when the whole island takes cover as nor'easter storms rage across the coast. It's taken deep pockets and vigilant zoning laws to maintain the island's character, though, and at times, Nantucket has a sanitized, exclusive homogeneity; enormous, identically colored houses line the coast in some places, and bone-deep preppiness may leave some visitors wishing for a bit of grit and color. In Melville's words, though, "these extravaganzas only show that Nantucket is no Illinois," and it's all part of the island experience.

Getting to Nantucket

Ferries leave for Nantucket Town from Hyannis on both the **Steamship Authority** (508/477-8600, www.steamshipauthority.com, round-trip tickets $41 adults, $21 children, $14 bicycles, $354 car, 2.25 hrs) and the passenger-only **Steamship Authority Fast Ferry** ($81 adults, $41 children, $14 bicycles, 1 hr). Also leaving from Hyannis: **Hy-Line Cruises High Speed Ferry** (800/492-8082, www.hylinecruises.com, round-trip tickets $89 adults, $54 children 5-12, $14 bicycles, 1 hr). You can also get to Nantucket from Oak Bluffs on Martha's Vineyard (late June-early Sept.).

During the summer, many flights a day are offered by **Cape Air** (508/771-6944, www.flycapeair.com) from Boston, Hyannis, and Martha's Vineyard.

Getting Around

Nantucket is a conveniently compact oasis at 47.8 square miles (124 sq km), which translates to only 14 miles (22 km) in length and 3.5 (5.6 km) across. A car ride across the island rarely takes longer than half an hour, which explains why

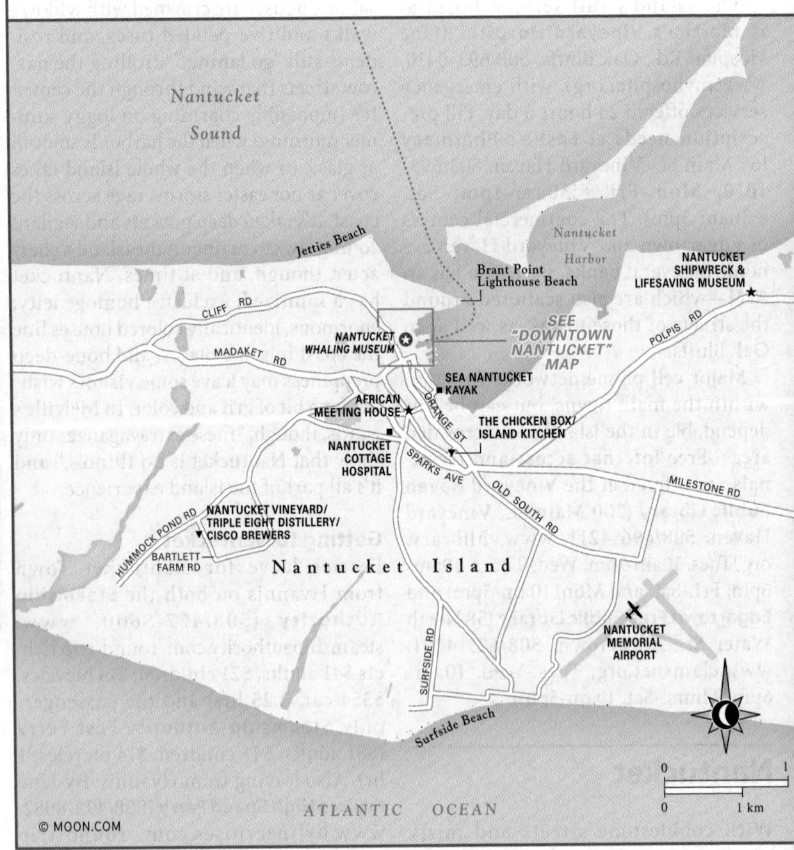

many visitors choose to leave their vehicles on the mainland and get around on bikes or the local buses.

The cost of traveling to Nantucket with your own car is prohibitive, and while several agencies rent vehicles from Nantucket Airport, a car isn't really necessary given the size of the island. A bicycle is a fun choice, as is a scooter: Rent a single- or double-seater at **Nantucket Bike Shop** (4 Broad St., 508/228-1999, www.nantucketbikeshop.com). The **Nantucket Regional Transit Authority** (508/228-7025, www.nrtawave.com) does continuous loops between Straight Wharf in Nantucket Town and Madaket, Surfside, Siasconset, and the airport.

Sights

★ Nantucket Whaling Museum

The world's whaling industries have a lasting legacy of destruction that obliterated some species of whale and left others teetering at the brink of extinction. Now that the oil in our cars, machines, and furnaces comes from below the ground it's easy to forget that it used to roll off whaling ships in great wooden

One Day in Nantucket

Nantucket Whaling Museum

Morning

Catch an early-morning ferry from Hyannis, then find a spot on deck to watch **Brant Point Lighthouse** appear at the mouth of Nantucket's sheltered harbor. Spend a leisurely hour going "laning," wandering the cobblestone streets and historic neighborhoods of Nantucket Town, with time for a hearty breakfast at **Island Kitchen.**

Afternoon

Explore the island's whaling history (and go nose-to-nose with a mammoth sperm whale) at the excellent **Nantucket Whaling Museum.** Pick up some wheels at **Nantucket Bike Shop,** then take to one of Nantucket's many bike paths to explore rolling, dunes, salt marshes, and scenic beaches.

Evening

If you've booked an evening ferry back to the mainland, you have time to visit the three-in-one **Nantucket Vineyard, Cisco Brewers, and Triple Eight Distillery,** which has live music on an outdoor patio to go with locally made wine, spirits, and beer. Snag one of the free shuttle buses leaving from the downtown visitor center during the summer, then watch the sun go down with a crowd of locals before catching your boat.

vats, the fruit of dangerous hunting trips that could last for years. Standing between a fragile, open whaleboat and the 46-foot (14-m) skeleton of a sperm whale puts it all in perspective at the wonderful **Nantucket Whaling Museum** (15 Broad St., 508/228-1894, www.nha.org, late May-late Oct. daily 10am-5pm, call or check online for off-season hours, $25 adults, $20 seniors, $5 children 6 and over, free children under 6).

Other Sights

The shoals around Nantucket have wrecked hundreds of ships throughout the years, and many more lives would have been lost without the islanders that plunged into the breakers to look for survivors. Hear their stories at the **Nantucket Shipwreck & Lifesaving Museum** (158 Polpis Rd., 508/228-1885, www.eganmaritime.org, late May-mid-Oct. Mon.-Sat. 10am-5pm, $12 adults,

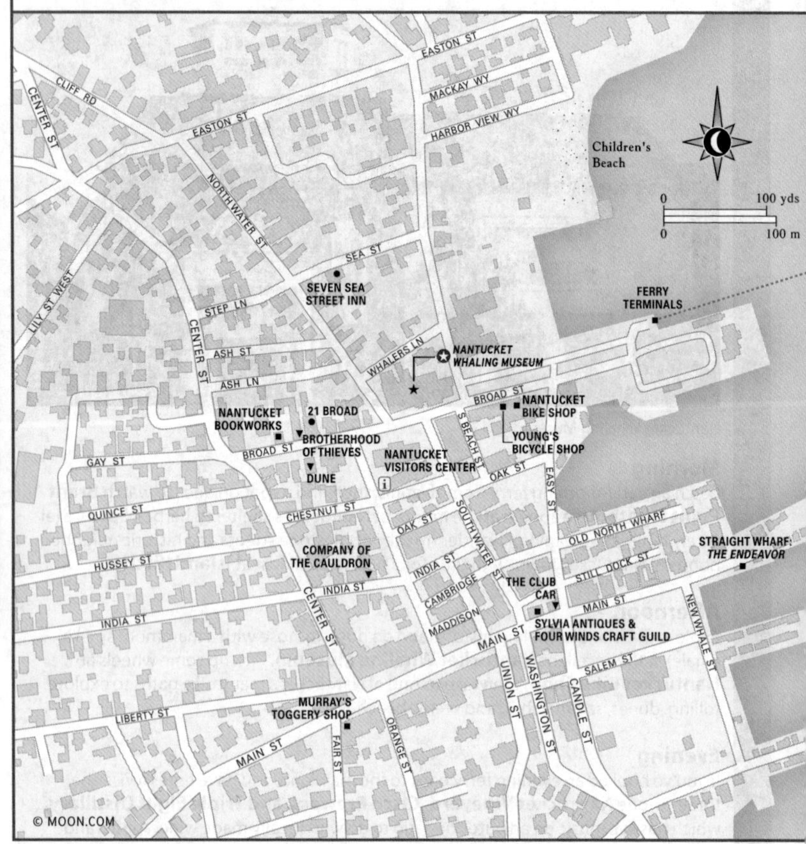

$9 seniors and students, $7 youth 6-17), which is 3.5 miles (5.6 km) from town by the Polpis bicycle path. The small **African Meeting House** (29 York St., 508/228-9833, www.maah.org/nantucket-location, June-Sept. Wed.-Thurs. noon-4pm, Fri.-Sun. 10am-4pm, $10 adults, $8 seniors and youth 13-14, under 13 free) dates to 1827, when it was used as a meeting place and schoolhouse for escaped slaves, Cape Verdeans, and Native Americans.

Entertainment and Events

With long, dark winters and party-fueled summers, it's no surprise that Nantucket has an on-island source of alcohol. Locally owned **Nantucket Vineyard, Cisco Brewers, and Triple Eight Distillery** (5 Bartlett Farm Rd., 508/325-5929, www.ciscobrewers.com, Mon.-Sat. 11am-7pm, Sun. noon-6pm, tours $20) produce everything from aged rum to pinot noir in a facility just outside of town, with a free shuttle service from the downtown visitor center that runs every 20-30 minutes during high season. Guided tours include tastes of spirits, wine, and beer, and this is the place to be in the late afternoon, when outdoor shows by regional and local bands attract a laid-back crowd of locals and visitors.

Later in the evening, things can get pretty raucous at **The Chicken Box** (16 Dave St., 508/228-9717, www.thechickenbox.com, daily noon-1am), a fried-chicken stand turned roadhouse with reggae and rock bands several nights a week; it's a hike from downtown, so plan to return in a cab. Tucked into a former train car, **The Club Car** (1 Main St., 508/228-1101, www.theclubcar.com, May-Oct. daily, dining 11:30am-3pm and 5:30pm-10pm, bar 11am-1am) is an atmospheric place to get a drink downtown, with a nightly sing-along piano show, elegant snacks, and a good selection of wine. Music starts at 9pm.

Nantucket lights up the first weekend in December for **Christmas Stroll Weekend** (www.christmasstroll.com), when the town goes all out with period carolers, nautical Santas, and lighthouses dressed for the holidays. Once the weather warms up, there's the **Daffodil Festival** (www.daffodilfestival.com) in April, which takes over with parades of blossom-festooned antique cars and a tailgating picnic.

Shopping

If you're searching for shops on Nantucket, you won't have to look for long; the entire downtown is lined with boutiques and stores, with the biggest concentration along Main Street. There are a few classic Nantucket souvenirs, though, that are distinct in the Cape Cod area. There's a fine selection of **Nantucket lightship baskets** at **Four Winds Craft Guild** inside **Sylvia Antiques** (15 Main St., 508/228-9623, www.fourwindscraftguild.com, Mon.-Sat. 10am-5pm, Sun. 1pm-4pm), and you can pick up all sorts of clothes in distinctive "Nantucket red"—actually a faded pink—at **Murray's**

Top to bottom: whale bones at the Nantucket Whaling Museum; Brant Point Lighthouse; *The Endeavor*

Toggery Shop (62 Main St., 508/228-0437, www.nantucketreds.com, Mon.-Sat. 10am-6pm, Sun. 10am-5pm), a longtime preppy pilgrimage spot. Legend has it that every inn on the island used to stock guest rooms with a copy of *Moby-Dick*, which is full of Nantucket references. Buy your own copy at **Nantucket Bookworks** (25 Broad St., 508/228-4000, www.nantucketbookworks.com, daily 10am-10pm), which also has an excellent collection of works by local authors.

Sports and Recreation

Beaches

Nantucket's beaches are soft and sandy, and they're the center of life on the island, when fine weather turns all eyes to the sea. The first one you'll spot as you approach the coast on the ferry is **Brant Point Lighthouse Beach** (on Brant Point, at the tip of Easton St.) at the mouth of Nantucket's sheltered harbor. It's a quiet and very small beach, about a 15-minute walk from town. As it has no facilities or lifeguard, it's frequented mostly by those looking for a brief stroll or a view of the lighthouse or town. A quick five-minute walk from town, just around the bend in the harbor toward Brant Point, is **Children's Beach.** With very few waves, a small park, a lifeguard on duty, and restrooms, it's a perfect spot to take the tykes. On the outskirts of town, equipped with lifeguards and restrooms, is **Jetties Beach** (www.nantucket-ma.gov). There's also a playground; a concession stand selling burgers, ice cream, and such; and boat rentals. Take a shuttle or ride a bike to the island's south side to reach **Surfside** (www.nantucket-ma.gov), a big, wide stretch of sand that catches a heavy swell and has an excellent snack bar.

Biking

With off-road paths, mellow traffic, and gentle terrain, a bicycle is one of the best ways to explore the island. You can pick up wheels just off the ferry at **Young's Bicycle Shop** (6 Broad St., 508/228-1151, www.youngsbicycleshop.com, daily 8:30am-5pm, $35 half day to $45 full day rental). They stock helpful maps of popular bike rides, and their website has links to a number of the best, with step-by-step instructions and maps. The 4.2-mile (6.75-km) self-guided tour of downtown takes in the lighthouse and Nantucket's most historic neighborhoods; other good choices are the flat, 3.5-mile (5.6-km) ride to **Surfside Beach,** or the scenic, 19-mile (30-km) ride that heads out to **Sconset** via Milestone and comes back on the Polpis bike path.

Boating

One of the most peaceful ways to see the island is from the water; **Sea Nantucket Kayak** (76 Washington St., 508/228-7499, www.seanantucketkayak.com, daily 9am-4pm, boats from $25/hr to $55 for all day) rents kayaks and stand-up paddleboards from a waterfront location that's walking distance from downtown, with tips on where to paddle.

To explore the harbor under sail, book a place on ***The Endeavor*** (Straight Wharf, Slip 1015, 508/228-5585, www.endeavorsailing.com, 1.5-hr daytime sails $110, sunset sails $175), a 31-foot (9-m) Friendship sloop that makes four trips a day with Captain Jim Genthner.

Food

Slipping into the basement door at **Brotherhood of Thieves** (23 Broad St., 508/325-5812, www.brotherhoodnantucket.com, daily 11:30am-1am, $16-30) feels like discovering a shined-up sailor pub, with brick walls, thick wooden beams, and long, dark wooden tables. Burgers, sturdy mains, and bar food are well-prepared (if unremarkable), and a seat at the bar is an excellent place for striking up conversations. When the basement is crowded, more seating is available upstairs, but the dining room seems a bit too brightly lit after the atmospheric gloom on the lower level.

Simple breakfasts and affordable lunch and dinner plates make **Island Kitchen** (1 Chins Way, 508/228-2639, www.islandkitchen.com, daily 7am-2pm and 5:30pm-9pm, $11-34) a year-round favorite, and the meal-sized salads are a refreshing break if you've been living off chowder and clam shack fare. Diner-like counter seating looks into the small open kitchen, and the tables at this casual joint fill up quickly, so arrive early on weekends or come prepared to wait.

A pale, minimalist dining room is a serene backdrop for the showstopping food at **Dune** (20 Broad St., 508/228-5550, www.dunenantucket.com, mid-May-Oct. daily 5pm-9:30pm, $37-60); the menu changes seasonally, but always features elegant seafood presentations with brightly flavored sides that lean French. The rich summer corn bisque is an evergreen favorite, and the pan-roasted coconut-lemongrass halibut is a melt-in-your-mouth bite of heaven.

Another destination-worthy restaurant is **Company of the Cauldron** (5 India St., 508/228-4016, www.companyofthecauldron.com, Mon. and Thurs.-Sat., call for seasonal dinner hours, $90-140), an intimate, romantic spot with fixed-priced dinners from chef and owner Joseph Keller that are among the best on the island. Fresh flowers and candles encourage a leisurely feel, and the restaurant has just one seating each evening, so reservations are essential.

Accommodations

With the exception of an excellent hostel, it is very challenging to find a place to sleep for under $350 during Nantucket's peak season, but prices drop dramatically in the shoulder season, when crowds start to thin. Simple rooms are available on Airbnb for less than the commercial options, but still start at $200 in the summer.

A five-minute stroll from the ferry and the heart of downtown Nantucket, the **Seven Sea Street Inn** (7 Sea St., 508/228-3577, www.sevenseastreetinn.com, $299-559) imbues a colonial seacoast house with bright colors and cosmopolitan comforts like memory-foam king beds, paintings by Nantucket artists, and local chocolate-covered cranberries presented in a bow box in each room upon check-in. The generous and hearty fireside breakfast features fresh pastries, which you can also enjoy on the flowering patio.

The airy decor at **21 Broad** (21 Broad St., 508/228-4749, www.larkhotels.com, $499-809) is a vibrant blend of modern lines and Nantucket style, both urban and beachy. Elegant extras are less stuffy than at other high-end hotels on the island: a mix-your-own cocktail bar, small-plate breakfasts, and complimentary beach bags, chairs, and towels are more fun than formal. During the summer, a deck with an outdoor fireplace is a haven in the heart of downtown Nantucket.

Information and Services

Get the lowdown on where to stay, where to eat, and how to get there from the centrally located **Nantucket Visitors Center** (25 Federal St., 508/228-0925, www.nantucket-ma.gov, Mon.-Sat. 9am-5pm), which maintains a list of the rooms that are available each day.

The island's only emergency medical facility is **Nantucket Cottage Hospital** (57 Prospect St., 508/825-8100, www.nantuckethospital.org), which offers 24-hour care. Fill prescription needs at the hospital-affiliated **Cottage Pharmacy** (10 Vesper Ln., 508/825-7300, www.nantuckethospital.org, Mon.-Fri. 9am-6pm, Sat.-Sun. 9am-3pm).

Nantucket is home to two banks, both with ATMs: **Nantucket Bank** (2 Orange St., 508/825-1120, www.nantucketbank.com, Mon.-Fri. 8:30am-4pm, Sat. 8:30am-noon) and **Cape Cod 5** (0 Main St., 508/228-1255). Be aware each charges a fee of $3-4 if you are not on its network. Cell phone service can be unreliable on Nantucket.

New
York City

Highlights

★ **Central Park:** The United States' most famous park is even bigger and more beautiful than you thought (page 398).

★ **The Metropolitan Museum of Art:** Explore everything from antiquities to the cutting edge in the largest art museum in the country (page 398).

★ **The Museum of Modern Art (MoMA):** Find the world's largest collection of modern art and world-class traveling exhibitions (page 400).

★ **The High Line:** Follow a trail of public art and modern landscape architecture over a reincarnated piece of railway (page 402).

★ **National September 11 Memorial & Museum:** Pay tribute to some of New York's most tragic stories at this moving monument (page 403).

★ **Ellis Island and the Statue of Liberty:** Get the iconic view of New York Harbor at this gateway to the United States, then see the famous French gift carrying a torch for freedom (page 405).

★ **Broadway Shows:** Watch the ol' song and dance on the Great White Way, the nerve center of New York's musical theater scene (page 405).

New York City

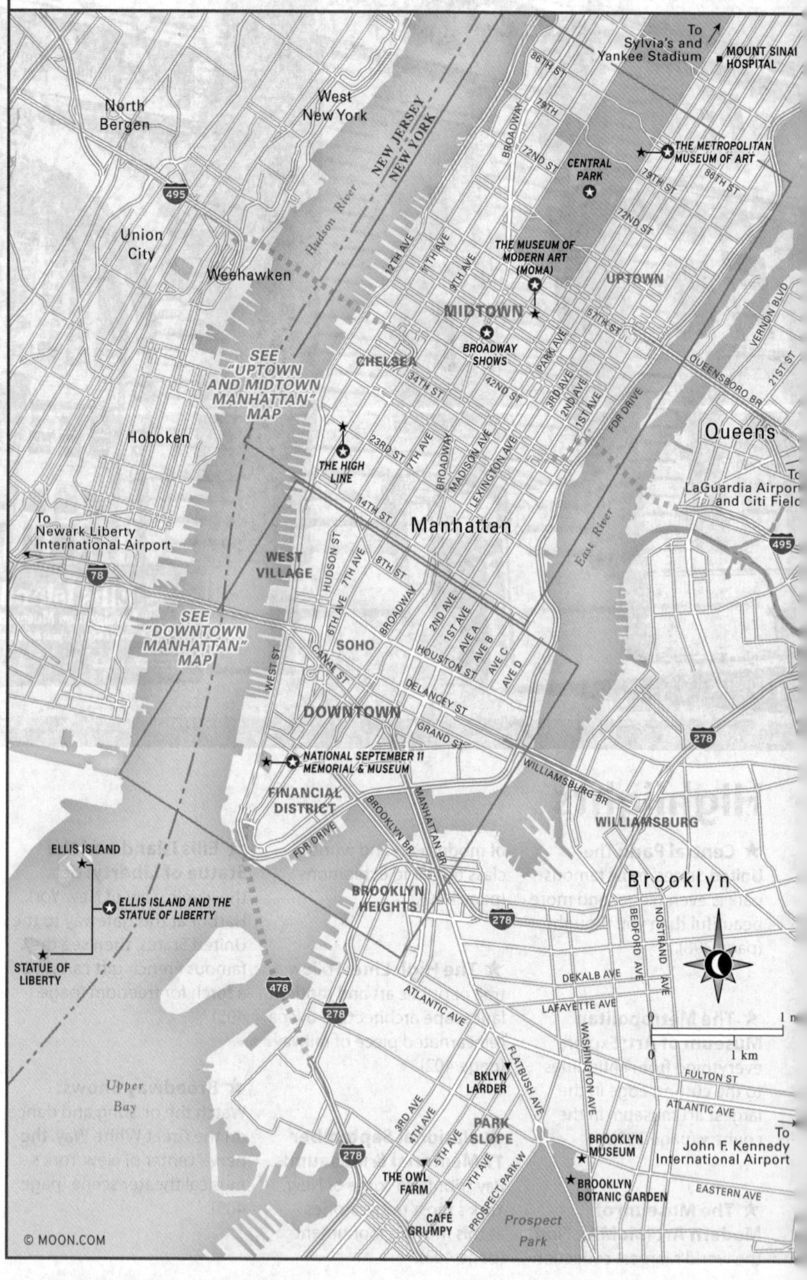

Best Restaurants

★ **Daniel:** The last word in New York City's fancy French dining, chef Daniel Boulud's eponymous restaurant is full of pomp and fine preparations (page 409).

★ **Sylvia's:** Grab an outdoor table at this soul food institution and tuck into fried chicken, smothered pork chops, and more as the world floats by (page 409).

★ **Despaña:** Hefty Spanish sandwiches laden with chorizo and manchego are the star attractions at this SoHo market, counter-service restaurant, and tapas bar (page 411).

★ **Russ & Daughters:** Visit the "appetizing" shop or café for Jewish deli classics, chewy bagels, lox, and caviar (page 411).

★ **John's of Bleecker Street:** Brave the lines to get the perfect New York pie from this simple landmark pizza joint (page 412).

The Big Apple needs no introduction, and while New York City is *not* part of New England, it's a grand place to launch or conclude an epic trip through the Northeast.

For most first-time visitors, passing through New York means sampling the classic sights: crossing the New York Harbor to Ellis Island and the Statue of Liberty, peering over the edge of the Empire State Building, ordering a pastrami sandwich, and immersing yourself in Times Square's gaudy chaos.

In between the "best-ofs," though, simply take in the city's unique rhythms and prepare for the unexpected. Duck into street-corner pizza joints, catch a Broadway show, and watch the world drift by from a bench in Central Park. The five boroughs of New York—Manhattan, Queens, Brooklyn, the Bronx, and Staten Island—sprawl over 303 square miles (785 sq km) of immigrant neighborhoods, glamorous avenues, and grit, but you can walk across Manhattan Island's widest section in under an hour. Because of this, Manhattan's bristling skyscrapers are easy to explore on foot and by public transport, and there's no better way to get a feel for New York life than by hitting the sidewalks and subway platforms.

Meet some locals along the way and you'll notice that, contrary to reputation, New Yorkers tend to be gregarious, kind, and funny. One piece of the NYC typecast hits home, however—many New Yorkers think their bright lights and bustling streets are the center of the known universe. To find out why, take a long walk down Broadway, head to Wall Street for the closing bell, or hit the town at 4am, when the "City that Never Sleeps" is still going full-steam.

Planning Your Time

If New York City is your New England gateway, plan to visit car-free, exploring the city before picking up your rental (or after returning it). Make a beeline for Manhattan, where you'll need at least two days if you'd like to see the primary sights, with additional time to get farther afield.

Orientation

New York City is divided into five boroughs: the Bronx, Queens, Brooklyn, Staten Island, and Manhattan. Most of the key tourist attractions are located in Manhattan, which is divided into a patchwork of smaller neighborhoods laid out on a grid.

Best Accommodations

★ **American Dream Bed and Breakfast:** Hostel prices meet bed-and-breakfast hospitality in this friendly Midtown option (page 412).

★ **The Pod Hotel:** Tiny rooms have techy touches and modern style for an up-to-the-minute feel (page 412).

★ **45 Times Square Hotel:** Design that evokes the hottest nightclubs and an atmospheric indoor pool make this place an especially swanky choice (page 413).

★ **citizenM:** Chic decor and a rooftop bar make this the hippest place to sleep in Midtown—and oversize beds ensure sweet dreams in the heart of Times Square chaos (page 413).

★ **The Nolitan Hotel:** These modern digs come with complimentary bikes and skateboards, and a rooftop bar with million-dollar views (page 413).

Uptown Manhattan generally refers to the area north of 59th Street. Downtown Manhattan, or Lower Manhattan, refers to the island south of 14th Street and encompasses neighborhoods including SoHo, the East Village, Greenwich Village, the Lower East Side, the Meatpacking District, the Bowery, and Nolita. Midtown Manhattan loosely stretches between these zones, and some of its more famous neighborhoods include Times Square, Hell's Kitchen, Chelsea, and Gramercy Park.

Avenues run north-south on Manhattan Island, from 1st Avenue on the east side to 11th Avenue on the west. While the avenues are laid out in numeric order, some named streets are interspersed: It's a four-block hike from 3rd Avenue to 5th Avenue, crossing Lexington, Park, and Madison Avenues.

Streets run (mostly) east-west; starting at Houston Street, numbered streets rise as you head uptown. When reading an address, note that 5th Avenue is the dividing line between east and west. Below Houston Street, streets begin to snarl and go off the grid—from there, a map is essential.

Getting to New York City

Driving from Boston

215 mi/346 km, 3.5 hr

Leave Boston on **I-93 South,** then use Exit 16A to merge onto **I-90 West,** which you'll follow for 55 miles (142 sq km, $7.05 toll). Take Exit 78 for **I-84 South,** following signs to New York City, continuing on I-84 for 41 miles (66 km). Take Exit 57 to **Route 15 South,** then Exit 86 onto **I-91 South.** After 17 miles (27 km), use Exit 17 to merge back onto **Route 15 South** for 30 miles (48 km).

Take Exit 52, merging onto **Route 108 South/Route 8 South** for 5 miles (8 km) before exiting onto **I-95 South.** Continue for 45 miles (72 km), then stay left to continue onto **I-278 West,** following signs for Manhattan. Use Exit 46 for Manhattan/FDR Drive, continuing onto the **Robert F. Kennedy Bridge** ($10.17 toll). Take Exit 10 for destinations in Midtown.

Driving from Newport

180 mi/290 km, 3 hr

Leave downtown Newport on **Route 238,** then turn west on Route 138 across the **Newport Bridge** ($6 toll). Exit onto **Route**

Two Days in New York City

One World Observatory

Day 1

Cue the Jay-Z, pull on some walking shoes, and see the hits in 48 hours: Grab a bagel (any bagel) and head to the **One World Observatory** to get your bearings from the tallest building in the hemisphere. Head back down to planet earth to visit the nearby **National September 11 Memorial & Museum,** commemorating the nearly 3,000 people killed in the 2001 terrorist attack. From there, pick up a hefty Spanish sandwich from **Despaña** and continue to **Battery Park** for a ferry to the **Statue of Liberty and Ellis Island,** making it back in time for sunset on New York Harbor and dinner—farm-to-table at **Gramercy Tavern,** barbecue ribs at **Sylvia's,** or just a hot dog at **Katz's Delicatessen?**

Day 2

Slow down for a morning of modernists and old masters at **The Metropolitan Museum of Art.** Once sated, head over to **Ess-a-Bagel** for jumbo kosher baked goods with smoked fish, and then find a bit of fresh air and greenery in nearby **Central Park.** Stroll the peaceful **Strawberry Fields,** climb to the top of **Belvedere Castle** and take a spin around the **Central Park Carousel.** You might want to take a nap by **The Pond,** so you can clap all the way through the final bow at a **Broadway show.** Call it a night with a velvety bowl of noodles at **Totto Ramen.**

1 North toward Providence after 8.5 miles (13.6 km), then stay left to continue onto **Route 4 North.** Take Exit 5 to turn left onto **Route 102 North,** staying on it for about 8 miles (13 km), then turn left onto **Route 3 South** for 4.4 miles (7 km), and merge onto **I-95 South.**

Continue for **137 miles** (220 km), then stay left to continue onto **I-278 West,** following signs for Manhattan. Use Exit 46 for Manhattan/FDR Drive, continuing onto the **Robert F. Kennedy Bridge** ($10.17 toll). Take Exit 10 for destinations in Midtown.

Driving from the Berkshires

135 mi/218 km, 2.25 hr

From **Great Barrington, Massachusetts,** leave town on **Route 7 South,** then turn right onto **Route 23 West** for 17 miles (27 km). Turn right to merge onto the **Taconic State Parkway**—among New

Driving the Connecticut Coast

Great piles of suburban wealth do little to dispel Connecticut's reputation as an NYC bedroom community, but the coast is dotted with pretty towns and sandy beaches that could easily fill a day or two of leisurely exploration. Follow Route 1 all the way down (or up) the coast between Rhode Island and New York, hopping off onto I-95 where you want to save time.

Mystic Seaport, Connecticut

Explore Sailing History

With a deeply sheltered harbor that straddles the Mystic River, lovely **Mystic** is all seaside charm, with colonial buildings and fields of bristling masts. Its showstopping attraction is the **Mystic Seaport Museum** (75 Greenmanville Ave., Mystic, 860/572-0711, www.mysticseaport.org, daily 10am-5pm, $28 adults, $26 seniors, $24 youth 13-17, $19 children 4-12, under 4 free), the largest maritime museum in the United States, which re-creates a 19th-century coastal village complete with costumed docents, ship smiths, riggers, and coopers in old buildings that were shipped from around New England.

Hit the Beach

The stretch of road from the **Connecticut River** (which divides the towns of Old Saybrook and Old Lyme) to **Guilford** is among the most appealing on the coast, a landscape shot through with inlets and marshland, dotted with ice cream shops and country boutiques. A crown jewel is breezy, beautiful **Hammonasset Beach State Park** (1288

York state's most **scenic** drives, passing through Hudson Valley farms and forest.

Follow the Taconic Parkway for about **85 miles** (137 km), then exit onto the **Saw Mill Parkway South** for 16 miles (26 km). Keep right at the fork to continue onto **Henry Hudson Parkway/Route 9A South,** which crosses the **Henry Hudson Bridge** ($8.25 toll, assessed and billed automatically). Turn left on surface streets for destinations in Midtown.

Getting There by Air, Train, or Bus

Air

Three airports serve New York City: **John F. Kennedy International Airport** (JFK, 718/244-4444), **LaGuardia Airport** (LGA, 718/533-3400), and **Newark Liberty International Airport** (EWR, 973/961-6000) in New Jersey. Coming or going, taxis between JFK and Manhattan have a flat rate of $70, plus a $0.50 New York state surcharge, not including bridge/tunnel tolls and tips. From LaGuardia, taxis charge regular metered fare, with the cost running approximately $32-40, not including tolls and tips to Manhattan, with meters starting at $2.50. From Newark, a taxi fare will usually cost around $52-75, plus tolls and tip.

For inexpensive transportation to and from JFK, the Port Authority operates the **AirTrain** (www.jfkairport.com/to-from-airport/air-train), a light-rail that connects all airport terminals to the subway system. You can access the AirTrain from the Sutphin Boulevard stop on

Boston Post Rd., Madison, 203/245-2785, www.ct.gov, $15 weekdays, $22 weekends). If the shore's too pretty to leave behind, there's a **campground** on-site ($30 primitive sites, $45 hookups, $80 primitive cabins).

Eat Classic Coastal Food

Another classic Connecticut coastal experience is stopping for seafood at **The Place** (901 Boston Post Rd., Guilford, 203/453-9276, www.theplaceguilford.com, late Apr.-Oct. Mon.-Thurs. 5pm-9pm, Fri. 5pm-10pm, Sat. 1pm-10pm, Sun. noon-9pm, $15-30), a rough-and-tumble outdoor joint in **Guilford** with tree stumps for chairs, smoky roasted clams, and big communal tables.

Go to College

Despite the blue-blooded university at the heart of **New Haven,** the sprawling seaport's reputation has always been more grit than glam. That's changed in recent years, and the city center is an energetic mix of new businesses and art galleries abutting older neighborhoods. The highlight is still **Yale University** (Sachem St., New Haven, 203/432-4771), whose campus displays Gothic and Victorian architecture. **Guided tours** (daily 1pm) last a little over an hour, or download a map and take a **self-guided audio tour** (http://visitorcenter.yale.edu). The campus also has several fine (and free) museums: Visit the **Yale University Art Gallery** (1111 Chapel St., 203/432-0600, https://artgallery.yale.edu, Tues.-Fri. 10am-5pm, Sat.-Sun. 11am-5pm, June-Sept. Thurs. 10am-8pm) to see a vast collection that includes works by Chuck Close and Dorothea Lange, along with pieces from around the world.

If you get hungry while in town, note that New Haven's other claim to fame is a distinctive take on thin-crust pizza known as "apizza." It's got a charred, slightly sour crust and an oblong shape, and the plain version comes topped with oregano, tomato sauce, and pecorino romano. If you want chewy strings of mozzarella cheese, order yours with "mootz." A great place to get your first pie is **Modern Apizza** (874 State St., New Haven, 203/776-5306, www.modernapizza.com, Tues.-Sat. 10:30am-10pm, Sun. 3pm-10pm, $13-25).

the E line or via the Howard Beach stop on the A line (take a train marked "Far Rockaway"). You can also take the Long Island Rail Road from Penn Station to the AirTrain at Jamaica Station. The cost of a one-way trip on the AirTrain is $8.25. You can pay the fare using a pay-per-ride MetroCard or purchase tickets in the station, and if you're catching the train from Jamaica or Howard Beach, you can simply tap your credit card at the fare gates. Newark also offers inexpensive rail service directly from the airport to Manhattan's Penn Station by way of the **NJ Transit** (973/275-5555, www.njtransit.com) train network. The ride takes just under half an hour and a one-way ticket costs $15.75, with the first train departing at 4:50am and the last at midnight.

The **Port Authority of New York and New Jersey** (www.panynj.gov) operates booths that provide information on rates and connections to private limousine and van companies. Its **Air-Ride service** (800/247-7433) provides recorded information about bus, shuttle, and private car services from area airports. Shuttle options include **Olympia Trails/Coach USA Airport Express** (866/912-6224, www.coachusa.com), **GO Airlink NYC** (212/812-9000, www.goairlinkshuttle.com), and **Supershuttle** (800/258-3826, www.supershuttle.com).

Train

Moynihan Train Hall (33rd St. between 8th Ave. and 9th Ave.) serves passengers arriving on **Amtrak** (800/872-7245, www.amtrak.com) as well as **NJ Transit** (973/275-5555, www.njtransit.com), **Long Island Rail Road** (718/217-5477, http://mta.info/lirr), and the subway's A, C, E, 1, 2, and 3 trains. Visitors arrive at New York's other main station, **Grand Central Terminal** (89 E. 42nd St.), via **Metro-North Railroad** (212/532-4900, www.mta.info/mnr) and the 4, 5, 6, 7, and S subway lines (NYC Transit, 511 or 718/330-1234).

Bus

The Midtown **Port Authority Bus Terminal** (625 8th Ave., 212/435-7000) is the main long-distance bus hub for the city, linking New York City with destinations all over New England. Carriers include **Greyhound** (www.greyhound.com), **Peter Pan** (800/343-9999, www.peterpanbus.com), and discount bus service **Megabus** (www.megabus.com). A good way to find fares to other destinations in New England is on the search site **Wanderu** (www.wanderu.com), which aggregates bus and train schedules with real-time fares.

Sights

Uptown

★ Central Park

Designed by Frederick Law Olmsted and Calvert Vaux in the mid-19th century, **Central Park** (between 5th Ave. and Central Park W., 59th St. and 110th St., 212/310-6600, www.centralpark.com, daily 6am-1am) was the first landscaped recreational area in the United States. Many of Central Park's most prominent attractions have been beloved landmarks since it opened in 1876, such as the wild-looking **Ramble,** tranquil **Central Park Mall,** and lovely **Bethesda Terrace and Fountain.** Today, it remains an impressively large and beautiful park, a beloved respite from the relentlessly urban landscape that surrounds it.

Though open year-round, the park truly comes alive in the warmer months. Each summer brings a host of outdoor performances, including free concerts by the New York Philharmonic, the Shakespeare in the Park festival, and the often-raucous SummerStage. Recreational activities abound, including softball on the **Great Lawn,** boating on the lake, tai chi on the North Meadow, and bicycling, jogging, and horseback riding. Squirrels and chipmunks run wild throughout, while the park's famous red-tailed hawks soar overhead. More than 130 species from polar bears to tropical toucans live in naturally designed habitats at the **Central Park Zoo** (off 5th Ave. near 64th St., www.centralparkzoo.com, daily 10am-4:30pm, $20 adults, $17 seniors, $15 children, free under 3, discounts with online purchase).

A wonderful way to explore the park is by bicycle: Multiple **Citi Bike** (www.citibikenyc.com) stations are located along 8th Avenue on the park's west side, but for a longer ride it's worth renting a bike at **Unlimited Biking: Central Park** (56 West 56th St., 212/392-6028, www.unlimitedbiking.com, rentals from $25).

Some favorite stops to visit by bike are the John Lennon memorial at **Strawberry Fields,** whimsical **Belvedere Castle,** and **The Pond,** where park views have a perfect backdrop of skyscrapers.

Visiting families shouldn't miss the **Central Park Carousel** (1802 65th St. Tranverse, daily 10am-6pm, $3.25), where 57 hand-carved horses and a pair of chariots have gone round and round since 1908.

★ The Metropolitan Museum of Art

Undisputed crown jewel of Museum Mile, a stretch of 5th Avenue that includes some of the city's most important collections, the **Metropolitan Museum of Art** (1000 5th Ave., 212/535-7710, www.metmuseum.org, Sun.-Tues. and Thurs. 10am-5pm, Fri.-Sat. 10am-9pm, $30 adults, $22 seniors, $17 students, free children under 12, NY residents, students

Uptown and Midtown Manhattan

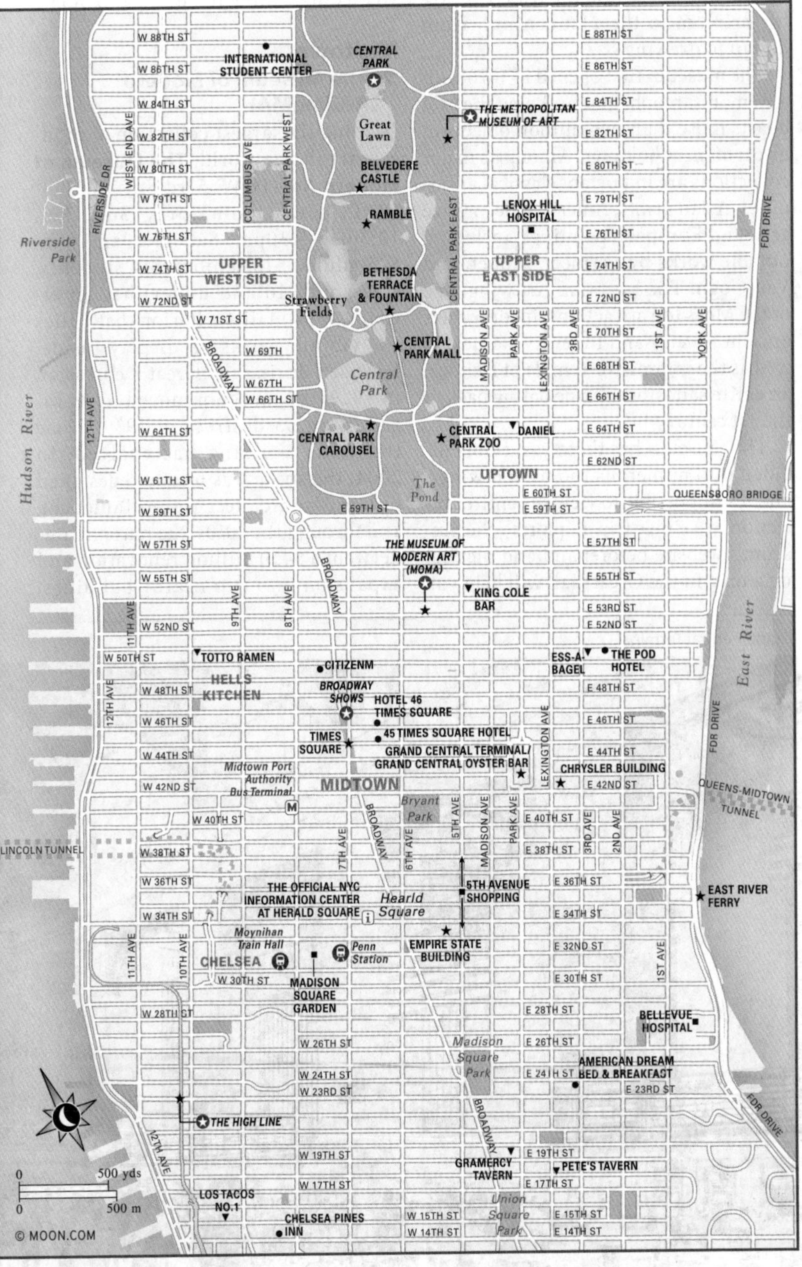

from NY, NJ, and CT) houses one of the world's largest and most diverse collections, with works ranging from the prehistoric era to the 21st century, from design to drawing.

The museum first opened in 1870 with a Roman sarcophagus, and now the Met boasts more than two million objects in its permanent holdings. Among its major collections are important classical antiquities, Asian prints, American decorative arts, and European paintings, including notable works by Vermeer, Monet, and Van Gogh. The Egyptian Art wing, one of the Met's top attractions, incorporates ancient jewelry and funerary statues, as well as the impressive Temple of Dendur, an entire sandstone shrine dating back to the 1st century BC.

The museum has three vast floors divided into numerous rooms and wings, and it's impossible to view the entire collection in a single trip. Exploring the museum's website beforehand and picking up a map in the Great Hall will help you prioritize. You can also use the interactive museum map on the website to chart your course through the ample exhibits.

Midtown

★ The Museum of Modern Art (MoMA)

Holding the largest collection of modern art in the world, **The Museum of Modern Art** (11 W. 53rd St., 212/708-9400, www.moma.org, Sun.-Fri. 10:30am-5:30pm, Sat. 10:30am-7pm, $25 adults, $18 seniors, $14 students, free youth 16 and under) has an elegant, minimalist exterior that belies the vibrant works on display inside. Founded during the Great Depression in 1929, the museum moved to its location on 53rd Street in 1939. Since then, the building has evolved; in 2004, the space was totally redesigned by Japanese architect Yoshio Taniguchi, and through the 2010s, the museum underwent a $450 million renovation and expansion into two nearby buildings,

Grand Central Terminal

including the former American Folk Art Museum.

MoMA's permanent collection and its temporary exhibitions are on display in galleries surrounding a six-story atrium, facing the museum's signature sculpture garden (which is free and open to the public). To view the permanent collection, head to the 4th and 5th floors' Painting and Sculpture galleries, where you'll find such iconic works as Van Gogh's *Starry Night,* among other modern masterpieces. Its temporary exhibitions from up-and-coming artists are almost always worth the trip in themselves.

Times Square

With its crowds, chaos, and iconic bright lights, **Times Square** (between Broadway and 7th Ave., W. 42nd St. and W. 47th St., 212/768-1560, www.timessquarenyc.org) is a massive commercial intersection, shimmering with all of New York's energy and electricity. Lured by the shopping, the theaters, the mega-restaurants, and the occasional street performances, people from all walks of life crowd the sidewalks along Broadway. Larger-than-life billboards have always been a hallmark of Times Square, and nowadays dozens of dazzling, multimedia "spectaculars" vie for attention. Even the police station and the subway stops sport glittering logos.

Named after the *New York Times* offices on 43rd Street and Broadway, Times Square was originally synonymous with theater, vaudeville, and cabaret. During the Great Depression, Broadway attendance dwindled, and seedier businesses moved in. By the 1960s, Times Square had developed a grungier reputation. However, after a cleanup effort in the 1990s, the area became far more tourist-friendly (if a bit generic), with new landmarks like the Hard Rock Café and Disney Store. More than 330,000 pedestrians are estimated to pass through Times Square every day.

One of the most visible new "attractions" in Times Square is the throng of characters—from grinning Lady Liberties to topless women and matted Sesame Street puppets—who charge visitors wanting photos with them.

Grand Central Terminal

Roughly 750,000 people pass through **Grand Central Terminal** (89 E. 42nd St., 212/340-2583, www.grandcentralterminal.com, daily 5:30am-2am) every day, headed for the city's busiest subway station (five lines pass through underground) and the Metro North commuter trains. Completed in 1913 under the auspices of transportation magnate Cornelius Vanderbilt, the station is all pomp and classical grandeur. The Beaux-Arts facade on 42nd Street looks more like the entrance to a Roman coliseum than a rail station, with its pair of Corinthian columns supporting sculptures of Hercules, Minerva, and Mercury (the Roman god of speed and commerce). With its towering ceilings and famous four-sided clock at the center, the station's Main Concourse is one of the most spectacular public spaces in the world. And it's almost always alive with activity. Grand Central has become a destination unto itself, with an impressive food hall and a range of shops along the lower concourse. Many locals stop in even without a train to catch, as the beloved Grand Central Oyster Bar is a longtime favorite restaurant.

Chrysler Building

What the Empire State Building has in stature, the **Chrysler Building** (405 Lexington Ave., 212/682-3070, Mon.-Fri. 8am-6pm) achieves in style. To keep his competitors guessing, the building's architect, William Van Alen, hid his final plans for the top of the structure, which included a seven-story spire. At the last minute, workers raised the spire right through what spectators had assumed was the roof and riveted it into place. It was the first human-made structure to reach over 1,000 feet (305 m).

From the outside, the 1,046-foot (319-m) granite-and-glass structure, with its protruding gargoyles (designed to resemble the hood ornaments of Plymouth cars), is topped by a distinctive crown ornamentation of stainless steel cladding. The luxurious lobby (once a car showroom) is the only interior space open to the public, giving visitors a chance to peek past the security gates at the marble walls, polished nickel chrome decorations that embellish the stairway railings, and mural by Edward Trumbull depicting early 20th-century technological triumphs.

Empire State Building

Completed in 1931, the 102-story **Empire State Building** (350 5th Ave., 212/736-3100, www.esbnyc.com, daily 10am-10pm, last elevator 9:15pm) is one of New York's most recognizable landmarks. A 1,454-foot (443-m) limestone monument to progress, it remains a fixture in the popular imagination, in part because of its long cinematic history. It served as a romantic rendezvous point in *An Affair to Remember,* only to be destroyed by aliens in *Independence Day.*

Taking the ear-popping elevator ride to the 86th-floor main observation deck means waiting in three interminable lines (metal detector, ticketing, and elevator) and shelling out $44 ($38 children 6-12, under 6 free), but visitors are rewarded with panoramic views of the city, stretching for up to 80 miles (128 km) in all directions. To experience the Empire State Building without a crushing crowd, buy tickets online before arriving and plan to come as the building opens at 10am, or midafternoon around 3pm.

★ The High Line

A triumph in innovative urban planning, **The High Line** (Gansevoort St. and Washington St. to W. 34th St., between 10th Ave. and 11th Ave., 212/500-6035, www.thehighline.org, daily 7am-10pm) is a picturesque 1.45-mile (2.3-km) stretch of public walkways, sundecks, and gardens, built atop an elevated rail bed that runs along Manhattan's west side. Cutting through the Chelsea gallery district and offering views of Midtown skyscrapers on one side and the Hudson River on the other, the park is open year-round and fully accessible by wheelchair. (And conveniently for rail commuters and visitors, it also features a connector path with direct access to Moynihan Train Hall.) A vestige of the neighborhood's industrial past, the elevated railway was built in the 1930s, replacing the street-level freight trains that carried goods from the Meatpacking District to the warehouses and docks farther north. After falling into disuse in the 1980s, the structure was threatened with demolition (most of the original 13 mi/21 km of track were destroyed in the 1960s). In response, a local community-based organization,

Friends of the High Line, launched a campaign for its preservation.

Since then, The High Line has become a focal point of the neighborhood, with trendy hotels, great restaurants, and shops opening along its route, in addition to ongoing public art projects throughout the park. **Free public tours** of The High Line offer a fascinating look at the park's design and artwork, and stargazing evenings take place during summer months; check the website for the schedule.

Downtown

★ National September 11 Memorial & Museum

Ten years after the tragedy on September 11, 2001, the former World Trade Center site was reopened as the **National September 11 Memorial** (between Church St. and West Side Hwy., Liberty St. and Vesey St., 212/266-5200, www.911memorial.org, daily 8am-8pm), an eight-acre (3.2-ha), tree-filled public plaza designed as the centerpiece to a new business and transportation complex. Two elegant pools were built in the footprints of the former Twin Towers, with the names of almost 3,000 victims from the terrorist attacks in New York City, Pennsylvania, and the Pentagon in 2001, as well as the 1993 World Trade Center bombing, etched in bronze panels surrounding them. Among the hundreds of white oaks filling the plaza is a lone pear tree that survived the collapse of the towers; after its rehabilitation, the "survivor tree" was returned to the site.

In early 2014, the **National September 11 Memorial & Museum** (180 Greenwich St., 212/312-8800, Wed.-Mon. 9am-7pm, last entry 6pm, closed Sept. 11, $33 adults, $27 seniors, American students, youth 13-17, $22 veterans, $21 youth 7-12, under 7 free) opened on the grounds. Filling a multistory belowground exhibition

Top to bottom: walking The High Line; National September 11 Memorial & Museum; SoHo shopping district

Downtown Manhattan

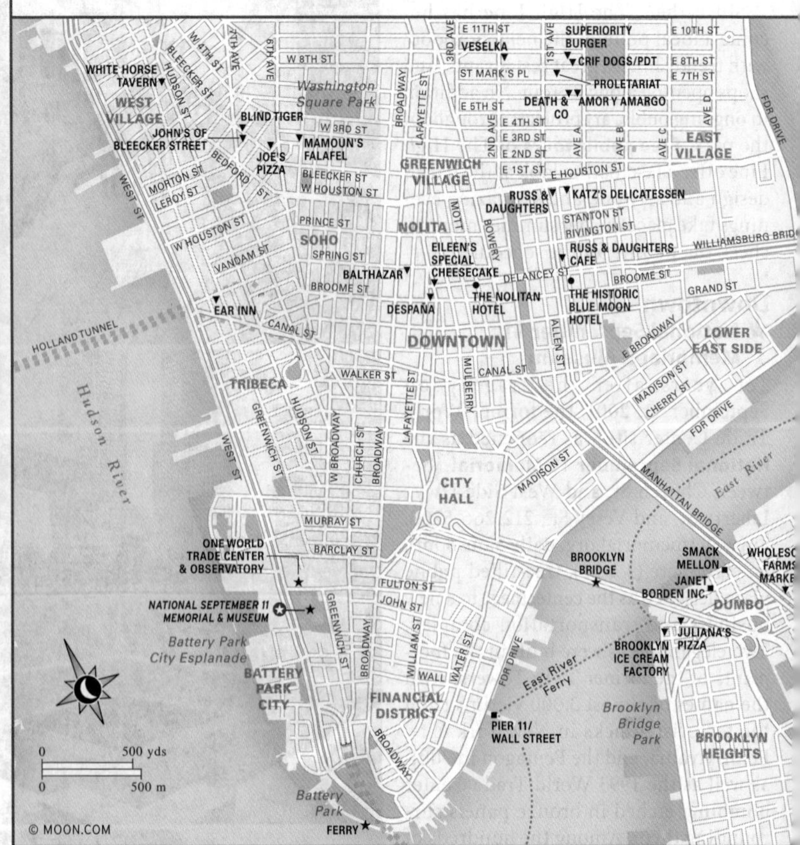

space, the museum chronicles the events on the day of the terrorist attacks, history of the Twin Towers, and geopolitical context of the time. Exhibits include artifacts recovered from the demolished towers, such as a mangled fire truck, and a more somber memorial room covered floor-to-ceiling with photos of the victims. Reserve tickets online to bypass the long line at the entrance.

One World Trade Center and Observatory

Built on the site of the original World Trade Center, the shining tower of **One World Trade Center** (285 Fulton St., www.onewtc.com, daily 9am-10pm) is the tallest skyscraper in the Western Hemisphere, rising above the Manhattan skyline to a symbolic 1,776 feet (541 m). Architect David Childs designed a footprint identical to the original Twin Towers, but the resemblance to the squared-off original buildings ends there: Freedom Tower, as it's often called, is sheathed in glass that reflects the sky and the surrounding buildings. Between floors 100 and 102 is **One World Observatory** (844/696-1776, www.oneworldobservatory.com, May-early

Sept. daily 9am-10pm, early Sept.-June daily 9am-8pm, $38 adults, $36 seniors, $32 children 6-12, under 6 free), which has stunning views of the city and multimedia presentations on the local history and landscape.

★ Ellis Island and the Statue of Liberty

A gift to the United States from France after the Union victory in the Civil War, the **Statue of Liberty** (board ferry at Battery Park/State St. at Battery Pl., visitor information 212/363-3200 or ferry 877/523-9849, www.nps.gov/stli, daily 9am-5pm, closed Dec. 25) has become a symbol of the country's finest aspirations. Designed by sculptor Frédéric Auguste Bartholdi, with internal structural engineering designed by Gustave Eiffel (of Eiffel Tower fame), the statue arrived in 1885 and was assembled and dedicated on Bedloe's Island, now known as Liberty Island.

Across the harbor, **Ellis Island** (www.ellisisland.org, daily 9:30am-4:30pm, closed Dec. 25) was once the nation's main immigration checkpoint. More than 12 million people passed through the site from 1892 until it closed in 1954, though immigration slowed considerably after the 1920s. After years of disuse, the main building of the former immigration complex was completely restored, reopening in 1976 as an interesting museum, displaying photos and artifacts from the island's past.

Statue City Cruises (877/523-9849, www.statuecruises.com, reserve, pedestal, and crown tickets $25 adults, $18 seniors, $12 children) is the only company authorized to provide transportation to Liberty and Ellis Islands. Ferries depart every hour from Battery Park in New York (and hourly from Liberty State Park in New Jersey), and include full access to both Liberty Island and Ellis Island. While tickets are sold on-site in Battery Park, it's worth booking ahead; tickets to the statue's pedestal are the same price as basic "reserve" access tickets to Liberty Island, but a limited number are given out, and crown tickets are booked months in advance for busy periods.

Entertainment and Events

★ Broadway Shows

The 41 historic theaters classified as Broadway houses are mostly located in the 10 blocks surrounding Times Square. Broadway shows all play in these houses (productions classified as off-Broadway run in smaller theaters), and most are performed six evenings a week, along with two matinees. Tickets run the gamut from the price of a fancy New York hamburger to the cost of a transatlantic flight.

Spending an hour or so in line at **TKTS** (in Times Square, at South Street Seaport, or in downtown Brooklyn) can get you a good deal on discounted same-day tickets for Broadway and off-Broadway shows that haven't sold out. Signs near the booth list the possibilities for that day, and the useful **TKTS app** (www.tdf.org) gives real-time updates about what shows are available. Some theaters release same-day tickets and sell day-of standing-room tickets. If you're between the ages of 18 and 35, you qualify for discounted tickets through the **Roundabout Theatre Company's HipTix program** (www.roundabouttheatre.org) and **Lincoln Center Theater's LincTix program** (www.lct.org/linctix).

Shows are constantly changing, but the most successful productions are long-running and spectacular: Favorites include ***Wicked*** (www.wickedthemusical.com), a musical retelling of the *Wizard of Oz* story, and ***Kinky Boots*** (www.kinkybootsthemusical.com), but the historical hip-hop show ***Hamilton*** (www.hamiltonbroadway.com) is still the hottest ticket on the street (prices for the breakaway success and Tony Awards monster broke records with $850 premium tickets).

Nightlife

Classic NYC Bars

The poet Dylan Thomas drank his last (18) whiskeys at the **White Horse Tavern** (567 Hudson St., 212/989-3956, www.whitehorsetavern1880.com, Mon.-Wed. 4pm-midnight, Thurs.-Fri. 4pm-2am, Sat. noon-2am, Sun. noon-midnight), an atmospheric Greenwich Village bar that's been frequented by a who's who of literary legends, from James Baldwin and Norman Mailer to an entire cadre of Beat poets. The food is dubious, but the beer and whiskey are cheap. Find something entirely different at **King Cole Bar** (2 E. 55th St., 212/753-4500, www.marriott.com, Mon.-Sat. 11:30am-midnight, Sun. noon-midnight) in the St. Regis Hotel, where you can sip a very expensive cocktail with a well-heeled Midtown crowd. The real highlight, though, is getting to take in the stunning Maxfield Parrish mural that provides the finest bar backdrop in the city.

All dark wood and pressed-tin ceilings, **Pete's Tavern** (129 E. 18th St., 212/473-7676, www.petestavern.com, daily noon-2am) is one of the oldest bars in New York City. The writer O. Henry was a regular here, and it remains a cozy place to duck off the sidewalk for a beer. Another bar that jostles for position as oldest in the city is the raucous **Ear Inn** (326 Spring St., 212/226-9060, www.theearinn.com, daily 11:30am-4am), formerly a sailor and longshore workers' bar, and a Prohibition-era speakeasy. Come here for a colorful cross section of the city and live music some nights.

Craft Beer and Cocktail Bars

Three of Manhattan's best cocktail bars are strolling distance apart in the East Village: Bartenders in suspenders and snappy bow ties serve lengthy apprenticeships before ever pouring a drink at **Death & Co** (433 E. 6th St., 212/388-0882, www.deathandcompany.com, Mon.-Wed. 6pm-1am, Thurs.-Sun. 5:30pm-1am), whose creative cocktail recipes are unusual and intensive—think eyedroppers, beakers, and unpronounceable ingredients. Tiny **Amor y Amargo** (95 Ave. A, 833/328-4588, www.amoryamargo.com, Sun.-Thurs. 5pm-midnight, Fri.-Sat. 5pm-1am) is just steps away and specializes in esoteric bitters and equally bitter amari aperitifs with Italian flair. In-the-know patrons enter **PDT**—it stands for "please don't tell"—through the vintage phone booth in the back of **Crif Dogs** (113 St. Mark's Place, www.pdtnyc.com, Sun.-Thurs. 5pm-2am, Fri.-Sat. 5pm-3am). Decor is updated speakeasy chic, cocktails are extraordinary, and reservations are a good idea.

Plenty of Manhattanites got their craft beer baptism at **Blind Tiger** (281 Bleecker St., 212/462-4682, www.blindtigeralehouse.com, Mon.-Fri. 11:30am-4am, Sat.-Sun. 10am-4am), an unpretentious-looking draft joint with a very respectable brew list and knowledgeable bartenders. Skinny as a pilsner glass, **Proletariat** (21 E. 7th St., 833/328-4588, www.proletariatny.com, Mon. 5pm-10pm, Tues.-Thurs. 5pm-midnight, Fri.-Sat. 5pm-1am, Sun. 3pm-10pm) is another craft beer gem that pulls offbeat brews from all over.

Festivals and Events

It's hard to find a weekend in New York without some kind of festival happening, from the massive and colorful **Puerto Rican Day Parade** (www.nprdpinc.org, second Sun. every June) to arts celebrations of all kinds, including the prestigious **New York Film Festival** (www.filmlinc.org/nyff, late Sept.-early Oct.). A few standouts include the iconic **Macy's Parade** on Thanksgiving Day (212/494-2922, www.macys.com/parade) and **Rockefeller Center Christmas Tree Lighting Ceremony** (212/632-3975, www.rockefellercenter.com, late Nov.-early Dec.). People from around the United

States watch the **Times Square New Year's Eve** (www.newyearseve.nyc) celebration, and the wonderfully energetic **NYC Pride** (212/807-7433, www.nycpride.org, June) event is one of the best in the country.

Unless you're planning a trip around one of these destination events, however, it's worth simply checking through the city's event listings. A good place to start is the ***New York Times* Arts and Entertainment Guide** (www.nytimes.com/spotlight/arts-listings). You can also pick up a free copy of the ***Village Voice*** (www.villagevoice.com/calendar), or check out **NYC.com.** Magazine ***Time Out New York*** (www.timeout.com/newyork) also offers extensive weekly listings.

Shopping

The classic place to shop New York's elegant department stores is **5th Avenue,** between 49th and 60th Streets, where behemoths like **Bergdorf Goodman** (754 5th Ave., 212/7533-7300, www.bergdorfgoodman.com, Mon.-Sat. 11am-7pm, Sun. 11am-6pm) and **Tiffany & Co.** (727 5th Ave., 212/755-8000, www.tiffany.com, Mon.-Sat. 10am-8pm, Sun. 11am-7pm) line the iconic street.

To experience the city's more creative side, head to **SoHo** (the shopping district is bordered by Canal and Houston Streets, and Sullivan and Lafayette Streets), where name brand and indie boutiques abound and a gallery-like minimalism recalls the area's past as an arts district. Two favorite stops for local fashionistas are **rag & bone** (119 Mercer St., 212/219-2204, www.rag-bone.com, daily 11am-7pm) and **A.P.C.** (131 Mercer St., 212/966-9685, www.apcstore.com, Mon.-Sat. 11am-7pm, Sun. noon-6pm), which share a minimalist aesthetic and a passionate following.

On the **Lower East Side** (Orchard St. and Ludlow St., between E. Houston St. and Rivington St.), small storefronts sell the latest in urban gear and cutting-edge fashion, like ultramodern sneakers and graphic tees. Producer and creative director Carlos Rodriguez, a veteran of the hip-hop scene, sells street culture-inspired fashion at **Option A** (147 Orchard St., 212/334-5444, www.optionanyc.com, daily 12:30pm-8pm), and NYC-based designers display their work alongside vintage apparel from luxury brands at **Pilgrim New York** (70 Orchard St., 212/463-7720, www.pilgrimnyc.com, Tues.-Sun. noon-5pm).

Meanwhile, pretty boutiques displaying sweet frocks are the norm along the tree-lined streets of **Nolita** (Mulberry St. to Elizabeth St., between Broome St. and Houston St.). Find beautiful welded bracelets and jeweled piercings at **Astrid & Miyu** (248 Elizabeth St., 646/864-0010, www.astridandmiyu.com, daily 11am-7pm), and a fragrance to match from the custom scents at **Le Labo** (233 Elizabeth St., 212/219-2230, www.lelabofragrances.com, daily 11am-7pm).

Sports and Recreation

Parks

Central Park is New York's most extraordinary green space, but there are parks scattered throughout the city. Occupying the southernmost tip of Manhattan, 25-acre (10-ha) **Battery Park** (State St. at Battery Pl., 212/344-3491, www.thebattery.org) is the jumping-off point for visitors headed to Liberty and Ellis Islands. The park itself features sculptures, harbor-facing benches, and the Castle Clinton National Monument, a small sandstone fort that was the first U.S. immigration center. Weary Wall Street workers jog off stress on the **Battery Park City Esplanade** (212-267-9700, https://bpca.ny.gov/place/the-esplanade) along the Hudson River.

Washington Square Park (between W. 4th St. and Waverly Pl., University St. and Macdougal St., 212/504-4115, www.nycgovparks.org) is a Greenwich Village

One Day in Brooklyn

Once a working-class enclave, Brooklyn today is a hipster darling and creative hot spot—a destination in its own right.

walking across the Brooklyn Bridge

Morning

Frequent subway trains link Manhattan and Brooklyn, but it's far more fun to arrive on the **East River Ferry** (844/469-3377, www.ferry.nyc, one-way $4 adults, $1.35 seniors, free children under 44 in.). For a sightseeing trip down the East River (a more direct boat departs from Pier 11/Wall St.), catch the ferry at East 34th Street/Midtown. If you've gotten an early start, hop off in **Williamsburg** (N. 6th St./N. Williamsburg ferry stop) to explore this legendary hipster haven en route to other parts of Brooklyn. Walk up **North 6th Street,** which is packed with restaurants and shops, and then, three blocks from the water, turn onto one of the neighborhood's trendiest strips, **Bedford Avenue.**

The other classic way to reach Brooklyn is by **walking across the Brooklyn Bridge,** a 1.3-mile (2-km) trip with amazing views. The longest suspension bridge in the world when it opened in 1883, the Brooklyn Bridge remains one of the city's most important landmarks. From Manhattan, access it from the Brooklyn Bridge/City Hall metro station. Budget an hour for the walk, as the pedestrian lane can be crowded.

Continue by foot or ferry (Brooklyn Bridge Park/DUMBO stop) to **DUMBO** (that's "down under the Manhattan bridge overpass"), the perfect place to take in Brooklyn's

institution, attracting dog-walking celebrities, boa constrictor-wearing locals, NYU students, and fire-juggling street performers. Its famous triumphal arch stands at the foot of 5th Avenue.

Spectator Sports

From the **Yankees** to the **Mets** and the **New York Knicks,** New York City's sports include some of the most recognizable, best-loved, and widely reviled teams in the United States (sometimes all at once). The baseball teams play a hectic schedule of up to five games a week, so it's often possible to get tickets a day or two before the game. Head to **Yankee Stadium** (1 E. 161st St., Bronx) in the Bronx to see the **Yankees** (718/293-4300, www.mlb.com/yankees, tickets from $33), one of the city's two Major League baseball teams. The **New York Mets** (718/507-8499, www.mlb.com/mets, tickets from $33) play at **Citi Field** (123-01 Roosevelt Ave., Queens), near LaGuardia Airport. When choosing seats, it's worth avoiding the very cheapest tickets in the stadium's 400 level, where the ball is barely visible, and spend the money to sit in the 100 or 200 level, where tickets start at $45.

The **New York Knicks** (877/695-3865, www.nba.com/knicks, tickets from $90), or Knickerbockers (technically), are one of just two founding NBA teams still based in their original city—the word *knickerbocker* refers to early Dutch settlers who wore their pants rolled up above their knees. This team plays home games at **Madison Square Garden** (4 Pennsylvania Plaza), and attending a game at this "Mecca of Basketball" is a

creative culture. The blocks between the Manhattan and Brooklyn Bridges afford plentiful places to stop, but don't miss **Janet Borden Inc.** (91 Water St., 212/431-0166, www.janetbordeninc.com, Tues.-Sat. 11am-5pm, by appt.), which specializes in contemporary photo art, or supercool nonprofit gallery **Smack Mellon** (92 Plymouth St., 718/834-8761, www.smackmellon.org, Wed.-Sun. noon-6pm).

Afternoon

Duck back under the bridge to reach **Brooklyn Bridge Park,** which has winding paths along the **East River** waterfront, an ideal spot for a picnic and people-watching: Find supplies at **Wholesome Farms Market** (108 Jay St., 917/909-1537, Mon.-Fri. 5:15am-midnight, Sat.-Sun. 7am-midnight), or call ahead for a thin pie from **Juliana's Pizza** (19 Old Fulton St., 718/596-6700, www.julianaspizza.com, daily 11:30am-3:15pm and 4pm-9pm, $18-34). Afterward, grab a locally made scoop at the **Brooklyn Ice Cream Factory** (14 Old Fulton St., 718/522-5211, www.brooklynicecreamfactory.com, daily 11am-10pm, $6-9), which you can lick on the way to **Brooklyn Heights,** an upscale neighborhood with some of the borough's classic brownstone houses (some of the best are along **Willow** and **Cranberry Streets**).

Hop a subway train (lines 2 or 3) at the nearby Clark Street station and get off at the Grand Army Plaza stop, continuing on foot into **Prospect Park,** a 585-acre (237-ha) enclave that holds its own against the grandeur of Central Park (Olmsted designed both green spaces.) Amble aimlessly or explore the park's attractions, like the wonderful **Brooklyn Botanic Garden** (990 Washington Ave., 718/623-7200, www.bbg.org, Tues.-Sun. 10am-6pm, $18 adults, $12 seniors and students 12 and over, under 12 free) or **Brooklyn Museum** (200 Eastern Pkwy., 718/638-5000, www.brooklynmuseum.org, Wed.-Thurs. 11am-6pm, Fri.-Sun. 11am-8pm, $18 adults, $12 seniors and students, youth 11 and under free), which has old-world masterpieces and contemporary art.

Once you've had your fill, ride the subway back over to Manhattan and tuck into some authentic Spanish tapas at **Despaña** or brasserie comfort classics at **Balthazar.**

---

classic New York experience. If you'd simply like to catch *any* sports game in the city, check the resale site **Stub Hub** (www.stubhub.com) for last-minute deals.

Food

New York City overflows with amazing food options, from roadside "street meat" carts slinging gyros and hot dogs to high-end institutions and foodie hot spots. Narrowing down the choices is almost impossible, as the restaurant scene seems to change daily. Some places, however, serve meals worthy of planning a trip around, whether you're splashing out for the dinner of a lifetime, finding wiseguy joints that feel like NYC movie sets, or just visiting New York's culinary touchstones.

Uptown

Artfully choreographed service, refined contemporary French cuisine, and a delightfully elegant atmosphere keep ★ **Daniel** (60 E. 65th St., 212/288-0033, www.danielnyc.com, Tues.-Sun. 5pm-9:30pm, 4-course prix-fixe menu $188) among the finest restaurants in the United States. This is an opulent, reserve-a-month-ahead destination for a memo rable evening.

A sweet-and-savory uptown classic, ★ **Sylvia's** (328 Malcolm X Blvd., 212/996-0660, www.sylviasrestaurant.com, Sun.-Tues. 11am-8pm, Wed.-Sat. 11am-10pm, $16-35) is the legacy of the late Sylvia Woods, who was dubbed "The

Queen of Soul Food" for her nourishing soul food. Over half a century since opening its doors, this edible institution still draws salivating crowds with its barbecue short ribs, fried chicken and waffles, and hearty side dishes that could easily constitute a meal on their own. Each day's menu usually features rotating specials, and the outdoor seating puts you in the vibrant heart of Harlem.

Midtown

The landmark **Grand Central Oyster Bar** (Grand Central Terminal, Lower Level, 212/490-6650, www.oysterbarny.com, Mon.-Fri. 11:30am-9:30pm, $23-40) serves the freshest of fish in a sprawling, subterranean space with vaulted ceilings. Bustling commuter noise is the backdrop as you cozy up to oysters on the half shell and a glass of champagne, but the most renowned dish is the oyster pan roast, a creamy stew with six Blue Point oysters ladled over triangles of toasted white bread. Not everyone loves it, but it's authentic old New York.

A pioneer of farm-to-table seasonal fare, **Gramercy Tavern** (42 E. 20th St., 212/477-0777, www.gramercytavern.com, daily 11:30am-10:30pm, tavern menu and dining room lunch $21-36, fixed menu $168) serves gorgeous seasonal food in a casual tavern and more formal dining room. For an affordable version of this exquisite New York destination, come at lunch to order off the à la carte menu, but the kitchen really shines on the nuanced multicourse dinners.

Some of New York's finest turn out at **Ess-a-Bagel** (831 3rd Ave., 212/980-1010, www.ess-a-bagel.com, daily 6am-5pm, $5-11), where police officers rub elbows with lawyers at tiny faux-marble tables. The smoked fish and spreads leave most competitors' versions in the dust.

On any given night in NYC, you'll

Top to bottom: Yankee Stadium; the "Mega Ramen" at Totto Ramen; Reuben sandwich at Katz's Delicatessen

observe countless diners lining up for steaming bowls of noodles. **Totto Ramen** (464 W. 51st St, 646/596-9056, www.tottoramen.com, daily noon-10pm, $16-27) is a legendary big fish in a vast pool of ramen shops. The creamy, collagen-rich chicken paitan broth is velvety heaven, especially when combined with a scoop of koji miso and blowtorch-finished char-siu pork. Prepare to sit shoulder to shoulder with diners at the counter, and brace yourself for a 30- to 40-minute wait during peak lunch and dinner hours. You can also order ramen to go if you'd prefer slurping your noodles outdoors.

Downtown

In 1971, falafel was pretty darn exotic for Greenwich Village residents, who took their first bite at **Mamoun's Falafel** (119 Macdougal St., www.mamouns.com, Mon.-Wed. 11am-2am, Thurs. 11am-3am, Fri.-Sat. 11am-4am, Sun. 11am-1am, $7-16), a friendly Middle Eastern restaurant that still draws crowds of locals. The food is fresh, flavorful, and cheap. Most come for the standards—falafel sandwiches, shawarma—but the menu also includes mambrumeh, a filo pastry that oozes honey and chopped pistachios. There are just a few places to sit in the eatery, but Washington Square Park is just a short walk away.

For the true hole-in-the-wall New York pizza experience, **Joe's Pizza** (7 Carmine St., 212/366-1182, www.joespizzanyc.com, Sun.-Thurs. 10am-3am, Fri.-Sat. 10am-5am, $6-18) is a wonderful option, with its thin, crisp-chewy crusts, an atmospherically grimy dining room, and melted cheese that stretches the length of your arm. Regulars love the pepperoni slice for a quick lunch (bring it to Washington Park for a very New York picnic).

It's easy to see why **Veselka** (144 2nd Ave., 212/228-9682, www.veselka.com, Mon.-Sat. 8am-midnight, Sun. 8am-11pm, $8-21) is a favorite for hearty Ukrainian fare and people-watching, open 24 hours a day. Eggs Benedict come on top of hefty potato pancakes and short rib pierogi are pillowy and rich, served alongside applesauce, sour cream, and cabbage.

When you step inside ★ **Despaña** (408 Broome St., 212/219-5050, www.despananyc.com, Sun. and Tues.-Thurs. 11am-6pm, Fri.-Sat. 11am-10pm, $13-54), you might confuse your surroundings for a market in Barcelona. Drool over the cured meats and Manchego cheese wheels behind the counter, order a hefty bocadillo sandwich to go, or indulge with a more decadent dinner of tapas, such as Amandia olives or garlicky white anchovies on toast.

From the gruff service to the melt-in-your-mouth pastrami sandwiches (on rye, of course!), **Katz's Delicatessen** (205 E. Houston St., 212/254-2246, www.katzsdelicatessen.com, Mon.-Thurs. 8am-11pm, Fri. 8am-midnight, Sat. 24 hrs., Sun. midnight-11pm, $18-29) is a legend. Since its 1888 opening, sandwiches have gotten a bit pricey, but they're enormous (although it's possible to order a half sandwich), truly delicious, and thoroughly old-school. Take a number, then guard it with your life until you leave the restaurant—pay on the way out. Alternatively, if you're willing to pay a little extra, you can place an order ahead of time for pickup.

Another Lower East Side behemoth, ★ **Russ & Daughters** (179 E. Houston St., 212/475-4880, www.russanddaughters.com, daily 8am-4pm, $5-15) is a shop, not a restaurant, but this is the place to go for a bagel-and-lox picnic to rule them all. Grab a ticket when you step in the door of the "appetizing store," which has smoked and cured fish, caviar, bagels from the Bagel Hole in Brooklyn, and enough babka and rugelach for a month of Sundays. The same family also runs the appealing **Russ & Daughters Café** (127 Orchard St., 212/475-4881, www.russanddaughters.com, Mon.-Thurs. 8:30am-2:30pm, Fri.-Sun.

8:30am-3:30pm) nearby, if you'd like your food on a plate.

A SoHo icon, **Balthazar** (80 Spring St., 212/965-1414, www.balthazarny.com, breakfast Mon.-Fri. 8am-11am, lunch Mon.-Fri. 11:30am-4:30pm, dinner daily 5pm-midnight, brunch Sat.-Sun. 9am-4pm, $23-49) serves wonderful bistro fare to a mix of celebrities, local power brokers, and ladies who lunch. The experience easily justifies the prices.

The coal-fired brick ovens at ★ **John's of Bleecker Street** (278 Bleecker St., 212/243-1680, www.johnsofbleecker.com, Sun.-Thurs. 11:30am-10pm, Fri.-Sat. 11:30am-11pm, pizzas $20-34) have been turning out thin, crispy pies topped with traditional ingredients for almost a century. It's a strong contender for best old-school pizza joint in the city, with wooden booths and pitchers of beer.

Vegetarian comfort food is infused with verve and a little of chef-owner (and drummer) Brooks Headley's punk rock spirit at **Superiority Burger** (119 Ave. A, 646/422-7707, www.superiorityburger.com, Sun.-Mon. and Wed. 5pm-11:30pm, Thurs.-Sat. 5pm-2am, $11-23), which has a tiny menu and colorful diner-style booths flanked with pieces of Headley's art collection. Since opening in 2015 it's won accolades from eaters of all stripes, and it's a bargain for some of the most creative meat-free food around.

In a city not known for great Mexican food, **Los Tacos No. 1** (75 9th Ave., www.lostacos1.com, Mon.-Sat. 11am-10pm, Sun. 11am-9pm, $8-14) is an island of authentic, street-style tacos. Adobada tacos and carne asada are favorites here, as are the giant vats of creamy, sweet horchata. No seating.

Anyone on a mission to find New York City's best cheesecake would do well to start at **Eileen's Special Cheesecake** (17 Cleveland Pl., 212/966-5585, www.eileenscheesecake.com, Sun.-Thurs. 11am-7pm, Fri.-Sat. 11am-8pm, under $10), where the slices are ultrarich and fluffy. Miniature versions make it dangerously easy to try all flavors, from a plain version topped with strawberries to the luscious salted caramel.

Accommodations

Uptown

Under $150

If you're between the ages of 15 and 35, the **International Student Center** (38 W. 88th St., 212/787-7706, www.nystudentcenter.org, 6- or 10-bed dorms $60-80) is a convivial budget option that recalls the early years of hosteling with a few modern tweaks: homey, ad hoc decor, a good-size kitchen and common space, and air-conditioning in all guest rooms. It's wonderfully convenient to Central Park and public transport.

Midtown

$150-250

Stylish, artful touches elevate the budget-friendly ★ **American Dream Bed and Breakfast** (168 E. 24th St., 212/260-9779, www.americandreamhostel.com, $139-154 s, $158-172 d, $168-200 t), which has minimalist private rooms and shared bathrooms. A surprisingly generous breakfast of fresh pastries, fruit, and cereal is served each morning, and snacks are available throughout the day. The rooms, which have a double-single bunk bed, all come with air-conditioning, television, and a heater, but try to book one with a window, as the windowless versions are a bit claustrophobic.

In the spirit of New York, ★ **The Pod Hotel** (230 E. 51st St. or 145 E. 39th St., 212/355-0300 and 212/865-5700, www.thepodhotel.com, $220-315) uses thoughtful design to compensate for cramped quarters. Super-small, economical guest rooms are clean and brightly decorated, and the cheerful lobby has a backpacker-cool vibe. Rooms all have televisions, safes, and individually controlled heating and cooling units.

$250-350
Just one block away from lights, cameras, and action at Times Square, **Hotel 46 Times Square** (129 W. 46th St., 212/221-2600, www.nycasa46hotel.com, $255-332) has an unbeatable location, particularly if you're planning to spend a late night out at the theater. The style is forgettable and the furnishings a bit staid, but all rooms have coffeemakers, televisions, air-conditioning, and safes, and some have a refrigerator and microwave. Continental breakfast is included.

Leaning into the glitz and color of the surrounding area, ★ **45 Times Square Hotel** (125 W 45th St., 212/354-2323, www.palladiumhotelgroup.com, $296-474) aims to dazzle guests with accents such as elaborate floral wallpaper, XL-size plush headboards, and walls of mirrors. The rooms are somewhat basic as far as practical amenities go, but the soft-lit indoor pool and swim-up bar sweeten the deal considerably.

Ultracool and filled with contemporary art, ★ **citizenM** (218 W. 50th, 212/461-3638, www.citizenm.com, $326-514) has free movies, 24-hour snacks, rain showers, and utterly enormous beds. The location right on Times Square is in the heart of the action downtown, but a gym, yoga terrace, and rooftop bar with panoramic views would make it easy never to leave the premises.

Downtown

$150-250
In trendy little Nolita, ★ **The Nolitan Hotel** (30 Kenmare St., 212/295-2555, www.nolitanhotel.com, $151-238) is one of the first boutique hotels to open its doors in this nook of Manhattan. The modern, industrial-influenced rooms boast great views of the neighborhood, which you can explore with the hotel's free bikes and skateboards. The hotel's on-site Italian-Japanese fusion restaurant, **Kimika,** offers a tempting seasonal menu, and the rooftop bar, **Somewhere in Nolitan,** is an ideal venue for savoring a New York sunset.

$250-350
A former tenement, **The Historic Blue Moon Hotel** (100 Orchard St., 646/787-5503, www.bluemoon-nyc.com, $259-489) has been transformed into a boutique hotel that retains bits and bobs of Victorian charm, such as pressed tin, newspaper clippings, and a lobby ideal for catching up on the *New York Times.* The rooms themselves are standard fare, and the continental breakfast is skimpy, but you're just around the corner from Russ & Daughters.

Vintage movie posters give the rooms at the **Chelsea Pines Inn** (317 W. 14th St., 212/929-1023, www.chelseapinesinn.com, $275-450) a whimsical feel, and the friendly owners make it a charming place to stay (if you can get past the brownstone's three flights of stairs). The guest lounge, indoor greenhouse, and enclosed patio garden are green havens in this bustling neighborhood, and they're always stocked with espresso, tea, snacks, and coffee. An ample cold breakfast is served.

Information and Services

Information

The Official NYC Information Center at Herald Square (151 W. 34th St., 212/494-3827, www.nycgo.com, Mon.-Fri. 10am-10pm, Sat. 10am-7pm, Sun. 11am-7pm) is the official tourism organization in the city. Maps, brochures, and other informational materials are available at the visitor centers.

Attraction Passes

A dizzying array of sightseeing passes are available for exploring New York, and choosing one that's well suited to your plans can offer substantial savings. The **New York City Pass** (www.citypass.

com/newyork, $138 adults, $118 youth 6-17) includes admission to five sites over nine days, so it is only worthwhile if you're in town for more than 48 hours. The first two included attractions are the Empire State Building and the American Museum of Natural History, and you can choose the other three from a list that includes the Guggenheim Museum and the 9/11 Memorial and Museum. For shorter trips to the city, a better option is the **New York City Explorer Pass** (www.gocity.com/new-york, from $79 adults, $69 children 3-12), which allows you to select all of the sites you're interested in.

Services

Emergencies

For immediate emergency medical and police service, dial **911.**

These hospitals operate 24-hour emergency rooms: **Lenox Hill Hospital** (100 E. 77th St., 212/434-2000, www.lenoxhillhospital.org), **Mount Sinai Hospital** (Madison Ave. at 100th St., 212/241-6500, www.mountsinai.org), and **Bellevue Hospital** (464 1st Ave., 212/562-5555, www.nychealthandhospitals.org).

Getting Around

Public Transit

The **subway** is the cheapest and often fastest way to get around. Riders can pay their fare via **MetroCards,** which are sold in machines in every subway station, or by simply tapping a contactless credit card at the fare gate. It costs $2.90 for a single-ride ticket. Both options come with a free transfer between the subway and bus, but the contactless credit card method offers an additional perk. Once you buy 12 rides within 7 days using the same card, you can get free rides for the remainder of that weeklong period by tapping the same card. You'll need to buy $34.80 worth of fares to unlock this perk, which is almost the equivalent of what you would pay for a weeklong MetroCard-based subway and bus pass ($34). For visitors planning a longer stay, a 30-day pass costs $132. Passes allow unlimited rides for one person.

Large route maps are mounted at all stations and are available for free at any subway station booth. Subway line and schedule information is also available at the **Metropolitan Transportation Authority** website (www.mta.info) and information line (718-330-1234), as well as via the MTA's smartphone app, MYmta.

MetroCards are accepted on city buses, as is exact change in coins (no pennies or half dollars), but you can also pay your bus fare by tapping a contactless payment-enabled credit card to the farebox, or by downloading the MYmta app (new.mta.info) and scanning your smartphone upon boarding. The fare for a single ride is $2.90 for local buses and $7 on express buses. Transfers to and from connecting buses or subways are free with use of a MetroCard, your credit card, or the app. On buses and subways, up to three children under 44 inches tall ride for free when accompanied by an adult. Most buses have maps posted and wheelchair lifts.

Taxi

Metered **yellow cabs** have an initial $3.00 fare, which increases at $0.70 increments for every one-fifth of a mile (0.3 km) traveled or 60 seconds idle. There is a $1 surcharge daily 8pm-6am and a $2.50 surcharge weekdays 4pm-8pm, plus a $0.50 New York state surcharge.

During **rush hour,** it's often faster to take the subway, as hailing a cab can be nearly impossible. At other times, especially at night, taking a cab is the most convenient way to get around. Open cabs tend to cruise for fares on avenues and crosstown arteries, and near hotels, nightclubs, and other crowded areas.

Cabs can be particularly scarce on busy nights like New Year's Eve or during storms. In these instances, it makes good

Transit Pro Tips

Beat the gridlock on the MTA.

In New York, you can avoid the headache of searching for parking by ditching your wheels and embracing the MTA's thrumming labyrinth of public transit. Squeezing into a subway car is one of the essential New York experiences. You might find yourself sharing a pole with an investment banker, a chef, or an actor from Spike Lee's latest joint. Sold yet? Here's how to make the most of New York public transit.

Step 1: Exit the Vehicle

If you'll be renting a car for your New England road trip, schedule the pickup at the end of your New York sojourn (or at the beginning, if NYC is your final stop). If you're bringing your own vehicle, consider staying at a local hotel that offers on-site parking and access to city trains and buses.

Step 2: Learn your ABC's

New York boasts a dizzying roster of trains. Odds are you'll catch several during your visit. For stops up and down Manhattan, the A train is your surest bet. The B, L, and M trains will take you east from Manhattan into the expanse of Brooklyn. And if you're exploring the tonier landscapes of Manhattan's Upper East Side, the Q train is the ticket. A guide to all the subway lines, with colorful maps, can be downloaded at https://new.mta.info/maps. These maps include the numbered trains that snake throughout the city, offering more localized stops. Speaking of which, before boarding any train, check the digital sign on the window to see if it's a local or express train. Taking express trains can save you a lot of time, but if done erroneously, it can mean overshooting your stop and having to backtrack.

Step 3: Consult the Cloud

Download the MTA's own app, **MYmta,** to plan custom transit routes and get real-time information on when trains and buses will be arriving or departing. If you want to go even further down the rabbit hole of multimodal transit, **Citymapper,** a third-party transit app, will show you not just MTA routes, but also Citi Bike kiosks, ferries, and rideshare prices.

sense to call a car service; rates tend to be comparable to a cab ride. App-based car services like Uber and Lyft are increasingly popular. Here are a few car service options:

- **Carmel Car Service** (845/225-5555, www.carmellimo.com)
- **Dial 7 Car & Limousine Service** (212/777-7777, www.dial7.com)
- **Uber** (www.uber.com)
- **Lyft** (www.lyft.com)

Bike

New and expanded bike paths have made Manhattan a much easier and safer place to traverse by bicycle. In 2013, New York's first bike-share program, **Citi Bike** (855/245-3311, www.citibikenyc.com), began operation, with over 1,700 stations located across New York's five boroughs. For riders over the age of 16, Citi Bike offers two short-term rental options, a **24-hour pass** ($19) or **30-minute single ride trips** ($4.49), which can be purchased with a credit card at any Citi Bike station. Note that the flat rate for Citi Bike single ride trips covers half an hour, and each additional minute costs $0.23, which can add up quickly if you're planning on taking a lengthier ride around the city. You can download the Citi Bike app to your smartphone to locate nearby stations.

Car

Driving around New York City is not for the faint of heart, and parking overnight in Manhattan can rival the cost of a cheap hotel. If you do need to park in New York, it's worth consulting the **NYC parking site** (www.nyc.bestparking.com), which shows fares in real time, or the free parking app **SpotHero,** which allows you to book discounted sites.

Essentials

Getting There

Getting to Boston

Air

With up to 1.5 million passengers moving through its gates each month, **Boston Logan International Airport** (One Harborside Dr., East Boston, 800/235-6426, www.massport.com/logan-airport) is the largest and busiest transportation hub in the region. The airport serves nearly 50 airlines, of which 13 are international, including Aer Lingus, Air Canada, Air France, Alitalia, British Airways, Iberia, Icelandair, Lufthansa, Norse Atlantic, Swiss, TAP Air Portugal, Virgin Atlantic Airways, and WestJet. International flights arrive in Terminal E. From the airport, a variety of options take passengers to downtown Boston, which is only a mile (1.6 km) away. The most efficient way to get into the city is via taxi, though expect to pay a minimum of $30 for downtown locations, or shared van service to downtown and Back Bay for $30-40 per person.

Far cheaper (and almost as quick) is the **Silver Line bus** (www.mbta.com); inbound rides on SL1 from Logan Airport to Boston's South Station are free and leave from stops directly in front of each terminal. Buses leave several times an hour, 5am-1am, and reach South Station in 15-25 minutes. Another good option is the **Blue Line subway,** which runs from 6am to 12:30pm daily. From each terminal, you can catch the free shuttle bus that offers direct service to nearby Airport station. Take the Bowdoin-bound train to State Street station ($2.40 fare, 10-15 minutes) for access to downtown Boston.

Train

Amtrak (800/872-7245, www.amtrak.com) runs frequent trains along the Northeast corridor to Boston, including the **Acela Express,** the United States' first high-speed service, from New York (3.5 hrs) and Washington DC (6 hrs). Unless you are in a rush, though, it can often make more sense to save $100 and take the **Northeast Regional** service, which also runs to Boston from New York (4.5 hrs) and Washington DC (7 hrs), stopping along the way in New Haven, New London, Providence, and several smaller cities on the Connecticut and Rhode Island coasts.

From the west, Amtrak's **Lake Shore Limited** route offers service to Boston from Buffalo, New York (12 hrs) and Cleveland, Ohio (15 hrs), stopping along the way in Springfield and Worcester in Massachusetts. Connecting to that route, Amtrak's **Adirondack** route offers service between New York City and Montreal, Quebec (12 hrs).

Bus

New England is accessible from many domestic and Canadian locations via **Greyhound Bus Lines** (800/231-2222, www.greyhound.com). Nearby major cities offering service to Boston include New York (4.5 hrs), Philadelphia (7.5 hrs), Montreal (7.5 hrs), Washington DC (10.5 hrs), Buffalo (10.5 hrs), Toronto (14 hrs), and Cleveland (16 hrs). The discount carrier **Flixbus** (www.flixbus.com) serves several major cities as well, and booking in advance (particularly on less popular days) can mean very cheap fares. While not the quickest way to travel, the bus can be an attractive alternative for those on a budget or traveling to more rural or remote regions not served by rail or air.

A good way to search public transport on different carriers is the site **Wanderu** (www.wanderu.com), which combines information about trains and buses.

Getting to New York City

Air

Three airports serve New York City: **John F. Kennedy International Airport** (JFK, 718/244-4444), **LaGuardia Airport** (LGA, 718/533-3400), and **Newark Liberty International Airport** (EWR, 973/961-6000) in New Jersey. Coming or going, taxis between JFK and Manhattan have a flat rate of $70, plus a $0.50 New York state surcharge, not including bridge/tunnel tolls and tips. From LaGuardia, taxis charge regular metered fare, with the cost running approximately $32-40, not including tolls and tips to Manhattan, with meters starting at $2.50. From Newark, a taxi will usually cost around $52-75, plus tolls and tip.

For inexpensive transportation to and from JFK, the Port Authority operates the **AirTrain** (www.panynj.gov/airtrain), a light-rail that connects all airport terminals to the subway system. You can access the AirTrain from the Sutphin Boulevard stop on the E line, or via the Howard Beach stop on the A line (take a train marked "Far Rockaway"). You can also take the Long Island Rail Road from Penn Station to the AirTrain at Jamaica Station. The cost of a one-way trip on the AirTrain is $8.25. You can pay the AirTrain fare using a pay-per-ride MetroCard, by purchasing tickets in the station, or by tapping a contactless credit card at the fare gate.

The **Port Authority of New York and New Jersey** (www.panynj.gov) operates booths that provide information on rates and connections to private limousine and van companies. Its **Air-Ride service** (800/247-7433) provides recorded information about bus, shuttle, and private car services from area airports. Shuttle options include **Olympia Trails/Coach USA Airport Express** (866/912-6224, 908/354-3330 or 877/863-9275, www.coachusa.com), **GO Airlink NYC** (212/812-9000, www.goairlinkshuttle.com), and Supershuttle (212/209-7000 or 800/258-3826, www.supershuttle.com).

Train

Moynlhan Train Hall (33rd St. between 8th Ave. and 9th Ave.) serves passengers arriving on **Amtrak** (800/872-7245, www.amtrak.com) as well as **New Jersey Transit** (973/275-5555, www.njtransit.com), **Long Island Rail Road** (718/217-5477, http://mta.info/lirr), and the subway's A, C, E, 1, 2, and 3 trains. Visitors arrive at New York's other main station, **Grand Central Terminal** (89 E. 42nd St.), via **Metro-North Railroad** (212/532-4900, www.mta.info/mnr) and the 4, 5, 6, 7, and S subway lines (NYC Transit, 511 or 718/330-1234).

Bus

The Midtown **Port Authority Bus Terminal** (625 8th Ave., 212/435-7000) is the main bus hub for the city, and services leave for destinations all over New England, including **Greyhound** (800/231-2222, www.greyhound.com), **Peter Pan** (800/343-9999, www.peterpanbus.com), and discount carrier **Megabus** (www.megabus.com).

A good way to find fares to destinations in New England is on the search site **Wanderu** (www.wanderu.com), which aggregates bus and train schedules with real-time fares.

Road Rules

Car Rental

The major car rental companies have branches at even small airports around New England. To reserve a car in advance, it's often better to use a car rental search aggregator (as with airline tickets), such as **Priceline** (www.priceline.com) or **Orbitz** (www.orbitz.com). Rentals can be found as cheaply as $25 a day, before taxes and fees, though more standard rates start at $50 a day. While searching for cars, be aware that one-way rentals often have a surcharge, especially when beginning or ending your trip in a smaller city. Most car rental companies offer several kinds of insurance: The collision damage waiver covers damage to the rental car, and liability covers damage to others, though personal car insurance may already cover this. (If you don't have primary car insurance, your credit card might include this benefit for car rentals.)

To rent a car, drivers must be at least 21 years of age with a valid driver's license. Drivers between 21 and 24 years of age may be limited to certain models, and some companies charge a "young driver" fee in addition to the rental price.

Inquire directly with major car rental companies for details: **Alamo** (888/233-8749, www.alamo.com), **Avis** (800/352-7900, www.avis.com), **Budget** (800/214-609400, www.budget.com), **Dollar** (800/800-5252, www.dollar.com), **Enterprise** (855/266-9565, www.enterprise.com), **Hertz** (800/654-3131, www.hertz.com), **National** (844/393-9989, www.nationalcar.com), or **Thrifty** (800/847-4389, www.thrifty.com).

RV Rental

Weeklong RV rentals start at $600, and mileage is generally a supplemental charge. Check with **Cruise America** (800/671-8042, www.cruiseamerica.com) and **Outdoorsy** (877/723-7232, www.outdoorsy.com) for availability. If beginning and ending your trip in New York City, camper rentals are available just across the Hudson River in Jersey City from **Escape Campervans** (877/270-8267, www.escapecampervans.com) from $150/day, including 100 miles (160 km) each day. An RV-accessible campsite can cost upwards of $50. Note that RVs aren't as well suited to New England driving as they are to the wide-open roads of the American West.

Many RV rental companies require that drivers be 25 years of age or above, though some allow drivers between 21 and 24 years old for an additional fee. A standard driver's license is sufficient for operating an RV.

Driving Rules

Seat belts are required in all New England states outside of "Live Free or Die" New Hampshire, where they're only required for those under 18 years of age. All states have child safety seat requirements—child safety seats are available as an add-on with any car rental. Talking on a **handheld cell phone** and **texting while driving** are illegal in all New England states.

All states in New England now have **move-over laws** that mandate slowing down and changing lanes (when safe) while passing stopped police cars and emergency vehicles.

Road Conditions

If traveling in summer and fall, the most challenging road issue is the extensive roadwork that takes place during the snow-free months. Find detailed information about roadwork and **traffic conditions** at www.newengland511.org. State by state information is available for **Massachusetts** (www.mass.gov/dot), **New Hampshire** (www.dot.nh.gov), **Maine** (www.maine.gov/mdot), **Rhode Island** (www.dot.ri.gov), **Connecticut** (www.ct.gov/dot), and **New York** (www.nyc.gov/html/dot).

The two-lane highways that connect much of rural New England can get clogged with traffic, but the only places where it's truly important to plan around the busy times are Boston and New York City. If renting a car, wait until you leave the city to pick it up, and try to avoid the weekday hours of 7am-10am and 3pm-7pm.

When traveling in rural areas, hitting a **deer** or **moose** on the road is a significant concern, especially when driving at dawn or dusk. Slow down, keep an eye on the edge of the road, and pay close attention to the "wildlife crossing" signs denoting animal corridors.

Parking

Outside the tourist hot spots and cities, parking is easy and inexpensive throughout New England. In Boston and New York City, it's worth planning ahead and either avoiding parking by leaving your car outside the city (both cities have long-term parking at commuter train stations) or booking a parking spot in advance.

The free app **SpotHero** (www.spothero.com) is a good choice for finding and booking discounted spaces in parking garages throughout both cities.

Many cities have now converted to credit-card meters—some require a ticket be left in the car, and some don't. Many (but not all) meters are free on Sundays. If you're driving an RV, note that large chain hotels often have parking spots that can accommodate the vehicles, but smaller inns and bed-and-breakfasts may not.

Tolls

Some of the interstates and bridges in New England and New York require tolls, and the state-run systems are a bit of a patchwork, with some requiring cash, a few accepting credit cards, and others using license-plate recognition software. Many toll stations have an express **EZ-Pass** lane (www.e-zpassiag.com), which uses electronic sensors to deduct the toll from a prepaid account; visitors with an EZ-Pass from elsewhere in the United States can use their EZ-Pass in New England with their own vehicle or with a rental vehicle of the same vehicle class.

A few toll locations are transitioning to cashless tolls, which operate using either the EZ-Pass or by taking a photo of your license plate and then forwarding on the bill. Unfortunately for rental car drivers, some rental agencies tack on a processing charge to this, adding as much as $5 a day to the tolls. Inquire directly with your rental agency.

International Drivers Licenses

International visitors need to secure an **International Driving Permit** from their home countries before coming to the United States. They should also bring the government-issued driving permit from their home countries. They are expected to be familiar with the driving regulations of the states they will visit. More information is available online: www.usa.gov/non-citizen-driving.

Maps and Tourist Information

Each of the destinations covered in this book has tourist information offices stocked with free maps that are great for navigating by car or bicycle. To obtain these maps (and other guides) in advance, contact the tourist offices for each state: **Massachusetts** (www.massvacation.com), **New Hampshire** (www.visitnh.gov), **Maine** (www.visitmaine.com), **Vermont** (www.vermontvacation.com), **Rhode Island** (www.visitrhodeisland.com), **Connecticut** (www.ctvisit.com), and **New York** (www.iloveny.com).

Roadside Assistance

In an emergency, dial **911** from any phone for police and emergency services. The **American Automobile Association** (800/222-4357, www.northernnewengland.aaa.com) offers roadside assistance including jump-start, towing, and flat tire services. Depending on your situation, it may be more cost-effective to join AAA on the spot than pay out of pocket for a tow truck. If traveling in a rental car, roadside assistance may be offered by your agency.

Visas and Officialdom

Passports and Visas

Visiting from another country, you must have a valid passport and a visa to enter the United States. The U.S. government's Visa Waiver Program allows tourists from many countries to visit without a visa for up to 90 days. To check if your country is on the list go to http://travel.state.gov. To qualify, you must apply online with the **Electronic System for Travel Authorization** (www.cbp.gov) and hold a return plane or cruise ticket to your country of origin dated less than 90 days from your date of entry. Holders of Canadian passports don't need visas or visa waivers. Even with a waiver, you still need to bring your passport and present it at the port of entry.

Embassies and Consulates

New York City and Boston are home to consulates from around the world. Travelers in legal trouble or those who have lost their passports should contact the consulate of their home country immediately. The **U.S. State Department** (www.state.gov) has contact info for all foreign embassies and consulates. The **British Consulate** (www.gov.uk) has offices in the **Boston** area (1 Broadway, Cambridge, 617/245-4500) and **New York City** (885 2nd Ave., 212/745-0200). The **Australian Consulate** has an office in **New York City** (150 East 42nd St., 34th floor, 212/351-6500), and the **Canadian Consulate-General** is in **Boston** (3 Copley Place #400, 617/247-5100) and **New York City** (466 Lexington Ave., 20th floor, 212/596-1628).

Customs

Foreigners and U.S. citizens age 21 or older may import (free of duty) the following: 1L of alcohol, 200 cigarettes (one carton), 100 cigars (non-Cuban), and $100 worth of gifts. International travelers must declare amounts that exceed $10,000 in cash (U.S. or foreign), traveler's checks, or money orders. Meat products, fruits, and vegetables are prohibited due to health and safety regulations.

Travel Tips

Conduct and Customs

The legal **drinking age** in the United States is 21. If you look younger than 35, expect to have your ID checked not only in bars and clubs, but also before you purchase alcohol in restaurants, wineries, and markets. Young-looking international travelers should bring their passports, as some locations may not accept other identification such as international driver's licenses.

Smoking is banned in many places, including bars, clubs, and restaurants. Many hotels, motels, and inns are also nonsmoking. Smokers should request a smoking room when making reservations.

Money

The currency is the **U.S. dollar ($).** Most businesses accept the **major credit cards** Visa, MasterCard, Discover, and American Express. ATM and debit cards work at many stores and restaurants, and ATMs are available throughout the region. You can **change currency** at any international airport or bank. Currency exchange may be easier in large cities and more difficult in rural and wilderness areas.

Banking hours tend to be 8am-5pm Monday-Friday, 9am-noon Saturday. Never count on a bank being open on Sunday. There are **24-hour ATMs** not only at banks but also at many markets, bars, and hotels. A **convenience fee** of $2-4 per transaction may apply.

Internet Access and Cell Service

Wireless Internet is available in most cafés, as well as many other businesses. Local libraries are good places to find computers with Internet access free of charge, as most make these services available to visitors. Most hotels and bed-and-breakfasts offer free wireless Internet, though some smaller, rural inns may not.

While all New England cities have full cell coverage, many rural areas do not, so it's worth having access to a paper map when traveling through the countryside.

Hotel and Motel Chains

Hotel and motel chains like **Best Western** (800/528-1238, www.bestwestern.com), **Motel 6** (800/557-3435, www.motel6.com), **Days Inn** (800/407-9832, www.daysinn.com), and **Super 8** (800/454-3509, www.super8.com) are easy to find in urban areas. Many offer discount rates (depending on season) and reasonable amenities. Expect higher rates during the summer (June-Sept.). For the most part, it's easiest and cheapest to book these through an online travel site such as www.expedia.com, www.booking.com, or www.hotels.com.

Traveling with Children

Travel all over New England is quite family-friendly. Most hotels offer cribs in the room upon request, and public transportation and attractions offer discounted fares for children. The majority of restaurants are happy to offer high chairs, and many have kids' menus. Some higher-end bed-and-breakfasts, though, do not welcome younger children, and upscale restaurants may look askance at small diners.

Children will enjoy aquariums, amusement parks, and, perhaps most of all, beaches. Many beaches and parks are equipped with bathrooms. You'll also find several good family-friendly restaurant and hotel options. Generally hotels allow up to four in a room, so be sure to inquire about a suite if necessary.

The main concerns when traveling the highway with children are that the long drive can make them antsy, and the twists and turns can cause nausea, even for parents. Make plenty of stops to allow your young ones to burn off some energy and for everyone to use the bathroom, stretch their legs, and breathe in the fresh air. Bring plenty of car-fun activities to keep your kids busy, like books and travel games.

Senior Travelers

If you are over 60 years of age, ask about potential discounts. Nearly all attractions, amusement parks, theaters, and museums offer discount benefits to seniors. Be sure to have some form of valid identification such as a driver's license or passport.

Access for Travelers with Disabilities

Public transportation in the vast majority of New England is wheelchair-accessible, as are most major hotels, museums, and public buildings. Even many beaches and campgrounds in Massachusetts are accessible, though the remoter the destination, the greater the possibility that it will not be. As common sense would dictate, call ahead and plan accordingly.

The greatest challenge for travelers in wheelchairs in New England may be accessing historic neighborhoods and inns that have not been retrofitted with wider doorways and elevators. Some inns have converted one or more rooms with roll-in showers, while others are completely inaccessible.

Those with permanent disabilities, including the visually impaired, should inquire about a free **Access Pass** (888/275-8747, ext. 3, or online at https://store.usgs.gov/access-pass, $10) from the National Park Service. It is offered as part of the America the Beautiful—National Park and Federal Recreational Lands Pass Series. You can obtain an Access Pass in person at any federal recreation site with the requisite documentation in hand, or by submitting a completed application online. The pass does not provide benefits for special recreation permits or concessionaire fees.

LGBTQ+ Travelers

Few regions in the country are friendlier to LGBTQ+ visitors than New England. Same-sex marriage is legal in every state, and cities like Boston, Portland, and Providence have significant and thriving gay and lesbian communities. Meanwhile, resort towns such as Provincetown, Massachusetts, and Ogunquit, Maine, are major destinations for LGBTQ+ visitors from around the world.

The extensive and free state-by-state guides offered by the **International LGBTQ+ Travel Association** (www.iglta.org) are a great resource for travelers to begin with. Visiting Boston, Provincetown, or Providence? Check out the more specific city travel guides from **Queer In The World** (www.queerintheworld.com). And if you're leaning toward a hike in the Berkshires or the Maine coast, consider attending one of the group events organized by the **Venture Out Project** (www.ventureoutproject.com), whose day trips are a portal into the regional community of LGBTQ+ outdoorspeople.

Travelers of Color

New England may have been a crucial sanctuary for abolitionists, but de facto racial discrimination and the notorious housing policy known as redlining led to cities and towns becoming palpably segregated by neighborhood, to the point where New England has long been perceived as a racist region. But the ground reality has changed significantly in recent decades, with big multiracial communities firmly rooted in Boston (now a majority-minority city), Providence, and more metro areas across the region. Vermont, Maine, and New Hampshire tend to be more monochrome, but with road tripping and outdoor recreation exploding in popularity, being a person of color in rural New England is becoming less conspicuous.

One terrific resource is **Travel Noire** (www.travelnoire.com), a travel media website whose extensive city and regional articles highlight PoC-owned businesses, events, and cultural landmarks across New England. For a deeper cut, **Black Boston** (www.blackboston.com) offers frequently updated event listings across the city's historically multiracial communities such as Jamaica Plain and Dorchester. And for experiential travel tips for the broader region, prolific blogger and road warrior **Franny the Traveler** (www.frannythetraveler.com) has compiled instructive documentation of her experiences as a Black woman visiting Vermont, Maine, and other destinations that are less racially diverse.

Environmental Concerns

Each state has environmental concerns that involve water pollution, disruption of fish and wildlife habitats, and emissions. You can do your part as a visitor and protect the natural environment by doing the following: Stay on trails and do not stomp on plantlife; utilize pet waste receptacles in pet-friendly campgrounds; protect water sources by camping at least 150 feet (46 m) from lakes and streams; leave rocks and plants as you find them; light fires only where permitted and use only established fire pits; pack it in, pack it out—check your campsite for garbage and properly dispose of it or take it with you.

Health and Safety

People travel to New England from all over the globe simply to receive care from the area's doctors and hospitals, which are widely regarded as among the best. That said, certain precautions will help you stay as safe as possible. If immediate help is needed, always **dial 911**, otherwise go to the nearest 24-hour hospital emergency room.

Compared with the rest of the nation, New England is relatively low in crime, and many of its rural areas are virtually crime-free. Cities are, not surprisingly, a different story. But even in Boston and New York, if you follow the basic rules of common sense (take precautions in watching your belongings, avoid walking alone late at night, and be aware of your surroundings), odds are safety won't be a problem.

In the New England countryside, one of the biggest threats to visitors' safety can be their own lack of outdoors savvy and preparedness. Whether summiting

Ticks and Lyme Disease

Forget snakes, bears, and moose—ask a New Englander what wildlife they're scared of, and they'll say **ticks.** The eight-legged creatures are tiny—from the size of a poppyseed to just under three millimeters—and easy to miss. Some are carriers of **Lyme disease,** a dangerous bacterial infection. Not all ticks can carry Lyme disease, but the deer tick sometimes does, and it's the most common species in the Northeast. Taking the following precautions will help protect against Lyme:

- Wear long pants tucked into your socks when walking through high grass and bushy areas.
- Use insect repellent that contains DEET, which is effective against ticks.
- Shower within a few hours of coming inside, and always check carefully for ticks after spending time outdoors. If you find a tick, use tweezers to grasp it near to your skin, and firmly remove without twisting. Don't worry if the mouth parts remain in the skin; once the tick is separated from the body, it can no longer transmit the bacteria that cause Lyme.

Carefully checking for ticks once a day is a good practice. Don't panic if you find a tick, as it takes around 36 hours for the bacteria to spread. The first symptoms of Lyme disease are often flu-like, and occur 3-30 days after infection. They're often accompanied by a rash or bull's-eye redness around the bite. If you experience these symptoms, it's smart to visit a doctor. Prompt treatment of Lyme disease is generally effective, but the disease can be fatal if untreated.

White Mountain peaks or on a day hike, it's important to stay aware of weather conditions and bring maps, extra clothes, and sufficient food and water.

Carry your **medical card** and a list of any **medications** you are taking. Keep a **first-aid kit** in your car or luggage, and take it with you when hiking. A good kit should include sterile gauze pads, butterfly bandages, adhesive tape, antibiotic ointment, alcohol wipes, pain relievers for both adults and children, and a multipurpose pocketknife.

Whether you're in a large city, resort area, small town, or even a wilderness area, take precautions against **theft.** Don't leave any valuables in the car. If you must, keep them out of sight in the trunk or a compartment with a lock if available. Keep wallets, purses, cameras, mobile phones, and other small electronics on your person if possible.

Internet Resources

The websites maintained by state tourism agencies can be surprisingly useful, with tips on finding scenic byways, events, and on-call staff.

New England

Discover New England

www.discovernewengland.org
This site highlights seasonal events and current happenings in every corner of New England, and suggests driving tours and weather information, plus gives a brief primer on each state.

NewEngland.com

www.newengland.com
Run by the folks behind *Yankee* magazine, this site is packed with local landmarks, recommended itineraries, foliage reports, event listings, and vacation planners.

New England Towns
www.newenglandtowns.org
Read selective, quirky histories of small New England towns, plus little-known facts and statistics.

Fall Foliage Reports

Get in-depth and up-to-date foliage reports on each state, starting in early September and throughout autumn, from the following websites: **Vermont** (www.vermont.com/foliage.cfm), **New Hampshire** (www.visitnh.gov/seasonal-trips/fall/Foliage-Tracker), **Maine** (www.mainefoliage.com), and **Massachusetts** (www.visit-massachusetts.com/state/foliage).

Destination Websites

Expect to find basic background information about the destination, plus essentials such as hours, locations, entrance fees, driving directions, and special deals or packages currently offered.

Massachusetts

Greater Boston Convention & Visitors Bureau
www.meetboston.com
The site provides a full a list of events throughout the year and visitor information on lodging, restaurants, sights, shopping, and transportation.

The Freedom Trail Foundation
www.thefreedomtrail.org
Find tourist info, historical background notes, and the latest news on tours and events for the 16 historic sites that make up Boston's Freedom Trail.

The Berkshires
www.berkshires.org
This site offers lots of advice on dining and lodging in the area, plus other diversions such as spas, concerts, family outings, and outdoor excursions, plus a list of current getaway deals.

Cape Cod Chamber of Commerce
www.capecodchamber.org
Find full business listings, information on where to stay and eat, backgrounds on the 15 towns that make up Cape Cod, help on getting around the area, plus information on golfing, baseball, football, and other sports in the area on this website.

Nantucket Island
www.nantucket.net
Plan your island vacation with this site's easy listings of local restaurants, hotels and inns, beaches, and museums. There's also plenty of information on where and how to go boating, fishing, golfing, and biking, plus a section on where to take kids around the island.

Martha's Vineyard Island
www.mvy.com
From diving and sailing to horseback riding and beachgoing, this site details all there is to do on and around Martha's Vineyard. It also lists accommodations and restaurants, posts a calendar of events and festivals, and provides information on car rentals and ferries, as well as vacation rentals. The last-minute lodging feature of this website is particularly useful.

Maine

Maine Tourism
www.visitmaine.com
This site offers information on everything to see and do in Maine, including fall foliage, outdoor recreation, family-friendly outings, restaurants, shopping, events, and accommodations.

Portland, ME
www.visitportland.com
With coverage that stretches across southern Maine, this site is an excellent resource for trip planning.

Acadia National Park, ME
www.nps.gov/acad
Maps, campground information and booking services, and online passes are available on this site.

New Hampshire

New Hampshire Tourism
www.visitnh.gov
Find all kinds of visitor information on the state, including local foliage reports, travel itineraries, online photo galleries, deals on seasonal travel packages, and lodging and restaurant listings.

Mt. Washington Valley, NH
www.mtwashingtonvalley.org
Just about anything happening in the valley shows up on this site: local events throughout the year, dogsledding and cross-country skiing—plus how to find the best local crafters and artists, as well as shopping, restaurant, and hotel listings.

Vermont

Vermont Tourism
www.vermontvacation.com
Here you'll find information on nightlife and dining, shopping, accommodations, ski resorts, local churches, and businesses, plus help on getting around the area by public transportation and finding local festivals.

Rhode Island

Providence Chamber of Commerce
www.goprovidence.com
This site offers information not just on visiting Providence, but also on moving there.

Newport, RI
www.discovernewport.org
Find full listings of local businesses on the site, along with useful visitor information on events, historic sites, and shows by area and neighborhood.

The Preservation Society of Newport County
www.newportmansions.org
The Preservation Society operates the majority of mansions open to the public in Newport. Find out more about the history and character of each one on this in-depth site—plus essentials such as events, hours, and online ticketing.

Connecticut

Connecticut Tourism
www.ctvisit.com
Built primarily for visitors to the state, this site lists weekend getaway itineraries and events happening throughout the year. It also offers help on getting to and around the different counties, and special deals on hotels.

Mystic, CT
www.mystic.org
The town's official site lists everything currently happening within it, from the aquarium's exhibits to the Seaport's presentations. Also find restaurant, hotel, and shopping listings.

Suggested Reading

Reference

Feintuch, Bert, ed. *The Encyclopedia of New England*. New Haven, CT: Yale University Press, 2005. A good book to read *before* you go, this 1,600-page, eight-pound tome will tell you everything you want to know about New England and then some, including entries on Walden Pond, fried clams, Ben & Jerry's, and the Red Sox. Instead of a disjointed alphabetical arrangement, the book cogently organizes contents by subject matter.

History

Cronon, William. *Changes in the Land: Indians, Colonists, and the Ecology of New England*. New York: Hill and Wang, 1983. The classic study of early New England history debunks myths and shatters preconceptions about Pilgrims and Native Americans and how each interacted with the landscape.

Fairbrother, Trevor. *Painting Summer in New England.* New Haven, CT: Yale University Press, 2006. From an exhibition of the same name at the Peabody Essex Museum, this beautiful art book includes dozens of paintings by American Impressionists, along with stories about the artists.

Gumprecht, Blake. *North to Boston: Life Histories from the Black Great Migration in New England.* Oxford University Press, 2023. The intersectional stories of New England's Black communities, from the Boston neighborhoods of Mattapan and Dorchester to the woods near Walden Pond, have long been due for the narrative spotlight that Gumprecht offers with this fascinating book.

Howard, Brett. *Boston: A Social History.* New York: Hawthorn, 1976. Detailing the impact of the city's leaders and most prominent families over the centuries, Howard shows the impact Boston Brahmins have had on local politics and cultural landscape.

McCullough, David. *1776.* New York: Simon & Schuster, 2005. Rather than writing a start-to-finish account of the Revolution, McCullough drills down to the pivotal year in which the fortunes of George Washington turned, from the tense standoff of the siege of Boston to the ultimate victories at Trenton and Princeton.

Paine, Lincoln P. *Down East: A Maritime History of Maine.* Gardiner, ME: Tilbury House Publishers, 2000. A look back at more than four centuries of pirates, privateers, lobstermen, and windjammers from a maritime historian and native Downeaster.

Rappeleye, Charles. *Sons of Providence: The Brown Brothers, the Slave Trade, and the American Revolution.* New York: Simon & Schuster, 2006. A fascinating journey into the heart of colonial America, told through the history of the most enlightened city in the New World—which nevertheless founded its fortune on the slave trade.

Vowell, Sarah. *The Wordy Shipmates.* New York: Riverhead, 2007. The popular essayist and National Public Radio contributor not only writes one of the most irreverent and entertaining histories of the early days of Puritan and Pilgrim New England, but also makes those ancient times surprisingly relevant to the present-day United States.

Woodard, Colin. *The Lobster Coast: Rebels, Rusticators, and the Struggle for a Forgotten Frontier.* New York: Viking, 2004. From early Scots-Irish woodchoppers to 20th-century oil painters, this clearly written account populates the map of Maine with colorful historical characters.

Natural History and Ecology

Albers, Jan. *Hands on the Land: A Natural History of the Vermont Landscape.* Boston: MIT Press, 2002. In a gorgeous oversized book, Albers details the various factors—geological, ecological, and economic—that have transformed the Green Mountain State.

Kessler, Brad. *Goat Song: A Seasonal Life, A Short History of Herding, and the Art of Making Cheese.* New York: Scribner, 2009. In this lovely and earnest little book, longtime writer Kessler sets out to live the dream that tugs at many of us: leaving the city to go back to live a simpler life out on the farm. What he finds in two years of raising goats is nothing short of a connection to our most mythic religious archetypes.

Kurlansky, Mark. *Cod: A Biography of the Fish that Changed the World.* New York: Penguin, 1998. The settlement and economic rise of New England is inseparable from the plentiful groundfish that once populated its waters in astounding numbers.

National Audubon Society. *National Audubon Society Regional Guide to New England.* New York: Knopf, 1998. The amateur naturalist would do well to pick up this guide, which details many local species of trees, wildflowers, reptiles, and mammals with 1,500 full-color illustrations.

Wessels, Tom. *Reading the Forested Landscape: A Natural History of New England.* Woodstock, VT: Countryman Press, 2005. A good read before heading off into the hills, this book helps put features of the landscape into their proper context.

Literature

Douglass, Frederick. *Narrative of the Life of Frederick Douglass, An American Slave: Written By Himself.* 1845, Signet Classics, 2005. The quintessential slave narrative includes details of Douglass's life as an abolitionist in Boston.

Frost, Robert. *The Poetry of Robert Frost: The Collected Poems, Complete and Unabridged.* Henry Holt and Co., 1979. The New England landscape infuses Frost's poetry, much of which was written in Vermont and New Hampshire.

Hawthorne, Nathaniel. *The House of the Seven Gables.* 1851, Signet Classics, 2001. The tragic story of several interlocking families is set in a house that still exists in Salem, Massachusetts.

James, Henry. *The Bostonians.* 1886, Modern Library Classics, 2003. Beacon Hill comes alive in this evocation of 19th-century Boston.

Jewett, Sarah Orne. *The Country of the Pointed Firs.* 1896, Dover, 2011. Maine's customs, dialect, and traditions come to life in this often-overlooked masterpiece.

Melville, Herman. *Moby-Dick.* 1851, Penguin Classics, 2002. From the opening scene in New Bedford, Massachusetts, this classic tale brings New England's grand, tragic whaling history to the page; it was written at Melville's country home in the Berkshires.

Stegner, Wallace. *Crossing To Safety.* 1987, Random House, 2002. A quintessential Western author tells a finely woven story of love and loss with the backdrop of northern Vermont.

Thoreau, Henry David. *Walden.* 1854, Modern Library Classics, 2000. The classic account of Thoreau's two years living a hermit's life on Walden Pond is a philosophical treatise, a timeless glimpse into 19th-century rural New England, and inspiration for the modern-day environmental movement. Look for an edition that includes *The Maine Woods* and *Cape Cod,* travelogues that blend the author's sharp eye and wry sense of humor.

Wharton, Edith. *The Age of Innocence.* 1920, CreateSpace, 2015. A stormy romance brings the Gilded Age New York and Newport society to life.

Contemporary Fiction and Memoir

Bergman, Megan Mayhew. *Birds of a Lesser Paradise.* Simon & Schuster, 2012. Writing from a farm in Vermont, Bergman draws New England's cows, chickens, and exotic birds into her intimate short stories.

Beston, Henry. *The Outermost House: A Year of Life on the Great Beach of Cape Cod*. New York: Owl Books, 1928. Beston's attempt to "go Thoreau" by living for a year in a small house in the dunes remains the most joyous evocation of Cape Cod's unique ecology.

Elder, John. *Reading the Mountains of Home*. Harvard University Press, 1999. With the company of Robert Frost's poetry, a Vermont writer watches a year unfold in the Green Mountains.

Fitzgerald, Issac. *Dirtbag, Massachusetts*. Bloomsbury Publishing, 2022. An unflinching, irreverent, and deeply empathetic story of growing up in poverty across the Bay State and discovering beauty in unlikely places and figures, Fitzgerald's unique memoir is as real and essential as contemporary New England writing gets.

Greenlaw, Linda. *The Lobster Chronicles: Life on a Very Small Island*. New York: Hyperion, 2003. The sword boat captain featured in Sebastian Junger's nonfiction book *The Perfect Storm* returns with a fascinating memoir of her return to her family's home on Isle Au Haut in Maine to try her hand at the lobstering business.

Hodgman, John. *Vacationland: True Stories from Painful Beaches*. New York: Viking, 2017. Digging deep into memories of family getaways to the Pine Tree State, Hodgman, a humorist and *The Daily Show* writer, presents a collection of side-splitting stories that showcase the weirdness, melancholia, and profundity of life in Maine.

Irving, John. Many of the most popular books of this cult American novelist are set in New England. For example, *The Cider House Rules* is centered around an orphanage in Maine, *The World According to Garp* takes place in part at a New England boarding school, and *A Prayer for Owen Meany* concerns several generations of a troubled New England family.

MacDonald, Michael Patrick. *All Souls: A Family Story from Southie*. New York: Ballantine, 2000. In writing his moving memoir of Irish American life, MacDonald does for South Boston what Frank McCourt did for Limerick, Ireland.

Stout, Elizabeth. *Olive Kitteridge*. Random House, 2008. Experience the hidden lives (and anguishes) of a small Maine coast town through the eyes of the titular junior high math teacher in Strout's haunting novel of short stories.

Guidebooks

Appalachian Mountain Club Books (www.outdoors.org/publications) publishes dozens of guides considered gospel by outdoors enthusiasts in the region. They are jam-packed with nononsense directions for hiking and canoeing every inch of the New England wilderness. Among them are the *White Mountain Guide* and *Maine Mountain Guide*, as well as several guides for canoeing and kayaking.

Corbett, William. *Literary New England: A History and Guide*. New York: Faber and Faber, 1993. An excellent guide to sights associated with poets and writers who called New England home, it includes detailed directions to hard-to-find graves, historic sites, and houses.

Dojny, Brooke. *The New England Clam Shack Cookbook*. North Adams, MA: Storey Publishing, 2003. In addition to providing recipes for stuffed quahogs and other favorites, this book offers a guide to some of the best clam shacks, lobster pounds, and chowder houses in all six states.

Hartnett, Robert. *Maine Lighthouses Map & Guide.* Howes Cave, NY: Hartnett House Map Publishing, 2000. A fold-out map that provides detailed directions to every lighthouse along the rocky fingers of the Maine coast. Hartnett also publishes a map to lighthouses in Massachusetts and New Hampshire (yes, there are two).

Kershner, Bruce, and Robert Leverett. *The Sierra Club Guide to the Ancient Forests of the Northeast.* San Francisco: Sierra Club Books, 2004. Despite centuries of human habitation and exploitation, a surprising number of old-growth stands still exist in New England. This guide takes you inside their mossy interiors, and explains what makes old-growth forests so unique.

Perrett, Kelsey, and Miles Howard. *Moon New England Hiking: Best Hikes plus Beer, Bites, and Campgrounds Nearby.* Berkeley, CA: Avalon Travel, 2020. From the same publisher that offers Moon Handbooks, this guide features plenty of hiking trails to get your boots muddy and watering holes to refuel with craft libations and munchies.

INDEX

C

D

E

F

G

H

I

J

K

L

M

N

O

P

QR

S

T

UV

WXYZ

LIST OF MAPS

PHOTO CREDITS

Title page photo: Hill Farmstead LLC and Bob M. Montgomery Images; page 4 © Serene Folding / Visit Portland; page 5 © N. Millard/GoProvidence.com; page 7 © (top) Visit Maine; (bottom) Visit Portland; page 8 © Miles Howard; page 10 © (top) Ogden Gigli; (bottom) Ben Nugent/Cape Cod Chamber of Commerce; page 11 © (top) Kirkikisphoto | Dreamstime.com; (bottom) N. Millard/GoProvidence.com; page 12 © N. Millard/GoProvidence.com; page 13 © (top) FabioConcetta | Dreamstime.com; (bottom) Mathew Trogner /Allagash Brewing Company; page 14 © Redwood8 | Dreamstime.com; page 15 © James Kirkikis | Dreamstime.com; page 17 © (top left) Miles Howard; (top right) Rabbitti | Dreamstime.com; (bottom) Ogden Gigli; page 19 © Visit White Mountains/Roger Marcoux Photography; page 20 © (top left) Martha's Vineyard Chamber of Commerce; (top right) Miles Howard; (bottom) Dobbs Productions and Bar Harbor Chamber of Commerce; page 23 © (top left) Dobbs Productions and Bar Harbor Chamber of Commerce; (top right) Linda Mohammad; (bottom) Kyle Klein Photo; page 25 © Alexander Grey | Unsplash.com; page 26 © (top left) Kittycat | Dreamstime.com; (top right) Josh Laskin; (bottom) Miles Howard; page 27 © William DeSousa-Mauk; page 28 © Miles Howard; page 31 © (top) F11photo | Dreamstime.com; (bottom) Visit White Mountains; page 32 © Discover Newport; page 33 © James Kirkikis | Dreamstime.com; page 34 © Kyle Klein; page 41 © Rodchron | Dreamstime.com; page 44 © (top) Aevang | Dreamstime.com; (middle) NPS; (bottom) BOAF/NPS; page 46 © Linda Cook | Dreamstime.com; page 47 © (top) Vodickap | Dreamstime.com; (middle) Kyle Klein; (bottom) Mbastos | Dreamstime.com; page 52 © F11photo | Dreamstime.com; page 57 © (top) Dyermh | Dreamstime.com; (middle) Phillip Reeves | Dreamstime.com; (bottom) F11photo | Dreamstime.com; page 61 © (top) Jiawangkun | Dreamstime.com; (middle) Studio Nouveau/Boston Museum of Science; (bottom) Mimi Katz | Dreamstime.com; page 64 © Sandrafoyt | Dreamstime.com; page 69 © (top) Teconley | Dreamstime.com; (middle) Miles Howard; (bottom) Appalachianviews | Dreamstime.com; page 71 © James Kirkikis | Dreamstime.com; page 76 © (top) Blackbird Doughnuts; (middle) Markzhu | Dreamstime.com; (bottom) Boston Harbor Hotel; page 80 © Killglenys | Dreamstime.com; page 82 © Miles Howard; page 85 © Sarawinter | Dreamstime.com; page 91 © Beruldsen | Dreamstime.com; page 93 © Miles Howard; page 98 © Kirkikisphoto | Dreamstime.com; page 108 © (top) Bdingman | Dreamstime.com; (middle) Portland Museum of Art; (bottom) Maine Historical Society; page 111 © Visit Maine; page 114 © Allagash Brewing Company; page 117 © Miles Howard; page 120 © Miles Howard; page 126 © Maine Maritime Museum; page 133 © Joe Sohm | Dreamstime.com; page 136 © (top) Lokinthru | Dreamstime.com; (middle) Dbvirago | Dreamstime.com; (bottom) Benjamin R. | Unsplash.com; page 146 © Visit Maine; page 148 © Miles Howard; page 152 © Luckydoor | Dreamstime.com; page 158 © Dobbs Productions and Bar Harbor Chamber of Commerce; page 160 © Friends of Acadia/National Park Service; page 162 © (top) Jlwhaley | Dreamstime.com; (middle) Lokinthru | Dreamstime.com; (bottom) Miles Howard; page 165 © Ujjwalstha | Dreamstime.com; page 167 © (top) Miles Howard; (middle) Phyllis D. Peterson | Dreamstime.com; (bottom) Visit Maine; page 174 © Dobbs Productions and Bar Harbor Chamber of Commerce; page 176 © Miles Howard; page 178 © Miles Howard; page 185 © Pxlman | Dreamstime.com; page 188 © Appalachianviews | Dreamstime.com; page 190 © James Wrigley; page 192 © (top) Miles Howard; (middle) Robert Kozlow; (bottom) Miles Howard; page 194 © Courtesy of AMC/Corey David Photography; page 199 © (top) Josh Laskin; (middle) Yggdrasill33 | Dreamstime.com; (bottom) Visit White Mountains; page 203 © John Anderson | Dreamstime.com; page 207 © Miles Howard; page 209 © Kirkikisphoto | Dreamstime.com; page 221 © (top) Jimdelillo | Dreamstime.com; (middle) Peanutroaster | Dreamstime.com; (bottom) Jlobo211 | Dreamstime.com; page 222 © 1miro | Dreamstime.com; page 224 © Vermont Maple Sugar Makers' Association; page 229 © Cllhnstev | Dreamstime.com; page 230 © (top) TheAmericanExplorer | Dreamstime.com; (middle) Miles Howard; (bottom) Cllhnstev | Dreamstime.com; page 231 © Jlobo211 | Dreamstime.com; page 236 © Jxander | Dreamstime.com; page 238 © Tabakmarko | Dreamstime.com; page 244 © (top) Sandrafoyt | Dreamstime.com; (middle) Jlobo211 | Dreamstime.com; (bottom) Igokapil | Dreamstime.com; page 248 © Hill Farmstead LLC and Bob M. Montgomery Images; page 250 © Ogden Gigli; page 257 © Berniephillips | Dreamstime.com; page 260 © Jeff Goldberg, Esto; page 265 © Haveseen | Dreamstime.com; page 267 © (top) Dylan Beckman/MASSMOcA; (middle) Miles Howard; (bottom) Miles Howard; page 272 © Boston Symphony Orchestra; page 275 © (top) Leesniderphotoimages | Dreamstime.com; (middle) Stockbridge Chamber of Commerce/Gross & Daley Photo; (bottom) Bratty1206 | Dreamstime.com; page 278 © Shanshan533 | Dreamstime.com; page 283 © Cllhnstev | Dreamstime.com; page 285

© Wirestock | Dreamstime.com; page 291 © Kirkikisphoto | Dreamstime.com; page 296 © (top) Discover Newport; (middle) Discover Newport; (bottom) Jiawangkun | Dreamstime.com; page 299 © Discover Newport; page 302 © Discover Newport; page 304 © N. Millard/GoProvidence.com; page 310 © (top) N. Millard/GoProvidence.com; (middle) N. Millard/GoProvidence.com; (bottom) N. Millard/GoProvidence.com; page 311 © Kevin Murray; page 312 © N. Millard/GoProvidence.com; page 314 © N. Millard/GoProvidence.com; page 317 © (top) N. Millard/GoProvidence.com; (middle) N. Millard/GoProvidence.com; (bottom) N. Millard/GoProvidence.com; page 320 © Trent Bell; page 322 © Jnevitt | Dreamstime.com; page 329 © Smitty411 | Dreamstime.com; page 332 © Elaine & Gordon Rondeau; page 336 © Falmouth Chamber of Commerce; page 338 © Bratty1206 | Dreamstime.com; page 343 © Cape Cod Chamber of Commerce; page 345 © Lydia May | Dreamstime.com; page 352 © Joe Rosetti; page 358 © (top) Bill Wakeley; (middle) Cape Cod Chamber of Commerce; (bottom) Vadim_777 | Dreamstime.com; page 360 © Barbara Kram; page 362 © Wickedgood | Dreamstime.com; page 366 © Rolf52 | Dreamstime.com; page 374 © Demerzel21 | Dreamstime.com; page 385 © Leesniderphotoimages | Dreamstime.com; page 387 © (top) Nantucket Historical Association; (middle) Sabberidgio | Dreamstime.com; (bottom) Nantucket Chamber of Commerce; page 390 © Rabbit75 | Dreamstime.com; page 395 © Palinchak | Dreamstime.com; page 396 © Monamakela | Dreamstime.com; page 400 © Alexandre Fagundes De Fagundes | Dreamstime.com; page 403 © (top) Agaliza | Dreamstime.com; (middle) Searagen | Dreamstime.com; (bottom) Andersastphoto | Dreamstime.com; page 408 © Pat138241 | Dreamstime.com; page 410 © (top) Littleny | Dreamstime.com; (middle) Totto Ramen/Jayna Kropas; (bottom) Fulcrumsf | Dreamstime.com; page 415 © William87 | Dreamstime.com; page 417 © Martinabirnbaum | Dreamstime.com

ROAD TRIP GUIDES

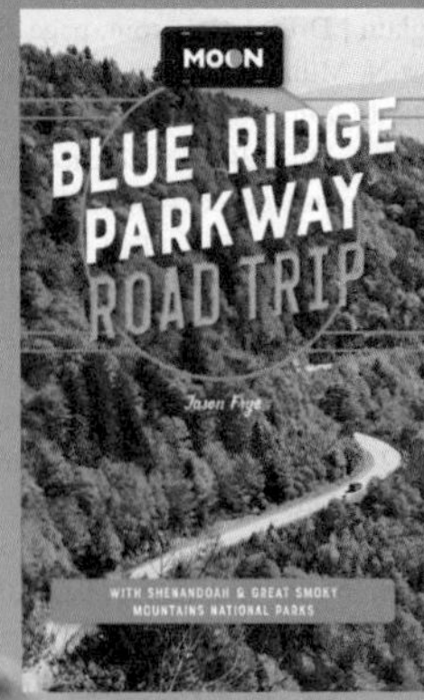

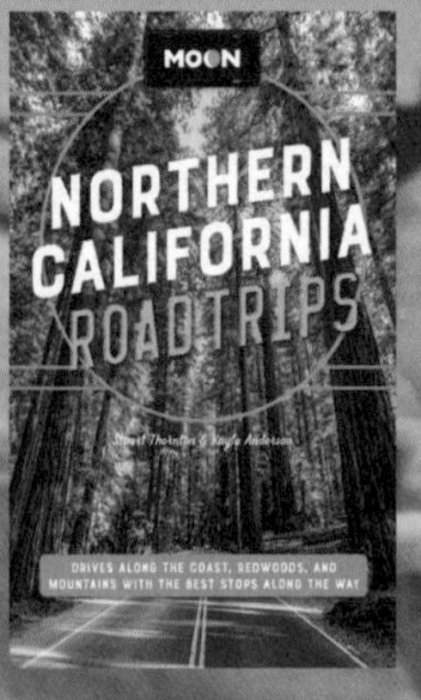

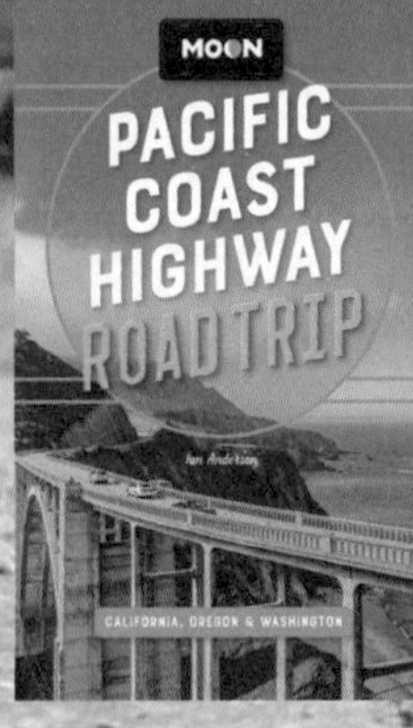

MOON.COM | ROADTRIPUSA.COM

MOON
SOUTH FLORIDA & THE KEYS
Road Trip
WITH MIAMI, WALT DISNEY WORLD, TAMPA & THE EVERGLADES
JASON FERGUSON

MOON
SOUTHERN CALIFORNIA
ROAD TRIPS
Ian Anderson
DRIVES ALONG THE BEACHES, MOUNTAINS, AND DESERTS WITH THE BEST STOPS ALONG THE WAY

MOON
SOUTHWEST
ROAD TRIP
Tim Hull
DRIVE THE LOOP FROM LAS VEGAS TO SANTA FE, VISITING 8 NATIONAL PARKS ALONG THE WAY

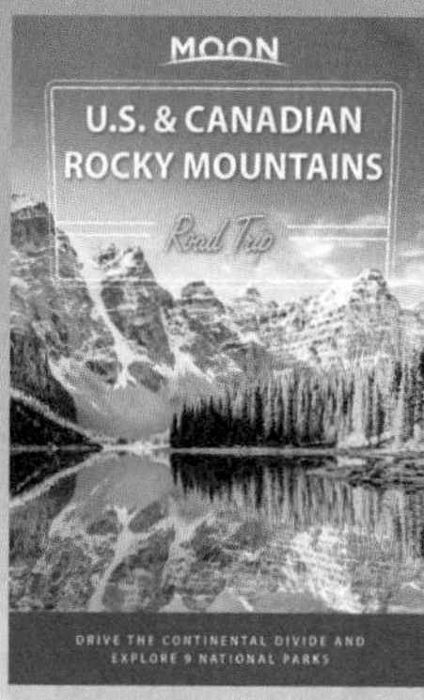
MOON
U.S. & CANADIAN ROCKY MOUNTAINS
Road Trip
DRIVE THE CONTINENTAL DIVIDE AND EXPLORE 9 NATIONAL PARKS
BECKY LOMAX

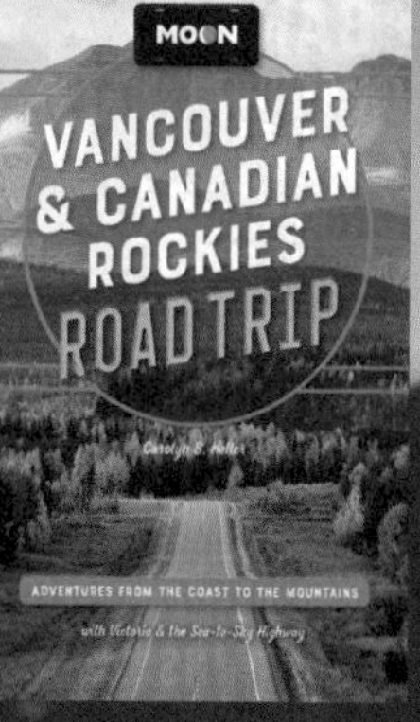
MOON
VANCOUVER & CANADIAN ROCKIES
ROAD TRIP
Carolyn B. Heller
ADVENTURES FROM THE COAST TO THE MOUNTAINS
with Victoria & the Sea-to-Sky Highway

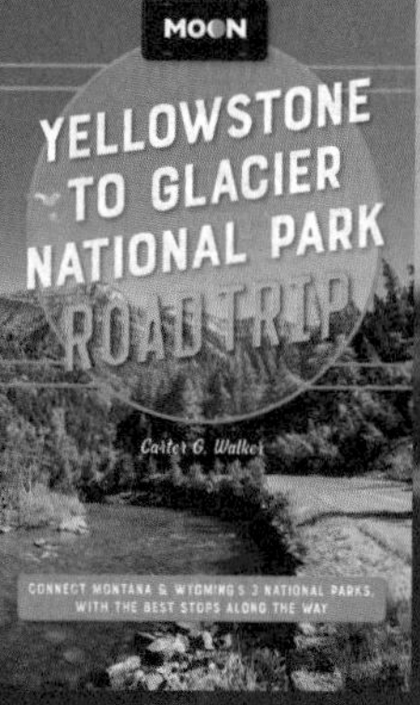
MOON
YELLOWSTONE TO GLACIER NATIONAL PARK
ROAD TRIP
Carter G. Walker
CONNECT MONTANA & WYOMING'S 3 NATIONAL PARKS, WITH THE BEST STOPS ALONG THE WAY

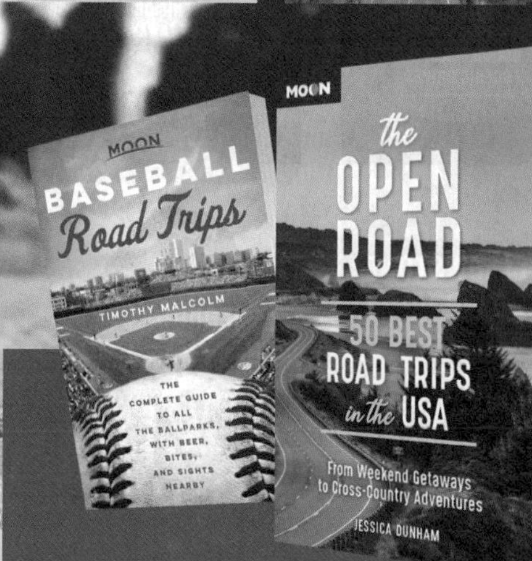
MOON
BASEBALL
Road Trips
TIMOTHY MALCOLM
THE COMPLETE GUIDE TO ALL THE BALLPARKS, WITH BEER, BITES, AND SIGHTS NEARBY
MOON
the
OPEN ROAD
50 BEST ROAD TRIPS in the USA
From Weekend Getaways to Cross-Country Adventures
JESSICA DUNHAM

MOON
Road Trip USA
CROSS-COUNTRY ADVENTURES ON AMERICA'S TWO-LANE HIGHWAYS
Jamie Jensen

MAP SYMBOLS

- Highway
- Primary Road
- Secondary Road
- Unpaved Road
- Trail
- Ferry
- Railroad
- Pedestrian Walkway
- Stairs
- City/Town
- State Capital
- National Capital
- Highlight
- Point of Interest
- Accommodation
- Restaurant/Bar
- Other Location
- Information Center
- Parking Area
- Place of Worship
- Winery/Vineyard
- Trailhead
- Camping
- Train Station
- International Airport
- Regional Airport
- Park
- Golf Course
- Unique Feature
- Unique Feature Hydro
- Waterfall
- Mountain
- Ski Area
- Glacier

CONVERSION TABLES

°C = (°F - 32) / 1.8
°F = (°C x 1.8) + 32
1 inch = 2.54 centimeters (cm)
1 foot = 0.304 meters (m)
1 yard = 0.914 meters
1 mile = 1.6093 kilometers (km)
1 km = 0.6214 miles
1 fathom = 1.8288 m
1 chain = 20.1168 m
1 furlong = 201.168 m
1 acre = 0.4047 hectares
1 sq km = 100 hectares
1 sq mile = 2.59 square km
1 ounce = 28.35 grams
1 pound = 0.4536 kilograms
1 short ton = 0.90718 metric ton
1 short ton = 2,000 pounds
1 long ton = 1.016 metric tons
1 long ton = 2,240 pounds
1 metric ton = 1,000 kilograms
1 quart = 0.94635 liters
1 US gallon = 3.7854 liters
1 Imperial gallon = 4.5459 liters
1 nautical mile = 1.852 km

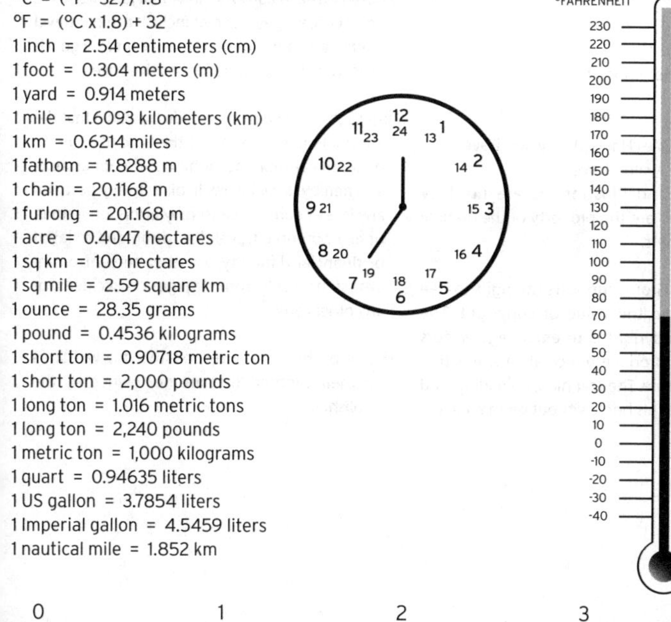

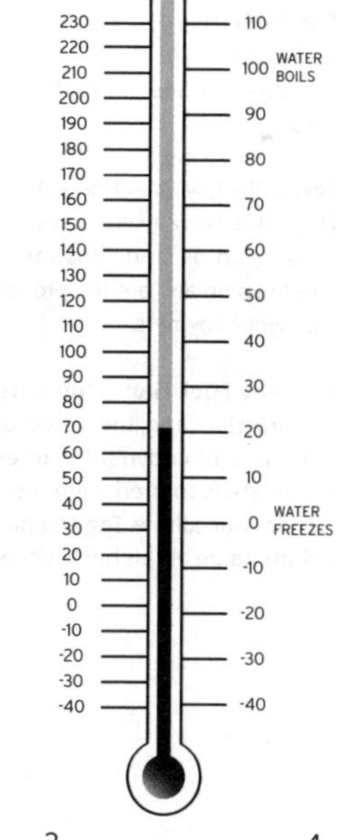

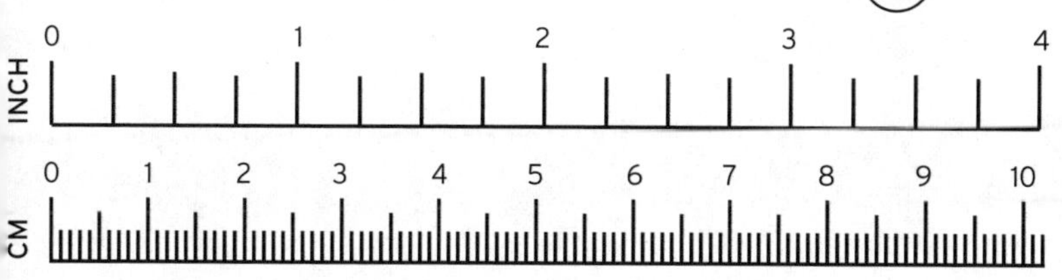

MOON NEW ENGLAND ROAD TRIP

Avalon Travel
Hachette Book Group
555 12th Street, Suite 1850
Oakland, CA 94607, USA
www.moon.com

Editor: Devon Lee
Managing Editor: Hannah Brezack
Copy Editor: Barbara Schultz
Graphics and Production Coordinator: Ravina Schneider
Cover Design: Erin Seaward-Hiatt
Interior Design: Darren Alessi
Map Editor: John Culp
Cartographers: John Culp, Abby Whelan
Proofreader: Brett Keener
Indexer: Greg Jewett

ISBN-13: 979-8-88647-060-4

Printing History
1st Edition — 2017
3rd Edition — September 2024
5 4 3 2 1

Front cover photo: Vermont, New England. James Kirkikis / Alamy Stock Photo

Printed in China APS